EDMUND WILSON ❖

Bibliography

T. E. Lawrence: A Bibliography
Catalogue of the Library of the Late Siegfried Sassoon
George Orwell: An Annotated Bibliography of Criticism

Edited Collections

George Orwell: The Critical Heritage
Hemingway: The Critical Heritage
Robert Lowell: Interviews and Memoirs

Edited Original Essays

Wyndham Lewis *by Roy Campbell*
Wyndham Lewis: A Revaluation
D. H. Lawrence and Tradition
The Legacy of D. H. Lawrence
The Craft of Literary Biography
The Biographer's Art
T. E. Lawrence: Soldier, Writer, Legend
Graham Greene: A Revaluation

EDMUND WILSON

A Biography ❖ ❖ ❖

Jeffrey Meyers

A PETER DAVISON BOOK

Houghton Mifflin Company

BOSTON   NEW YORK   1995

For information about permission to reproduce selections from
this book, write to Permissions, Houghton Mifflin Company,
215 Park Avenue South, New York, New York 10003.

Library of Congress Cataloging-in-Publication Data
Meyers, Jeffrey.
    Edmund Wilson : a biography / Jeffrey Meyers.
        p.   cm.
    "A Peter Davison book."
    Includes bibliographical references and index.
    ISBN 0-395-68993-7
    1. Wilson, Edmund, 1895–1972 — Biography.   2. Authors.
American — 20th century — Biography.   3. Critics — United States —
Biography.   I. Title.
PS3545.I6245Z76   1995
818'.5209 — dc20   94-37574
    [B]   CIP

Excerpts from the following works are reprinted by permission of Farrar,
Straus & Giroux, Inc.:
The Twenties by Edmund Wilson, edited by Leon Edel. Copyright ©
1975 by Elena Wilson
The Sixties by Edmund Wilson, edited by Lewis M. Dabney. Copyright
© 1993 by Helen Miranda Wilson
Letters on Literature and Politics 1912–1972 by Edmund Wilson, edited by
Elena Wilson. Copyright © 1977 by Elena Wilson

Excerpts from the unpublished letters of Edmund Wilson are used with
permission of his estate, copyright © 1995 by Helen Miranda Wilson

Printed in the United States of America

MP 10 9 8 7 6 5 4 3 2 1

Contents

Illustrations

Helen Wilson and her son Edmund, c. 1900 (*Nathaniel Hartshorne*)

Edmund Wilson, Sr. on the steps of the Old Stone House (*Courtesy of the Estate of Edmund Wilson*)

Edmund Wilson, 1920 (*Nathaniel Hartshorne*)

Christian Gauss at a Princeton football game, 1940s (*From* The Papers of Christian Gauss, *Katherine Gauss Jackson and Hiram Haydn, ed. Copyright © 1957 by Random House, Inc. and renewed 1985 by Alice Gauss. Reprinted by permission of Random House, Inc.*)

Scott Fitzgerald, Nice, 1925 (*Courtney Vaughan*)

Edna St. Vincent Millay, c. 1927 (*Vassar College Library*)

John Peale Bishop, c. 1922 (*Jonathan Bishop*)

Mary Blair, 1921

Elinor Wylie, 1926 (*Yale Collection of American Literature, Beinecke Rare Book & Manuscript Library, Yale University*)

Ted Paramore, 1930s (*Anna Paramore Brando*)

John Dos Passos, 1924 (*Elizabeth Dos Passos*)

Margaret Canby, 1920s (*Mary Canby*)

Louise Fort Connor, 1930s (*Peter Connor*)

Léonie Adams, c. 1930 (*Blackstone Studios. Courtesy of Marian McAllister*)

Louise Bogan, 1937

Edmund Wilson, 1930

Edmund Wilson and Mary McCarthy, Wellfleet, 1942 (*Reuel Wilson*)

Mamaine Paget, 1937 (*Celia Goodman*)

Elena Wilson, 1940s (*Courtesy of the Estate of Edmund Wilson*)

Vladimir Nabokov, 1957 (*Cornell University Library*)

Isaiah Berlin, 1950s (*Sir Isaiah Berlin*)

W. H. Auden, 1945 (*Robert Wilson*)

Robert Lowell, 1950s (*Doris Eyges*)

Reuel, Elena, Helen, Rosalind, Edmund and Henry Thornton, with Recki and Bambi, Wellfleet, 1948 (*David Chavchavadze*)

Rosalind Wilson, 1968 (*Rosalind Baker Wilson*)

Dawn Powell, 1950 (*Robert Offergeld. Courtesy of Anne Yarowsky*)

Edmund Wilson, 1952 (*Courtesy of the Estate of Edmund Wilson*)

Mary Pcolar, c. 1970

Edmund Wilson, three days before his death (*Nicolas Sapieha /Art Resource, New York*)

Acknowledgments

Biography is a cooperative venture, and it is a pleasure to acknowledge the generous assistance I received while writing this book. Edmund Wilson's daughter Rosalind and his editor Leon Edel encouraged and helped from the beginning, and the University of California appointed me a Visiting Scholar. My friends were extremely helpful. William and JoAn Chace, Mary and Howard Berg, Jackson and Mary Bryer provided splendid hospitality while I was working at Yale, in Boston and on Cape Cod. I had stimulating talks with Arthur Miller about Penelope Gilliatt, with Joseph Frank about Vladimir Nabokov and with Barnaby Conrad about James MacInnes. Iris Murdoch and Francis King sent their memories of Wilson. Alfredo and Barbara Bonadeo, Morris Brownell, Bill Daleski, Michael Howe, Rachel Meyers, Michael Millgate, Dr. Mario Papagni, Thomas Pinney and Michael Scammell sent valuable information.

For personal interviews I would like to thank: Daniel Aaron, Sir Isaiah Berlin, Mary Canby and Catherine Canby Day, Loran and Mary Crosten, Walter Edmonds, Barbara Epstein, Jason Epstein, William Fenton, Celia Paget Goodman, Albert and Macklin Guerard, Paul Horgan, Stuart Hughes, Mable Hutchins, Simon Karlinsky, Alfred Kazin, Harry and Elena Levin, Eva Marcelin, Sheldon Meyer, Dr. Edgar Miller, Eleanor Perenyi, Richard Pipes, Arthur Schlesinger, Jr., Elizabeth and Robert Stabb, Roger Straus, Henry Thornton, Adelaide and Daniel Walker, Richard and Charlee Wilbur and Rosalind Wilson (who spent two days with me); for telephone conversations: Nicholas Alaga, Anna Paramore Brando, Clelia Carroll Carey, Philip Carroll, Peter Connor, Mrs. Edwin Grabhorn, Robert Hartshorne, Andrew Hoyen, Dr. Robert Jackler, Anne Miller Kellogg, Ellen Lifschutz, Dr. John Miller, Edwin Newhouse, Edward Paramore III, Jacqueline Rice, William Matson Roth, Ruth Schorer, Robert Silvers, Dr. Robert

Smith, Mary Struve, Frances Nevada Swisher, Robert Swisher and Helen Wilson.

For letters about Wilson I am grateful to: Lord Annan, Frances Bebis, Saul Bellow, Frank Bergman, Kate Berryman, John Biggs III, Jonathan Bishop, Marie-Claire Blais, Mina Brand, Mrs. Henry Brandon, Austin Briggs, Barry Callaghan, David Chavchavadze, John Crichton, Elizabeth Dos Passos, Suzanne Hughes Dworsky, Monroe Engel, Leonor Fini, David Flusser, Donald Gallup, Robert Giroux, John Golden, Edward Gorey, Philip Hamburger, Elizabeth Hardwick, Henry Hardy, Sir Rupert Hart-Davis, Nathaniel Hartshorne, Lincoln Kirstein, Charlotte Kretzoi, Cecil Lang, Alison Lurie, Kenneth Lynn, Michael Macdonald, Nancy Macdonald, John Marks, Malachi Martin, Marian McAllister, Kevin McCarthy, Mary Meigs, Edward Mendelson, Thomas Mendenhall, Glyn and Barbara Morris, Helen Muchnic, Charles Nash, Sherman Paul, Marlene Pcolar, Norman Podhoretz, Anthony Powell, Willard Quine, Philippe Radley, Richard David Ramsey, Paul Roazen, Alan Ross, A. L. Rowse, Marian Schlesinger, Jeffrey Simmons, William Jay Smith, Eliot Stanley, Rebecca Stickney, William Styron, Walter Sullivan, Diana Trilling, David Turner, John Updike, Ed Victor, John Wain, Reuel Wilson, Nancy Tate Wood, Anne Yarowsky, Thomas Daniel Young and Geraldine Zetzel.

The main collection of Wilson's papers—thousands of pages—is in the Beinecke Library at Yale University. I also received copies of Wilson's letters and other information from the following libraries: Amherst College, State University of New York at Binghamton, Boston University, Brown University, State University of New York at Buffalo, University of Calgary, University of California at Berkeley, University of California at Los Angeles, University of Chicago (and University Archives), Columbia University, Cornell University, University of Delaware, University of Edinburgh, Harvard University (and University Archives and Poetry Room), The Hill School, Indiana University, University of Iowa, Lyndon Baines Johnson Library, John Fitzgerald Kennedy Library, Library of Congress (and Recorded Sound Division), University College, London University, University of Maryland, University of Michigan, University of Minnesota, National Library of Scotland, Newberry Library, New York Public Library, New York University Archives, University of Oregon, University of Pennsylvania, Princeton University (and University Archives), Radcliffe College, University of Reading, St. Lawrence University, Smith College (and College Archives), Stanford University: Hoover Institution, Swarthmore College, University of Texas, University of Tulsa, Vassar College, University of Virginia and Wesleyan University Archives; and from various institutions: American Academy of Arts and Letters, American Academy of Arts and Sciences, Candlewood Valley Care Center, New Milford, Connecticut (on Léonie Adams), Federal Bureau of Investigation, Guggenheim Foundation (Thomas Tanselle), Harcourt Brace (Julie Bade), Houghton Mifflin, Internal Revenue Service, Alfred Knopf (Robin Swados), Lewis County Courthouse (for Wilson's will), *London Review of Books*, MacInnes, Donner & Kaplowitz, Macmillan UK (Katie Owen), National Archives and Records Administration: Military Personnel Records, *New Republic*, New York State Power Authority (on Robert Moses), *New Yorker*, *Provincetown Arts* (Christopher Busa), Red Bank Public Library, San Francisco Bar Association, Scribner's, the Society of Jesus (on Martin D'Arcy) and State Bar Association of California.

As always, my wife, Valerie Meyers, scrutinized each chapter and compiled the index.

Preface

This first life of Edmund Wilson completes my trilogy on modern American writers that began with the biographies of Hemingway and Fitzgerald. When I told a learned friend that I was writing about Edmund Wilson (1895–1972), he replied with an adversarial, half-accurate and deliberately provocative letter: "He seems an *idiot savant* of literature, knowing little else, and being of a saturnine, alcoholic and belligerent disposition. And how quickly now he has faded, yet how eminently sensible and balanced he always is when he writes on books. He terrified every one and today his books are unread. What, if anything, do you find redeeming in him as a man?" Wilson, a heavy drinker, certainly had a melancholy streak, a contentious character and a frightening demeanor. All this helps make him a fascinating man.

But Wilson, whom Gore Vidal called "America's best mind," also had extraordinarily wide interests and ranged far beyond literature. He wrote about art, theater, music, film, popular culture as well as political events, foreign travel, the revolutionary tradition in Europe, the Dead Sea Scrolls, the Zuni and Iroquois Indians, the American Civil War, the culture and politics of Canada. He was the master of the biographical essay and the autobiographical memoir, and was the greatest diarist of his time. Far from fading into obscurity and being ignored by contemporary readers, eleven of his fifty books are still in print, and his publishers have brought out eleven new works since his death—more than most *living* authors have written in the last twenty years.

As for his redeeming features—if, indeed, he is in need of redemption—I admire his curiosity, energy, intelligence and erudition, his clear thought, pure style and good taste, his personal courage, defense of the underdog and constant struggles against mindless authority, his loyalty to friends and generosity to many writers, his independence and integrity.

Even John Updike, an astute admirer of Wilson, mistakenly writes that "after 1930 his biography becomes largely bibliography." From the beginning of his literary career Wilson seemed thoroughly bookish, respectable, even conventional, and this image was reinforced in his rotund and dignified old age. But Wilson's life was as interesting as his books and—in its own way—as romantic and chaotic as Scott Fitzgerald's. He lived in bohemian poverty in the 1920s and 1930s, suffered a nervous breakdown and the tragic death of his second wife, had three other wives (including Mary McCarthy), attracted an astonishing number of beautiful mistresses (including Edna Millay) and was a compulsive chronicler of his sexual adventures.

Wilson had always engaged in controversy, which intensified as he grew older and more combative. He witnessed and reported the Harlan County coal-miners' strikes in 1932, quarreled with the Communists after his disillusioning visit to the Soviet Union in 1935, fell out with Evelyn Waugh in 1945, had his vividly erotic *Memoirs of Hecate County* burned and suppressed in 1946, threw himself into the scholarly battles about the Dead Sea Scrolls in 1955, and defended the Iroquois against dispossession by the New York Power Authority in 1959. After being prosecuted and heavily fined by the United States Government for not paying his taxes, he fought a spirited campaign against American involvement in Vietnam in *The Cold War and the Income Tax* (1963), bitterly disputed the Russian prosody of Pushkin's *Eugene Onegin* with his old friend and protégé Vladimir Nabokov in 1965, and opposed academic pedantry and dullness with his own humane learning in *The Fruits of the MLA* (1968).

Despite the chaos, Wilson had an enviable life. He came from a privileged background, had an excellent education at The Hill School and Princeton, and continued his studies until the end of his life. He learned Greek, Latin, French, Italian, German, Russian, Hebrew and Hungarian. He traveled widely, in western Europe as well as in Russia, Greece, Hungary, Haiti and Israel. He knew Lawrence, Joyce, Eliot, Wyndham Lewis, O'Neill, Hemingway, Faulkner as well as Igor Stravinsky and Charlie Chaplin. He was a close friend of Fitzgerald, Dos Passos, Allen Tate, Malraux, Nabokov, Isaiah Berlin, Auden and Robert Lowell; and was universally recognized as the most distinguished American man of letters in the twentieth century. He had a fertile imagination, and wrote novels, stories, poems and plays as well as seminal works like *Axel's Castle* (almost continuously in print since 1930), *To the Finland Station* (1940), *The Wound and the Bow* (1941) and *Patriotic Gore* (1962). Wilson's life became more interesting as he got older. His reputation continued to rise throughout his long career, he received many honors and prizes, and died peacefully in his ancestral home. Wilson showed that it was possible, between 1920 and 1970, for an independent and contentious thinker to write learned books and succeed as a professional writer.

Wilson's reflection on the artistic qualities of Igor Stravinsky applies with equal force to himself: "It is inspiring for any kind of craftsman to have the spectacle of such a sustained career—the artist always himself and always doing something different, but always doing everything intensely with economy, perfect craftsmanship and style." If Wilson is somewhat out of fashion today, it is only because the impressive intellect, knowledge and humane insight that illuminate his books have been lost through the onslaught of rigid ideological conformity, which he opposed throughout his life. As he prophetically wrote in the *Nation* in January 1938: "The young . . . are today not enthusiastic . . . about books: they merely approve when the book suits their politics. . . . I think it is a pity that they do not learn to read for pleasure. They may presently find that an acquaintance with the great works of art and thought is their only real assurance against the increasing barbarism of our time." The qualities exemplified in Edmund Wilson must be valued and restored if our literary culture is to survive.

There is something more to our interest in the private lives of great men than the mere desire to pry into other people's personal affairs. A great writer, for example, represents a special concentration both of purpose and of sensibility. He is more conscious than other people of the things that are going on in his time, and he is more articulate about them. He is driven to formulate more clearly some attitude toward the world that he lives in. But the works that he gives to the public do not tell the whole of his story, for they must always be artificial arrangements in the interests of ideal values. The real struggle of the ideal with the actual can only be seen at close range in the relationships and vicissitudes of the man's own life.

—EDMUND WILSON,
Foreword to Ada Nisbet's
Dickens and Ellen Ternan (1952)

EDMUND WILSON ❖

ONE

Red Bank, 1895–1907

I

Edmund Wilson's ancestors served the altars of learning and committed murders in the name of God. He was descended from Cotton Mather, seventeenth-century puritan divine and zealous witch hunter during the Salem trials, and shared many characteristics—intellect, bookishness, linguistic ability, temperament, energy, productivity and multiple marriages—with his eminent forefather. The prodigiously learned Mather, more widely read than any other American of his time, had entered Harvard at the age of twelve and spoke seven languages. Known for his arrogant manner and aggressiveness in controversy, he overtaxed his nerves by indefatigable industry, poured out more than 450 works on an enormous range of subjects and still managed to acquire three wives.

In *Patriotic Gore*, Wilson quotes Harriet Beecher Stowe's rapturous praise of Mather's masterwork, *Magnalia Christi Americana* (1702). Stowe felt, after reading this ecclesiastical history, that "the very ground I trod on [in New England was] consecrated by some special dealing of God's providence." Wilson, however, found the Calvinistic Mather a tormented and extremely neurotic man. "When anything goes wrong with Mather," he observed, "from a toothache to the death of his wife, he is likely to fall into a panic lest he not be, after all, elected, and to be stricken by a paroxysm of guilt." The poet Allen Tate believed that the ghost of Cotton Mather had burrowed into Wilson's conscience like a mole. Mather surfaced in Wilson's most diabolic work, *Memoirs of Hecate County*, when the autobiographical narrator remarks: "Maybe the Devil was in Cotton Mather . . . when he got people to hanging one another as witches."

Wilson's maternal ancestors, the Kimballs and the Bakers, sailed from England soon after the *Mayflower* and settled in New England in the middle of the seventeenth century. The Wilsons came from Londonderry in northern Ireland a century later, and all four grandparents were born in New York State. Like Henry James, Wilson identified himself as a New Yorker, and told an Italian journalist, to whom he had granted a rare interview: "my mother's family emigrated from New England to New York State at the end of the eighteenth century, and my father's family were among the first settlers in central New York."[1] During the first westward migration from Connecticut and Massachusetts, these settlers drove ox-carts into the northern wilderness below the St. Lawrence River and Lake Ontario, and established, between the Adirondacks and the Finger Lakes, a cultivated extension of New England.

Like his much-admired Oliver Wendell Holmes, the subject of the finest chapter of *Patriotic Gore*, Wilson, a solid member of the Eastern gentry, maintained the scholarly traditions of the preachers, lawyers, doctors, professors and men of letters in his family. His maternal grandfather graduated from Hamilton College in Clinton, New York, and became a physician. He practiced homeopathic medicine in Eatontown, New Jersey, and encountered considerable opposition from the more orthodox doctors. In 1887 he delivered the future critic and playwright Alexander Woollcott, who was born in the North River Phalanx, a socialist community near Red Bank, New Jersey. In 1971 Wilson dedicated *Upstate: Records and Recollections of Northern New York* "To the Memory of My Grandfather, Walter Scott Kimball, 1828–1890"—who died five years before Wilson was born. Walter's sons Reuel and Paul also became physicians.

Wilson's paternal grandfather, Thaddeus, a graduate of Amherst College and Princeton Theological Seminary, became the Presbyterian minister in Shrewsbury, New Jersey. Wilson inherited from his family a profound hostility to the commercial mentality of the capitalistic class. He felt that he and his forebears represented the idealistic spirit that studies and understands, and opposed the materialistic spirit that acquires and consumes. In four different books he emphasized that "the commercial development [following] the Civil War extinguished the old enthusiasm for culture along with the republican ideals and made cultivated people in general ashamed of the United States."

His father, Edmund Sr., born in Shrewsbury on December 15, 1863, was educated at Exeter, Princeton and Columbia Law School. At Princeton, in the class of 1885, he edited the *Princetonian* and was forcefully drilled in French by an exiled Polish general, who cursed at his students as if they were troops. He was admitted to the bar in 1888, and became attorney general of New Jersey under Governor J. Franklin Fort in 1908. Though a lifelong Republican, he continued to serve under the Democratic governor, Woodrow Wilson, until 1914. Woodrow Wilson (no relation), whom Edmund Sr. called "an animated corpse," often came to the house and impressed the rest of the family. A member of local debating, fishing and shooting clubs, Edmund Sr. was a popular after-dinner speaker, whose printed addresses were piously preserved by his son. In a front-page obituary, the *Red Bank Register* stated: "With his eloquence he combined a great deal of common sense and an acute mind as to the intricacies of the law. He stood in the front rank of New Jersey lawyers."

A tall, good-looking man with an intense expression, a trim moustache and an air of worldly superiority, Edmund Sr. was, like his son, never snobbish about race or class. But he gave orders (as his son later did) with a dictatorial tone and a barely restrained impatience. His law firm, Nevius and Wilson, was modestly located above a liquor dealer (he himself never drank) in the Hendrickson Building on Front Street in Red Bank. He maintained a modest standard of prosperity, provided his family with good food, private schools and extensive travel. "But his love of independence and his distrust of big business," his son wrote, "were so great that he stuck all his life to his miscellaneous local practice and resisted all temptations to become a corporation lawyer in a state governed by corporations."[2]

A crack trial lawyer, Edmund Sr. lost only one case, early on in his legal career, and successfully defended several murderers in highly-publicized trials. Woodrow Wilson, who wrongly thought that his attorney general was allied with the corrupt political machine of his opponents, "tried to embarrass [Edmund Sr.] by demanding that he investigate Atlantic City, a huge Republican racket, which he imagined my father would not dare to touch." Using an obscure law, he brought in honest jurors from another county, tried several hundred men and sent most of them, along with the boss, to jail.

Lawyer Wilson, sometime attorney for the Pennsylvania Railroad (which he despised), also did some war work. At President Wilson's request, he sorted out the complex affairs of the sequestered North German Lloyd shipping line. Edmund Jr. recalled, in a poignant essay (one of his finest) about his father: "The President had sounded him out as to whether he would fill the next Supreme Court vacancy. This, he felt, would be interesting enough to reconcile him to living in

Washington, and he said that he would accept. But no vacancy occurred during Wilson's term." A vacancy did, in fact, occur and Louis
Brandeis was appointed to the Supreme Court by Woodrow Wilson in
1916.

Edmund Jr. used thwarted idealism and antipathy to materialism to
explain the unusual career of his brilliant but ill-adjusted father. He
thought that his father's traditional education and learning had estranged him from the ruthless exploitation that characterized the
Gilded Age. Old-fashioned Americans like his father, who rejected the
mad pursuit of money, suffered an intolerable strain. In his essay on
the eccentric critic John Jay Chapman, whom Wilson identified with
his father, he expanded the idea he had first expressed in his autobiographical essay "The Case of the Author" (1932): "By the later years of
the eighties, the industrial and commercial development which followed the Civil War had reached a point where the old education was
no longer an equipment for life. It had, in fact, become a troublesome handicap. The best of the men who had taken it seriously were
launched on careers of tragic misunderstanding. They could no longer
play the role in the professions of a trained and public-spirited caste:
the new society did not recognize them." Twenty years later, in "The
Author at Sixty," Wilson concluded that men like his father "had to
deal with a world in which this kind of education and the kind of ideals
it served no longer really counted for much."[3] During the boom of the
1920s, the high-minded Edmund Jr. would find himself in a similar
dilemma.

Wilson's mother, Helen Mather Kimball, was born in Eatontown,
New Jersey, on April 20, 1865. Only five feet tall, she had brown eyes
and the same sharp pointed nose, thin mouth, round plump face and
small receding chin as Queen Victoria. She was called Nelly, attended
Abbot Academy in Andover, Massachusetts and wrote sentimental poetry (which her son also saved). While on holiday in Asbury Park,
Wilson's mother had met Stephen Crane's mother, a public lecturer
and journalist who wrote on religious and social subjects. Crane published *The Red Badge of Courage* the year Edmund was born.

Helen Kimball, who could (like her son) be tactlessly blunt, occupied herself with dogs, gardening, bridge-playing and antique-col-
lecting. A voracious but indiscriminate reader of popular novels, she
was lively and shrewd. But she was rather prejudiced against the more
intellectual members of the family, and liked to say: "I can't bear 'em
bright." Lawyer Wilson, who had been Dr. Kimball's chess partner for

many years, was attracted (Edmund Jr. wrote) "by her positive, self-confident, determined nature, because he had been used to depending on the support of his mother's strong character. . . . But my mother, I think, married my father only because there was no one else. Aside from their professional parents, they had nothing whatever in common, and the longer they were married, it seemed to me, the more they became estranged." Helen married Edmund Sr. shortly before her twenty-seventh birthday, on March 9, 1892. After his death, she ignored the realities of their marriage and fondly recalled: "I was a funny, fat little thing, who married the best man who ever lived."

Edmund Sr. paid a great deal of attention to his clothes and was photographed in a high wing-collar, a necktie transfixed by a shiny pearl pin and a creamy striped waistcoat under a conservatively cut jacket. He loved to travel but could never agree with Helen about their destination. She wanted to go to lively, fashionable and luxurious resorts, which he found tedious, while she was bored by his earnest quests for culture. Their other principal disagreement concerned her desire for an elaborate new house. When she cancelled his itinerary, he retaliated by cancelling her architectural plans. The contrast in their characters was reflected in their very different sense of humor. Helen played a joke on her husband by going to the window and exclaiming that she had just seen an accident. When her husband rushed to look, she cried "April Fool!" and he solemnly declared: "Madame, I don't think that's funny."[4]

The mental illness on both sides of the family was much more serious than their temperamental differences. Uncle Paul Kimball suffered from terrible depressions, and Edmund Sr. spent all his later years in and out of mental homes. His son noted that by the time Edmund Sr. was thirty-five (three years after his son was born) he "was subject to neurotic eclipses, which came to last longer and prove more and more difficult to cope with. He suffered from hypochondria." He elaborated on this illness when describing the narrator's father in his novel, *I Thought of Daisy*: "He was nervous and hypochondriacal, and used to shut himself up for days in his room, and refuse to see anybody. . . . He finally had the whole household so that it was just like some kind of sanatorium—the doors were all muffled with felt, and he couldn't stand to have a light burning or to hear a sound after he'd gone to bed himself."

Edmund Sr., terrified of disease and obsessed with the idea that his gall bladder had to be removed, endured the unnecessary operation in

order to save himself from insanity. After two more superfluous surger-
ies, the family found it difficult to prevent him from excising all his
expendable organs. While under the care of a nurse at home, lawyer
Wilson pathetically asked his son if he thought his career was finished.
Though his father spent more and more time shut up in his room
behind the felt-covered door, he could, when necessary, summon up
hidden sources of energy: "When he felt that the money was running
low, he would emerge from his shadow or exile and take on a couple of
cases, enough work to retrieve the situation."

During one of his "rest cures" in Europe, Edmund Sr. was examined by an eminent London neurologist, who rather brutally told his
wife: "Your husband is mad." This announcement had a traumatic
effect. On the boat back from Europe "she became deaf—literally
overnight—and never regained her hearing." Helen could only grasp
certain words if she used an ear trumpet or if someone shouted directly
into her ear. Though there was no physical cause for Helen's deafness,
she claimed to have "gout of the ear," a disease which would, in any
case, have affected her outer ear but not her hearing. It seems clear that
she developed "hysterical deafness" so that she would never have to
hear any more bad news and that "gout" was merely a polite explanation which prevented embarrassment about her deeper psychological
problems.[5]

II

Edmund Wilson, the son of a neurotic and hypersensitive lawyer, was
born in Red Bank, New Jersey, on May 8, 1895 and baptized on August
31 at his grandfather's First Presbyterian Church in nearby Shrewsbury. Though the stability and progress of the nineteenth century were
still taken for granted, contemporary events were eating away at the old
order. In 1895 the Jameson Raid, which foreshadowed the Boer War,
took place in South Africa and the Turks practiced genocide by massa-
cring the Armenians in Constantinople. Röntgen invented the X-ray
and Marconi the wireless telegraph. Friedrich Engels, whom Wilson
would write about in *To the Finland Station*, died and Freud, whose
insights he would employ in *The Wound and the Bow*, published *Studies
in Hysteria*. Henry James, Joseph Conrad, Oscar Wilde and H. G.
Wells all brought out important books that influenced the course of
literary modernism.

Red Bank, New Jersey, about thirty-five miles south of Manhattan and five miles from the ocean, was built on high terraces, green and sheer, overlooking the Navesink River. According to Wilson's cousin, "Red Bank was where the nearby Rumson people went shopping or took their Irish maids to mass. Rumson was the place where Wall Street millionaires built mansions and enjoyed playing in their clubs."

The large, gloomy, ugly and uncomfortable Wilson house, built in a typical middle-class suburb in the 1880s, was located quite near the run-down part of town. The black jazz pianist Count Basie—the other eminent citizen of Red Bank—was born there in 1904. The Wilsons' yellow and brown residence at 100 McLaren Street stood on a big corner plot that bordered on a large estate. It had shuttered windows on the first two floors and dormer windows on the top floor, a covered porch around the front and side, and a prominent stained-glass window. In "A House of the Eighties" (1935) Wilson later recalled:

> The ugly stained-glass window on the stair,
> Dark-panelled dining-room, the guinea fowls' fierce clack,
> The great grey cat that on the oven slept—
> My father's study with its books and birds,
> His scornful tone, his eighteenth-century words.

Wilson's mother nicknamed him "Bunny" in the nursery. When he later asked her where she got the name, she explained that as a black-eyed baby he "looked just like a plum bun." The shy, sensitive and nervous young man retained the childishly apt Bunny throughout his life; and in middle age—all pink and white and round—seemed to grow into his name. His oldest friends, from schooldays through the twenties, always called him Bunny. After that, he became more formidable and was known to more recent friends as Edmund.

Though Bunny came from a long line of ministers, he reacted against the old-fashioned Bible-worship and recoiled from the rigors of Calvinism. His grandfather was a moderate Presbyterian, and he remembered: "When my parents went to church on Sunday, they would leave me with my formidable [paternal] grandmother, who undertook my instruction in the Scriptures. These bleak and severe Sunday mornings, though they left me with a respect for the Bible, had the effect of antagonizing me against it, and this attitude was tacitly encouraged by the moral sabotage of my mother, whose family, once-rigorous New Englanders, had scrapped the old-time religion and still retained a certain animus toward it."

Bunny, a spoiled and egoistic only child, felt safe and invulnerable in his own domain. But his apparent security was undermined by troubled dreams and by tense relations with his self-absorbed and difficult parents. Though he received a great deal of attention, he also felt dominated by his lonely mother, who tried to control the lives of those she loved. He once had an Oedipal dream about going to bed with his mother; and also dreamt that his father was not only a sexual rival but even a threat to his life: "[I] had a childhood dream that I saw my father in the kitchen in his maroon dressing gown . . . sharpening a carving knife in order to kill us all."

Though his father threatened to whip him, he never actually touched the boy. His mother was much tougher than the high-strung invalid. "She was brusque and gruff like my uncle," Wilson recalled, "and her reprimands were always intended and not due to loss of control. In childhood, she would spank me with a silver-backed brush, which she would then complain had been dented." Starved for affection, Wilson later complained to his wives that his mother had never kissed him. His third wife, Mary McCarthy, hated her mother-in-law and gave a savage description of the old lady. She also explained the deeper reasons for the mother's hostility toward her son, who (Helen felt) had prevented her from having other children: "She was a stumpy downright old lady with an ear trumpet and a loud, deaf voice. She looked like a warthog. . . . [Wilson] believed that she held it against him that his large head had torn her vaginal tissues as he was being born. There was not much love lost between them."[6]

His relations with his father were also troubled. Wilson was thinking of Edmund Sr. when he wrote in "Woodrow Wilson at Princeton" that the father's "influence upon his son seems to have been profound—perhaps the most important of Wilson's life." But the influence of Edmund's father, unlike Woodrow's, was largely negative. Edmund Sr. was either shut up in a sanatorium for "neurasthenics" or let loose to play the martinet at home, where he crushed his son with the same dictatorial tone that he used to intimidate witnesses in the courtroom. Bunny, who later unconsciously adopted his father's mode of conversation (an uneasy mixture of cross-examination and didactic pronouncements) was both humiliated and terrified in childhood:

> A permanent antagonism existed between my father and me, [and] I was always, in tastes and opinions, on the opposite side from him. . . . He was not an easy man to talk to: he almost eliminated

give-and-take, for his conversation mostly consisted of either asking people questions in order to elicit information or telling them
what to think. Our dinners at home, when we had no guests and
there were only my parents and I, were likely to turn into lectures. . . . My conversation with him usually took the form either
of his asking my view of some question, then immediately squelch-
ing this view and setting me right on the subject, or of explaining
at length, but with an expert lucidity, some basic point of law or
government.

Wilson's unhappy childhood was reflected in *The Wound and the
Bow*, where he formulated one of his most important ideas. He believed
that superior strength is inseparable from disability, "that genius and
disease, like strength and mutilation, may be inextricably bound up
together."[7] The "wound" of Wilson's childhood led directly to the
"bow" of his art, and to the nervous breakdown—at the same age as
his father's—which made him such a difficult husband and father.

Bunny, a selfish and demanding child, was trapped in the gloomy
old house with a severe, remote and melancholy father and a prosaic,
philistine and strong-willed mother. He found it very difficult to talk to
either parent. In any case, his mother was so remote and so deaf that he
had to think up things to say and then write her long letters, which she
could not always read. Emotionally strangled, cut off from both parents
and isolated from the outside world, Bunny lacked normal human
relations. He withdrew into books, was more interested in ideas than in
people, and always remained rather insensitive to the feelings of others.

Like many emotionally starved children, Wilson turned for affection to servants, cousins and friends. Jenny Corbett, a sixteen-year-old
girl, was hired by his parents soon after their marriage. Intelligent,
sensitive and affectionate, she taught Bunny to walk, became essential
to everyone in the family and remained with his mother for more than
fifty years. Bunny was also fascinated by the coachman, who looked
after the chickens, the guinea fowl and the single cow that gave the
house a rural touch. The sober and serious young man was the illegitimate mulatto son of a local white judge.

Bunny's closest friend and constant companion was his slightly
older first cousin, Sandy Kimball. The two restrained and generally
well-behaved lads were also capable of occasional mischief. One July 4,
the firecrackers they were playing with suddenly exploded and Edmund completely lost his eyelashes and eyebrows—making him more

Bunny-like than ever. This, however, proved advantageous to the red-headed boy, for his singed pink eyebrows eventually grew back in a darker and more manly fashion.

Sandy later became a terrifying example of the dangers of mental illness that lurked on both sides of the family. He went to prep school and college, spoke enthusiastically of his homosexual experiences, was rejected by his girlfriend, failed his medical school examinations and worried about not taking part in the war. He then became schizophrenic, passed into eclipse in the state mental hospital in Middletown, New York (just north of New Jersey) and was confined there for the rest of his life.

Bunny spent a good deal of time with Sandy at their grandfather's house in Lakewood, New Jersey, about twenty-five miles south of Red Bank. In his revealing essay, "At Laurelwood" (1939), Wilson contrasted this comfortable house—with its doctor's office, library and conservatory—with the fabulous mansion of their neighbor, Jay Gould, Jr., son of the railroad baron and one of the richest men in America, to show the difference between families with culture and those with money. The young Bunny was shocked when the Gould boy ordered the footman to get out of the pony cart and fetch some green apples, and then explained: "These men must do their duty." Though Bunny's family also had servants, he would never have been allowed to behave in so arrogant a manner. At Lakewood, Bunny developed two interests that would last a lifetime: a taste for yellow lady's-slipper orchids and for Richard Barham's fantastical *Ingoldsby Legends*.

Wilson later remarked that until he left for prep school, the members of his family were the only people he knew really well. But he did have at least one close childhood friend outside the family, Margaret Edwards. Since her mother did not believe in germs, the little girl used to be brought to his house to amuse him when he had a cold. In her seventies, Margaret could still recall their early years in Red Bank, their education at dame schools, Bunny's shyness and the beginning of his lifelong interest in the theater—a notable occasion that once again provoked Mrs. Wilson to dent her silver-backed hairbrush:

> Red Bank was a cultural center in those days. There were several theaters and opera houses here, like the Gilbert and Sullivan theater at Pleasure Bay. . . . Both children attended private schools that were then a part of the Red Bank social scene. They went first to Miss Ella Venderveer's elementary classes on Broad Street,

then to The Shrewsbury Academy on Leroy Place run by a Professor Talmadge. They also attended a dancing school located on the second floor of the borough hall.

"Edmund couldn't dance in those days, and he told me many years later that it made him lonely. . . . Edmund and I loved to put on plays. He would write the story and I drew the scenery and figures. I can't remember what they were about, they were so spontaneous. We would get very dramatic, and jump up and down on the beds and turn lights on and off for thunder and lightning effects. One day, Edmund and I went in the clothes closet with matches to make better lightning, and Mrs. Wilson came home. When she caught us, she spanked us both."

Wilson, who always kept in touch with his charming companion, sent her amusing and flirtatious poems:

A valentine greeting to Margaret Edwards,
Whom at three years of age I could sometimes lead bedwards
With much leaping about and ebullient laughter.
A pity it never happened after.[8]

But in childhood he approached sex, like most other experiences, through books. At an early age he had secretly read the perverse case histories in Havelock Ellis' voluminous *Studies in the Psychology of Sex* (1897–1910) in the medical office of Sandy's father. Bunny saw a naked little girl for the first time when a playmate called Betty Fox undressed in a bathhouse in Sea Bright, near Red Bank, on the Jersey shore.

Helen Wilson, aware of her son's isolation, tried to encourage him to lead a more normal life and to play with other children. On one occasion, while staying with his mother in a hotel in Atlantic City (where his father had fought the racketeers), he recited Longfellow's "The Ride of Paul Revere" during a performance with the other boys and girls. One of them politely said of Bunny: "He may be a very nice little boy even if he doesn't come from Philadelphia."

Helen was, rather surprisingly, passionately interested in collegiate athletics, and cherished the ill-founded wish that her scholarly son would turn into a jock: "She had hoped I would be an athlete, a change from my cerebral father—something more like her sportsman brother who had played on the football team. She was an enthusiastic follower of collegiate sport, and even in her old age she continued as long as she was able to go to football and baseball games at Princeton, and in the off season attended basketball for want of anything better."

According to Tom Matthews—who worked under Wilson on the *New Republic* in the 1920s and later became an editor of *Time* magazine —"His parents once tried to lure him out of doors and into the normal companionship of other boys by buying him a complete baseball outfit; he appeared at the baseball field with this equipment and made himself popular with the other boys by giving it all away, after which he retired underneath the nearest tree with his book." Wilson later denied the truth of this *ben trovato* anecdote, which contributed to his image as a perpetual old man, by maintaining: "It could not have been my 'parents,' in any case, who presented me with the equipment: my father was as unathletic as I was."

But this was not quite true. His father, unlike Bunny, was a keen outdoorsman. At the end of the day, still dressed in his lawyer's suit, he would go fishing in the Navesink River, and often dragged his unwilling son on hunting and fishing trips in Canada and northern New York. Helen's hopes for her son's sporting career were never to be realized. He himself wanted to be a professional magician (another lifelong interest) and had already discovered, when still quite small, that he was "a poet . . . or something of the kind."

Bunny attended Shrewsbury Academy, in the town where his grandfather was minister, and returned there in 1910, during his prep school years, to pay tribute to his wonderfully named old teacher, Lyttleton Sleeper. The local newspaper reported Wilson's somewhat priggish speech, which praised the spiritual values and idealistic influence of his genial master:

> Edmund Wilson, who was one of the pupils of the school, was the orator of the evening. His address was at times touching, humorous, and thoughtful. He dwelt largely on the impress which Mr. Sleeper had made on his pupils by his broad mind and kindly spirit, rather than on the definite rules of grammar and arithmetic which he taught. Of all his pupils, it was said, there were few, if any, who had strayed from the path of usefulness and righteousness. The standard of citizenship [in his former pupils was] . . . largely due to the spirit which prevailed in the little schoolhouse at Shrewsbury.[9]

Later on Wilson, always a devoted pupil, would write two of his finest essays on his prep school and college teachers.

III

The Wilsons spent nearly every summer in Talcottville, north of Utica, in the wilderness of upstate New York. The house that Helen had inherited from her maternal ancestors was to play an important part in the last two decades of her son's life. The family maintained its roots, Wilson wrote, and had "never really departed very far from the old American life of the countryside and the provincial cities with its simpler tastes and habits."

The town was named for Hezekiah Talcott, a Tory veteran of the American Revolution. With his son Jesse, born in Middletown, Connecticut, in 1775, Hezekiah came to the town of Leyden, Lewis County, in about 1798 to take up extensive lands and water rights on the Sugar River. In 1800, he built the Old Stone House with thick walls of Georgian limestone. The impressive three-story dwelling had high shuttered windows and two identical front porches, one above the other, supported by six elegant white pillars. In the stagecoach days the house had been acquired by the innkeeper Thomas Baker, who turned it into a high-class tavern and hotel that also served as town hall and post office, social center and source of supplies.

Helen Wilson was bored and depressed by the place. Despite her deafness, she was still gregarious and preferred fashionable resorts where there were things to do and people to meet. But Bunny, released from the constrictions of his immediate family, loved it in boyhood as much as he did in middle and old age. Happily united with his cousins, he biked and read, fished and swam in the river, played games, went on picnics and took excursions. He had an attractive, though much older cousin, the pretty Dorothy Furbish, whom he was always hoping to kiss. She later married Wilson's upstate friend, the law professor Malcolm Sharp. As he became more self-sufficient, Bunny came round for a time to his mother's gloomy view of Talcottville. As he told the poet Louise Bogan: "When I got older, I used to get depressed and irked when my parents came back every summer. It seemed like moping around in a tomb when life was going on elsewhere."

His father tried to alleviate the dullness by teaching him how to shoot a rifle, which Bunny refused to learn, and by arranging trips around New York and into Canada. Though he felt closer to his father in Talcottville, which seemed to relieve his intense anxieties, "it bored me [he said] to travel with him alone. But Sandy's presence made it great fun. He was actually very indulgent, and Sandy, with his willingness to play up to him, got on better with him than I did."

In the summer of 1908 the Wilsons, along with their extended family of cousins, uncles and aunts, sailed to Europe on the North German Line ship, *König Albert*. After stopping at the Azores, Gibraltar and La Linea in Spain, they disembarked in Naples. Bunny—in a diary, presented to him by Margaret Edwards—disdainfully called it "a very dirty place, full of howling dagoes."[10] They pressed on to Pompeii, Capri and Rome, where he threw a coin into the Fontana di Trevi and wished his pet dachshund was doing well without him. Continuing their precipitous pace, they traveled to Florence, Venice, Vienna and Karlsbad, in the Czech part of the Austro-Hungarian Empire, where, for the first time, they paused. At that stuffy spa, where most of the guests were being treated for internal disorders, they sat at outdoor cafés, listened to the band pump out waltzes by Franz Lehar and consumed quantities of good Pilsner beer. His father, who kept laughing in an unusually wild and hysterical way, drank the sulphurous waters and was treated for neurotic depression. His uncle Reuel, by contrast (foreshadowing Bunny's later life), went on alcoholic binges, suffered stupendous hangovers and was confined to bed for detoxification.

After a restful month in Karlsbad, they turned west to Nuremberg, where Bunny was fascinated by the medieval torture instruments, then visited Frankfurt, journeyed up the Rhine to Cologne, and saw Paris. Finally, they crossed the Channel to London, where Bunny went to three plays by Somerset Maugham (whom he came to despise), visited the mummies at the British Museum and saw Maskelyne's magic performance before returning home to start prep school.

During his formative years Wilson grew up with a secure place in upper-middle-class society (a position he was unable to maintain for most of his writing career) and became attached to his ancestral home. He was shy and sensitive; interested in flowers and in drama, fantasy and magic, and always absorbed in books. He felt alienated from his parents, developed a difficult, demanding character, and inherited from his father an irritable disposition and a peremptory mode of discourse. He learned something about sex, but would have no sexual experience until he was twenty-five. He endured the "wound" of his childhood, inherited a strain of melancholia and was highly susceptible to mental illness. But he discovered the delights of European travel, and had already chosen his literary vocation.

TWO

The Hill School and Princeton, 1908–1916

I

Though Wilson's father had gone to Exeter, he thought his old school left the students too much on their own. Sandy Kimball had entered St. Paul's in 1907, but Edmund was sent to The Hill, which then had a great academic reputation and seemed more suitable for a sensitive and immature adolescent. The school had been founded in 1851 on a hill in Pottstown, Pennsylvania, forty miles northwest of Philadelphia. The headmaster, Matthew Meigs, was a Presbyterian minister who came from Michigan but had recently served in Southern parishes. When the thirteen-year-old Wilson entered in 1908, just after returning from his first tour of Europe, the school was run by Matthew's son John, who had made extraordinary additions and improvements to the buildings and curriculum.

In his fine essay "Mr. Rolfe," Wilson contrasted the school with the town, which had more in common with D. H. Lawrence's coal-mining village in Nottinghamshire than with the placid suburban life of Red Bank. The school "rose like a segregated plateau in the midst of the little steel town—the narrow and cobbled streets where the greenery showed meagre in the spring, the slag pits and the blast furnaces that startled the new boys and kept them awake at night by blazes that would light up the whole room." To the young Wilson, the atmosphere of The Hill seemed to reflect the roughness that characterized industrialized areas of eastern Pennsylvania.

Helen Wilson, with typical tactlessness, called her son "Bunny" when she first brought him to the dormitory, and this name was gleefully taken up by the boys to mock the vulnerable newcomer. Wilson tried to fight the boys who derided him with "Bunny," but he could not take on the whole dorm and soon resigned himself to the burden of this childish nickname. He found the school, especially during his freshman year, as rigid and regimented as the army and a terrifying contrast to his comfortable life at home. He later described it in a series of emotionally charged words:

> The first days of my first fall at prep school were passed in complete confusion. We were always being shrieked at by bells, which uprooted us from what we were doing and compelled us to report somewhere else. We had to get there while the bell was still ringing, and I used to be swamped by the mob of boys pouring in and out of the classrooms and pushing along the corridors and porches, and finally arrive late in a panic. . . . Every moment of our time was disposed of; our whole life was regulated by bells; and—till we reached the Sixth Form, at any rate—we had hardly an hour of leisure.

The students managed, nevertheless, to do a certain amount of mischief, as Wilson (no longer the victim) boasted in a letter to his mother during his second year at The Hill. A professor had complained, with ironic exaggeration, of "gross indecency" when forty boys had failed to put their underwear in the weekly wash. And an unfortunate boy, who had been secretly reading in the toilet and could not therefore complain to the master, was locked in and "will have to stay there until we choose to let him out. Last night we threw a half dead mouse into Wilcox's room through the transom."[1]

The pressure at school was intensified by the moralizing speeches of visiting evangelists, who turned Wilson decisively and permanently against religion. As the grandson of a Presbyterian minister he had attended church and learned the Bible, but (influenced by his sceptical mother) had never felt a deep and vital faith. When he began to think independently about religion, he concluded that it was merely an absurd delusion, that there was not a shred of evidence for the survival of the human soul.

At that age, however, it took a certain stubborn self-sufficiency to resist these unremitting exhortations. Even the strong-minded Wilson was intimidated by the fanatical condemnation of sex. He later told his upstate friend Glyn Morris how Mrs. Meigs, the headmaster's wife, would counsel the boys against the endemic plagues of all prep schools —masturbation and homosexuality—which not only caused tell-tale black rings under the eyes but inexorably led to insanity. "She always expected," Morris wrote, "the boys to fall on their knees, confess all, be forgiven, and admonished never to do it again. Edmund didn't do this and was crushed because she told him, 'Your temptations will only be intellectual ones.'"

Wilson's story "Galahad" (1927) describes his reaction against the prevailing religious and moral attitudes at The Hill, and—influenced by a dominant theme in the works of D. H. Lawrence—portrays the clash between sterile religious principles and the fervent reality of sexual experience. In this schoolboy's fantasy, a repressed prig, who at first rejects the bold overtures of his school friend's rich and beautiful sister, is transformed into an awakened sensual being. When his friend's sister crawls into bed with him while he is a guest in her house, "Hart had a glimpse of her firm round breasts; he was surprised to find them so big: he had always supposed that girls' breasts were little low dotted things. He was shocked and recoiled from the sight, as if from something indecent; it drove him back into himself." Though he refuses to sleep with the girl, he belatedly changes his mind, escapes from the school and secretly returns to her home. But—in this stereotyped plot—she now rejects her newly-ardent admirer, who is tormented by disillusioned romanticism and frustrated love.

His French uncle André Champollion, noting Wilson's virginal innocence, crudely tried to encourage a more realistic attitude toward sex. While he was still at The Hill, André shocked him by referring to an imaginary girlfriend and suddenly exclaiming: "I don't mind you fucking Sally on the sofa, but I won't have you wipe your cock on my best lace curtains!"

Wilson's two outstanding teachers at The Hill balanced the religious and sexual fanaticism with humane values and learning. His English instructor, Dr. John Lester, drilled the students in grammar, sentence structure, prosody and rhetoric as thoroughly as if he were teaching them a foreign language. He taught Wilson a fundamental principle: one must develop a prose style with three essential qualities —"lucidity, force and ease." In a letter to Lester, written more than forty years after he graduated from The Hill, Wilson specified what he had absorbed from his old instructor: "The work you made us do, for example, in diagramming sentences gave me a grasp of the structure of the language which I regard as one of the most valuable things I learned at school. . . . I think it is a great advantage, at this stage of one's education, to be taught English by an Englishman."[2] In 1910 the young

Wilson had praised his master at Shrewsbury Academy for his "kindly spirit" rather than for his teaching "the definite rules of grammar." But in middle age he realized that the rigorous instruction he had received at The Hill from Dr. Lester and Mr. Rolfe was much more important.

Wilson's father wisely decided that he would learn Greek, just as he had decided he would go to The Hill rather than to Exeter. Alfred Rolfe, his beloved Greek teacher, was born in Concord, Massachusetts, in 1860, graduated (like Grandfather Thaddeus Wilson) from Amherst and studied classics in Dresden in the late 1880s. Wilson described Rolfe's attractive Germanic appearance and ambiguous expression, which "was full of an unusual sort of kindliness and humor pleasantly tempered with irony": "He was blond, with drooping-lidded blue eyes and a high-domed oval head, which was very inadequately thatched with strands of thin yellow hair, and he wore a yellow drooping moustache of the kind that was supposed to be English. . . . His expression remained enigmatic, and you could never be sure whether he was smiling at you or withering you with mock sweetness."

Wilson identified with Mr. Rolfe, recognizing in his teacher as well as in himself—before this aspect of his character had fully emerged— "a certain strain of the sybarite [that] coexisted with rectitude and discipline. . . . I [too] incurably disliked athletics, carried myself very badly, and loved to read in bed." Wilson also admired—though he was sometimes victimized by—Rolfe's pungency and sarcasm as well as his merciless demands, for "Mr. Rolfe shed on everything he dealt with a peculiar imagination and charm, and this held you even while you resented him." Rolfe once glared at a student named Fairfax Downey, who was slouching in his seat, and characteristically remarked: "Fairfax, slip up one vertebra and recite."[3]

In September 1908, just before leaving home for prep school, the rather lonely and withdrawn Wilson had wondered if he would ever find friends to share his intellectual interests. The Hill School engendered such friendships with Alfred Bellinger (who became a professor of classics at Yale), Stanley Dell (future translator of Jung), Walker Ellis (soon to be President of the Triangle Club at Princeton), Larry Noyes (his postwar roommate) and Ted Paramore (a close companion and sexual rival in the 1920s). Like Wilson, Bellinger, Dell and Ellis went from The Hill to Princeton, while Noyes and Paramore attended Yale. "For such students," Wilson proudly wrote in the *Hill School Bulletin* of 1958, "The Hill was providing an encouragement and a training which

I imagine were not surpassed—if, indeed, they were ever equalled—by any other school at that period."

Wilson admired the intellectual independence of Alfred Bellinger (with whom he frequently corresponded between 1912 and 1918), who once skipped a football game so he could read in The Hill library. Though Wilson hated the rough, brutal games on the cold autumn afternoons, and the wild cheers that intruded on his own more placid reflections, he never dared to miss the game and always went along with the crowd. Bellinger, however, believed that Wilson was "much better read, more independent of thought, much more of a literary person" than his classmates. Wilson's favorite childhood reading had been the Raffles books by E. W. Horning and "The Lady and the Tiger" by Frank Stockton. In prep school he came to admire George Borrow's *Lavengro*, Francis Thompson's poetry, Browning's *The Ring and the Book*, George Meredith's works and the major English and French nineteenth-century novelists. The entry on Wilson in *The Dial*, the Hill yearbook of 1912, gave his nickname as "Bunny," implied that he was a dull fellow and called him "exceedingly well read."

His grades, however, did not reflect his intellectual ability. Like many bright students, he preferred to pursue his own interests rather than study the prescribed curriculum. During the three terms of his sophomore year (1909–1910), for example, Wilson took a formidable array of classes: English, English Composition, Latin, Latin Composition, Greek, French, Algebra and Declamation. He earned his best (though not very good) grades during the spring term: dismal lows of 58 in Latin Composition and 59 in Algebra, highs of 81 in English and 84 in Declamation (the easiest course). This led to an overall average of 67.2 percent and placed him twenty-eighth—in the middle of a class of sixty. In the spring term of 1911, he took English, Latin, Latin Composition, Greek (where, under Rolfe's tutelage, he went up from 62 to 75), Greek Composition, French and History. In his junior year he earned his highest grades—75—in Latin Composition and French, which led to an overall average of 70 percent and put him only twentieth in a class of fifty-seven.

Wilson was a member of QED, the school debating club. But he really shone on the editorial board (along with Ellis and Dell, the editor-in-chief) of the *Hill School Record*, in which he first had the pleasure of seeing himself in print. He contributed a number of essays about prep school literary magazines in his "Exchanges" page; and also wrote on the poor quality of prep school poetry, on the influence on college writers of O. Henry, W. W. Jacobs, Conan Doyle and G. K. Chesterton; on the eighteenth-century authors Crabbe and Burke; and —predictably enough—on the pleasures of the library. In this school-prize essay, he described in loving detail "the library of a pleasant old-fashioned house where I used often to visit." This was primarily based on his grandfather's library, which he later evoked in "At Laurelwood."

Wilson also wrote eleven stories for the school magazine, two of which, influenced by the Raffles books, had charming Edwardian titles: "Mr. Holcrest and the Burglar" and "The Daring Flight of Addison Thinbridge." His other fiction included "The Conjuring Shop" (March 1910) about a couple who kept a magic store, and a rather recherché piece on the works of Aphra Behn. His most important story at The Hill, Wilson later told an interviewer, was ignited after reading *Tristram Shandy* and then an essay by the French critic Hippolyte Taine. "That was really the thing that started me off, my first literary stirrings. I did a paper on Sterne for my English master. What I produced was not a critical essay but a fictional study of Sterne, a psychological study."[4] In "The Successful Mr. Sterne: 'Lives of Great Men All Remind Us' " (April 1911), Wilson first found, under Taine's influence, the biographical method he would later employ in *To the Finland Station* and *The Wound and the Bow*.

II

The precociously learned Wilson—fortified by the discipline and idealism of The Hill—had no trouble gaining admission to Princeton, and followed his father and uncles to the university in 1912. Princeton had been founded in 1746 as a Presbyterian college and Jonathan Edwards, the Yale-educated theologian, had been an early president. In the 1770s its students included Aaron Burr, who later killed Alexander Hamilton in a duel; James Madison, who became the fourth president of the United States; the novelist H. H. Brackenridge and poet Philip Freneau. Booth Tarkington had founded the Triangle Club in the early 1890s; and Eugene O'Neill (whom Wilson would meet in the 1920s) had failed out, after a rebellious and dissipated year, in 1907.

The spire-filled college, surrounded by luxurious estates, rose out of the flat midlands of New Jersey. "The loveliest riot of Gothic architecture in America" was modeled on the Oxford quads just as the system of preceptors, founded by young Edmund's hero Woodrow Wilson (who had been president of the university before becoming governor of New Jersey and then wartime president of the United States), was based on the Oxford tutors. Anglophilia prevailed at Princeton, whose fifteen hundred male students followed a tradition of gentility, charm and honor. Princeton men carefully cultivated an easy grace and debonair irony, and tended to frown on seriousness and striving.

In his essay on the unpromising subject of New Jersey, written six years after he graduated from college, Wilson condemned the dingy towns, the seedy people and the boring landscape. But he gave an idealized picture of Princeton, frozen in a perfect present: "Here where clear windows and polished knockers are still bright on Colonial houses, where Nassau Hall, in dry grace of proportion, still wears the dignity of the eighteenth century, the eternal lowland haze becomes charming, the languor a kind of freedom. . . . It is as if life were on the point of stopping, turning no face to the future, not caring if the future ever comes." "In Princeton," Wilson later wrote in *A Prelude*, "almost everything was amenity: green campus, flowering shrubs, new buildings with Gothic fancywork, agreeable eating clubs, undergraduate elegance and gaiety."[5]

But Wilson, especially as a student, was quite critical of Princeton's narrow Presbyterianism and wealthy suburbanism, and exasperated by the meaningless laxity of the place. Woodrow Wilson had stiffened the academic standards. But his successor, the current president John Grier Hibben, was in Edmund's view a barely competent mediocrity. The professor who taught Wilson the Bible and treated Jesus from the "historical point of view," was dismissed by Hibben as soon as his book appeared. Though the preceptorials, or small discussion groups that supplemented the formal lectures, were designed to establish a more intimate relation between student and instructor, many of these young teachers were dull and disappointing. Wilson agreed with his friend and classmate John Peale Bishop that most of the English professors were "old boys with a weakness for pedantry." Wilson thought Alfred Noyes, a popular minor poet and author of "The Highwayman," "was a smug middle-class Englishman of the kind that Shaw liked to caricature and the Sitwells lived to shock. I always thought his poetry a fake." And the pompous ass Duncan Spaeth made himself ridiculous by including Whitman in his course on nineteenth-century poetry and then demeaning his achievement by stating: "Walt Whitman—born on Long Island, died in Camden—found life beautiful!"[6]

The charming but philistine students, with few exceptions, were no better than the teachers. Bishop pointed out that though "the entrance requirements of Princeton are as high as those of any university in the country, the average boy at entrance is little better than literate." Such a boy would not progress very far under the tutelage of Noyes and Spaeth. The "exceedingly well read" and studious Wilson, fresh from the rigors of The Hill, was a far cut above his fellows. In "Disloyal Lines to an Alumnus," written in 1934 when the stock and bond markets were in a desperate state, Wilson satirically described Princeton nestled amidst

> Deep woods, sweet lanes, wide playing fields, smooth ponds —Where clean boys train to sell their country's bonds.

In his essay on John Jay Chapman three years later, Wilson (who had no desire to enter his father's law firm) repeated his disdain for the base aspirations of his classmates. They "had no higher object, on graduating, than to qualify for selling bonds or to slip behind some desk in a family concern and present a well-brushed appearance."

The life of a freshman was hedged about with the same sort of restrictions that Wilson had chafed against at The Hill. Daily chapel was compulsory until September 1915. In "The Fettered College," published in the *Nassau Literary Magazine* in February 1915, Wilson objected to the fact that first-year students were forbidden to walk on Prospect Street, where the social clubs were grandly housed, and had to wear black shoes, black jerseys, black ties, hard collars and little black caps. Wilson was also forced to participate in brutal and loathsome ordeals, supposed to engender class spirit, like "the big freshman rush, in which the sophomores would hold the doors of the gym and try to prevent the freshmen from charging into it."

Another irritating regulation of the college required Wilson to take courses for which he had no aptitude, interest or use. He failed coordinate geometry and got a low grade in chemistry, where he tended to attach the Bunsen burner to the water pipe instead of the gas pipe and (as in a Chaplin comedy) get a spurt of water in his face. In June 1915, at the end of his junior year, he earned a dismal C in English, a surprisingly higher grade of B in Plane Geometry as well as in his courses on Virgil and Homer, and only one A: in Greek Composition. Still inspired by Alfred Rolfe, Wilson was one of the very few students who loved the classics enough to take Greek and Latin throughout his college career. He liked to ride around the countryside on his spiffy new bike and once threw himself off balance, just after buying Liddell and Scott's heavy Greek dictionary, by swinging the book with one hand. In "Princeton, April, 1917," he recalled how he was stimulated by reading the classics and would "Wear out the night with Plato in my room / To meet the morning with a crystal mind."

At Princeton, unlike most major universities, professors cultivated the brightest students and often invited them to dinner. In this way, Wilson came to know his two outstanding teachers—Norman Kemp Smith and Christian Gauss (both of whom became lifelong friends) —both socially and intellectually. Kemp Smith, born in Dundee in 1872, taught for many years at Princeton and then returned to Britain when the Great War broke out to take up the Chair of Moral Philosophy at the University of Edinburgh. In his tribute to Kemp Smith in *A Prelude* (whose title evoked Wordsworth's major poem on the "Growth of a Poet's Mind"), Wilson praised not only his teaching but also his character, his intellect and his wide range of interests: "He was one of the most admirable men I have ever known and one of the most rewarding. He had written on Descartes, [Hume] and Kant and was a master of technical philosophy, but philosophy meant for Kemp Smith the study of everything that men had thought about themselves and their world, so that he was interested to talk about anything. . . . Swaying from side to side and regarding us from under that solemn brow, [he would] explain, in his full deep Scotch, the closely linked chain of philosophic thought through the centuries."[7] Wilson traveled to London and to Edinburgh to see Kemp Smith when he visited Europe in 1921 and in 1945.

The most important influence on Wilson at Princeton was Christian Gauss, who became a surrogate father and gave him the emotional and intellectual companionship he never received from the remote and austere Edmund Sr. Gauss' father, who came from Baden, emigrated to the United States after participating in the abortive German revolution of 1848. Gauss himself, born thirty years later in a German-speaking household in Ann Arbor, graduated from the University of Michigan at the age of twenty. The highly respectable Gauss had once enjoyed a bohemian phase as foreign correspondent, literary reviewer and would-be poet in the Paris of the late 1890s. He had grown long blond hair, worn a green velvet jacket with a flowing Latin Quarter tie and bought drinks for Oscar Wilde during his homosexual exile. Gauss taught Romance languages at Michigan and Lehigh until 1905, when Woodrow Wilson invited him to Princeton as a preceptor. He built up the modern languages department, was dean of the college from 1925 to 1945 and retired the following year.

Wilson's superb memoir of Gauss, which complements his tribute to Mr. Rolfe, was written in 1951 (after Gauss' fatal heart attack in Penn Station) and opened Wilson's best collection of literary reviews, *The Shores of Light*. In this memoir Wilson affectionately describes Gauss' "pale cheeks and shuttered gaze, his old raincoat and soft felt hat, and [his] shabby mongrel dog named Baudelaire," and suggests that Gauss stood at an oblique angle to the college: he "seemed to meet the academic world in a slightly constrained self-consciousness at not having much in common with it. . . . He wore golf stockings and even played golf. He interested himself in the football team." Though Gauss was a superficial writer, he had—like Kemp Smith—unusual moral and intellectual qualities. Like Wilson himself, Gauss "lived in an intellectual world of which he was perfect master, which included many centuries and countries, the past and the immediate present." His "infinite learning, infinite range of interest, infinite intelligence and sympathy" made him an inspiring teacher. In his poem on Gauss, written in 1920, Wilson,

> Watching his clear green eyes, as hard and as fine as gems,
> Heard him speak of books and politics and people,
> With his incredible learning and his cloudless mind.[8]

Gauss' essay on Wilson at Princeton, published in 1944, provides a nice balance to Wilson's memoir of Gauss. Like Wilson, Gauss describes Princeton as static and fixed in the past, as a pleasant and isolated place where the students "lived outwardly at least in a kind of campus dream world which had come down to them with little change from the Golden Nineties" and which was scarcely affected by the European war that broke out in the summer of 1914. Gauss met Wilson that year and found him "red-haired, eager, tireless" and bubbling with ideas. Countering the prevailing view of Wilson as a solemn grind, Gauss emphasized his sense of humor and remarked: "There was nothing of the 'esthete' or the 'gloom' about him. He loved a good joke."

Wilson, "a brilliant student of classics, philosophy and modern languages," took Gauss' classes in Italian and French literature during his junior and senior years, and learned to study every word when reading a foreign language. Under Gauss' guidance, he developed an intense and lasting admiration for his two literary idols: Dante and Flaubert. Wilson acknowledged Gauss' powerful intellectual influence in his generous dedication to *Axel's Castle* (1931), his innovative study of modern Symbolist poets and novelists: "Dear Christian Gauss: You will see how these essays have grown out of your lectures of fifteen years ago. But it is not merely on that account that I have felt I owe you a debt in connection with them. It was principally from you that I acquired then my idea of what literary criticism ought to be—a history of man's ideas and imaginings in the setting of the conditions which have shaped them."[9] Thus Wilson, following Gauss, expressed his literary credo.

III

Outside of class, Wilson's life focused on his social club, on the Triangle musicals and on the *Nassau Literary Magazine*. Wilson "stuck together" with Stanley Dell and other friends from The Hill, and joined Charter. It was a respectable choice but not—like Ivy, Tiger, Cottage, Cap and Gown—one of the elite clubs. After being elected to Charter in his sophomore year, Wilson realized he had very little in common with the rich and handsome blockheads in the club and scarcely knew what to do there. Since he had no interest in sports, did not play billiards or bridge, did not dance or drink, and did not know any girls to bring to the parties, there was nothing to interest or occupy him. In fact, he had joined Charter only because he did not want to be left out. He actually considered the clubs "the most undesirable of Princeton institutions—not so much because they are snobbish . . . but because they are hopelessly dull. Nothing interesting is ever done in them." Haughty and aloof, at odds with both the wealthy students and the athletes, and still essentially a loner, he much preferred to read by himself in his room.

But even reading could be troubling to the young man who was supposed to have only "intellectual" temptations. During his senior year, sitting in his favorite Morris chair with a serious book in his hand, he would suddenly have a spontaneous ejaculation. He naturally longed for girls and fantasized, when he stayed in hotels, about amorous adventures with chambermaids. But he was terribly shy with both servants and girls of his own class; and was bored by the conventional young ladies, whom many of his college friends would marry and divorce. "My feminine ideal at this time," Wilson recalled, "was not the kind of girl that I saw at the proms, but one of those lively and slender brunettes, capable of serious interests, for whom the heroes in H. G. Wells' [*The New Machiavelli*] abandoned their passive wives." But such girls, while Wilson was at Princeton, seemed as distant as the stars. In the yearbook of 1916, the man who would have four wives was rated "the most eligible bachelor" in his class.

"Outside of athletics," wrote John Peale Bishop in his essay on Princeton, "the most powerful organization is the Triangle Club, an unwieldy and smart assemblage, which each year tours a dozen cities, presenting a musical comedy written, book and music, by the undergraduates on a lively but slightly antiquated model."[10] During the Christmas vacation, the Club performed the play—with chorus, orchestra and scenery, and men in the female parts—throughout the country. In 1913 Wilson told a friend that he was writing Triangle Club songs under the influence of Gilbert and Sullivan. Two years later, Wilson wrote the book, Scott Fitzgerald did the lyrics and John Bishop acted in the Triangle Club musical, *The Evil Eye*.

The villain of the play is named Count La Rochefoucauld-Boileau (after two major authors in Gauss' French Literature course), the setting is a Normandy fishing village called Niaiserie (silliness) and the plot concerns the survivor of a shipwreck, who has lost her money and is rescued by a man reputed to have the evil eye. On November 6, 1915, the *Princetonian* explained: "The taking of the girl by Boileau and the arrest of Jacques on the instigation of the peasants form a tangle from which the hero and heroine are able to extricate themselves only in time for the last curtain." Though some of the audience found the musical a bit too exotic and literary, the *Princetonian* of January 7, 1916, proudly reported: "At the Chicago performance of *The Evil Eye* three hundred young ladies occupied the front rows of the house and following the show, gave the Princeton locomotive and tossed their bouquets at the cast and chorus." *The Evil Eye: A Comedy in Two Acts*, published as a twenty-six-page pamphlet in 1915, was Wilson's first book.

Wilson's work on the *Nassau Literary Magazine*, like that on the *Hill School Record*, reflected his new interests and discoveries, and prepared him for his journalistic career in the early 1920s. Wilson contributed his first essay as a freshman, was put on the editorial board that year by T. K. Whipple (later a professor at Berkeley) and became managing editor during his senior year. While at Princeton Wilson, always versatile and prolific, wrote parodies, theater reviews, editorials, short stories, poems on Swift and on Whistler, and appreciative essays on Stendhal, George Meredith, Henry James, Arnold Bennett, Max Beerbohm and Compton Mackenzie. (Later on, he would visit the last two writers and express his admiration in person.) He also reviewed Gauss' lightweight *Through College on Nothing a Year* and wrote a parodic memoir, "Edward Moore Gresham: Poet and Prose-Master," which he later felt was good enough to reprint in *Vanity Fair*. Disdainful of his literary efforts, the philistines in the class retaliated by voting Wilson "the worst poet."

Gradually emerging from his shell, Wilson formed many rich and lasting friendships at Princeton. Since his cousin Sandy Kimball was a year ahead of him and belonged to a different club, they drifted apart and saw very little of one another. Walker Ellis, the dashing figure from New Orleans, who had been the most showily brilliant fellow at The Hill, became president of the Triangle Club. But he quickly faded in the 1920s, when Wilson found his outwardly genial smile quite arrogant and offensive. Always grateful for T. K. Whipple's recognition and help, Wilson later wrote an introduction to his book, *Study Out the Land* (1941), in which he described his old friend as "a long-legged, loose-jointed fellow, with pale blond hair and a Missouri drawl, whose expression, with its wide grin, seemed at once sad and droll."

John Biggs, whose grandfather had been governor of Delaware and whose father was (like Wilson's) attorney general, had a booming voice, an impressive head and a powerful build. He published two novels with Scribner's in the 1920s, and became the youngest judge named to the Third U.S. Circuit Court of Appeals. Wilson turned to Biggs for advice and help during his divorces and tax troubles, when both men had become solidly pear-shaped. In 1953 Wilson wrote a fine tribute to his old classmate: "The kind of American to whom I am really closest is someone—very rare—like John Biggs."[11]

Stanley Dell and John Peale Bishop both served with him on the editorial board of the *Nassau Lit*. The monkey-faced Dell had been, like Bishop, handicapped by poor health in his youth; and had spent a great deal of time in Europe, where he mastered French and German. Dell won the Croix de Guerre during the war and later became a disciple of

Jung. Dell, again like Bishop, never quite fulfilled his promise. But, Wilson later wrote, he was more at home with Dell, who had absorbed European culture, than with any of his old friends.

Born in West Virginia in 1892, Bishop, an invalid in childhood, attended Mercersburg Academy in Pennsylvania and entered college a few years after his contemporaries. Christian Gauss praised Bishop's exquisite poetry and sophisticated character: "He came to Princeton with a more carefully thought out and more accomplished mastery of the technique of English verse than any other undergraduate of that talented group. Even as a freshman John had a self-possession and self-mastery which gave him the poise and bearing of a young English lord." Scott Fitzgerald, intrigued by Bishop's scholarly and aesthetic persona, found him anachronistic and decadent. In his first novel, *This Side of Paradise*, he portrayed the sandy-haired, crack-voiced, foxy-faced Bishop as Thomas Parke D'Invilliers, an "awful highbrow . . . who signed the passionate love-poems in the *Lit*. He was, perhaps, nineteen, with stooped shoulders, pale blue eyes, and . . . without much conception of social competition."

Bishop won all the literary prizes as an undergraduate. After college he continued to cultivate his precious persona, and later told an editor: "As to my tastes, I like to eat and drink, and above all to talk; I am fond of looking at paintings, sculpture, architecture and formal gardens; in a very modest way, I paint and garden myself. In particular, I like the architecture of humanism and the music of the eighteenth century. I prefer the ballet—at its best—to the theatre. I no longer care very much for reading, except for information."[12] Bishop published his first volume of poems in 1917, served overseas as a lieutenant in the infantry, and was Wilson's colleague and collaborator in the early 1920s.

Wilson's most charming and talented friend at Princeton was his lyrical co-author of *The Evil Eye*, Scott Fitzgerald. Born in St. Paul, Minnesota, in 1896, Fitzgerald was the son of a genteel father, who had failed in the furniture and the soap business, and an embarrassingly eccentric daughter of a self-made Irish-immigrant grocer. He attended Newman, an obscure Catholic prep school, failed out of Princeton (without even learning to spell) during his junior year, and spent the war years pursuing his social life and writing career while stationed in American army camps.

The stocky, plain, auburn-haired Wilson was a contrast in every way to the blond, green-eyed and dazzlingly handsome Fitzgerald.

Repressed and self-conscious, the rather solitary Wilson spent most of his time on his studies and the *Nassau Lit.*, while the spontaneous and romantic Fitzgerald ignored his classes and devoted himself to getting into the best club, achieving success with the Triangle musicals and courting wealthy debutantes.

At Princeton Wilson had the advantages of distinguished lineage, professional background and superior education. A year ahead of Fitzgerald, he corrected Scott's one-act play "Shadow Laurels" and his story "The Ordeal" and published them in the college magazine in 1915. To Fitzgerald, Wilson appeared smug and arrogant, a well-dressed and withdrawn grind, while to Wilson, Scott seemed ignorant, shallow and foolish. It was understood between them that Fitzgerald was the brash superficial upstart, destined to make a splash but perhaps also doomed to failure, while Wilson was the solid intellectual who would set him straight.

In January 1916 Wilson and Bishop published in the *Nassau Lit.* a rather cruel satiric poem designed to put the cheeky Fitzgerald in his proper place. They contrasted his shallowness to their learning, and deflated his flashy cleverness, superficial reading, derivative cynicism, unworthy ambition and failure to graduate by having Fitzgerald exclaim:

> I was always clever enough
> To make the clever upperclassmen notice me;
> I could make one poem by Browning,
> One play by Shaw,
> And part of a novel by Meredith
> Go further than most people
> Could do with the reading of years;
> And I could always be cynically amusing at the expense
> Of those who were cleverer than I
> And from whom I borrowed freely,
> But whose cleverness
> Was not of the kind that is effective
> In the February of sophomore year. . . .
> No doubt by senior year
> I would have been on every committee in college,
> But I made one slip:
> I flunked out in the middle of junior year.

Fitzgerald, still as sexually innocent as Wilson, was capable of upholding moral standards, though he could not resist boasting about his virtue. In June 1916 Wilson, Bishop and Alex McKaig (soon to be a close observer of Fitzgerald's early married life) were walking on Nassau Street. "Two girls passed us," Wilson recalled. "Alex said, 'They're hookers!' I had not known we had hookers in Princeton, and, in fact, had never heard the word before. John and Alex went off with the girls, while Scott and I took a walk down the hill to the lake. 'That's one thing,' exclaimed Scott, 'that Fitzgerald's never done!'"

In 1914 Wilson broadened his education by spending the summer in England. With Stanley Dell and three other college friends, he took a ship to Liverpool and bicycled from Edinburgh to Tintagel, on the north coast of Cornwall. During the era of the Anglophile expatriate, Wilson thought of England "with awed ecstasy." He read Wordsworth's *Prelude* in the Lake Country and visited many cathedral towns; saw Bernard Shaw's *Pygmalion*, with Mrs. Patrick Campbell, three times and made a pilgrimage to George Meredith's house in Box Hill, Surrey. He also attended a reading by Rupert Brooke in Harold Munro's Poetry Bookshop, and was surprised to find that the handsome idol had a weak and effeminate voice. When the Great War broke out on the August 4 Bank Holiday, Wilson felt annoyed that it prevented him from traveling to France. He was also astonished by the popular enthusiasm and frivolous excitement of the crowds standing outside Buckingham Palace and calling for the King and Queen. He returned on the American liner *Minnehaha* (later torpedoed by the Germans), and shocked his father by admitting that he had failed to visit Parliament.

The next summer Wilson, together with Stanley Dell, decided to balance his emphasis on the humanities by taking a course in labor relations at Columbia University. He was then rewarded by a train trip with his parents—through Canada, with stops in Winnipeg and Seattle—to San Francisco. Wilson was impressed by the musical performances and the elaborate displays of art and architecture at the Panama-Pacific International Exposition. But he was deeply suspicious of the romantic hedonism of Southern California (indeed, of all tropical places, like Florida and Jamaica). With Eastern urbanity, he wrote Stanley Dell: "California, by the way, would be just as well suited for a honeymoon as Lake Como. It is the only place I have seen in the United States where romance seems pervasive and inevitable. The trouble is that you would have to pass through the Middle West on the way, and I wouldn't be sure of the felicity of any union inaugurated under those auspices. The children of such a union would be morose and deformed."[13]

When he graduated in 1916, his father, paralyzed by one of his neurasthenic "eclipses," did not attend the ceremony. Back in Red Bank and anxious about his uncertain future, Wilson was surprised by his emotional attachment to the university that had deepened his knowledge of the classics, modern languages and literature, brought gratifying friendships and developed his ability as a writer. "Coming away from Princeton," he told Dell, "was a hard break: can you believe that? I haven't been so blue before since I went to college as when I came back after a hilarious motor trip to New York . . . and found all the rooms locked and the Club deserted, with chairs piled on tables in the dining-room." Wilson later spoke at Princeton and gave the Christian Gauss lectures. Despite his lasting friendship with his old mentor, he rejected Princeton's religious and social values and never felt the same loyalty to his college as he did to The Hill. In March 1956 he told Dell that he did not pay his class dues and disapproved of the whole concept of class get-togethers.

After graduation and before enlisting in the army, Wilson had an important discussion with his father. Though Edmund Sr. had usually been dictatorial and censorious, he now, after some characteristic cross-examination, sympathetically supported his son's idealistic aims:

> I told him I should like to go to Washington to try my hand at political journalism. "At Princeton," he answered, "you specialized in literature; then you went to Columbia Summer School to study sociology and labor. Now you want to do political journalism. Don't you think you ought to concentrate on something?" "Father," I replied, "what I want to do is to try to get to know something about all the main departments of human thought. I don't know anything about politics yet, and I'd like to see something of it at first hand." He did not even smile at this. "That's a possible ambition," he said. "Go ahead if you're really serious."[14]

THREE ❖

War, 1916–1919

I

The war, as Gauss pointed out, had almost no impact on university life. Wilson responded to the opening of hostilities with little more than personal irritation. He had resisted his father's attempts to teach him to shoot, and had no desire to kill either birds or animals. Yet he spent the summer of 1916, just after graduating from Princeton, at an army camp in Plattsburgh, New York—near the Canadian border, on Lake Champlain. Though the United States had not yet entered the war, the camp had been set up, as part of the "preparedness" program, to train young men for eventual military service. Wilson found this experience terribly boring and became convinced, he said, that "I was incapable of becoming an officer and that, in general, I loathed the Army. I could not imagine commanding men, and I could not imagine killing them." He was so nervous on the rifle range that he never even hit the target.

Life at the camp was enlivened by two college friends—Edgar Woodman from Princeton and his cousin Charley Walker, who had been editor of the *Yale Literary Magazine*. Walker recalled that Wilson, hopeless in practical matters, could not find his pup tent during an overnight exercise, fell asleep on the ground and woke up the next morning to discover that he was lying right next to it. Walker—who became an expert in labor relations, translated the plays of Aeschylus and taught at Yale—was, later on, Wilson's neighbor and close friend in Wellfleet.

In the fall of 1916, Wilson's father—who had chosen Edmund's prep school, Greek course and university—persuaded the owner of the *New York Evening Sun*, a New Jersey neighbor, to hire his son as a cub reporter at fifteen dollars a week. On September 1 Wilson moved into a small apartment at 15 West 8th Street in Greenwich Village with three Yale friends. David Hamilton and Morris Belknap studied painting at the Art Students' League, and Larry Noyes worked in an architect's office. Though his father said he would have to support himself and gave him very little money, Edmund managed to live well on slightly more than his weekly salary. The four roommates were able to hire a Chinese servant and often had friends to dinner.

The *Evening Sun*, once a distinguished newspaper, had lost its reputation by the time Wilson joined the staff. The work, as he told Bellinger, was not difficult: "writing up little stories about people being almost killed under trucks, being fined for buying partridges, attempting suicide in hospitals, and things like that—or rather, rewriting most of them. The work is really quite varied, though, and so intermittent that I have a great deal of time to read and write in the office."

Wilson cultivated a fine style that was inappropriate for a factual newspaper. When an editor called him in and suggested: "You don't want to write like Dr. Johnson," Wilson cheekily replied that he would be very happy if he could. His well-modeled sentences, enhanced by Flaubertian irony, did not, as he admitted, add to the excitement of his news stories. He was then "much too shy to be any good as a reporter."[1] Later, he became an expert at probing interviews, wrote effective accounts of poverty, strikes and suicides during the desperate years of the Depression, and reported on the political and cultural life of American Indians, French Canadians, Haitians, Hungarians, Russians and Israelis.

II

In adult life Wilson was usually quite decisive. But in the spring of 1917, after America entered the war, he agonized for several months about what to do. His uncle André, who had crudely joked with him about sex, was a naturalized American citizen. But he enlisted in the French army, was sent to the front in March and killed in April 1915. Wilson did not believe the patriotic propaganda, had no enthusiasm for combat and knew from his experience at Plattsburgh that he could never be an officer. Rejecting the traditional imperatives and privileges of his class, he decided to volunteer as a common soldier.

As he explained in "The Case of the Author," his military service was more an escape than a commitment: "When America went to war, I enlisted . . . as a soldier instead of going to an officers' training camp as most of my friends from college were doing, partly at any rate because I wanted to get as far away from that old life as possible." Wilson did not, like most of his noncombatant college friends, join the fashionable ambulance corps. Instead, like Walt Whitman, who dressed wounds during the Civil War, he became a nurse and dealt directly with the worst horrors of the war: with the shell-shocked and the wounded, the mutilated, the dying and the dead.

Described in his army records as five feet, six inches tall, with brown eyes, red hair and fair complexion, Wilson enlisted as a private in August 1917. In Base Hospital Unit Three, he was always called "Ed" or "Woodrow." He served first in Detroit and then, after sailing from Canada to Southampton in late October, in a military hospital at Vittel, in the Vosges region of northeastern France. Serving in a military hospital, he told Bellinger, would suit his qualified patriotism: "I have never yet really felt it my duty to fight in this war. I consider myself well provided for in a branch of the service which commits me to nothing except a desire to repair damage and do something for my country—which I hope later to serve more effectively in other fields."

After only two months of fatigue, orderly and guard duty in Michigan, Wilson felt blighted by army life. He was not only exhausted by the tedious work, but also—like his hero Rimbaud, marooned in the wilds of Abyssinia—encircled by barbarians, severed from familiar reality and threatened by complete degeneration. In 1888 Rimbaud declared: "[I am] obliged to chatter their gibberish, to eat their filthy messes, to endure a thousand and one annoyances that come from their idleness, their treachery, and their stupidity. But that is not the worst. The worst thing is the fear of becoming doltish oneself, isolated as one is, and cut off from any intellectual companionship." Thirty years after Rimbaud, Wilson complained to Dell: "you have no idea how introspective one becomes during guard duty on the long, cold autumn nights, sitting in the adjutant's tent, companioned only by the bugs, or pacing the old familiar well-worn path between the latrine and the camp gate. You have no idea, seriously, how isolated and inward you become, surrounded by and dealing with people with whom you cannot talk the real language, whose habits and manners you detest. . . . This is not the absence of charity on my part, it is only the reaction of intelligence."[2]

His embarkation for the war in Europe was delayed several times during October and November while the Unit received some minimum training. These postponements frayed the nerves and increased the brutal behavior of the soldiers, some of whom had graduated from

Gauss' old university in Ann Arbor. "Every time this bogus departure takes place," Wilson told Dell, "the morale of the unit goes down and the men, many of them immature high school and University of Michigan fellows, dull their disappointment by whoring and surreptitious liquor."

Wilson, neither a fornicator nor a drinker, sublimated his desires by devouring the *New Republic* "with an almost sensual appetite" and spending as much time as possible in the elegant Grosse Pointe home of the pleasant but (he felt) boring family of his New York roommate David Hamilton. These refined and cultured people, Wilson told Dell, were the exact antithesis of the army camp Yahoos, who both repelled and fascinated him: "The Hamiltons . . . represent the other pole from the class of society where men seem to be familiarized with the most obscene perversions and horrors of life from their earliest years and to spend a large part of their leisure conversing about them with unflagging delight."

Finally, on October 30, Wilson sailed to England on an overcrowded, asphyxiating and lice-ridden ship, a sharp contrast to the luxurious vessels he had traveled on with his family and friends during his previous visits to Europe. He told Dell that "the greater part of the unit (including myself) has been consigned to a filthy unventilated hold formerly used to contain the baggage of the passengers, which was stored away on tiers of racks. . . . We are, of course, expected to sleep on the baggage racks, but as no one could do this without suffocating during the night and having his body devoured by vermin, most of us sleep on deck or double up with those of our friends who were fortunate enough to get staterooms in the steerage." The food on the ship was so vile—he told his mother, in a letter signed "Yours lovingly" —that he avoided the mess and subsisted on a weird diet, purchased at the canteen, of oranges, chocolate and peanut brittle.

While aboard ship, the irrepressible writer occupied himself by starting a magazine and by writing editorials for the first issue of *Reveille* (November 9, 1917), "published by Base Hospital Number 36 for the members of the unit and the folks back home." At the "rest camp" in Southampton, Wilson slept in a water-flooded tent and first heard about the Russian Revolution (which would occupy his mind throughout the 1930s) from bits of information printed in the English newspapers.

Toward the end of November Wilson's unit was transported across France, for two straight days, in freight boxcars that made the ship seem positively comfortable. The soldiers, packed forty to a car, got completely drunk and fell upon one another in the postures of the dead. Vittel was a fashionable French version of the spa he had visited at Karlsbad. Once there, the exhausted Wilson flopped on a narrow army cot in the palatial *salle* of the Casino, situated at the edge of a fine park, and gazed up at the dreamy clouds and classical figures that were painted on the lofty ceiling. The room was so cold that his breath puffed out like steam; and he later remembered the stark winter light, "the cold mists, the bad French stoves, the nights with everything darkened on account of German planes, the eating of hot soup through smothering colds," as well as the red wine that warmed him at dinner and the acid smell of the tiled toilet.[3]

In December 1917 Wilson wrote to Fitzgerald, who was then a lieutenant in the infantry, training at Fort Leavenworth under a young captain named Dwight Eisenhower. In a rare positive letter about the army, Wilson described the brief respite he enjoyed, after the dreadful trip overseas, in a quiet corner of France that remained isolated from the war until the first wounded soldiers began to arrive:

> [We are] only near enough to hear the guns, which do not sound as loud as thunder. We are stationed in what was once a popular summer resort but has now been turned over to the American hospital service. . . .
>
> Our life here, with its round of marvelous French dinners at little cafés and of walks and bicycle rides to the ancient villages that are all around us, would be perfectly idyllic, if it were not for the fact that the unseen, unrealized reality of the war and one's own prolonged inactivity makes it more ghastly than you can believe.

He thought of volunteering as a litter-bearer at the front so that he could experience the reality of battle, but eventually decided that the wounded brought as much reality as he could bear. Though he heard the rumbling guns from Verdun, about sixty miles away, he never saw the front until after the war.

In the last weeks of 1917 Wilson discovered in the museum of Nancy, handsomely situated on one of its ornamental squares, the work of two seventeenth-century artists who came from that town. He was fascinated by the subtle and mysterious chiaroscuro paintings of Georges de La Tour; by the satirical and sinister engravings of burning, beating, torture and executions in Jacques Callot's *Miseries of War* (1653). Callot's work, which had a profound influence on Goya, matched Wilson's mood during the war and provided a certain emotional support.

Before the wounded came in, Wilson shifted about in various menial jobs. He began as an interpreter at headquarters. He was next transferred, at his own request, to the X-ray department, where he carried in firewood and kept the stove warm. He was then involuntarily transferred to the dental department, which needed an interpreter to speak to the French patients. In this sinecure he tended the fire and kept the water pitcher warm, and spent the rest of his time either reading or talking to the dentist's assistant. In a letter to his mother of December 23, he expressed the enlisted man's traditional hatred of his incompetent and, in this case, barbaric superior. "[The dentist] treats his patients like dogs. Yesterday he broke three instruments trying to extract one man's nerve. . . . He never fills or doctors the teeth, but always pulls them out; and I can say without fear of exaggeration, that he is lazy, clumsy, and cruel."[4]

The long-awaited casualties of war were much more horrifying than anything in Callot. There were many delirious cases of pneumonia; and Wilson, dressed in white cap and gown to help protect him from infection, patrolled the hall at night to keep the wild men from jumping out the windows. In July 1918, the first mass of wounded Americans poured in after the major battle at Château-Thierry and included many cases of syphilis and shell-shock. Wilson spent a month dressing the raw burnt skin of the screaming victims of mustard-gas. He recalled that "their penises were spongy and raw and swollen to enormous size, and bandaging and unbandaging them was extremely painful. There was one doctor, known for his sadism—he liked to kick the enlisted men—who would rip the bandages off. . . . One patient had three-quarters of the surface of his body burned and his lungs partially destroyed."

The hospital was permeated with the stench of rotten flesh and the death-rate was appallingly high. In his novel, *I Thought of Daisy*, Wilson vividly described his numbed response to the macabre duties, which resembled the hideous work in an extermination camp: "After a time, after his first physical sinkings of nausea and fear, he had been able to line up corpses on the floor of the field hospital with less emotion than he had once arranged books on the shelves of his bookcases at college, and had incinerated amputated legs with less of real regret than he had once burnt discarded manuscripts." In a bitter letter to Stanley Dell, Wilson rejected the arguments for America's participation in the war and agonized about the ineffectuality of the hospital. His experience confirmed his isolationist politics and made him long to "follow that art which is more real to me than anything else in life":

> I am horribly depressed by an all but compulsive skepticism. The illusion of nationalism, the private interests of politicians, and the ignorance and stupidity of most of the men who do the fighting make the ideals which are said to be the goals of this war seem as dubious as the ideals which we know to have proved false in earlier wars. The hospital business, besides, exposes so many of the wretched and ghastly ironies of war—men dying (in large numbers) through pneumonia and improper care, before they so much as see the front, and being buried perfunctorily before their families know they are dead. . . . I feel, what I have long felt, a fool, a cipher. I am too young to have made myself a place in the only field in which I have ever expected to win any distinction and the regime of the army seems to abort all my literary plans for the present.[5]

III

Wilson described the people of Lorraine as dry and hardbitten, but very amiable. The most amiable person in Vittel was a pretty young girl, Ninette Fabre. She had black hair, large green eyes under delicately penciled eyebrows and a charming oval face, and liked to wear a fashionable cloche hat and loose coat. Her bearded and bad-tempered father owned the local café where Wilson took his meals, but he guarded her strictly and threatened any American who dared to take liberties with his daughter. Nevertheless, since she wrote romantic poetry and seriously studied English, Ninette soon became quite friendly with the twenty-two-year-old Edmund. Entranced by her tubercular condition, by her burning cheeks and pale skin that made her resemble the poetic and pathetic heroines of *Traviata* and *Bohème*, Wilson became for the first time in his life seriously interested in a woman.

When Ninette's condition deteriorated, she was sent to recuperate in the warm climate of Cannes. Wilson met her there during his trip to

Europe in 1921, and she continued to correspond with him in French for another year. In a typical love message of October 1921, she emphasized her anxious wait for the postman, expressed her joy at reading his letters, regretted that she had not allowed him to kiss her more freely and reaffirmed her desire to be with him. In February 1922 she apologetically told him that she was going to marry a rather conventional man. Since she had always wanted to live in Paris on her own, she scarcely knew how to explain her decision, which was undoubtedly influenced by family pressure and by an invalid's need to have someone to care for her. Breaking off their mildly passionate correspondence for reasons of decorum, Ninette concluded their *amitié amoureuse* by explaining: "All the charming things you said gave me pleasure; and if I ever had any regrets about marrying, you would be one of them."

After almost a year of war, the high-strung Wilson had reached the limits of endurance and appealed to his father for help. In September 1918 Edmund Sr. arranged his promotion to sergeant and his transfer to General Headquarters at Chaumont, forty miles west of Vittel. At Headquarters Wilson—grateful for the change, especially after the departure of Ninette—translated documents from French into English for the Intelligence Corps. After reading many books on the subject, he prepared a report on political and military conditions in Poland, and moved colored pins on a large wall to mark the movements of the Allied troops who were fighting for the Czarists in the war against the Bolsheviks.

Just before Christmas he was sent to Trier (birthplace of Karl Marx) on the mistaken assumption that he knew German, and joined the Army of Occupation on the Moselle River, near the border of Luxemburg. In Trier he met George Perkins, a friend from The Hill and Princeton, whose young wife had just died in the flu epidemic that ravaged both Europe and America right after the war. Wilson later visited Perkins' house and family and portrayed them in "Galahad," his story of religious fanaticism and sexual frustration in prep school. Perkins was then living in the house of the mayor and Wilson found the defeated enemy quite congenial: "I used to go out there in the evenings and we would have parties, with younger members of the family in a little café—and they were most amusing parties, very mixed, with the *Burgomeister's* little cousin in pigtails, who played the piano." Wilson's duties in Trier were as light as in Chaumont. He helped to censor newspapers, to disarm the inhabitants and to billet Allied troops, and had free time to read French novels, take German lessons, drink the fruity Moselle wine and go to the opera. Unlike most soldiers, he avoided the temptation of prostitutes.

He portrayed his experiences in Trier in his short story "Lieutenant Franklin."[6] After the armistice of November 1918, Lieutenant Franklin, who does not know German, is sent by mistake from Nancy, through the northern landscapes of Metz and Luxemburg, to occupied Trier. Uncomfortable in the role of conqueror, he tries to stop the Allied suppression of a moderate German newspaper, which has mildly criticized the British. Bored in Trier, Lieutenant Franklin befriends a German family, like the one Wilson had met through Perkins, and kisses a pretty war widow. But, after being ordered to stop fraternizing with the enemy, he is relieved of his duties and immediately sent back to France. The story criticizes the pervasive muddle of the army, the incompetence of the American officers and the foolish attempt to prevent humane relations with the Germans, which would help smooth the way to peace.

Once the war was over, Wilson went on leave and made his first extended visit to Paris. He stayed at the American University Club in the rue de Richelieu and went to the Guitry theater, and also journeyed south to Toulouse and Perpignan, near the Pyrenees. Like Fitzgerald's Jay Gatsby, who went to Oxford in 1919, Wilson wanted to attend a European university after the war, but could not get released from the army. Writing to John Bishop, a lieutenant in the infantry, in January 1919, Wilson expressed his preference for the Sorbonne over Oxford, praised his two mentors at Princeton (Kemp Smith had been sending him "piles of British propaganda") and longed for his release from military duty: "I should certainly choose the University of Paris, if it is possible to go there, and should avoid Oxford, which, I warn you, is, in spite of all its amenities, in many ways a deadly place. I should not expect to get much valuable instruction, in the event of availing myself of this university scheme, knowing all too well how few the Gausses and Kemp Smiths are and how sterile most university teaching is—and it must still be worse since the war—but, if I went to Paris (or Bordeaux), I should at least expect to learn some French, and, in any case, anything would be a relief from the galling yoke of the army."

Wilson sailed back to America on the cruiser *North Carolina*, reached New York on July 2 and was discharged at Mitchell Field, in Southampton, Long Island, on July 9, 1919. His parents visited him separately at the military camp; and he was gratified when his father, impatiently throwing his weight around, "first complained of the army's inefficiency in not letting him in to see me sooner, then when the officer in charge warned him that that way of talking was treasonable, telling him [quite emphatically] that there was nothing in what he had said that violated any law."[7] Wilson was shocked to hear from his father that his cousin Sandy had become insane.

Wilson's story "The Death of a Soldier," published in his first book, *The Undertaker's Garland* (1922), expressed more forcefully and effectively than "Lieutenant Franklin" his attitude toward the war. During the appalling two-day journey from Le Havre to Vittel, a sick soldier, cruelly neglected by the medical officers, dies of pneumonia before he reaches the front and is quickly buried before his far-off family even knows that he is dead. Like most intelligent and sensitive soldiers, Wilson was maddened by the monotonous obscenity of the army, revolted by the boorishness and truculence, shocked by the horror of the hospital. But worst of all, he wrote in "The Death of a Soldier," was the loss of individuality. He "felt always the oppression of being handled like a thing without a will. They could do absolutely anything they liked with him; he had felt that in the barracks as he had never felt it before." Later in life, he often remembered the strange places he had seen during the war, the contact with French and Germans, the intense pleasures of escaping from the war and the flirtation with Ninette. But his most powerful memory was of the loss of personal control.

Though Wilson loathed the army, he had a relatively "good war." He returned physically unharmed, yet toughened up and forced into manhood. When he left Princeton he lacked experience in the ordinary working world, but his two years as an enlisted man put him into close contact with lower-class men and awakened his curiosity about how they lived. The war cut him off, in a healthy way, from his conventional upper-middle-class existence, which he had always assumed he would follow.

The war also made Wilson question the political and economic system that had made it possible. In the 1930s he would become a social as well as a cultural critic and join the attack on capitalism. Looking back on the person he was in 1919, he later dramatized his disillusionment and made the hero of his play declare: "I suddenly realized that I couldn't go back to the way I'd lived. The war made me see what a fraud it all was and that everything that was worth anything had to be done outside all that. The respectable life is a living death!"

This Nietzschean rejection of the comfortable bourgeois world,

Wilson felt, would help him achieve the idealistic goals that he had developed at The Hill and at Princeton and would pursue throughout his career. In "The Case of the Author," he described his feelings and beliefs after the war, which marked the first great turning point of his life: "I swore to myself that when the War was over I should stand outside society altogether. I should do without the comforts and amenities of the conventional world entirely, and I should devote myself to the great human interests which transcended standards of living and conventions: Literature, History, the Creation of Beauty, the Discovery of Truth."[8] In retrospect, Wilson no doubt idealized his ambitions and disguised with high-sounding abstractions his natural desire to achieve fame as a writer. Though he cared little about money and lived very modestly for years, he could never have pursued his literary goals by standing outside society. His work as editor, critic and reporter repeatedly led him to subjects, people and cultures in the actual world.

The war exposed Wilson to real wounds and suffering, which inspired the theme of his best critical book, *The Wound and the Bow*. More importantly, his war experience transformed him into a lifelong pacifist. It provided the ethical basis not only for his sympathy with the defeated South in the Civil War, but also for his opposition to America's foreign policy: the participation in World War Two, the Cold War ideology that justified vast military spending and the disastrous involvement in the war in Vietnam.

FOUR

Vanity Fair and
Edna St. Vincent Millay,
1919–1921

I

Edmund Wilson, unlike most writers of the 1920s, never had an expatriate period and remained in the American grain. Greenwich Village, whose bohemian life he captured in *I Thought of Daisy*, was his Paris and his Rome. In September 1919, after a month at home in Red Bank, Wilson began to reconstruct his life by moving into an apartment with his three Yale roommates of 1916 at 114 West 12th Street, where they hired a West Indian cook. His frequent shifts of residence had a discernible pattern. Throughout the 1920s he rented a number of small shabby apartments or cheap furnished rooms in the Village. In the 1930s, restless as ever during and between marriages, he tended to live in midtown in the East and West 50s. In the late 1930s he borrowed a secluded house in Stamford, Connecticut. During both decades he spent as many summers as possible in Provincetown, where he went swimming and bicycling and led a much healthier life than in New York.

In 1941 he bought his first house, in Wellfleet, on Cape Cod. But he continued, during the 1940s and early 1950s, to spend winters in Manhattan at more fashionable uptown addresses in the East 80s and 90s. From the late 1950s to the early 1960s he resided in Cambridge, Massachusetts, during the winter. After inheriting the Old Stone House in Talcottville in 1951, he lived in upstate New York in the summer and returned to Wellfleet in the fall. These frequent moves put him in touch with different settings and people, and stimulated his incessant work.

After the war, the more sophisticated Wilson took a harsher view of his old friends, who still inhabited a world he had vowed to reject. David Hamilton, coddled by an indulgent mother, was languid and ineffectual. Morris Belknap, a good-natured fellow from Louisville, was ultimately rather dampening and sour. Larry Noyes, a homosexual from St. Paul, was a terrible snob who looked down on the shabby-genteel family of Scott Fitzgerald. Their ménage broke up when Hamilton and Belknap married. The energetic Wilson saw very little of these idle friends in later life.

But Wilson was fascinated by one of their Yale classmates—the handsome, witty and charming Phelps Putnam—whom he met in 1919. Born in Boston in 1894, Putnam graduated from Exeter and Yale, and was (Wilson wrote) "rather like E. E. Cummings—fatally irresistible to women: the women's ideal poet, attractive and unreliable." In 1927 Wilson told Putnam: "You have knocked off one of the best books of English poetry of the time," and his enthusiasm was shared by sound critics like Paul Rosenfeld and Allen Tate. Wilson must have been struck by the final couplet of Putnam's poem on the male sexual organ, which had crude Restoration wit: "You lead us, master, sniffing to the hunt, / In quest forever of the perfect cunt."[1] But Putnam, who suffered from asthma and drink, became a casualty of the 1920s and quickly deteriorated. By 1937 he was being "de-alcoholized" at a rehabilitation center in Hartford. After Putnam's death, Wilson wrote an elegiac Introduction to his *Collected Poems*, edited by Charley Walker.

In 1919, when Wilson began his assault on the cultural citadel, the salient aspects of his appearance and character had already been formed. Unless he experienced a sudden spurt of growth in his mid-twenties, he must have added a gratifying two inches on his passport of 1921. On this document he listed his height as five feet, eight inches, and described himself as having a high forehead, straight nose, small mouth, fair complexion and red hair. Matthew Josephson, who knew Wilson at *Vanity Fair* in the early Twenties, described his collegiate clothes, splashed by colorful ties, as well as his temperament and intellect. The short, plump, pink-cheeked young man "looked spruce in a brown Brooks Brothers suit, and wore a brilliant yellow necktie; his hair was reddish brown, his eyes dark brown and keen looking, his manner shy but sometimes brusque. . . . Wilson had learning, a wide-ranging curiosity, and, at the same time, a hard-headed skeptical spirit. He was forward-looking and all for 'stunning' the American bourgeoisie"—in the iconoclastic style of H. L. Mencken.

According to Tom Matthews, a Princeton graduate who was his assistant on the *New Republic,* the imperious Wilson had by the mid-1920s acquired some of the attributes of middle age. He was "a short, sandy-haired youngish man, at thirty already inclining to stoutness and baldness, with pale, blinking eyes and a high, strained-tenor voice; his profile as regular as a plump Roman emperor's but his expression like an absent-minded cantankerous professor's."[2] By the 1930s Wilson had adopted a more conservative style of dress, and wore dark suits, rusty wool ties and a broad-brimmed black Stetson.

In the early Twenties Wilson had his first sexual experience, but had not yet exorcised his puritan heritage. E. E. Cummings, that enviable ladies' man, called him, in a memorable phrase, "the man in the iron necktie." One of Wilson's girlfriends said, when he refused to dance with her, that he read too much, and the former wound-dresser admitted: "Maybe you have death in you somewhere that keeps you from enjoying things." He also had a saturnine imagination and a powerful melancholic streak, which made him recognize the tragic element in the lives he wrote about. But in his own letters and diaries he described the most intense emotional events of his life—sexual encounters, love-affairs, marriages, nervous breakdowns, death of his father and mother—in the most clinical and matter-of-fact way.

Though Wilson could sometimes be nervous, impetuous and quick-tempered, he usually managed to keep himself under control. The poet Schuyler Jackson once attacked Wilson at the beginning of a dinner. Wilson attentively finished his soup and then masked his anger with a sudden and extremely formal farewell: "I'm sorry that such excellent liquor should have produced such a disagreeable conversation, and I shall now take my leave."[3]

Wilson had never taken a drink or gone out with a girl at Princeton, but he had seen a lot of swilling and whoring in the army. After the war he plunged into the bohemian social life of Greenwich Village. Under the influence of Prohibition (which paradoxically encouraged drinking), and of libidinous friends like Ted Paramore and Edna Millay, Wilson was liberated from his repressed and constricted existence. When he defined himself as a man of the Twenties, he meant that he liked "something exciting: drinks, animated conversation, gaiety; an uninhibited exchange of ideas"—and a promiscuous sex life.

Sedentary by day and drinking at night, Wilson occasionally grew concerned about his health. In January 1921 he tried to establish a rigorous regime that included daily exercise at the Yale Club and a return to work in the evening from nine until midnight. But, as he explained to Stanley Dell, this sound schedule had a terrible effect: "I followed out this system with admirable consistency the first few days of the week, with the result that I soon fell ill and have been obliged to take to my bed with indigestion, a tumultuous headache, and general debility. I think it must have been the exercise that did for me: when I don't exercise I'm all right, and when I dissipate in the evenings I never have a headache."

The hedonistic Ted Paramore, who felt Wilson read too much and lived too little, believed a little more ribaldry would prevent him from becoming a parasite on the books of other men. Wilson eagerly took his advice. The journalist Burton Rascoe met Wilson, strangely attired in dressing gown and top hat, in the company of Tallulah Bankhead (a childhood friend of Scott Fitzgerald's new wife), and was surprised to see that normally solemn young man try out a few magic tricks: "Bunny performed some feats of legerdemain and conjuring. It was all refreshing and amusing and I pondered the happy circumstances which allow so serious and studious a young man as Bunny to forget himself in a riot of giddy nonsense and absurdity." Rascoe once became Wilson's victim during a characteristically drunken party. Matthew Josephson remembered a lively "gathering at Edmund Wilson's, in the course of which several of the guests fell to brawling in various corners of a rambling apartment he had in the Village. On this or perhaps a later occasion our host himself was engaged in combat with Mr. Burton Rascoe and bit him in the calf."[4]

When Wilson was sober, he could be extremely charming, lively and interesting. Most people were eager to enjoy his company and cultivate his friendship. He was both intensely American and extraordinarily cosmopolitan, combined high purpose with moral seriousness, had read everything and soon came to know almost everyone in the world of letters. He got on well with a wealthy patron of the arts like Margaret de Silver, who told him: "You are so *stimulating* and so entertaining in your somewhat bossy irascible way," and with Louis, the servant of his New Orleans friend, who always asked about "that pretty-looking gentleman that talks so nice."

The center of Wilson's life, from early childhood to the day of his death, was the reading and writing of books. For Wilson—the most bookish author since Montaigne—the reality in books often came before the actual experience of life. He not only, like many writers, compulsively corrected the errors in the books he read, but also mentally rewrote the sentences to make them conform to his own style. One of his greatest pleasures was telling his friends about books, especially hard-to-get books in a language they did not know, which he had read and they (of course) had not. Like the French historian Jules Michelet, whom he praised in *To the Finland Station*, Wilson's soon-to-be-realized goal was to have "read all the books, been to look at all the monuments and pictures, interviewed all the authorities, and explored all the libraries and archives of Europe."

Dürer's engraving of the scholarly St. Jerome, translating the Bible in his secluded and well-ordered study, engrossed in his writing and his thoughts, became for Wilson, especially during tumultuous periods when he had no privacy or quiet, the image of an ideal life: "the sight of that solid old man sitting there in that clean solid room, with its thick walls and heavy beams, while the sun of a whole long day was moving the panes of light across his desk and the floor, and with a lion, which apparently he kept as a pet, contentedly dozing beside him, used really to affect me deeply."[5]

When Wilson emerged from the study, his idiosyncratic and didactic way of conversing combined the lectures he had heard in college with the cross-examination he had learned from his father. In a rather high-pitched, resonant voice, which had evolved from shouting to his deaf mother, and a stutter (or splutter) that developed when he got excited, Wilson, as straightforward in his conversation as in his prose, would ignore all small talk and come directly to the point. He was always writing about something, and while telling friends about his current enthusiasm, would work out his essays in his head. But he was also endlessly curious and voracious for knowledge. Less interested in people than in what he could learn from them, he would pick their brains in a gratifying way. One day in Cambridge, later in life, he asked Leon Edel, an authority on Henry James, to take him to James' grave and discuss the life of the novelist on that sacred spot.

Wilson had an empirical, rationalistic mind, ready, like a ship with her steam up, to set out at once on the sea of thought. Though obstinate and impractical about the details of everyday life, he was morally courageous and extremely idealistic. He once told an interviewer that though he had experienced many disillusionments in life, he still cherished the tenets of the Victorian age: "like most people born in the nineteenth century, I still have—entirely instinctively—the belief in human progress, the conviction that the world won't fall apart, the faith in the value of reform." The minister's grandson, who had rejected religion in childhood, did not believe in God, but (defining Him self-reflectively) identified God with "a vigorous physical persistence, a rectitude in relation to others and to one's work in the world, and a faith in the endurance of the human mind."[6]

Wilson had great energy and capacity for work, and a formidable appetite for exploring difficult subjects. Though he traveled widely, he never took a complete vacation and his journeys were always related to his writing. In the early 1920s (and throughout his life) he wrote numerous reviews, essays, poems, plays and stories, and devised an effective system, based on solid self-confidence, for getting all his work into print: "I made a list of all possible magazines and another of all my pieces which I could imagine being accepted. I did not allow myself to be unnerved or discouraged by rejection slips but tried with each of my products every one of the magazines on the list, and when I had sent each of them out and got it back, I began sending them out again. This proved to be a good idea."

Wilson's work was partly fueled by drink, but he did not pay much attention to food. When he could no longer afford Chinese and West Indian cooks, and had to shift for himself, he ate whatever was cheapest to buy and easiest to prepare. When he lived on Lexington Avenue, his slapdash housekeeper would rush in, open cans of tomato soup and peaches, cook a hamburger and then disappear. His first two wives did very little cooking. Though his last two were good cooks, he was quite happy with a substantial breakfast, which propelled him into the study at nine o'clock, a fried egg sandwich (his great standby, even at the Boston Ritz) and the creamiest desserts he could find. His strange diet made him pot-bellied while still in his thirties.

Wilson was much more catholic in his taste for alcohol. Despite the example of Uncle Reuel Kimball, who became a hopeless alcoholic and had to be periodically dried out, Wilson was transformed in the early Twenties from the Presbyterian teetotaler at Princeton and in the army into a heavy, indiscriminate guzzler. As William Drummond said of Ben Jonson: "Drink [was] one of the elements in which he liveth." Wilson variously drank, whenever the occasion offered, champagne, sherry, wine, beer, Scotch, bourbon, Canadian whiskey, cocktails, bath-tub gin and (if necessary) pure alcohol. He liked Château d'Yquem or Liebfraumilch with dinner, and preferred Molson beer and Johnnie Walker Red Label whiskey. When Alfred Kazin once asked him if he would like a drink, Wilson eagerly replied: "My tongue is hanging out." Stephen Spender recorded that "at the Princeton Club he would order six Martinis at a time and drink them one after another." On one spectacular and solitary occasion, Wilson noted, "I drank a whole bottle of champagne and what was left of a bottle of Old Grand-dad and started in on a bottle of red wine. I was eating Limburger cheese and ginger snaps. . . . Felt queasy for the next twenty-four hours."[7]

Though Wilson consumed enormous quantities of liquor (and liked to ply others with drink), he rarely became more than congenially high. Though his speech slowed down, he could still make sharp and coherent comments about others—until he finished everything in the bottles, fell into a stupor and had to be helped into bed. He was not physically strong, but had tremendous stamina. Unaffected by the night's heavy drinking, refreshed and clear-headed after his sleep, Wilson always resumed work at the usual time the next morning.

Wilson drank because everyone drank in the Twenties; it made him more convivial with friends and helped overcome his shyness with women. When the Twenties had vanished, Wilson took alcohol to help him recapture the enchanted world of his youth. The Greenwich Village characters in *I Thought of Daisy* drown themselves in drink and he explained in *Memoirs of Hecate County:* "One drank to go back there, where one's friends were, where life was irresponsible and daring, where it was passionate, amusing and frank." Though Wilson (like Hemingway) usually did not drink until after he had finished his work, it sometimes helped to stimulate his writing. As Graham Greene observed: "The profession is very hard on the nerves; one catches fire at the beginning of the day and burns out by the end of it." But when he did not catch fire, a glass of whiskey would help him start a piece—and sometimes finish it. When he was burnt out at the end of the solitary day, whiskey eased him into tranquil unconsciousness. In one of his dialogues with himself Wilson's interlocutor remarks: "You seem to me very vigorous," to which he replies: "It's these drinks that produce the illusion."[8]

II

Wilson began as a free-lance writer after the war, but soon had the opportunity to join the staff of one of the most sophisticated magazines of the time. In January 1920 Dorothy Parker wrote a caustic review in *Vanity Fair* that wounded the actress Billie Burke. Her husband, the theatrical producer Florenz Ziegfeld, complained to the owner of the magazine, Condé Nast, and Parker was prohibited from reviewing plays. She resigned in protest and her close friends, Robert Benchley and Robert Sherwood, went with her. This left the editor Frank Crowninshield with no staff but his secretaries. Wilson—fortified by his experience on the *Hill School Record* and the *Nassau Lit.*—was recruited to fill the gap. He started at $45 a week, and hired John Bishop as his assistant. When he returned in July 1922 for another ten months, with a rising reputation, he began at $75 and ended at $82 a week.

Vanity Fair—a cross between today's *Esquire, Paris Review* and *New Yorker*—covered contemporary topics, published avant-garde art and humor, and appealed to clever and cultured people: "Its pages were filled with pertinent references to the customs of the time, parodies of its pretensions, serious discussion of its intellectual interests (or the lack of them), and, in the advertisements, appeals to the wealthy and the snobbish. . . . The subscribers were introduced to the latest in the arts: there were discussions of futurism, of modern music . . . of *vers libre*, of the symbolists, of Joyce's new 'Work in Progress,' of Apollinaire, of *The Waste Land*."

Frank Crowninshield, the editor, was born in Paris in 1872, the son of an artist, and educated in France and Italy. He had worked on several other magazines before taking charge of *Vanity Fair* in 1914. Wilson considered Crownie—a tall, elegant, grey-haired man with brown eyes and a surly moustache—a clever and entertaining fellow with a frivolously amusing side: "In his well-pressed gray suits that harmonized with his silvering hair, [he] would travel around the office with a gait at once strutting and mincing, with the upper part of his body bent forward." Though Crownie seemed to be homosexual, Wilson suspected that he had a girl secretly hidden away.

But Crownie's affected manner soon got on Wilson's nerves. He was shallow as well as unreliable, capable of unscrupulousness and occasional meanness. "I never knew anyone who talked as much as Crowninshield," Wilson wrote, "about being and behaving like 'a gentleman' and one who exemplified this less in his own relations." Crownie, on his part, was rather intimidated by Wilson and surprised (like Burton Rascoe) by the playful side of his nature. Though Wilson was more than twenty years his junior, he wrote: "I always regarded him with a certain degree of awe, a feeling inspired, perhaps, by his extraordinary fund of knowledge, his gift for writing poetry, his mastery of four languages." Wilson had a "penchant for charades . . . a pleasant sense of humor, and an easy style in writing French prose."[9]

When things got slow in the office, Crownie encouraged Wilson and Bishop to play delightful games like "The Rape of the Sabine Women." Bishop would pick up one of the secretaries, Jeanne Ballot, and dash across the room with her; Wilson would then pick up the other one and dash madly at Bishop with her. The Princeton friends kept up the classical spirit of the game by passing notes to each other. One of them, in Latin, alluded to Catullus' *Illa Lesbia*. After a year of such stimulating frivolity, Wilson boasted to Stanley Dell that Miss Ballot, "a nice little half-French girl who has been respectably brought up in Brooklyn, is in a continual state of rut, having reached the age for amour, and lays formidable siege to John from morning to night (having broken her teeth on me)."

Wilson was always keenly aware that "literature demands not only all one can give it but also all one can get other people to give it." He brought all his talent and intellect to *Vanity Fair* at a time when American literature was experiencing a great renaissance. He gave the poet Elinor Wylie a part-time job and published the work of Edna St. Vincent Millay. He introduced the magazine's readers to Freud, Proust, Henri Bergson, Jean Cocteau, T. S. Eliot, Gertrude Stein, and brought out the work of new writers like Bishop, Fitzgerald, Dos Passos and Cummings. Influenced by Mencken, Wilson also wrote several amusing articles on things he considered overrated: afternoon tea, the sea, the comedian Eddie Cantor, youth, movies, summer, weddings, motoring, crocheted ties, the country and Kipling (about whom he later wrote a major essay) as well as on those he considered underrated: ruffs and satin breeches, the human body and Edith Wharton.

Though Wilson was sympathetic to literary modernism, and admired innovators like Eliot and Cummings, he disliked the poetry of Frost, Williams, Stevens, Pound and Hart Crane. He wittily described the arch aesthete and insurance executive, Wallace Stevens, as "the voice of a helpless pierrot imprisoned in a functioning businessman." Stevens, apparently unaware of this hostility, praised in his *Letters* Wilson's incisive analysis of both political and literary issues.

Just before his discharge from the army, Wilson had asked his mother to bring him a copy of Pound's *Lustra* (1916). Three years later he complained to Bishop that he had just received Pound's idiosyncratic "ill-spelled, ill-written, ill-phrased, idiotic letter enclosing an incoherent and all but illegible article." Echoing criticism that was sometimes directed at himself, Wilson later categorized Pound, who was Eliot's mentor, as derivative, parasitic and bookish: "He still seems to me to be a writer at second-hand who lives almost exclusively on other people's literature. . . . Except technically, he's rather an un-grown-up fellow who, falling victim to the American cultural disease, has stuck too close to books." The perennial outsider, Pound later resented Wilson's position in the literary establishment and returned his disdain. The year before *Axel's Castle* was published, Pound felt Wilson was too superficial and conventional for an avant-garde journal like *Hound & Horn*, and compared him to the mainstream editor of the *Dial*. "Cheapens the periodical," Pound exclaimed. "Anyone can buy him for ten cents in *Nation* or wherever it is he 'edits' and he has there plenty of room for his suds. I think he is a bit of a [Gilbert] Seldes, floating with the current."[10]

In February 1921, proud of his success during his first year on *Vanity Fair*, Wilson asked Crownie for a raise, pointing out that he was earning less than the tyro who wrote about men's fashions. When Crownie tactlessly replied that there were many people who could do Wilson's job but it was hard to find someone to do men's fashions, Wilson got enraged and quit.

III

In the early 1920s Wilson resumed his uneasy friendship with Fitzger-ald, the first of his friends to achieve literary success. In 1916, when Wilson was working for the *Evening Sun* and Fitzgerald was an under-graduate, Scott had spotted Wilson, wearing a tan raincoat over his inevitable brown suit, carrying a cane and walking confidently through the crowds of New York. To Scott, who always hero-worshiped Ed-mund, "the shy little scholar of Holder Court" had turned into a promising symbol of cosmopolitan sophistication and seemed to em-body the literary life. "That night, in Bunny's apartment," Fitzgerald recalled, "life was mellow and safe, a finer distillation of all that I had come to love at Princeton."

Soon after they left college, Fitzgerald had presumptuously de-clared: "I want to be one of the greatest writers who ever lived, don't you?" Wilson reacted to this remark by adopting a Johnsonian persona to match Fitzgerald's naive and provincial Boswell. He never dreamed that Fitzgerald would actually begin to realize his ambition by learning the techniques of fiction from his older contemporaries—like Compton Mackenzie and H. G. Wells—instead of, like Wilson, studying the works of Plato and Dante. While Wilson held fast to his rigorous intellect, Fitzgerald gave way to his romantic impulse.

At this stage in their lives neither young man understood the nature of the other's talents. In August 1919, while Wilson was trying to instill some critical sense in Fitzgerald, Scott warned Edmund, who never completed his projected collection of war stories but would, with *The Shock of Recognition*, become an accomplished anthologist: "For God's sake, Bunny, write a novel and don't waste your time editing collections. It'll get to be a habit."[11] Wilson longed to be an imaginative writer, but his emotional repression, his scholarly cast of mind and his thorough knowledge of the literature of the past inhibited his creative urge. He was working as a journalist and editor but, like Fitzgerald, aspired to be a novelist, and assumed that fiction was an altogether higher and more valuable kind of writing than literary criticism.

In college Wilson had been the older, wiser and more sophisticated student, and with Bishop, a scornful critic who deflated Fitzgerald's illusions. He now became Fitzgerald's literary mentor, discussing the art of the novel with him, urging him to pay more attention to literary form. Fitzgerald eagerly sought his comments on the manuscript of his first novel, *This Side of Paradise*. In November 1919 Wilson responded with his characteristic mixture of friendly derision, backhanded compliments and faint praise. He compared Fitzgerald's novel to the trivial best-seller by the pre-adolescent Daisy Ashford, spotted the influence of the hero of Mackenzie's *Sinister Street* and mocked Fitzgerald's pretensions: "I have just read your novel with more delight than I can well tell you. It ought to be a classic in the class with *The Young Visiters*. . . . Your hero is an unreal imitation of Michael Fane, who was himself unreal. . . . As an intellectual [Amory Blaine] is a fake of the first water and I read his views on art, politics, religion and society with more riotous mirth than I should care to have you know." At the same time he offered sound criticism and warned Fitzgerald against adopting the cheap effects of commercial stories instead of doing serious work. "It would all be better if you would tighten up your artistic conscience and pay a little more attention to form. . . . I feel called upon to give you this advice because I believe you might become a very popular trashy novelist without much difficulty."

In the years to come Wilson's private and public comments helped Fitzgerald define and develop his art. Fitzgerald constantly deferred to

Wilson's literary judgment, called him his intellectual conscience and retained him as a mentor long after he had established himself as a serious novelist. Wilson, however, envied the enormous and apparently arbitrary financial success that followed Fitzgerald's first novel. He was exasperated by the way Fitzgerald wasted his talent and sacrificed his integrity by writing inferior stories for popular magazines.

In his composite review of Fitzgerald's first two novels, Wilson repeated some of the points he had made in his letter (written before *This Side of Paradise* was published in March 1920), and established the critical approach to Fitzgerald's work that many others would follow: "He has been given imagination without intellectual control of it; he has been given the desire for beauty without an aesthetic ideal; and he has been given a gift for expression without very many ideas to express." Though Wilson's judgment was sound, it also expressed irritation. It seemed unjust that *he* had the intellectual control, aesthetic ideals and abundant ideas, while Fitzgerald, the dim student, had somehow blundered into the creation of a phenomenally popular novel. Trying to account for its astonishing critical success, Wilson praised the book's vitality: "I have said that *This Side of Paradise* commits almost every sin that a novel can possibly commit: but it does not commit the unpardonable sin: it does not fail to live. The whole preposterous farrago is animated with life."

By 1920 Fitzgerald had become a famous spokesman for the postwar generation, and fulfilled Wilson's prediction that his very shallowness would make him a popular success. Still toiling as a journalist and book reviewer, Wilson now became as critical of Fitzgerald's personal faults as he was of his literary defects. In April, just after his marriage, Fitzgerald went down to Princeton, introduced the teenaged Zelda Sayre as his mistress and got a black eye during a rowdy party at his club. Six days later he returned with Wilson and Bishop for a *Nassau Lit.* banquet. The three friends, in a classical tribute, gathered laurel wreaths to crown Christian Gauss. When Fitzgerald went to the Cottage Club to continue the celebrations, he found he had been suspended for drunken behavior. Wilson could not resist the opportunity to mock him in a poem:

> Poor Fitz went prancing into the Cottage Club
> With his gilt wreath and lyre,
> Looking like a tarnished Apollo with the two black eyes

That he had got, when far gone in liquor, in some unintelligible
  fight,
But looking like Apollo just the same, with the sun in his pale
  yellow hair.

When Wilson and Bishop (whose thin volume of poems had also
been eclipsed by Fitzgerald) saw his first novel piled high in the publisher's handsome shop window on Fifth Avenue, they drew up a satiric
catalogue (like their satiric Princeton poem) for a "Proposed Exhibit
of Fitzgeraldiana for Chas. Scribner's Sons." These items—which
summed up their contemptuous view of Fitzgerald's immaturity, vanity, narcissism, shallowness and undistinguished military career—consisted of three double malted milks, a bottle of hair tonic, a yellow silk
shirt, a mirror, his entire seven-book library (including a notebook and
two scrapbooks) and an "overseas cap never worn overseas."[12] Though
emotionally vulnerable, Fitzgerald tolerated these jabs with humility
and good-natured resignation. Had he become angry and broken with
Wilson, he would have lost the benefit of his criticism.

In 1921 Fitzgerald solicited Wilson's comments on the typescript
of his second novel, just as he had done two years earlier with *This Side
of Paradise*. Wilson must have been pleased by his brief but flattering
appearance in *The Beautiful and Damned* as Eugene Bronson, "whose
articles in The New Democracy [the *New Republic*] were stamping him
as a man with ideas transcending both vulgar timeliness and popular
hysteria." In February 1921 Wilson told Dell that he was impressed by
Fitzgerald's ability to describe the seeds of destruction in his recent
marriage to Zelda: "I am editing [not merely reading] the MS of Fitz's
new novel, and though I thought it was rather silly at first, I find it
developing a genuine emotional power which he had scarcely displayed
before. . . . It is all about him and Zelda." Wilson also reported that
alcohol had aged Fitzgerald's handsome profile at the same time that
maturity had tempered his mind: "He looks like John Barrymore on the
brink of the grave . . . but also, somehow, more intelligent than he used
to." Later on, when his friend's drinking got out of control, Wilson
referred to "This Side of Paralyzed by F. Scotch Fitzgerald."

Wilson showed Fitzgerald his rather cruel composite review in the
Bookman when it was still in typescript. Appreciating the penetrating
analysis, Scott modestly accepted his comments on the unconvincing
characters, the lack of discipline and poverty of aesthetic ideas, and

even told a friend that he had enjoyed reading them. Though he asked Wilson to delete damaging references to his drinking and his criticism of the war, he conceded: "It is, of course, the only intelligible and intelligent thing of any length which has been written about me and my stuff—and like everything you write it seems to me pretty generally true. I am guilty of its every stricture and I take an extraordinary delight in its considered approbation. I don't see how I could possibly be offended at anything in it." Fitzgerald, mining every scrap of praise, was particularly pleased by Wilson's conclusion that "*The Beautiful and Damned*, imperfect though it is, makes an advance over *This Side of Paradise*: the style is more nearly mature and the subject more solidly unified, and there are scenes that are more convincing than any in his previous fiction."[13]

IV

While working on *Vanity Fair* and editing Fitzgerald's novels, Wilson formed the first of many friendships with attractive and talented women writers. Elinor Hoyt Wylie had come from the same distinguished background as Wilson and combined, in her bizarre life, an unusual mixture of respectability and scandal. Her family came to America in the seventeenth century; her grandfather, a general in the Civil War, was governor of Pennsylvania; and her father, a Yale graduate and successful government lawyer, became solicitor general during Theodore Roosevelt's administration. Wylie was born in New Jersey in 1885 and brought up amidst the aristocracy of Washington. But the insanity in her family was more pervasive than in Wilson's. Her brother and sister committed suicide, and another brother, who married Tallulah Bankhead's sister, attempted suicide by jumping off a boat.

Wylie was high-strung and temperamental. When she was thirty-five and married, she abandoned her son and husband (who also became insane) and ran off with a much younger married lawyer, Horace Wylie. Since Horace was unable to obtain a divorce, they were—like Vronsky and Anna Karenina—socially disgraced and exiled to Europe. But their illicit relations were inevitably discovered, and they left a trail of scandal behind them. Elinor left Horace Wylie, after two miscarriages, when they returned to America in 1915 and he became the model for the clever and unscrupulous hero of her first novel, *Jennifer*

Lorn (1923). Finally, in 1923, she married the poet William Rose Benét. When Wilson expressed doubts about this union, Elinor callously exclaimed: "Yes, it would be a pity that a first-rate poet should be turned into a second-rate poet by marrying a third-rate poet."

Edna Millay, her friend and rival, wrote six poems about Wylie and dedicated *Fatal Interview* to her in 1931. Thomas Wolfe wrote a flattering portrait of her as the glacial Rosalind Bailey in *The Web and the Rock* (1937): "Her neck and the carriage of her head were young and proud and beautiful, her dark hair was combed in the middle and framed her face in wings, her eyes were very dark and deep, and her glance was proud and straight. Anyone who ever saw her would retain the memory of her lovely, slender girlishness, her proud carriage, the level straightness of her glance, and a quality of combined childishness and maturity, of passion and of ice." But she was also extremely touchy, her vanity and egoism demanded constant flattery, and she made a terrible impression during her visit to England in the summer of 1926. The novelist Rosamond Lehmann called her "pathologically neurotic and self-centered." Virginia Woolf, writing to Vita Sackville-West, was quite cruel about her physical appearance: she is "a solid hunk: a hatchet minded, cadaverous, acid voiced, bareboned, spavined, patriotic, nasal, thick legged American."[14]

Wilson met Wylie between her second and third marriages, when they became colleagues on *Vanity Fair*. She had by then lost her beauty, become skeletally thin and spoke with the harsh voice of a peacock. But he seemed willing to play the courtier to this difficult and fascinating woman, and they sent each other whimsical and devoted poems. The title of her unpublished "Impromptu Sonnet: To Bunnius Augustus" alluded to his nickname as well as to his Roman senatorial aspect. The opening lines tried to stimulate the more frolicsome side of his character: "O thou sublime and four-square visaged boy! / What still solemnities enwreathe thy brow?" Wilson gallantly and flirtatiously responded with the unpublished "Queer Doings: To Elinor" and with "Nocturne: Impromptu to a Lady," which he published in *Poets, Farewell!* and *Night Thoughts:*

> Then rise! In some deep-sunken hole
> Below the drifts you shall be kissed;
> Or, crouching in some hollow bole,
> Snow-cushioned for the winter tryst.

By the early 1920s Wylie had already "decided, my excellent Bunny, that among members of the sterner sex you are my favorite friend in N. Y." She lent him her apartment at 68 Bank Street in the Village when she traveled to Europe in 1926 and aroused the wrath of Virginia Woolf.

Wylie would accept severe criticism from Wilson that she would not take from anyone else. "His slightly sour attitude toward life and letters," her sister wrote, "appealed to her as a valuable astringent." But, influenced as he always was by personal friendship, Wilson consistently overpraised—in his diaries, letters and essays—the style and technique of her hot-house lyrics. Indifferent to the leading male poets, Wilson believed that women as a rule were better poets than men. Reviewing Wylie's *Black Armour* in *Vanity Fair* of July 1923, he generously called her "one of the most consistently interesting of American poets. Even when her poems are not suffused with beauty, they are alive with intelligence." In an "Imaginary Dialogue" the following year, he compared her to a major writer: "Elinor Wylie is the Edith Wharton of our poets. Her pride, her submerged passion and her museum showcase culture are all characteristically American."[15]

After Wylie's death in 1928, at the age of forty-three, Wilson wrote that "I missed her extremely when she died of a stroke—she had refused to take any precautions and continued to drink against the doctor's orders." He told her husband that Wylie, the first of his friends to die, "leaves the impression undimmed of her almost supernatural brilliance and energy." Wilson loyally maintained his high opinion of her work and eight years later, in *Travels in Two Democracies*, observed: "As I reread Elinor Wylie, I kept thinking, what a marvellous language! What crystalline colors, what palpable textures! What resource, what felicity, what wit!"[16]

V

Wilson's relations with Edna Millay, who came from a very different background, were much more intense and passionate. She was born in Rockland, on the coast of Maine, in 1892, and grew up in small New England towns. Her parents were divorced when she was eight years old, and her mother worked as a practical nurse to support her three daughters. Millay published her precocious poem "Renascence" in

1912. After a semester at Barnard, she transferred to Vassar and graduated in 1917. She acted with the Provincetown Players in Greenwich Village and published her first poem in *Vanity Fair* in July 1920, shortly after Wilson joined the staff. During the next three years she brought out all her poetry and prose in that magazine and reached a much wider audience.

Wilson first met Millay at a party in the Village, after her performance on stage, early in 1920. As with Dora Carrington of the Bloomsbury Group, the photographs of Millay fail to capture and convey the strange magnetism that attracted and inspired so many men. Though Wilson fell deeply in love with her—she, more than any of his wives, was the most passionate love of his life—his description of her seems rather flat. He wrote that she could, when excited, "become almost supernaturally beautiful. She was small, but her figure was full, though she did not appear plump. She had a lovely and very long throat that gave her the look of a muse, and her reading of her poetry was thrilling."

Wilson's friend John Dos Passos came closer to distilling the essence of her poetic aura and sexual eagerness when he said that she had "violet eyes and the loveliest hair in the world. . . . The curious glint in her coppercolored hair intoxicated every man who saw her." The handsome Max Eastman, another of her ardent admirers, emphasized more coolly her theatrical quality, her intense eyes (a different color than in Dos Passos' description), her dramatic voice—and her impressive intellect:

> Her frequent effect on people was to make them a little tense and self-conscious as though because she was there, life, which had been flowing along naturally enough, had become an enacted drama.
>
> She was not voluptuously beautiful like her sister Norma; she had the legs and, at times, the expression of a maiden aunt. But her eyes were of an incredible wild gray-green out of the forest, and they had bewitching crinkles around them. Her torso was shapely, and her voice as thrilling as a violin. . . .
>
> Edna had as clear, hard, alert and logical a mind as I have encountered in man or woman. She surprised me continually too with her large and accurate knowledge about many things—about nature, about language, about everything relating to her art.[17]

Millay's greatest attractions were her intriguing bisexuality and her enchanting promiscuity. She loved sex and, in the true style of the bohemian Twenties, seemed willing to sleep with everyone. Wilson's Princeton friend Alex McKaig said that Millay had had—as early as 1920—eighteen love affairs, and Wilson suggested they form an alumni association. Millay's biographer attempted to tabulate the members of the concupiscent club, but listed only fourteen men, including Wilson, Bishop, the revolutionary John Reed, the radical novelist Floyd Dell and several more obscure figures. But some of these members, like Frank Crowninshield, seemed dubious; and others—like the poet Witter Bynner, the editor Alan Macdougall and the musician Harrison Dowd—were well-known homosexuals. Millay enhanced her own legend with a poem that emphasized her sensuality, her iconoclasm and her fatal provocations:

A large mouth,
Lascivious,
Asceticized by blasphemies.
A long throat,
Which will someday
Be strangled.

When Wilson met Millay he was still a sexually inexperienced and innocent young man who had not yet succumbed to the awful daring of a moment's surrender. He had the great good fortune to lose his virginity to Millay. She, more than anyone else, enabled Wilson to make that crucial leap from the intellectual experience of books to the sensual experience of life. After he had made love, with her, for the first time ever, Millay sadly but poetically reminded him of the transient nature of all amorous pleasure: "I know just how you feel: it was here, and it was beautiful, and now it's gone." But the effect on the repressed young man, astonished that such a desirable woman would want to sleep with *him*, was overpowering. He declared that "Edna ignited for me both my intellectual passion and my unsatisfied desire, which went up together in a blaze of ecstasy that remains for me one of the high points of my life."[18]

But the well-ignited Wilson did not merely want to be a member of the Gang of Eighteen: he wanted Millay all for himself. In the summer of 1920 he followed her to Truro, on Cape Cod (she also introduced him to that delightful peninsula) and made a formal proposal of marriage. She said she would think about it, but suggested his unsuitability with a witty riposte. When he flatteringly remarked: "By the time we're fifty years old, we'll be two of the most interesting people in the United States," Millay, who probably thought she had already achieved that eminence, sharply replied: "You behave as if you were fifty already."

Doomed to frustration and anguish with Millay, Wilson wrote that he had made allowance for her genius, "had 'understood' and forgiven her everything, had seen her simply as a creature too noble, too courageous and too brilliant for the ordinary mind." In August 1920, returning to his fiery imagery, he lamented:

> I who have broken my passionate heart
> For the lips of Edna Millay
> And her face that burns like a flame
> And her terrible chagrin.

He finally decided that Millay and Crowninshield were the two most cynical people in the world. Both believed that everyone, especially intelligent and superior men like Wilson, could be fooled by clever flattery.

Crownie found it inconvenient when two of his staff—Wilson and Bishop—fell in love with one of his leading contributors. Millay cynically encouraged their simultaneous courtship. Wilson, on his part, felt it was sexually exciting to compete for the woman he loved with a friend who was bonded to him by the same intense emotions. He would repeat this psychologically significant pattern—a congenial triangular ménage —with several other men and women in his life. While competing for Millay, Wilson dreamed that he had shed his masculine accoutrements by shaving off his beard and getting rid of his uniform, and had weakly handed over his girl to Bishop, who was wearing civilian clothes.

Bishop—who was three years older than Wilson, had pursued hookers in Princeton while Wilson held back and had seen combat in the war—was a much more vigorous and successful ladies' man. Though fastidious in taste and intellect, Bishop also had a touch of eighteenth-century coarseness. In fact, he had to disengage himself from one lady poet before he could fully devote himself to his principal prey. While at *Vanity Fair*, Wilson wrote, Bishop had "already established a fairly intimate relationship with Elinor Wylie, and it was sometimes thought that he would marry her. But she was much older than he and, although immensely amusing and clever about poetry, so self-centered that she could hardly have supplied for him the solicitous attention he needed."[19]

Alex McKaig, who loved to chronicle the sexual adventures of his Princeton friends, recorded on August 20, 1920, that Wilson (whose proposal had been rejected) still thought he would win Millay and, making allowances for her genius, would tolerate her inevitable adultery: "Lunch with Bunny Wilson at Yale Club. He gave me to understand that he was going to marry Edna St. Vincent Millay in spite of her 18 love affairs. Also hinted she might continue her amours, says she is the greatest woman he ever met—a genius. This is the girl John is in love with, the old eternal triangle. Bunny hinted John had been a boob in the whole affair. John says the girl loves him. Bunny said not. Bunny hinted at extraordinary events." But McKaig, when discussing Bishop's relations with Millay, also condemned his egoism and vanity, which seemed to match those of Elinor Wylie: "I've come to think he's damn stupid—interested only in himself, and women, and loves most the sound of his own voice, liquor, and adulation (when he can get it)."

In the fall of 1920 Wilson fulfilled his fantasies by accepting an amiable arrangement, suggested by Millay herself, that he take the lower half of Millay and John take the upper while they exchanged pleasantries about who had the better share. Though Wilson's diaries often provide intimately detailed accounts of his sexual relations, he remained vague about how he and Bishop made simultaneous love to Millay. Delmore Schwartz, knowing nothing of their peculiar relations, alluded to her famous lines ("My candle burns at both ends; / It will not last the night") and wittily suggested the perverse but intriguing possibility of approaching her from two directions. During "the implicit Bohemianism of 20 years ago," Schwartz wrote, artists asked, "let us live, write poems, be free, sleep with Edna Millay and use her candle on both sides."

Millay's letters to Wilson, which drove him into a frenzy of expectation and disappointment, now seem pretentiously poetic, intolerably arch and rather insincere. On August 3, 1920, a week before McKaig recorded his conversation with Wilson, she wrote apologetically from Truro: "I feel that you rather hate me. . . . Which is false of you. . . . I have thought of you often, Bunny, and wondered if you think of me with bitterness." She also suggested that Wilson needed alcohol to express his tenderness by asking: "is it only when you're tight that you want to be friends with me?" In January 1921, when Millay, supported by *Vanity Fair*, had moved to Paris, she again expressed contrition and suggested the possibility of a reconciliation: "Poor Bunny—it will never be right between us, will it, my dear?—I have wronged you greatly. I know that. Whatever my motives may have been, as far as you are concerned it is all a great wrong."

Millay, who felt her whole life had been ruined by men and women falling in love with her, when she only wanted to sleep with them, portrayed her tumultuous relations with Wilson in a poem called "Portrait." The lighthearted lovemaking that had brought her tranquility roused Wilson to tears and anger because he wanted so much more than she was willing to give him:

> I could not ever nor can I to this day
> Acquaint you with the triumph and the sweet rest
> These hours have brought to me and always bring. . . .
> Always, and even now, when I rise to go,
> Your eyes blaze out from a face gone wickedly pale;
> I try to tell you what I would have you know—
> What peace it was; you cry me down; you scourge me with a
>   salty flail;
> You will not have it so.[20]

On June 11, 1921, after quarreling about his salary with Crowninshield and resigning from *Vanity Fair*, Wilson sailed to Europe in pursuit of Millay. He shared a stateroom with an unpleasant Belgian, who corrected his French, and arrived in Paris on June 20.

Enticed by her letters, Wilson must have hoped, with Bishop safely on the other side of the ocean, to have both halves of Millay to himself. But his hopes were dashed when he found she had yet another lover, the journalist George Slocombe. Two weeks after his arrival, Wilson gave Bishop a full report. He described her distinguished appearance and more serious behavior, and mentioned her desire to reform her turbulent life. But Wilson also announced that he had finally cured himself of the destructive love that had caused more torment than pleasure. The end of his letter bears a striking resemblance to her melancholy statement after they first made love ("it was here, and it was beautiful, and now it's gone"):

> I found her in a very first-rate hotel on the Left Bank and better dressed, I suppose, than she has ever been before in her life. . . .

She also seems to be in very good health, the phase of being run down that Crownie hated has passed. But she looks older, more mature—at least she has on the occasions when I have seen her; she assured me that perhaps the next day she would be like a little girl again. She was very serious, earnest, and sincere about herself —inspired, I suppose, by my presence; no doubt, *ça passera*—and told me that she wanted to settle down to a new life: she was tired of breaking hearts and spreading havoc. She loved, she was very happy with her present lover, a big red-haired British journalist named Slocum [*sic*]—the Paris correspondent of the London *Herald*. . . . But she can no longer intoxicate me with her beauty or throw bombs into my soul; when I looked at her it was like staring into the center of an extinct volcano. She made me sad; it made me sad, curiously enough, that I had loved her so much once and now did not love her any longer.

Wilson's entry in his journal, at about the same time, was less poetic and more practical, and mentioned her mercenary aspect, which he omitted in the letter to Bishop. Though he was sad about the end of the affair, he also felt liberated and relieved when he finally managed to escape from her pernicious influence:

I found Edna very much allied with the Bohemians of the Left Bank, with whom I was not much at home. . . .

She was very broke at the moment and she asked me to take her to the South of France; but I knew that she was not to be relied on and would leave me for anyone who seemed more attractive. I did not want to have to worry and suffer again. . . . I declined to go away with Edna, and lent her money instead. . . .

Actually, of course, I would not love her again for anything; I can think of few more terrible calamities; but I felt that, impossible and imperfect as she is, some glamour of high passion had gone out of life when my love for her died.[21]

VI

Though Wilson managed to break with Millay, he retained a high opinion of her poetry and she left a permanent mark on his work. She provided the inspiration for Rita Cavanaugh in his novel, *I Thought of*

Daisy (1929), for Ellen Terhune in his collection of stories, *Memoirs of Hecate County* (1946), and for his long, poignant memorial essay, one of his finest in this genre, which was written after her death in 1950 and closed *The Shores of Light* (1952). Millay became his muse; but she had a more profound impact on his life than on his art. When a significant number of his Princeton class thought even casual kissing was morally wrong, she freed him from sexual repression as well as from the constraints of conventional behavior, and transformed the "man in the iron necktie" into one of the great literary fornicators of all time. Like Dr. Walter Robie's guide book to sex, *The Art of Love* (1921), which Wilson lent to girlfriends so he could more easily seduce them, the unconstrained and sensual Millay encouraged him to do anything that gave him pleasure. Though restrained in his behavior (except when drunk), Wilson was sexually uninhibited and seemed to enjoy all forms of sexual activity with all kinds of women—from prostitutes to socialites.

Once liberated from his puritan heritage, Wilson found that he was extremely responsive to sensual experience. While listening to a concert at Carnegie Hall, he "realized that violin music was intensely sexual and feminine, even when produced by a man, in the sense that it represents the feeling for a woman of the underpart of the penis lingeringly passing in and out and eliciting exquisite music."

Wilson's appetite for attractive women was, as he wrote of the American novelist Harold Frederic, indomitable and persistent. He defined his own cyclical behavior as dedicated toil followed by an orgy. Like Bertrand Russell and H. G. Wells, he was a physically unattractive intellectual whose hyperactive sex life fuelled his work. Wilson was bold in his approach, indifferent to rebuffs and astonishingly successful with women. Sex for him did not merely provide pleasure, but was also a way to experience new feelings and gain new understanding. For Wilson, as for Pepys and Boswell, no seduction was complete until he had recorded its details in his diary.

When asked by a friend how he managed to convince so many women to go to bed with him, Wilson, whose strongest card was his impressive intellect, replied that he talked them into it. His seductive line, though effective, was rather banal. "Do spend the night here," he would formally suggest, "I won't molest you—much as I should like to." Once, when he wanted to kiss a woman "inside the thighs," she coyly said: "Closed for the day." When he succeeded in winkling a lady out of her foundation garments, her slippery body and the crustacean-like smell of her parts reminded him, in a commonplace way, of eating shellfish.

The most idiosyncratic aspect of Wilson's sexual taste was his obsessive foot-fetishism. He was once attracted to a Russian mistress by "the thickness and neatness of her feet," and held another woman's foot in his armpit while gazing at her sexual parts. When married to his second wife he would—as Leopold Bloom does with Molly in *Ulysses*—lie with his head at the bottom of the bed and his face against her feet: "it would make her nervous, even hysterical, [for me] to kiss her feet, she would pull them away." With another woman, Louise Fort Connor, Wilson wrote that "I picked up her foot in my lap, took her shoe off and kissed her foot, then put my hand up her dress and my fingers in her cunt. . . . She rubbed my member in my trousers with the tip of her foot."[22] Feet must have played a significant part in his sexual relations with Millay as well as with all his other women.

Wilson's obsession found its way into his imaginative work. In his play about the Twenties, *This Room and This Gin and These Sandwiches*, the woman (based on his first wife) remarks: "My feet aren't little," to which the man replies: "Yes, they are: they're darling." His most striking simile, noted by many reviewers and readers, appeared in *I Thought of Daisy* and connected feet with food: "I held her firm little insteps for a moment in my hands: in pale stockings, her tired and sweaty [waitress'] feet were like two little moist cream cheeses encased in covers of cloth." Wilson's foot-fetishism, instead of perversely displacing his interest in normal sex, intensified the pleasure he got from it.[23]

VII

Wilson was pleased by his moral resolution when breaking with Millay, but unhappy about losing the romantic journey with her to the South of France. Alone in Paris, he turned to other friends. He tried to persuade Scott and Zelda Fitzgerald, who had married in April 1920 and were currently traveling in Italy, to join him in France: "Take my advice, cancel your passage [home] and come to Paris for the summer! Settle down and learn French and apply a little French leisure and measure to that restless and jumpy nervous system." But the Fitzgeralds, who had been traveling in Europe since May and had already visited Paris, were not attracted by Wilson's sober suggestions. Though Scott would actually spend more time in France than Bunny, he never learned much more French than *"Très bien,* you son-of-a-bitch!" Besides, though Wilson did not know it, Zelda was pregnant and they were eager to get home. So Wilson, using Crownie's introduction to a *Vanity Fair* author, looked up the poet and playwright Jean Cocteau, who was gratified by his admiration.

A more promising possibility was the beautiful and (like Millay) bisexual Djuna Barnes. Born in New York three years before Wilson, she lived in Europe and would later publish the much-admired introspective novel, *Nightwood*. Barnes adopted a teasing and tempting attitude toward him. When a friend told her that Wilson worked harder than they did, Barnes (thinking of his pampered weekends in Red Bank) replied: "Oh, no, he lives like a pet pony!" Provoked perhaps by Barnes' witty comment: "I spent all summer looking for a night to go with that nightgown," Wilson took her to dinner at a Montmartre restaurant and suggested that they travel together to Italy. Barnes refused the seductive offer.

Disappointed by Millay, Fitzgerald and Barnes, Wilson chose a more sober alternative and flew to England to see his fifty-year-old philosophy teacher, Norman Kemp Smith. His first flight was terrifying. One of the engines on the Goliath plane broke down and then stopped completely; after flapping around at a lopsided angle for fifteen minutes, it made an emergency landing on the French coast. The next morning Wilson crossed the Channel by ferry and made a depressing visit to Kemp Smith in Haslemere, Surrey. His old friend had aged considerably during the war and, Wilson suspected from long experience with his father's nervous illness, seemed about to crack up. Most alarming of all, Wilson told Gauss, was that the former disciple of the rationalist David Hume now seemed preoccupied with religion: "I was really worried about him, not only from his appearance—he looks very gray and haggard and his eyes are bloodshot: all his old freshness and ruddiness were gone—but especially from the general tone of his talk: he spoke like someone who has been under a long strain and has been on the verge of a breakdown; he seemed full of strong fears about himself, about degenerating in middle age. But the thing that shocked me the most was the fact that he . . . [was] disposed to turn to Catholicism!"[24]

Wilson traveled from London to Venice and Florence, which also failed to meet his expectations. Though Venice usually enchants most visitors, it provoked Wilson's puritan disapproval. He found the city constricted, gaudy and Byzantine, and tired of it after only a week.

Since Wilson knew no one in Florence (on later trips he would confidently seek out the leading writers), he reverted to his old habits and spent most of his time in his hotel room reading Dante, Vasari and Leopardi. He planned to go from Florence to Naples, but when his pocket was picked in the railroad station before the train had started, he abandoned the trip and returned to France.

Just after the war Wilson had set out on his sexual odyssey (after making sure no ladies were present in the drugstore) by buying his first contraceptive: "The clerk withdrew to the back counter and produced a condom of rubber, which he highly recommended, blowing it up like a balloon in order to show me how reliable it was. But the condom, thus distended, burst, and this turned out to be something of an omen. I soon got over my shyness with women but I was the victim of many of the hazards of sex—from which I might have been saved by previous experience: abortions, gonorrhea, entanglements, a broken heart." The abortions and gonorrhea were the result of his entanglement with a Ukrainian waitress whom he met in 1927, but his heart had been broken by Edna Millay.

In mid-August 1921, just after he had severed his relations with Millay, Wilson told Dell that he was suffering a sort of retribution for his long years of virginity. Desperate (like Millay) for a more settled mode of existence, he thought he might have to follow his friends' example and find reluctant refuge in marriage: "My affairs of the heart (confidential) are badly entangled. I suppose it is old mother nature's revenge for my long period of freedom from these troubles that I should have spent this last year occupied with women at the expense of everything else; just now I am reduced to a state where I am anxious to find a modus vivendi which will enable me to live and let live. I really don't want to marry but—."[25] Though Wilson held out for the next two years, he became involved with his future wife when he returned from Europe in September 1921 and took up the job of managing editor at the *New Republic*.

FIVE

The *New Republic* and
Ted Paramore, 1921–1922

I

In mid-February 1921—shortly before Wilson set off for Europe—
the political journalist Walter Lippmann, an occasional contributor to
Vanity Fair, offered him a job on the *New Republic*. Wilson accepted at
once. The journal had been founded by Herbert Croly in 1914 with
money provided by Willard Straight, an idealistic partner in the Mor-
gan bank. When Straight died, his widow, Dorothy, who had an even
greater fortune and later married the Englishman Leonard Elmhirst,
continued the subsidy. Though its stipends were modest and its circu-
lation down to 30,000, the *New Republic*, located in two old houses on
West 21st Street near the Hudson River, was the outstanding liberal
weekly in America.

Lippmann thought Wilson's youth, energy and intellect would
help rescue the magazine, which had become rather stale and was
losing its readers. As Wilson explained to Dell: "They offer me more
money, more chance to write than I get here, and the prospect of
becoming a regular editor some day. Lippmann got them to take me
on. They are really in quite a bad way. The magazine has become so
dull that the editors themselves say they are unable to read it and the
subscribers are dying off like flies. The editors, who started out as gay
young freethinkers, have become respectable to the point of stodgi-
ness." When he dined out with the Lippmanns, Wilson was depressed
by their extreme conventionality, immediately saw what he was up
against and realized how comparatively lively his old magazine had
been. He was amused to discover that Lippmann, whom Wilson regarded as utterly bourgeois, found Herbert Croly hopelessly old-
fashioned and dull.

The club-like atmosphere at the *New Republic* was very pleasant. There were no regular office hours and lunch was served at one in the dining room, where the staff frequently entertained political and literary celebrities. Wilson dealt with many illustrious writers, for in the 1920s Bertrand Russell, John Maynard Keynes, H. G. Wells, Rebecca West and Virginia Woolf all contributed to the magazine. Yet several colleagues at the *New Republic*, like Crowninshield at *Vanity Fair*, felt intimidated by Wilson's patrician manner and dyspeptic temperament. Though there was no jolly "Rape of the Sabine Women" at the *New Republic*, the job had immediate advantages as well as future prospects. If Wilson became a regular editor, he could draw a large salary, stay away from the office and write his books at home. In 1929, when he was thinking of leaving, Croly suddenly had a stroke and Wilson was asked to stay on. When Croly ran the magazine, the younger editors had been his satellites; after his death in May 1930, they all had equal power. Since the *New Republic* was endowed by the Elmhirsts (who lived in England), it had a sound financial basis. But, Wilson would later discover, its contents had to reflect the owners' political views.

Wilson contributed more than 350 articles and reviews to the *New Republic* between 1921 and 1941. Though the magazine has not kept records of these decades, some sketchy details of his payments have survived. By the end of 1929 he had earned $5,450; in the late 1930s his salary as literary editor was $144 a week; in 1937 he was paid $60 for a review of Kipling's *Something of Myself* and $520 each (half in cash and half in credit against unearned advances) for several 5,000-word essays on the forerunners of socialism, which became part of *To the Finland Station*.

The *New Republic*, casual about schedules, gave Wilson generous leave and in the summer of 1921 he sailed to Europe in pursuit of Edna Millay. When he returned to New York in September, he lived for a time at 136 West 16th Street. In February 1922, he took a railroad apartment above a furrier's loft at 777 Lexington Avenue, near 62nd Street, with his Hill School friend Ted Paramore. Born in the fashionable summer resort of Manchester, Massachusetts, north of Boston, a year after Wilson, and raised in Santa Barbara, California, Paramore was voted the most brilliant and versatile man in the Yale class of 1917. He had been in the U.S. Embassy in Petrograd in 1917, and during the Revolution had guided a trainload of 124 American refugees through Siberia and safely out of the country. Paramore's exciting adventures and acute understanding of the country aroused Wilson's interest in the language, literature and history of Russia.

Paramore's father, a rakishly jovial yachtsman and son of a railroad millionaire, always kept Ted well-supplied with money—which he sometimes lent to the hard-up Wilson. In the *New Republic* of July 25, 1928, Wilson wrote a lively tribute to Ted's colorful father, whom he called one of the most attractive and admirable men he had ever known. Ted Paramore had visited the Fitzgeralds in St. Paul when Zelda was pregnant in the summer of 1921. The following year, while Ted was living with Wilson, Fitzgerald satirized him in *The Beautiful and Damned* as the rather boastful Frederick E. Paramore, who had been to Harvard with the hero of the novel, Anthony Patch. When the fictional Paramore, a social worker at a settlement house, is asked what he has been doing since college, he casually replies: "'Oh, many things. I've led a very active life. Knocked about here and there.' (*His tone implies anything from lion-stalking to organized crime.*)" Paramore became a successful journalist, playwright, poet and screenwriter. In 1921 he wrote the extremely popular "Ballad of Yukon Jake," which parodied the vigorous frontier verse of Robert Service; in 1938 he collaborated with Fitzgerald on the screenplay *Three Comrades,* based on the novel by Erich Remarque; in 1951 he planned a screenplay based on Fitzgerald's life.

Wilson wrote that Paramore, a year behind him at The Hill, had gone around "with the air of an alert bull terrier who might become scrappy. But I now found him agreeable and great fun. . . . He was . . . so sensitive, so infectiously amusing and so apparently well-intentioned." Handsome, hard drinking and a great ladies' man, Paramore —like the heroes of Fitzgerald's early novels—loved "pretty girls, riding, tennis, dancing, and lots of licker." "Santa Barbara," he told the solemn and envious Wilson, in one of his scandalous and diverting letters, "is a continuous round of panics and gin bouts, interspersed with wild wrastling on the beach and more serious rogering, covering, fluttering, and playing the two-bakked beeste in the canyons."[1] The only woman who ever intimidated Ted was the witty Hollywood writer Anita Loos. He was attracted to her, but feared his passes would provoke her ridicule.

Wilson adored the rich, cynical, hedonistic, fornicating and alcoholic Paramore, who invented fantastic dishes like "sweetbreads smothered in aspirin tablets—veal cutlet with sauce veronal." At the start of

Wilson and Paramore's ghastly party on May Day 1926, Ted provocatively announced: "I've got enough stuff here for a brawl that'll bring out four fire companies:—punch bowl as big as a man!" During the party Wilson tried to shut the bathroom door while a macaw was perched on top, and then went to bed still wearing his garters and socks. Untroubled by Wilson's puritan conscience, Ted led the kind of insouciant and pleasure-filled life that Edmund hoped to have. Paramore became, along with Edna Millay, Wilson's tutor in the art of seduction.

Though he loved to hear about Ted's escapades, Wilson disapproved of his heavy drinking, which sometimes brought on delirium tremens. In December 1924 Wilson told a mutual friend that if Paramore won his suit against the film director Mack Sennett, who had stolen Ted's Yukon joke, he would come east and drink himself to death on the damages. Fond of yet worried and annoyed by Ted, Wilson felt he was wasting his talent in Hollywood. By middle age Paramore, who had married three times and had become a financial success, responded to Wilson's concern with a bantering and slightly superior attitude. In 1948, after Edmund had had his third child, Ted replied to one of his Christmas poems with a "Yuletide Riposte" of his own:

> Just turn the knob of Wilson's door,
> Then stand aside and cower,
> While children fathered by this man
> Stream out for half an hour.[2]

John Dos Passos, whom Wilson met in the offices of *Vanity Fair* while he was living with Paramore, was a near-sighted, shy, intellectual artist. He had a temperamental affinity with Wilson and appealed to the more serious side of his character. Born in Chicago a year after Wilson, Dos Passos was the grandson of an immigrant shoemaker from Portuguese Madeira and the illegitimate son of a highly successful New York lawyer, who wrote legal books that were owned by Wilson's father. Dos Passos had been educated in Europe and at the Choate School. After graduating from Harvard, he served as an ambulance driver during the war in France and Italy. He had traveled widely in Spain and the Middle East; and his war novel, *Three Soldiers* (1921), had been favorably reviewed by Fitzgerald. Sensitive and insecure about his parentage, Dos Passos was also self-conscious about his stammer and slight lisp. E. E. Cummings, his Harvard classmate, liked to mock Dos Passos' peculiar speech and sentimental politics by exclaiming: "Isn't it dweadful of me to lie here in this luxurious warm bath while human welations are being violated all over the countwy—stwikers are being shot down!" Wilson's third wife, Mary McCarthy, found Dos Passos, their neighbor on Cape Cod, "terrifying" because he was so difficult to talk to and so shy about mentioning anything to do with sex.

Dos Passos at first assumed that Wilson was the conventional "slight sandyheaded young man with a handsome clear profile" that he seemed to be. He was startled when, as they waited for the elevator at *Vanity Fair*, the unathletic Wilson suddenly executed a neat somersault. He was also surprised to discover that Wilson, who did not drive a car, rode a motorcycle from New York to his parents' home in Red Bank. When they swam on the Jersey shore Wilson, though buffeted by rough seas, maintained his dignity and continued his elaborate discourse: "He was an unexpectedly strong swimmer; once when I went out to see him at Red Bank we went into the surf in heavy weather. We had been talking about Henry James' novels as we trotted down the beach. The waves pounded us. Though I was coughing and spluttering and hard put to it to keep from drowning, Bunny kept unreeling one of his long involved sentences in a quiet conversational tone. Except when he was interrupted by a wave's breaking over his head, he didn't miss a single dependent clause."[3]

Until their political quarrel erupted during the Cold War, Dos Passos was one of Wilson's closest friends. Wilson admired his amiable personality, his gentlemanly demeanor, his knowledge of other cultures, his stimulating conversation, his willingness to take a stand and fight for the underdog. During the 1930s Bishop's poem "No More the Senator" urged Wilson "to give up serious political activity and to withdraw into private virtue." In the first chapter of *I Thought of Daisy* he portrayed Dos Passos as Hugo Bamman and praised "his good manners, his integrity, and his cultivated intelligence" as well as his "true social idealism which cut under capitalistic politics."[4] In 1929, the year the novel was published, Dos Passos married the vivacious Katy Smith, who had been a childhood friend of Hemingway during their summers in northern Michigan. Her father taught physics at Tulane University and wrote a book (which would have appealed to Wilson) arguing that Christ had never actually existed. The slim, blond Katy, a college roommate and close friend of Hemingway's second wife, was a superb cook and sympathetic companion in Provincetown.

II

After his first years on the *New Republic*—where he wrote book reviews, theater criticism, literary essays as well as articles on film, vaudeville, the circus, night clubs and jazz—Wilson had established his reputation as a significant and influential critic. He had also proved to his somewhat sceptical family that a writer could become a successful professional. In the early 1920s the avant-garde *Little Review* identified him as foremost among those engaged in "trying to steal up and sneak Matthew Arnold's cloak off Eliot." But Wilson's principal models, as he freely acknowledged, were Edgar Poe, Hippolyte Taine, George Saintsbury, Van Wyck Brooks and H. L. Mencken.

Like Poe, whom he consistently praised, Wilson was torn between writing popular journalism or ambitious books, and exemplified the difficulty of surviving in philistine America as a serious author. We have seen that Wilson's discovery of Taine's chapter on Sterne in his *History of English Literature* (1873), while he was a student at The Hill, gave him the first glimmerings of the biographical and critical method he would later adopt as his own. In his autobiographical essay "A Modest Self-Tribute," Wilson observed that Taine "had created the creators themselves as characters in a larger drama of cultural and social history, and writing about literature, for me, has always meant narrative and drama as well as the discussion of comparative values." Echoing the credo expressed in the dedication to *Axel's Castle*, Wilson accurately wrote that "I have tried to contribute a little to the general cross-fertilization, to make it possible for our literate public to appreciate and understand both our own Anglo-American culture and those of the European countries in relation to one another."

The immensely learned and far-ranging George Saintsbury, Professor of English Literature at the University of Edinburgh from 1895 to 1915, came closest to fulfilling Taine's—and Wilson's—cross-cultural ideals and to achieving first-rate stature as a professional critic. Wilson particularly admired Saintsbury's mastery of all literatures, independent judgment, catholic taste, genial personality and lucid expression. As he wrote in his tributes to Saintsbury:

> Academic fashions and categories, conventional assumptions and beaten trails, meant very little to him: he had to explore every inch

for himself, see everything with his own eyes and formulate his own opinions.

He seems to make us want to feel that we are under some obligation to gratify the literary palate with everything that can possibly be relished.

He had read everything. He was able truly to boast that he had never judged any of his subjects until all the evidence was in and that he had never uttered a second-hand opinion. The principal thrill of reading Saintsbury is the sensation of looking down on literature as with the comparative eye of God. And he had an original and most attractive literary style.[5]

Wilson's older contemporary Van Wyck Brooks was one of the first critics to devote himself to exhaustive study of American literary and cultural life. Like Taine and Saintsbury, Brooks had great erudition, curiosity and enthusiasm. "He is very much interested in everything," Wilson wrote, after a stimulating visit from Brooks, "likes to tell you about artists and writers he knows and loves to discover the unpublicized interconnections between well-known literary figures."

Wilson also met and admired the controversial and iconoclastic H. L. Mencken. An intensely Germanic, beer-drinking, cigar-chomping man, notorious for his savage satires on philistine life in America, Mencken had a squat proletarian face, a pudgy nose, and hair plastered down and parted in the middle. Wilson contributed to Mencken's *Baltimore Evening Sun* and invited him to write for the *New Republic*. Both men were interested in dictionaries and in the meaning of words, and Wilson supplied Mencken with a list of army slang that was used in later editions of *The American Language*.

Both men focused on American literature, but also had a keen awareness of European culture. They avoided generalizations and emphasized specifics, wrote essays about social as well as literary issues and were opposed to prudishness in print. Both writers were hostile to Christianity. Fitzgerald, who shared Wilson's high opinion of Mencken, called him "The Baltimore Anti-Christ." "Anti-Christ" was also John and Katy Dos Passos' affectionate nickname for Wilson. Mencken rejected one of the stories Wilson sent to the *American Mercury*, but offered valuable suggestions about how to improve it and explained that "we have enough [material] in our Hoboken warehouse to last until the Second Coming."

Wilson wrote that Mencken was, "since Poe, our greatest practic-ing literary journalist." Thinking of himself as well as of Mencken, Wilson remarked that it seemed "astonishing that one independent critic, writing mainly in newspapers and magazines, should have fought so many successful fights and grown to be so powerful a figure." Mencken returned his admiration. When Wilson was hired by the *New Yorker* in 1943, Mencken told the editor, Harold Ross: "You have found a highly competent critic and perfectly honest man. The combi-nation is not too common in this great Republic."[6]

All five critics, like Wilson himself, had a clear and accurate expos-itory style, expressed themselves in plain, direct statements and were extremely prolific. Wilson's criticism, like that of his masters, conveys a strong sense of his own personality and traditional values, his rectitude and humane learning. There is little technical or formal analysis in his criticism. Instead, Wilson emphasizes the study of personalities and ideas, which, as he pointed out in his Preface to *The Confessions*, "had its first important expression in Rousseau." The eminently readable Wil-son always described things in concrete detail. "His virtues," wrote one of his most appreciative critics, John Updike, "were old-fashioned American ones: industriousness, enthusiasm, directness, integrity."

In his major essays Wilson described the historical background and the life of the subject, provided an analytic summary of the principal works and offered a judicious appraisal. Wilson told Vladimir Nabokov that he saw in Flaubert's *Madame Bovary* a reflection of the two stages of his own critical approach: "It is as if he first assembled his data and then at a given point turned on the music and magic. I am especially interested in this because it is more or less my own method."[7] Wilson often revealed his own character while writing about others, and had the uncanny ability to make his reviews more interesting than the books he wrote about.

Wilson's writing habits were extremely efficient, enabling him to produce a prodigious quantity of books and articles. He regularly began work at nine in the morning and continued, with a lunch tray at his desk, until three or four in the afternoon. He always answered letters by return of post, and would draft his response, for an office secretary to type, at the bottom of the letter. He usually took notes from his voluminous reading on the endpapers of the books. Following a priest-like ritual, he could not begin writing without washing his hands. He invariably wrote in longhand with a lead pencil on legal-size yellow pads. According to his upstate friend Glyn Morris, "the pencil was held between forefinger and the fourth finger in a very peculiar manner."

Wilson's pragmatic and purposeful way of writing was the same as Max Beerbohm's: "First I write one sentence: then I write another. That's how I write. And so I go on." Wilson elaborated on his method of pouring out and then refining his prose when he told Glyn Morris: "I just put down everything hodge-podge, then I make a second draft, then a fair copy which is typed and edited again. I made eleven drafts of *The Dead Sea Scrolls*. Then I read the proofs and edit them. . . . You have to set a goal for each day and stick to it. I usually try to do six pages."

Despite his heavy drinking and tumultuous life, Wilson never seemed to suffer from writer's block. Part of his success was due to his absolute absorption in the task. In a self-interview, he described how he wrote one of his longest essays, on the little-known novels of a Victorian poet: "I'm in Cambridge, Mass., imprisoned in an upstairs room, with the complete works of Swinburne and the six volumes of his correspondence and a lot of books about him on my desk, on the windowsill, on the bureau, and on the empty bed next to mine. I sleep with them, work with them, eat with them. It's a possible mode of escape" from the unpleasant realities of the world.[8]

Wilson (as he said of the English author Maurice Baring) "seemed to make books of everything he wrote, and some of them overlap." The key to his achievement was the ability to write about what interested him and then get editors to pay for it. In the revealing essay "Thoughts on Being Bibliographed," he noted how he successively worked up and revised pieces, as if he were constructing a monument with rocks and stones and boulders, from reviews to essays to chapters in books: "My own strategy . . . has usually been, first to get books for review or reporting assignments to cover on subjects in which I happened to be interested; then, later, to use the scattered articles for writing general studies of these subjects; then, finally, to bring out a book in which groups of these essays were revised and combined." Wilson's close connection to a number of important magazines—from *Vanity Fair*, the *New Republic* and the *Dial* to the *Nation*, the *New Yorker* and the *New York Review of Books*—enabled him to get the plum assignments and promptly publish all his work. He could bring out any book he had assembled, and took this process one step further when he made new books from sections of old ones.[9]

In the 1920s Wilson was brilliant at analyzing the meaning and estimating the value of the extremely innovative and difficult new works of Joyce and Eliot, and his reviews and essays on these writers eventually became chapters in *Axel's Castle*. His perceptive reviews of Joyce's *Ulysses* in July and August 1922—which emphasized the Homeric parallels, the realistic characterization and the unexpected humor—earned a gratifying commendation from the master. That summer the half-blind Joyce wrote, with punctilious formality: "Your articles in the *New Republic* and [Baltimore] *Evening Sun* about *Ulysses* have been read to me, and I desire to express my thanks for your very appreciative and painstaking criticism." Wilson was so far ahead of most critics, who were generally baffled by these works, that the originality of his interpretations was not fully recognized. In December 1929 the *New York Times* was moved to editorialize about him with obtuse and heavy-handed irony: "The quickest road to the comprehension of the Joycean method is 'to note what goes on in one's own mind when one is just dropping off to sleep.' To less subtle and imaginative minds than Mr. Wilson's that is a moment of jumbles, grotesqueries, absurdities."

Wilson reviewed Eliot's *Waste Land* in the *Dial* and *Vanity Fair*. His essay "The Poetry of Drouth," a classic of criticism on Eliot, was often quoted by subsequent reviewers. Moved by Eliot's subtle thought and striking images, Wilson immediately recognized its puritan sensibility and called it "the most considerable poem of any length yet produced by an American poet." Just after the poem appeared, Wilson, who had some inside information (perhaps from the indiscreet Ezra Pound) about Eliot's private life, pursued an illuminating biographical approach. He told John Bishop that *The Waste Land*, written while Eliot was under psychiatric treatment in Lausanne, is "certainly a cry *de profundis* if ever there was one—almost the cry of a man on the verge of insanity."[10]

In an equally acute review of *Ash Wednesday*, Wilson wrote of Eliot: "even at the moment when his psychological plight seems most depressing and his ways of rescuing himself from it least sympathetic, [the poem] still gives him a place among those upon whose words we reflect with most interest and whose tones we remember the longest." But his psychological approach offended the very canons established by the apostle of impersonality and the New Critics who followed him. They focused on the text itself, tried to exclude all other considerations and had a strong influence in academic circles. Allen Tate, ignoring Wilson's shrewd insights, wrote a thoroughly unconvincing protest: "Edmund Wilson's review of 'Ash Wednesday' seems to me to be very unsound; it ends up with some very disconcerting speculation on Eliot's private life which has no significance at all."

Wilson actively sought out every American author who interested him and eventually came to know nearly all the important writers in the country. His major fault as a critic, throughout his career, was a generous one: he frequently reviewed (or introduced) books by close friends and allowed his personal feelings—his loyalty and love—to influence his literary judgment.[11] He did not, however, use reviews to pay off personal grudges and almost never reviewed a book he knew he would dislike.

Wilson, though well disposed to women writers, would sometimes indulge in a misogynistic remark. Once, when discussing an obscure contributor with the editor Malcolm Cowley, he said: "I thought at first it must be a woman, on account of the hysterical character of the stuff and a kind of bad taste that women routinely develop when they decide to be outspoken." But he usually tended to inflate the reputations of the women he knew and liked. In the *New Republic* of October 12, 1927, for example, he expressed his current literary taste and declared that the most "distinguished American writers who have emerged during the last seven years [are]: John Dos Passos, Ernest Hemingway and Lewis Mumford in prose; in poetry, Louise Bogan, Elinor Wylie, Léonie Adams, Allen Tate and John Crowe Ransom" (whose technical skill he admired). This admittedly arbitrary list was notable for the authors it left out. There was no mention of O'Neill, Fitzgerald and Faulkner in prose, or of Stevens, Williams, Marianne Moore, Cummings or Hart Crane in poetry. Tate and Wylie were friends; Adams already was and Bogan soon would be Wilson's lover.

Wilson tended to overpraise (as we have seen) the work of Phelps Putnam, Elinor Wylie and Dos Passos. But the most extreme example of his partiality, which hurt his critical reputation, was his attitude toward Edna Millay. In July 1923, after she had returned from Europe, Millay married a conventional Dutch coffee importer, Eugen Boissevain. When Wilson saw her four years later, he was shocked and disillusioned by her physical decline. At thirty-five she appeared to have lost a great deal of her poetical aura and to have absorbed some characteristics of a solid Dutch burgher: "She seemed well and normal again, almost robust—no make-up, a dreary white-flecked gray dress, which, however, she insisted, had come from a very expensive and good place. Her hands and feet and ankles were so much larger than they used to be that I could hardly believe they were the same ones I had loved. Nor did her throat seem so beautiful—I think her putting on flesh had spoiled its contour—and her mouth, which seemed thicker than it used to, revealed two big square front teeth." In his long memorial essay, published in 1952, two years after her death, Wilson insisted that "my estimate of Edna Millay's work has never been much affected by my personal emotions about her." He then immediately contradicted himself by equating her with titanic writers like Proust, Mann and Joyce: "Edna Millay seems to me one of the only poets writing in English in our time who have attained to anything like the stature of great literary figures in an age in which prose has dominated."[12]

Though Wilson's estimate of Millay now seems wildly inflated, it is worth noting that his opinion was shared by the severe and judicious poet-critic A. E. Housman. In mid-January 1932, Housman told his friend Sydney Cockerell that Millay was "the best living American poet" and that her latest book, *Fatal Interview*, was "mighty good." Nevertheless, after writing a highly favorable notice of Millay's *Conversation at Midnight* (1937), Wilson received a letter from the poet Horace Gregory, which exposed a vulnerable point in his critical armor: "If you accept Miss Millay as your criterion, I don't see how you can write intelligently of Auden or anyone of the younger group today."[13] Though Gregory was certainly right about Millay, Wilson would, later on, shrewdly appraise the poetry of Elizabeth Bishop, John Berryman and Randall Jarrell, and write penetrating essays on both Auden and Robert Lowell.

III

During the early 1920s Wilson remained on close terms with John Peale Bishop, who combined Paramore's rakishness with the seriousness of Dos Passos. Bishop continued to work on *Vanity Fair* after Wilson had left; and his departure for Europe, after his marriage in June 1922, brought Wilson back to the magazine from July until the following May. On May 26, 1922, three weeks before Bishop's marriage to Margaret Hutchins, Wilson expressed his dislike (shared by all Bishop's friends) of his future wife and accurately predicted that she would soon extinguish John's poetic talent:

I regard it as more or less of a calamity, as she has always seemed to me a prime dumbbell, but I suppose it was inevitable. The suddenness of the whole thing—while Crownie is abroad—may make it necessary for me to go back to the old madhouse [*Vanity Fair*] and take his place till some new young man can be found to be groomed for managing editor. . . . Contemplation of John's impending married life with a strong-willed, unintelligent woman of passionate gentility and correctitude was what put the lid on [for] me. She has a great deal of money, to be sure, and theoretically will enable John to serve the muses undisturbed by the necessity of earning a living, but actually I am afraid that she will set out to stifle poesy, and all the experience that goes to make it, with relentless jealousy.

Bishop, comfortably imprisoned in an old château outside Paris, lived mostly in France until 1933, and wrote many tedious letters to Wilson. Fitzgerald, whose career had taken off while Bishop's remained stagnant, criticized his dullness and weakness in a report to Wilson: "Yes, John seemed to us a beaten man—with his tiny frail moustache—but perhaps only morally." Fitzgerald continued to see his friend for nostalgic reasons and remarked two years later that Bishop "was here [on the Riviera] with his unspeakably awful wife. He seems anemic and washed out, a memory of the past so far as I'm concerned." Archibald MacLeish, who had an affair with Margaret Bishop in 1924, called her a misplaced clubwoman whose money had emasculated her husband. Allen Tate compared Bishop to "a man lying in a warm bath who faintly hears the telephone ringing downstairs" and lacks the energy to answer it.[14]

But in 1922, before Bishop's marriage, the two old friends—who had been sexual collaborators with Edna Millay—now collaborated on Wilson's first (and Bishop's second) book, *The Undertaker's Garland.* Wilson had previously written the Princeton musical *The Evil Eye* with Fitzgerald and throughout his career continued to produce joint efforts with many of his friends.[15] He found the comradeship of fellow writers a welcome relief from the long solitude of individual effort.

The Undertaker's Garland, his most ambitious collaboration, was brought out by Knopf in September 1922—the year *Ulysses* and *The Waste Land* were published—as the use of classical mythology in literature became fashionable. This rather bizarre work, which had been rejected by Scribner's, was written in alternating chapters of both verse and prose by Bishop and "Edmund Wilson Jr." It combined Bishop's fantasy and elegant dandyism with Wilson's pronounced taste for the macabre.[16] The book was inspired by their experiences in the war and contained—as the ironic title suggests—the same kind of mortuary poetry as in Edward Young's *Night Thoughts* (1745) and Thomas Beddoes' *Death's Jest Book* (1850).

Wilson was well trained in the classics in prep school and college. In the course of his career he wrote essays on Sophocles' *Oedipus Rex*, *Antigone* and *Philoctetes*, on Lucian and Plato, Virgil and Persius. He composed a poem on Quintilian, translated Latin poems by Petronius and A. E. Housman, published "Reflections on the Teaching of Latin" and "A Note on Elegiac Meter." The learned, Eliot-like epigraphs in Latin and Italian at the beginning of the book, and the long quotation in Greek at the head of the first chapter by Wilson, though academic and decorative, do suggest certain themes. Wilson quotes Lucretius to evoke the living-dead soldiers in the war who vainly tried to avert their inevitable doom: "And will *you* kick and protest against your sentence? You, whose life is next-door to death while you are still alive and looking on the light?" He uses a bitterly ironic passage from Canto VII (not Canto III, as printed in the book) of Dante's *Inferno* to suggest the damned souls in the trenches as well as those who managed to survive but still bear psychological wounds: "Fixed in the slime they say, 'We were sullen in the sweet air that is gladdened by the sun, bearing within us the sluggish fumes; now we are sullen in the black mire.'"[17]

The Undertaker's Garland was a handsome book with mauve labels pasted on the front cover and spine and morbid Beardsley-like decorations by Boris Artzybasheff. Though Wilson was in close touch with modern literary movements, this book—with its nostalgia for a lost and better world—seemed deliberately old-fashioned, even archaic. Scholarly, disillusioned and decadent, the rather mannered exercise was a catalogue of mortuary moments, influenced by the classics, fin-de-siècle poetry, Housman's world-weariness, and the traditional forms of the Georgian poets. In "The Funeral of a Romantic Poet" Wilson writes, in unbearably stilted diction:

> "The Lake"? The Lake forgets? While mortal kind
> Keep close the songs where Beauty's hand is set—
> Ah, night with words of sorrow in the wind!
>   Ah, rocks that speak!—the Lake shall not forget!

The book attacks the enemies of life: bourgeois society, materialistic industry and the war that has been justified by lies. Wilson and Bishop saw the skull beneath the skin and decided, they said, "to interpret our country in a book devoted to death." The various chapters concern the death of a centaur, a dandy, an efficiency expert, a soldier and God as well as the funerals of Mary Magdalene, a Romantic poet, an undertaker and a madman. The settings range from Greenwich Village, Jerusalem and Paris in 1840 to wartime France and Hades. In Wilson's "Emily in Hades"—the first fictional expression of his urge to escape from repression and experience passionate life—a woman dies of influenza, is bored in Hades and regrets that she had "never known love." The best chapter of the book is Wilson's "The Death of a Soldier," which (we have seen) was based on his actual experience in war, and describes a young man's death from pneumonia on a troop train in France.

The critics were inevitably puzzled by the eclectic elements in the book, and so was his mother. H. L. Mencken praised the "acrid and devastating humor" of the two bold young men "who had undertaken to spit in the eye of Death, treat it as a joke." Gilbert Seldes, in an unenthusiastic review in the *Dial,* found the book dull, but admired its clever technique: "[the pieces in] verse are almost always without exception too long, the procession of ideas and the procession of images fail often to coincide, and lengths turn into *longueurs.* But nothing in the book gives evidence of haste or indolence or contempt for the practised art, and nearly everything in it has something of an alert, a sophisticated and watchful intelligence." Speaking for herself as well as her highly intellectual husband, Helen Wilson remarked: "Edmund's written a book and I can't understand a word of it and neither can Ed."

In September 1923, five months after the book was published, Wilson regretfully informed Bishop that the sales were down to zero: "Knopf tells me that the difficulty has been to sell or advertize a book which does not fall into any obvious category. I have a feeling that when we have become more famous it will be reprinted and greatly admired."[18] Though he did become famous, only "The Death of a Soldier" was reprinted—by Wilson himself—and *The Undertaker's Garland* has never been admired. Nevertheless, by the end of 1922 he had worked on two important magazines, established his critical reputation and published his first book. He was now ready to find a wife.

SIX

Mary Blair, 1923–1926

I

Wilson first met Mary Blair, his future wife, in about 1920 when she was acting in Eugene O'Neill's play *Diff'rent*. The following summer, after refusing Edna Millay's request to take her to the French Riviera, he recorded in his diary: "I felt committed to Mary Blair, who had promised to try to join me in France." Though Blair did not come to Europe that summer, Wilson continued to court her in New York while working on *Vanity Fair* and the *New Republic*.

The daughter of a printer in Pittsburgh, Mary was born in 1895. Her Irish family were followers of Emanuel Swedenborg, and she continued to see mystical visions until she was well into her twenties. Malcolm Cowley's father was the Blairs' family doctor, and Mary was a classmate of Cowley and the future critic Kenneth Burke at Peabody High School. She graduated from the drama school at Carnegie Tech and had been married for a time to a fellow student, Charles Meredith.

Small and slim, with auburn hair and dark brown eyes, Blair had a warm, deep voice and wore exotic jewelry. She had leading roles with the Provincetown Players, in New York and on tour, from 1918 to 1930, and starred in Eugene O'Neill's *The Hairy Ape* (1922), *Desire Under the Elms* (1924) and *All God's Chillun Got Wings* (1924). O'Neill's biographer described her volatile presence on stage: "A thin-faced girl with an intense quality about her, Miss Blair compelled attention more through her personality than her technical ability; an uneven performer, her acting could vary widely from one evening to the next; it all depended on her emotional state and frame of mind at the time."

Blair became notorious when she played opposite Paul Robeson in *All God's Chillun*. She was quoted in the Brooklyn *Daily Eagle* as saying: "I deem it an honor to take the part of Ella. There is nothing in the part that should give offense to any woman desiring to portray life, and portray it decently." But her comment was considered inflammatory, and she received obscene letters and bomb threats from outraged racists after "a national news syndicate, emphasizing one transient moment in the script, sent out a rehearsal photograph of Blair entitled 'WHITE ACTRESS KISSES NEGRO'S HAND.'" Toward the end of her life, Blair wryly but accurately predicted that the obituaries would characterize her as the actress "who kissed a Negro's hand." O'Neill praised her talent and courage, and was always "grateful for her appearing with Robeson when no other actress would."[1]

In Wilson's play, *This Room and This Gin and These Sandwiches* (1937), which he dedicated to Mary long after their marriage had ended, Arthur Fiske, modeled on Wilson, is a reserved architect who wants to marry Sally Voight, based on Blair, an attractive, neurotic actress with the Beech Street (that is, Provincetown) Players. But she is involved with another man, wants to retain her independence and is reluctant to marry. Arthur tells Sally that she embodies his romantic ideal: "The first time I ever met you after I'd seen you act, I knew that you were the person I'd been waiting for—you were the thing I wanted that I'd never found." Their friends agree that Sally has made Arthur more easy-going and more human. Though she finally agrees to marry him, she fears that "he wants me to make up for some lack in himself."

Wilson's strong-willed mother opposed the marriage, probably because of Mary's Swedenborgian background, dubious profession and delicate health. She also thought that a man with his nervous temperament should not marry an unstable, itinerant and egoistic actress. But his father loyally said that "any woman Edmund married would be accepted completely." Wilson, despite the declaration of the character in his play, was extremely unromantic. He did not want his wife to be his muse, but to release him from his inhibitions, to provide sexual pleasure, to look after him and his household, and to contribute an element of order and stability. Wilson's daughter later noted that he "demanded of any wife that she perform the same duties as my grandmother's staff, which is what he was used to."

On February 14, 1923, when she was two months pregnant, Wilson married Mary Blair. During the first chaotic year together, they moved four times. They first lived in an apartment above Elinor Wylie at 1 University Place, near Washington Square. They spent from mid-May to mid-August in Brookhaven, on eastern Long Island, in an idyllic house, at the edge of a wood, with a brook running through the front yard. During the quiet evenings they amused themselves by reading Restoration comedies. In August they shifted to 15 Willow Street, near a maternity hospital in Brooklyn, where they suffered from the fumes of a nearby candy factory and from their uncongenial neighbors. Their daughter Rosalind was born on September 19. Weakened by the birth, Mary became ill with whooping cough and pleurisy, and Rosalind was taken from the hospital to Red Bank. For her first eighteen years, she was brought up by her grandmother in the same town, in the same household and in the same way that her father had been.

Though Blair was a versatile actress, she was not suited to play the role of wife. She continued to work in the theater, despite her illness, performed at night and was often absent on long road tours. She earned more money than Wilson, which made him feel guilty. Her sister destroyed Wilson's letters after her death, but he kept Mary's rather gloomy letters to him, written while she was traveling with her plays. She was sorry that she bored him with her talk about the theater, urged him to stop drinking, worried about money and the new baby, and was bitter about his interest in other women. Mary also drank heavily. When drunk, she would "go into one of her acts" and behave even more outrageously than Edmund.[2]

Wilson took a keen interest in her theatrical career, became acquainted with Eugene O'Neill and persuaded the Provincetown Players to produce his first play, *The Crime in the Whistler Room*, which opened in October 1924. Wilson's mother had told him, "at an early age, that I 'didn't have it in me to write a play,'" and her discouraging prediction made a deep impression. Like his father, he loved the theater and was determined to prove his mother wrong.

From the early 1920s until the 1950s, O'Neill was the leading American playwright. In 1922, soon after they met, Wilson described him to Fitzgerald as "an extraordinarily attractive fellow" who was surprisingly modest about his success: "I find with gratification that he regards *Anna Christie* as more or less junk and thinks it is a great joke that it won the Pulitzer Prize." Three years later, however, Wilson found it difficult to make contact with O'Neill, despite his appealingly boyish charm: "I found conversation with him impossible. He was then completely on the wagon, and you were cautioned not to offer him anything to drink. But I got so bored with his nonresponsive silence that . . . I decided to prime him with some wine," and they talked about Greek tragedy and homosexual sailors. When they returned to Wilson's flat O'Neill, once having started, could not stop talking. But his talk, which had no connection with Wilson or Blair, was an unbroken monologue. Worst of all, however, "he drank up everything we had in the house: when a bottle was set before him, he simply poured out drinks for himself, not suggesting that we might care for any." Ignoring all hints by his hosts, O'Neill did not leave until four in the morning. Wilson finally decided that he disliked O'Neill's plays, which "depend too much upon hatred."[3]

The Crime in the Whistler Room, like all Wilson's plays, now seems over-intellectual, undramatic and rather dull. But it is one of the three plays (out of the eight he wrote) that was actually produced on stage, and he admired it enough to reprint it in 1937 and again in 1954. It portrays the clash between the genteel and bohemian traditions, and has a certain biographical (if not theatrical) interest. In this satiric play Bill (a nickname for Elizabeth) McGee, a waitress, has been rescued by Miss Clara Streetfield, a YWCA do-gooder, and taken into her upper-class house. Decorated with Victorian paintings by Whistler, it represents the bankrupt bourgeois tradition and decayed gentility of the past. Bill is again rescued, from this house of the living dead, by the brilliant but ambitious, brash and unstable writer Simon Delacy. He likes to speed in roadsters and romantically elopes with Bill, uniting the artist and the working class—the only elements in society that are still alive. Simon expresses the Lawrencean theme of "Galahad" and "Emily in Hades" when he tells Bill: "Remember you're alive and they're dead! Remember every moment of pleasure is a triumph against the forces of death!" Wilson, who at the end of the war believed: "I could never go back to the habits and standards of even the most cultivated elements of the world in which I had lived," explained that his play "is a fantasy of our first liberation from the culture and convention of the previous era."

The Streetfields are based on the De Forests, the family of a Hill School friend, who lived amidst elegant splendor in Cold Spring Harbor, Long Island. As Wilson wrote in *A Prelude* (without connecting this family to his play): "At the De Forests', everything was perfect: house and grounds, pictures, furniture and dinners. The only questions that seemed to disturb them—and that only in a very quiet way—were the displacement of an etching or a rearrangement of furniture."[4]

Mary Blair starred in the play that Wilson wrote during their brief marriage. The character of Bill McGee, like Sally Voight in *This Room and This Gin and These Sandwiches*, seemed modeled on her own life. Like Mary, Bill comes from Pittsburgh and wants to be an actress. When Bill unexpectedly announces: "I'm going to have a child!,"

Simon Delacy's response expresses Wilson's own attitude toward the pregnancy that forced him into marriage: "I don't want to seem cold-blooded about it, but we might as well face the situation. It can't be done, can it? I haven't got any money—or at least not enough—and neither of us wants to get married."

Delacy, who marries Bill and stands for the promise of life, was clearly based on Scott Fitzgerald. Wilson describes him as handsome, stylish and dissolute; socially insecure, self-centered and immature: "He is an attractive young man with a good profile, who wears a clean soft shirt and a gay summer necktie, but looks haggard and dissipated. . . . His manner in the presence of the Streetfields alternates between too much and too little assurance, but there is something disarmingly child-like about his egoism." Like Fitzgerald, Delacy is from the Midwest, gets into drunken brawls in nightclubs, writes film captions for silent movies and identifies with the most dissipated author in American literature: "I'm going to be the most amazing American writer since Edgar Allan Poe—a Poe with a social conscience!" Delacy's novel *The Ruins of the Ritz* echoes the title of Fitzgerald's major story, "The Diamond as Big as the Ritz" (1922). Scott had discussed his new novel with Wilson and was completing the *The Great Gatsby* when Wilson's play was produced. Delacy's description of his evening with a bootlegger clearly foreshadows Jay Gatsby: "Fleischman was making a damn ass of himself, bragging about how much his tapestries were worth and how much his bathroom was worth and how he never wore a shirt twice. . . . I told him I wasn't impressed by his ermine-lined revolver: I told him how he was nothing but a bootlegger, no matter how much money he made."[5]

The critics, recognizing the seriousness and intelligence of the play as well as its radical defects, gave it mixed reviews. In the *Nation*, Joseph Wood Krutch dismissed it by concluding: "In spite of all his elaborate machinery Mr. Edmund Wilson achieved little more than a fairly conventional satire on stale culture." But in the *Bookman*, Stephen Benét was extremely enthusiastic about its literary qualities: "Expressionistic, chaotic, full of obvious flaws from the point of view of the commercial theatre, it yet displays moments of harsh power and crippled beauty that are simply astonishing. We know of no more fascinating experiment in recent years than this acrid, violent, gorgeous nightmare. There is superb writing in it—not only shrewd and bitter dialogue but a poetic intensity and imagination of a high and unusual order."[6] Despite Benét's commendation, the play was not a success. Wilson received five percent of the gross receipts, but earned very little for his efforts.

Blair and Wilson were attracted to each other. But they had very different minds and temperaments, and led incompatible lives. In his early diaries he matter-of-factly recorded that "Mary Blair and I had separated. I had found it impossible to be married to an actress. She was always at the theater at night and I was out on the town. I took Rosalind down to my mother's and went to live alone at 229 West Thirteenth St in one room with a bathroom." Though the phrase "out on the town" hints at problems, Wilson does not specify the most significant reason for the collapse of his marriage. Edna Millay had married her sturdy Dutchman in July 1923, five months after Wilson's marriage, but they continued to meet and resumed their romance. According to Rosalind, "My mother always told me it was not she who had wanted the divorce. Her story was that she was the breadwinner and would come home from the theater to find a DO NOT DISTURB sign on the door and that my father was still seeing Edna Millay, with whom he was in love for many years."

Wilson and Blair separated in 1925, like many of his friends of the 1920s, and got divorced five years later. The legal costs were two hundred dollars. In 1930 Wilson married his second wife and Mary married her third husband, Constant Eakin, the wealthy New York manager of the Frigidaire Corporation. She always remained on good terms with Wilson, and after her third marriage told Rosalind that she was still in love with him. In 1930 Wilson expressed a rare warmth of feeling as their divorce became final: "When I finally left her in her apartment, after dinner, she gave me a human intelligent look, as she said good night, which made me feel her friendliness and her strength —a look of understanding between us on a level away above our wrangling—I could count on her, she counted on me."

Blair retired from the theater in 1935 and entered a tuberculosis hospital in Pittsburgh the following year. She wrote Wilson that she did not know how she had caught the contagious disease, bravely describing the course of her illness and agonizing operations. Wilson made several trips to Pittsburgh to visit her. In June 1945, Rosalind, who had seen very little of her mother during her childhood, told Wilson that Mary and her husband looked as if they would disintegrate at any moment. They drank all day and night and rarely ate meals.

Soon after Blair's death on September 18, 1947, at the age of fifty-two, her sister Lois wrote that Mary had suffered terribly during the final phase of her life: "These last years for her must have been so very miserable. . . . Her doctor said: 'it's a damn good thing your sister's dead.' I think she has wanted to die for a year—in fact for twelve years. But her dogged determination not to be an invalid was sometimes too pitiable."[7]

II

Wilson's father was a distant, oppressive and sometimes pathetic man, who was too neurotic to provide emotional support. But he did help his son get on in the world. He gave him a first-rate education, supported Edmund's idealistic ambition "to know something about all the main departments of human thought," got him a job on the *New York Sun*, arranged his promotion and transfer to the Intelligence Department of the army, went to the military base on Long Island to expedite his discharge, shared his love of the theater and approved of his marriage to Mary Blair.

In mid-May 1923, three months after Wilson got married, his father became ill in Utica, on the way home from Talcottville, and suddenly developed double pneumonia. The last words of the fifty-nine-year-old chronic valetudinarian were: "What does the doctor say about my condition?" Just after he died in Red Bank on May 15, Wilson's mother "gave a little cry." But as soon as they had gone downstairs she astounded Edmund by declaring that she would at last be able to realize her long-standing ambition: "Now I'm going to have a new house!"

Wilson did not, as he had hoped, inherit any money from his father, who left everything to his wife. He could not, as a high-brow journalist and serious writer, earn enough to live at his customary standard, was constantly pressed for funds and sometimes descended into squalor. He remained financially dependent on his deaf, disapproving mother, who had assumed parental responsibility for his daughter, and was often reduced to begging her for what he considered to be his rightful inheritance. His legacy, including possession of the Old Stone House in Talcottville, was delayed for nearly thirty years until her death in 1951.

Wilson told Burton Rascoe that he was both weakened by the loss of his father, who symbolically stood between him and death, and strengthened by his new independence and by his freedom from a lifetime of competition and censure: "Your father's death makes a big psychological difference to you, I think—robs you of something, and gives you something new at the same time—at least it did in my case." He explained his feelings in a letter to Bishop, in which he resolved to make use of every moment for either work or pleasure. His father's sad example had taught him that sexual and alcoholic indulgence were the best antidotes to depression: "My father's death gave me a sudden conviction of the shortness and unsatisfactoriness of life. . . . There is probably no other form of idling so profitable as dissipation. I feel that it was partly through an insufficient capacity for dissipation that my father suffered his melancholia; but at the same time he got more results with his nervous energy than I have yet got with mine, and it is high time for me to even the balance."[8]

Soon after her husband's death Helen moved from the gloomy old house in McLaren Street to a more convenient and much lighter home at 36 Vista Place in Red Bank. The smaller, two-story white house had cement steps with brick borders and a black railing leading to a glassed-in entrance. Pleasant and typically suburban, it had shuttered windows in front, a large back porch, and a flower and vegetable garden fenced in with high rose trellises. Across the street, big houses stood on the bank of the sailboat-filled Navesink River.

Freed from her husband's constraints, Helen lived more affluently than ever. She owned a custom-built Cadillac with "her initials on the doors, flasks of brandy in the side pockets, fur lap robes on a rack and fresh flowers in the side vases." Her first chauffeur, Oscar Breckenridge, was succeeded by a tall black driver named William. Glyn Morris summarized the widow's uneasy relations with her son: "She treated Edmund as a child till she died when he was fifty-six. On his birthday she sent him ten dollars; and never read a thing he wrote"—though she kept his books in a glass case near her bed. Wilson may have been alluding to Helen when the heroine of one of his stories condemns her husband's mother: "I think she's a spoiled, vain old woman. She expects to be treated with homage as if she were a dowager empress."[9]

After the birth of Rosalind, four months after his father's death, Wilson usually spent weekends in Red Bank. He was met at the station by the car and chauffeur, enjoyed the comfortable house and garden, and escaped from the tensions of the city. Dos Passos claimed that Wilson boldly traveled between New York and Red Bank on a motorcycle. But Edmund, in a more accurate version of the story, revealed his mechanical ineptitude: "he bought a motorcycle, wrecked it the first time he rode it, and then was arrested for driving without a license."

Wilson went to Red Bank both to see his daughter and to extract money from his mother. Rosalind later recalled that during her childhood he would read to her and take her for walks. Though she naturally resented the women in his life, she was also glad they were looking after him in New York. He wanted to be a good father, but the role did not come easily to him. He once tried to take away Rosalind's doll house and give it to his mistress' daughter.

Hard-working, and always pressed for money, Wilson was moody, tense and unpleasant when he came to Red Bank. Rosalind did not look forward to his visits and was relieved when he left. He would arrive at the house, shout the week's news to his mother, then complain about the dinner and demand money. During his financial crises, especially when Rosalind's welfare was concerned, his mother would either send a check or cover the ones he bounced at the local bank. Like his mother, Wilson never offered Rosalind money, but always made her ask for it.[10]

III

On May 5, 1923, having filled the gap created by Bishop's absence, Wilson resigned for the second time from *Vanity Fair*. In January of that year he had become the drama critic of the *Dial*, and in 1924 he rejoined the more serious and congenial *New Republic*, remaining on the staff until 1931. Right after leaving *Vanity Fair*, Wilson became the press agent for the Royal Swedish Ballet, which was then touring the United States. The following January he enthusiastically announced to Bishop that he had completed a modern ballet, with captions, a silent film and music by a Russian-born avant-garde composer:

> I have written a great super-ballet of New York for the Swedish Ballet—a pantomime explained by movie captions and with a section of movie film in the middle, for which [Leo] Ornstein is composing the music and in which we hope to get Chaplin to act. It is positively the most titanic thing of the kind ever projected and

will make the productions of [Darius] Milhaud and Cocteau sound like folk-song recitals. It is written for Chaplin, a Negro comedian, and seventeen other characters, full of orchestra, movie machine, typewriters, radio, phonograph, riveter, electromagnet, alarm clocks, telephone bells, and jazz band.

Though Wilson's description seems quite wild and suggests why his work was never performed, this kind of eclectic, cacophonic music was fashionable in the 1920s. Three years later George Antheil's *Ballet Mécanique*—scored for anvils, aeroplane propellers, electric bells, motor horns, player pianos, pieces of tin and steel—achieved instant notoriety in Paris.

In February 1924, after convincing the Swedish Ballet to pay his expenses to California, Wilson attempted to persuade Chaplin to take the starring role. He stayed in Santa Barbara with Ted Paramore, who arranged the introduction. Their meeting was cordial, but Chaplin refused the invitation:

> We found him on the set where he was making *The Gold Rush*. He was wearing the make-up of his character and, while he talked to us, stood quietly swinging his cane. I had already met him at *Vanity Fair*, when he came to have a photograph made, and he had shown me how to perform the trick of pulling his derby down on his head and having it pop up into the air. . . . He was good-mannered and perfectly natural. . . . He laughed appreciatively at my ballet—later published as *Cronkhite's Clocks*—but explained that he always had to do everything himself, invent and play his own character.

The title *Cronkhite's Clocks: A Pantomime with Captions* not only suggests the god Chronos and the theme of time, but also the sickness (*Krankheit*) of a society dehumanized by machines. Wilson's postwar theme was also expressed in more famous and successful works: Karel Čapek's Expressionist play *R. U. R.* (1920), films like René Clair's *A Nous la Liberté* (1931) and Chaplin's *Modern Times* (1936), and D. H. Lawrence's prophetic poem "The Gods! The Gods!": "and all was dreary, great robot limbs, robot breasts, / robot voices."[11]

After talking to Chaplin, Wilson went to San Francisco to visit Ted's mistress Margaret Canby, who was sharing an apartment with her friend Paula Gates while both young women were waiting for a divorce. Wilson, always attracted to exotic looks, at first assumed Paula was Jewish, but he soon learned that she was Mexican and, like Mary Blair, an actress. On March 10, after Wilson had returned to New York, Ted playfully reported: "You made a tremendous hit with Paula, whom I suspect of having amorous designs on you. . . . It is too bad you could not have stayed longer and studied this extraordinary woman at closer range."

Ted was right about Paula's amorous designs, but did not realize that the apparently shy Wilson had managed to study her at very close range indeed. Paula had warned Wilson that Margaret Canby was "fickle and faithless." Then, in a letter written five days before Ted's, she praised (as many other women would do) Wilson's passionate love-making and confirmed that he had made a powerful impression: "I doubt if you and I could ever repeat the wonderful experience we had. . . . You have made me so very hungry and given me a feast. You have crucified me and given me new birth. . . . Oh Bunny, dear dear thing, so still and so vital, and destructive and reviving." She also told him that she had backed out of a play in San Francisco because she lacked "the stimulus of your extraordinary personality. You are still like a lovely strange dream. A young God come down to me for a moment and then vanishing into the ether. Ted has been here a week and it hasn't worked out so well. I didn't tell him about us but he started imitating you and I burst into tears!!"[12] Wilson's brief affair with Paula Gates increased his restless dissatisfaction with Mary. It also enhanced his sexual confidence, and proved that the "young God" had learned Ted's hedonistic lessons and could compete with him in his own territory.

IV

During his marriage to Mary, Wilson maintained an independent existence and sought out the best writers of his time. Between 1924 and 1926, he met E. E. Cummings, Paul Rosenfeld, D. H. Lawrence and Sherwood Anderson, and discovered a major new talent, Ernest Hemingway. Wilson probably met Cummings, who also lived in the Village, through his college classmate, John Dos Passos. Wilson described the young poet as slipping out of a local restaurant "with his spirited crest of hair and his narrow self-regarding eyes." In a review, he described Cummings' lyrical but immature style as that of "an eternal adolescent, as fresh and often as winning but as half-baked as boyhood." Maintaining his typical schoolmasterly stance, Wilson told Bishop that the undisciplined Cummings, who seemed to pour out his poems, needed correction rather than encouragement. He had a genuine gift, but no discrimination about the strengths and weaknesses of his own work.

In August 1929 he visited the poet in New Hampshire and told Allen Tate about Cummings' aesthetic viewpoint, which was very similar to the one Wilson was then writing about in *Axel's Castle:* "He has been sober for weeks, and I found him more interesting and satisfactory to talk to than I ever had before. He certainly has the most extraordinary point of view. It is 100 percent romantic. The individual is the only thing that matters, and only the gifted individual—in fact, only the poet and artist. The rest of the world is of no importance and has to take the consequences." Despite his apparent retreat to the Ivory Tower, Wilson noted, Cummings was also unusually perceptive about what was happening in the world. Later on, Wilson was so appalled by Cummings' Christian phase that he lost all interest in seeing him. In his shrewd estimate of the sparkling but insubstantial poet, Wilson called Cummings "A fixed point of effervescence, / With a touch of deliquescence."[13]

Wilson was extremely fond of the now-forgotten music critic Paul Rosenfeld, a round little man, plump as a partridge, with a sad jowly face and a Chaplinesque moustache. Shy, cultured, generous with praise and money, he wrote in the tradition of James Huneker for the *New Republic* and the *Dial,* and was a passionate partisan of contemporary music, painting and literature. Rosenfeld, heir to the Rheingold beer fortune, was born in New York in 1890, graduated from Yale and served in the army during the war. He had several close writer friends in common with Wilson—Cummings, Tate, Cowley, Waldo Frank and Louise Bogan—and edited *The American Caravan*, which published Wilson's story "Galahad" in 1927.

In 1929 Rosenfeld expressed his gratitude for Wilson's intellectual comradeship and suggested that their warm friendship was based on "the happy give and take, and a great community of interests, and the confidence that the culture of the heart persists." Rosenfeld's death in middle age in 1946 followed the unexpected deaths of Wilson's Princeton friends—T. K. Whipple in 1939, Fitzgerald in 1940 and Bishop in 1944—and was a great emotional shock. Wilson, the survivor, wrote memorial essays on all four friends. As usual, he loyally overpraised Rosenfeld's writing. He was "one of the most exciting critics of the

'American Renaissance,'" Wilson wrote, and his work "had a kind of fullness of tone, a richness of vocabulary and imagery, and a freedom of the cultural world."[14]

Like D. H. Lawrence, Wilson rebelled against his puritan background. In August 1923, in the apartment of the publisher Thomas Seltzer, Wilson met the English novelist, who was then going through an extremely difficult and unhappy period of his life. Lawrence had just come from Mexico, where he had exhausted himself by completing the first draft of *The Plumed Serpent*. His rootlessness, isolation, confusion about the future and financial problems with Seltzer (who had not paid Lawrence his royalties) as well as Frieda's longing for her mother, her children and a settled home, exacerbated their eternal conflicts about dominance and submission.

Though he noted Lawrence's working-class origins, Wilson recognized his courage and tremendous vitality, and commented on his petulant and typically unconventional behavior:

> I found Lawrence's appearance disconcerting. He was lean, but his head was disproportionately small. One saw that he belonged to an inferior caste—some bred-down unripening race of the collieries. Against this inferiority—fundamental and physical—he must have had to fight all his life: his passionate spirit had made up for it by exaggerated self-assertion.... On this occasion, he suddenly became hysterical and burst out in childish rudeness and in a high-pitched screaming voice with something like: "I'm not enjoying this! Why are we sitting here having tea? I don't want your tea! I don't want to be doing this!"... Mrs Lawrence sat silent, her feet in rather large shoes or sandals, one beside the other and flat on the floor, as if she were the anchor that held him down, the Mother *Erde* on whom he depended.

Wilson was ambivalent about Lawrence. He told Lawrence's friend Witter Bynner that he admired him but never had much appetite for him. Though Wilson disliked most of Lawrence's fiction, he called *Studies in Classic American Literature* (1923) "one of the few first-rate books that have ever been written on the subject" and included the entire book in *The Shock of Recognition*. In *The Triple Thinkers* he called Lawrence the last of the great Romantic poets and one of the most original modern novelists. He thought the gamekeeper in *Lady Chatter-*

ley's Lover talked too much, and wrote an extremely perceptive review after that novel was privately published in 1928. "D. H. Lawrence's theme is a high one," Wilson observed, "the self-affirmation and the triumph of life in the teeth of all the sterilizing and demoralizing forces—industrialism, physical depletion, dissipation, careerism and cynicism—of modern English society."

Wilson would also satirize these destructive forces in *I Thought of Daisy*, which was published the year after Lawrence's last novel. Though Wilson was vague about Frieda's footgear, he had, characteristically, noticed and commented on her feet. She reappeared in Wilson's novel as Professor Grosbeake's wife, who has a daughter named Frieda and plays the same solid role that Wilson thought Frieda played in Lawrence's life: "She was a broad, handsome, placid German woman, very thoroughly educated and very practical. One always felt that she was a kind of base upon which Grosbeake's metaphysics rested."[15]

Wilson got on much better with Sherwood Anderson, Lawrence's leading American disciple, whom he met during his visit to New Orleans in March 1926. Just after he left Louisiana, the sensual and intuitive Anderson affectionately commented on Wilson's extremely mental approach to life—his main limitation as a novelist. But he also perceived the gentle side of Wilson's character, which he usually kept hidden: "He is a likeable man, very much the intellectual. It is amazing how these men can walk about seeing little. They go instinctively to books. Everything must be got at second hand. In this man there is a kind of sweetness." Wilson, also very fond of Anderson, enjoyed his company and admired his work:

> For him the inhabitants of a little Ohio town were just as important and on just the same level as the people with names that he afterwards met in Chicago and New York. He and Dreiser were, in my opinion, the only really first-rate men who came out of the Middle West in that period. I liked him very much. . . . He was not irritating at all personally, but one of the most agreeable men I have ever known. It is only in his writing that he is sometimes irritating. He had a humorous racy quality that was very Southwestern and that hardly ever got into what he wrote. He had a kind of reverence for literature which made him a little stilted in a peculiar way when he "took pen in hand," in the old phrase that is very appropriate to his attitude.

While in New Orleans Wilson, now separated from Mary Blair, took the opportunity to sample the local product. He had sex with a no-frills young prostitute, who was eager to finish the business as quickly as possible. She had crudely formed feet and a long big toe, would not take off her clothes, "simply threw herself on her back across the bed with her feet hanging down at the side and pulled her skirts up over her stomach."[16]

Wilson's relations with Anderson's sometime friend Ernest Hemingway were more complex and long-lasting. Both men came from the same professional upper middle class, were hard drinkers, frequently married, and had a number of friends in common: Fitzgerald and Dos Passos, who were close to both of them, as well as Anderson, Bishop, Tate, Cowley, Maxwell Perkins and Morley Callaghan. But the Eastern, college-educated, scholarly, reserved and unathletic Wilson was very different from the tough and handsome Hemingway.

Their relationship began when Wilson had established his reputation as a critic and the unknown expatriate Hemingway was still publishing with little presses in Paris. Wilson was, early and late, the most influential critic on Hemingway. He was the first to recognize Hemingway's talent (in the *Dial* of October 1924), emphasized his moral qualities, established the authoritative view of his work and, in *The Wound and the Bow*, wrote the most penetrating long essay about him. Wilson picked a winner, but Hemingway also chose the critic best able to advance his reputation. Despite Wilson's generous encouragement of Hemingway's early work, they never became intimate friends. But they continued to see each other for nearly ten years.

In November 1923 Hemingway, writing from Toronto, sent Wilson his first book, *Three Stories and Ten Poems*. When Wilson expressed his admiration, Hemingway, suitably modest and flattering, said: "I am very glad you liked some of it. . . . Yours is the only critical opinion in the States I have any respect for. . . . It is very sporting of you to offer to help me get a book before the publishers. I don't know any of them." They met during Hemingway's next trip to New York in January 1924; and in October of that year Wilson wrote a brilliant review of *Three Stories* and *in our time*, which recognized the essence of Hemingway's talent and helped to establish his serious literary reputation. Wilson stated that Hemingway's prose "is of the first distinction," linked him with Anderson and Gertrude Stein, and noted that his colloquial diction conveyed "profound emotions and complex states of mind." He also perceived that in *in our time* Hemingway "is remarkably successful in suggesting moral values by a series of simple statements," and that his "harrowing record of barbarities" has the sharpness and elegance of lithographs by Goya. When this review appeared Hemingway wrote to Wilson that "he was 'awfully glad' his early books had pleased so good a critic" and praised Wilson's review as "cool, clear-minded, decent, impersonal and sympathetic." Such intelligence as Wilson had displayed was "a damn rare commodity."

In his review of Hemingway's second book of stories, *Men Without Women*, in the *New Republic* of December 14, 1927, Wilson, who still championed Hemingway at this stage of his career, castigated the superficial reviews of his colleagues and provided some shrewd insights about the stories. He defended Hemingway's characters as "highly civilized persons of rather complex temperament and extreme sensibility" and observed that "his drama usually turns on some principle of courage, of honor, of pity" that reveals serious moral values.

In 1930, when both writers were publishing with Scribner's, Hemingway called Wilson "of all critics or people, the one who has understood best what I am working at." He asked Wilson, through their mutual editor, Max Perkins, to write an introduction to a reprint of the enlarged trade edition of *In Our Time*; and Wilson, drawing on his previous reviews, did so. Two years later, Hemingway told Dos Passos that Wilson's *The American Jitters* was "*wonderful* reporting" but wished he had not tried "to save his soul" by espousing Left-wing causes. Writing to his Russian translator in August 1935, Hemingway (just before Wilson's first negative review of his work) anticipated later criticism by calling Wilson "the best critic we have, but he no longer reads anything that comes out."[17]

V

In 1926, the same year as Lawrence's *The Plumed Serpent* and Hemingway's *The Sun Also Rises*, Wilson published *Discordant Encounters: Plays and Dialogues*. His first book, *The Undertaker's Garland*, had alternating chapters in different voices by Bishop and Wilson. The dialogues in his equally odd second book were written in different voices by Wilson himself.[18] *Discordant Encounters*, presumably rejected by Alfred Knopf, was brought out by the small but adventurous firm of Albert and Charles Boni. (Boni and Liveright had published Sherwood Anderson's work as well as Hemingway's first trade book, *In Our Time*.) Wilson was unhappy with the physical appearance of the book and exaggerated its defects in a witty letter to the novelist Hamilton Basso, whom he had also met on his trip to New Orleans: "A wretched-looking volume it is. The cover looks like a strip of bathroom linoleum . . . and the pages are printed on paper something like that used in patent-medicine almanacs. There are also a good many misprints, repeated lines, etc., which give a smart modern effect something like Gertrude Stein."

Like Wilson's other works in mixed genres, the plays and dialogues in *Discordant Encounters* have no unity. Nevertheless, Wilson was inordinately fond of this work and later reprinted four of its chapters in four different books.[19] We have already discussed *The Crime in the Whistler Room*, in which Mary Blair played the leading role, and *Cronkhite's Clocks*, the ballet Wilson wrote for Charlie Chaplin. "In the Galapagos: Mr. William Beebe and a Marine Iguana" (which has absolutely nothing to do with *Cronkhite's Clocks*) opposes a scientific and an instinctive view of the world, and includes a boring lecture on molecules that puts the iguana to sleep. In "Mrs. Alving and Oedipus: A Professor of Fifty and a Jurist of Twenty-Five," two figures, based on Gauss and Wilson himself, debate the environmental and moral aspects of Ibsen's *Ghosts* and Sophocles' *Oedipus Rex*. Both plays, Wilson wrote, portray the victims of "impossible moralities and oppressive institutions." In "The Poet's Return: Mr. Paul Rosenfeld and Mr. Matthew Josephson," the former (speaking for Wilson and advocating traditional culture) attacks the latter's negative review of Elinor Wylie's *Black Armour* (1923) as well as Josephson's Dadaist view that both life and art are absurd.

Fitzgerald not only inspired the hero of *The Crime in the Whistler Room* but was also the subject of the most important chapter of the book: "The Delegate from Great Neck: Mr. Van Wyck Brooks and Mr. Scott Fitzgerald." In May 1922, while Fitzgerald was actually living in Great Neck, Wilson tried to persuade Mencken to publish this imaginary dialogue, a genre popularized by Walter Savage Landor in the Victorian era. The dialogue, Wilson said, considered "the joylessness and lack of vitality in American life. It has just struck me as ironic that while Fitz and Zelda were revelling nude in the orgies of Westport (summer before last), Brooks, in the same town, probably without ever knowing they were there, should have been grinding out his sober plaint against the sterile sobriety of the country."[20]

In this conversation Wilson attributes his *own* ideas about artistic integrity to the learned, scholarly and rather withdrawn Brooks, who knows far more about American literature than anyone else in the world, and gives him all the best lines. Speaking for Wilson, Brooks freely censures Fitzgerald for haste, superficiality and commerciality; for writing too much and too fast; for allowing himself to be corrupted by high-paying magazines like the *Saturday Evening Post*. This influential and frequently reprinted essay contained some valuable criticism, but it portrayed Fitzgerald as foolish, shallow and outclassed by the heavyweight critic.

Though Wilson was attracted to the dramatic dialogue, he did not have a dramatic talent and the debates in the book were too one-sided to provoke much interest. The critical and cultural essays he wrote in the 1920s and collected in *The Shores of Light* and *The American Earthquake* were far superior to the rather limp and labored plays and dialogues. *Discordant Encounters* received only a few lukewarm reviews and sank from sight even faster than *The Undertaker's Garland*.

VI

In the mid-Twenties, after he had separated from Mary Blair and was writing *Discordant Encounters*, Wilson, clearly pressed for money, rented a sordid furnished room on Ninth Avenue. Tom Matthews, who came from a wealthy family, was horrified to find that Wilson had abandoned his customary comfort and respectable life, and was living in "helpless, squalid bachelorhood: an unmade bed, empty gin bottles on the dirty floor, no carpet, one naked light bulb." Wilson rarely entertained friends in his room, but sometimes met them for drinks and meals at the Princeton Club at Park Avenue and 39th Street. Though he consoled himself with prostitutes, he was then quite lonely. "Having, as a rule," he told Dell in 1925, "no one to talk to at the highball hour, I have formed the habit of pouring it all into my correspondence to avoid the necessity of talking to myself." Wilson used letters, as he used conversation, to explore the ideas he was trying to express in his work.

During 1925–26 Wilson laid prolonged siege to Katze Szabo, a pretty, lively German-American girl. Despite strenuous efforts, he never quite managed to seduce her or pry her away from her boyfriend. Wilson's diary revealed her flirtatious nature, his techniques of seduction, his excitement at her passivity and his continuous obsession with feet: "Her body in her new thin black dress as she lay in the armchair with her feet in another chair, *en faisant valoir* [making the most of] her breasts and thighs and crotch. She went to sleep, and I carried her in and put her on my bed, kissing her voraciously but respectably on her beautiful neck and on her feet at the low instep of her shoe, before I left her."

When Katze awoke, she was pleased by his appreciation of her beauty, admired his persistence and was unexpectedly responsive to his love-making. But, Wilson recorded, "when I carried her to the couch—we both had been drinking—she succumbed completely till I began to address myself to her bloomers, when she made me stop— 'Why?'—'Because we're both being foolish—we're neither of us in earnest.'" The tone and diction of "began to address myself to her bloomers" suggests that he was earnest in the wrong sense. The frustrating affair finally petered out when Katze unkindly remarked on his woodchuck cheeks and shoe-button eyes, told him that she disliked him intensely and never wanted to see him again. Licking his wounds, Wilson concluded that she was a cruel, self-centered and perverse (though not perverse enough) girl.

Wilson had better luck with Marie, a part-time model and call girl, whom he picked up outside a midtown hotel. When he first saw her in the street he was repulsed by her hard-boiled, whore-broken look. But when he began to talk to her he learned that she was another exotic type (her father was from Barcelona). Beneath her tough exterior, she had a pleasing simplicity and gentleness, soft tragic eyes and thick sensual lips. Marie, who came from Brooklyn and had a strong local accent, had been educated in a convent school, where she was molested by the priests, and married at fifteen to a brutal man who was currently in jail for rape.

When he took Marie to his latest apartment at 229 West 13th Street, Wilson discovered that

> She was broad and had olive skin when she took off her bandeau, [and] disclosed large full breasts of which the nipples were spread from pregnancy . . . Her cunt, however, seemed to be small. She would not, the first time, respond very heartily, but, the second, would wet herself and bite my tongue, and when I had finished, I could feel her vagina throbbing powerfully.—Thrust my naked cock up into those obscure and meaty regions.[21]

Wilson's detailed, objective and characteristically clinical description emphasizes the woman's body and his own sexual activity, but excludes his feelings (if any) about her. He closely questioned Marie about her background and current life. Learning all about her (for later use) was as important to him as achieving sexual pleasure.

Wilson had a more significant relationship with the young poet Léonie Adams, whom he probably met through her friend and fellow-poet Louise Bogan. In December 1925 Bogan reported, with heavy irony, to the poet and translator Rolfe Humphries: "A missive from Léonie informs us that the Great Wilson made some hearty passes at her, inviting her to stay at his house, and all. Are we to allow this sort of thing to happen to our blond Nordic females?" Part of the joke was that Adams, far from being blond and Nordic, was very short, wore bangs, had fine porcelain-like features and slightly slanting eyes. She attracted Wilson by what he called her purity of spirit and her "Latin-American prettiness." Leon Edel, who knew Adams, remembered her as delicate and articulate, "bird-like in gesture, brief and vivid in speech. Her lyric quality and her reticences appealed to Wilson."[22] Though not especially attractive, she was a strange, ethereal and intelligent woman, with an unusual mixture of New England and Spanish blood.

Léonie was born in Brooklyn in 1899 and belonged to Margaret Mead's circle of friends at Barnard, where she was a brilliant student, edited the college magazine and had poems accepted in literary magazines while still an undergraduate. Wilson called her first volume of poems, *Those Not Elect* (1925), "a very remarkable work" and said "the language, which seems to branch straight from the richest seventeenth century tradition, strikes music." Adams and Allen Tate traveled together, along with Tate's wife and child, in England and France, where they met Ford Madox Ford and Gertrude Stein. Léonie married the critic William Troy in 1933. Though she published very little after her second book, *High Falcon* (1929), she had a successful career. After World War Two she taught at Bennington and several universities; was Consultant in Poetry at the Library of Congress during 1948–49; and shared the Bollingen Prize with Louise Bogan in 1954.

In May 1927 Wilson puffed both Adams and Bogan, who were rivals as well as friends: "Miss Léonie Adams, in the past year, has published in magazines a considerable amount of work brilliantly up to her best; and Miss Louise Bogan, a set of poems which surpass her best previous work." The poet William Jay Smith, who knew both women, said that Léonie had a crush on Louise, was jealous of her greater reputation, and felt bitter toward Bogan when Adams stopped writing and became (like her husband) an alcoholic. Bogan tended to be slightly condescending to Adams, but in October 1929, pleased by Léonie's homage, she told the poet John Hall Wheelock: "*High Falcon* is dedicated to [my husband] Raymond and me. . . . It is full of extraordinary loveliness—and a sharpness that I, for one, could not put a name to. She has the greatest talent in the really grand manner of anyone writing in America today."[23]

Léonie had many qualities that Edmund found attractive in women. She was exotic-looking, intellectual, talented, passionate, neurotic and a heavy drinker. "Either you'd given me too much gin," she told Wilson in December 1925, "or that is a revolving bed." She used to astonish Ford Madox Ford by drinking great quantities of brandy and remaining cold sober. In October 1928, after their affair began, Wilson told Bishop: "I have seen a good deal of her in the last winter and have found her by far one of the most interesting girls in New York. She is a little shy at first, but extremely intelligent and amusing when you get to know her."

In fact, their friendship was much more intense than Wilson's gentlemanly reticence had suggested. Léonie appeared as "Winifred" in his diaries, where he described their timorous, nervous, sometimes painful love-making as if she were a virgin:

> Her little moth-flutterings and rabbit-startings, her soft tender cheeks, arms and neck, her little vibrating limbs, seized with the tremor of fear and excitement when I embraced her—"You mustn't mind if I'm frightened"—nervously, spasmodically contracted—it hurt a little, but not much or long, because when I asked her later whether it had hurt, she said that she was sorry that she'd said it hurt. Her little pansy or violet face, with its touch of Spanish sensuality that made me desire her. Her obedience and readiness, in spite of her fear. Her little whispered exclamations, begun and not finished unless I urged her, and not always then: "It seems very strange! I don't understand! . . . I'm not sure it's right to make love! . . . You don't know me!". . . She was so sweet, so dear.[24]

The relatively innocent Léonie, his social and intellectual equal, evoked a tenderness and depth of feeling that was completely absent from his much cruder descriptions of Katze and Marie.

While in France, Léonie sent Wilson a number of highly-charged letters that made him feel guilty. He had been drunk when he took her to bed and later reflected that he should not have slept with her. Her letters were very emotional—whining, self-pitying, apologetic, sometimes even apologizing for her apologies—and, in the demands they made upon him, apparently unwelcome. She praised his writing, enclosed her poems, admitted her jealousy of his other women, asked if he wanted to see her and when they could meet. When Wilson uneasily tried to withdraw from her by expressing his need for independence and isolation, she reasonably but rather obtusely responded: "I mean to say that if you wanted my love those objections would probably not appear to you at all, or you would know that they were of no importance to me." When she returned from Europe in 1929 they had "harrowing interviews" and their affair came to an inevitable end.

Wilson kept in touch with Adams, as he had with Millay. Though Bogan reported, in 1963, that Adams never stopped talking and had also become a fanatical Catholic Rightist, Wilson looked her up and had a disillusioning meeting with Léonie in New York that year. "She had lost her looks," he recorded, "so that it shocked me. I felt she had become brutalized by living with that lowgrade Irishman [William Troy]! But she later told me that she had just had 'a virus,' so she was probably not looking her best. She seemed to me, when we were first talking, to be just like a middle-aged English teacher—which is what she is at Columbia."[25]

In the mid-1920s Wilson continued his successful career on the *New Republic* and developed a wide range of friendships with both men and women. But the death of his father, his lack of money, the difficulties with his mother, the break-up of his marriage, the isolation from his daughter, the failure of *Discordant Encounters*, his transient existence, and his frenetic and often frustrating sexual life made this a very difficult and unhappy period. He would also have trouble with his next two books and experience a severe mental crisis before finding his true literary vocation as a critic.

SEVEN

Nervous Breakdown, 1927–1929

I

The years between Wilson's first two marriages were the most emotionally unstable period of his life. His marriage had left him with a sense of failure and some responsibility for a small child. Although his position on the *New Republic* widened his acquaintance with writers and built his reputation as a journalist and critic, he craved the fame and financial reward that only successful books could bring. He turned out essays, fiction and poetry, but failed to have the impact he hoped for. It was a time of painstaking literary work and relative poverty, varied by hard drinking and the pursuit of sex.

Recognizing his own instability, Wilson in 1927 made his first will. He owned nothing, but he was thinking of his mother's sizable assets, which he would eventually inherit, when he left one third of his estate to his legal wife, Mary Blair, and two thirds to his only child, Rosalind. He bequeathed books and personal possessions to the closest friends of his youth, Alfred Bellinger, John Bishop, Charley Walker and Phelps Putnam; to the journalists Burton Rascoe, Paul Rosenfeld, Gilbert Seldes; to the English lawyer Sylvester Gates and his first lover and muse, Edna Millay. Two years later he sent out copies of his first novel to Bishop, Millay, Christian Gauss, Scott Fitzgerald, Allen Tate and Léonie Adams. In 1929 his list for an "ideal party" included Bishop, Millay, Rosenfeld and Seldes; Fitzgerald, Tate and Adams, Dos Passos and the essential Ted Paramore. He relied on this educated and literary circle of friends to share his ambition, his friendship, and whatever pleasure it was possible to secure.

During these years Wilson continued to move frequently, and lived in several apartments in or near the Village, on West 13th Street, East 9th Street and Washington Square. He worked at the *New Republic* office, was anchored to Red Bank on weekends, and spent most summers with Rosalind and her nanny on Cape Cod. In 1927 he rented the Old Coast Guard Station in Provincetown, which had once belonged to Eugene O'Neill. The house was so isolated, standing alone near sand, sea, ships and lighthouses, that Wilson felt as if he were living in the Atlantic Ocean.

The following summer Terence Holliday, the owner of a bookshop in the Village, invited Wilson to lunch at the Algonquin to meet Wyndham Lewis, who had come to New York to sell some paintings and meet American publishers. Wilson had read his Vorticist magazine *Blast* in 1914, and was interested in Lewis' promotion of avant-garde art and literature, the connections he made between culture and political systems, and his views on the function of writers in modern society. But an obtuse review of his novel *Tarr* in the *New Republic* of July 15, 1918, had persuaded Wilson that the bitter tone and jagged style were calculated to set his teeth on edge, and he tended to dismiss Lewis as a novelist.

During the past five years, Lewis had published five major books—including *The Art of Being Ruled* and *Time and Western Man*—and expected some recognition. Lewis' reputation, based on the aggressive persona of his books, had preceded him to New York and Wilson expected him to behave like a monster. But, Wilson told Tate, he was surprised to find Lewis quite congenial: "He isn't really peevish, however, but a very agreeable person and quite interesting to talk to when his own personal egoism, though even this is not of a very poisonous kind, doesn't get into the discussion." Wilson liked Lewis well enough to see him several times during this visit.

Wilson took a more negative view of Lewis during a second trip to New York in the winter and spring of 1940. Under a political cloud for his Right-wing stance of the 1930s, impoverished and marooned in North America for the duration of the war, Lewis was even more prickly than usual. Wilson later told Lewis' biographer that he had been put off by Lewis' aggressive and unbalanced personality: "I did not particularly like him, and did not like his writings, though I thought some of his pictures were very good when I saw the exhibition at the Tate Gallery [in 1956]. His delusions of persecution, which he would never seem to shake off, were a nuisance, and I always had an uncomfortable feeling that I was dealing with someone not completely sane." They continued to correspond, despite Wilson's coolness, after Lewis returned to what he called the "sanctimonious ice-box" of Toronto. When writing about a political meeting, Wilson noted that one of his theatrical friends reminded him, uneasily, of Lewis: "Phelps Putnam, the poet, with his black clothes and his monocle, hanging around the conference—a little too much like Wyndham Lewis in his menacing fascist make-up."[1] The rebarbative personality and Right-wing political views of Lewis, the first English writer Wilson ever met, prejudiced him against British authors and contributed to his hostile attitude during his later journeys to London.

Wilson's friendship with Scott Fitzgerald kept him in touch with the prankish undergraduate humor they had shared when they collaborated on *The Evil Eye* at Princeton. In the early Twenties Wilson was still stagestruck. He read with delight the typescript of Fitzgerald's farcical political satire on the stupidity and corruption of the Harding administration, *The Vegetable, or From President to Postman: A Comedy in Three Acts*. Though usually very critical of Scott's work, Wilson told him this rather feeble fantasy of a working man who dreams he has been made President was "one of the best things you ever wrote" and "the best American comedy ever written." Wilson urged him to "go on writing plays," and tried, with Mary Blair's help, to place the play in New York. In gratitude for his support, Fitzgerald dedicated the work partly to Wilson. When it was published in April 1923, a few months before its disastrous try-out in Atlantic City, Wilson opposed the negative reviews it had received and called it "a fantastic and satiric comedy carried off with exhilarating humor. . . . I do not know of any dialogue by an American which is lighter, more graceful or more witty."[2]

Although his appreciation of *The Vegetable* was misplaced, Wilson was perceptive about *The Great Gatsby*, which had graceful, witty dialogue in a superb dramatic context. In April 1925, just after it was published, Wilson recognized its merits and wrote Fitzgerald: "It is undoubtedly in some ways the best thing you have done—the best planned, the best sustained, the best written."

In his imaginary conversation between Fitzgerald and Van Wyck Brooks, Wilson parodied Fitzgerald's inexhaustible appetite for parties and had him exclaim: "Think of being able to give a stupendous house party that would go on for days and days, with everything that anybody could want to drink and a medical staff in attendance and the biggest jazz orchestras in the city alternating night and day!" In 1928, Fitzgerald continued in this festive role when he wrote to invite Wilson for a weekend at Ellerslie, a rented thirty-room mansion on the banks of the Delaware River: "All is prepared for February 25th. The stomach pumps are polished and set out in rows and stale old enthusiasms are being burnished." The two friends had not seen much of each other since Scott's extended trip to Europe in 1924. Their relations had suffered a certain chill when Wilson, always keen on getting the work done, began to question him about the progress of his new novel and Fitzgerald preferred admiration to advice.

Wilson arrived at the local train station with the playwright Thornton Wilder. As Fitzgerald's chauffeur drove them to the house, they had a lively discussion about the latest volume of Proust. Fitzgerald seemed determined to tease and provoke his guests instead of providing the relaxing and civilized weekend they had expected. He proudly took them on a tour of inspection while the butler, hiding behind the heavy doors, obediently rattled a chain and groaned like a ghost. He played records of Stravinsky's discordant *Rite of Spring* and made them look at a book of photographs showing horribly mutilated soldiers from the recent war.

Like most of Scott's friends, Wilson was attracted to Zelda, who had several of the qualities he admired in women: Southern exoticism, beauty, wit, recklessness and hysterical unpredictability. He was especially charmed by her sparkling but often incoherent talk: "she had the waywardness of a Southern belle and the lack of inhibitions of a child. She talked with so spontaneous a color and wit—almost exactly in the way she wrote—that I very soon ceased to be troubled by the fact that the conversation was in the nature of a 'free association' of ideas and one could never follow up anything. I have rarely known a woman who expressed herself so delightfully and so freshly."

Zelda had once intrigued Wilson by declaring that hotel bedrooms made her sexually excited. Later on, in a letter to her daughter Scottie, Wilson recalled that the bohemian Zelda used to fascinate Fitzgerald's bachelor friends: "It was a smart thing in the twenties for attractive young married women to hold levees in their bath. . . . I believe your mother did it, though of course only casually with her and your father's friends." When corresponding with Fitzgerald's biographer, Wilson defended Zelda's artistic ability and urged him to "make clear that even when her mind was going, the writing and painting she did had her curious personal quality of imaginative iridescence and showed something of real talent."[3] But Zelda's charms could not entirely make up for her slapdash hospitality.

Wilson was impressed when Fitzgerald read a dazzling passage from the manuscript of *Tender is the Night*, which he had been working on, without making much progress, for the past three years. But he was embarrassed and annoyed when he heard Scott asking his chauffeur to report the hostile remarks his guests had made about him on the drive back to the station. "It's only very seldom," he insisted, "that you get a real opportunity to hear what people say about you behind your back." "The aftermath of a Fitzgerald evening was notoriously a painful experience," Wilson concluded, in a vivid memoir that captured the essence of Scott's feckless character and zany behavior. "Nonsense and inspiration, reckless idealism and childish irresponsibility," he wrote, "were mingled in so queer a way." The weekend did nothing to revive their flagging friendship. Scott's absurd antics, his strenuous efforts to amuse and the enormous contrast between Scott's magnificent house and his own squalid room in New York jarred on Wilson's nerves.

Their relations remained cool for the next five years, while Zelda suffered her first mental breakdowns and Fitzgerald struggled to complete *Tender is the Night*. In January 1933—after Wilson had published *Axel's Castle*, Hemingway had achieved great success with *A Farewell to Arms* and Fitzgerald's career had become stagnant—Scott turned up drunk in New York for a dinner with his two friends. Wilson and Hemingway, both hardened drinkers, were shocked by Fitzgerald's willingness to humiliate himself in public. Wilson thought Fitzgerald used childishness and cunning to excuse his own failings and attack others without provoking retaliation: "Hemingway [with the help of Wilson's reviews] was now a great man and Scott was so much overcome by his greatness that he embarrassed me by his self-abasement, and he finally lay down on the restaurant floor, pretending to be unconscious but actually listening in on the conversation and from time to time needling his hero, whose weaknesses he had studied intently, with malicious little interpolations."[4] At regular intervals Wilson and Hemingway would take Scott to the toilet and hold his head while he vomited. When he recovered, Scott insulted his friends and then asked if they still liked him. Though Fitzgerald apologized to Wilson the following month, the weekend at Ellerslie and dinner in New York made Wilson lose respect for his old friend and doubt if Scott could ever recover his reputation as a serious writer.

II

Wilson wrote that in 1926, the year after he separated from Mary Blair, he had no regular girlfriend and thought constantly about sex. Reluctant to begin another affair that could lead to marriage, and unhappy with his solitary writing life, he thought a lower-class girl would provide sexual companionship without emotional complications. Just after returning from a summer in O'Neill's house in Provincetown, the unlikeliest of dance-partners went to the Tango Gardens, a cheap dance hall on 14th Street, where he met Frances, a Ukrainian waitress. Thus began a long relationship, which lasted from September 1927 until he married Mary McCarthy in 1938.

The small, dark Frances had a broad Slavic face, a wide nose, light green "foreign" eyes and reddish-blond hair parted in the middle. She was remarkably similar to Marie, the model and call-girl he had picked up in New York the previous summer. Both were sensual, lower-class Catholic women from Brooklyn, married to brutal men who were serving time in jail. Frances was attracted to the gentlemanly and generous Edmund, and established with him the same sort of connection that Myrtle Wilson had with Tom Buchanan in *The Great Gatsby*. Although the relationship was based entirely on sex, which Wilson rewarded as far as his slender means allowed, it was accompanied by warm and tender feeling on both sides.

Frances' wretched existence was the basis for Anna Lenihan's life in Wilson's story "The Princess with the Golden Hair." Her aunts and her mother, Sophie, were born in Stanislav, near Lvov, in what was then Austrian Galicia and is now southwestern Ukraine. Born around the turn of the century, Frances never knew her father. Her mother—a hard creature whom Wilson compared to "a mother pig, [with] round glittering green eyes, rather handsome, round flat face, round flat nose, no neck"—had tried to abort both Frances and her sister, and had placed Frances in an orphanage between the ages of two and four. Her sister had become deaf from being beaten as a child; and Frances attributed her own poor health as an adult to the rough treatment she had suffered all her life.

Frances' family were fur and textile workers, living on relief in Coney Island. She had left home as soon as possible and married—after attempting suicide—when she was only seventeen. Her husband, Albert, had told her that he was an automobile salesman, but he actually stole cars and was sent to Sing Sing. Her daughter, Adele, about the same age as Rosalind, was also put in an orphanage by her paternal grandparents when Frances was sick and unable to look after her.

While Albert was in jail, her mother and step-father, Alex Litwood (anglicized from Litvak), mistreated Frances, made her do all the cooking and sleep in the filthy basement. "Please don't come here to see me," she begged Wilson. "This basement is so dirty and looks awful—I'd die of embarrassment." Alex turned their apartment into a speakeasy and whorehouse, pimped for the girls he hired and paid them three dollars for each customer.

In March 1928 Frances went up to Oswego, New York, on Lake Ontario, to visit her husband. He had served his prison sentence and was supposed to be dying of a blood clot on the brain. She stayed on East 3rd Street with the family of A. T. Minahan—who may have been her in-laws and whose name is close to the fictional Lenihan. Albert eventually recovered and moved into the Brooklyn flat with Frances. But he could not get a job, drank heavily, beat her up and eventually left her.

Frances had waited on the marble tables in Childs', where, Fitzgerald wrote in "May Day," "a crowd of poor people with sleep in the corners of their eyes [try] to look straight before them at their food so as not to see other poor people."[5] Wilson thought she looked cute in her yellow uniform. But after her husband beat her, her face was so black and blue that she could not go back to work there. She later got a waitress job at Schrafft's for twenty dollars a week.

Frances' thirty-four letters to Wilson during their years together were surprisingly well written. She addressed him as "Dear Ed" (no one ever called him "Eddie") or "Hello Darling," signed her letters "Lovingly" or "All my love and kisses," but never wrote her surname on the letter or envelope. She complained about physical illness, family problems and marital strife; often asked Edmund for money and thanked him when he sent it; expressed concern for his welfare; and was sexually provocative. As in Wilson's story, she had to write and see him secretly to avoid enraging her jealous husband and lovers. Nevertheless, their relations were well known and when she returned home at night her brother-in-law would jeeringly ask: "Did Mr. Wilson get it in tonight?—Why don't you let poor Mr. Wilson get it in?" Edmund, embarrassed by this exploitative liaison, also tried to keep Frances well hidden from his friends.

Frances was often threatened with eviction, and there was high tension when she was forced to live with her sister. "I think I'll swear out a warrant," she once threatened, "and shut up her filthy mouth." The most dramatic and dangerous event took place in November 1933 when her apartment was attacked by thieves and murderers. She described the action in the words of a grade-B movie of the 1930s: "There's been plenty of trouble here yesterday. Holdup men came in here to rob us. Alex ran to the window to call the police and the gunmen shot at Alex—missed him and the bullets almost killed a woman across the street. . . . If things get too hot here, I'll take Adele to your place and we'll stay until this blows over. These gangsters are out to get Alex and we have police protection."

Her letters also contained some tender domestic concerns. "I wish you were back," she declared. "Let me help you fix up your place—I'd love it." Like Mary Blair, she repeatedly urged him to cut down on alcohol, which often brought out the worst in Wilson and made him ill: "Darling, I wish you'd stop drinking until you are better. I'm sure you wouldn't be having this [nose infection] if you didn't drink."

She tried to tease and provoke him when he was out of New York. She reported that she had caught a cold from sleeping in the raw; missed him and got lonely because she had not yet found a new boyfriend. While Wilson was courting his second wife in glamorous Santa Barbara, Frances wrote: "Wonder if there is anyone taking up your time or do you sit on the beach all day watching the bathing beauties? . . . I'm so lonesome without you—there's no one to fuss over me the way you did. . . . I'm thinking seriously of staying with you when you get back—if you still want me." While Wilson was in Provincetown in August 1932, she told him: "If you were only here I'd love you to death. . . . Don't stay there too long."[6]

In his diaries Wilson provided, as usual, a very precise account of his sexual relations with Frances (whom he calls Anna). Only in sex, especially sex with working-class women, could Wilson finally overcome his extreme repression and find an intensely gratifying connection and release. With Frances, who (Wilson said) "used to sleep curled up to fit my back and with my cock in her hand," he was completely uninhibited and took polymorphous pleasure in all aspects of sexuality. He walked around without any clothes on, liked kissing her all over—

especially on her feet—tried unusual sexual positions, enjoyed fellatio and practiced cunnilingus. This made Frances weak with pleasure and so preoccupied him that he would almost forget to pass on to the "warm and mucilaginous moisture of ordinary intercourse." He seemed to get an additional thrill by writing about sex after he had experienced it and could become quite lyrical about their love-making: "Her little mouth under the moist kisses of my mouth and my finger on her little moist cunt rubbing its most sensitive spot—I felt that I was in contact with her two tenderest places—tiny, infinitely delicious, those two little spots on her slight small body where flesh, where personality melted into magic and delight." But Wilson never fell in love with Frances, and their sexual relations remained separate from the rest of his life.

Their delight was sometimes spoiled by poor health. Frances—plagued by venereal disease and gynecological problems—aborted Wilson's child in September 1929. She had another abortion after her husband got out of jail and needed an operation for a fallopian cyst in the early 1930s. Wilson noted that her shaved sexual parts, the night before she entered the hospital, were "far from being ready for any love." Though Frances was devoted to him, she gave him body lice and a case of gonorrhea, which fired him up with a five-day fever that inspired his poem "Infection":

> I thought, bad whiskey, manners, plays,
> Bad talk abroad, bad work alone,
> Bad damp apartments on bad days,
> Have poisoned me from brain to bone—

till he discovered that she had unwittingly caught the clap from her husband and passed it on to him.

In the spring of 1934, between his second and third marriages, his long affair with Frances threatened to come to an end. In April she complained that she had seen very little of him recently, asked if he was getting tired of her and then announced that she had a new boyfriend with "serious intentions." Jerry was insanely jealous when he spotted her telegram to Wilson. She tried to keep Wilson secret from him and continued to see both men. But on June 25 she declared she had to choose between them: "He's here every night now and stays quite late. He's madly in love with me and very jealous of you—proposes regularly every night. . . . Jerry wants me to write you that I'll never see you again." Three days later she said: "I can't see you any more. . . . So this is goodbye." The jealous rivalry, however, must have stimulated Wilson's interest, for they continued to meet secretly until September 28, when she temporarily decided to commit herself to the more ardent lover and the supposed security of marriage: "He's crazy about me and only wants to be with me all the time. I'm going to be very happy with him—I think. I've been happy with you too—but this is different."[7] Her last letter, two days later, announced her imminent marriage. But when her marriage did not work out she returned to Wilson and continued to have sex with him.

Frances appeared in his play, travel book and poetry as well as in his fiction. In *Beppo and Beth* (1934) June Macy, the hero's girlfriend, is based on Frances. She comes from a large family in Brooklyn, her former husband is a criminal and "she's a natural woman. . . . She has no education at all, but she's never for a moment cheap. It's because she's got Europe so close behind her—her people were Polish peasants." When traveling alone in Russia in 1935, Wilson often thought of Frances and mentioned that he had first been attracted by her "Russian voice": "Her parents were Ukrainians from the neighborhood of Lemburg [Lvov], and she had grown up among Slavic Americans. I had always attributed the sadness of her voice to the hardships and tragedies of her life, and her quietness and patience and sweetness to the gentleness of her own personality." In his final tribute, "Home to Town: Two Highballs" (1940), he commemorated his love for Frances and praised her "slim pale body,"

> The little drooping breasts, the cigarettes,
> The little cunning shadow between the narrow thighs. . . .
> They will never have a girl so pale and blue-veined and quick and
>   passionate as you.[8]

Wilson had sought a sexual connection without complications. But he could not help becoming involved with the tawdry drama of Frances' life and infected by her sexual disease. Poor, sickly, downtrodden and dependent on the whims of her family and her lovers, Frances was very different from the attractive, educated, poised and stylish women he thought of marrying. Yet in some vital way Frances represented for him an essentially feminine spirit, a source of sensual renewal that fascinated him all his life.

III

During his years with Frances, Wilson continued his association with the *New Republic*, strengthened his considerable reputation as a literary journalist and inevitably made a number of enemies, who resented his powerful position in the world of letters. The ingrate Edward Dahlberg, who resented the substantial help that writers like Lawrence and Wilson had given him, offered a sneering portrait in his autobiography: "Wilson had thin leafy hair of a rusty-colored hue, a lisp, a caustic chin, a mouth too niggardly closed for his vocation, literature."

Wilson's round-up review "The Muses Out of Work," published in the *New Republic* in May 1927, provoked cries of wounded outrage from the Imagist poet, cynical novelist and bohemian drinker Maxwell Bodenheim, and from the equally touchy and suicidal Hart Crane. Wilson wrote that Bodenheim's poetry had "many ingenious figures, but little emotion. . . . His books are rather disappointing when we set out to read them through." Bodenheim replied by calling him a "fatuous policeman, menacingly swinging his club."

Wilson categorized Crane as a kind of misguided Rimbaud. He criticized his vague imagery and even vaguer meaning, and dismissed his first book, *White Buildings*, with a military metaphor: "His poetry is *disponible* [available], as they say about French troops. We are eagerly waiting to see to which part of the front he will move it: just at present it is killing time in the cafés behind the lines." Crane failed to roll with the punches and wrote a furious self-pitying letter to the critic Yvor Winters. Though Crane came from a wealthy family—his father had invented "Life Savers" candy—he had rebelled against his background, had not gone to college and was living hand-to-mouth in New York. Ignoring the soundness and substance of the criticism, and unaware of Wilson's own poverty, he illogically attacked his privileged background and elite education: "Wilson's article was just half-baked enough to make me warm around the collar. It's so damn easy for such as he, born into easy means, graduated from a fashionable university into a critical chair overlooking Washington Square, etc., to sit tight and hatch little squibs of advice to poets . . . as though all the names he had just mentioned have been as suavely nourished as he."

Crane once spotted Wilson, hard at work as usual (and very much as Wilson would later describe himself, imprisoned with Swinburne), in his study at 3 Washington Square North. Like Dahlberg, Crane vented his anger in heavy irony, mocked Wilson's physical appearance and suggested that the Johnsonian icon was not quite up to his task as a critic. "Let's take a look at Number 3," Hart told a friend. "We'll probably see Bunny sitting at his work table in the front window, heavy learned tomes stacked high at both elbows, his hair ruffled and face red from expenditure of pure intellectual energy, scribbling away, giving his fine mind no week-end of respite, oblivious to the outside world." Crane may have been mollified when Wilson recommended him for a Guggenheim Fellowship, which he won in 1931.

Wilson confronted rather than ignored this sort of ad hominem criticism with a Swiftian *saeva indignatio*. "For a worker in ideas," Wilson declared, "it is dangerous, it may prove fatal to one's effectiveness, to betray that one's feelings have been hurt. The critic must remain invulnerable. When goaded, he should show himself not peevish, but indignant, with a background of scorn." Wilson defiantly quoted and thus defused these attacks (Crane's letter had been quoted in Philip Horton's 1937 biography) when he reprinted his review of Bodenheim and Crane in *The Shores of Light*.

Wilson had admirers as well as detractors. Unlike Hart Crane, the young Lionel Trilling, who moved to Greenwich Village in 1929, found Wilson, living on East 9th Street and studiously involved in his work, a truly inspiring figure: "To validate its present dignity, to suggest that what the Village stood for in American life was not wholly a matter of history, Edmund Wilson lived just across the way. Someone had pointed out his apartment to me and I used to take note of his evening hours at his desk. . . . He seemed in his own person, and young as he was, to propose and to realize the idea of the literary life." Malcolm Cowley shared Trilling's admiration for his older colleague on the *New Republic*. In February 1929, before Wilson had published his first major book, Cowley praised his ability to survive as a serious writer: "you have a special distinction: you're the only writer I know who has been successfully leading a double life—that is, who has been earning a living out of literature and at the same time writing good books."[10] Trilling and Cowley knew that Wilson's life was difficult, isolated and financially precarious.

IV

Though he later dealt with social issues in essays, in the late Twenties Wilson was still trying to express his ideas in fiction. In August 1927 he went to Boston during the last appeal on behalf of the condemned Anarchists Sacco and Vanzetti. Leon Edel wrote that "he went actually to see friends [Louise and Henrietta Fort]; but the drama of the celebrated case, the tense atmosphere, the tragic overtones of every step in the appeal, the arrest of the liberals on the Common, impinged heavily on Wilson's feelings and colored the mood of his entire stay." In 1920 two Italian immigrants, Sacco and Vanzetti, had been accused of committing murder during a payroll robbery in South Braintree, Massachusetts. Though the evidence against them had been discredited during the long judicial process, their death sentences were upheld by a distinguished committee appointed by the governor of the state, and they were executed in August 1927.

Wilson turned his reaction to these events into an ironic, well-controlled story. First published in the *New Republic* a month after the execution, "The Men from Rumpelmayer's" was his best work of fiction in the 1920s. The title came from a line of dialogue, which alludes to the firm of expensive caterers, on the first page of Virginia Woolf's novel *Mrs. Dalloway* (1925).

The story opens in a country club north of Boston on the day the Supreme Court decides the final appeal. The narrator—the guest of a Harvard friend, his Californian wife and his sister-in-law—mentions the committee appointed by Governor Fuller: a judge and the presidents of Harvard and MIT. But the subject is too volatile to discuss among friends, even though one of the sisters—quoting Vanzetti's statement: "I am innocent of these two harms"—agrees with the narrator that he is not guilty. So they decide to avoid politics, and drive down to Boston to buy lobsters for dinner. On the way south, however, they are constantly reminded of the case, which permeates their lives even as they try to escape from it. They smell condemned clams in the slimy mud of a beach, consider driving past Charlestown Prison where the condemned men are held, boil the lobsters alive and discuss the broken, violent marriage of some close friends.

On his return home the narrator reads that the appeal has been denied. He also receives two telegrams: a flirtatious one from the unmarried sister and an urgent appeal from the Sacco-Vanzetti Defense Committee. He ignores both. By returning to his ordinary, unreflective life, the sensitive and intelligent narrator illustrates how easy it is to be indifferent to suffering. Wilson illuminated his theme when he told Bishop, a year later, that during the Sacco and Vanzetti case, "all the different kinds of Americans, eminent and obscure, had suddenly, in a short sudden burst of intensified life, been compelled to reveal their true characters."[11]

During the summer of 1927 Wilson had also begun to use his experience of literary life in a novel, *I Thought of Daisy* (1929). As in his previous stories, he used a first-person narrator, revealing its autobiographical origins. Wilson's novel traces the development of the narrator's awareness as he tries to decide what to do with his life. From the first Wilson acknowledged that he had imposed a dangerously schematic structure on his story. As he told Max Perkins, Fitzgerald's close friend and Wilson's new editor at Scribner's: "I have made characters, incidents, and situations subordinate to a set of ideas about life and literature, and unless the ideas are really put over, unless they are made interesting enough to compensate the reader for what he is missing in action and motion, for what he ordinarily gets in a novel, the whole performance will fail."

In his Foreword to the 1953 edition, Wilson explained that each of the five chapters is dominated by a different mood and a different point of view: "In the first, it is Hugo Bamman, with his revolt against bourgeois society and his social revolutionary ideas. In the second, it is Rita the Romantic poet. In the third, the narrator is adrift in the void . . . the world in which he finds himself now appears to him anarchic and amoral, and the point of view is more or less materialistic, with an emphasis on animal behavior. . . . In the fourth section, my hero recovers himself under the influence of the metaphysician Grosbeake, who instils into him a certain idealism and induces a certain serenity." In the final section, Daisy becomes the dominant character and tells about her own life; and the hero, at last, makes "connections with the common life."

Wilson's plan led to a rambling novel that lacks clear focus and dramatic action. Instead of vivid scenes and characters, he provides digressive lectures that are not nearly as interesting as his own literary criticism. In the midst of chapter three, for example, he includes a long, static discussion of Dostoyevsky, lifted from his *New Republic* essay of October 1928, in order to expound the idea that suffering can inspire great art. Proust, whom Wilson had been writing essays about in preparation for the chapter in *Axel's Castle*, influenced Wilson's alternation between reverie and narrative, and his essayistic meditations on his major characters. The passage toward the end of Proust's *The Captive*, on Dostoyevsky's fictional technique and portrayal of character, influenced the Dostoyevskyian discussion in Wilson's novel.

Retrospectively, Wilson realized the defects in the form and characters of the novel: "I have sometimes been rather appalled by the rigor with which I sacrificed to my plan of five symphonic movements what would normally have been the line of the story. There is no very full account of the narrator's relations with Rita, though the reader must have been led to expect it." Daisy's involvement with the four men in her chaotic life provides a kind of structure: her first husband Phil Meissner, a photographer who eloped with her on a motorcycle in order to induce an abortion; the tabloid journalist Ray Coleman; the minor poet Pete Bird, with whom she lives in a country idyll; and the narrator himself, who takes her on a trip to Coney Island and finally becomes her lover. There are also two lyrical fireside scenes—with Rita, and with Daisy and Pete Bird—in which the narrator achieves a rare sense of communion with both women. Wilson's portrayal of the bohemian men and women who practiced free love in Greenwich Village in the late Twenties is quite different from Fitzgerald's depiction of relatively chaste and conventional cocktail-drinking debutantes and beaux in *This Side of Paradise* (1920). *I Thought of Daisy* reveals the great change in drinking habits and sexual mores that took place in that hedonistic decade.

In 1937 Wilson misleadingly wrote to Mary McCarthy that "*I Thought of Daisy* is not autobiographical, though it is told in the first person. There is hardly anything in it that ever actually happened to me." Yet the unnamed first-person narrator of the novel is clearly a satiric self-portrait and embodies the paradoxical characteristics of Wilson's fictional heroes. As Stanley Edgar Hyman wrote, in a hostile criticism of Wilson's work: "The fictional man is coldhearted and repelled by human contact, yet exacerbated by a rampant sexuality; lacking in creative talent, yet impelled to produce imaginative work; committed to commercialism and admiring only integrity; 'democratic' and 'socialist' while bitterly chauvinistic, snobbish and contemptuous of people; almost without humor and addicted to parody and satire; aware of the complex and oversimplifying everything, from literature to human relations, in a series of false 'either-ors.'"[12]

More significantly, all the main characters in *I Thought of Daisy* are based on Wilson's family and friends. We have seen that Hugo Bamman was modeled on Dos Passos, that Bamman's neurotic father resembled Edmund Wilson Sr. and that Mrs. Grosbeake was a portrait of Frieda Lawrence. Wilson said that Daisy was based on the lively and amusing chorus girl Florence O'Neill, a friend of Ted Paramore and Katze Szabo, who was married to a man called Ted Leisen. Florence never became Wilson's lover. But his diaries reveal that Florence, like Daisy, had a father who was "ruined by being indicted for manslaughter; he and another man had hit each other (both's fault) when father was coming out of garage; man killed and father in hospital for a month." Like the fictional heroine, she tried to commit suicide by cutting her wrist, and she took a pleasant trip to Coney Island with Wilson.

Rita Cavanaugh, who speaks with passionate vehemence and inspires the narrator by her dedication to art, is a portrait of Edna Millay. The narrator is in love with her, and his exalted description of Rita in the novel is similar to Wilson's later portrait in his memorial essay on Millay: "Her cheeks were fiery now—all her face was suffused with fierce pink, and I saw that there was red in her hair. I saw now for the first time that she was beautiful. Her brow was very high and wide, and the resonant voice with which she recited—so different from her quick dry speech, a mere pizzicato of those strings—seemed the full-toned and proper music of what I saw now also for the first time was a long and lovely throat."

In early 1929 Wilson, eager for Millay's reaction, asked her opinion of the manuscript of the novel. Dissatisfied with both the artistic quality of the book and with the portrait of herself, she sent him an emotional response: "I swear that you will do yourself a great injury if you publish it just as it is—it is very uneven—I like much of it tremendously—but it is not a whole—it needs a whole lot of working on still. . . . It really isn't good enough, yet, Bunny, I swear it isn't.— You can make a grand book of it, but it's not finished." But by then Wilson was suffering a nervous breakdown and about to go into a nursing home. He never received this crucial letter and, thinking she no longer cared about his work, fell out of touch with Millay for nearly twenty years.

Christian Gauss, who had three beautiful blond daughters, inspired Professor Grosbeake, a modern sage who advocates and exemplifies order and harmony, and who enables the narrator to stabilize his life and get back in proper touch with Daisy. Bamman represents idealism, Daisy life, Rita art and Grosbeake intellect.

Following his schematic plan, Wilson expounds rather than dramatizes the themes of the book. In his all-night discussion with Rita, the narrator learns that "any great strength or excellence of character . . . carries with it weaknesses and ignominies inseparable from excellence and strength"—an idea that Wilson would fully develop in *The Wound and the Bow*. Another theme runs through all his major works of the 1920s: the Lawrencean need to break out of self-contained repression, "say *Yea* to life," and embrace the emotional and sexual possibilities of human existence. Finally, Wilson alludes to and then reverses an idea in Eliot's "Tradition and the Individual Talent" and argues that there should not be a "gulf between the self which experiences and the self which writes!" He believes that literature, "a reality as deep as life itself," can lead the narrator toward rather than away from life, which is exemplified by Daisy. At the end of the novel the narrator realizes that through his revitalizing contact with Daisy he now can "save myself at last from that dreadful isolation of the artist which had appalled me in Hugo and Rita . . . [and] by the way of literature itself . . . break through into the real world."[13]

The sales of the novel were so meager that when a young woman told Wilson: "I got your book and enjoyed every moment of it," he replied: "Oh, it was you who bought it." The critical response was also extremely disappointing. Paul Rosenfeld had loyally praised its "crispness" and "sharp impressionism," but the biographer George Painter (reviewing the reprint) pointed out the uneven nature of the book. Wilson had admitted that it lacked "vividness and excitement," and Painter, conceding that it had good ideas, images and phrases, concluded: "alas, it had nothing else." In August 1929, the month the book was published, Fitzgerald finally had the opportunity to judge Wilson's fiction. He wrote Hemingway that the book was interesting to those who knew Wilson and his close friends, but despite (or perhaps because of) Wilson's carefully thought out plan, it was formless: "Bunny Wilson's book has a fascinating portrait of Dos in it, and it is full of good things, and to me interesting throughout. Oddly enough, what it lacks is his old bogey, form. It is [as] shapeless as Wells at his wildest."

Christian Gauss had inspired Wilson to "want to write something in which every word, every cadence, every detail, should perform a definite function in producing an intense effect." But he failed to achieve this ideal. The month after the novel appeared Wilson recognized the artistic flaws he later acknowledged in the Foreword and told Phelps Putnam: "I'll never undertake anything of the kind again —hereafter, will confine opinions and ideas to essays, and in fiction hew straight to the line."[14] The cool reception of *I Thought of Daisy* led Wilson to concentrate on "opinions and ideas," and he did not publish another book of fiction for seventeen years.

Poets, Farewell!, published by Scribner's two months later, in October 1929, continued this renunciatory tone. Like all Wilson's books of the 1920s it lacks structure and unity. It is a grab-bag of poems in traditional forms, descriptions of landscapes in prose, translations from Latin and Italian, comic verse, satires on Henry James and Edwin Arlington Robinson, and bitter memories of the war. It also includes a social protest poem about a young girl indicted for murder, whose case Wilson had discussed in "The People v. Dorothy Perkins" in July 1925. Its settings were the places Wilson had lived in and traveled to during his first twenty-five years: upstate New York, the Jersey coast, Cape Cod, Southampton, Venice, the Boboli Gardens in Florence, Nancy, Vittel and Chaumont.

Many of the poems allude to Wilson's friends, but they do not transcend the private situations that inspired them. He dedicated poems to John Bishop, John Amen, a lawyer friend, and Stark Young, the drama editor of the *New Republic*. "Nocturne" was written for Elinor Wylie, "Infection" described the disease he caught from Frances, "Shut Out the Square!" and "Copper and White" were love poems to Edna Millay. The third poem concludes with a beautiful phrase from Lucretius and from Virgil's *Georgics* (II: 47), *in luminis oras*—"the shores of light"—which Wilson later adopted as the title of his literary chronicle of the Twenties and Thirties. The last one recalls his tender love-making with the copper-haired woman:

> So warm we lie—ah, now! and now! we meet,
> All in our mouths—and now and now and now!—
> I knew that passionate mouth in that pale skin
> Would spread with such a moisture, let me in
> To such a bareness of possessive flesh!

The main theme of this book, as of *I Thought of Daisy*, is the call to the sensual life. It is celebrated not only in the poems to Millay, but also in his apostrophe to the vagina in "Americanization": "And that voracious maw, profound and warm, / I still feel throbbing after it was fed," and his paean to pleasure in the Venetian "Lido":

I strip you of your shining sheath,
Crowd wide your thighs with steady knee,
Stab flesh with flesh and sharply breathe,
Exhaled from open flanks, the sea.

The title poem describes Wilson's visit to Louise Bogan's house in Hillsdale, upstate New York, and concludes with a valedictory to poetry and a passing of the lyre to his poet-friend: "Voices, farewell!—the silver and the brass— / I leave that speech to you who have the tongue." But the farewell was only temporary and Wilson continued to publish his minor verse in two more books and six pamphlets throughout his life. Bogan responded loyally to Wilson's gracious gesture by over-praising his work to John Hall Wheelock: "I think there are eight or ten fine poems in it—poems full of great style and really noble thinking—noble in the passionate sense, like music." John Bishop, who was mentioned in "Quintilian," gave a more judicious appraisal in a letter to Allen Tate, when he called the poetry prosaic: "Certainly the fault of much of Bunny's poetry is that . . . there are too many lines of direct statement, in which whatever is being conveyed to the reader is conveyed at once and by the shortest cut."

Wilson felt that the most disappointing feature of publishing a book was the dullness of the reviews, even when favorable. After laboring for months and years "to focus some comprehensive vision or make out some compelling case," he was appalled and disgusted to find "his book discussed by persons who not only have not understood it, but do not even in some instances appear to have read it."[15] He therefore devised the gratifying habit of composing in his head enthusiastic reviews of his own books.

V

By the end of the 1920s Wilson had reached a crisis in his personal and professional life. He had always been frightened by the strain of mental illness that troubled his family. His childhood friend and cousin, Sandy Kimball, was schizophrenic and Wilson had often visited him in the insane asylum where he was confined until the end of his life. Sandy's father, Dr. Reuel Kimball, had collapsed, become quite helpless and regressed into a second childhood. And there was always the ghastly specter of his own father. He had "passed into the shadow," just after

Edmund was born, at exactly the age, thirty-three, that his son would also suffer a nervous breakdown. But Edmund Jr., much tougher than his father, fought his way out of his illness instead of retreating from the world.

In *A Prelude* Wilson observed: "The most painful moments of my life have been due to indecision. I usually know exactly what I want to do, and it has been only when I could not make up my mind that I have really gone to pieces." Wilson's indecision about the direction of his writing career was not a cause of his breakdown, but a symptom of his anxiety and insecurity about the future. Poor as usual, living in a cheap furnished room, "a narrow stale-smelling little hole," he not only felt the letdown a writer often experiences after completing a book, but was full of doubts about *I Thought of Daisy*. Elinor Wylie, his first close friend to die, suffered a fatal stroke in December 1928, and Herbert Croly, the editor of the *New Republic*, had a paralytic stroke in January 1929.

Wilson led the strenuous double life of literary journalist and creative writer. And his loneliness and emotional hunger had also involved him in multiple entanglements with women. He needed Frances, but was ashamed of his liaison with her. He felt guilty about his love affair with Léonie Adams, who was writing anguished letters from Europe, and apprehensive about meeting her demands when she returned. He had come back from California, where he had been courting Margaret Canby, and missed her terribly. He loved her, but wondered if they had enough in common to sustain a marriage. He still felt loyal to Mary Blair, who supported him during this nervous crisis, as well as disloyal to Ted Paramore, who had also wanted to marry Margaret.

When the strain became too intense, Wilson drank more heavily than ever and fell into a depression. "One of the symptoms of certain neurotic states," he wrote from personal experience in *Memoirs of Hecate County*, "is an irrational drop of morale, a depression that may suddenly descend on you and absolutely flatten you out." The symptoms were terrifying. During his nervous breakdown, Rosalind later recalled, Wilson, always working furiously against journalistic deadlines, "thought there was a pencil writing for him all by itself." He told Glyn Morris, as if describing a story by Poe: "I couldn't get over the idea that I was being followed. Eventually, every time I had this feeling, I would turn around as though to confront my follower. By doing this repeatedly I convinced myself that it was an illusion."[16]

Wilson knew something was seriously wrong when he could not face the weekly confrontation with his dominant and disapproving mother. He set out for Red Bank, but "found myself seized with panic as soon as I got into the taxi. . . . I began to tremble violently, and I realized that I could not go down to my mother's." He consulted a doctor, who thought he had merely been drinking too much, put him in the hospital for a few days and drugged him with morphine. When the symptoms returned, Wilson, afraid of becoming insane, asked his aunt to find him a psychiatrist. He saw Dr. John McKinney (who was two years older than Wilson and had earned his medical degree at the University of Michigan), a young neurologist at St. Luke's Hospital. But the panics and depressions continued. In January 1929, Wilson wrote with cool objectivity, he began to feel suicidal: "The weeks when this was at its worst were the most horrible experience of my life. I told McKinney one day that I felt I could not live through my crises of depression, when it seemed to me I was condemned, by some power I could not control, to destroy myself in some violent way."

Finally, like his father before him, Wilson took refuge in a sanatorium. He spent three weeks—from mid-February to early March 1929—in the Clifton Springs Sanitorium and Clinic, west of his ancestral home in upstate New York, between Rochester and Syracuse. He ate and slept properly, took baths and massages, and had electric treatments. They helped fill up the day, but also irritated him. As Theodore Roethke wrote, with frightening brevity:

> Swift's servant beat him.
> Now they use
> A current flowing
> From a fuse.

At the clinic, Wilson also became addicted to paraldehyde, a form of ether, which had an offensive odor but produced an exhilarating effect.

He spent most of his time, as usual, working and writing letters to friends—Gauss, Perkins, Tate, Burton Rascoe, Gilbert Seldes and Seward Collins, editor of the *Bookman*. The tone of his letters was consistently stoic and amusing, making light of his illness and suggesting that he was essentially all right. "I came back from California in excellent form," he told the fatherly Gauss, "but, soon after arriving in New York, passed into a nervous decline and have been sent to this sanatorium—not, I hope, for long." Within a week, the place had become a god-forsaken lazar-house from which he was eager to escape. Wilson also occupied himself with a therapeutic and satisfying revision of *Poets, Farewell!* and of passages in *Axel's Castle*. This literary work strengthened his confidence and helped him recover.

Sceptical about his treatment and angry that the clinic did not want to release him, Wilson finally insisted on leaving. But his nerves were still bad and he returned to McKinney, who "psyched" him. Wilson continued to refill his prescription for paraldehyde until, after McKinney suggested he was in danger of becoming an addict, he used his tremendous will power to break the habit abruptly. Wilson gained certain insights about his illness, but resented his dependence on McKinney. Despite the doctor's reluctance, he eventually detached himself from treatment. It took several years, however, to recover from his manic-depressive mood swings, which would make him shudder and twitch, and fly into sudden rages. Fearful of losing control after his nervous breakdown, Wilson constantly tried to master himself and dominate others.

The conflict between his emotional repression and his desire for imaginative expression led directly to Wilson's breakdown. Though he achieved a sexual breakthrough, he lost the artistic struggle. Unlike Fitzgerald, Wilson lacked warmth and did not have sufficient sympathy and imagination to portray living characters in his fiction. As Allen Tate perceptively told him, during one of their intellectual disputes: "There is a sense in which, as Arnold said of Gray, *you have never spoken out*. There is an area of your sensibility that you have never completely come to terms with."[17]

By the end of the 1920s Wilson realized that his career was running on two divergent tracks. His weekly essays for the *New Republic* enhanced his reputation as a major critic. But he wanted to be an imaginative writer rather than a literary journalist. However, *The Crime in the Whistler Room* did not succeed, his four discordant books did not sell and he publicly said farewell to poetry. Wilson needed an entire decade to define his role as a man of letters and realize that his talents were critical rather than creative. He did not achieve his first literary success until *Axel's Castle* was published in 1931. Before that transitional book appeared, he embarked upon a second marriage.

EIGHT

Margaret Canby, 1930–1932

I

Wilson first met Margaret Canby (née Waterman) during his trip to San Francisco in March 1924. A wealthy California socialite, Margaret was very different in background and temperament from Mary Blair. Margaret's family, originally from Philadelphia, had made a fortune (now greatly diminished) in Pennsylvania coal fields and lived on a grand estate in Montecito, near Santa Barbara. Her family also had an artistic side. Margaret's cousin was the lesbian artist Romaine Brooks; her father (who had left her mother) had been painted by Mary Cassatt; and her stepmother had been Daisy of the Floradora Sextet.

Margaret, born in Santa Barbara and one of three sisters, was the same age as Wilson. A small, attractive woman, barely five feet tall, she was carefree, fun-loving, down-to-earth and unintellectual. When her convertible top blew off as she was driving back from Los Angeles, she said: "Oh, well, there it goes"—and drove on. She was very musical, interested in clothes, owned a hat shop called "Margot's," and loved to go swimming and ride horses. Charley Walker's wife, Adelaide, thought her rather frivolous and foolish. But Margaret was also intrigued by the literary world and attracted to Wilson's bohemian side.

Wilson, for his part, was drawn to her lively good spirits, her warmth and dignity, her breeding and elegance. Her mother was a Scotch-Canadian Presbyterian, and he particularly admired the characteristics of this heritage: a cool, imperturbable shell and a thoroughbred sense of propriety. In his diaries, he contrasted Margaret's refinement to Frances' careworn body, and praised her femininity, sensuality, figure and, of course, her feet: "Her skin was so smooth—she seemed so smooth and soft, after [Frances], with her hard high bones—her own hard pointed chin . . . the gray in her hair—her amiable face—

her Scotch matter-of-factness and composure, occasionally broken by some severe remark—surprise at seeing her blush—powder which removed odor—discrepancy between ordinary manner and way of talking and passionate enjoyment (groaning)—strong neck and back from horseback riding—small feet contrasting with rather thick torso—small hands, but with rather blunt thickish fingers."

Wilson was sexually stimulated by competition with close friends and male rivals, and by sharing or stealing the woman who attracted both of them. He competed with John Bishop for Edna Millay and Léonie Adams, with Ted Paramore for Margaret Canby and, later on, with Philip Rahv for Mary McCarthy, with Arthur Koestler for Mamaine Paget and with James Thornton for his (and then Wilson's) wife Elena. The timid and thoughtful Paul Rosenfeld once shrewdly observed that Wilson's "typical friend was someone clever but dissipated who looked rather the worse for wear. He was evidently thinking of Phelps Putnam, Scott Fitzgerald and Ted Paramore, the last of whom was a perfect example of this. For all his cleverness, Paramore never got anywhere with the projects—usually theatrical or connected with the movies—which always kept him sanguine and allowed him to assume an air of having important business."[1]

Ted and Margaret belonged to the privileged class of Santa Barbara and had known each other since their teens. He had danced with her at the Yale proms and taken her up the coast to the lavish parties at Hearst Castle. She had become engaged to Ted while he was still in college. But her sisters thought he was a bad influence, and her mother blamed him for driving her into a bad marriage and "ruining her life." Margaret finally gave up the idea of marrying Ted when he escorted her to a dance, got very drunk and behaved outrageously. She no longer felt she could trust Ted but was, nevertheless, fatally attracted to "bounders."

By revealing his sexual relations with Margaret to Wilson—who was at first his secret sharer and at last her triumphant husband—Ted aroused his interest and his competitive instinct. While Ted was at Yale, Wilson reported, Margaret informed Ted that "she was going to marry [James] Canby and he had written and told her not to, that he loved her, and then he lay awake all night thinking about it and in the morning went out and got the letter back from the post office and sent her another letter telling her he hoped she would be very happy and all the regular conventional stuff—and as soon as he got back from Russia, as soon as they were together again—he was taking her home from a party—they both [Ted said] 'swooned away' together—'as soon as we got together, it was like an electric current—it used to come over me periodically while I was away—I used to miss her terribly.'" After hearing such stimulating stories, Wilson had "vivid fantasies" about Ted and Margaret. Though he had better sex with Frances than with Margaret, he later found Ted "getting into" his fantasies about his mistress as well as about his new wife.

In the early 1920s Ted resumed his affair with Margaret and still hoped to marry her after her divorce from Canby. Even before Wilson had met Margaret, Ted sent dramatic accounts from Santa Barbara about the impending collapse of her violent marriage. In September 1922, seventeen months before Wilson's first trip to California, Ted portrayed James Canby as an abusive drunkard and Margaret as an unfaithful wife who had become a tragic victim:

> Her lovely husband has latterly taken to beating her up when drunk, so that I have seen black and blue marks on her arms the size of a grapefruit. This he varies with the clever gesture of sobbing, sulking, melancholia, and threats of suicide, so that Margaret, having a sweet nature and a genuinely kind heart, cannot decide in which direction to move and is slowly being driven towards a nervous collapse. . . . I used to feel sorry for Canby, who seemed to be getting a rotten deal, and had neither the intelligence nor the stamina to cope with the situation, but he has behaved so badly, with his nasty drunks, his fights in public cafés . . . his humiliation of Margaret in public, and his indulgence in obscene language to her before the servants that . . . I have to put him down as a blue vitriol son-of-a-bitch.

Shortly before Wilson first met Margaret, Ted described her as a "glutton for punishment." He awakened Wilson's sympathy by reporting that Canby had been driven to desperate measures to keep her, that his violence had intensified, that Ted himself had had a fist fight with her husband and that she had now been pushed to the breaking point: "It has been a miracle that it has not already ended in tragedy: three attempts [by James Canby] (bogus, I believe) at suicide, several more beatings up, and a free for all, knockdown and drag out between two males (both drunk). . . . The final break came when he slammed a glass door at Margaret and cut [a vein in] her foot." Wilson used the last incident in "The Men from Rumpelmayer's." When the narrator asks:

"What's become of Lois and Ed?," the Californian sister replies: "She's in love with somebody else, and he doesn't want to give her a divorce because he's still so in love with her. He finally disappeared, you know, and went on a terrible bender. . . . Finally he turned up, looking haggard and wan and as if he hadn't changed his clothes for weeks. . . . Afterwards he slammed a glass door, you know, and it broke and cut her arm."[2]

In March 1924 Margaret moved up to San Francisco, where Wilson first met her during his affair with Paula Gates. That month Ted, who used Paula as a bait to distract Wilson's attention from Margaret, wrote Wilson an unusually sober and solemn letter expressing his feelings for the woman he had loved for more than ten years: "I wanted Margaret. It may be difficult for you to realize or believe the seriousness and importance of this but it is absolutely true. At the present time I do not seriously desire anything else in life." Despite Ted's heartfelt declaration, when she came to New York later that year Wilson began his love affair with her.

Edmund and Margaret were often separated during their long courtship and brief marriage. Margaret's divorce agreement did not allow her to take her son Jimmy (born in 1918) out of the state and she usually spent at least half the year with the boy in Santa Barbara. Her chatty, rather superficial letters to Wilson discussed her plans, travels, house arrangements and hat shop, and were mildly spiced with conventional expressions about how much she missed him. Wilson disliked Southern California, felt it encouraged hedonism and sapped the will to work, and urged Margaret to come east as often as possible. "I was glad to leave California," he told Allen Tate in January 1929, after revising *I Thought of Daisy* at Margaret's sister's beach house, "because there is a sort of insipidity about everything there, in spite of the superficial brilliance—that is, the brightness and coloring of both man and nature—which ends by taking the savor out of life." He much preferred the grey mists and dunes of Cape Cod.

When they were with each other they drank, made love, had a good time and recovered together from hangovers. In November 1929 Margaret, whom Wilson considered the best woman drinking companion he had ever known, promised that they would get drunk the night she arrived in New York. She was impressed by his "sexy" description of riding in the sidecar of a motorcycle. But, aware of his mechanical ineptitude, she warned him not to kill himself. He nearly came to disaster when he borrowed a car in Santa Barbara and drove it to Ted's house in Hollywood. When he arrived at his destination he did not know how to stop, and kept driving round and round the block until the car finally ran out of gas.

In *Memoirs of Hecate County* (1946) the narrator, who is having affairs with several different women (one of them based on Frances), coolly considers marriage to Jo Gates, who is clearly modeled on Margaret. He describes their enforced separation and decides that he would actually prefer, while married to her, to be on his own for half the year:

> It was a question of whether or not I ought, finally, to marry Jo. It was now a little less than a week before she would have to go out to the Coast to do her six months a year with her children, and our relations were now at the point, after a love affair that had lasted six years, where it seemed the inevitable thing for us to marry and live together. . . . [But] it was difficult for me to go out to California with her (her former husband had made it impossible for her to bring her children East). . . . The old arrangement had had the advantage for me that it had combined a dependable girl, available half the year and never left on my hands too long, with six months of entire freedom. . . . She had just inherited securities which, even on the shrunken market, would bring her ten thousand a year.[3]

Though he had complained about Mary Blair's absence at the theater, Wilson came to like solitude, independence—and sexual freedom —during marriage.

Wilson matter-of-factly announced to friends, like Tate and Rascoe, that he and Margaret had married on May 9, 1930 in Washington, D.C. at the house of the lawyer John Amen. A few years behind Wilson at Princeton, Amen had married the daughter of President Grover Cleveland and former wife of Stanley Dell, and had become a close friend. While on his honeymoon Wilson, nearly always at work, attended the Senate hearing on the international naval treaty, which had been negotiated that year at the London Conference. As soon as the school term was over, they gathered the twelve-year-old Jimmy Canby and the seven-year-old Rosalind Wilson, and spent a happy summer in Eugene O'Neill's old house in Provincetown. Rosalind adored Margaret and considered her the most "normal" of Wilson's four wives.

When the children returned to Santa Barbara and to Red Bank in the autumn, Edmund and Margaret rented an apartment at 52 West 58th Street. After Margaret's return to California and Wilson's extensive travels for the *New Republic* in 1931, they met that July at a dude ranch in Bland, New Mexico, once a gold prospecting center and now a ghost town in the wilderness west of Santa Fe. In the fall of 1931 they lived in Margaret's house at 7 Lingate Lane in Montecito.

Living together emphasized their temperamental and intellectual differences. Margaret's mother suggested they have children but Wilson, who could not even take care of Rosalind, did not want any more responsibilities. Margaret's father, uncles and first husband had all had independent incomes, and before she met Wilson she had never been intimate with men who actually worked. She liked gaiety, was jovial and gregarious, expected a great deal of attention and wanted an active social life. She was rather bored when Wilson compulsively worked all the time. Hating his melancholy streak, she called him "Old Man Gloom himself."

Malcolm Cowley said that Margaret, bored by Wilson's increasing interest in politics, "complained to the girls that he used to wake her in the middle of the night to discuss the political situation. 'You see it's this way,' he would tell her as he paced up and down the bedroom and his wife, who had no opinions, tried hard to keep awake." Matthew Josephson described a party the Wilsons gave in May 1932 for W. Z. Foster, the Communist candidate for president: "Dos Passos was there, among others, and during an animated conversation with Foster made a sweeping gesture with his arm, overturning a large tray of gin cocktails which Wilson was carrying into the crowded parlor."

Wilson loved to relax in a warm bath—reading, drinking, musing —but he could not stay calm for long and also seemed to enjoy a tempestuous married life. The most vivid account of the Wilsons' arguments, heated by alcohol, came from the theater director Harold Clurman. He lived above them on West 58th Street and reported that Wilson, a year after his breakdown, often went completely out of control: "He was a tormented man, capable of hysterical fits of anger, even of violence. There were the savage and sometimes drunken quarrels I overheard from my bedroom window directly above his—quarrels that ended with his tearing the curtains from their rods and with the frightened cries of his wife, Margaret. . . . Both she and Wilson drank nonstop; once he came upstairs . . . spoke a few hurried words and fell down drunk in front of us." When Wilson found Margaret kissing a friend, he made a jealous scene and she left to spend the night in a hotel. She hated quarrels, he seemed to enjoy them. She called him "a cold fishy leprous person." He wondered if he was irrationally, cruelly and "deliberately turning on her, treating her brutally" in order to destroy the woman he loved and "drive her out."[4]

By the summer of 1932 James Canby had lost so much money in the Depression that he could not pay Jimmy's train fare and expenses to the East Coast. So Margaret went to California to spend the summer with her son, and Wilson left the *New Republic* to complete his second play, *Beppo and Beth*. He stimulated himself by playing Beethoven on the phonograph and drinking copious quantities of gin. Bored and frustrated on his own, he looked up Frances and invited her over to his place. But, Wilson said, with curious punctilio, "I would not let her go into the bedroom, but made love to her on the couch." Frances, experiencing new horrors in her marriage to the criminal, was glad to see Wilson. On August 25 she urged him to seize the day: "Your wife will be back soon and I won't be able to see you so often." Wilson ambiguously reported that Margaret forgave his infidelity because "she'd be hypocritical not to—she'd done the same thing herself"[5]— either with Ted during her marriage to Canby or with another lover in Santa Barbara while married to Wilson.

On September 30, 1932, while Wilson was still seeing Frances, Margaret died (as would Ted Paramore) in a freak accident. The previous evening, just before she was to go east to spend the autumn with Wilson, she went to a farewell party in El Paseo, an elegant Spanish Colonial building. The party took place in the studio of the artist Clarence Mattei, who had painted Margaret's portrait, on the second floor above the open central courtyard. It was foggy and driz-zling as she descended the worn, unevenly tiled open staircase (which is still there) that led from the studio to an outside passage. Wearing high heels and almost certainly drunk, Margaret tripped or slipped at the top of the steep stairs, fell all the way down and fractured her skull.

In an obituary of October 1 the *New York Times* inaccurately reported that "Mrs. Wilson was injured last night when she slipped and fell on a wet paving at the entrance of a café." The *Santa Barbara News Press* on that date, providing more precise and extensive details, ex-plained that she had remained unconscious for several hours while the doctors struggled to save her life:

> [Mrs. Wilson] died in a local hospital yesterday morning of inju-ries received when she slipped and fell the night previous on the

steps of El Paseo, fracturing the base of her skull. . . . [She] entered El Paseo shortly after eight o'clock Thursday evening with a party of friends. She slipped on the wet tiles, or her heel caught on the steps, for she fell suddenly, her head striking the pavement. She was rushed to the hospital, but never regained consciousness.[6]

On September 30 one of Margaret's friends telephoned Wilson and told him she "had fallen downstairs and fractured her skull and was dead." When he heard the news, Rosalind recalled, he began to sob, "the only time I ever heard him cry." Three weeks later Wilson told the California writer Upton Sinclair about her death as matter-of-factly as he had previously told Tate about his marriage: "My wife was killed in Santa Barbara last September by falling down a flight of stairs—she had just gotten out of bed with the flu."

Wilson's apparent objectivity masked lacerating emotions and overwhelming guilt. If he had brought Margaret and Jimmy across the country for the summer of 1932, she would never have gone to the fatal party. If he had spent the summer with her in Santa Barbara, he could have protected her by controlling her drinking and guiding her down the steps. His jealous quarrels and deliberate cruelty, his sexual encounters with Frances when Margaret was in California, tormented his puritan conscience. During his long propeller flight across the country —from Newark to Cleveland, Chicago, Salt Lake City and Los Angeles—and while mourning with Margaret's family in Santa Barbara, Wilson composed a forty-page monologue that is the high point of his journals. Mixing memory and desire, he frankly revealed his eroticism and devotion, his remorse and despair. He also attempted, by reaching a new understanding, to recover part of his loss. "This was all he had left of Margaret," wrote Leon Edel, "these memories—and he seems to have clung to them."[7]

In this extraordinary memoir, Wilson expressed his gratitude, described her physical presence, recalled their love-making, with its sado-masochistic element, focused on her death and analyzed his dreams about her. Margaret's love had fortified him, but he had used his new strength against her: "I felt for the first time how she'd given me all my self-confidence, the courage that I hadn't had before to say what I thought—all her natural smartness, fine quality, taste—social self-confidence which I'd use to repudiate conventional society and make her uncomfortable in doing so." When they slept together, he recalled, they seemed to achieve an unspoken harmony: "how sweet and pretty and darling she had been, all soft and cunning, so affectionate and gentle . . . she always turning with me, no matter when or how many times I wanted to turn."

Sexually excited by unusual clothing and situations, they had made love when Margaret was wearing an evening gown, a strawberry girl costume for the Beaux-Arts ball, riding breeches in New Mexico or nothing at all in the dunes of Provincetown. He remembered her witty response when "she took off her dress and her underthings came with it so that she was naked: we both laughed—I'm one of those ready girls she said." But Margaret, more inhibited and less compliant to his needs than Frances, was more difficult to calibrate to his tastes. "She would never bite my lip as hard as I wanted her to or as hard as I would hers," Wilson wrote. He also complained that "she would bite my tongue too hard, [but] it was hard to get her to bite my lip while I bit hers, bringing on the orgasm."[8]

He could see, retrospectively, that he had ignored some danger signs. Her feet were very small for her sturdy body and she had always been afraid of falling when she wore high heels. She had once fallen down the stairs when rushing to answer the telephone in their New York flat and covered herself in bruises. Since Margaret had often spoken of suicide, Wilson was at first afraid she had killed herself. Her death meant that he "could have nothing in common with her any more." Only after she was dead did he realize how much he loved her. Obsessed by guilt and struggling for several decades to accept her death, Wilson wrote in 1954 that "my impulse to free myself from relationships with women had something to do with my letting Margaret go off to Santa Barbara, where she died. Now in dreams I want her back."

When Katy Dos Passos died a violent death in 1947, Wilson inevitably thought of Margaret and tried to console Dos Passos by explaining his own feelings: "I know what you must have been going through from my own experience after Margaret was killed. . . . I can tell you that you will get over it and get over the morbid feelings of guilt connected with it—though I never did quite till I remarried [in 1938], when, in spite of my difficulties with Mary [McCarthy], I began to function normally again." Dos then recalled his own response to Margaret's death, his affection for Edmund and the limitations of even the most sympathetic understanding: "Thinking back to my feelings when Margaret died:—Though I didn't know her well, I was particularly fond of her and I had been fond of you since a day many many years ago when you turned a modest somersault while waiting for an elevator in an office building—I forget which—in New York;—and felt her loss keenly but I never have for a moment imagined what I now know you were going through."[9] Their similar tragedies brought the two old friends together for a poignant moment before their final quarrel.

While in Santa Barbara, Wilson examined the scene of the accident at El Paseo and cast a clinical eye on Margaret, who had been processed by a cosmetic mortician before cremation: "Her cheeks were full of paraffin and hard, they had made them seem too big—lips cold and hard—also, breasts—a look of pride, almost of scorn." Wilson paid the funeral home $433, destroyed all the letters he had sent to Margaret and, though poor himself, generously assigned his interest in her estate to her son Jimmy. In 1946, when Jimmy brought his new wife to meet his step-father, they found Wilson kissing *his* new wife on their couch. He was still paternal toward Jimmy, asked if he was happily married and took a serious interest in him.[10]

Margaret's death was one of the great turning points of Wilson's life. It convulsed his existence and threw him back to the wild drink and sex he had indulged in during the 1920s. He lost his wife's income, which had given him more freedom to write his books, and had to return to the weekly grind of journalism at the *New Republic*. He tried to exorcise his guilt by his marriage to Mary McCarthy, which led to the most bitter quarrels of his life.

II

While traveling through America and reporting for the *New Republic*, Wilson visited the poet Allen Tate and his novelist-wife Caroline Gordon at their peeling and pillared house, "Benfolly," near Clarksville, Tennessee. Wilson had known Tate, who had a bulging forehead and a sharp tongue, since the early 1920s and had invited him to review for the *New Republic*. Tate also had a young daughter, and was a close friend of John Bishop and Léonie Adams. In April 1931, two months after his visit, Wilson sent a positive report to another mutual friend, Katherine Anne Porter: "The Tates in their native Tennessee, however, looked healthier and more in tune with things than I have ever seen them. Allen seems an inch and a half taller and much robuster. I think they find it a little dull—they seem to want to get back to New York for next winter." Tate, equally enthusiastic in his letter to John

Bishop, praised Wilson's insight about local conditions: "Edmund's visit—it was his first to the South except New Orleans and Charlottes-ville some years ago—was very brief, but with characteristic energy he took in all that we showed him, and classified his information so well that he can tell me things I never dreamed of."

Caroline Gordon, however, introduced an acerbic note that suggested all was not well between them. Given the opportunity, she took advantage of her innocent guest. "It was mean, I know," she maliciously told a friend, "but I let him nibble the tiniest tip of a [tobacco] leaf. Not a chew, you understand, just a nibble. He went into a slight convulsion."[11]

When Wilson recovered and returned to New York, he published "The Tennessee Agrarians." In this essay he mildly criticized their pretentious decay and reactionary way of life, and included an unmistakable allusion to the unnamed Allen Tate, who had published lives of Stonewall Jackson in 1928 and of Jefferson Davis in 1929: "the products of a classical education, they come back to marry girls at home, to renovate family mansions, to do some farming with the aid of a share-cropper, to write books about the Civil War. . . . As lacking in a religion or a common ideal as their compatriots of New York or Paris, they try to find one in ancestor-worship." Infuriated by Wilson's criticism as well as by his ingratitude for their convulsive Southern hospitality, Tate told Wilson that he found the essay "a slick piece of journalese which falsifies everything we stand for. . . . Can you really with such unblushing glibness reduce our position to *ancestor-worship?* . . . You like to think that we are wistful boys mooning over the past."

Their friendship soured after this exchange. Despite Tate's unrestrained bitterness (most people who wrote to Wilson were extremely deferential), they continued to correspond for the next thirty years. In May 1944 the fiercely competitive Tate abandoned his pose of cool detachment and lit into Wilson's formidable egoism. "You know, Edmund," he exclaimed, knowing his letter would do no good but unable to contain his exasperation, "I have sat around for nearly twenty years listening to you talk, often about the novel. I don't think it ever occurred to you during that time that I might possibly have something interesting to say."[12]

Their friendship (or what was left of it) reached a crisis in January 1951 when Wilson learned from Malcolm Cowley that Tate (who once lacked religion) had now converted to Catholicism. "Hiram K. Antichrist," always adamantly opposed to religion, considered it a medieval superstition for gullible minds. When the Yiddish novelist Isaac Bashevis Singer once expressed his belief that the human soul was immortal, Wilson tartly replied: "Why immortal? I do not wish to be immortal. One life is enough." Wilson, who had been shocked by Kemp Smith's Catholic leanings, tied Tate's conversion to his reactionary political views. Since Tate grew up believing an impossibility—that the South should not have been defeated in the Civil War—and was used to looking back to the past instead of forward to the future, his mind was softened up and intellectually prepared to accept the "impossibility" of Catholic dogma.

Instead of ignoring Tate's conversion or offering polite good wishes, Wilson bluntly told him, on January 4, that he was particularly angry at the Catholic Church for interfering with free speech and helping to suppress his book of stories, *Memoirs of Hecate County* (1946). He then let loose a diatribe against the doctrines of Christianity: "I hope that becoming a Catholic will give you peace of mind; though swallowing the New Testament as factual and moral truth seems to me an awful price to pay for it. You are wrong, and have always been wrong, in thinking that I am in any sense a Christian. Christianity seems to me the worst imposture of any of the religions I know of. Even aside from the question of faith, the morality of the Gospel seems to me absurd."

When discussing belief in the doctrine of the Resurrection in his poem "Causerie" (chat), published in 1925, Tate had suggested that though Wilson played the devil's advocate, he was really a secret Christian:

> I have known men in my youth who foundered on
> This point of doctrine: John Ransom, boasting hardy
> Entelechies yet botched in the head, lacking grace;
> Warren thirsty in Kentucky, his hair in the rain, asleep;
> None so baptized as Edmund Wilson the unwearied,
> That sly parody of the devil.[13]

Writing to Cowley the following day, Wilson condemned Tate's defense of his conversion, repudiated the imputation that he himself was a believer and mocked Tate's hopeless attempt to cultivate the gentle spirit of his faith:

[Allen's is] a very odd letter, because, though couched in a facetious vein, it shows a determined-effort-to-adapt-himself attitude. He makes against me, however, a malicious, libelous, and baseless charge of crypto-Christianity. It is strange to see habitually waspish people like Allen and Evelyn Waugh trying to cultivate the Christian spirit. . . . I hope, though, that conviction will soften Allen, who has lately been excessively venomous about his literary contemporaries. He could never forgive any kind of success.

Wilson's letter also included a satiric squib (omitted from the printed version), which poked fun at Tate's reactionary views as well as his sequential marriages to Caroline, whom he would later divorce for the second time:

> Allen Tate
> Is out of date
> Caroline Tate
> Is his indivisible mate
> and his ineluctable fate.

A week later Tate sharply replied to Wilson's letter of January 4, returning to the charge that Wilson was indifferent not only to his work but also to his life: "I am perfectly reconciled to your almost total lack of interest in what I write; but it is a little difficult to contemplate a certain coldness, an inattentiveness to what one is, without feeling a little discouraged about it." Wilson seemed to compound his crime by making negative remarks about Caroline's books. This provoked Tate to exclaim that she would always be polite to Wilson, but that his visit to their home "would not in the end give her pleasure."[14] Tate's conversion to Catholicism did not prevent him from divorcing both Caroline and his second wife, and then marrying an ex-nun.

III

With his fifth book, *Axel's Castle: A Study in the Imaginative Literature of 1870–1930* (1931), Wilson made a quantum leap from his imaginative failures of the 1920s to a major critical work that solidified his position as grandee of the literary establishment. Like his earlier books (and many of his later ones) *Axel's Castle*, published in installments in the *New Republic*, was structurally weak. After a useful introduction to Symbolism, which he defined as "an attempt by carefully studied means —a complicated association of ideas represented by a medley of metaphors—to communicate unique personal feelings," Wilson devoted the central chapters to six Irish, French and American poets and novelists: Yeats, Valéry, Eliot, Proust, Joyce and Gertrude Stein. Stein came out of chronological order and was not in the same class as the other supreme artists; she was treated more critically and received only eleven pages.

When the book was published in February 1931, five of the six authors were still alive (Proust had died in 1922) and in the midst of their prolific careers. No biographies then existed, though there were some memoirs and letters, and very little criticism had been written about them. Diana Trilling remarked, for example, that "in 1927, two years out of [Radcliffe] College, I had not yet heard of Proust or Yeats or T. S. Eliot." One of the first to explore this unknown territory, Wilson defined a major literary movement and revealed the core of meaning in these obscure and difficult works. His aim was to give popular accounts of these authors in order to show their importance and convince people to read them. But he made no concession to the general reader and did not translate the poems in French by Mallarmé, Valéry and Laforgue. Christian Gauss, to whom he dedicated the book, thought he had succeeded brilliantly and declared: "the book will impose you upon the literate public as the most intelligent and penetrating critic of our time." If Wilson's book now seems familiar, it is because we have so completely absorbed its ideas.

Axel's Castle was influenced by Arthur Symons' *The Symbolist Movement in Literature* (1899), which had considered some of the major poets of nineteenth-century France: Nerval, Villiers de L'Isle-Adam (whose work inspired Wilson's title), Rimbaud, Verlaine, Laforgue, Mallarmé and Huysmans.[15] All these writers, except Huysmans, were briefly described by Wilson, who picked up where Symons left off. Wilson did not discuss English, German or Russian writers (though he might have included Conrad, Lawrence and Wyndham Lewis); but later on—when he had improved his German and learned Russian— he thought of bringing out an expanded edition (as Symons had done) that would treat Hopkins, Rilke, Stefan George, Mayakovsky and Blok. Wilson in turn inspired a stream of books. The first one, Maurice

Bowra's *The Heritage of Symbolism* (1943), did not mention Wilson, dealt with Yeats and Valéry, and also included Rilke, George and Blok.[16]

The title of *Axel's Castle*—like the titles of *To the Finland Station* and *The Wound and the Bow*—appealed to the reader's imagination and suggested the theme of the book. In contrast to *I Thought of Daisy*, which moves toward an engagement with life during the narrator's trip to Coney Island and love-making with the heroine, the hero of Villiers' *Axel* tries to live in a world of pure fantasy, escapes from reality and retreats to his hermetic castle. "His moral triumph," Wilson explained, "consists in his killing himself and his sweetheart, in his rejection of life itself, which can never be so satisfactory as his exquisite and intense imaginings."

In the opening chapter on Symbolism, Wilson takes up A. N. Whitehead's idea, in *Science and the Modern World* (1925), that the Romantic movement was a reaction against Newtonian science and argues that Symbolist poetry expressed the same kind of reaction against the biological science of the nineteenth century. Wyndham Lewis' *Time and Western Man* (1927) had attacked Whitehead's beliefs as well as the obsessional Time-philosophy of Joyce, Proust and Stein, which Lewis associated with the pernicious subjectivity of romanticism, impressionism, relativism and the Freudian unconscious. *Axel's Castle* attempts to challenge and answer Lewis' fierce attack on the excessive subjectivity of literary modernism.

Wilson's discursive chapters on Yeats, Valéry and Eliot all move from their poetry to an analysis of their prose. The chapter on Yeats includes an extended contrast to Bernard Shaw. The chapter on Valéry digresses to criticism of his attack on Wilson's old hero Anatole France, whom Valéry had succeeded in the French Academy. Wilson's interpretation of *The Waste Land* as a criticism of the faithless modern world established the direction of criticism for many decades. Wilson also perceived, as early as 1922, that the poem was intensely personal, nothing more "than a most distressingly moving account of Eliot's own agonized state of mind during the years which preceded his nervous breakdown." Eliot's breakdown had been precipitated by his intensely unhappy first marriage and his subsequent revulsion from sexuality. He later confirmed Wilson's insight by praising I. A. Richards' acute remark that in *The Waste Land* his "persistent concern [was] with sex, the problem of our generation, as religion was the problem of the last."

The discussions of Proust and Joyce were the best in *Axel's Castle*.

In a representative passage Wilson suggests how Joyce's style and technique reveal his characters and themes: "Joyce has undertaken in *Ulysses* not merely to render, with the last accuracy and beauty, the actual sights and sounds among which his people move, but, showing us the world as his characters perceive it, to find the unique vocabulary and rhythm which will represent the thoughts of each. . . . Joyce has attempted in *Ulysses* to render as exhaustively, as precisely and as directly as it is possible in words to do, what our participation in life is like—or rather, what it seems to us like as from moment to moment we live."[17]

Wilson met Eliot, Joyce and Stein in the 1930s, and had also heard about Stein from his cousin Dorothy Reed Mendenhall, a fellow student at Johns Hopkins Medical School. According to Dorothy—who gave a very different account from the official version in Stein's *Autobiography of Alice B. Toklas*—Stein worked at medicine in a half-hearted way, earned poor grades, failed her final exams and was refused her degree. Using this revealing information, Wilson, always very keen on completing his work, later concluded that Stein "was evidently very lazy and afterwards succeeded in evading a serious literary career by acquiring a reputation on the accomplishment, after *Three Lives* [1909], of very little at all exacting work." In *Axel's Castle*, Wilson criticizes the "fatty degeneration of her imagination and style" and concludes that most of what she "publishes nowadays must apparently remain absolutely unintelligible even to a sympathetic reader." Grateful for his attention, Stein was surprisingly tolerant of Wilson's criticism. Using his familiar nickname, she told Carl Van Vechten: "Yes I have seen Bunny Wilson's book, thanks so much, I was not born in Baltimore [but in Allegheny, Pennsylvania], and I am not *german* [though her father was born in Bavaria], and I do make poetry which can be read otherwise I was pleased."

Wilson met Stein in New York in January 1935 and published his impressions, after her death, in *The Shores of Light*. Though intrigued by her personality, he was appalled by her egoism. Wilson had "an agreeable first impression of a quick and original intelligence dealing readily from the surface of the mind with the surfaces presented by life—the responses so direct and natural, the surfaces seen so unconventionally, that one did not at first feel anything wrong; but a chilling second impression of . . . a great iceberg of megalomania that lay beneath this surface and on which, if one did not skirt around it, conversations and personal relations might easily crash and be wrecked."

Wilson spoke more frankly in a letter to Dos Passos that mentioned Stein's lesbian relationship with Alice Toklas: "I like Gertrude Stein and found her stimulating to talk to; but the whole setup is rather creepy and I don't think I could ever become a habitué. It is the most complete example of human symbiosis that I have ever seen."[18]

In the final chapter Wilson contrasts Villiers' Axel, who had withdrawn into a world of the imagination and declares: "Live? our servants will do that for us," with Rimbaud, who renounced poetry to become a trader in Abyssinia. But this opposition does not quite work. Rimbaud was not an artist in action like D'Annunzio, T. E. Lawrence and Malraux. Though he managed to escape from mechanized Europe, he had a disastrous career in the wilds of Africa.

The reviewers, both early and late, admired *Axel's Castle*. It has remained in print until the present day and has probably been, for the last sixty years, one of his best-selling books. Allen Tate, before he had become testy with Wilson, perceived the major theme and called it "a brilliant history of the increasing cross-purposes of the artist and his industrialized society." Stanley Edgar Hyman, in a generally hostile essay of 1948, conceded that Wilson had fulfilled his ambition and "had an effect in our time, in opening up a whole new area of literature to a wide audience, second only to T. S. Eliot's *The Sacred Wood* [1920]." Frank Kermode, a major critic writing in 1961, used Matthew Arnold's phrase about the task of the great critic to describe Wilson's penetrating insight. It is "a testimony to the author's flexibility and diagnostic power at a time when his subject as a whole was considerably more obscure than it is now. . . . His real achievement was to identify, even if he could not completely describe, the master-spirit of an age." In 1967 the poet Karl Shapiro offered a fine synthesis of Wilson's achievement: "Wilson's critical triumph is that he situated literature in the landscape of the human condition, stealing the fire back from the critical analysts and abstractionists. . . . He is perhaps the only modern critic who has unselfishly, learnedly, and studiously brought into single focus the scientific, sociological, aesthetic, and creative sensibilities of our age."[19]

Like many authors, Wilson felt empty and unemployed after finishing his major work. Despite the favorable reviews, the book did not sell briskly at first, though it did well in the long run. He joked that he might earn more money by selling it to the movies and wanted to cast "Adolphe Menjou as Proust and the Marx Brothers as Joyce." But even before he had completed the book, Wilson came to believe that "any literary movement which tends so to paralyze the will, to discourage literature from entering into action, has a very serious weakness; and I think that the time has now about come for a reaction against it."[20] Having booked his readers into Axel's Castle, he then decided to move them out of that comfortable lodging. At the beginning of the Depression literary aestheticism gave way to social realism and a concern with the struggles of the working class, and Wilson's book seemed politically out of date as soon as it appeared. Having survived a nervous breakdown and the death of his wife, he began to look beyond his private concerns and to study social conditions during the worst years of the Depression. He stabilized his life with political commitment and now devoted himself to Karl rather than to Groucho Marx.

NINE

Marxism and Russia, 1932–1935

I

After Margaret's death Wilson gave up the flat on West 58th Street and moved to a shabby wooden house near the East River, at 314 East 53rd Street, which cost fifty dollars a month. Grieving for Margaret, he became absorbed in his work, saw few people and scarcely left the house. He was tended by a Japanese servant, a parody of a gentleman's gentleman, with a drooping lower lip, a cough, a nervous limp, "cold and watery eyes, chirping voice, practically no English," who smelled stale and persisted in wiping his nose on the back of his hand. Wilson sometimes escaped to Rosa's, a cheap local restaurant, where he ate at a common table with strangers. He continued to see Frances, who still had problems: drunken lodgers and gangsters at home, no job, gyneco-logical illness and serious operations.

Katy Dos Passos' friends Edith and Frank Shay, living downstairs in Wilson's house, reported that he was drinking heavily. He had now become even more violent than when living below Harold Clurman on West 58th Street. One night the Shays were awakened at two in the morning by

> a pealing doorbell and the shouts of Frank's name from the street. . . . Then came a great splintering crash and Wilson surged in carrying the frame of the front door on his back. . . . Wilson scarcely knew what he was doing. After his striking entrance, he just scuttled past us upstairs on all fours and gaining his room threw a lot of furniture over the floor, and today is so pale and wan as to hardly be recognizable as a living man. . . . On coming down to lunch, he asked *if we had heard him come in.* . . .
>
> [Wilson] rarely rises until late in the afternoon. He is more restless and crazy than ever, drinking himself into frenzies nearly

every night and tearing up newspapers with his teeth, and then so pitiful and sick and despondent in the brief period of sobriety that occurs between the time when he gets up and when he darts out again.

Edith thought Wilson desperately needed some order and restraint in his life, that "some good woman ought to take him in hand."

Wilson continued to spend long summers in a rambling and musty old house in the center of Provincetown at 571 Commercial Street, with the harbor right outside the back window. In the early 1930s, when he cycled south to Truro, the novelist Waldo Frank described him as "a short, soft-bodied man with fine features stamped sharp within the surrounding contours of his face, already heavy jowled." Imperious in manner and always old for his years, the heavy, ruddy, breathless Wilson is usually remembered—despite his motorcycle, somersaults and swimming—as an elderly man. But even in Province-town, where life was much more relaxed, his rage kept surging to the surface and he again went out of control.

In the summer of 1934 Wilson got into a heated argument about Emerson with the critic Matthew Josephson (the subject of one of his "discordant encounters") and left the house in anger. When Jean, the wife of Joyce's first biographer, Herbert Gorman, tried to stop him as he mounted his bicycle, he "hauled off and gave her a tremendous slap in the face." As Wilson rode off, Jean angrily urged Josephson to run him down. "In low gear, at about three miles an hour, [Josephson] inched forward a bit, just snubbed his rear wheel, then stopped. At once bicycle and rider fell over sideways with a crash. . . . As Jean, now all concern, bent over him, he stood up, blinking in the light of the car and gave her another mighty slap in the face."[1]

Wilson's main source of income during these troubled and rela-tively impoverished years was, as usual, the *New Republic*. In October 1933 he owed the journal the considerable sum of $1,441 (about ten weeks' salary) for advances on work not yet completed. The following summer he suggested that the magazine pay him at half his old rates— four cents a word for articles, two cents a word for reviews—and charge the other half against his debt. In 1937 the *New Republic* pub-lished his play *This Room and This Gin and These Sandwiches* in a cheap paperback edition that included *The Crime in the Whistler Room* and *Beppo and Beth*, and paid a small royalty. By 1942 sales had dwindled to only fifty copies a year, which earned the princely sum of $5.11. His contract for the play stipulated that he would receive twenty-five dollars a week for the first six weeks of the run and fifty dollars thereafter —but the play was never produced.

Scribner's paid Wilson a thousand dollars advance against fifteen percent royalties for his novel, *I Thought of Daisy*, probably offered about the same for *Axel's Castle*, and undoubtedly gave much less for *Poets, Farewell!* and *The American Jitters* (1932), which sold about 1,270 copies during the first year. *Axel's Castle* sold only three to six hundred copies a year between 1937 and 1944, reaching a total of 3,131. But its reputation continued to grow, and during 1962–63 it sold 2,040 copies and earned four hundred dollars. Wilson did not have an agent and bargained hard for decent advances; but he usually did not earn them and in the early 1930s had a running debt with Scribner's.

In October 1938, after Wilson had moved on to Harcourt Brace, he ignored the fact that Fitzgerald had written several best-sellers and bitterly complained to Perkins: "You wouldn't do anything for me on either occasion [when he had asked for funds] at a time when you were handing out money to Scott Fitzgerald like a drunken sailor. . . . Harcourt has given me $1,700 on *To the Finland Station* [which took six years to write] and Norton has given me $800 for my next book of literary essays." Norton never published *The Triple Thinkers* (though Wilson presumably kept the $800), and that book was eventually brought out by Harcourt, which had paid an advance of $750 in November 1933.

Wilson's royalties from Harcourt were especially dismal. *Travels in Two Democracies* (1936), *The Triple Thinkers* (1938) and *To the Finland Station* (1940) all had small sales and left Wilson with a debit for his unearned advances. "A few weeks ago I was down to my last dollar," he told Louise Bogan, a year and a half into his third marriage, and eleven months after his second child was born. "I've spent the better part of two weeks in New York on two separate trips for the purpose of shaking down editors and publishers."

As book sales dwindled during the Depression, Wilson could never earn enough to live on—no matter how hard he worked. Necessity sometimes drove him to capitalize on his reputation and sign contracts with several publishers for books he was unable to complete. Since publishers existed to support good writers, Wilson believed, their money was spent on a good cause. In 1932 he summed up his precarious financial situation and explained how he managed to procure essential luxuries: "I have worked mostly for highbrow magazines: my top salary was $7,500 a year, and I didn't get that very long. I have always managed, however, to live slightly beyond my income, and have been rescued by small family inheritances which have allowed me a margin for classical reading, liquor, and general irresponsibility."[2]

II

Wilson had inherited from the generations of doctors, lawyers and ministers in his family a strong sense of justice and social responsibility. His own financial insecurity heightened his concern about the desperate economic situation of most Americans in the early 1930s. Crops had failed in the Midwest, and the stock market crash led to widespread unemployment. He was drawn to Marxism, like most intellectuals of the time, in response to the social disaster that was visible all around him. He briefly became a Communist but, no less sceptical in politics than in religion, espoused his own particular brand of Communism. He never joined the Party, though he studied Marx and the history of the Russian Revolution with passionate interest.

Disgusted with the capitalist system that had caused so much suffering, and fascinated by the great idealistic enterprise that Marx and Engels had set in motion in Russia, Wilson believed that America, with its democratic traditions and industrialized economy, could create a classless society more readily than the Soviet Union. Tracing the permutations of Wilson's intellectual roles, Daniel Aaron observed that he "had played at being the Menckenian ironist, the old native-stock American, the liberal capitalist, the enthusiast for American energy, the ivory-tower solitary, the mad hedonist. . . . Now, in 1932, he sided with the 'cool-headed revolutionists' who looked to Russia."

Since Marxists believed the decay of capitalism was inevitable, the Crash now seemed a welcome consummation. In "The Literary Consequences of the Crash" (1932)—whose title echoed Maynard Keynes' *The Economic Consequences of the Peace* (1919)—Wilson wrote that the past three years "were not depressing but stimulating. One couldn't help being exhilarated at the sudden unexpected collapse of that stupid gigantic fraud. It gave us a new sense of freedom." E. E. Cummings, who ran into Wilson in October 1931, found him "broke but cheerful—expects a revolution."[3]

Wilson made the clearest statement of his political position in "An Appeal to Progressives," published in the *New Republic* on January 14,

1931. Although he opposed the Communist assumptions about the greed and corruption of people driven by economic motives, the inevitability of Marxist dogma, the failure of American democracy and the bankruptcy of capitalism, he wanted to refine the doctrine and create an American socialism: "I believe that if the American radicals and progressives who repudiate the Marxist dogma and strategy of the Communist Party still hope to accomplish anything valuable, they must take Communism away from the Communists, and take it without ambiguities, asserting that their ultimate goal is the ownership by the government of the means of production."

Calling himself a "progressive," Wilson—like Dreiser, Dos Passos, Sherwood Anderson and Waldo Frank—voted for William Z. Foster, the Communist candidate for president in 1932. Wilson had held a reception for Foster in his apartment, praised Foster's courage when he appeared before the House Committee investigating Communism and (with Cowley) sent a long letter to Theodore Dreiser explaining why he supported Foster:

> We are convinced that both the Republican and Democratic parties represent the interests of the moneyed classes, that is, of the big manufacturers, capitalists and bankers, and not the interests of the people at large; that there is no way out of the crisis through either of them. Both parties are hopelessly corrupt, and both will try to save the profits of the rich at the expense of the rest of the population. . . .
>
> The Communist Party alone is working to educate and organize the classes dispossessed by the present system, so as to make them an efficient instrument for establishing a new society based on equal opportunity to work, equable distribution of income, and ownership by the people of the natural resources.

As Leon Edel has noted, in 1932 the American Communist Party had not yet made its major blunders and Roosevelt's New Deal had not yet been implemented; so Wilson's choice seemed more reasonable that August than it seems today. Foster, no great danger to Roosevelt, got only 103,000 out of forty million votes.

Wilson's conservative Southern friends, Bishop and Tate, privately expressed their disapproval without coming up with a serious alternative of their own. Twenty years before Tate's religious conversion,

Bishop lamented that "Edmund's going over to Communism is as sad as Eliot's passage to Christianity." Tate opposed Northern industrialism with Southern agrarianism while (as Wilson had pointed out) perpetuating feudal conditions and exploiting both black and white sharecroppers on his own land. But Tate complained that Wilson, by moving to the Left, "has succumbed to all those degradations of values that are tearing society to pieces." Max Perkins, who published Wilson's reportage in *The American Jitters* but did not agree with his politics, also voiced his regrets in a letter to Bishop: "He is so completely committed to Communism now that it's hard to see how he can ever get it off his mind, even if it comes to seem something remote as it probably will. He doesn't seem at all happy and I do not think he is writing as well and just because he is all mixed up in this Marxism."[4]

His friends were unduly concerned about Wilson. His politics did not affect his literary judgments; always more of an observer than a man of action, his active involvement in politics was short-lived. By 1933 he had severed relations with organized movements, though he still supported A. J. Muste—a Congregational minister, social reformer and peace activist—who took part in many of the labor struggles of the Thirties. Suspicious of Franklin Roosevelt, Wilson voted from 1936 through 1948 for the Socialist candidate for president, Norman Thomas (Princeton '05). "He is the old-fashioned kind of Socialist," Wilson wrote as the election approached in September 1940, "but he has come through this period of confusion on the Left with a record that shines in the dark night."

Wilson's life was closely bound up with his books. He lived to study, to observe, to think, to write, and sought out political conflicts and different cultures in order to describe them. Like William Dean Howells, he exerted himself "to cover a considerable area, to observe and report at first hand." The 1929 textile strike in Gastonia, North Carolina, first aroused his interest in labor disputes. While married to Margaret he had given up his office job at the *New Republic*, but continued to report for them on urban poverty and industrial unrest in Michigan, Kentucky, Tennessee, West Virginia and Massachusetts. His travels around the country took him out of the narrow New York literary world, and showed him the struggles of ordinary people. Engels' *The Condition of the Working Class in England in 1844* (1845) was a model of this kind of investigation. Wilson's political journalism was also similar to Orwell's *The Road to Wigan Pier* (1937), which used first-hand accounts of the industrial working class to persuade people to change the political system. Wilson's reporting, like Orwell's, relates the political to the ethical life of the nation.

In February 1932, when thirteen million people were unemployed during the severest winter of the Depression, Wilson (whose wife's money came from coal mines) joined the labor barricades during a coal miners' strike in Pineville, Kentucky. He accompanied Waldo Frank, Malcolm Cowley, the International Labor Defense lawyer Allen Taub and several other committed Leftists on the Independent Miners' Relief Committee. They brought food supplies and hoped to assist the miners, whose wages had been cut and who were being starved into submission. They met the county attorney, who assured them they were free to distribute food, but threatened that "as soon as you buck the law, it will be my pleasure as well as my duty to prosecute you."

When the Committee members tried to fulfill their mission, they were seized, taken to the Tennessee state line and badly beaten up. Cowley later testified: "In the darkness, I heard someone shrieking about thirteen feet away. When I reached the spot I heard Waldo Frank say that they could beat him again if they wanted to, but he would not swear to a falsehood. . . . When the lights were turned on, I saw Taub's face was a mass of blood. Waldo Frank was bleeding profusely from a bad cut on the back of his head." Cowley and Taub confirmed that Wilson, though not beaten, was an active participant, and he devoted thirty pages of his diaries to this disillusioning experience. He told Dos Passos how they had been duped and exploited by the Communist Party, which was looking for martyrs and had sent them to Kentucky to be arrested and beaten:

> That night [the deputies] came to the hotel and got us and took us in cars to the state line. There they turned off all the lights and slugged Waldo Frank and Allen Taub, the lawyer, in the head —evidently with the butts of guns. Waldo, who was chairman of the committee, played his role with great sang-froid and tact. . . .
>
> I came back convinced that if the literati want to engage in radical activities, they ought to organize or [do] something independently—so that they can back other people besides the comrades and so that the comrades can't play them for suckers.[5]

Like Orwell, who described himself as a "Tory anarchist," Wilson was sufficiently objective to alienate people on the Left as well as on the

Right. The Communist Mike Gold, for example, doubted Wilson's sincerity and described him ascending "the proletarian 'band wagon' with the arrogance of a myopic, high-bosomed Beacon Hill matron entering a common street-car." The novelist James Farrell, however, gave a more accurate account of Wilson's politics: "In the early thirties, he joined the spiritual and intellectual migration of writers to the Left. However, he retained his judgment, perception, and independence. When new questions were posed, he investigated them in all serious-ness. He did not accept ready-made slogans simply because a radical brand was put on them."

Wilson collected his reportage for the *New Republic* in *The Ameri-can Jitters* (1932). The twenty-nine essays, written between October 1930 and October 1931, express compassion for the poor and outrage for their suffering, and show that Wilson had moved a long way from the artistic isolation of *Axel's Castle* (1931). The earlier book describes an aesthetic approach to life and a withdrawal from the world; the later concerns the human condition itself. In order to write it, Wilson had to leave his study, travel around the country and talk to the people.

The three most substantial chapters are an exposé of labor condi-tions at the Ford factory in Detroit, a description of the Red Cross' attempt to relieve poverty in rural Kentucky and an impassioned de-fense of the black Scottsboro boys, who were falsely accused of raping two white girls in a freight-car in Alabama. Earlier in the book Wilson had described three suicides in Brooklyn. Toward the end of the book he reaches San Diego, which had the highest suicide rate in the coun-try. He concludes his essay "The Jumping-Off Place" (which refers both to the Pacific and to death) with a catalogue of desperate men who seem to epitomize the anguish of the age and turn Wilson toward the Communist solution:

> Ill, retired, or down on their luck, they stuff up the cracks of their doors and quietly turn on the gas; they go into their back sheds or back kitchens and eat ant-paste or swallow Lysol; they drive their cars into dark alleys, get into the back seat and shoot themselves; they hang themselves in hotel bedrooms, take overdoses of sulphonol or barbital; they slip off to the municipal golf-links and there stab themselves with carving-knives; or they throw them-selves into the bay.[6]

III

In the early 1930s Wilson's relations with his mainstay, the *New Republic*, changed for the worse. In the summer of 1930, when he went on leave to complete *Axel's Castle*, Malcolm Cowley temporarily replaced him as literary editor. The following year—when he resigned from the editorial board, shifted his interest from literature to politics, and left the office to report on social and economic conditions in the Depression—Cowley permanently took over his job. In 1933 the Elmhirsts became alarmed at Wilson's "excessive Leftism," which had influenced the politics of the magazine after Herbert Croly's death in 1930, and stopped sponsoring his trips around the country. He therefore began work on *To the Finland Station* in 1934 and the following year went to Russia to do research.

When Cowley was promoted to editor and Wilson reverted to contributor, a certain friction developed between them. As early as 1924 Wilson told Bishop that Cowley had ability but was an ass, and Cowley also had reason to dislike Wilson. In December 1926 Cowley and especially Tate became angry when Wilson published an essay, "Poe at Home and Abroad," which was based on his conversations with them and had appropriated their ideas. Tate told Cowley that "Wilson's shameless exploitation of 'the economic value of an idea' was 'really humiliating.'"

Over the years Wilson had soothed and scolded Cowley. In October 1927, when Cowley complained that another editor had mucked about with his work, the more experienced Wilson patiently explained that one could not hope to receive an intelligent or efficient response:

> Reviews of the kind which publish the work of writers like you and me are always edited by persons of essentially the same sort—that is, unbusinesslike people who are subject to all kinds of manias, absent-mindedness, metaphysical prejudice, partisan feeling, sinking spells and whims. As a contributor to the *New Republic* and its kindred magazines, I have myself had dozens of experiences of the kind you describe, and have long ago resigned myself to them.

Wilson himself stood out as an editor because he never behaved in this whimsical way. He offered his friends and contributors painstaking revision and expert advice.

Twelve years later, Cowley felt obliged, for commercial reasons, to interfere in a way that Wilson would never have sanctioned. He asked Wilson to delete a hostile reference to Random House in his review of Christopher Isherwood's *Goodbye to Berlin:* "The last time you lit into Random House, Bennett Cerf swore he would never advertise again in the *New Republic.* He actually did stay out for more than six months, costing us about four hundred bucks." Wilson refused to delete the remark, and Cowley ran the piece as Wilson wrote it. "The designers of Random House," he said, "who pride themselves on their fine editions, have turned out for Mr. Isherwood a thing that looks like a Gideon Bible with a cheap nickel clasp on the wrong side."[7]

At about this time Wilson wrote "A Libel Against Malcolm Cowley," which, Bishop told Tate, was "even wickeder" than his savage satire "The Omelet of A. MacLeish." In his "Libel" Wilson suggests, in limping verse, that Cowley used his political influence and editorial position to extract sexual favors from naive women, and that his physical performance was unimpressive:

> The next on my list is Malcolm Cowley
> Who edits *The New Republic* so foully
> To the beautiful offices, cheerful and chic,
> There come brisk little Stalinist girls every week.
> They ply him, they prod him, they prate about Spain;
> They play with his penis while praising his brain—
> Till—heavy and slow—with a grunt and a scrunch—
> In the amplified hours allotted to lunch
> He fondles them, follows them, lays them at leisure.

Cowley patiently weathered Wilson's assaults and maintained close contact with him until 1948. He became upset that year by one of Wilson's characteristically curt letters, written from the *New Yorker,* and thought: "hell, there's no use keeping this up."[8]

Though Wilson focused on politics, he did not desert literature. In the early Thirties he met Nathanael West and T. S. Eliot. He admired West's *Miss Lonelyhearts* and recommended his next novel, *A Cool Million,* to Max Perkins. After West was killed in a car crash, Wilson wrote an affectionate description of his appearance, character and wit, and linked him to the tradition of Russian fantasy:

> He also used to show me his gun, of which he was very proud, but I had a feeling that his hunting was largely a following of the

Hemingway fashion. . . . He had a sad quiet Jewish humor, and the quality of his imagination was, I think, both Russian and Jewish. There was something of Chagall about him and even something of Gogol. He was well-dressed and good-looking and had an extremely pretty girl friend who was a model.

Wilson, a leading interpreter of Eliot's work, had been instrumental in establishing the poet's reputation in America, for which Eliot was grateful. In January 1923, three months after the appearance of his ambitious poem, Eliot, with his usual mock modesty, had congratulated Wilson on his perceptive analysis and deprecated his own work:

> Please accept my cordial thanks for your more than generous appreciation of the *Waste Land*. I think you have understood it remarkably well, perhaps a little over-understood it. I mean read more into it than it contains here and there. I am very sensible of its fundamental weaknesses, and whatever I do next will be, at least, very different; I feel that it is merely a kind of consummation of my past work, not the initiation of something new, and it will take all my courage and persistence, and perhaps a long time, to do something better. The *Waste Land* does not leave me well satisfied.

In February 1933, Fitzgerald met Eliot, who was lecturing at Johns Hopkins University. Fitzgerald stayed sober for this august occasion and they had a successful encounter. But, he told Wilson, he was somewhat disappointed with the great man and felt that the forty-four-year-old Eliot, who had just escaped from a devastating marriage, was "very broken and sad and shrunk inside."[9]

In May, when Eliot reached New York, Wilson heard him read his poems and thought he had put on an even better show than Shaw's recent performance at the Metropolitan Opera House. Wilson was as shrewd about Eliot's character as he had been about his poetry. Praising Eliot's acting ability and noting the spooky masks he used to disguise his real self, he told Dos Passos: "I suppose that a kind of dramatic resonance he has is one of the things that has made his stuff carry so. He gives you the creeps a little at first because he is such a completely artificial, or rather, self-invented character—speaking English with a most careful English accent as if it were a foreign language which he has learned extremely well." Eliot's studied performance piqued Wilson's desire to penetrate his mask. In July Eliot spent the night at Wilson's house on East 53rd Street, ate at the common table in Rosa's humble restaurant and got "very drunk." "He's much nicer when drinking," Wilson explained to Louise Bogan, "of which he seems to do a great deal, as the million snobberies, poses and prejudices which he thinks he has to cultivate then drop off." But Wilson, guilty about Eliot's terrible hangover, felt as if he had wantonly broken some rare and exquisite vase.

Wilson continued to be intrigued by Eliot's character. He noted the striking contrast between Eliot's judicious opinions and his "incoherent" personality, and felt "he was probably the most highly refined and attuned and chiselled human being that I had ever met and I couldn't help being rather awed by him." In May 1942 Wilson urged the critic Maxwell Geismar to write about Eliot from the social and human as well as the literary point of view. On a trip to London in 1954, Wilson saw Eliot's *The Confidential Clerk* and considered it a weak play with unconvincing characters. He also quoted Isaiah Berlin's belief that Eliot, playing a Christian role, had adopted John Hayward, his crippled housemate, as the leper he felt obliged to embrace. Three years later, writing to Van Wyck Brooks, Wilson again emphasized the different, even contradictory, images that Eliot cunningly employed to hide his true self from the world: "I think there is a scoundrel and actor in Eliot. It was the young scoundrel who wrote the good poetry and it is now the old scoundrel who is putting on the public performance. In private, he is humorous and disarming about his reputation, but the performance still goes on. . . . He is absurd in his pretensions to pontificate."[10]

IV

Like the learned Eliot, Wilson had (especially for an American) an impressive knowledge of classical and modern tongues, and always read books in their original languages. Learning foreign languages, he told Alfred Kazin, was like having a love-affair. "I have always been greedy for words," Wilson declared. "I can never get enough of them. I love Elizabethan plays, dictionaries of slang and argot, lists of Americanisms. . . . I always find a pleasure almost sensual in attacking a new language, especially if it has a strange alphabet whose barrier I find I can penetrate." Since there was no longer a single universal language, like medieval Latin or eighteenth-century French, Wilson, with his universal interests, had mastered Greek and Latin in prep school, French and Italian in college; and had studied German and Russian in the 1930s, Hebrew in the 1950s and Hungarian in the 1960s.[11]

The only blind spot in his study of European languages was Spanish. He did not know the language and literature, disliked the cult of death and the bullfights, and criticized Hemingway's *Death in the Afternoon* (1932). Wilson's hostility to the country was influenced by Mario Praz's *Unromantic Spain* (1929), which opposed the French tradition—Hugo, Merimée, de Musset and Gautier—that had romanticized Iberia. In 1965—citing Praz, by then a good friend—Wilson frankly acknowledged his limitation: "I have also been bored by everything, with the exception of Spanish painting, that I have ever known about Spain. I have made a point of learning no Spanish, and I have never got through *Don Quixote;* I have never visited Spain or any other Hispanic country. But Mario Praz does know Spanish and *has* visited Spain, and his report on it confirms me in my prejudices."

Wilson's antagonism to Spanish culture was balanced by his infatuation with Russian. He had learned German (by studying Heine) in order to read Marx and Engels in their original language. Marx was his heroic model for the study of Russian, which Wilson—inspired by D. S. Mirsky's *Pushkin* (1926)—began to learn on his trip to the Soviet Union in order to read that poet. In *To the Finland Station* Wilson wrote that when he was fifty, Marx learned Russian, "read up Russian literature and history, and had documents sent him from Russia. . . . If he devoted hours and weeks to reconstructing from documents in Old Slavonic the history of the land system in Russia, he also found it necessary to learn Rumanian in order to follow what was happening in the Balkans."

When he returned from the Soviet Union, Wilson lived for a time with Russian friends in order to study the language; when he moved to Wellfleet in 1941, he took lessons from his Russian neighbor Nina Chavchavadze. While traveling in the Soviet Union, Dos Passos had become weary of trying to hack his way through the dark thicket of Russian. But Wilson loved the challenge and compared the cunning little sounds of spoken Russian to "the language of mice."

Wilson's knowledge of languages was more literary than colloquial. He liked to practice French with the children of Talcottville friends, the Crostens, who thought his pronunciation and spoken French was "pretty bad." Though Wilson had a good grasp of the vocabulary and grammar, his spoken Russian was even worse. During a performance of *Swan Lake*, he tried to say in Russian that his daughter had a crush on Rudolf Nureyev. But his accent was so abominable that Richard Pipes, a professor of Russian history at Harvard, could not understand him. Though keen on taking lessons, Wilson would remain obstinate when he misunderstood a Russian text and when Elena Levin, a native Russian, tried to correct him.[12]

Nina Chavchavadze's son David defined the difference between Wilson's literary and colloquial Russian. "Every time he attended a party at our house," David recalled, "he used to sign the guest book, in Russian, 'N. N. Chernokhvostov,' which means 'black tail' and refers to the devil." David, agreeing with Richard Pipes and Elena Levin, also wrote:

> He had learned Russian well enough to read all the classics in the original, even feeling capable of arguing with Vladimir Nabokov on fine points of translation. The only trouble was that he could not speak it. My mother gave him lessons with little effect. Only once did he speak a Russian phrase to me. I had brought a very pretty girl into his home, and he was always aware of pretty girls. He came out with a phrase praising her looks, grammatically correct, mid-nineteenth century in style, and hideously pronounced.

Inspired by the success of Allen Tate, Léonie Adams and Matthew Josephson, who had all won Guggenheim travel grants, Wilson decided to apply for a fellowship to visit Russia. He proposed to study Russian history at the Marx-Lenin Institute, but discovered, once in Russia, that it was closed to all foreigners. Recommended by Christian Gauss and Robert Morss Lovett, an associate editor of the *New Republic*, Wilson was "appointed for the completion of a book dealing with the study of history during the past hundred years, to be entitled *To the Finland Station: An Essay on the Writing and Acting of History;* tenure, twelve months from May 1, 1935."[13] His $2,000 tax-free award was supplemented when he became seriously ill in Odessa; and he received an additional $800 when his fellowship was renewed for three months in 1939. Wilson later became a good friend of Henry Allen Moe, a Minnesota-born Rhodes scholar and lawyer, who directed the Guggenheim Foundation for forty years.

During the Twenties and Thirties many eminent people traveled to Russia to see the Communist experiment and to report on social and economic conditions. Most went with a distinctly Socialist perspective, conscious of the hardships of the Depression, hopeful that they would find a superior social system, interested in a relatively unknown culture, idealistic and eager to put the best interpretation on whatever they saw. Wilson, who shared these assumptions, also had a romantic fascination with Russian language and literature. He planned to write a book which combined political discussion with descriptions of his travels.[14]

Wilson's book was similar in tone to Dos Passos' "Russian Visa: 1928," an essay which he published in *In All Countries* and *Journeys Between Wars.* Though not very perceptive or profound, Dos Passos' impressionistic and generally sympathetic travelogue covered a lot of ground. He arrived in Leningrad, sailed down the Volga to the Caspian Sea, visited Baku and the Caucasus (where he dropped into the eleventh century), and ended up in Moscow. Dos Passos emphasized the material progress of the Soviet Union, but was well aware of the State-organized terror that raged throughout the land and was very glad to leave. Anticipating departure, he wrote, was like "waiting for the cage that's going to haul you out of the mine."

Ignoring his history of mechanical disasters, Wilson actually thought of riding a motorcycle through Russia. He prepared for his trip by reading on the subject at the New York Public Library, and naturally relied on Dos Passos' advice and introductions. Wilson wanted to root Communism in American soil, but Dos Passos had seen enough of the Russian system to realize that it was quite incompatible with democracy. In a letter to Wilson of January 1935, he stressed his extreme disillusionment and named the political events that had led to what Trotsky had called "the Revolution Betrayed":

> About Russia I should have said not politically useful rather than politically interesting—I suspect that a vast variety of things are going on in Russia under the iron mask of the Kremlin, but I don't think that any of them are of use to us in this country—if our aims are freedom and the minimum of oppression. . . . My enthusiastic feelings about the U. S. S. R. have been on a continual decline since the early days. The steps are the Kronstadt rebellions, the Massacres by Bela Kun in the Crimea, the persecution of the Socialist Revolutionaries, the New Economic Program, the Trotsky expulsion, the abolition of factory committees, and last the

liquidating of the Kulaks and the Workers and Peasants Inspection—which leaves the Kremlin absolutely supreme.

The Stalinist Terror was far more entrenched when Wilson visited the Soviet Union. On December 1, 1934, Sergei Kirov, the liberal head of the Communist Party in Leningrad, had been assassinated by Stalin's *agents-provocateurs*. This murder changed the course of Soviet history. It halted the temporary relaxation in cultural and political affairs, and initiated the political persecution that sent armies of people to prison or death. As Robert Conquest wrote in *The Great Terror:* "Kirov's death was the keystone of the entire edifice of terror and suffering by which Stalin secured his grip on the Soviet peoples. . . . Over the next four years, hundreds of Soviet citizens, including the most prominent political leaders of the Revolution, were shot for direct responsibility for the assassination, and literally millions of others went to their deaths for complicity in . . . the vast conspiracy."[15] Despite Dos Passos' suspicions and the evidence of Russian oppression, Wilson, like many other observers, failed to grasp the true nature of Soviet society.

V

After some delays with his visa—which were reported in the *New York Herald Tribune* on the day of his departure—Wilson sailed on the Cunard Line's *Berengaria* from New York to Southampton on May 10, 1935. A week later he took a Soviet ship, the *Siberia*, to Helsinki and arrived by train at the Finland Station in Leningrad on May 23. Five days later he went to Moscow; then traveled east to Gorki and southeast to Lenin's hometown, Ulyanovsk; sailed down the Volga to Stalingrad and along the Don to Rostov; and took a train west to Kiev in the Ukraine and south to Odessa on the Black Sea, which was pleasantly associated with Tolstoy and Chekhov. Finally, in late September, he journeyed by train through Warsaw and Berlin (without stopping to investigate the Nazi régime) to Paris, and sailed home from Cherbourg on October 9.

In Leningrad Wilson visited the usual tourist sites: St. Isaac's Cathedral (now an anti-religious gallery), the Winter Palace, the Hermitage Art Museum, the Peter and Paul Fortress. In Moscow he rented the comfortable flat at 53 Bolshaya Ordinka that belonged to the *New*

York Times correspondent Walter Duranty, who was away for the summer. Always intensely curious, he saw St. Basil's Cathedral, palaces, museums, theaters, parks, dachas, parades, the attractive subway, collective farms and the Troitsk-Sergievsky Monastery, "a delirium of Byzantine ornament and barbaric magnificence."

In Moscow, Wilson met, but did not identify in his book, the distinguished intellectual Prince Dmitri Mirsky. His book on Pushkin had inspired Wilson's serious study of Russian and he later became the subject of Wilson's superb essay. Mirsky, a White Russian officer during the Civil War that followed the Revolution, had been driven into exile. But he had converted to Marxism in England and, with Maxim Gorki's help, returned to Russia. A tall, erect, bearded, bald and bespectacled man, he wore old but elegantly cut English clothes, had the same intellectual range and erudition as Wilson, and "would comment on an expensive and very *soignée* white beard as a relic of the old régime, or point out, as we walked at night behind the Kremlin wall, the scene of one of the episodes of *War and Peace*." In August 1935, the month after Wilson saw him in Moscow, Mirsky was sent into exile. Arrested during the purges of 1937, he was confined to the brutal prison camp at Kolyma in Siberia, went insane there and died in January 1939. "He was a gifted and heroic person," Wilson later observed, "and his fate was one of the tragedies of the Stalin dictatorship."

Wilson had a strong constitution and, until he reached old age, was rarely sick. In January 1926 he had had a bad case of the measles. In April 1934 he succumbed to a serious nasal infection, caused by a barber cutting the hairs in his nose, which led to necrosis and put him in the hospital. For the rest of his life he suffered from severe nosebleeds, caused by high blood pressure and by alcoholism, which dilated the peripheral veins and arteries and made them bleed very easily. After Wilson had traveled across the flat steppes to Kiev, he became extremely ill and developed a high fever. Though eager to escape the country, he was forced to stay on for treatment that was both barbaric and tender.

When he was finally examined in Odessa, the doctor told him that he had scarlet fever. Usually a children's disease, it causes throat infection, high fever and a severe rash. The treatment during Wilson's six-week quarantine in the old and dirty hospital, built in the time of Pushkin, was crude and primitive. He told Louise Bogan how he was cupped "with 20 brass cups, twice a day" and said "it was like being buried under a pile of horse shoes. Then the doctor, to cheer him up, gave him *Little Women* in German to read, and Edmund suddenly remembered that Beth, in that book, dies of scarlatina."[16]

Wilson was nursed with great warmth and sympathy. He had all his expenses (including telegrams abroad) paid for by the state and was allowed to study in the operating room at night. Just as he was ready to be discharged, he suffered an acute kidney attack. By the time he got out of the hospital, the ships had stopped sailing in the Black Sea and he could not use the return passage he had bought from Istanbul. So he wired Henry Moe at the Guggenheim Foundation: "Can you lend hundred six weeks hospital scarlatina nephritis cable American Express Paris," and Moe added a hundred dollars to the stipend. The description of his illness, which put Wilson into close contact with ordinary Russians, was the most interesting part of his book.

Wilson's *Travels in Two Democracies*, his first book in four years, was published by Harcourt Brace in June 1936 and contains a journalistic record of his tours through America and Russia. The strange title is meant to equate American political with Russian social democracy, and the book contrasts American poverty and despair with Russian economic progress. The first part, a continuation of his reportage in *The American Jitters* during the dawn of the New Deal in 1932–34, includes random essays on Hull House in Chicago, a miners' strike in Illinois, the Radio City Music Hall, Roosevelt's inaugural, Bernard Shaw's lecture, the dishonest president of National City Bank, the Old Stone House in Talcottville, a milk strike in upstate New York, an evangelical meeting, cherry blossoms in Washington and his World War One story, "Lieutenant Franklin." All this, of course, had nothing to do with the second part, which describes his trip to Russia.

Wilson offers no explanation of why he went to Russia and what he planned to do there, and does not mention the Marx-Lenin Institute. Apart from his time in hospital, his experiences are fairly commonplace. He has, as usual, an eye for the ladies, but does not record his seductions in that sexually free society. His sketchy journalistic entries, taken down on the spot, are never fully developed into the scenes and chapters one expects to find in a finished work. By the time the book was published, the Purge Trials had started on their murderous course and Wilson's title was unintentionally ironic—even absurd.

Throughout *Travels in Two Democracies* Wilson vainly struggles to rationalize the difference between what he actually sees and what he desperately wants to believe, and presents a series of confused, unresolved and apparently unrecognized contradictions. He admits that it is "peculiarly difficult to write calmly about the Soviet Union" and wonders "whether any given disaster is [really] due to sabotage or incompetence." Pointing out the negative aspects of the country, he mentions the dingy hordes in Leningrad, admits that Communism makes little progress and concedes that the Revolution has not changed the sadness of the people, who are cold-bloodedly manipulated by the government. When Wilson asks a Pole who had worked in Detroit why he had come to Russia, he frankly states: "I t'ink I'm crazy." The Soviet state, Wilson acknowledges, systematically falsifies history, pays an army of informers, engenders an atmosphere of fear and suspicion, and carries out a policy of official terror.

At the same time, and without even noting the discrepancies in his account of Russia, Wilson states that literature has more prestige than in any other country; ignoring Bely, Blok, Akhmatova, Mayakovsky and all the other writers who were suppressed or killed after the Bolsheviks secured power, he maintains that "the great writing of the Russian Revolution was done by Lenin and Trotsky."[17] He idealizes, in an agitprop passage, Lenin's character and his wife; and even praises Stalin's energy, positiveness and shrewdness—just as the great dictator set out to murder millions of his countrymen. Wilson finds the Russians modern and energetic, "natural, decent and humane," heroically engaged in the struggle to build a new society. But he confuses the decency and warmth of individual Russians with the brutal political system. He vaguely claims that the government is "based on a scientific view of history"; that the people have freedom and human dignity. Wilson incongruously accepts the Party line and concludes that the Soviet government, by opposing Nazism, is "the only guarantee in Europe against another receding tide of civilization," that it represents "the moral top of the world." Wilson's description of his actual experiences in Russia clashed with his idealistic expectations.

Eager for publication in England, Wilson offered *Travels in Two Democracies* to T. S. Eliot at Faber and Faber. In April 1936, two years after their friendly meeting, Eliot noted the striking lack of coherence between the two parts of the work, stated it would be "of little interest to people who are not acquainted with the American scene," and rejected the book, which never appeared in England. John Bishop sharply disapproved of Wilson's naive adherence to a preconceived ideology and refusal to confront the reality of Russia: "I greatly disliked Bunny's book on his travels. . . . The book reveals his incredible ignorance of himself. The story of Lieutenant Franklin is immensely revealing, the naiveté of the approach to the war is beyond my comprehension. And he is just as naif in his approach to Russia, if it is true that he thought, as he says, that Russia would be just like the USA with the added advantage of socialism. And the conclusions, arrived at before he started on his travels, are therefore valueless."[18]

After writing his book, Wilson continued to cling to his illusions about the Soviet Union. Reviewing André Gide's critical account of his visit to the U.S.S.R. in the *Nation*, he took issue with Gide's disillusionment. Like Wilson, Gide had originally been idealistic about Russia and attracted to the idea of a society without religion. But, unlike most Left-wing writers, Gide emphasized Communist oppression. "I doubt whether in any other country in the world," he concluded, "even Hitler's Germany, thought be less free, more bowed down, more fearful (terrorized), more vassalized." Wilson attributed Gide's disappointment to "his habitual perversity and malice. He had approached the Soviet Union with something of the unconscious utopianism of one who has been using his conception of the anti-religious morality of Russia as a switch to sting the French bourgeoisie."

In Paris in October 1935, on his way home after five months in the Soviet Union, Wilson met James Joyce, who had praised his discerning review of *Ulysses*. But the taciturn and hypersensitive Joyce was completely unresponsive to Wilson's forthright approach. As Leon Edel wrote: "It was characteristic of Wilson, when he met someone, to look at him with a sharp direct glance—shrewd, inquiring, lively, and even diagnostic. He remembered being greeted by Joyce in the entrance to his apartment, but the Irish writer fell at once into a total silence. Nothing Wilson did could break it. They had drinks; everyone talked. Joyce seemed lost in gloom and blankness. Wilson fired questions; no answers."

Wilson himself later provided a partial explanation for Joyce's strange behavior. After his first silent meeting, he thought he would try again and invited the Joyces to dinner. Nora appeared alone and said Joyce had a terrible headache. Wilson and Nora got on well and at the end of the evening, she said: "I may as well tell you the truth. Jim did not have a headache. He said, 'I don't want to see that Wilson. All that he does is keep staring at my tie.'"[19]

VI

After returning to America, Wilson took up the study of Russian and plunged into work on *To the Finland Station*. He felt closer to Russians than to any other Europeans, and would later form many close friendships with Russian émigrés: Vladimir Nabokov, Isaiah Berlin, Igor Stravinsky, Svetlana Stalin, Paul and Nina Chavchavadze, Helen Muchnic of Smith College, the literary editor Roman Grynberg, the literary scholar Gleb Struve, the ballet director Evgenia Lehovich, and Harry Levin's wife, Elena. Wilson's fourth wife was part Russian and his son became a professor of Slavic languages.

Wilson, too independent to submit to the discipline of the Communist Party, became increasingly critical of Soviet policy. By 1938 he declared: "the Stalin régime in its present phase is pretty hopelessly reactionary and corrupt." But Malcolm Cowley, still literary editor of the *New Republic*, remained an adamant Stalinist and Wilson attacked his blind faith in the Soviet régime. In the spring of 1937 he tried to correct Cowley's ignorance about the Purge Trials that were then taking place: "all the trials have been fakes since the time of the Ramzin sabotage trial [in January 1937]. They have always been intended to provide scapegoats and divert attention from more fundamental troubles. In the case of these recent trials, I imagine that not a word of these confessions was true. The victims had, I suppose, been guilty of some kind of opposition to the régime." Leon Trotsky, the intellectual commander of the Red Army during the Civil War that followed the Revolution, had been driven into exile and would in 1940 be murdered in Mexico by Stalin's agent. Wilson told Cowley that Trotsky's writings were incompatible with the charges of treason brought against him, that "Trotsky in the publicity of the Soviet Union is simply what the Jew is to the Nazis."

Wilson wrote *To the Finland Station* during the Spanish Civil War but, partly because of his lack of interest in Spain, never published anything about the most momentous conflict of the late 1930s. In a letter to his New York neighbor Muriel Draper, whom he had seen in Russia, he condemned the Soviet use of terror against the working-class Left, who had refused to follow the Communist line. Wilson had met Dos Passos' friend and Spanish translator, José Robles, in Provincetown. In another strong letter to Cowley, Wilson defended Robles' loyalty to the Spanish Republic, attacked the Communists for executing him on a false charge of treason and explained why they did so: "When I knew him, his Left position was quite clear, and he was certainly a man of excellent character. When the war started, he thought he ought to go back, and by the time Dos had arrived, he had been shot. . . . He was one of the few Spaniards who knew Russian, so that he may have known too much. He was personally aristocratic and not at all the sort of person who would be likely to suppress his disapproval. What finished him was probably his enthusiasm for the social revolution, which the Russians were putting down."

When interviewed in 1951 by the F.B.I.—which was supposedly investigating a job applicant—Wilson expressed his past and present views of Stalinist Russia. According to the F.B.I. report, Wilson said that he "had been interested in the future of the Soviet Union, 'tried to give STALIN the benefit of the doubt' and visited Russia in 1935. Although he, WILSON, was impressed by the unpopularity of STALIN, he also realized that STALIN had used the Soviet Red Army and the trick of purges and smears to cause unrest and preserve his own power as head of the Soviet Union. WILSON said he realized that the Soviet Union under STALIN could never improve the plight of the masses and that the Russian Revolution had failed."[20]

TEN

Mistresses, 1936–1937

I

After returning from Russia, as restless as ever, Wilson careened about for a year in various rented or borrowed hotel rooms, flats and houses. He stayed with a Russian family, lived in a penthouse near Union Square and had a place at 234 East 15th Street. Finally, in October 1936, following a long summer in Provincetown, he was offered a house on Westover Road, a few miles south of Stamford, Connecticut. The house belonged to the wealthy and widowed patron of the arts, Margaret de Silver. A cultured and liberal daughter of Philadelphia Quakers, Margaret lived in New York with the anti-Fascist editor, Carlo Tresca.

"Trees," where Wilson settled for the next three years, was a large, isolated, rustic cottage, with a screened-in porch, just above the small Mianus River. Rosalind, then in prep school in Connecticut, often stayed in the house. She found it "a depressing place set in acres of thick boring woods. . . . It was surrounded by spooky rocks and a nasty unswimmable river running below." Louise Bogan, another frequent guest, agreed that it was dreary, but thought it would be a good place for Wilson to write his next book, *The Triple Thinkers:* " 'Trees' is a stone house, rather gloomy, and full of bad liberal-anarchist attempts at decoration, and its situation, among saplings, with no real lookout, depresses me, but it is completely equipped with all modern conveniences . . . oil burner with thermostatic control, bath, telephone, electric stove and God knows what else. Edmund will be happy working here throughout the winter."[1]

Living alone and buried in the forest with no other house in sight, Wilson reverted to his old habits. He worked through the night and went to bed at four, put himself to sleep with slugs of gin and got up for lunch at noon. Rarely visiting New York, he walked in the woods, fished the river and, he told the Tennessee squire Allen Tate, was as rural as any Agrarian. He was at first looked after by a young mulatto woman called Celeste, but she could not bear the loneliness and soon took off for the city.

Celeste was replaced by Wilson's old black servant Hatty. She had come North after her husband died and had worked for Wilson since the early 1930s. Without asking his permission, she smuggled into the house several of her small grandchildren, whose mother had gone insane and been committed to Bellevue. Hatty was as eccentric as Wilson's Japanese butler. She once used an embroidered linen napkin as a diaper for her granddaughter. On another occasion, wanting an advance on her salary when Wilson was subletting Muriel Draper's apartment on First Avenue, she pawned Draper's sealskin coat and silver fox jacket and then lost the tickets. But Hatty was also extremely capable. She was a dab hand at fried-egg sandwiches, prepared home remedies for Wilson's hangovers, altered his old evening clothes, re-paired the hot-water heater and lent him money when he was hard up. Poised, soft-spoken and tactful, she always agreed with what he said. Wilson came to feel a deep sympathy and affection for her.

II

In March 1938, while living at "Trees," Wilson brought out his second book of literary criticism, *The Triple Thinkers*. The ten chapters had been previously published in the *Atlantic Monthly*, the *New Republic*, the *Partisan Review* and *Hound & Horn* between 1933 and 1938. Ten years later he revised the book extensively, dropped the chapter on Samuel Butler's *Erewhon* and included three new ones—on Ben Jonson, Mr. Rolfe and "The Historical Interpretation of Literature"—from the 1940s. The suggestive title, which came from Flaubert's letter to Louise Colet, was not explained until the chapter on Flaubert, where Wilson writes that "the artist should be triply ('to the nth degree') a thinker." This phrase could also mean that the great artist, to achieve his complex vision, must keep in mind, at the same time, three different thoughts or three aspects of one idea.

The Triple Thinkers, unlike *Axel's Castle* and *The Wound and the Bow*, has no unifying thesis. It concerns the five literatures which most interested Wilson: Russian, French, English, Irish and American. But the contents of the book—which were not in thematic, logical or chronological order—would have been more effectively divided into three parts: first, the personal memoirs of his Hill School teacher Mr. Rolfe and of the Princeton professor Paul Elmer More (which includes a fine portrait of More's friend Christian Gauss); then, the chapters on individual writers in chronological order: Jonson, Pushkin, Flaubert, James, Shaw, Housman and John Jay Chapman; and finally, the three general essays: "Is Verse a Dying Technique?," "Marxism and Literature" and "The Historical Interpretation of Literature." Wilson did not carefully plan and structure his books. He wrote his essays separately, then gathered them up, and his various editors did not provide much help.

The charming memoir of More, published after his death, describes Wilson and Gauss' visit to his Princeton home in December 1929, and presents as intellectual opponents, Gauss, the expounder of French Romanticism, and his close friend More, the great anti-Romantic. Their serious and stimulating conversation—which ranged from pagan and Christian religions to Joyce and Eliot—is like a modern-day Platonic symposium. "Morose Ben Jonson" argues that his plays (like the work of James and Housman) lack organic life, yet have influenced a great many writers. Wilson explains Jonson's works with an innovative but reductive psychoanalytical theory and claims that he is an "anal erotic" type.

"In Honor of Pushkin" and "John Jay Chapman" introduce these authors to readers who are unfamiliar with their work. Wilson tries to show that Pushkin was the greatest poet of the nineteenth century by interpreting his major work, *Eugene Onegin*, and by analyzing and translating his poem *The Bronze Horseman*. Wilson was attracted to the intense individualism, aristocratic attitude and eclectic tastes of Chapman's essays on American literature, and identified Chapman with his own father. He describes how Chapman had once held his hand in the fire until it became so charred that it had to be amputated, but never fully explains his manic need for self-punishment. He briefly mentions but does not comment on Chapman's anti-Catholic and anti-Semitic writings for the Ku Klux Klan, and overestimates this nearly-forgotten figure by calling him the "best writer on literature of his generation." Chapman was delighted by Wilson's attempt to resurrect his work. Like Joyce and Eliot, he wrote to express his gratitude: "The manner in which you introduce and expound bits from my essays seems to bring out the meaning in a way that startled me and certainly brought tears to my eyes a good many times. . . . It takes my breath away—I have not lived in vain—I don't want anybody else's praise. One man is enough. And this reminds me, that I had always said to myself, while writing anything—'I am writing for one imaginary man.'—You must have been he."

"The Politics of Flaubert" offers a Marxist reading of *Sentimental Education*, and concludes that Flaubert shifts the blame for the evils of the world from a social class to the human race.[2] The longest, most ambitious and influential essay, "The Ambiguity of Henry James," searches for the "hidden" author beneath the surface of his most difficult and intriguing story, "The Turn of the Screw." Wilson identified with James, as he had with Chapman, noting that his family "were not New Englanders, even by ancestry, but New Yorkers of Irish and Scotch-Irish stock," and that by writing plays James—like Wilson himself—had "sacrificed not only his time but also all the strength of his genius for work that was worse than mediocre."

Wilson's starting point was a 1924 article by Edna Kenton, which had pointed out that the governess in James' story was the only one who saw the ghosts. Taking a Freudian approach (as in the chapter on Jonson), Wilson argues that the story portrays the governess' neurotic sexual repression and that "the ghosts are not real ghosts but hallucinations of the governess." By 1948, however, James' recently-published *Notebooks* revealed that he had consciously intended "to write a *bona fide* ghost story." Ignoring Lawrence's admonition: "Never trust the artist. Trust the tale," Wilson recanted his theory. In any case, as A. J. A. Waldock had stated the previous year, the governess could not possibly have imagined "a perfectly precise, point-by-point image of the man, then dead, whom she had never seen in her life and never heard of."[3] Though Wilson may have been mistaken about "The Turn of the Screw," he did draw attention to the complexity of the story and suggest how James used narrative technique to disguise rather than reveal meaning.

"Bernard Shaw at Eighty," a retrospective survey of his long career, expresses Wilson's disillusionment with the windy speeches and absurd politics of his former hero. "A. E. Housman" focuses on his brilliant classical scholarship and concludes that he has managed (as Hemingway said of Fitzgerald) "to grow old without in a sense ever knowing maturity." Wilson argues affirmatively in "Is Verse a Dying Technique?," maintaining that "the technique of prose today seems to be absorbing the technique of verse." But in a 1948 addition he again recanted his argument by conceding that Auden's recent work had, on the contrary, returned "to the older tradition of serviceable and vigorous English verse." The weakness of this essay, as F. O. Matthiessen remarked in a *New Republic* review, was a certain lack of discrimination. Wilson regarded "with equal seriousness the talents of Hopkins and Edna Millay, or the dramatic verse of Maxwell Anderson and T. S. Eliot."

"Marxism and Literature" considers an important question: "what sort of periods are most favorable for works of art?" It argues that though Marxism cannot help us to judge the value of a literary work, it can "throw a great deal of light on the origins and social significance of works of art." The concluding and closely related essay, "The Historical Interpretation of Literature," was originally delivered as a lecture at Princeton in October 1940, a month after the publication of *To the Finland Station*. Exploring the political role of the man of letters, Wilson discusses the intellectual contribution of the heroic figures of his latest book: Vico and Taine, Marx and Engels, Lenin and Trotsky.

The Triple Thinkers returned to the idea—first discussed in *Axel's Castle*—that the artist must stand above politics and remain true to his own moral vision. After renouncing Communism and while writing *To the Finland Station*, Wilson adopted—even as he questioned—a Marxist approach to show the close connection between literature and society. As Frederick Dupee observed in an appreciative notice in the *Partisan Review*, Wilson's book combined "esthetic maturity with the insights of social history,"[4] and strengthened his reputation as the leading literary critic of his time.

III

Though Wilson was more deeply involved with women during the mid-1930s than at any other time of his life, he also had important connections—not always friendly—with men: the university teacher Lionel Trilling, the poet and bureaucrat Archibald MacLeish and the novelist Ernest Hemingway. Wilson and Trilling, who was a decade younger, were often linked toward the end of their careers. Both published fiction (though Trilling's was more distinguished) and were considered the preeminent American men of letters. Trilling, who had a much narrower range of interests, remained cloistered at Columbia. Wilson, who encouraged Trilling to seek an audience outside the university, fostered the cultivation of humane letters in a wider world.

In 1929, when he first saw Wilson at work in his Greenwich Village flat, Trilling had found him an inspiring model. He urged Trilling to complete his long-delayed book on Matthew Arnold, telling him that it would be useful and that he wanted to read it. Wilson showed, by his own example, that an involvement in contemporary life was quite compatible with serious scholarship. "It is impossible to overestimate the liberating effect which this had upon me," Trilling gratefully recalled, "the sudden sense that I no longer had to suppose that I was doing a shameful academic drudgery." When *Matthew Arnold* finally appeared in 1939, Wilson reviewed it in the *New Republic.* He called it a valuable and interesting book, and wrote that Trilling "justifies our instinctive faith in Arnold and even makes us respect him more. . . . [His] book is a credit both to his generation and to American criticism in general."

After Wilson's notice was published, Trilling went round to the *New Republic* to ask him for books to review. He was surprised to discover that his formidable hero "was terribly shy and rather withdrawn and self-defensive, by no means as assertive and forceful as in later years. Wilson appeared to me then as very gentle and rather dim." In the course of their unpublished twenty-year correspondence Wilson congratulated Trilling on his academic promotion, mentioned his own classes at Chicago and asked about a temporary teaching stint at Columbia. He praised Trilling's review of Fitzgerald's posthumous collection, *The Crack-Up* (edited by Wilson); thanked Trilling for testifying on his behalf at the *Memoirs of Hecate County* trial; discussed Jane Austen's *Mansfield Park*, the meaning of Edward Lear's word "runcible" and the poetry of Robert Frost. Wilson also considered his long career at the *New Republic* and the curious way in which their work and reputations were frequently linked in England.

In his amusing poem, "The Mass in the Parking Lot," Wilson wrote, apropos of Trilling's essay on Henry James' *The Princess Casamassima:*

> "I've made a discovery! Isn't it thrilling?
> He's as good as Stendhal," cried Lionel Trilling.

Trilling, whose essay "Art and Neurosis" was influenced by the theme and psychoanalytical approach of *The Wound and the Bow*, concluded that Wilson brought "an enormous lucidity and intelligence and commonsense to the study of literature. . . . He, more than anyone else, taught me the virtues of simplicity in writing. . . . He gave me the desire to communicate not only with professionals but with intelligent people generally."[5]

Archibald MacLeish—a friend of Bishop, Tate, Dos Passos and Hemingway—was a successful government official and an ambitious but depressingly mediocre poet. He provoked Wilson's wrath by his affair with Margaret Bishop; by his echo-chamber vulgarizations of Yeats, Pound and Eliot; by the high-sounding banalities of his verse; by his sellout to slick journalism and to the man Wilson called "Il Luce"; by his ever-changing, all-purpose role as public spokesman; and by the undeserved honors that he gathered with such ease. Moreover, Wilson considered "The Hamlet of A. MacLeish" (1928) "a prime piece of bathos" and believed he had been satirized in the poem as "Rosencrantz and Guildenstern and Osric, the water fly, all rolled into one."

In 1932 MacLeish sent his long and exceptionally dull poem *Conquistador*, about Cortés' conquest of Mexico, to Ezra Pound. Pound bluntly told him that it was "damn bad," but *Conquistador* won the Pulitzer Prize in 1933. In the *New Yorker* of January 14, 1939, Wilson, egged on by Louise Bogan, published his most brilliant poem, "The Omelet of A. MacLeish." He took the title and italicized marginal comments from MacLeish's earlier poem, and cruelly parodied the Poundian lines, the hollow incantations and the solemn portentousness of *Conquistador*. MacLeish, who got wind of the poem before it appeared and realized he was about to be scalped, told Wilson: "I shall await your parody in the *New Yorker* with terror. You take all my hair off or only the little I have left?"

The deadly poem cut to the heart of MacLeish's poetic defects. Wilson satirized his intrusive catch-all colons: "And my colons went out on the air to the clang of a gong"; his absurd self-questioning: "And the questions and / questions / questioning / What am I? O"; and his awkward attempts at hard-nosed proletarian speech. In *Frescoes for Mr. Rockefeller's City* (1933), MacLeish wrote: "She's a tough land under the corn, mister," which Wilson mocked as "He's a tough lad under the verse mister." Writing in *Frescoes* in his minority/diversity vein, MacLeish said: "Niggers we were, Portuguese, Magyars, Polacks," which Wilson turned into: "And the Polacks and Dagoes and Hunkies undoubtedly dead." In Wilson's parody, MacLeish prepares his poetical omelet and stuffs it with eclectic ingredients from Greek tragedy, alliterative Anglo-Saxon, Dante, Valéry, Pound, Eliot, Saint-John Perse, Cummings: "Nimble at other men's arts how I picked up the trick of it." MacLeish, in Wilson's view, not only stole from his betters, but also changed his convictions to curry favor with the Left. When Wilson's poem appeared in book form, Robert Penn Warren called it "a brilliant combination of parody and criticism and butchery."[6]

MacLeish replied privately with a feeble scatological poem, which he enclosed in a letter of January 1939 to Hemingway. Wilson had mocked the solemn occasion when the undergraduates of MacLeish's college were selected for the senior societies: "Men of Yale: and the shudder of Tap Day." Alluding to *The Triple Thinkers*, MacLeish attributed Wilson's motive to a wounded ego, called him a coldly rational "Princeton Aristotle" and attacked his opposition to World War Two:

> As one on whom
> The Triple Stinker publicly hath stunk
> I claim the usual convenience. Room! . . .
> The wounded ego of a man gone rotten
> Sticks to the pant-leg and will stain the stuff. . . .
> The strong intelligence that should have won
> A Princeton Aristotle's decent fame
> But quibbled when the fascists pulled a gun:
> I got it all with the shamelessness of shame.

In the *New Republic* of June 19, 1940, MacLeish widened his attack on opponents to the war and sternly insisted that Dos Passos and Hemingway—who had contemptuously rejected, in *Three Soldiers* and *A Farewell to Arms*, the propagandistic attempts to justify World War One—"must face the fact that the books they wrote in the years just after the [last] War have done more to disarm democracy in the face of fascism than any other single influence." In an essay on MacLeish, which was originally published on July 1, 1940 and later opened *Classics and Commercials*, Wilson attacked the pomposity and malign implications of MacLeish's criticism of Dos Passos and Hemingway, and declared: "He has surely in the course of his career struck a greater variety of attitudes and been ready to repudiate them faster than any other reputable writer of our time."[7] Wilson was so aesthetically and morally disgusted by MacLeish that he refused to shake hands with him when they met in Dos Passos' hospital room in September 1947.

In 1926 MacLeish had said: "[Wilson's] a damn fine critic and I wish I could please him." But even MacLeish, whose work was based more on industry than artistry, recognized his own limitations and confessed to Amy Lowell: "This rhythm and vocabulary which my intelligence knows for second rate are me, my 'style,' all that I have." Toward the end of his long, much-honored life he trimmed his sails yet again, and bitterly exclaimed: "Bunny Wilson was far from being the critic he's supposed to be. He was a very small-minded, petty, jealous, mean man and a stinker of the first order, and if I'm saying these words for all eternity, I mean them."[8]

Wilson had not seen Hemingway since their unpleasant dinner with Fitzgerald in January 1933. But he maintained an active interest in Hemingway's work, and now became as perceptive about his defects as he had once been about his strengths. Wilson's evaluations of Hemingway are a touchstone of his fine critical judgment. His review of *Green Hills of Africa*, published in the *New Republic* in December 1935 and translated into Russian, marked the beginning of Wilson's disenchantment with Hemingway, which culminated in his major critique of 1939. Wilson called this self-indulgent account of a big-game hunting expedition "certainly far and away his weakest book," maintained that he was losing interest in his fellow men and only wanted to kill the animals, and "has become progressively more sterile and less interesting . . . as he has become more detached from the great social issues of the day." Wilson noted another weakness, first revealed in *Death in the Afternoon* (1932), which became increasingly prominent as Hemingway's work declined: "he seems to lose all his capacity for self-criticism and is likely to become fatuous or maudlin . . . as soon as he begins to write in the first person."

Three years later, in another severe review, Wilson asserted that Hemingway's play about the Spanish Civil War, *The Fifth Column*, was almost as bad as *To Have and To Have Not* (1937) and did not do "very much either for Hemingway or for the revolution." But Wilson shrewdly observed that the best work in Hemingway's early stories, in contrast to the play, represented "one of the most considerable achievements of the American writing of our time." In 1938 Hemingway, risking his life by reporting the Spanish War, was committed to "the great social issues of the day" while Wilson was becoming increasingly critical of the Communists. In a bitter letter to Wilson, written just after his review had appeared, Hemingway began with moderate praise, but then attacked Wilson for his indifference to the fate of the Spanish Loyalists: "You were the first critic to take any interest in my writing and I have always been very grateful and have always looked forward to reading anything you write about what I publish. I know that all of you who took no part in the defence of the Spanish republic must discredit those who did take part and I understand human beings enough to appreciate your attitude and the necessity for it."

Wilson's "Hemingway: Gauge of Morale," published in the *Atlantic Monthly* of July 1939, was the most important and influential study of Hemingway, and marked a turning point in his contemporary reputation. Drawing heavily on his previous reviews, he offered an analytical account of Hemingway's strengths and weaknesses during the first two decades of his career. Wilson contrasted the successful artist of the 1920s with his radical decline in the following decade, emphasized his personal and literary exhibitionism, and criticized his lack of objectivity, craftsmanship, taste, style and sense. Instead of concentrating on his art, Hemingway had been occupied with building up his personality. Wilson wrote that the "arrogant, belligerent and boastful [Hemingway] is certainly the worst-invented character to be found in the author's work." Yet Hemingway's recovery of his artistic integrity in the two brilliant African stories of 1936 allowed Wilson to conclude his damaging essay on a positive note: "His whole work is a criticism of society: he has responded to every pressure of the moral atmosphere of the time, as it is felt at the roots of human relations, with a sensitivity almost unrivaled."[9]

In 1940 Wilson defended Hemingway against MacLeish's political attack and wrote a generally favorable review of *For Whom the Bell Tolls*. He stressed its moral qualities and added this review to his long essay when he revised it for *The Wound and the Bow* (1941). But when he submitted the book, which he had contracted to write for Scribner's, they refused to publish the chapter on Hemingway. When Wilson refused to withdraw it, they broke their contract and forfeited their considerable advance, and he resold the book to Houghton Mifflin. Wilson explained to a friend that Max Perkins, fearful of losing his most profitable author, "was afraid of publishing anything about Hemingway, no matter how appreciative, because he carries on like a madman about everything that is written about him. . . . Hemingway has been getting worse (crazier) of late years, and they are scared to death that he may leave them." Charles Scribner, Jr. later confirmed Wilson's account of the incident: "Perkins and my father knew that if they published this, Hemingway would be out the door. (In fact, Ernest was so outraged that he wanted to kill Wilson.)"

Wilson took mild revenge for the profitable rejection of his book with two satiric references to Hemingway in *Memoirs of Hecate County*

(1946). Alluding to early stories like "Now I Lay Me" (1927), about the effects of shell-shock, Wilson remarked that one of his characters "liked to dramatize his insomnia with a kind of diluted *Weltschmerz* that had a flavor of both Hemingway and Spengler," whose *Decline of the West* had been published in English that year. Wilson also mocked the romantic attitudes to Spain expressed in Bizet's opera, as well as Hemingway's irritating *Death in the Afternoon* and one of his fashionable hangouts in New York: "The piano splashed out a passage from *Carmen* and a high distinct cultivated voice began mincing out a song about a beautiful cigarette girl at the Stork Club and a man named Don José Hemingway who wanted to be a toreador."[10]

After the dispute of 1941, Wilson and Hemingway continued to snipe at one another, but their comments revealed a certain ambivalence. In May 1950, while Arthur Mizener was writing his biography of Fitzgerald, Hemingway warned him about Wilson's malign influence: "He is an excellent critic about many things but he has strange leaks in his integrity and his knowledge leaks so bad that if he were an aqueduct he would run dry." To Hemingway, Wilson's critical acuity was counterbalanced by his disloyal and destructive criticism. In a letter of 1953 to Hemingway's future biographer, Carlos Baker, Wilson, mocking the novelist's machismo, sharply commented that Hemingway's wife had to have an awed and innocent appreciation of his exploits. Wilson thought she had to be "the female bird, shy and retiring, entirely devoted to the splendid and brave and adventurous cock-pheasant."

After Hemingway had miraculously survived two African plane crashes in January 1954, Wilson felt relieved that he had not been killed but dreaded the inevitable boasting about his dangerous exploits in the bush. Six years later, when Hemingway's articles on bullfighting, "The Dangerous Summer," appeared in *Life*, Wilson, in a letter to their mutual friend, Morley Callaghan, mocked the most recent exhibition of his public personality: "Have you seen our Ernest in *Life*? The matadors are out-bulked by Ernest; the bulls have the faces of Ernest; and one of the principal settings of the story seems to be the room in Spain in which Ernest started writing it. Second installment: more pictures of Ernest towering over his spunky little matador."[11]

Like everyone else, Wilson was shocked by Hemingway's violent death in July 1961. Though it had been announced as an accident, Wilson instinctively knew it was a suicide. "Of course he often made a fool of himself," Wilson observed, "but it is as if a whole corner of my generation had suddenly and horribly collapsed. I knew that the desperation in his stories was real. . . . It makes it more understandable to know that he had been taking shock treatments and was part of the time quite out of his mind." After reading Baker's biography eight years later, Wilson emphasized the negative side of Hemingway's character that had emerged from the book—his ingratitude, self-punishment, compromised principles and sense of self-betrayal: "Hemingway's always turning nasty and picking a quarrel with anyone who has ever done anything for him—I see I am not spared; and his repeated self-injuries through clumsiness give somewhat the impression of self-inflicted wounds. He had a high sense of honor, which he was always violating; and this evidently gave him a permanent bad conscience, which I suppose contributed to his drinking."

Wilson, who had written the first serious notice of Hemingway's work in the *Dial* in 1924 and had been consistently illuminating about his achievement, had virtually the last word on his last novel, *Islands in the Stream*, in the *New Yorker* nearly fifty years later. Wilson made two important points about the public and private Hemingway. He had triumphantly satisfied two typical American ambitions: "that of becoming an accomplished outdoorsman and that of making a great deal of money." And the major theme of his last four novels—from *A Farewell to Arms* to *Islands in the Stream*—was that of a "crucial game played against invincible odds."[12]

Wilson's relationships with these representative figures reveal his central role in American cultural life. He encouraged Trilling to write literary criticism that could be appreciated by an intelligent audience outside the academic world; he saw through MacLeish's specious verse and pointed out the injustice of his public awards; aware of the dangers of fame and wealth to a creative artist, he held Hemingway to the highest standards of his early work.

IV

"Trees" became the site of Wilson's sexual adventures during the mid-1930s. His first wife was slowly dying of tuberculosis, his second wife was dead and his relations with the physically ill and newly-married Frances had deteriorated, though he continued to see her until his third marriage. Wilson was uninhibited only when he was having sex, and seemed to take great pleasure in every part of it. Instead of relaxing him, sex made him want to talk, read poetry, sing songs in a foreign language. He had a bull-like physical stamina, and his numerous mistresses often praised his sexual performance.

Wilson was not only drawn to a certain type of male friend, who was "clever but dissipated [and] looked rather the worse for wear," but was also attracted to a particular kind of woman: good-looking, witty, sharp-tongued, often intellectual, a heavy drinker, usually childless, unhappily married or recently divorced, extremely neurotic and mentally unstable. Paula Gates (whom he had known in San Francisco) as well as Betty Huling, Louise Fort, Helen Augur, Elizabeth Waugh and Louise Bogan all fit this general pattern.

Betty Huling played the same sort of comradely role at the *New Republic* as Jeanne Ballot had played at *Vanity Fair*. She was born into a wealthy suburban family in Larchmont, New York, in 1901, graduated from Vassar, was the efficient copy-editor at the *New Republic* from 1934 to 1950, and then worked for *Atlas* magazine, which was also supported by the Elmhirsts. Betty—who never married—had an ugly nose, thick lips and a bad stutter. But she was witty and warm, with blond hair, electric blue eyes and beautiful legs that she often displayed on the tennis courts. She lived near Elinor Wylie on Bank Street in the Village, had a thorough knowledge of books and often burst into explosive laughter. Betty appears in *Memoirs of Hecate County* as Helen Hubbard, who gives the narrator "her wide boyish grin and her frank and fun-loving laugh that could be heard above the crashing uproar," while Imogen remarks that "She'll never get married now. . . . All she cares about is playing tennis."[13]

Wilson began his affair with Betty in 1934 and resumed relations with her in 1945, after his separation from Mary McCarthy. They gossiped about their sex lives in their letters, swam on the Connecticut coast, "made mincemeat" out of their friends (Betty called Caroline Gordon Tate "a venomous woman"). They also got drunk on Betty's potent cocktails made from gin, applejack and pink grenadine. Mary Blair, who heard the news about Wilson from Rosalind and kept a friendly eye on his adventures, wrote: "Far be it from me to pick on your girl friends but I'll bet Betty Huling just tries to arrange your life for you." The lonely Paul Rosenfeld was more perceptive about their liaison. "You sound as though you have been having a good summer on the Cape," he wrote in September 1936. "Betty plus a good cook must have been an altogether rare and happy situation."

Always intensely curious about people's lives and still nostalgic about his old loves, Wilson kept in touch with Betty—as he had done with Edna Millay and Léonie Adams—and was saddened when he saw her four months before her death in 1969. She had been in and out of mental hospitals, had been subjected to electro-convulsive therapy and was depressingly moribund: "Awful to see such a vigorous, outgoing and extroverted woman reduced to such a state of helplessness. . . . Still suffers from her depression. . . . She went through a horrible operation with her lung. I don't think they have told her her cancer is fatal."[14]

Louise Fort, the daughter of a Boston railroad executive, was born in 1900. Once engaged to the Washington lawyer John Amen, she had married Peter Connor. She worked briefly as a real estate agent in Chicago and was the mother of two children; but she had a miserable marriage, drank heavily and suffered a nervous breakdown in 1935. Wilson once gave her a copy of *The Waste Land* with the admonitory inscription: "If you would read more poetry you wouldn't have to drink so much." Drunk or sober, Louise's behavior could be quite eccentric. She was once arrested for peeing in public, then weaving her car back and forth across the road.

When he first became her lover in 1933, Wilson described Louise as affectionate and witty, sensual and responsive: "Full lips, smelled like strawberries, almost too rich. In the total dark—began to crawl on me. Afterwards, 'Well, that's something nobody can take away from you! . . . I'd like to be married to you.' I asked her if she liked me, and she said, 'I must love you. . . . Some people can sleep with people they don't like, but I love you. . . . This is the last time you ever get such service.'" Two years later, as she arranged to come down from Boston to spend the weekend with him in New York, her letters were full of expectation and endearments. She was accommodating about the party to be given by the *New Yorker*, where her sister Henrietta then worked, and flattering about their previous encounter: "I can arrive Friday afternoon in time for the party if you want me enough. I do not mind missing it, however, if your other girl can go as it will cut my stay here rather short. . . . I might meet you in Albany again—I hope with greater success, more leisure and *some* moderation. I will come to New York if you would really like to have me."

The following spring Wilson traveled to Chicago for another rendezvous and in the hotel room was shocked to discover that Louise —like Proust's Baron de Charlus—wanted to be beaten. He spanked her with his bare hands and slapped her face, but was not harsh enough to please her. Two months later, however, he got into the swing of things and began to realize the potential of their sado-masochistic encounters: "I tried a little violence the first day, but she couldn't give herself up to it. I asked why she thought she liked this, and she answered that she thought it was because [her husband] had never subdued her. Although I enjoyed it myself, I had some sort of inhibition about hitting her and could only seem to do it clumsily, not landing my blows squarely. I used to look forward to it and wonder how and where to buy a whip."[15] In February 1937 Louise, having thrown away his phone number "in a fit of common sense," was unable to find it again. Recalling their tense, furtive liaison, she called him "my dearest love" and wrote: "I would dearly love to see you but could no longer go through the nerve strained strategies to do so."

Wilson resumed relations with Louise, as he did with Betty Huling, after his marriage to Mary McCarthy had ended, and was inevitably disappointed by the change in her appearance. Comparing her, as before, to sensual fruit, he recorded that "her face was sallow and seemed almost leathery—so different from her old strawberry-and-cream lusciousness, with its flushing of high color." Conducting his usual post-mortem in 1958, Wilson found that Louise (like Millay, Adams and Huling) was in bad shape. She had been in a sanitorium for addiction to narcotics and alcohol, and was no longer debauched and hysterical. But she continued to take drugs and was still "quite out of her head."

Wilson continued to indulge in erotic fantasies about Louise. In her last letter to him, she recalled that he had threatened to expose her in his diaries, had disingenuously suggested that he could not stop their publication and had rather cruelly forced her to plead for mercy: "I dined with you at the Princeton Club that summer preceding my divorce. We had many cocktails. You said 'You are in my memoirs.' I was flattered. 'Good God' you said, striking your forehead, 'I hope I'm dead when it's published.' You stared at me for a moment and added, 'I hope we're both dead.' Please, can't you change that or delete it? My children read many of your books. Quite a few people know how long our friendship has lasted. You wrote something pretty bad or why must we both die before publication?"[16]

Wilson had a brief affair with his second cousin and childhood companion, Helen Augur, in January 1937. They remained friends, she knew his last two wives and she lived in his Talcottville house in the

1950s. Divorced from her rich husband, Warren, she owned a penthouse in Stuyvesant Square and wrote historical novels. Wilson once arranged her invitation to the writers' colony at Yaddo in Saratoga Springs, New York.

Helen was small, blond, blue-eyed and very pretty. She was also sharp-tongued and spiteful, a mixture, Wilson said, of "self-delusion and practical sense, intelligence and utter idiocy." Helen wrote emotionally intense letters to Wilson, while he was in Stamford and she was in New York, the morning after their love-making. Though they sometimes fought bitterly, she said he could be both tender and passionate. Ecstatic yet frightened by her newly-found passion, she gratefully expressed her love:

> Darling, I'm too sleepy to say anything to you except what I could say better in non-conversation. . . . It's all so strange . . . that curious combination of sheer pleasantness and the brute tides underneath.—It's so good to be at peace with you at last, and to know that never again will I have to be venomous to you, whatever happens.—We're awfully either-or people.—Goodnight. —I miss you. H.

> I go wild wanting to tell you and tell you—just about, I don't know—it's too soon and I'm too scared.—I thought I wasn't, having plunged into the center of my main terror and found my angelic joy.—But it's terrifying being away from you.—Nothing seems right now but having you again.—All these years I've tricked myself and wasted myself (and you have too). . . . When you come I'm going to love you and make up for all those days of this long week.

In the summer of 1953—when Wilson, then married but on his own in Talcottville, shared the house with Helen—they fought angrily and sometimes comically. In his diaries and in the autobiographical *Upstate*, he dissected her character and criticized her neurotic complaints, demands for attention, aggressive manners, intolerable bossiness, catty remarks, blatant egoism and inevitable physical decline:

> [She has] a warm and vital voice, bustlingly capable and energetic, ambitious in a worldly way and instinctively tending to dominate a household. What is pathetic is that she has no household and has

neurotically doomed herself not to have one. . . . She eventually became so tyrannical, undoing everything I did and thwarting whatever I tried to do, putting away things that I needed and snatching other things out of my hands, that I began having acrimonious scenes with her. . . .

The vigorous practical side (except when she was a foreign correspondent) has never been effectively integrated with the moony and cerebral one. She seems to live a good deal of the time in some self-centered adolescent fantasy. . . . Helen's combined self-indulgence in her dreams and something like a certain lack of self-respect, due, I think, to her failure as a woman, now appear in her slumping figure, the cigarette always hanging out of her mouth and her yellow upper lip. . . . How well she looked when I first got to know her, then married to Warren Vinton: blond, plump, pinkcheeked, smiling, *pimpante* [spruce] in her bright clean clothes.[17]

While seeing Frances, Betty Huling, Louise Fort and Helen Augur in the mid-1930s, Wilson carried on his most agonizing affair with the "incomparably beautiful" Elizabeth Waugh. She appeared in his diaries as "D." and inspired Imogen, the "Princess with the Golden Hair," and the sexual descriptions in the story that led to the suppression of *Memoirs of Hecate County*. About the same age as Edmund, Elizabeth, a would-be painter, had married Coulten Waugh in 1918 and owned the Hook Rug Shop and art gallery in Provincetown. She corresponded with him from 1935 to 1940 (sometimes writing from Mexico), describing her gynecological problems and her psychoanalysis with Sandor Rado—who also treated Mary McCarthy. Besides being psychologically troubled (like Betty and Louise), Elizabeth had nose problems, which made her speak in an odd way, and back problems, which probably suggested Imogen's strange back brace in Wilson's story.

Elizabeth, the prettiest woman Wilson had ever seen, had reddish-blond hair and "great open liquid female brown eyes." Her open-work shoes disclosed her reddened toenails and when they met in town Wilson recognized, as if they were independent of her body, her small feet "'trotting' along the street." During their love-making she excited him by uttering "little low incoherent phrases, which seemed to come out of her inmost woman's nature." Afterwards, she hurt Wilson's feelings by remarking that he looked like a monk in Boccaccio. Confronting himself in the mirror, he was forced to admit that his face was all too fat and debauched.

Elizabeth's letters to Wilson were abject, hysterical, out of control. She said that she had never before been carried along on such a flood of passion, that she loved him deeply but had never suffered such heartbreak, and connected their violent love-making with his other mistresses: "[When] I took out my night-gown to wash I found it covered with blood stains. It was as if you had been sleeping with a virgin. Are all the others like that too?" She apologized for her personal shortcomings and feared, as he came to know her, that there would be nothing left in her to please him. She asked to spend as much time with him as possible and begged Edmund not to put her out of his life. But she also pleaded to be released from the affair, which had taken four years to consummate and could only end in despair: "It appears that I have thought only of you for four years. . . . Let me go! no good will come of it—you can see the tragedy under my eyes. . . . I know that you need me—I need you too—but it would be terrible for you too because you love me and you would regret your past [behavior] as you have never regretted anything before."

In the most extraordinarily dramatic letter he ever received, written in March 1937 from Fort Myers on the Gulf coast of Florida, Elizabeth (like Helen Augur) said that Edmund had awakened her sexually. But she described their affair in a tragic, even feral way, and accused him, as his wives would do, of trying to destroy the women he loved. She portrayed herself as a wounded animal, wanted to bite him in revenge, and even suggested that his literary work had somehow penetrated her internal organs. Finally, comparing her mental anguish to the pains of childbirth, Elizabeth seemed to hint that she had given birth to his dead baby:

> You once said to me "don't ever do this to anyone else.". . . I feel like an animal you stepped on—I want to bite—you have hurt me so much more than I could ever have hurt you—I lived in an unawakened state. . . . My whole life ahead did not seem a boring stretch of years. . . .
>
> See what you have done? Spoiled my life and Coulten's— though he doesn't know it—and won't if I can help it—you are ruthless—you like to hurt people. . . . I hope you are really sorry about me—My mental agony is more unceasing than birth

pains. . . . I am writing because I want you to know about the damage you have done—I want to bite—Even your damn plays get into my fallopian tubes. . . .

I had no idea that pain like this existed—Just as I didn't know anything about what it would be like to have a still born child.[18]

After patiently laying siege to Elizabeth Waugh and finally overcoming her resistance, he found it difficult to deal with her grief and remorse.

V

Wilson's close friendship with the poet Louise Bogan was more like his intellectual companionship with Elinor Wylie, Edna Millay and Léonie Adams than his sexual relationships with Betty Huling, Louise Fort, Helen Augur and Elizabeth Waugh. But Bogan was also mentally unstable. She had three nervous breakdowns, spent long periods in mental hospitals and was always threatened by that terrifying darkness. Louise Bogan, who came from a poor Irish-Catholic family, was born in 1897 in a mill town in Maine. She married a professional soldier in 1916, had a daughter the following year and left him in 1919, when she was twenty-two. Wilson, then working on *Vanity Fair*, was the first friend she made after coming to New York in 1920. He became her literary mentor and she dedicated her third book of poems, *The Sleeping Fury* (1937), "To Edmund Wilson in gratitude."

They would drink, gossip about friends, discuss and even write poetry together. Her friend May Sarton said that Louise would "drink a martini down as though it were a glass of water and demand another at once. After a third, she was knocked out and sometimes even fell asleep." Wilson was so close to Louise that Mary Blair had felt excluded. She later told Wilson that when she first met Bogan in April 1923, shortly after their wedding, Louise "never acknowledged my existence. You were the host but I just wasn't there. . . . I never could like her." When Rosalind quoted some popular verse, Edmund, over-solicitous about Louise, harshly reprimanded her: "You mustn't recite things like that in front of Miss Bogan. She's a lyric poet. It will trouble her." In 1924, when Louise was about to marry a fellow-Princetonian, Raymond Holden, Wilson recalled the dull consorts of Wylie and Millay as well as Elinor's comment about William Benét. He told

Bishop that if Holden succeeded in his suit, "all the remarkable women of the [poetical] kind in New York will be married to amiable mediocrities."[19]

Louise had her first mental breakdown in April 1931. Wilson, who had been through the same torment two years earlier, recommended his own doctor, tried to ease her out of her suffering and assured her that she would recover:

> I'm terribly sorry you've been in a bad state—I sympathize profoundly, having been there myself. But it is an excellent thing to go to bed on these occasions and [John] McKinney is really an awfully good man. . . .
>
> Everything is changing so fast and we are all more or less in a position of having been brought up in one kind of world and having to adjust ourselves, socially, sexually, morally to another which is itself in a state of flux. . . .
>
> My affection and admiration for you are deep—have been from way back, as you know. You are one of the people that I value most and count most on.

In the spring of 1935—between her separation from Raymond Holden and her love affair with the poet Theodore Roethke—Edmund and Louise spent a great deal of time together. They drank heavily, studied German, read Heine and, for a brief time, became lovers. On May 13, three days after sailing for Russia, Wilson wrote another tender letter, thanking Louise for her friendship and intellectual stimulation, and mentioning what a good time he had had with her: "I want you to know how appreciative of you and how fond of you, my dear, I really am: I never had this kind of companionship with a woman for any length of time before in my life, and I became so addicted to it this winter that maybe it's just as well that I'm going away: you and I really have too much fun together. I'm afraid that if I had a little more money I'd decide to spend all the rest of my life drinking beer and stout with you." On October 16 Louise told the "bearish and St. Bernardish" Roethke that "My pal Edmund W. returned from Russia last night and ran around town frantically trying to find me. . . . He's much thinner [after scarlet fever], poor dear, and looks rather hunted. . . . He's staying at the Lafayette, having been evicted or sold up or something while away."

As soon as Wilson was settled in "Trees," Louise visited his rural retreat and gave Roethke a lively account of his hopeless attempts to reduce his consumption of electricity and liquor:

> Bunny kept turning the ice-box off, every night, in some mistaken hope that it would stay cold by itself, and in the morning the food smelled like a charnal house, and there was never enough gin, because he ordered, out of a desire for work and sobriety, only one bottle at a time, and then he and I would polish that off, and it would only be ten o'clock in the evening, and we'd be in the middle of an argument, with no gin to help us carry it on, and Edmund would sit there and say: "I'll get a case of it; that's the thing to do: get a case of it!"

Two months later, writing to their mutual friend, the poet and translator Rolfe Humphries, Louise said she would never dream of marrying Edmund and was quite happy with their present friendship—except for the fact that he still counted on Frances to take up the slack in his love-life.

In February 1937 Louise noted that their deep affection was marred by bitter quarrels, fuelled by drink: "I don't know why I fall for your epistolary gifts, and am willing to make up with you.—You do give me such a pain, sometimes, that I'd like to cut your throat. But I suppose I have given, and still give, you pains too, so, if we can't really break each other down, let's build each other up, as you say." When *The Sleeping Fury* appeared that April, Wilson, immensely pleased and touched by the dedication, told Louise: "I can only say, my dear, that I derived deep aesthetic satisfaction from it and that I was deeply proud—a feeling that I really don't often have—to be associated with it by your dedication."[20] In July, after Louise had returned from a trip to Ireland, another mutual friend, the critic Morton Zabel, told Wilson that he was worried about her sanity and wondered if she was heading for her third mental breakdown: "She seems to have got into some weird mess on the boat going to Ireland and to have been followed by spectres and irrational obsessions all around the British Isles. They have followed her back to America, and I've actually feared for her mind."

Though their friendship peaked in the Thirties, they always remained on good terms. They became colleagues in 1944 when Wilson joined the *New Yorker*, where Bogan was poetry critic from 1931 until

1969. In 1955 Wilson suggested that he and Louise compose a poem in alternating lines for Auden's birthday, and began with an uninspired imitation of the first line of Wordsworth's sonnet "London, 1802." Wilson's affection for Louise was linked with his admiration of her work. She once thanked God that Wilson had never reviewed her, but had somehow forgotten that he had noticed her first book, *Body of This Death* (1923), in *Vanity Fair*. Echoing Keats, he praised its "deep vibrating full-throated tone with a faint metallic sharpness which only makes it more definite and more telling." In 1961 Bogan acknowledged her debt to Wilson, as Fitzgerald had done, and remembered "in the beginning, sitting at that desk with the tears pouring down my face trying to write a notice. Edmund Wilson would pace me and exhort me to go on. He taught me a great deal, at a period when I needed a teacher."[21]

Wilson remained on friendly terms with his mistresses after their sporadic sexual relations had ended. He liked to analyze their personalities as well as their sexual response. When he saw them late in life, he fondly recalled their love-making and mourned their loss of beauty. He enjoyed the excitement and pleasure of a succession of mistresses, but none of them could ever lead to a permanent connection. Toward the end of the Thirties, exhausted and unsettled by this emotional turbulence, he longed for a more stable existence. Though he married the beautiful Mary McCarthy, he would be unhappier with her than with any woman he had ever known.

ELEVEN

Mary McCarthy, 1938–1945

I

When Edmund Wilson met Mary McCarthy in 1937 he was forty-two, an established author, a powerful literary critic and political reporter. She was twenty-five, clever and ambitious. Already divorced, she was living with Philip Rahv, one of the editors of a new Left-wing journal, the *Partisan Review*, and beginning to make her way as a critic. When Wilson married Mary he took on, like Leonard Woolf with Virginia Stephen, a brilliant but sexually troubled and mentally unstable woman. But Wilson, unwilling to be a devoted caretaker, expected a sexual partner and amenable wife. McCarthy competed with him intellectually, tormented him with jealousy and portrayed their quarrels in her books for the rest of her life.

Mary McCarthy—the daughter of a sometime lawyer, heavy drinker and ne'er-do-well—was born in Seattle in 1912 and moved with her family to Minneapolis in 1918. That year, when she was six years old, both her parents died suddenly in the influenza epidemic that followed the Great War. She was brought up by a great-aunt and uncle, who beat her and treated her cruelly. In 1923 she returned to Seattle and attended the convent school that she described in *Memories of a Catholic Girlhood*. She lost her faith at twelve, her virginity at fourteen. After graduating from Vassar in 1933, she married Harold Johnsrud, an actor and aspiring playwright. She divorced him in 1936, when she began to work for the publisher Covici-Friede, and to write scathing book and theater reviews for the *Nation* and the *Partisan Review*. She was, by her own account, extremely promiscuous and once slept with three different men in one day.

She had heard Wilson lecture on Flaubert at Vassar in 1932. In her late satiric vein, she described him as a puffy, nervous public speaker

—the worst she had ever heard—and compared him to a fish out of water: "After a few sentences, he had floundered, mouth ajar, gasping for air." But she was much more impressed than she cared to admit in her revisionary memoir. In an essay on current criticism in the *Nation* of December 1935, she stated that only Wilson "had made any extended effort to relate what is valuable in modern literature to the body of literature of the past."[1]

Philip Rahv and the other editors of the *Partisan Review* were desperately trying to recruit Wilson to their new magazine. They told McCarthy that he was a great figure in the literary world and used her as bait to lure him into their circle. William Phillips, echoing Lionel Trilling's respectful attitude, recalled: "Of the established figures who associated themselves with us, the one whom we respected most was Edmund Wilson, a strange, remote, impressive figure. . . . I really felt legitimized only when he praised something I had written."[2]

McCarthy first met Wilson in the *Partisan Review* offices near Union Square in October 1937. She must have reminded him, with her wit, brains and sexual freedom, of Edna Millay (also from Vassar) and of the attractive women he had known in his youth in the 1920s. She describes herself in *A Charmed Life*, giving Martha Sinnott blond rather than dark hair, as "a strange, poetical-looking being, with very fair, straight hair done in a little knot, a quaint oval face, very dark, wide-set eyes, and a small, slight figure. . . . [She has a] tapering neck and gold knot of hair, like a girl in a locket." "The Monster's" physical defects, by contrast, are savagely depicted in her memoir, where he appears as "short, stout, middle-aged, breathy . . . with popping reddish-brown eyes and fresh pink skin." When Donald Ogden Stewart—who had roomed with Phelps Putnam at Yale and befriended Fitzgerald in Hollywood—read one of her stories, he was struck by the similar Irish good looks and witty style of McCarthy and Fitzgerald. He told Wilson that he had suddenly sat up in bed and thought: "Jesus Christ, [you] married Scott."

In the photographs of Wilson and McCarthy, taken on the porch of their Wellfleet house in 1942, the curtains, shutters and outdoor furniture look old and shabby. Though the day is warm, Wilson is dressed with characteristic formality in a hat, jacket and tie, baggy trousers and scuffed brown shoes. Mary, her long scraggly hair hanging down the sides of her finely-shaped face, wears a childish, pinafore-like summer dress and shoes enticingly open at the top. They smile at each other while Wilson—jovial, contented and apparently old enough to be her father—leans on a pile of newspapers and seems to be picking his teeth. "The pictures of me are downright disgusting," he told Mary, "and have given me quite a turn. I seem to be taking snuff in one of them." No wonder, then, that Mary's handsome brother Kevin described Wilson as "formidable and obnoxious-looking." Arthur Schlesinger, Jr. was also struck by the indelicacy of such a pretty young girl married to a stout old man, with an old man's manners, who always looked much older than his actual age.[3]

In his essay on Giacomo Casanova, Wilson wrote that the great lover had discovered that "you could go a long way with girls if you took them to masquerades in pairs." So he invited Margaret Marshall, the literary editor of the *Nation*, to accompany McCarthy on their first dinner date. Mary got drunk in the private dining room of an Italian restaurant, went on a talking jag, passed out and woke up, next to Margaret, in a strange bed in the Chelsea Hotel. For the moment, all was well. On their second joint date, Wilson and the two ladies took a taxi all the way from New York to Stamford. After Margaret had obligingly fallen asleep in the guest room of "Trees," Mary followed him into his study to continue their intense conversation. Misunderstanding her intention (or perhaps reading it correctly) Wilson—in McCarthy's account—took her into his arms. She gave up the battle and they made drunken love on the couch. "*Anything*, sex included, to avoid retiring," she wrote in her version of this event.

It was exciting to have two men in love with her at the same time, even though she had to deceive one of them. McCarthy assured Rahv that nothing had happened that night, and he guilelessly believed her. She continued to see Wilson secretly about once a week until the end of December 1937. When she finally wearied of her duplicity and told Rahv the truth, he gave her a wounded look and solicitously asked: "What do you want to do?" By trying to satisfy Mary's wishes, rather than attempting, like Wilson, to coerce her into marriage, Rahv intensified her guilt. She tried to compensate for this by idealizing Rahv and comparing him to "a bambino in an Italian sacred painting."

In her memoirs, McCarthy gave some rational reasons for marrying the retrospectively repulsive Wilson. They came from a similar privileged, upper-class background (whereas Rahv was an impoverished Russian-born Jew) and "there was a certain feeling of coming home, to my own people." She was naturally attracted to Wilson's intellect and, with their solid training in Latin, planned to read Juvenal together. They were going to live at "Trees" in the country and would enjoy the world of nature and the outdoors—riding horses, fishing for trout, picking wildflowers: "It was an idyl he was offering me, and not wholly false." Wilson, unlike Rahv, wanted to have children, and Mary became pregnant as soon as they were married. But the principle of self-interest was paramount. Marriage to Wilson would "do something" for her literary gift, and an alliance with an influential figure would certainly help to satisfy her ambition and advance her career. Some wit in the *Partisan* circle even suggested that she had left Rahv because Wilson had the better prose style.

Making her wedding seem as grim as possible, McCarthy claimed that they married in the Red Bank city hall, without any family or friends, and with two town employees as their witnesses. Leon Edel writes more convincingly that "the wedding took place at Wilson's mother's home in Red Bank" on February 10, 1938.[4]

II

Wilson inspired male characters in McCarthy's first five works of fiction. She kept driving nails into him, as if he were a pagan fetish, in order to exorcise his evil influence. Her first version of their marriage, written while she was still living with Wilson, appeared in her short story "Ghostly Father, I Confess" (1942). After their bitter divorce in 1946, she continued to fictionalize their marriage in "The Weeds" (1950), in *The Groves of Academe* (1952), in a crucial chapter of *The Group* (1963) and especially in *A Charmed Life* (1955). Though her relations with Wilson inspired a great deal of her work, she always denied that the characters in her stories and novels had anything to do with him.

At the end of her life, McCarthy, who survived Wilson and had the last as well as the first word, gave the same version of their marriage in her autobiography *Intellectual Memoirs* (1992) as she had in her fiction. This supposedly factual account attempted to validate the earlier imaginative transformations of their courtship and married life. The fundamental question about her marriage is the same one that every divorced woman faces, and that she had confronted, for therapeutic reasons, earlier in her fiction: how could she possibly have married, let alone loved, the Monster she now loathes? Her solution in the memoir is to deny that she had ever fallen in love with him. In an attempt to assuage her guilt, she claims that she continued to love Philip Rahv, whom she had betrayed during the first months of her affair with Wilson. Refusing to face the fact that she had indeed chosen Wilson, she cruelly attacks Wilson to punish him for her fateful decision to marry him and for the subsequent failure of their marriage. In the memoir, as in the fiction, she idealizes herself as young, beautiful and full of promise, her potential threatened (rather than enhanced) by a monster. The self-portrait of the victim of male oppression is a response to the *Zeitgeist* of the 1980s, not an accurate reflection of her relations with Wilson in the 1940s.

In "Ghostly Father, I Confess," her first fictional version of their marriage, the heroine Meg Sargent finally settles down and marries a bullying architect named Frederick. But she does not love him and has married him for all the wrong reasons: for his incomprehension, his blunt severity and his egoism. When, after a short time together, she tells him that she cannot go on with the marriage, he advises her, with icy, self-interested pragmatism: "Give up worrying about your imaginary sins and try to behave decently. You use your wonderful scruples as an excuse for acting like a bitch. Instead of telling yourself that you oughtn't to have married me, you might concentrate on being a good wife."

Meg's unhappy situation and irrational behavior lead to a psychiatrist's couch. Her doctor authoritatively explains that she has chosen precisely the kind of man who has forced her into the stifling pattern of her childhood and who makes her feel isolated and helpless: "[You] marry Frederick and imitate, as much as it's possible for a grown woman, your own predicament as a child. You lock yourself up again, you break with your former friends, you quit your job; in other words, you cut yourself off completely. You even put your money in his bank account. . . . His own insecurity makes him tyrannical and over-possessive; his fear of emotional expenditure makes him apparently indifferent." Her psychiatric treatment exacerbates rather than relieves the tensions of her marriage.

Instead of responding to these new insights, Frederick justifies his own actions and condemns Meg's behavior, using her shaky emotional history and her current mental illness to patronize and control her: "he was always talking about what he called her 'bad record,' a divorce, three broken engagements, a whole series of love affairs abandoned *in medias res.* . . . The fact of her illness . . . was invaluable to him as a weapon in their disputes. He was always in a position to say to her, 'You are excited, you don't know what you are saying,' 'You are not a fit judge of this because you are neurotic,' 'We won't discuss this further, you are not sane on the subject,' and 'I don't want you to see your old friends because they play into your morbid tendencies.'"[5] Though Frederick's statements have a certain validity, McCarthy, her finger on the scale, tilts the balance in Meg's favor and discredits it.

"The Weeds" (1950) was the first time-bomb to explode under Wilson after their marriage had ended. In this story the woman, oppressed by her husband's jealous hostility, wonders how many wives have poisoned their husbands "out of sheer inability to leave them." She does eventually leave him and flees to a hotel, but her husband finds her and brings her back home. She then discovers that he has neglected the garden in the same way as he had neglected her, that the weeds have taken over and that the garden—a symbol of her life—is ruined. Finally, she realizes that though part of her had dreamed of flight and deliverance—a recurrent motif in McCarthy's fiction about Wilson—"it was also this part which had created for itself the small mirages of duty and pleasure which had held her to him for five years." Though McCarthy portrays herself as a victimized heroine, she also acknowledges that she had once wanted the "duty and pleasure" of a secure marriage to a famous writer.

McCarthy's pen-portraits of Wilson became increasingly caustic. In *The Groves of Academe* (1952) she recreates Wilson as the Irishman Henry Mulcahy—contributor to the *Nation*, Guggenheim Fellow, man of superior intellect and specialist in Joyce, Proust and Marx—who is fired from his lowly position at a third-rate college. As usual, however, pretty Mary pitilessly emphasizes his physical defects and gross appetites—his pear-shaped body, drooping trousers and "sand sprinkling the lashes of his nearsighted, glaucous eyes." McCarthy not only describes him as unattractive, but also makes him quite conscious of his own ugliness. A "soft-bellied, lisping man with a tense, mushroom-white face, rimless bifocals, and graying thin red hair, he was intermittently aware of personal unattractiveness that emanated from him like a miasma." She also savages Wilson's taste for starches and sweets that accentuated his ovoid shape. He dearly loved "candy bars, frosted cupcakes, nuts and pickles, second helpings of mashed potatoes; he was defiantly conscious of a porous complexion, bad teeth, and occasional morning halitosis." Accustomed to admiration, McCarthy often judged people by their physical appearance. In her novel, she suggests that external ugliness is a direct reflection of internal evil.

When Louise Bogan read this novel, she disapproved of McCarthy's portrait. Remembering Wilson's descent from Cotton Mather, she told May Sarton: "it's a pity she had to disguise Edmund into such a *caricature*—with a *Jesuit* education: he is the most early American Protestant character I have ever known." After their divorce, Wilson kept his personal feelings apart from his literary judgment and praised Mary's work. When her novel appeared, he ignored the satire and gallantly told Vladimir Nabokov: "Mary's new book is very good—in some ways, the best thing she has done."[6]

In chapter thirteen of *The Group* (1963)—McCarthy's Memoirs of Vassar County—Kay Petersen accuses her drunken husband Harald, a failed playwright, of committing adultery. (In real life, *McCarthy*, not Wilson, was the adulterous one.) After Harald beats her and kicks her in the stomach—as McCarthy accused Wilson of doing in her legal deposition—Kay cracks up and Harald commits her to the Payne-Whitney Clinic, a private mental hospital in New York. Kay later admits that she never should have provoked Harald when he was drinking. In her fiction, McCarthy portrays herself as the victim rather than the instigator of the violence, and is put in the hospital to punish rather than to help her. Wilson made no attempt to defend himself against the libel in *The Group*. But, when discussing the best-seller that had catered to popular taste, he told Glyn Morris: "I'm not impressed with her writing. Her last book was not too favorably reviewed. I don't read her anymore."

McCarthy executed her most vitriolic portrait of Wilson in *A Charmed Life* (1955), where he appears as the heavy-drinking Miles Murphy—a grotesque version of Henry Mulcahy. (Both names are variants of the typically Irish "McCarthy.") Like Wilson, Murphy always reads books in their original language and has a weakness for intellectual women. He also had "three wives and innumerable mistresses and a couple of illegitimate children." Like Edward Dahlberg and Hart Crane, McCarthy exaggerates, with an explosive simile, Wilson's unattractive appearance: "He was a fat, freckled fellow with a big frame, a reddish crest of curly hair, and small, pale-green eyes, like grapes about to burst." In addition to being physically repulsive, which makes his marriage to the innocent Martha Sinnott (Sin-not) weirdly improbable, Murphy is also bad-tempered, gluttonous, selfish and demanding: "Miles, of course, thought only about his own comfort; he ate and drank like an Elizabethan . . . never considering for a minute that it was a human being who waited on him and catered to him and kept his things in order."

In *A Charmed Life* McCarthy, less willing than in her previous work to acknowledge Wilson's intellectual power, now emphasizes her own superior imagination and prose style: "he was forceful and energetic, with a gift for amassing information that was like his prodigies at the table. . . . He had no facility of expression. She herself, she now perceived, had qualities Miles envied: a sharp ear and a lively natural style. . . . She knew him, moreover, to be selfish, brutal, and dishonest in his domestic life."

Having established Murphy's appearance and character, McCarthy then takes up the vexing question of why Martha had slept with and married him. Murphy, reasonably enough, "supposed that she must love him because she had let him seduce her on the very first meeting and because she did not leave him though she continually threatened to do so." Martha repeatedly says she "had no explanation," she married him "without knowing why" and remained "totally mystified" about her motives. But her friend Dolly Lamb insists: "You *must* have been attracted to him." Dolly says that he reminded her of "everybody's father" and Martha admits that sleeping with him was "like sleeping with your wicked uncle." Yet Martha, recalling her love-making with Miles on a deserted beach, also admits that "she had a lot of sexual defenses" but "always liked it, in the end."

Though Martha does not understand the "deep urge in herself," McCarthy's conclusion—first stated in the novel and unconvincingly repeated in her memoirs forty years later—is that she was browbeaten into marriage, "violently against her will," in order to pay for sleeping with Wilson when she was drunk and when she was still in love with Rahv. In *A Charmed Life*, she writes:

> [He] started bulldozing her into marriage before she really knew him. It was what she needed, he assured her, appraising her with his jellied green eyes when she woke up, for the second time, in bed with him, after a lot of drinks. . . . He knew what was the best for her, doubtless—she needed a steadying force, a man, as he said, with a mind. . . . She would never, surely, have yielded to his

embraces, shrinking, as she did, from his swollen belly and big, crooked nose, if some deep urge in herself, which *he* seemed to understand, had not decreed it. The fatalistic side of her character accepted Miles as a punishment for the sin of having slept with him when she did not love him, when she loved, she still felt, someone else.[7]

McCarthy does, however, shed some light in this novel on another bizarre episode connected to Wilson. In the summer of 1953, when both of them had remarried, McCarthy returned to live in Wellfleet with her third husband, Bowden Broadwater, who liked to refer to Wilson as "my father-in-law." McCarthy casts a cold eye on Wilson's fourth wife, Elena Thornton, and portrays her as Martha's antithesis, a subservient *Hausfrau:* "This tall placid brunette girl simply worshipped Miles, which was what Miles always needed. Everything about him, apparently, was sacred to her, including his ex-wives."

But why, having embarked on a new—if not charmed—life, did McCarthy return to that small village where her ex-husband still lived, where everyone knew their past history and which was filled with so many unhappy memories? In the novel, Martha admits that her return was certainly risky and "in poor taste." Yet she feels that Murphy does not own the peninsula, wants to compete with him again and wishes to show the Murphys "how tawdry they are in comparison to us."

In 1980 McCarthy involved herself in a libel action by remarking during a television interview that every word Lillian Hellman "writes is a lie, including 'and' and 'the.'" But McCarthy herself could lie when it suited her. When her novel appeared in 1955 she tried to defuse Wilson's irritation by telling him: "I hope that you don't think that you're portrayed in *A Charmed Life*. My denials are fervid, if only on artistic grounds; I trust that I would not make such a bad likeness if I set out to do one." But she disingenuously contradicted herself on two other occasions. She told her biographer Doris Grumbach that her portrait was merely a comical exaggeration: "In some sort of joking way, it was as if I were saying to Edmund: 'Look what would happen to you if you were transposed by an evil fairy into this ghastly red-headed, self-analytic, jargon-speaking Irishman. This is what you'd be like.'"[8] Finally, in November 1955 she admitted to their mutual friend Arthur Schlesinger, Jr. that her gross caricature *was* meant to represent Wilson's worst qualities and reveal to the world what it was like to be married to a monster: "to the extent that Edmund is a boor and a four-flusher . . . Miles is a kind of joke extrapolation of him—minus the talent, minus the pathos. . . . I've used certain episodes, altered from my married life with E., as the raw material to create him, and I've drawn on my own feelings quite directly, in the chapter where Martha remembers her marriage. . . . Edmund has in common with Miles a capacity for behaving *incredibly*." McCarthy—famous for her clear-sighted intelligence and logical, penetrating mind—did not, after years of psychoanalysis, show much insight into her own motives and behavior.

Even in old age, after a lifetime of reflection, McCarthy was still unclear about if and why she had wanted to marry Wilson, and remained astonishingly imperceptive about one of the crucial emotional decisions of her life: "I could not accept the fact that I had slept with this fat, puffing man for no reason, simply because I was drunk. No. It had to make sense. Marrying him, though, against my inclinations, *made* it make sense." But according to her friend Eleanor Perenyi, "nobody could make Mary do what she didn't want to do." Following her inclinations, she frequently and eagerly slept with Wilson, drunk or sober. Though "St. Mary's wrath," in Norman Mailer's words, "was limned with brimfire," her Authorized Version of their marriage has remained unquestioned.[9]

III

McCarthy's letters to Wilson, the suppressed passages in his diaries and his legal deposition give a very different picture of their marriage. When Wilson first met McCarthy he was the most important man of letters in America and she was, by her own account, "a young, earnest, pedantic, pontificating critic, cocksure and condescending." Despite her close association with the Left-wing writers on the *Partisan Review*, all her "habits of mind were bourgeois." She had a sharp intellect and a clear prose style, but had not yet become a satirical observer of social nuance and had not yet produced the books that would make her famous.

Wilson's early letters to Mary—written when he was in Stamford and she in New York—mention the problems of his daily life, his sadness and his dreams. He writes that he misses her and wants to see her, but he is always matter-of-fact, never passionate. Mary's letters to Wilson were written during their courtship, during a visit to her family in Seattle and during her psychoanalysis in New York. After their legal separation, she wrote about their divorce, their financial arrangements and their child. In later years, she discussed her books and their mutual friends. Her retrospective view of their marriage ignored and denied her own powerful feelings. After re-reading her letters to Wilson she conceded: "Apparently I liked him much more than I remember, more than I ever would again." But she immediately added a disclaimer: "what I hear in the letters is not love, though—I never loved Wilson —but sympathy, affection, friendship. Later I grew to think of him as a monster; the minotaur, we called him in the family."[10] This image made her the captive and sacrificial maiden, trapped in his maze.

Yet her letters reveal that she *did* love Wilson, married him willingly and was, at least at first, quite happy with him. In November 1937 Wilson laconically wrote: "You left your book again.—I miss you." But on December 1, McCarthy described, in an exciting and flattering way, the powerful effects of their love-making:

> I am still *distraite*. My stomach bounces around and does odd, terrifying things, and my movements are jerky, my will relaxed, and I am full of dreamy abstraction. . . . I know I do miss you. You have dislocated me, in a way. I should like to hear from you so as to get some new bearings. At the moment, I feel out of touch on all fronts, suspended. . . . You are nice. I like you. I think about you pleasantly. I want very much to see you.

A week later, she said she was very amenable to his wishes: "What made you insist on my staying in bed with you? I am grateful to you for it now, for I did sleep a little." In mid-December she frankly expressed her feelings and told him exactly what he wanted to hear: "My dear, I miss you so much. I hope you will come to New York. I had a lovely time with you last night. . . . Kisses, Mary" and "I think you're wonderful. I miss you. Love, Mary."[11]

Soon after Christmas, sleeping with both men and torn by her own duplicity, Mary suddenly told Rahv that she was having an affair with Wilson and that he wanted to marry her. Her revelation, which Rahv accepted with surprising equanimity, strengthened her relations with Wilson. Throughout January, as Wilson won her by word as well as action, she told him that she loved him and was committed to him: "I am full of such lovely things to say to you. . . . Your letters make me dreamy. I think I must be a little bit in love. . . . I think you're wonderful. I can't resist saying it, naively, like that. . . . You mean more and more to me. It's perfectly dreadful. . . . I've missed you and thought about you all the time—have thought constantly how I wanted to tell you things, talk over people with you." Mary, the only one of his wives who was his intellectual equal, developed an uncanny instinct for knowing how his mind worked, and they felt so close at times that they even had parallel dreams.

As soon as they married and returned to "Trees," Wilson—who knew, before Mary did, that she had a talent for writing stories—set her up with a typewriter in the spare room. He encouraged her writing career as he had done with Wylie, Millay, Adams and Bogan. Always grateful for his recognition and encouragement, she later said: "I would never have written fiction, I think, if it hadn't been for him."[12] Their marriage, though tempestuous, was extraordinarily productive for both of them. Wilson edited Fitzgerald's *The Last Tycoon*, brought out a massive anthology of American literature and published five books, including three major works: *The Triple Thinkers*, *To the Finland Station* and *The Wound and the Bow*. McCarthy, who had a baby and went into analysis, still published sixteen articles, five stories, a memoir and a novel. They even collaborated on a poem about Spain, which Wilson published in *Note-Books of Night*.

Despite Mary's sexual entanglement with Rahv, both she and Wilson continued to publish in the *Partisan Review*. By May 1940, however, relations were strained. Wilson wrote to one of the editors, Frederick Dupee, defending his wife and complaining about the way they both had been treated: "I've thought there was something wrong in your shop ever since you passed up that short story of Mary's. You people owed her a chance to develop, since she was one of your original group." He was also intensely irritated when Dwight Macdonald first begged for a piece on Lenin and then rejected it and asked him to do something else. Drawing on his own experience at the *New Republic*, Wilson maintained: "You are developing all the symptoms of the occupational disease of editors—among them, thinking up idiotic ideas for articles that you want the writers to write instead of printing what they want to write." But the marriage of two talented writers also provoked tension and rivalry. His observation about Elinor Wylie and William Benét applied with equal force to McCarthy and himself: "I did not know then what bad results can follow from the competition of two writers or artists on anything like a plane of equality."

Though he realized that Mary was his temperamental opposite, he found her provocative and amusing. Their marriage was sometimes "nightmarish," but he always remained fond of her. He exacerbated her bad temper, however, by criticizing her cooking and the way she ran the house. "Mary longed for the constant reassurance that everything was perfect," Rosalind observed, "and my father was the last person to give it to her."

When their marriage was over and he sought consolation from other women, he told Anaïs Nin: "With Mary it was war. Even sex was a belligerent affair. It could never happen naturally and joyfully, in a relaxed way. There had to be some play-acting. There had to be a battle." He blamed their fights on her "fits of alienation" which "made life very difficult. I was always having to cover them up. I could not bear to write about it."[13] Wilson did not recognize Mary's emotional needs and could not respond to them. When he failed her, she fled to New York and found other lovers.

In addition to competing as writers, they fought about his dominance, his control of their money and his drinking; about her pregnancy, her mental problems and her infidelity. Wilson, completely absorbed in his work, tended to lecture rather than converse, and would sometimes lecture all through dinner. He would say to one friend: "I must give you my seminar on Dante" and ask another: "Have I told you about Swinburne?," and then talk brilliantly for an hour or more. He liked to control human relations, and at his own parties would retreat to the rear of his house and summon his guests, one by one, for individual talks. Soon after he met Mary, he threatened to give her a long lecture, if she agreed to submit, on Byron. This kind of talk was fascinating on occasion, but became quite intolerable when she had to listen to it every day. Nancy Macdonald, for one, was horrified at how Wilson dominated Mary and talked to his friends as if she were not there.

Mary had a private income of fifteen hundred dollars a year and that money, along with what she earned from her writing, was deposited in Wilson's bank account—to which at first she had no access. Though Wilson was stubborn and difficult to oppose, she took a stand on this issue and persuaded him to let her have her own account.

Though he rarely had hangovers, Wilson's heavy drinking often caused and intensified their quarrels, and he drank more when he was unhappy with Mary than ever before. He usually began to drink when his work day was over and continued after his guests had left at the end of the evening. He would play his favorite records, write up his diary and finish whatever liquor was at hand. But he would also strike out at Mary and with cruel words destroy her love for him.

Three of Wilson's friends gave vivid accounts of the consequences of his hard drinking during his marriage to Mary. Adelaide Walker said he was a binge drinker who would turn cruel when he was not stupefied: "He'd finish a piece of work and start drinking in a perfectly civilized way, and then he'd just go on and on. He'd drink everything in the house. This would last sometimes for several days. And he'd go to bed and be sick, and then wouldn't drink for a fairly long time. And he could also drink more or less normally at times. He didn't always go on and drink himself into a stupor. But Mary had a very difficult time because he'd be very mean and satirical." In December 1939 Allen Tate, whose tongue was as sharp as Mary's, told Bishop: "Dr. Wilson has never been quite human, and I am not surprised to hear that he has become a metabolic machine for the transformation of alcohol." Three years later, Bishop related a story he had heard from John Biggs, who was staying with Wilson and disapproved of his Leftist politics: "John and Bunny sat up late and did a good deal of drinking. After he got to bed—around 1:30—John heard Bunny fall down the cellar stairs. He sat up in bed. 'Is that Edmund Wilson, the critic?' he asked himself, preparing to rush to his rescue. 'No,' he said, 'that's the lousy communist to whom I have just been talking,' and went promptly to sleep. Communist or critic, Bunny was knocked out by the fall and didn't revive for some time."[14]

McCarthy later called Wilson a "tyrant and paranoid." But *she* was the one who had the mental breakdown and then accused him of persecuting her by seeking medical assistance. When they fought she certainly behaved irrationally. She once, by her own admission, set fire to a sheaf of papers and swept them under the locked door of Wilson's study. Her defense was that "one of his favorite ploys was to hit me and then run into his study and lock the door to escape retaliation: Wouldn't that drive you mad?"

Their first violent conflict took place four months after their marriage, on June 8, 1938. The night before, after heavy drinking with the Tates, Wilson, angry about the blue sheets she had put on their bed "as a surprise," tore them off and "bounced" her onto the floor. The following morning, after the Tates had left, "she claimed that Wilson had really hit her hard, striking her breasts and stomach," and she broke down "in a fit of uncontrollable weeping and vomiting." Wilson called the local doctor, who suggested she enter a New York hospital for a "rest." They took a taxi into Manhattan and Wilson committed her to the Payne-Whitney Clinic.

Mary was the only witness to the beating, which Wilson firmly denied. She may have wanted to explain what she felt was a shameful nervous breakdown by blaming it on him. If she was so terrified of the brutal Wilson, why did he have to run away from her and lock himself into his study? Wilson was capable of violence when he was drunk. But he was not drunk the next morning when he allegedly beat her, and there is no evidence that he ever struck any other wife or girlfriend (though he did slap Jean Gorman). Moreover, Mary's letters to Wilson during the three weeks she was in Payne-Whitney do not at all suggest that he had beaten her up and driven her into a breakdown. These letters, like the ones written during their courtship, express her love for him and suggest that he had the same sympathetic concern about her mental illness as he had for Louise Bogan's in 1931.

At first Mary assumed a chirpy attitude and compared her own experiences to his nervous breakdown in 1929: "Tonight we are going to have a Community Sing. I bet you didn't have that in *your* insane asylum." She also showed deep feeling for Wilson, who did not seem to be the villain in this episode: "I miss you and want you terribly. I'm awfully happy that I'm married to you and that we're going to have a baby.... I absolutely adore you. I think I should be extraordinarily fortunate if only I could be with you."

The doctors thought her illness was sufficiently serious to keep her under observation in the clinic for three weeks. She was discharged on June 29 with a vague diagnosis: "Without psychosis; anxiety reaction." Just after she returned from the hospital, they moved out of the gloomy "Trees" to a larger house at 233 Stamford Avenue on Shippen Point. Rosalind, who joined them for the summer on Long Island Sound but did not feel that Mary made her welcome in the house, witnessed their frequent quarrels. She thought that Mary did a great deal to provoke Wilson, who threatened to strike her but held back his hand. In any case, Rosalind said, "Mary was more than a physical match for my father."[15]

McCarthy's analysis with Sandor Rado, a Hungarian émigré, began in June 1938 and continued with several other doctors at least until 1942. Wilson wanted a child, but did not think they should have one when Mary was still mentally unstable. Recalling the unwanted pregnancy of Mary Blair, Wilson wrote to McCarthy while she was in

Payne-Whitney and urged her not to have the baby. He thought it would hurt their marriage and her treatment, that it would impoverish them, oppress her and interfere with her work:

> About the pregnancy question, I have thought it all over again and I can't come to any other conclusion but that you mustn't go through with a child at this time. It's a disappointment because we'd counted on having one but, after all, we can always have one; and in the meantime it will land you in a situation that you are really unprepared for. You want it very much when you are feeling good about things; but you are still in a generally stirred-up condition and I think you are somewhat confused about this as about other things. You oughtn't to be let in for relationships and responsibilities which you're not ready for at the present time and which might ruin your relationship with me as well as interfere with your psychoanalysis. . . . There are also the possible difficulties: with a baby you would be badly tied down and the expenses of baby and psychiatrist, too, would certainly be more than we could afford. I think, too, that you and I will get along better with the question out of the way: you won't find your situation with me closing down over you in so oppressive a way as I'm afraid you have.

Since they had both wanted the child *before* her breakdown, her claim that he kicked her in the stomach when she was pregnant seems doubtful. Her accusation may have been prompted by the fact that he wanted her to have an abortion *after* her breakdown.

But McCarthy, like Blair (and like Bill McGee in *The Crime in the Whistler Room*), decided to oppose Wilson and have the baby. Frances had aborted his child and Elizabeth Waugh had apparently given birth to his still-born infant. But his second child and only son, Reuel Kimball Wilson, was born on Christmas Day, 1938. The obscure name Reuel—which appears in Exodus 2:18, and means "friend of God" —had been in the family for generations. Wilson hired a nursemaid for the baby so Mary could get on with her work. They were drawn together by the infant and their marriage went more smoothly after his birth.

Pressed for money because of his new wife and child, Wilson reluctantly took a teaching job at the University of Chicago in the

summer of 1939. He watched with pleasure as the tomboyish Mary
—with "long legs, straight figure, olivish skin"—played baseball with
amused young men against the vivid green background of the university park. Twice during the summer the neighbors called the police
during their furious arguments. But when Mary left with the baby to
visit her family in Seattle, their letters were characteristically affectionate. Wilson was certain that "part of my decline has been due to the
trauma caused by your departure." He also teased her by writing:
"Maybe one reason your grandmother has been doing more for you is
that you have been so immensely improved under my guidance."

During their temporary separation, a financial crisis revealed their
very different ideas about money. The poet Elizabeth Bishop, who had
been at Vassar with McCarthy, emphasized how Mary and her first
husband had "worried about their *clothes;* endless discussions of new
spring outfits and pathetic interior-decoration schemes." Though it
was natural for an attractive young woman to want pretty clothes, both
Bishop and Wilson disapproved of Mary's bourgeois materialism,
which clashed with their own values—and with Wilson's lack of cash.
McCarthy complained that Wilson spent his money "on taxis, liquor,
long-distance phone calls. There was nothing left for clothes or furniture or jewelry, all of which I cared about." She was delighted that her
grandmother had bought her a fur coat. But when she told him she had
spent all her money in Seattle and mentioned how much money the gift
had "saved," Wilson, struggling to find their train fare back to the East
Coast, wrote her, with barely restrained anger: "You are not saving
anything on the fur coat, as I shouldn't have been able to buy it now in
any case. You have very strange ideas of economy. I am down to my last
dollar."[16]

After the summer in Chicago, the Wilsons rented a house in Truro,
on Cape Cod, for a year. They then returned to "Trees" from October
1940 until they moved into their house in Wellfleet in July 1941. The
following summer, while visiting John and Katy Dos Passos in Provincetown, Mary began to bleed and had a miscarriage. In late July, when
Wilson was staying at a hotel in Boston, he said that he had a particularly fine room and was longing to cheer her up and entertain her. But
when Mary spent four days a week in New York to see her psychiatrist,
Wilson felt abandoned and blamed all their troubles on her absence. As
Hemingway told Martha Gellhorn when she went abroad as a reporter:
"What old Indian likes to lose his squaw with a hard winter coming
on?"

Wilson had reason to be concerned. Though Mary, a good hostess, loved to have the Wellfleet house filled with literary luminaries, she flirted provocatively with all men, "behaved like a bitch" and was extremely unfaithful. According to Rosalind, she tried to seduce Dos Passos and the Harvard professor Theodore Spencer, became pregnant (and presumably aborted the child) with the translator Ralph Mannheim and had a well-known affair with the art critic Clement Greenberg. In September 1942 she wrote apologetically from New York: "Let us not try to rasp so much when I get back. I feel very sad about everything. . . . Dear Edmund, I am sorry about everything."[17]

Wilson's diaries cast some light on their marital relations in the early 1940s. His editor, Leon Edel, told Rosalind that "McCarthy's madness was implied in various passages of the forties diaries, but all this was cut out [at her insistence] by the lawyers who checked the ms for Roger [Straus] and I also removed some pages that seemed to me unpublishable." When Wilson visited Edna Millay and her husband, he noticed that Eugen Boissevain habitually babied her just as he himself used to do with McCarthy. The age difference, Mary's instability and her need for a strong father figure, forced Wilson into a paternal role. This made McCarthy confuse him with the hated uncle who had treated her terribly during her orphaned childhood: "I was cast as the horrid false father, her uncle, and the things that, in her hysteria, she would accuse me of were usually his crimes and not mine." He said she was childish, and in an unpublished passage from *The Forties*, described her paradoxical character as irresponsible yet dutiful, willful yet submissive. He also suggested the difficulty of living with her: "She was capable of much dignity of character, and this made her collapses tragic."

For McCarthy, in 1982, the most objectionable part of *The Forties* was Wilson's claim that she had identified him with her "wicked uncle." In this suppressed passage he called her "an hysteric of the classical kind who makes scenes. . . . She would accuse me, in her fits, of imprisoning her and of other offences which were quite inappropriate." Another suppressed passage of January 1, 1943, which Leon Edel (and no doubt McCarthy) felt was unpublishable, begins with his description of what seems to be cunnilingus and reveals that their sex life, throughout the turmoil of their marriage, was still pleasurable to both of them:

> *With Mary at the Little Hotel.* I invented, first, a trick of running my tongue around on the inside of her lips—then, a smooth unbro-

ken rotary motion that didn't have the element of jerkiness that brought you down to the ground—it was wonderful, almost like flying in a dream, and it carried her along, too. I began to intensify it by speeding up a little and pressing in—and she came before I did. Then I doubled up her knees and put her legs back over her body and drove in from above. I asked her if she enjoyed it, and she answered, "Couldn't you tell?" A wonderful transporting discovery. Afterwards my penis did not lose its stiffness and still felt as if it had some kind of enchantment on it, as if it had been dipped in an invisible magic fluid that could prolong in the organ withdrawn the magic that was in her—only gradually fading off. I am happy tonight.[18]

Their good sexual relations—"she had always liked it in the end"—as well as their weekly separations and his tolerance of her infidelity, defused their conflicts and enabled their troubled marriage to survive for seven years.

IV

In November 1946, when reviewing the plays of Eugene O'Neill and recalling the aggressive and violent effects of alcohol that had led to the greatest crisis in their marriage, McCarthy remembered "those rancorous, semi-schizoid silences," the obscurity of thought, dark innuendoes, flashes of hatred and "terrors of drink." Her legal deposition of 1945, which was repeated almost verbatim in chapter five of *A Charmed Life*, gives the fullest account of the most drunken fight of their marriage, which took place in Wellfleet in July 1944:

We had about eighteen people at the party. Everybody had gone home and I was washing the dishes. I asked him if he would empty the garbage. He said: "Empty it yourself." I started carrying out two large cans of garbage. As I went through the screen door, he made an ironical bow, repeating, "Empty it yourself." I slapped him—not terribly hard—went out and emptied the cans, then went upstairs. He called me and I came down. He got up from the sofa and took a terrible swing and hit me in the face and all over. He said: "You think you're unhappy with me. Well, I'll give you something to be unhappy about." I ran out of the house and jumped into my car.

Years later she gave an intensified version of the fight by stating that he had beaten her in Reuel's bedroom and that when Mary and Rosalind jumped into the car, which later ran out of gas at Gull Pond, "he had pursued them and crashed through a window in the front door." According to Rosalind, both Mary and Edmund were drunk, he was certainly not able to "throw her around" and their physical fight was an equal contest. Rosalind drove the old Plymouth to Gull Pond, where she and Mary had a midnight swim and—without running out of gas—returned home. Only then did Wilson accidentally put his hand through the glass near the front door.

McCarthy transformed this incident into an effective dramatic scene and portrayed herself as a victim. But she did not suggest what *she* had said or done at the party or afterwards—apart from slapping him in the face when he was drunk—to provoke Wilson's violent behavior. In *A Charmed Life*, however, Martha provokes a quarrel by waking Miles up from a sound sleep, telling him she is in love with another man and daring him to put her out of the house. It is quite possible that such a scenario occurred in real life. Perhaps McCarthy had flirted with the men at dinner and then, exhausted by her work at the party and infuriated by his mocking refusal to help her, enraged the jealous Wilson by taunting him about his unattractiveness and her love affairs.

This incident, coming on top of everything else, was almost—but not quite—enough to doom the marriage. McCarthy filed suit for "extreme cruelty" and sent Wilson a farewell note that blamed herself for the quarrels and for running away instead of trying to resolve their problems: "I'm afraid I don't see what else there is to do. Perhaps the fighting is mostly my fault, but that's not a reason for our staying together.... I'm sorry. This could probably be managed with less éclat, but the only way I can ever break off anything is to run away."

On July 13 Wilson tried to win her back by using the persuasive words that had always been the key to his success with women. Arguing in a poignant letter that it would be best for Reuel if they remained together for the rest of the summer, he promised to renounce sexual relations and give up alcohol. He too blamed himself for their quarrels. He reaffirmed his love for her, referred (in an unusual display of feeling) to his own childhood fears and gave his own explanation for the failure of their marriage:

> I make this suggestion: come back up here for the rest of the summer on a purely friendly basis. I promise you that I will not

drink anything all summer. I think it is hard on Reuel to wreck the family in the middle of the summer like this. . . .

I feel terribly badly about this, and I know that it was my fault that things got into such a mess. . . . It may be that you and I are psychologically impossible for one another. . . . I have really loved you more than any other human being. . . . It is true that, as lovers, you and I scare and antagonize each other in a way that has been getting disastrous lately (though sometimes I have been happier and more exalted with you than I have ever been with anybody). And when you make me feel that you don't want me, all my fears of not being loved, which I have carried all my life from child-hood, come out in the form of resentment.

I know that the difference in our ages is a real difficulty between us. I prevent you from doing things that are no longer to my taste but that are perfectly natural for you to want to do; and you don't sympathize with my miseries—like the death of old friends, bad habits and diseases of one's own, and a certain inevita-ble disillusion with the world that has to be struggled against. . . .

It wouldn't work out in the long run; but we could make other arrangements in the autumn. . . . I will do my best to be consider-ate and not nag you.[19]

Moved by his arguments, McCarthy returned to Wellfleet and somehow lasted until the end of the summer. In the autumn, when Wilson finally agreed to a separation, she returned to New York, to Clement Greenberg, to her psychiatrist and to her lawyer. Wilson was spending the winter in an old house on Henderson Place, at the end of East 86th Street, which had been stripped bare by McCarthy, "right down to the toilet paper." In mid-January he promised that he would not force her to live with him or fight for custody of Reuel, and said he always missed her terribly when they were on bad terms. John Biggs III wrote that his father, Wilson's Princeton classmate, "was called to arbitrate by both. . . . Each had a separate room in a New York hotel and father shuttled between rooms. They later wrote stories about how rotten the other was." In February they lined up their witnesses and began to prepare legal depositions that were virtually antithetical.

McCarthy emphasized Wilson's violent temper and ridiculous jeal-ousy. She stated that in front of their son Wilson had publicly (and truthfully) accused her of infidelity. She also swore that Wilson had repeatedly assaulted her when drunk: "Directly after our marriage I discovered that he was addicted to drink and our life together became a series of violent episodes. After I became pregnant, he began beating me with his fists, he would kick me out of bed and again when I was on the floor. A short time before our son was born he knocked me down in the kitchen and kicked me in the stomach. At times he would hold me down on the bed and when I opened my mouth to scream he would hit me in the face and about the body. I was distraught and did not know what to do in my condition."[20]

Wilson challenged her view of their marriage in a letter to a friend in February 1945: "Her way of seeing herself in a drama doesn't always make connection with reality. Lately she has been acting out a novel when she ought to be writing one." By September Wilson had changed his mind about Reuel and decided to fight for half-time custody of his son. Edmund had remained faithful to Mary and was bitterly hurt by her adultery. His eight-page deposition emphasized Mary's traumatic childhood, her hysteria and derangement, her violence and infidelity. Soon after they married she "began to have outbursts of temper and fits of hysterical weeping" and revealed her "double personality." She admitted that she talked "like a guttersnipe," and was very jealous of Rosalind. She identified Wilson with her tyrannical German uncle and committed many violent acts against *him*. She broke into his study, tore the pages of his books and "threw the paper and ink on my desk and all over the room." Several times "she broke things over my head, and once she drove a fork into my eye." Reduced to animalistic behavior, she would also "scratch me, bite me, and kick me in the testicles." She also gave Wilson "plenty of cause for jealousy. On one occasion, she went to New York by herself, slept with a young man she knew [Ralph Mannheim] and presently announced to me that she was pregnant, but she did not know whether by him or by me . . . [and] arranged to have an abortion performed." Wilson also swore, in February 1945, that "she seems to believe that I have attacked her and struck her on occasion when nothing of the sort has happened. . . . At no time did I ever attack her."[21]

Witnesses were unable to resolve the striking contradictions in their statements or determine who was telling the truth. Neither Hatty—the maid who had lived with them at "Trees"—nor Rosalind appeared in court. But Rosalind later agreed with her father that Wilson did not beat Mary and that her charges were based on delusions: "My father's lawyers wanted me to testify at his divorce trial, which I really didn't want to do. It wasn't until I got to the trial that I realized Mary was claiming I'd seen my father kick her in the stomach, which I hadn't. Mary was a big girl and strong physically. On occasion, her childhood trauma made her think she was about to be beaten, when she wasn't. She would wake up screaming, 'Don't hit me' when my father wasn't in the room."

Though none of Mary's witnesses had actually seen Wilson's alleged violence, two of her friends testified against his character in order to substantiate her charge of "extreme cruelty." Philip Rahv's wife Nathalie, though critical of Wilson, made accusations that were far less serious than McCarthy's: "[Wilson] appeared to take delight in scolding and upbraiding his wife for petty matters. He humiliated her in my presence and in the presence of other friends by attempting to belittle her efforts at running the household and performing her wifely duties. He was constantly asking her where his things were when it was perfectly obvious where they were." And Charley Walker's wife Adelaide, one of his oldest friends, hurt Wilson bitterly by appearing against him. Adelaide later wrote Wilson to explain her behavior. She could not understand Wilson's hostility to her friendship with Mary, felt loyalty to the weaker party in the dispute and believed she had acted on principle: "I would, of course, have preferred to make it all none of my business. I can't tell you how little anxious I was to be involved. But Mary was very much alone, and in many ways much weaker than you, and it seemed cowardly just to run away entirely. I would like to say that I am sorry if I wronged you, that it was not through ill-will, that I was wrong not to see you before I acted, and that I hope we can some day again be friends."[22]

Harry and Elena Levin said that McCarthy *did*, as Wilson claimed, have a mental breakdown. And Mary was certainly afraid that his testimony would convince the court that she was not fit to be a mother. But in the final divorce agreement of December 1946, she was awarded custody and agreed that Reuel would spend the summers with Edmund on the Cape. He retained the right to choose his son's schools (which led to some conflict when she changed the boy's school at the last minute in September 1945), and paid her "maintenance" of eighty-five dollars a week (later reduced to sixty dollars). Though McCarthy was very hard up in the 1950s, she tried to be a good mother and was always conscientious about Reuel's health, schools, tutoring, clothing and social life.

V

Wilson and McCarthy had agreed to settle their affairs in an amicable way. But in March 1946, when he received a divorce bill from Baer and Marks for $1,525, he adopted a caustic tone and became threatening about the custody of Reuel:

> I have seen almost nothing of him for more than a year and his grandmother has hardly seen him at all. I know how much satisfaction this kind of thing gives you, that you are always able to find excellent reasons for the unpleasant things that you do, and I know that I must be prepared to settle down to a lifetime of unpleasantness with you whenever Reuel is concerned. But I want to remind you that I am also in a position to make things difficult and uncomfortable for you, and that it is not a good thing for Reuel to be made an object of continued hostilities between us.

Both Wilson and McCarthy later revealed in conversations with friends that their wounds were still bitter. She often discussed Wilson with Arthur Schlesinger, Jr. and, using wry humor, narrated atrocity stories about how he had beaten her and tried to have her committed to an insane asylum. But she was always grateful for what he had done to help her as a writer. Whenever Walter Edmonds, a Talcottville friend, mentioned McCarthy, Wilson would contemptuously hiss. Mentioning McCarthy's aristocratic Polish lover to the Harvard historian Stuart Hughes, Wilson, who used vulgar expressions in a refined way, observed: "I have the impression that Mary has him by the balls." When discussing McCarthy with another upstate friend, who naively asked: "Didn't he think it was lucky when a couple shared similar interests?," Wilson tersely replied: "It was hideous."[23]

In November 1945 their mutual friend Katy Dos Passos, using her familiar name for Wilson, reported that he had always encouraged Mary's writing, while she had always tried to ruin his work: "poor Antix [Antichrist] talked all evening about his domestic sufferings which may have indeed been frightful beyond belief. He told me about his life with Mary from the beginning—it was hideous for years I guess and a good thing they have parted. Antix said she wanted to destroy him and his work. She has indeed undermined his work. (I thought so myself some time ago.) She kept telling him it was worthless and getting worse."

McCarthy frequently wrote about Wilson both during and after their marriage, but he "could not bear to write" about her. When Wilson published his fictional *Memoirs of Hecate County* in 1946, the year of their divorce, John Cheever reported that Mary was extremely anxious about whether she had been satirized in that book. Though McCarthy does not appear directly in the stories, her unhappy relations with Wilson inspired his belief that "all American women are Harpies," and he portrayed all the women in that misogynistic book—except Anna and possibly Jo Gates—as witches.

Four years later, in his play *The Little Blue Light*, Wilson portrayed McCarthy as Judith, an aggressive, cold-blooded career-girl and unfaithful wife of Frank, the crusading journalist. Wilson's psychological explanation of Judith's character matches the one he gave in his deposition. Her parents had died when she was six and she had never recovered from the shock of that loss; she irrationally identified her husband with her dead father and worked off her grudge against the parent who had rejected her by dying. She tries to humiliate Frank and break down his confidence. Another character exposes Judith's spurious feminism by stating: "She's one of these modern women who want to have an equality for the sexes, but they *don't* have the same sense of honor as men." He also tells her: "You want to compete with men, yet you expect them to treat you with chivalry, and what a horrid yowl you set up when anybody tries to slap you down." Finally, he condemns her for emotional and sexual frigidity: "You're incapable of loving anyone—I'm sure you've never had even a single moment of genuine physical passion."[24]

Wilson's motives for marrying (after a brief courtship) the young, beautiful and intelligent McCarthy are obvious. But her motives for "the most dangerous action she had ever performed as an adult" have been distorted rather than illuminated by her writings about him. Delmore Schwartz, a member of the *Partisan Review* group, who could always be relied on for a sardonic remark, "told everyone that Rahv had been so vehement in praising Wilson's critical acumen that the ambitious McCarthy was impelled to switch allegiance." In her deposition of February 1945, which sounds like a cross between a love-lorn advertisement and a marriage manual, McCarthy gave several good reasons for her decision: "Before we married, he gave the appearance of a man of quiet habits with an interest in books, pictures, and music. He was well-known as a literary critic and I had admired his work even before I met him. During his courtship he held out great promise of a quiet settled life and the rearing of a large family."

Like Hemingway's third wife, Martha Gellhorn, the young McCarthy was talented, ambitious and recently divorced. Both women wrote extensively about their famous husbands and used them to advance their careers; both claimed their marriage was over as soon as it began. Martha competed with Hemingway as a writer, refused to accept a submissive role and finally left him. Mary, however, was more tolerant of Wilson's vexatious behavior and lasted much longer than Martha. But McCarthy persistently attacked Wilson: in Wellfleet, where they had lived when married; in conversations with mutual friends; in her fiction and memoirs. Her fiction was a form of therapy in which she continued to fight the old battles. Though full of rancor against Wilson, McCarthy's fiction is a tribute to the power of his personality and a testament of her feeling for him.[25]

Despite considerable unhappiness, McCarthy gained many advantages from her marriage to Wilson, who had an upper-class background, a first-rate education and formidable intellect. Like Martha Gellhorn, she benefited greatly from her husband's wide circle of friends as well as from his prestige in the literary world, which carried her far beyond the narrow backbiting of the *Partisan Review* circle. He recognized her talent and gave her valuable encouragement at the start of her literary career and inspired the fictional characters in five of her books. Despite her later denials, she fell in love with Wilson, enjoyed their sexual relations and had with him her only child. When they met in Paris in 1963 they summed up their essential problem. She regretfully said, "I was too young," and he sadly answered, "I was too old."[26]

TWELVE

Wellfleet, 1940–1942

I

Wilson's constant battles with Mary McCarthy seemed to stimulate him. While married to her in the early 1940s he taught at the University of Chicago and at Smith College, bought a house in Wellfleet, planned and wrote part of an unfinished novel, edited two posthumous works by Scott Fitzgerald and brought out five other books.

Wilson warmly praised the learning and dedication of his favorite teachers, but was generally hostile to academics, who failed to meet his high standards. The academy was respectful and gave him some recognition. In the early Thirties he had twice judged the Avery Hopwood Awards at the University of Michigan and served on the literary committee of the Guggenheim Foundation. He had lectured at Vassar when McCarthy was a student in 1932 and, after the successful reception of his recent books, gave talks in the late 1930s and early 1940s at Princeton, Columbia, Yale and Middlebury College.

He loathed teaching but, burdened by a family and pressed for money, reluctantly turned to universities as a source of income. He tried for a job at Cornell and turned down an offer from Yale; taught in the Gauss Seminars at Princeton (fall 1952) and at the Salzburg Seminar in Austria (February 1954); was the Abbott Lawrence Lowell Professor at Harvard (1959–60) and a Fellow of the Center for Advanced Studies at Wesleyan (1964–65). Plagued by debts in the mid-1960s, he spoke at the YMHA in New York and at Utica College, near his home in upstate New York.

Several of Wilson's prep school and college friends were professors: T. K. Whipple was at Berkeley, Alfred Bellinger and Charley Walker at Yale. Later on, his upstate friends included John Gaus from Harvard, Malcolm Sharp from Chicago and Loran Crosten from Stanford. Wilson certainly admired a few outstanding scholar-teachers:

Gauss and Kemp Smith, Saintsbury and Whitehead among the older generation; Morton Zabel and Newton Arvin, Harry Levin and Mario Praz among the younger critics.

With these rare exceptions, Wilson believed that teaching in universities put writers to sleep. He thought English professors were lazy, read only what they had to study for their courses, knew nothing outside their specialty, were devoid of taste and had no real interest in literature. Worst of all were the Oxbridge dons, who were recognized as authorities without ever publishing anything at all. Irritated by their fraudulence, Wilson devised an effective method of revealing their limitations. He would "cut in with some opinion, offhandedly and freely expressed, which is quite outside the scholar's gambits and would cause him to gasp and sulk." Wilson especially disliked the pretentious academic journals, like *Sewanee* and *Kenyon*, which returned the compliment by rejecting his work. His blunt condemnations—as well as his plain style, wide-ranging interests, copious publications and historical approach to literature in the age of New Criticism—did not endear him to the professorial sodality.

Yet Austin Briggs, an upstate professor, thought that Wilson, "for all his well known antagonism to the academic world . . . was actually very happy when he visited Hamilton College from time to time and got a good dose of academic shop talk. When I once asked Wilson why he had not enjoyed teaching, he told me that he hated being asked by students about books he had not read." Ironically, though much more widely read than most professors, Wilson felt somewhat insecure among the dull grey mass of Ph.D.'s.

Wilson also disliked the classroom because he was, by his own admission, a poor public speaker. He felt anxiety and even panic when he had to perform, would stutter nervously and become emotionally exhausted. He usually refused invitations from respected friends like William Fenton, explaining that he did not "do that sort of thing."[1] Wilson had a strong didactic streak and loved to lecture, address, correct, stimulate, exhort and encourage his friends—but he was not a good teacher. Though effective with his intellectual equals, his personal reserve and aloofness, the sense of his own integrity, prevented him from taking the steep descent to the level of his pupils.

In February–March 1939, a few months after Reuel was born, Wilson told Gauss that the University of Chicago had offered him $1,200 to teach two five-week terms during their summer session. He taught courses on "Varieties of Nineteenth-Century Criticism," including Taine and Marx; on Charles Dickens; and on "Research in English Literature, 1800–1900." At Wilson's urgent request, he was paid $600 in advance, and rented a flat at 5707 South Kimbark Avenue in the Hyde Park section of Chicago. The chairman of the department was the eighteenth-century scholar Ronald Crane. But Wilson probably got the job through Morton Zabel—a close friend of Louise Bogan—whose work he had published in the *New Republic* in 1938. The shy and gentle Zabel was born into a Catholic family in Minnesota in 1901, had taught at Loyola University before coming to Chicago and was an editor of *Poetry* magazine.

Wilson's first impressions were favorable. He contrasted the intense intellectuals at Chicago to the stagnant old dullards at Princeton and thought that the students were more serious, lively and up-to-date than the ones on the East Coast. He told Louise Bogan that he was having a good time and lecturing pretty well, and gave a more detailed tyro's report to his old mentor Christian Gauss: "I had a very good time at Chicago and got on very well with my classes (I liked the Middle Western students). I got used to talking on my feet and could hold them all right through my double classes of an hour and a half at a stretch. I made it all more or less informal."

Saul Bellow, who had studied Wilson's works, noticed the generosity beneath his gruff exterior: "Wilson had opened my eyes to the high culture of modern Europe, and on that account I was in his debt. I had met him in Chicago when he was hauling a heavy Gladstone bag on Fifty-seventh Street near the university, hot and almost angry, shining with sweat and bristling at his ears and nostrils with red hairs. . . . His voice was hoarse and his manner huffy, but he was kindly and invited me to visit him."

Most of the students, however, thought the incorrigible monologuist "was boring. One complained that Wilson did not seem to like the intellectual give-and-take, a trademark of the Chicago method." By mid-August, when McCarthy was in Seattle, Wilson's attitude changed from enthusiasm to disgust. He disliked spending time on teaching instead of on writing. He hated the flat more than any other place he had ever lived in. Apart from Zabel and the novelist Norman McLean, he was bored and exasperated by his colleagues in the English Department and could not wait to pull out.

While Mary was with her family, the sixteen-year-old Rosalind moved into his flat. She had just graduated from Wyckham Rye school in Connecticut, and had spent the summer living in a University of

Chicago dormitory, drinking milkshakes and going to the movies. When Wilson tried to teach her to memorize a poem every day, she stubbornly resisted; they both became emotional and there was a great deal of shouting at each other. She would soon enter Bennington College in Vermont, where Léonie Adams was teaching. At Bennington Rosalind waited on tables, won a *Mademoiselle* story contest, felt restless amidst all the arty talk during the war and—against her father's wishes—left without graduating.

Wilson tried his best to be a good father. He went swimming, bicycling and horseback riding with Rosalind, took her to the movies, the circus and the zoo, and to some deadly dinners with colleagues in the department. Despite strenuous efforts, he was distant and demanding, and felt he was not giving Rosalind the kind of normal family life she ought to have. Their most successful excursion was a visit to his cousin Dorothy Mendenhall, a pediatrician in Madison, Wisconsin. She had graduated from Smith College the year Wilson was born, and earned a medical degree at Johns Hopkins, where she was a classmate of Gertrude Stein. He was immensely curious to see her and, he told McCarthy, "She turned out to be wonderful. It is a pity we didn't go up together. She is very handsome, very intelligent and an excellent talker —keeps a marvelous house with marvelous meals—the most attractive house I have seen for ages—I wish we had one like it. . . . I had long conversations with her on politics, academic affairs, Gertrude Stein, Auden & Co., marriage and child rearing, and the family—about whom she is more illuminating than anybody except myself." Ruth Schorer, who grew up in Madison, took a much more critical view of Wilson's cousin. She thought that Dorothy was dominant, opinionated and self-righteous, and that she strongly disapproved of Edmund's bohemianism.[2]

Though Wilson did not want a permanent job, he continued his flirtation with universities. In early December 1941, shortly after he had bought and renovated the Wellfleet house, he had an offer of $6,000 to teach for a year at Cornell. The job would solve his financial problems, but he knew from his experience at Chicago that he could not teach two courses and write at the same time. While he was pondering his decision, America entered the war, Cornell cut back its budget and Wilson had to look for another job.

In the spring of 1942 Mina Curtiss, who later edited Proust's letters, took a leave of absence from Smith, a small women's college in central Massachusetts, and suggested that Wilson replace her for the fall semester. The two American literature scholars on the faculty, Newton Arvin and Daniel Aaron, supported her recommendation, and Wilson was hired for twelve weeks as Lecturer in English for $1,500.

Dividing his time between Wellfleet and Northampton, Wilson each week gave a public lecture, a two-hour seminar and a three-hour course, with nineteen students, on James Joyce. His over-ambitious plan for the undergraduate class was to approach *Ulysses* and *Finnegans Wake* through a preliminary study of Virgil, Dante, Shakespeare, Pushkin and the history of the novel, which took up the first half of the course. The Russian poet fascinated Wilson but had nothing to do with Joyce, and he could not possibly have covered Joyce's long and complex novels in the remaining six weeks.

Wilson's lectures and seminar concerned a rather abstract subject —"the representative powers of language"—which he illustrated with examples from Virgil, Milton, Pope, Flaubert and Joyce. Daniel Aaron, who became a friend that year, was dismayed by Wilson's performance in the classroom. He lost his natural eloquence, and would huff and puff when he read aloud. He could not break through his own formal reticence, and had no idea how to reach, interest and influence students.

At Smith, as at Chicago, Wilson at first liked teaching, though it took up more time than he had expected, and then turned against it when his classes became unbearably tedious. In April 1943, soon after he left Smith, he told Helen Muchnic, a colleague in Russian literature: "I am strongly reacting against academic communities after trying to do something with teaching and rather enjoying it at first. Now I've decided that the whole thing, for a writer, is unnatural, embarrassing, disgusting, and that I might better do journalism, after all, when I have to make money."[3] This attitude was tested, two months later, when he was asked to lecture on Russian literature at Yale, which had expanded their Slavic courses as the Red Army defeated the Nazis on the eastern front. They offered him a full-time job, but he wanted to concentrate on his writing and refused.

II

Wilson conceived the idea of *To the Finland Station: A Study in the Writing and Acting of History* (1940) while walking the streets of New York in 1934. It suddenly seemed to him that "nobody had ever presented in intelligible human terms the development of Marxism and the other phases of the modern idea of history." Just as the title "The Men from Rumpelmayer's" came from *Mrs. Dalloway*, so the title of *To the Finland Station* was influenced by Virginia Woolf's *To the Lighthouse* (1927).

The Finland Station, like Axel's Castle, was a symbolic monument. Lenin came through Germany to the St. Petersburg terminal, where the trains arrive from Finland, to start the Bolshevik Revolution in April 1917. Wilson saw the building on his trip to Russia in 1935 and found it rather disappointing. It was "a little shabby stucco station; rubber-gray and tarnished pink, with a long trainshed held up by slim columns that branch where they meet the roof." In the decade between *Axel's Castle* and *To the Finland Station*, his quintessential books of the Twenties and Thirties, Wilson shifted his interest from Modernism to Marxism, and moved from the inner to the outer world, from withdrawal to engagement. In doing so, he paid his debt to the Socialist movement of the 1930s and sparked the subject of Marxism into life.

Wilson did not write a much-needed preface to guide the reader through the complex argument of his most ambitious book. Part I, on the tradition and decline of bourgeois revolutionary ideas in nineteenth-century France, deals with the lives and historical writings of Jules Michelet, Ernest Renan, Hippolyte Taine and Anatole France. Part II—on the development of Socialist thought in France, England, America and Germany—concerns François Babeuf, Saint-Simon, François Fournier, Robert Owen, Prosper Enfantin, Ferdinand Lassalle, Michael Bakunin, Karl Marx and Friedrich Engels. In Part III of this dialectical structure, the ideas discussed in the earlier parts of the book achieve a synthesis in the revolutionary personalities of Lenin and Trotsky, who arrived in Russia to take charge of History. *To the Finland Station* revealed how ideas were transformed into action and showed that the Russian Revolution was an intellectual as well as an historical event.

Wilson was not admitted to the Marx-Lenin Institute in Moscow and did no original research on unpublished material in libraries and archives. He relied on printed matter in four languages, and specifically acknowledged his debt to Max Eastman's *Marx, Lenin and the Science of Revolution* (1926), Sidney Hook's *From Hegel to Marx* (1936) and E. H. Carr's *Michael Bakunin* (1937). Like Samuel Johnson, Wilson "turned over half a library to make one book." Louise Bogan told Morton Zabel that "he has read every word Michelet ever wrote, including his letters:

the 86 volumes (or so) are neatly piled along his study." Wilson's exhaustive research, his inclusive range, his mastery of complex ideas, his vigorous prose style, his effective alternation between biographical and political analysis, enabled him to surpass his predecessors and write the authoritative history of the revolutionary tradition in Europe.

In 1934, when Wilson began writing the book, he explained his historical method to Malcolm Cowley, who would publish many parts of it in the *New Republic*. The difficulty, Wilson found, was to offer a Marxist interpretation of certain writers while allowing them to maintain their own intellectual integrity: "About Michelet, my problem in the first section of the *Finland Station* is to present the non-Marxist French Revolutionary bourgeois writers from the point of view of my own Marxist lights and yet give an illusion of how the world looked to them and what they thought they were doing—so that I don't overtly bring the Marxist analysis to bear at all except when it is absolutely necessary."[4]

Wilson had an uncanny ability to find the vivid details that would —"in intelligible human terms"—bring the characters and their books to life. Saint-Simon "led a life of dissipation, from motives, he said, of moral curiosity," and when "dying in 1825, he declined to receive one of his relations for fear of breaking his train of thought." Lassalle "had a low opinion of his mother, whom he once described as 'the goose that had hatched out an eagle's egg.' " After years in solitary confinement, "Bakunin had scurvy, lost all his teeth, became stupefied and flabby." Lenin "crossed from Sweden to Finland in little Finnish sleighs." Wilson is especially good on Marx's poverty and desperate family life, and on the deaths of his children. "The pride and independence," Wilson writes of Marx, in an eloquent passage, "the conviction of moral superiority, which gave his life its heroic dignity, seem to go back to the great days of Israel and to be unconscious of the miseries between." Wilson is also capable of packing the essence of the *Communist Manifesto* into a few sentences: it "combines the terseness and trenchancy of Marx, his logic which anchors the present in the past, with the candor and humanity of Engels, his sense of the trend of the age.... It compresses with terrific vigor into forty or fifty pages a general theory of history, an analysis of European society and a program for revolutionary action."[5]

To the Finland Station, one of Wilson's greatest achievements, also has certain limitations. Michelet is given a disproportionate amount of space while Hegel, who should have been a central figure in the book, is scarcely discussed. Wilson admitted this weakness in a letter to Gauss of June 1937. Since Wilson disliked abstract ideas (the works he discussed in the book were rooted in historical reality), he simply avoided the subject instead of following his usual practice and working it up: "My great handicap, I find, in dealing with all this is my lack of grounding in German philosophy. Dialectical Materialism, which was in revolt against the German idealistic tradition, really comes right out of it; and you would have to know everybody from Kant down to give a really sound account of it. I have never done anything with German philosophy, and can't bear it, and am having a hard time now propping that part of my story up."

Wilson's attitude to Russia changed dramatically during the six years he spent writing the book. In 1934 he was still sympathetic to the Communists; after his trip to the Soviet Union in 1935 he became quite disillusioned; the Purge Trials that began in 1936 and Stalin's treacherous role in the Spanish Civil War made him increasingly hostile. Yet Wilson could not abandon his romantic and idealistic view of Lenin —based on the myth-making memoirs published by Trotsky and many others in the Soviet Union—which had originally inspired his own work. Though his Lenin "was one of the most selfless of great men," Wilson finally saw Russia as a land of oppression, murder and bloodshed. As he wrote in the Introduction to the 1971 reprint of *To the Finland Station:* "[I] did not foresee that the new Russia must contain a good deal of the old Russia: censorship, secret police, the entanglements of bureaucratic incompetence, an all-powerful and brutal autocracy. . . . I had no premonition that the Soviet Union was to become one of the most hideous tyrannies that the world had ever known, and Stalin the most cruel and unscrupulous of the merciless Russian tsars."

In order to maintain a positive view of the men and ideas that led to the Revolution, Wilson had to conclude the book when Lenin arrived in Russia, in April 1917, at the height of his idealistic ambitions. But the logical conclusion of his book was Stalin, not Lenin. In October 1939 Wilson regretfully told Bogan: "I am about to try to wind up the Finland Station (now that the Soviets are about to annex Finland)."[6] It would have been more convincing and meaningful to describe the current history of these Marxist ideas—which, perverted by the Soviets, were among the most pernicious in the history of mankind—and to conclude the book in 1939 with the Russo-Finnish War.

The long-gestated book appeared at the wrong historical moment. The thesis of *To the Finland Station*, which came out between the

Hitler-Stalin Pact (August 1939) and the German invasion which brought Russia into the war (June 1941), seemed as obsolete in September 1940 as *Axel's Castle* had been at the beginning of the Depression. During the month the book was published, Germany, Italy and Japan signed military and economic pacts, the Italians triumphed in Libya, the French failed to occupy Dakar, London was heavily bombed and Britain lost 106,000 tons of shipping. The heirs of the Russian Revolution, which Wilson praised as one of the great moments of history, quietly watched the Nazis invade, occupy and destroy most of Europe.

The Communist *New Masses* predictably attacked Wilson's essay on Marx, which deviated from the Party line and appeared in the *New Republic* before the book came out. It condemned as defeatist his "pseudo-Marxist counsel of despair and retreat" and called the essay "a specialized literary service to fascism." Throughout the late 1930s Wilson was frequently excoriated by the Left for turning against Communism. But the more impartial reviewers recognized his superior intellect and scholarship. Sidney Hook stated that he was "acquainted with nothing in any language which equals the insight, the eloquence and essential justice of Mr. Wilson's biographical account of Marx." Leonard Woolf observed that though Wilson was more interested in men than in ideas, his study of Marxist thought "got hold of an important historical fact or principle, and widened your knowledge of past, present and future events."

Harcourt Brace paid a $1,700 advance for *To the Finland Station* —less than $300 for each year he worked on it—and Wilson had spent the money long before he finished the book. The sales of his last three books with that firm had all been disappointing and he felt it was time to move on. By January 1947, Harcourt had sold 1,831 copies of *Travels in Two Democracies*; 2,337 copies of *The Triple Thinkers* (for which they paid an advance of $500); and 4,527 copies of *To the Finland Station*. The following month Harcourt, which still had 350 copies of Wilson's last book, sold the rights of all three works to Doubleday for $770: $500 for plates and rights, $270 for an outstanding loan to Wilson. Doubleday reprinted *To the Finland Station* in 1947, but it did not really take off until it was published by Anchor Books in 1953 and reprinted in 1955 and 1958. In 1963 Wilson noted that during the Cold War it had been circulated abroad by the State Department, in both English and Italian editions, to reveal the Communist threat. In 1971 he wrote an Introduction to a Farrar, Straus reprint of the book, whose value seemed to increase with the passing years. But by then he had lost interest in the ideological wars of the Thirties. As he wrote in "On Excavating My Library":

The Marxism I mastered at Stamford, Conn.,
Now bores me, though once deeply brooded upon.[7]

III

During the early 1940s Wilson once again became involved in editing Fitzgerald's work. On October 25, 1938 Fitzgerald, who had been working in Hollywood for the past year, had visited Wilson at Shippen Point in Stamford and introduced him to his new English girlfriend, Sheilah Graham. Struck by the dramatic change in Scott's character, Wilson attributed his new normality and tameness to Sheilah, who had persuaded him to give up alcohol. At the same time, Wilson held Zelda, now confined to a mental hospital, responsible for Scott's crazy behavior. He told Gauss that Fitzgerald, though calm, had lost a good deal of his old vitality: "He doesn't drink, works hard in Hollywood, and has a new girl, who, though less interesting, tends to keep him in better order than Zelda. . . . He seems mild, rather unsure of himself, and at moments almost banal."

Mary McCarthy, seven months pregnant with Reuel, was astonished by Fitzgerald's ignorance about politics. She found him boring and was struck by what she regarded as Wilson's arrogant condescension toward his old friend. Fitzgerald seemed to accept this and, after their meeting, resumed his youthful role as Wilson's disciple. "Believe me, Bunny," he wrote, stressing as always Wilson's superior intellect, "it seemed to renew old times learning about Franz Kafka and latter things that are going on in the world of poetry, because I am still the ignoramus that you and John Bishop wrote about at Princeton." Wilson's intellectual influence continued until the end of Fitzgerald's life. Budd Schulberg recalled that Fitzgerald, influenced by Wilson's study of Marx, would sit in the California sunshine reading *The Eighteenth Brumaire* "like an eager sociology student bucking for an A in Bunny Wilson's class in social consciousness."[8]

If Wilson seemed prematurely old in his thirties, Fitzgerald in his mid-forties still looked quite young. Wilson was deeply shocked when Fitzgerald died of a heart attack on December 21, 1940. Just after he had heard the news, Wilson told Zelda how closely he identified with

Fitzgerald, who had the emotional sympathy and intuitive understanding so lacking in his own character. The following month, Wilson associated Fitzgerald with the great masters—Yeats, Freud, Trotsky and Joyce—who had died since 1939. Remorseful that he had not fully reciprocated Scott's friendship and appreciated his genius, Wilson compensated for scorning Scott in his lifetime by single-handedly reviving his reputation after he died. "I patronized Scott," he admitted, "and said a lot of things about him that *The Great Gatsby* was to prove false. . . . I have always greatly admired that passage at the end of *The Great Gatsby*. In fact, I think the whole last ten or twelve pages are one of the best things in the American prose of this period. His unfinished novel about Hollywood is most remarkable—returns to the more concentrated and objective vein of *Gatsby* rather than to his romantic vein." In February and March 1940 Wilson published in the *New Republic* five commemorative essays and poems on Fitzgerald. He edited and supplied the title for *The Last Tycoon* (1941), and also edited Fitzgerald's uncollected essays, notebooks and letters (more than half of them to Wilson) in *The Crack-Up* (1945).

His death led Wilson to revaluate Scott's works. When he saw a revival of *The Vegetable*, he changed his mind and decided it was "terrible." Writing to Perkins in February 1941 and forgetting the psychiatrist-hero of *Tender is the Night*, he said that *The Last Tycoon* was "the only one of Scott's books that shows any knowledge of any field of human activity outside of dissipation." His two-page Foreword said it was "Fitzgerald's most mature piece of work" and, rating it higher than West's *The Day of the Locust*, called it "the best novel that we have had about Hollywood." For Wilson, the unfinished work had almost the look of a classic. Unlike most critics of the 1940s, he thought Scott would "stand out as one of the first-rate figures in the American writing of the period."[9]

In a letter to Gauss, Wilson praised the seriousness and technical skill of *The Last Tycoon:* "I think it would have been in some ways his best book—certainly his most mature. He had made some sort of new adjustment to life, and was working very hard at the time of his death. He had written the last pages the day before he died of a heart attack. In going through his MSS and notes, I was very much impressed to see what a conscientious artist he had become." Wilson not only wrote a Foreword to the novel, but also disentangled the manuscript and summarized the unfinished part of the book. His reconstruction of Fitzgerald's notes, which suggested how the fragmentary novel would develop and conclude, was absolutely brilliant. When the novel was published in October 1941, Sheilah Graham told Wilson: "It seems to me that you have described *exactly* all of Scott's ideas and schemes for the rest of the book. It clarifies everything he ever said to me on the novel." Wilson did not accept payment for his considerable work, but asked Scribner's to credit $500 to Fitzgerald's account for the benefit of his daughter Scottie.

Wilson's editorial work on *The Crack-Up* was also extensive and important. He told Max Perkins that he had hated Fitzgerald's confessional essays when they first appeared in *Esquire* in 1936. They must have reminded him, in a frightening way, of his own alcoholism and nervous breakdown in 1929. After Fitzgerald's death, however, he admitted that "there was more truth and sincerity in it, I suppose, than we realized at the time." But the strait-laced Perkins felt Fitzgerald had damaged himself with his self-autopsy and funeral sermon, and Scribner's refused to publish the book. Wilson then offered *The Crack-Up* to William Matson Roth at the Colt Press in San Francisco, who had brought out two of his own minor works in the early 1940s and also wanted to publish Fitzgerald.[10] Eventually the book was accepted by James Laughlin at New Directions, who had published Vladimir Nabokov's *Nikolai Gogol* in 1944.

Wilson not only edited *The Crack-Up* and negotiated with three publishers, but also had to deal with John Biggs, with the agent Harold Ober and with Scottie, all of whom represented Fitzgerald's estate; try to arrange permission to publish letters from Eliot, Stein, Hemingway and the film director Joseph Mankiewicz (he failed with the last two); and determine the fees of the writers who had paid tribute to Fitzgerald.

Wilson's work was made even more difficult by his conflict with Laughlin. Wilson told Biggs, with considerable exaggeration, that Laughlin—who could be exasperating and was known more for his good taste than for his efficiency at business—"has a mental age of about 14 and is considered by those who knew him to be on the verge of dementia praecox." He also wrote Edward Dahlberg, who hated all publishers, that Laughlin had "behaved so badly about Scott Fitzgerald's *Crack-Up* that I announced to him that I would never have any more dealings with him." Under pressure from Biggs and Ober, Wilson had made a number of cuts in the text that were restored by Laughlin, who convincingly argued that "Your trust consists in giving the world an un-tampered-with version of what [Fitzgerald] left. How would you like to have somebody scissoring your notes when you were dead?"[11] After much bad feeling, Laughlin eventually prevailed. (When Wilson arranged his own diaries for posthumous publication, he instructed his executors, as Laughlin had predicted, to publish every word he had written.)

Wilson's work on Fitzgerald led to thoughts on his intimate relations with the man and his work. In Wellfleet in February 1942 he wrote one of his most ambitious poems, "On Editing Scott Fitzgerald's Papers," and used it as the Dedication to *The Crack-Up*. The opening of the elegy, influenced by the description of the Atlantic gale in Yeats' "A Prayer for My Daughter," mentions that Wilson had edited his friend's manuscripts from the very beginning until the very end of Fitzgerald's literary career. His life's work, it seemed, was to correct and improve that errant genius. But even in the memorial poem, Wilson inappropriately portrays him in a vulgar and narcissistic moment. At Princeton he had once found Scott at what Wilson called "pretty nearly his favorite sport":

> Intently pinching out before a glass
> Some pimples left by parties at the Nass;
> Nor did [he] stop abashed, thus pocked and blotched,
> But kept on peering while I stood and watched.

In earlier poems, the brown-eyed Wilson had mentioned Gauss' "clear green eyes as hard and fine as gems" and Millay's "bright green eyes / That shine like jewels of the mind." He now concluded his poem on Fitzgerald more sympathetically by moving from rivalry to reverence, and returning to the once-emerald and now-dead eyes of his lost friend:

> Those eyes struck dark, dissolving in a wrecked
> And darkened world, that gleam of intellect
> That spilled into the spectrum of tune, taste,
> Scent, color, living speech, is gone, is lost.

Wilson remained keenly interested in preserving his friend's reputation when he was approached by Fitzgerald's first biographer, Arthur Mizener. In the late 1940s he carried on an extensive correspondence with Mizener, reading his typescript, correcting errors and putting forth his own more positive view of Fitzgerald. Though Wilson himself had often drawn attention to the more discreditable aspects of Scott's life, he was shocked by Mizener's conscientious revelations and delivered a harsh judgment of the biography: "The thing that worries me most is the general tone of the book. Five people who have read it—here [at the *New Yorker*] and at Houghton Mifflin—get the impression that you really dislike Scott and almost everybody connected with him and have made the most of every opportunity to put them in a bad light. . . . In dealing with his life you seem to dwell on everything that is discreditable or humiliating, almost to the point of ghoulishness." But Wilson was constructive as well as critical, and Mizener responded to his extraordinary efforts to improve the book. In March 1950 Wilson wrote to Mizener's editor at Houghton Mifflin asking if she would increase his advance so that Mizener could revise his biography according to Wilson's elaborate suggestions. "My own interest in it," Wilson wrote, "is in seeing that Scott Fitzgerald is presented as appreciatively and accurately as possible."[12]

Wilson also read the other books about Fitzgerald and kept in touch with Scottie. Though Zelda criticized Sheilah Graham after Scott's death, Wilson remained sympathetic to her. He published a surprisingly favorable review of her gossipy book on Scott, *Beloved Infidel* (1958), which Dorothy Parker had savaged as "an all-time low in American letters"; and wrote a short Foreword, which was not used, to Sheilah's *College of One* (1967). Irritated by Sara Mayfield's *Exiles in Paradise* (1971), Wilson told Glyn Morris that he was tired of books about the Fitzgeralds: "Mayfield makes Zelda as brilliant or more so than Scott, which is also nonsense."[13] He told Sheilah that Hollywood would probably have Katharine Hepburn play both Scott and Zelda.

Fitzgerald remained a living presence in Wilson's mind. He had always disapproved of Scott's connection with Hollywood and thought its "golden air of death" had made him lose faith in his own work. But Fitzgerald had imaginatively transformed the drama of his life in his books and "the struggle to be a good artist—which had a tragic ending—was one of the principal elements in Scott's career." In a long, fascinating letter of August 1953 to Lionel Trilling, Wilson said that the lack of proper training in Fitzgerald's youth gave him an inordinate respect for money and social prestige, and compromised his attitude to his art:

> The trouble about Scott's case . . . is that he didn't, in his early days, at home and in the third-rate Catholic school he went to, get

enough of the right kind of education to sustain him in his absolutely first-rate ambitions. He was early bedazzled by the pluto-
cratic society of St. Paul and Chicago, and could never quite get
over the idea that serious literature did not provide a real, or
sufficient, career. Yet his curious vocation was inescapable: he
could never really get away from it to do anything else successfully; and you have to compare him with the great wits and poets
that he wanted to emulate, not with the half-baked naturalists or
the moderately distinguished popular writers that are so common
here.

While preparing *The Crack-Up* Wilson, referring to Fitzgerald and
Bishop, honestly told Gauss: "I was more fortunate than either of them,
not in gifts, but in the opportunity to survive." "Men who start out
writing together," he told Bishop after Scott's death, "write for one
another more than they realize till somebody dies." Late in life, when
discussing whom he would summon up from the dead, Wilson suggested the importance of his old friends by naming Scott and Zelda,
Edna Millay, Plato and Baudelaire.[14]

IV

Wilson had been spending most summers and an occasional winter on
Cape Cod—a salty peninsula that juts into the Atlantic and then curves
backward like a scorpion's tail—since he first visited Edna Millay in
Truro in 1920. The Cape, still a maritime community, had foxes, deer,
rabbits and pheasants. Wilson loved the bluish ponds, the pine forests
filled with mushrooms, the grey dunes and salt marshes, the white
bluffs above the empty beaches. He was drawn to the cool clear light,
the changing colors of the swirling sea and cloud-streaked sky, the
wildness and isolation, the moody assaults of the ocean. "It is incomparably beautiful on the Cape," he told an English friend in 1946, "one of
the most marvellous places in the world: a mixture of woodland and
dunes: with any sort of swimming—ocean, bay and little fresh-water
lakes—and a climate that is never too hot and only in midwinter too
cold."

Wellfleet, on the narrow Bay side of the upper Cape, had a number
of colorful characters in its history. In 1870 Lorenzo Baker brought the

first bananas to America and founded a banana empire that later became the United Fruit Company. Luther Vrowell invented the first machine to manufacture brown paper bags. Sarah Atwood was one of the first women lighthouse keepers. Contemporary Wellfleet also had congenial intellectuals and bohemian freedom, and the isolated residents of the Cape formed a closely connected community. Wilson captured the mood when he recalled "all the parties, the days at the beach, the picnics, the flirtations, the drinking spells, the interims of work between trips, the moldy days of winter by the stoves, the days of keeping going on a thin drip or trickle of income."

Wellfleet, which tried to perpetuate the unconventional life of Provincetown in the 1920s, had a good deal of heavy drinking and emotional chaos. Everybody tried to be artistic, but few were real artists. Wilson, who frequently urged his friends to get on with their work, complained about the unreal and somewhat pretentious atmosphere: "In Wellfleet, we see so much of artists whose pictures are never seen, composers whose music is never heard, writers who do not write or who are not really writers." "You must remember," he once told Rosalind, referring to his fourth wife and to many of his close friends, "they're all exiles here."[15]

Wilson had lived mainly in the country, where he worked more efficiently, since moving to Stamford in 1936. In March 1941 he borrowed $1,500 from his mother, took out a mortgage for the rest and bought a $4,000 house in Wellfleet from the eccentric sister-in-law of Admiral Chester Nimitz. The rambling, green-shuttered, white clapboard farmhouse, built in the 1820s, stood on Money Hill—outside the center of town—only a few yards from Route 6. In those days the road was still fairly quiet and had not yet become the thundering main highway on what Wilson later called "the fucking Riviera."

The old three-story house had a gravel driveway to the right, a front porch with four white pillars and a railing on the second floor above the porch. The living room was in the front, an L-shaped kitchen and dining room were behind it, an "extremely pleasant middle room" behind that, then Wilson's study, with a bathroom and woodshed. Two bedrooms, filled with books, were upstairs. An old windmill used as a toolhouse and an old barn stood behind the house. A few shrubs afforded some protection from the main road and the big garden on the left side was mostly a jungle. Wilson borrowed another thousand dollars from his publishers to heat and renovate the house, and moved in, with Mary, Reuel and Rosalind, on about July 1, 1941. He lived there until the end of his life and it is now the home of his younger daughter.

Until he bought the house at Wellfleet, Wilson had very few possessions—apart from his books and papers, some old clothes and scraps of furniture. But first Mary and then his fourth wife, Elena, gradually fixed up the place and decorated the "yellow living room with a few engravings and Victorian mahogany pieces, including a sofa covered with lemony, striped silk." But the bohemian still mingled with the bourgeois elements in his character. A later visitor recalled that Elena painted the living room sofa, when they could not afford to buy a new one, and made it look awful. He did not have a telephone in Wellfleet for many years because he refused to pay a ten-dollar deposit.

Despite these odd touches, Wilson played the eccentric country squire in Wellfleet as he would later do in Talcottville. He carved like a paterfamilias when the Sunday roast was served and gave peremptory orders to the local workmen. When a contractor dug a big pit and asked Wilson what to do with the dirt, he instructed him to "bury it." In 1947 he bluntly told Dwight Macdonald: "I hear you're driving my car this summer." "'But Edmund, I bought the car from Mary for a dollar,' Dwight replied, recalling how she'd won the 1938 Chevrolet in a local raffle. 'But I gave her the money for the ticket,' Wilson replied—the money being a quarter." In the early 1950s Wilson enhanced his prestige by inheriting one of his mother's custom-built Cadillacs and hiring a black woman to drive him around in it.[16]

The Wellfleet house became well provided with animals. Wilson's pets included Bambi, the deer-and-caramel-colored cocker spaniel, and Recki, short for Rex or Reckless, the half German shepherd, half English setter. Recki ran wild, slept in the middle of the road and liked to eat ice cream cones. There were also invaders. Writing from personal experience, in his essay on *Finnegans Wake*, Wilson quoted Joyce on "copious holes emitting mice." The editor Jason Epstein, who sometimes exchanged houses with Wilson, remembered the many rats, which came from the old barn and headed for the garbage cans. They would begin to scratch the walls at sunset and then emerge on their predatory quest. But Wilson, who was fond of rats and had six books on the subject in his library, did not want them killed. He once rescued a mouse, "desperately swimming" in the toilet, by picking it up by the tail and putting it outside the house.

In June 1946 Wilson told Elena that he had found the maid in a state of hysteria because rats were running around the kitchen. He tried to reassure her by promising to poison them, but was reluctant to carry out his threat. The rats, which ate the straw place mats and gnawed the covers off his books, he celebrated in verse:

> Then, it's sad to see those with the covers so scarred
> By the plumbing that burst, which will always be marred,
> And the ones with glued backs eaten off with their titles
> By rats when keen hunger was eating their vitals.

He destroyed one large brown rat with poison, but could not bear to drown the young ones. In his comic Christmas poem, "The Rats of Rutland Grange," he conceded that the enemy had outwitted him: "These rats had come to know too well / All death-baits that the druggists sell."

Rats aside, Wilson took his civic duties seriously. In 1951, when the army tried to extend its gunnery range near Wellfleet, Wilson—with his neighbors Waldo Frank, Paul Chavchavadze and a dozen others —protested, in a letter to the *New York Times*, that the missiles "would gravely damage the fishing industry and vacation trade, which provide the livelihood of most Cape Codders."[17]

Wilson's appearance was as eccentric as his habits. Only five feet, six inches tall, in 1945 he weighed two hundred pounds. Friends commented on his dishabille at home and on his formal dress when he sallied forth in that unbuttoned community. Comfortably working in his study, Wilson, like the idle character in the Russian novel, wore "his Oblomov garb of light gray pajamas and a salmon bathrobe" until it was time to change for dinner. Repeating McCarthy's characterization of Wilson as a minotaur, Dwight Macdonald's son Michael noted that he "seemed buried in his labyrinth, at the end of a hallway lined by tall, black-bound Diaries—and bellowing from deep within his literary lair at lunchtime." David Chavchavadze "used to see him at the beach in Wellfleet wearing a hat and a white suit with a necktie. He never seemed to wear sportshirts." He usually wore "a white suit and plain wool tie, usually maroon. It stuck out on the Cape where *no* men . . . wore ties." Alfred Kazin also saw Wilson as a throwback to an earlier era, as a man who looked completely out of place among the bohemians on the Cape: "With his round bald head and that hoarse, heavily breathing voice box coming out of the red face of an overfed fox-hunting squire, Wilson looked apoplectic, stiff, out of breath." Yet Kazin was also impressed and even overwhelmed "by a certain seediness, the great bald dome, the lack of small talk, the grumpy concentration on every topic he came to."

Dos Passos had described Wilson's conversation when breasting the Jersey surf in the early Twenties. Michael Macdonald recalled his equally idiosyncratic swimming style two decades later on Cape Cod: "He called it the 'one-arm treadle.' Only his right arm was used for propulsion in a kind of semi-crawl, with Edmund occasionally surfacing to gasp some air—before resuming his head-down, straight-ahead progress, sawing the air with one arm, as his unseen left arm stabilized his body."[18]

Wilson's son Reuel was two-and-a-half years old when they moved into the Wellfleet house and six when his parents separated. He was raised by Mary and her third husband, Bowden Broadwater, both of whom referred to Wilson as "Monstro." Accustomed to the more easy-going régime of his mother, Reuel complained, during his summers in Wellfleet, that each household expected him to behave in a different way. When he first arrived in his father's house, he would cry himself to sleep. A stern and demanding part-time parent, Wilson had uneasy relations with his son. He was troubled by Reuel's behavior, complained that Mary had spoiled him and told her that "when Reuel first got up here, he wouldn't obey anybody and said and did many mean things to people." Reuel disappointed the expectations of his brilliant parents. Wilson thought of sending him to Exeter, though he was not terribly enthusiastic about the school, because so many members of his family had gone there. But Reuel's grades were poor and he was not admitted to the best prep schools.

As Reuel grew older, Wilson showed off his magic tricks, performed elaborate puppet shows and took him to Walt Disney films, which the father enjoyed as much as the son. When Wilson visited Edinburgh in 1945, he wrote Reuel a charming Stevensonian letter about the ghosts and pets in that spooky town: "The city is full of gloomy houses, and there is one street where every house is supposed to be haunted. In one of the houses they say there is a ghost who helps you on with your coat when you leave. In this house where I am staying there is a large cat named Betty and a black cocker spaniel named Jean, and they sleep in a basket together. The old Scotch housekeeper calls them 'beasties.'"[19]

Helen Wilson and her son Edmund, c. 1900: A "positive, self-confident, determined" woman, with the same sharp pointed nose, thin mouth, round plump face and small receding chin as Queen Victoria.

Edmund Wilson, Sr. on the steps of the Old Stone House: "He was nervous and hypo-chondriacal, and used to shut himself up for days in his room, and refuse to see anybody."

Edmund Wilson, 1920: "A slight sandyheaded young man with a handsome clear profile."

Christian Gauss at a Princeton
football game, 1940s: He had
"pale cheeks and a shuttered
gaze, [an] old raincoat and soft
felt hat, and a shabby mongrel
dog named Baudelaire."

Scott Fitzgerald, Nice, 1925:
"When his eyes sparkled and
his face shone with that powerful interior animation it was
truly an exciting experience."

Edna St. Vincent Millay, c. 1927: "The curious glint in her copper-colored hair intoxicated every man who saw her."

John Peale Bishop, c. 1922: An "awful highbrow, who signed the passionate love-poems in the *Lit.*, with stooped shoulders, pale blue eyes."

Mary Blair, 1921: Small and slim, with auburn hair and dark brown eyes, she had a warm, deep voice and wore exotic jewelry.

Elinor Wylie, 1926: She had "a quality of combined childishness and maturity, of passion and of ice."

Ted Paramore, 1930s:
"He was so sensitive,
so infectiously amus-
ing and so apparently
well-intentioned."

John Dos Passos, 1924:
Wilson admired "his
good manners, his in-
tegrity, and his culti-
vated intelligence."

Margaret Canby, 1920s: "Her skin was so smooth . . . with her hard high bones, her amiable face— her Scotch matter-of-factness and composure."

Louise Fort Connor, 1930s: She had a "strawberry-and-cream lusciousness, with its flushing of high color."

Léonie Adams, c. 1930: "Bird-like in gesture, brief and vivid in speech, her lyric quality and her reticences appealed to Wilson."

Louise Bogan, 1937: "My affection and admiration for you are deep," Wilson said. "You are one of the people I value most and count most on."

Edmund Wilson, 1930: "He was a short, soft-bodied man with fine features stamped sharp within the surrounding contours of his face, already heavy jowled."

Edmund Wilson and Mary McCarthy, Wellfleet, 1942: "The pictures of me are downright disgusting and have given me quite a turn. I seem to be taking snuff in one of them."

Mamaine Paget, 1937: "A young English girl, one of the brightest I have ever known and—need I say?—rather neurotic."

Elena Wilson, 1940s: "Rhine daughter, northern princess, always with fresh surprise."

Vladimir Nabokov, 1957: "He is a brilliant fellow and considered by the Russians the most important talent among the émigrés."

Isaiah Berlin, 1950s: Wilson said, "I tended to react to him a little as if he were an attractive woman whom I wanted to amuse and please."

W. H. Auden: "He is really extremely tough —cares nothing about property or money, popularity or social prestige."

Robert Lowell, 1950s: "Someone who talked like an old friend of the Twenties . . . accelerating conversations, going off in all directions."

Reuel, Elena, Helen, Rosalind, Edmund and Henry Thornton, with Recki and Bambi, Wellfleet, 1948: A patriarchal portrait.

Rosalind Wilson, Wellfleet, 1968: "She gets on my nerves, then I speak sharply to her and she flares up childishly."

Dawn Powell, 1950: "She was no classical beauty, and not chic in dress, and yet she had great attraction for women friends as well as men."

Edmund Wilson, 1952: "He was in true-to-type fighting mood, almost truculent, and riding his usual hobbyhorse."

Mary Pcolar, c. 1970: "I read Hungarian with a handsome young woman who is something of a prodigy."

Edmund Wilson, three days before his death: Slumped in a soft chair in the Old Stone House, he gazes stoically out toward nothingness.

V

The always-social Wilson craved release after a day of intense work. He widened his circle of friends when he moved to Wellfleet, and renewed relations with both Dos Passos and Bishop, who lived on the Cape. The Bishops had returned to America from France in 1933, and lived in New Orleans and Connecticut before building a house in South Chatham. Their new "colonial plantation–château," which cost six times more than Wilson's renovated house and was staffed by half a dozen servants, was tasteless and pretentious. While John was away in France, Margaret had cut his study in half to enlarge her bathroom. Seeing Margaret more frequently made Wilson loathe her more than ever. She was rigid, dogmatic, rude and unpleasant. Though obsessed with fine food, she served scant rations. She dominated her husband, was short-tempered with her children and impatient with Rosalind. During the war, Margaret said, her job was to "go around with a stick and make people do things they don't want to do," which Wilson called "very congenial work!" Only when Margaret was absent could he talk to John about literature and art.

Bishop's exceedingly dull letters to Wilson substantiate McCarthy's view that he was "'a dreadful, dreadful bore, a monologuist.' She could have '*died* of boredom' listening to him tell her how to grow sweet peas." Wilson, naturally more tolerant of his old friend, described Bishop, a keen bird-watcher, as "slight, rather bird-like, sensitive." But he was critical of Bishop's derivative poetry and appalling lack of discipline. In the summer of 1940 Wilson and Tate collaborated on a poem that satirized his respectability and self-indulgence: "So, Bishop, still malingering at Chatham, / You grow at once correct, corrupt and gray." Wilson thought the crab, "crawling but never destroyed," symbolized Bishop's self-enclosed and unproductive married life.

Though illness had forced Bishop to resign his government job in 1942, Wilson was as shocked by his death in 1944 as he had been by Fitzgerald's four years earlier. He told Millay he had not realized "that the gloom of his poetry had a real and serious cause or [been able] to guess that it announced the approach of death." He wrote Gauss that Bishop had experienced a rapid and dreadful decline toward the end and was prematurely senile when he died. Remembering the gaiety and glory of the Twenties, which seemed to intensify as that period receded, Wilson pondered the numerous casualties: "What happened to Louise and Henrietta [Fort], Ted Paramore, the Fitzgeralds, [John] Amen, Phelps Putnam, John Bishop, Edna . . . all the 'glamorous' personalities of that period?"[20] In 1948 Wilson paid tribute to Bishop, as he had done to Fitzgerald, by collecting and introducing his essays.

Wilson had happier relations with newer friends in Wellfleet. The cultured and charming Paul and Nina Chavchavadze, who combined an exalted heritage with a great capacity for fun, taught Wilson Russian and introduced him to Elena and to Svetlana Stalin. Rosalind wrote that "Nina's maiden name had been Romanov and she was a grand duchess of Russia. Her father, the tsar's uncle, had been shot by the Bolsheviks as he was leaving Russia. Her mother had been queen of Greece." Paul was a Georgian prince who grew up in the Caucasus, had gone into exile in Romania, became the interpreter of an advisor to the Queen, worked in a shipping office in America, returned to Europe with the Red Cross during the war and dealt with Russian refugees in Germany. Their son David adopted McCarthy's nickname and playfully addressed Wilson as "Sir Monstro," for he could, when stomping about in anger, be quite fierce.

When McCarthy was away or Wilson between marriages, he became a frequent dinner guest of the Chavchavadzes and of Charley Walker, his old army friend who had become a professor at Yale. He would knock on the Walkers' door with his gold-topped cane and when they said, "How nice to see you," would bluntly reply: "There's no one at home to feed me." He would also say, with mock portentousness, when knocking: "Guess who I am? I'm God."

In 1942 Wilson also met the young critic Alfred Kazin, who had just published *On Native Grounds*. Kazin was deeply hurt when McCarthy made a devastating attack on his book and Wilson looked on in amusement. "My high respect for his work was not reciprocated," Kazin later recalled. "He was too proud and temperamentally self-bound to take seriously any other American critic, or for that matter novelists and poets of a later generation."[21] Though Wilson was not keen on Kazin's work and tended to intimidate him, he certainly admired the criticism of John Jay Chapman, Van Wyck Brooks and H. L. Mencken, and also praised several of his younger contemporaries.

VI

During the 1940s Wilson published seven books (including an enlarged edition of *The Triple Thinkers*) and more than a hundred articles. In the early Forties he also spent considerable time planning and partially writing an unfinished novel that was called, as in a fairy tale, *The Story of the Three Wishes*. Leon Edel writes that Wilson's novel, which took place in Red Bank and Moscow, concerned three recent phases of his life: "his 1920s experiences in the period of 'boom and bust'; the subsequent economic depression and his flirtation with Communism; and then the period of his life in Provincetown. The story would have been a kind of H. G. Wells 'time machine' story . . . in which a character goes back in time." One character in this projected novel, based on McCarthy, was trying "to live up to the moral code of the Middle Western town she had come from and of the convent—she had some Irish blood—where she had been sent for a few years in her girlhood."

Wilson's publisher Roger Straus later wrote a report of the book and concluded that it was too incomplete to bring out as a separate work: "This uncompleted novel of Edmund Wilson's is clearly autobiographical. The 168 pages of written text are excellent and give an interesting picture of American life in the twenties. . . . The story of these four marriages covers at least fifteen years. . . . The outline and notes are copious and detailed. Perhaps it could all be published with something else of Wilson's."[22] After abandoning this novel, Wilson turned his attention to *Memoirs of Hecate County*. He used the "time machine" technique in "Ellen Terhune," and later portrayed Mary McCarthy as Judith in *The Little Blue Light*.

In the early 1940s the small Colt Press in San Francisco published two of Wilson's works: *The Boys in the Back Room* and *Note-Books of Night*. William Matson Roth, heir to a shipping fortune, and Jane Grabhorn, a well-known printer, had founded the press. She designed the books and they brought out about twenty titles—including Henry Miller's account of Greece, *The Colossus of Maroussi* (1941), and Paul Goodman's only novel, *The Grand Piano*—in finely printed editions. *Publishers Weekly* praised "the care, taste and warmth in the selection of binding patterns, papers, and placement of type and illustrations, which have always distinguished the Colt Press."

After Fitzgerald's death, Roth wrote to Wilson about publishing "The Crack-Up" essays and extracts of his diaries, along with the tributes by Scott's friends in the special issues of the *New Republic*. Roth got permission from *Esquire* to reprint the essays, but in July 1942, when he enlisted in the army and was shipped to Alaska, the Colt Press closed down. Wilson later met Roth in New York and encouraged him to write a life of Edith Wharton.

The title of Wilson's first Colt Press book came from a song, "See what the boys in the back room will have," about tough cowboys and gamblers. The phrase later took on political connotations and came to mean a group of men making secret decisions. Wilson's essay considered five novelists: James M. Cain, John O'Hara, William Saroyan, the now-forgotten Hans Otto Storm and John Steinbeck, who all were influenced by Hemingway, lived in California—though Cain and O'Hara were born in the East—and wrote about that state. (Wilson did not mention that the party scene in Cain's *Serenade*, 1937, "in which the heroine stabs the villain under cover of acting out a bullfight," came right out of Hemingway's story "The Capital of the World," 1936.) In the last section of the essay Wilson emphasizes the strange spell of unreality in California, which he had previously mentioned in his letters from Santa Barbara. Wilson reprinted his essay, with a Postscript on Fitzgerald, Nathanael West and Budd Schulberg, in *Classics and Commercials* (1950).

Extremely pleased with the appearance of the book, Wilson told Roth: "Mrs. Grabhorn has done such a beautiful job of it that I am embarrassed, as the format seems to me better than the contents."[23] He asked Roth to send complimentary copies to Sheilah Graham, Ted Paramore and Vladimir Nabokov. Wilson received an advance of $200 against ten percent royalties for each book. By May 1945 *The Boys in the Back Room* (1941) had sold only ninety-nine copies and *Note-Books of Night* (1942) eighty-nine copies, which earned an additional $71. Wilson got a £60 advance from Secker and Warburg for the English edition of his poetry book. It was published in 1945, and by 1948 sales had dwindled to three copies.

Wilson's second book of poetry, *Note-Books of Night*, was similar to *Poets, Farewell!* Both randomly combined poetry and prose, elegiac and satiric verse, mainly in couplets. Both used precise rather than suggestive language, described familiar settings and included poems to unnamed friends. "Provincetown, 1936" and "Home to Town: Two

Highballs" (his poem about Frances) in the second book echoed "Provincetown" and "Highballs" in the first.

Wilson imitated Hemingway's title "The Gambler, the Nun and the Radio" (1933) in "The Woman, the War Veteran and the Bear," and the dreamlike scenes in Joyce's *Finnegans Wake* in "Three Limperary Cripples." He wrote a comic pastiche in "Bishop Praxed's Apology, or the Art of Thinking in Poetry." He satirized scholars, Stalinists, Princeton in "Disloyal Lines to an Alumnus," Thoreau in "The Extrovert of Walden Pond" and MacLeish in "The Omelet"—the most important poem in the book. He alluded to Millay in "My dear, you burn with bright green eyes," Bogan (and himself) in "The Voice: On a Friend in a Sanitarium": "I who have been among them and who know / The spirit shrunken to its shuttered cell." In Wilson's story "Emily in Hades" (1922) a woman dies and is bored in hell. In "Lesbia in Hell," written in Swiftian octosyllabic couplets, Satan falls in love with Lesbia and wants to act out his sado-masochistic fantasies:

> He would have yielded trust and throne
> To make her moistened mouth his own,
> To bite her lips until they bled,
> To crush her on a secret bed.

But he fears Lesbia's sexual power and orders his soldiers to destroy her.

The Wound and the Bow: Seven Studies in Literature, Wilson's third critical book, was published by Houghton Mifflin, after Scribner's had broken their contract because of the chapter on Hemingway, in August 1941. The Boston publisher printed 3,000 copies and paid an advance of $1,000 against fifteen percent royalties. The title, like *Axel's Castle*, came from a work of literature (Sophocles' *Philoctetes*) and suggested the theme of the book: that a work of genius may draw its power from the vulnerability of its creator. The theme would have been clearer if Wilson had retained the original subtitle: "Studies in the Literature of Trauma." Thinking of his own childhood wounds, breakdown and psychoanalysis as well as of the mental problems of Zelda, Louise Bogan, Mary McCarthy and so many of his friends, he told Lionel Trilling that he had seen a good deal of the wound-and-bow combination.

The theme of the wounded artist began with Plato's *Ion* and evolved, from Neo-Platonic thought in the Renaissance and the sufferings of the Romantic poets, to the ideas of Dostoyevsky, Rimbaud and Nietzsche in the late nineteenth century and to Mann and Gide in the modern era.[24] Wilson had explored this idea in his journals of the 1920s when he wrote that art tries to resolve the discord between "pain and tranquility." Using the metaphor of disease, he speculated that "if the critic, having already been invaded by the measles, the diphtheria, the tuberculosis or the syphilis of maladjustment and suffering, is further infected by works of art . . . he may himself produce further works of art." In the book, Wilson did not state his theme until the final chapter —which should have come first—on Philoctetes. He then expressed the idea that superior strength was inseparable from disability by calling the hero of Sophocles' play a "victim of a malodorous disease which renders him abhorrent to society . . . [but] also the master of a superhuman art which everybody has to respect."

Trying to pry open some of the haunted chambers of literature, Wilson used the biographical and psychoanalytical approach to define the wound, which corresponded to the suppurating ulcer of Philoctetes, in each of his subjects. Dickens was traumatized by being forced as a child to work in a blacking factory. Kipling, who felt deserted by his parents, was sent from India to school in England, treated cruelly and driven to a nervous breakdown. Casanova was illegitimate. Edith Wharton also had a mental breakdown. Hemingway was seriously wounded in the War. Joyce was nearly blind.

In addition to the essay on Hemingway, the two most successful chapters—which take up three-fifths of the book—are on Dickens and Kipling. The chapter on Dickens, which Wilson thought "extraordinarily good," surveys Dickens' entire career, shows his development, emphasizes his artistic skill, illuminates his themes and suggests a plausible ending for his last, unfinished novel, *The Mystery of Edwin Drood*. In doing so, Wilson demonstrated, for the first time, the complexity and depth of Dickens' work, and argued that he is the greatest dramatic writer in English since Shakespeare.

In 1941 Kipling, like Dickens, had a poor reputation. By concentrating on his late stories, which often describe war neurosis and show "the heroism of moral fortitude on the edge of a nervous collapse," Wilson reveals that Kipling's work—linked thematically to Hemingway's—becomes continually more skilled and intense. Like his essay on Henry James in *The Triple Thinkers*, Wilson's penetrating chapters on Dickens and Kipling, on Hemingway and Joyce's *Finnegans Wake* changed the current perception of these authors.

After reading *The Wound and the Bow*, Delmore Schwartz—misquoting Shakespeare's Sonnet 29—revealed the immediate impact of the book:

> Shall I go there tonight, not Dickens read
> Who is so large, says Wilson, almost Avon's
> Great height (desiring this man's gift, and that
> Man's scope and hope) who might teach much,
> And give much joy. (He also had bad taste,
> Was maudlin and, says Wilson, "pretty bad"
> Are the short stories shoved in *Pickwick Papers*.)

In a letter to Zabel of August 1940, Wilson enclosed his own humorous quatrain about Kipling's dominant wife and overwhelming imperialism:

> Whereas my grievance against Rudyard Kipling
> Is that he let Mrs. K. control his tippling,
> And served the world adulterated brandy,
> Creating an immense sympathy for Gandhi.[25]

In June 1943, two years after the publication of *The Wound and the Bow* and a year after *Note-Books of Night*, Wilson tried to earn some money during the book-starved war by bringing out a thirteen-hundred-page anthology, *The Shock of Recognition: The Development of Literature in the United States Recorded by the Men Who Made It*. Fitzgerald had warned him as early as 1919 about wasting time on editing collections. Wilson himself, whose works had often been reprinted in anthologies, repeated Fitzgerald's warning in a letter to Morton Zabel of November 1936: "I'm a great hater of anthologies anyhow, and much regret to see you taking what I hope may not be the first false step on the road to [Louis] Untermeyer"—a minor poet and professional anthologist. Ironically, Wilson's *Shock of Recognition*, a collection of criticism on American literature written mainly by novelists and poets, was modeled on and complements Zabel's fine, two-volume *Literary Opinion in America* (1937), in which one major writer comments on the work of another. Though Wilson disliked anthologies, he had to sacrifice consistency to make a living.

The striking and oft-quoted title, which suggests the illuminating moments when artists become aware of their kin, came from Melville's observation: "For genius, all over the world, stands hand in hand, and one shock of recognition runs the whole circle round." In his Foreword Wilson wrote that this collection of literary documents "is an attempt to present a chronicle of the progress of literature in the United States as one finds it recorded by those who had some part in creating that literature. . . . What I am trying to present, in fact, is the developing self-consciousness of the American genius from the moment in the middle of the last century when we first really had a literature worth talking about to the moment toward the end of the second decade of ours when it was plain that . . . a new movement had got under way."

Keenly interested in the personal relations of writers and the rise and fall of reputations, Wilson also contributed twenty-two brief but acute Introductions to essays from James Russell Lowell and Poe to Mencken, Dos Passos and Anderson. (There was nothing in the book by or about Fitzgerald, Hemingway or Faulkner.) Wilson wrote that Poe "manages to be brilliant and arresting even about works of no interest." Long before Poe's genius was recognized in America, Wilson perceived that "his literary articles and lectures, in fact, surely constitute the most remarkable body of criticism ever produced in the United States." Wilson admired Henry Adams' stealthy and elusive malice, said Mencken "had the temerity to put his foot through the genteel tradition" and recognized, when Lawrence's reputation was unusually low, that his *Studies in Classic American Literature* "remains one of the few first-rate books that have ever been written on the subject."[26] Brilliant as an editor as well as a historian, biographer and critic, Wilson—like Lawrence—opened the field of American literature to serious study. *The Shock of Recognition* stimulated his interest in this subject and paved the way to *Patriotic Gore*.

When the book appeared, Wilson asked his editor at Doubleday to send copies to some of the contributors—Eliot, H. G. Wells, Mencken, Van Wyck Brooks—as well as to F. O. Matthiessen at Harvard, Daniel Aaron at Smith and the widows of Lawrence and Anderson. Wilson, who received a $1,000 advance but had to pay considerable permission fees, counted on a brisk sale. The book received favorable reviews from Aaron, Newton Arvin, Mark Schorer, Delmore Schwartz and Robert Penn Warren. But by September 1943 only 1,407 copies of the expensive book had been sold, out of a first printing of 3,500, and Doubleday bluntly told him they had lost a good deal of money.

In the early 1940s Wilson had a troubled marriage, money problems and two tedious teaching stints at Chicago and Smith. But he settled comfortably into the house at Wellfleet, kept in close touch with his friends and managed to accomplish an astonishing amount of first-rate work. An unexpected offer from the *New Yorker* would soon solve his financial problems, enhance his prestige and send him round the world as a roving reporter.

THIRTEEN

At the *New Yorker,* 1943–1944

I

In the early 1930s, Wilson's Leftist politics had alienated him from the Elmhirsts, and he resigned from the editorial board of the *New Republic.* During most of the Thirties, he concentrated on his books, tried to survive on publishers' advances and journalist's fees, and lived a difficult and at times degrading hand-to-mouth existence. Though no longer an editor, he maintained close ties with the *New Republic* and continued to publish most of his work there. But, having experienced at first hand the horrors of the Great War, Wilson, in contrast to most Left-wing intellectuals, adamantly opposed America's participation in World War Two. His isolationist position put him into direct conflict with the political views of the *New Republic.*

When its British patron, Leonard Elmhirst, visited America in 1940, Wilson's resentment about the policy of the magazine exploded into an open quarrel with the editors. When Michael Straight, Elmhirst's step-son, became editor later that year and took a strong pro-British line, Wilson "insisted that *The New Republic* had been betrayed by its founder," resigned on December 1, 1940 and never again wrote for the magazine. Wilson later explained that "the old *New Republic* was in effect suppressed by Leonard Elmhirst at the time of the war, when he arrived in this country and took over the paper, firing almost all of the old staff and reversing the editorial policy in regard to foreign affairs. The paper became at this point an organ of British propaganda." Wilson felt so passionate about this issue that he sacrificed his principal source of income.

After America entered the war following the attack on Pearl Harbor, Wilson mistakenly believed that the whole thing had been deliberately engineered by the malign Franklin Roosevelt and his devious Secretary of War, Henry Stimson. In his 1957 Postscript to *The Ameri-*

can Earthquake, Wilson declared that in November 1941, a month before Pearl Harbor, "the Japanese had presented to our government proposals of a decidedly conciliatory kind." But as his friend, the historian Arthur Schlesinger, Jr. pointed out in his review of the book, the Japanese proposals, "far from being 'decidedly conciliatory,' were, as the Japanese Foreign Minister himself described them, an ultimatum."[1] "It seems to me pretty clear," Wilson later told an editor, "that the government knew the attack was coming and did nothing to warn the fleet. Do you know about the entry in Stimson's diary in which he says that we have got to arrange for Japan to strike the first blow?" But Schlesinger again disagreed. Had the navy merely intercepted the Japanese task force en route to Hawaii, there would (he believed) have been sufficient outrage to get America into the war.

Wilson's opposition to the war was so extreme that he even tried to ignore the humanitarian issues. Usually pro-Semitic, he once argued —in what was certainly the most foolish sentence he ever wrote— that "American Jews had the motive of wanting to save their own people. . . . But the extermination of six million Jews was already very far advanced by the time the United States took action." In fact, the death camps did not become operational until *after* America entered the war in December 1941 and American intervention saved thousands of Jewish lives. In 1957 Wilson still maintained that "we should never, for all Hitler's crimes, have sent our soldiers to Europe at all." Referring to the fire-bombing of civilians in German cities, Wilson insisted that America's war crimes were even more horrible than Germany's: "The Nazis smothered people in gas-ovens, but we burned them alive with flame-throwers, and, bomb for bomb, we did worse than the Nazis."

His greatly admired friend Carlo Tresca, who was the leading Italian anti-Fascist in America and seemed "absolutely indestructible," was assassinated in New York by Mussolini's gunmen in January 1943. But even this shocking event failed to convince Wilson that an Axis victory would extinguish democracy and destroy the civilized world.

Wilson had been attacked by the Communists in the late 1930s. Now, his isolationist views and break with the *New Republic* made it very difficult to place his work in the liberal journals where he felt most at home. Alfred Kazin heard Wilson was so pressed for money that he had even asked for a job on the despicable *Time* magazine. His marriage was extremely unhappy, and when Kazin first met him in 1942 Wilson "was an embittered, impoverished, increasingly self-willed man of forty-seven whose seedy appearance shocked admirers who came upon him in New York."[2]

Wilson's fortunes were suddenly transformed in October 1943 when the *New Yorker* asked him to succeed Clifton Fadiman as their weekly book reviewer. Though the job meant he would have less time for his own books, he accepted it in order to pay the debts he had incurred on his new house and when writing *Memoirs of Hecate County*. He also wanted to save some money in case he had to publish this book at his own expense. In the fifth story in the book, "The Milhollands and Their Damned Soul," Wilson satirized his predecessor and intellectual antithesis, the bland and boring Fadiman.

Wilson agreed not to write for any other magazine, but also stipulated that the *New Yorker* would promptly print whatever he wrote. He told the editor, Harold Ross, that he wanted $10,000 a year for 1,200- to 1,500-word reviews and $3,000 for expenses; and actually began on January 1, 1944 at about $8,250 a year, with an office and secretarial help. In 1945 he earned $800 and expenses for each of his much longer "Reporter at Large" articles on postwar Europe, and later reported from Arizona, from upstate New York, from Canada and from Israel.

Immensely pleased with his new situation, Wilson told friends that he was rich for the first time in his life and had the publishers eating out of his hand. After the first year, he decided to review books only every other week and proudly declared: "The *New Yorker* is really at the present time one of the best-edited and best-written magazines in this country." The magazine gave Wilson a regular salary, an outlet for all his work, expenses to travel and time to write long pieces. Since the *New Yorker* allowed many sets of proofs, he got used to making elaborate corrections after his work had been set up in print. This became an expensive habit, and he often had to pay publishers for excessive changes in the proofs of his books. Most of all, the magazine enhanced Wilson's considerable authority and prestige, and his literary reviews were the most widely respected in America.

One young staff member was surprised to find that the formidable Wilson was "a short, overweight man in floppy dark clothes." He was not, like Fadiman, interested in timely reviews or in keeping his readers up to date on the newest books, but preferred to write at length and to express his individualistic view of works he found significant. As with Hemingway's work, he immediately recognized the merits of Saul Bellow's first novel, *Dangling Man* (1944). He called it "an excellent document on the experience of the non-combatant in time of war. It is well written and never dull. . . . It is also one of the most honest pieces of testimony on the psychology of a whole generation who have grown up during the Depression."[3]

By contrast, Wilson's fierce review of Carson McCullers' *A Member of the Wedding* (March 30, 1946)—which he called formless, pointless, undramatic and unreal—had a devastating effect on the sensitive writer. At Yaddo "the wounded and distraught author dissolved into tears . . . and sobbed hysterically. It was many minutes later—and with great effort—that she was able to recover enough to tell the group hovered about her of . . . Wilson's review. Both infuriated and desolate over *The New Yorker* piece, as well as embarrassed by her own actions and vulnerability, she vowed never to read another review of her works."

Charles Jackson, author of *The Lost Weekend* (1944), a best-selling novel about his alcoholism, had a very different response to Wilson's negative review. After he had recovered from the blow, he was grateful for Wilson's harsh but salutary criticism. Wilson wrote: "The book has so much that is good that it ought to have been . . . a really satisfactory piece of fiction," and then analyzed its faults: it was formless and repetitious, the flashbacks were boring, the minor characters had no individuality and the hero lacked depth. "All I needed was for you to point it out," Jackson told Wilson, "and what a pity that I had to wait till the book was in print, and too late." Wilson's famous attack on Dorothy Sayers and other detective writers, in "Who Cares Who Killed Roger Ackroyd?" (January 20, 1945), aroused the wrath of many *aficionados*, who sent him a mountain of hostile letters. One woman declared that she had never liked men named Edmund. The poet Rolfe Humphries tried to puncture what he took to be pomposity in the "Ackroyd" essay:

> Come off it Edmund: you were one
> Who used to like some foolish fun.
> Does turning out a weekly column
> Force you to be so god-damn solemn?[4]

After the first honeymoon years, Wilson became more critical of the smug, over-cautious atmosphere and the meddlesome editorial policy of the magazine. He complained that the *New Yorker* was afraid of political controversy, preferred a bland, soothing style, and tried to suppress any poetic or audacious form of expression. Like all authors, he had to repel officious editors who tried to justify their existence by interfering with his work. As he told Ross, with considerable irritation: "It simply amounts to other people trying to rewrite my copy who don't know as much about writing as I do and engaging me in long arguments and pleadings that are a waste of time and energy." In January 1948, after four years as a book reviewer, Wilson felt the editors were making things more difficult for him. He got fed up and suddenly quit—though he continued to write regularly for the magazine until the end of his life.

In 1958, after James Thurber published the reverential *Years with Ross*, Wilson blasted his old editors. He had never much liked the prissy and respectable Katharine White. He did not much care for Ross or his high-handed way of dealing with people, and found him suspicious, ignorant and resentful. Ross never understood anything at all about Wilson's writings, and, Wilson felt, "the assumptions about personal and business relations that decent people usually go on did not hold in the *New Yorker* office."[5]

II

Wilson's crusty public persona began to emerge during his early years at the *New Yorker*. He even developed an old man's disease to go with it. "I've come down with gout," he told Bogan in March 1944, "an affliction in my family which I'd so far escaped, and have been enacting the role of irascible old man with one foot up on a chair." His persona was reinforced by a famous printed card—a witty catalogue of bothersome requests—which he sent to importunate strangers who demanded his help:

> Edmund Wilson regrets that it is impossible for him to:
>> Read manuscripts,
>> Write articles or books to order,
>> Write forewords or introductions,
>> Make statements for publicity purposes,
>> Do any kind of editorial work,
>> Judge literary contests,
>> Give interviews,
>> Conduct educational courses,

Deliver lectures,
Give talks or make speeches,
Broadcast or appear on television,
Take part in writers' congresses,
Answer questionnaires,
Contribute to or take part in symposiums or "panels"
     of any kind,
Contribute manuscripts for sales,
Donate copies of his books to libraries,
Autograph books for strangers,
Allow his name to be used on letterheads,
Supply personal information about himself,
Supply photographs of himself,
Supply opinions on literature or other subjects.

This apparently rude and arrogant card was purely defensive, and gave an entirely misleading impression of his real character. In fact, Wilson performed almost all of these tedious tasks—though not for strangers. With people he knew, he was extraordinarily kind and generous.

Once Wilson was securely connected to the literary power structure, his friends began to consider him a one-man agent and employment bureau. We have seen that he went out of his way to encourage and praise his friends' work, recommended Nathanael West's novels to Scribner's, did extensive editorial work, without pay, on Fitzgerald's posthumous books and read the typescript of Arthur Mizener's biography. Wilson still had a sharp eye for talent and helped many young writers at the beginning of their careers. He gave Randall Jarrell books to review for the *New Republic*, and recommended his poetry to the *Atlantic Monthly* and the *New Yorker*. "His writing interests me more," he wrote one editor, "than that of any of the younger poets." He was also keen on the poetry of Elizabeth Bishop. He published her in the *New Republic*, told the Colt Press and New Directions about her work, and recommended her for a Houghton Mifflin poetry prize. He regarded her, Wilson told the publisher, "as one of the two or three really first-rate poets of her generation in this country."[6]

In June 1942 Wilson wrote three detailed pages of suggestions, corrections and errata—the sort of thing a conscientious teacher might do for a rather dim graduate student—for Maxwell Geismar's book on the contemporary American novel, *Writers in Arms* (1942), and also helped him place the book in England. Immensely grateful for this fundamental tuition, Geismar called Wilson "a good angel who arrives at the most opportune moments. . . . I really owe the whole business to you; and your touch has been magic on the whole course of the book."

The sometimes soft-hearted Wilson was even willing to back some persistent losers. Between 1938 and 1941 Harry Roskolenko, an obscure poet, asked Wilson to do almost everything he had refused to do on the printed card. He wanted Wilson to publish his verse in the *New Republic*, send him books to review, write a blurb for his book, contribute to a symposium he was planning, and recommend him to movie producers, foundations, publishers and employers. Instead of ignoring his requests, Wilson answered all his letters, published his review in the *New Republic* and referred him to the Gotham Book Mart for a job. Wilson's patience with H. H. Lewis, a proletarian poet and ardent Stalinist who vehemently defended the Purge Trials, was even more surprising. After extracting from Wilson two futile recommendations for a Guggenheim grant, Lewis had the cheek to ask for a third. Lewis seemed, from his letters, truly awful and Wilson was generous indeed to back such an inferior parasite. Both before and after he won his Guggenheim Fellowship in 1935, Wilson—a power in the land and apparent key to success—was asked to write recommendations for an astonishing number of candidates, and forty-six out of his ninety-seven recommendations were successful.[7]

III

Wilson made four significant new friendships in the early 1940s. Helen Muchnic, who taught Russian at Smith, was a notable recipient of his benefactions. He first met her when he lectured at Smith in the fall of 1942 and their friendship deepened during the disintegration of his marriage to McCarthy. After he married Elena and inherited the house in Talcottville, he usually stopped overnight, en route from Wellfleet to upstate, at Muchnic's convenient and hospitable home in Cummington, Massachusetts.

The daughter of a Russian-Jewish businessman who emigrated after financial failures, Muchnic was born in Odessa in 1902, moved with her mother and brother to Brussels in 1911, and joined her father three years later in America. She graduated from Vassar, studied at the School of Slavonic Studies in London and earned her doctorate at Bryn

Mawr. She joined the Smith faculty in 1930, taught soldiers at Yale during World War Two and helped organize the Russian department at Smith after the war. Smith College published her run-of-the-mill dissertation as *Dostoyevsky's English Reputation* (1939).

Muchnic, a short, buxom brunette, had curly hair, small widely-spaced eyes, a prominent nose and large straight teeth. Though not an attractive woman, she was bright, lively and graceful, with a soft feminine side, a European manner and a slight accent. She shared a house with an amusing and sardonic colleague, Dorothy Walsh. She found the academic atmosphere somewhat oppressive and, since she had her own income, kept an apartment in New York and spent many weekends there.[8]

Helen Muchnic disliked Mary McCarthy, another Vassar graduate. They had opposite views on everything and rubbed each other the wrong way. She also, according to Nabokov's editor Simon Karlinsky, hated Nabokov because he would not let her, as Wilson had suggested, translate his novels into English. Nabokov thought that since there were no good women novelists in Russian, she would not be suitable for the job. But Helen absolutely adored Wilson. He was also very fond of her and, while on his own at Smith, had drinks and dinner with Helen and Dorothy almost every night. "You should hear her talk about you," Rosalind told Wilson, after his separation from McCarthy, in June 1945. "Next to Dostoevsky, she is obviously in love with you." Daniel Aaron, another colleague at Smith, found Helen thoughtful, unusually sympathetic and solicitous. He thought that Wilson may have come close to a romance with Helen and that she believed Wilson would marry her. Harry Levin agreed that they were drawn together by a common interest in Russian, that she expected to marry Wilson and was heartbroken when he chose Elena.[9]

In January 1943 Wilson, recommending Muchnic to Nabokov, mentioned that she had been the student of his eminent friend: "I met while I was lecturing at Smith an extremely intelligent Russian woman who speaks and writes English absolutely perfectly. She has been over here ever since she was about eleven but has kept up her Russian and studied Russian literature with Mirsky in London. I have read her doctor's thesis on the influence of Dostoevsky in English, and it is interesting and well written."

Wilson corresponded with Muchnic for almost thirty years. Though he was only a few years older, she assumed a humble manner and wrote to him as a disciple. Her unexciting letters, which usually praised his current work, asked and thanked him for many favors ("Once again I have a request to make of you"). He often asked her to Wellfleet; pleading work, she refused the invitations—possibly because she felt jealous of Elena and uneasy as her guest. Helen discussed her reading, mentioned her depressed moods, and described the academic politics and problems at Smith, "my Siberia." Wilson's letters to her mainly concerned Russian literature. But he also, over the years, made extraordinary efforts to advance her professional career. He recommended her to publishers (including Graham Greene at Eyre and Spottiswoode), advised her about the terms of her contracts, encouraged editors to review her books, proposed her for a job at Bennington College and eased her into the Slavic slot at the *New York Review of Books*.

In March 1947, when Muchnic was about to publish *An Introduction to Russian Literature*, Wilson warned her about literary log-rolling: "Since I want to review your book in the *New Yorker*, it might be a good idea for you not to dedicate it to me, as this might make it rather awkward for me to praise it as highly as I should like." The following June, Wilson compared her to one of his idols and (as he had done with Millay) gave a highly inflated appreciation of her admittedly introductory work: "She is one of those rare teachers—like Christian Gauss at Princeton—whose mastery of ideas and languages has qualified them to deal with comparative literature at the same time that a gift of human insight enables them to interpret the classics in terms of the general problems of life." Later on, however, Wilson contradicted his earlier letter to Nabokov about her perfect English and told his wife that he had been correcting a manuscript by Muchnic, "who is more trouble than Paul [Chavchavadze] because she has something to say but hasn't mastered English."[10] Yet the *Smith Alumnae Quarterly* quoted Wilson absurdly declaring that on Russian literature "she is perhaps the best writer in the English-speaking world." If true, this would make the humble disciple an even greater critic than Nabokov or Wilson himself.

Muchnic dedicated her last collection of articles, *Russian Writers: Notes and Essays*, to Wilson and after his name quoted two lines in Russian from Anna Akhmatova: "I'm dreaming of your work / Your blessed work." In his book *A Window on Russia*, Wilson praised a chapter in Muchnic's book as "the best treatment I have seen of Solzhenitsyn." Early and late, Wilson expressed his devotion to Helen, with whom he was always tender and on his best behavior. In 1946 he told her: "It meant a lot to me to know you in those years when Mary and I were disintegrating, and it still means a lot to me, dear Helen." Twenty-two years later, after stopping off in Cummington, he wrote: "Our visit to you, as usual, was a restorative surcease from a world of anxiety."[11]

IV

In January 1945, during his separation from McCarthy and at the height of his friendship with Muchnic, Wilson met another—extremely attractive—European-born woman, who had a round face, a small chin and delicate features. This time, he lavished unwarranted praise on her work—not to repay friendship, but to gain sexual favors. Anaïs Nin, born in France of Spanish-Cuban parents, came to America at the age of eleven and still rolled her "r's" in the charming French manner. She was a close friend of Henry Miller and had brought out a rapturous study of D. H. Lawrence just after his death in 1930. Nin had also published a strange "prose poem," *The House of Incest* (1936), about narcissism (her specialty) and *Winter of Artifice* (1939), a psychological study of the relations between a father and daughter.

In the *New Yorker* of April 1, 1944 and (most unusually) again on December 2, 1944, Wilson reviewed her book, *Under a Glass Bell.* Unable to place it with a publisher, Nin had printed it herself. Noting that Nin had been influenced by Virginia Woolf and the Surrealists, Wilson called her "a very good artist" and wrote: "They are half short stories, half dreams, and they mix a sometimes exquisite poetry with a homely realistic observation." Though grateful for the unexpected attention in high quarters—Gore Vidal said "she was overnight a celebrity"—Nin felt Wilson had not done justice to her genius and dismissed his review as "well intentioned but inept and inadequate."

After their brief love affair, Nin urged him to be a bit more enthusiastic about her next privately printed book, *This Hunger.* But his style seemed to be infected by her own and he produced, on her behalf, one of the worst sentences he ever wrote: "She has worked out her own system of dynamics, and gives us a picture, quite distinct from that of any other writer, of the confusions that result to our emotions from the uncertainty of our capacity to identify the kind of love that we tend to imagine with our actual sexual contacts, and of the ambivalent attractions and repulsions that are so hard on contemporary nerves." It seemed, from this review, that Nin was hard on *Wilson's* nerves. Yet when her next book inexorably appeared the following year, he once again tried his best on her behalf. He wrote of the even more awful *Ladders to Fire* that Nin was "expert at her characteristic blending of exquisite poetic imagery with psychological portraiture." Still hard to please, Nin laconically recorded: "Edmund Wilson writes obtusely about *Ladders of Fire.*"[12]

Nin's unpublished letters to Wilson reveal the most acute case of literary megalomania since Gertrude Stein's. Nin was so completely self-absorbed and egoistic, so brazenly bent on exploiting Wilson's prestige, so eager to use his power to advance her reputation, that even a phrase like "how are you?" seemed, for her, immensely self-effacing. Nin did, however, include some essential flattery about his greatness as a critic. Wilson immediately recognized her motives, but was willing to play her little game as long as there was a chance of bedding her.

He had always been drawn to exotic types, like Paula Gates, Léonie Adams and the prostitute Marie, and later told lady friends about his keenness for the ruthless and yet rather fey Anaïs. She is "more amusing and attractive than she would seem to people who didn't know her. She has a very Latin-comic sense. . . . She is a practical little Franco-Spanish housewife on one side of her personality, and yet I always felt about her that I was dealing with a lovely little nymph who was not quite a human being. . . . I like to talk to her—especially about people and books, which is all she is really interested in."

Nin's diary of 1945 offers, amidst the endless crochet-work, a grossly distorted account of their personal relations. She assumed the role of poor bohemian, but was actually married to a wealthy banker. She implied that she never slept with Wilson, but did, in fact, have a brief affair with her literary father-figure. It was true, however, that Wilson, desperately unhappy after the break-up of his marriage to McCarthy, turned to Nin for consolation: "Edmund Wilson invited me for lunch. I felt his distress, received his confession. Even though not an intimate friend, Wilson senses my sympathy and turns toward it. He is lonely and lost. He is going to France as a war correspondent. He asks me to accompany him while he buys his uniform, his sleeping bag. We talk. He tells me about his suffering with Mary McCarthy. . . . He seems lonely. He portrays himself as a man who has suffered because he loves clever women and 'clever women are impossibly neurotic.' " In September Nin noted a paradoxical element in Wilson's character: "Contrary to his academic, formal, classical work, and the cold intellectual criticism, he himself is fervent, irrational, lustful, violent." She said Wilson terrified her and represented unknown dangers, and ambivalently concluded: "Wilson, if he ever tastes of me, will be eating a substance not good for him."[13]

Wilson had flattered her by saying that she was the most exquisite woman he had ever seen and had aroused McCarthy's jealousy by praising Nin's beauty and talent. Nin, by contrast, remembered that Wilson looked like a solid burgher in a Dutch painting. He told her, as he had undoubtedly told McCarthy: "I would love to be married to you, and I would teach you to write." To Nin—as to McCarthy—Wilson represented "force, authority, power . . . a strong, determined, palpable, positive man."

After extracting whatever benefits she could from Wilson, Nin finally criticized his lack of imagination and rejected his paternal power. She believed he would destroy her, called him the enemy of what she believed in and—like Dahlberg and Crane—attacked his literary dictatorship and unquestioned authority. "Rather than engage in a belligerent friendship with Edmund Wilson," she concluded, "I broke with him. I do not want to live again and again the father-and-daughter drama. . . . In the world of Wilson there was no magic and no poetry. No sweet delights of intimacy, admission of doubts. . . . There was in Wilson a harsh absolutism and literalness."

Recalling his old love affairs later on, Wilson fondly thought of Frances, Margaret Canby, Louise Bogan and Anaïs Nin. He got back in touch with her in 1966, as he usually did with his favorite women, and, using a military metaphor, told her: "I forgot all the causes for the crossness (I wanted you to give me the faith, love and praise I needed) but now I can enjoy friendship without expecting unconditional surrender." In his diary he recorded that Nin revealed she was "miffed," despite his strenuous efforts, because he had failed to "plug her reputation." But he was very glad to experience once again "her fine-boned prettiness and her amusing conversation, so Latin, and hence so exotic in New York." Wilson and Nin, briefly drawn together for mutual advantage, represented antithetical modes of style and thought. "At no point is she aware," Gore Vidal observed, "of having been in the presence of America's best mind. But then Wilson represents all that she hates: history, politics, literature. To her, mind and feeling must be forever at war. Thus she has systematically unbalanced both art and life."[14]

V

Contrasting Anaïs Nin and Dawn Powell in *The Forties*, Wilson remarked that "this continual complaining and having to be comforted is
one of the most annoying traits of women writers: Elinor Wylie, Louise
Bogan, Anaïs Nin (Dawn Powell the only woman I know, I think, who
doesn't have it)." For this reason—and for her charm, liveliness, wit
and congeniality as a non-stop drinking companion—Wilson felt
closer to Dawn than to any other woman friend. Unlike most friends
who met Wilson after the 1920s, Dawn called him Bunny.

Born in Ohio in 1897, Dawn graduated from Lake Erie College
and in 1920 married Joseph Gousha, a prosperous advertising executive
from Pittsburgh. The following year she gave birth to a brain-damaged
son, who was eventually placed in an institution. Dawn's patron was
Wilson's sometime landlady Margaret de Silver, and her long-time
lover was the heavy-drinking editor Coburn Gilman. But she remained
married to her husband (who could pay her son's expensive medical
bills), lived in the Village and drank at the Hotel Brevoort.

Dawn was a short, plump, buxom woman with dark bangs and
brown eyes, puffy cheeks and a rosy complexion. A Midwestern Anita
Loos or Dorothy Parker, she saw the comic side of life, punctured the
afflatus of the pompous and liked to flirt with men. She claimed to do
all her work in the Children's Room of the New York Public Library,
which had the only chairs that fit her. When Carlo Tresca, who had
been attacked by an assassin, dramatically pointed to his scar and asked
Dawn how she thought he got it, she brightly asked: "Helena Ruben-
stein?" Matthew Josephson defined her life-enhancing qualities:

> She was no classical beauty, and not chic in dress, and yet she had
> great attraction for women friends as well as men. Her expression
> was at once puckish and alert, her eyes never stopped moving,
> dancing. She drank copiously for the joy of living, but seldom
> appeared overborne by drink even in the small morning hours.
> While busily occupied day and night with her café and party-
> going . . . she managed, nevertheless, to turn out thirteen novels,
> one book of short stories, and several plays, two of which were
> produced on Broadway.

Dawn's letters to Wilson were familiar, gossipy, silly, joking. She described her dreams and illnesses, her trips to the Yaddo and Mac-Dowell writer's colonies, to Haiti and Paris; sent macabre news of mutual friends, and bitchy bulletins about Elizabeth Bishop and Jean Stafford. She enclosed humorous drawings and absurdly captioned postcards; thanked him for help with publishers and visited remote Talcottville; praised his work and wrote a rave review of *Night Thoughts*. For years Dawn and Bunny carried on a correspondence in which she took the part of the respectable Victorian novelist Mrs. Humphry Ward and he was a seedy Grub Street hack named Ernest Wigmore. Later on, tiring of these comic roles, they became a sophisticated French pair: Aurore and Raoul. (Raoul was the lover in *Sweets of Sin*, the pornographic novel that Molly Bloom reads in *Ulysses*.) Dawn kept up the fairly tedious joke as late as August 1962 when she enclosed a pink garter and wrote on pink stationery, sending up one of Wilson's favorite targets: "Must you destroy me utterly with your selfish jealousy? Can't you understand that for you I have always been a plaything but for Cowley I am a *Woman*. Aurore. P. S. I cannot bear to leave you without the petit souvenir—the garter you loved."[15]

A mutual friend told Wilson in 1949 that Dawn seemed to get increasingly malicious as her personal life became more difficult, and began to insult her companions after one or two drinks. But Wilson particularly admired her cheerfulness and bravery in the face of adversity. When Dawn was hospitalized with a lung tumor, Wilson noted that "she looked fresher and younger than I think I had ever seen her . . . was beginning to be proud of 'being a freak'—the doctors were all excited about her case and eager to see the operations." When she came to Talcottville near the end of her life, Wilson was alarmed to see her collapse on the couch—looking emaciated, yellow and haggard. But Dawn never complained, and after a few drinks always revived and started shooting out wisecracks. Wilson admired her as "an old-fashioned American woman not far from the pioneering civilization: strong-willed, stoical, plainspoken, not to be imposed upon."

As with Muchnic and Nin, Wilson overvalued Powell's quite readable but rather thin and carelessly written novels. In November 1944 he called *My Home Is Far Away* "touching without sentimentality and amusing only with rare lapses into caricature and farce. . . . An odd blend of sharp sophistication with something childlike, surprised and droll." In a major retrospective essay of November 1962 he compared her bizarre and amusing novels to the work of Anthony Powell and Evelyn Waugh, and declared that she has "a wit, a gift of comic invention and an individual accent. . . . The mind, the personality behind them, with all its sophistication, is very stout and self-sustaining, strong in Middle Western common sense, capable of toughness and brusqueness."[16] Wilson could always count on Dawn to cheer him up and sustain him in an alcoholic friendship that never became complicated by sexual entanglements.

VI

Wilson found in Vladimir Nabokov, his closest friend for more than twenty years, a rare combination of qualities. Handsome, charming and witty, sophisticated, cosmopolitan and multi-lingual, he had a charismatic personality and a brilliant intellect. A wide-ranging man of letters with catholic interests in science and art, Nabokov was also a major novelist whom Wilson could respect and assist. Simon Karlinsky observed that the two men had a great deal in common: "They came from cultivated upper-class homes within their respective cultures. Each had an interest and an involvement in the other's literature and native traditions. Both were at home in French literature and language. Both had a skeptical, albeit divergent, view of religion and mysticism. Both were sons of jurists who were involved in politics." Indeed, Nabokov's father would have become the Russian minister of justice if the short-lived democratic government had not been destroyed by the Bolsheviks in 1917, and Wilson's father would have been a justice of the Supreme Court if another vacancy had occurred after Woodrow Wilson appointed Louis Brandeis in 1916.

Nabokov was born in 1899 into a wealthy, aristocratic and powerful St. Petersburg family, who lost everything and were forced into exile in 1919. Having been tutored in French and English since childhood, he took a degree at Trinity College, Cambridge. After graduation he settled in Berlin—where his father was assassinated in 1922—and married three years later. His son was born in 1934 and the Nabokovs moved to Paris in 1937. During the Twenties and Thirties he published ten novels in Russian and became the leading émigré writer. In May 1940, nine months after the war had broken out in Europe, Nabokov, having lived for two decades in exile, arrived unknown in America.

At the suggestion of his cousin, the composer Nicolas Nabokov, Vladimir first wrote to Wilson on August 30, 1940. Wilson recognized Nabokov's extraordinary talent, and Nabokov soon replaced Scott Fitzgerald—who died the following December—in his emotional and intellectual life. Wilson generously helped Nabokov establish himself at the beginning of his American career at the same time that he was reviving Fitzgerald's reputation by editing his posthumous works.

During the next few years Wilson used his valuable contacts to commission Nabokov's reviews for the *New Republic* and place his work in the *Atlantic Monthly* and the *New Yorker*. He tried to get Nabokov teaching jobs at Bennington, Yale and Princeton (while he himself lost his chance for a position at Cornell) and recommended him for a Guggenheim Fellowship to prepare an edition of Pushkin's long poem *Eugene Onegin*. He introduced his new friend to editors at the Colt Press, New Directions and Doubleday, and advised him on how to get the most favorable terms for his books. Wilson read and made useful suggestions about Nabokov's manuscripts, and also wrote a blurb for his first novel in English, *The Real Life of Sebastian Knight* (1941). He compared the "absolutely enchanting" novel to the work of Proust, Max Beerbohm, Virginia Woolf, Kafka and Gogol, and stated that "Nabokov is as completely himself as any of these writers—a man with a unique sensibility and a unique story to tell." He tried to find a translator for Nabokov's Russian novels, and loyally promoted those books, though he did not actually like them. Though poor himself, he offered to lend Nabokov money (which was politely refused).

Wilson and Nabokov—like two bishops speaking *ex cathedra*—had a strong didactic streak, a stubborn tenacity of opinion, a fierce pride and a grand manner that rejected challenges and contradictions. Despite differences in their literary and political ideas, they were intellectual equals and sympathetic soulmates. With Nabokov, Wilson abandoned his characteristic aloofness, courted his immensely attractive friend and frequently invited him for stimulating visits. Nabokov, chafing under yet grateful for Wilson's valuable patronage, responded with wary warmth and affection.

Despite their formality and reserve, their friendship, during the course of many visits, flourished and deepened. Within eight months Nabokov was addressing Wilson as "Bunny"; he was calling Nabokov "Vladimir" and then the even more familiar "Volodya." In November 1940, Wilson told Gauss about Nabokov's English education and stylish reviews, artistic reputation and political beliefs: "His point of view is neither White Russian nor Communist. The family were landowning liberals, and intellectually the top of their class. His father was a prominent leader of the Kadets. [But] Vladimir is in pretty bad straits." Significantly, Wilson at first grasped Nabokov's political position and then, as his sympathy waned during their arguments about Communism, forgot what he had once perceived. Tremendously impressed by his new friend, Wilson told the Houghton Mifflin editor Robert Linscott that Nabokov was "the most brilliant man he had ever met."

When they first met, Wilson was still married to Mary McCarthy, who recalled their exhilarating conversations and the unusual depth of emotion: "Edmund was always in a state of *joy* when Vladimir appeared; he *loved* him."[17] His visit to the Wilsons in Stamford on June 6, 1942, inspired Nabokov's witty poem "The Refrigerator Awakes." It also involved some cagey fencing and Beckett-like incongruities. The atheistic Wilson asked Nabokov if he believed in God. When Nabokov countered with "Do you?" Wilson muttered, "What a strange question!" When Wilson's marriage broke up two years later and McCarthy moved from Wellfleet to New York, his resident cook, afraid that she would be named co-respondent in the divorce case, threatened to leave. Wilson turned to the Nabokovs at this desperate moment, and they moved into his house—before the cook moved out—for a transitional week in July 1944.

The following March, shortly after the death of John Bishop, Wilson, who found it difficult to express his deepest feelings, told Nabokov: "Our conversations have been among the few consolations of my literary life through these last years—when my old friends have been dying, petering out or getting more and more neurotic." Nabokov responded warmly. In the 1940s he wrote Wilson: "I simply must see you both. I miss you a lot. . . . You are one of the very few people in the world whom I keenly miss when I do not see them." He later told his first biographer that Wilson was a "very old friend, in certain ways my closest."[18]

Wilson's first review of Nabokov's work, in the *New Yorker* of September 9, 1944, was a favorable notice of his eccentrically perceptive study *Nikolai Gogol*. Though Wilson was "annoyed by the frequent self-indulgence of the author in poses, perversities and vanities," an annoyance that would intensify as Nabokov persisted in this habit, he said it "takes its place with the very small body of first-rate criticism of Russian literature in English."

In November 1947 Wilson used his authority to protect Nabokov from an officious *New Yorker* editor who wanted to flatten out the peaks of his idiosyncratic style. "I have read Nabokov's stories," Wilson imperiously told Katharine White, "and I think they are both perfect. Not a word should be changed." That same year, as Nabokov later wrote in his Introduction to the *Time* paperback edition of *Bend Sinister*, Wilson read the typescript of the novel and recommended it to Allen Tate, then an editor at Henry Holt, who published the book. The proud Nabokov, who did not find it easy to express his gratitude, freely acknowledged throughout his life his enormous debt to Wilson. In March 1943, for example, he gratefully told Wilson: "I have noticed that whenever you are involved in any of my affairs they are always successful."

Their passionate common interest led Wilson, in November 1943, to suggest that they collaborate on a "Siamese" book on Russian literature: Wilson would write the critical essays and Nabokov would do the translations. Though they signed a contract with Doubleday (which Nabokov called "Dayday") for this joint project in 1944 and received an advance of $750 each, the book was never completed. "The only time I ever collaborated with any writer," Nabokov told an interviewer, "was when I translated with Edmund Wilson Pushkin's [short verse-play] *Mozart and Salieri* for the *New Republic* [in April 1941] . . . a rather paradoxical recollection in view of his making such a fool of himself . . . [by] questioning my understanding of *Eugene Onegin*."[19] In September 1948 Wilson revived the idea of a collaboration and helped to inaugurate Nabokov's massive edition by suggesting that they work together on a prose translation, with scholarly notes, of *Eugene Onegin*. Yet when Nabokov took up this idea on his own, and devoted more than a decade to this project, Wilson admonished him (as Fitzgerald had once admonished Wilson) for spending so much time on editing instead of writing his own novels.

Though Wilson and Nabokov admired and respected each other, they always had radically different views on life and art. During their protracted disputations, the critic with a biographical and historical approach opposed an avant-garde artist. But their quarrels also turned into a duel, fought on various points of honor, between the patrician American critic who had great prestige and influence in the Anglo-American literary world, and the uprooted, dispossessed Russian novelist who quickly established a considerable reputation with his magical English prose.

For thirty years they argued, in person and by mail, gently and harshly, about punning, pronunciation, approaches to literature, taste in authors, pornography, the meaning and value of Nabokov's works, and Russian politics. They also fought about two issues that would recur in their late quarrel about Pushkin: the fine points of English and Russian versification and Pushkin's knowledge of English. Commenting as an editor on Nabokov's first *New Republic* review, Wilson advised him, in his very first letter, to give up his lamentable propensity to pun. Twelve years later the incorrigible Nabokov was still referring to Pushkin's poem as "You gin? One gin." In the course of their friendship, the precise and pedantic Wilson ticked off Nabokov about the correct way to pronounce "nihilist" in English and about the correct meaning of the French *faux ami, fastidieux.*

Their different—indeed, antithetical—approach to literature was a more serious problem. In his diary as well as in his essay on Nabokov, Wilson compared his convoluted novels to an old-fashioned decorative object of the Czarist era. He condemned the fabulous artificer's idea of a literary work as "something in the nature of a Fabergé Easter egg or other elaborate knickknack." The historically-minded Wilson, who emphasized the author's psychology and milieu rather than his technique and style, condescendingly asked Nabokov how he could "pretend that it is possible to write about human beings and leave out of account all question of society and environment." He severely concluded that Nabokov had mindlessly taken over "in your youth the *fin de siècle Art for Art's sake* slogan and have never thought it out."

Nabokov, carefully replying to his "fellow magician," argued, on the contrary, that "a critic's duty should be to draw [the reader's] attention to the specific detail, to the unique image, without which . . . there can be no art, no genius." In his Commentary on *Eugene Onegin,* he hit directly at Wilson's influential approach by regretting that Pushkin "is treated by Russian pedants as a sociological and historical phenomenon typical of Alexander I's regime (alas, this tendency to generalize and vulgarize the unique fancy of an individual genius has also its advocates in the United States)." In 1959 Nabokov asked his editor not to seek an endorsement of his novels from Wilson, whose "symbolico-social criticism and phoney erudition in regard to *Doctor Zhivago*" inspired his "utter disgust."[20]

Their letters became bitter and even insulting when the two intensely dogmatic, competitive and contentious friends disagreed about the merits of both classic and contemporary writers. Wilson would enthusiastically recommend his favorite authors and Nabokov—who had an exalted idea of his own work and loved to demolish the reputations of great artists—would attack them and condemn Wilson's crude taste. When Wilson called André Malraux "the greatest contemporary writer," the bristling Nabokov (who probably thought he himself was the greatest) asked Wilson if he was kidding and called *Days of Wrath* and *Man's Fate* "a solid mass of clichés." When Wilson praised Faulkner's genius, Nabokov found it incredible that he could take Faulkner seriously and dismissed *Light in August* as "trite and tedious." Wilson, however, disliked Stevenson and Kafka, whom Nabokov admired for their artistry. "You and I differ completely," he told Wilson, "not only about Malraux [and Pasternak and James], but also about Dostoevsky, Greek drama, Lenin, Freud, and a lot of other things —about which, I'm sure, we will never be reconciled." Wilson finally persuaded him to include Jane Austen in his course on the novel at Cornell, and they did manage to agree about a few immortals: Pushkin, Flaubert, Proust and Joyce.

Both men had a taste for "indecent" literature, from Pauline Réage's *Histoire d'O* to Jean Genet; and Wilson once suggested an obscene, Genet-like interpretation of the title of one of his books, *The Bit Between My Teeth*. When, on the beach at Wellfleet, "two large, Monarch-like butterflies went all-atangle in the air," Wilson exclaimed: "Ah, look at those butterflies! They're, they're copulating. Volodya would love this!" Wilson's *Memoirs of Hecate County* and Nabokov's *Lolita* were considered pornographic and ran into trouble with contemporary censorship. Yet both authors—like Joyce and Lawrence—criticized that aspect of each other's work. Wilson complained to Louise Bogan that Nabokov, ignoring the serious intent of his book, thought he had tried to imitate the pornography of John Cleland's eighteenth-century novel *Fanny Hill*. Using a masochistic image, Nabokov tactlessly told Wilson that his book had failed to arouse erotic interest: I "derive no kick from the hero's love-making. I should have as soon tried to open a sardine can with my penis. The result is remarkably chaste, despite its frankness." Eight years later Wilson offered an imperceptive and similarly cutting response to *Lolita* (which his last two wives admired much more than he did): "I like it less than anything else of yours I have read. . . . Nasty subjects may make fine books; but I don't feel you have got away with this." Both writers had a scrupulous, but very different sense of what was appropriate in literature.

Their political arguments were also intensely personal and bitterly contested. "In historical and political matters," Nabokov told him, stressing Wilson's ideological rigidity, "you are a partisan of a certain interpretation which you regard as absolute. This means that we will have many a pleasant tussle and that neither will ever yield a thumb . . . of *terrain*." Wilson had forgotten that the *intellectual* tradition in Russia, with few exceptions like Gogol and Dostoyevsky, was always liberal; that an important democratic tradition—which Nabokov's father had belonged to and died for—stood between the Czarists and the Communists. Strongly influenced by his long study of Marxism, Wilson tended to misjudge Nabokov as a reactionary monarchist. "Your conception of Russian history is all wrong," he told Wilson, with his usual bluntness, "being based on the stale Bolshevist propaganda which you imbibed in your youth. . . . [You have] a complete ignorance of the . . . liberal movement that started in the time of Alexander I"—who reigned from 1801 to 1825.[21]

Despite these strictures, Wilson naively sent him a copy of *To the Finland Station* and inscribed it "to Vladimir Nabokov in the hope that this may make him think better of Lenin." Loathing the man who had destroyed his country and ruined his life, Nabokov was appalled by Wilson's portrayal of Lenin (fatally based on Soviet sources) as a warm-hearted humanitarian and freedom-loving democrat. In 1971 Wilson recanted his views and admitted that Nabokov had been right. Alluding to Nabokov as well as to other critics, Wilson wrote in his new Introduction: "I have been charged with having given a much too amiable picture of Lenin, and I believe that this criticism has been made not without some justification." Provoking, stimulating, offending, even outraging each other was an essential element in their friendship, which survived for twenty-five years despite profound disagreements. "We have always been frank with each other," Nabokov told him, "and I know that you will find my criticism exhilarating."[22]

Wilson's position at the *New Yorker* gave him new security and power, and enabled him to exercise his influence on behalf of Nabokov and many other friends. His very different relations with Helen Muchnic and Dawn Powell revealed that he developed deeper and more lasting friendships when he was not sexually involved with women. Like Powell, Nabokov became an intimate friend, but the seeds of their future quarrel were germinating from the start.

FOURTEEN

Postwar Europe and Mamaine Paget, 1945

I

At the beginning of 1945, after his separation from Mary McCarthy, Wilson lived alone in the almost empty house in Henderson Place. In March, as World War Two was coming to an end, the *New Yorker* gave him his first plum assignment and sent him to report on conditions in Europe. They advanced him a few thousand dollars and paid a bountiful $1,000 for his biweekly 3,000-word articles. After attracting attention in the magazine, they would then be published in a book. Wilson had finally achieved, in a big way, his goal of writing about what he was interested in and getting editors to pay for his expenses as well as for his work.

Familiar with the principal countries and languages of Europe, Wilson had taken a grand tour with his family in 1908 and a bicycle trip through England with college friends in 1914; he had spent two war years in France, followed Millay to Paris in 1921 and traveled to Russia in 1935. Wilson sailed from New York on a small Norwegian steamer on March 14, 1945. He arrived two weeks later and stayed for a month at the Hyde Park Hotel in London. He then flew on a military plane to Naples and, after a few days there, spent six weeks at the Albergo della Città and the Hôtel de la Ville in Rome. He returned to London for two weeks on June 17 and put up at the Green Park Hotel in Piccadilly. Back in Rome for three weeks on July 1, he took a second trip to Milan and also visited the Abruzzi. In late July he flew from Naples to Athens, lived at the Grande Bretagne Hotel, and during the next three weeks visited Delphi and Crete. In late August he went back to Naples and returned from there to America.

Wilson's press credentials failed to come through in time for him to witness the destruction of Germany, but several momentous events occurred while he was in Europe. President Roosevelt died in Warm Springs, Georgia on April 12, Mussolini was executed in Milan on April 28 and Hitler committed suicide in Berlin two days later. The Nazi extermination camps were exposed after the Allied victory in Europe on May 8; Truman, Churchill and Stalin met at the Potsdam Conference in July; and the atomic bomb was dropped on Hiroshima on August 6.

Wilson had grown up reading Scott and Dickens in an era when Americans looked to England to illuminate their own history and culture. His ancestry, background and education were all extremely pro-English. He thought Eliot's decision to live in London "was quite a natural thing to do," and told an Italian journalist: "In my youth, we always looked to England or France—I was first an Anglophile, then a Francophile." Wilson had respected Kemp Smith at Princeton, befriended the English lawyer Sylvester Gates in 1927, admired D. H. Lawrence and got on with Wyndham Lewis in the late 1920s.

But Wilson was also hostile to England as only an American of English ancestry could be. He had told Van Wyck Brooks that during the American Revolution one of his ancestors had been shut up in a British prison ship. For Wilson, the emotions of the Revolution were still real. He hated the English monarchy, the House of Lords and the Established Church. He regarded their literary critics—apart from Cyril Connolly and V. S. Pritchett—as "unadventurous, belles-lettristic, snobbish and class ridden." Their rigid hierarchies, class distinctions and studied reticence, their arrogance, rudeness and cutting remarks grated against his more democratic manner and provoked him to bait the British. "I have become so *anti*-British over here," he admitted, "that I have begun to feel sympathy with Stalin because he is making things so difficult for England."

Wilson particularly disliked the intellectual dishonesty in what he called "the Oxford brush-off: getting rid of importunate and troublesome questions by laughing gently about some aspect of the country or class or person which is totally irrelevant to the question in hand."[1] The supercilious Oxford don Maurice Bowra exemplified this condescending and exasperating mode of discourse. When Wilson emphatically declared that Walt Whitman was the greatest American writer, Bowra said he had never read him and claimed he was a great writer in *South* America. Then, conflating Whitman and Melville, Bowra deliberately confused them with the Victorian author of sporting novels,

Whyte-Melville. Bowra's campy conversation infuriated the earnest Wilson.

Wilson's intense anglophobia was based more on principle than on personal hostility. He had experienced the horrors of World War One and had rejected the attempts to justify it. He agreed with Pound's "Hugh Selwyn Mauberley" (1919):

> There died a myriad,
> And of the best, among them,
> For an old bitch gone in the teeth,
> For a botched civilization.

As Europe moved toward war in the late 1930s, Wilson, strangely blind to the dangers of Fascism, had failed to see that it represented a much greater threat than the German aggression of World War One. "Bombarded by British propaganda," he later wrote, "we went in on the side of England and made her struggle for supremacy our struggle, when we might well by abstaining have shortened the war and left Europe less shattered and more stable." He did not explain, however, what could have induced the Axis powers to shorten the war (unless they won it) without American intervention and what ideology or country could have provided such stability. The decadent yet power-hungry England, who lost her empire after the war, was ruined and forced for many years to live in humiliating austerity. At a London Labour meeting in 1945, a woman's gaunt and wolfish face suggested to Wilson that England had indeed passed into a lower phase of civilization than anything he had ever known in modern life.

II

Despite his hostile attitude and contentious behavior, Wilson was recognized as the leading American man of letters and was warmly received by his publisher and by many distinguished authors. As V. S. Pritchett, speaking for most of his colleagues, later wrote, "You have long reigned in my mind as the Master, the only American critic indeed." On this trip to London Wilson met Henry Green, Elizabeth Bowen, Graham Greene, Stephen Spender, Cyril Connolly, Evelyn Waugh and George Orwell, all of whom were about ten years his junior.

Roger Senhouse of Secker and Warburg, Wilson's first English publisher, had brought out *To the Finland Station* in 1940, *The Wound and the Bow* in 1942 and even *Note-Books of Night* in July 1945. Armed with Doubleday's page-proofs of *Memoirs of Hecate County*, Wilson was now trying to sell him English rights of that controversial book. During lunch at the Travellers' Club on Wilson's second visit to London, the reserved Englishman, alarmed by the wild American, told a fellow publisher that "He was in true-to-type fighting mood, almost truculent, and riding his usual hobbyhorse. . . . He is in danger of running amok." The following week, in a memo to his own firm, the exhausted Senhouse described Wilson's devious yet confrontational approach: "The author [was] in good training and rather too flashily parading his own powers of negotiation. . . . He clearly suffers a deep torture of the soul as soon as he brings himself to face a publisher. . . . Clearly he must get a kick from his impenetrable methods, which are more devilish than the ordinary, clear-thinking, logical, ruthless mind behind the poker face of an inveterate gambler."[2]

Wilson naturally discussed the war with Bowen, Greene and Spender. Bowen had, apart from the buzz bombs, enjoyed wartime London and wittily remarked: "Everything is very quiet, the streets are never crowded, and the people one dislikes are out of town." By contrast, the rather saturnine Greene, addicted to the peculiar excitement of pursuit and persecution, felt a morbid nostalgia for "the hum of a robot bomb!" Wilson portrayed Spender and Peter Quennell (unnamed in *Europe Without Baedeker*) as fatuous fellows, corrupted by the repugnant social attitudes of their old school. As the two literary types compared their experiences in the volunteer fire brigades, "they agreed that it was quite different from 'school.' I gathered that what was lacking was the spirit of the school team: the cockneys who were sometimes in command merely counted on people to do the right thing in a more matter-of-fact way."

Cyril Connolly—the son of an army officer, educated at Eton and Oxford—was a porcine and self-indulgent gourmand. He was also a wit, a passionate bibliophile who sometimes stole books from his friends and, as editor of the innovative magazine *Horizon*, at the center of literary life in London. Wilson admired Connolly's books and praised their elegance, observing that, like other Irishmen, he seemed "born with a gift of style, a natural grace and wit, so that his [books] have the freshness of *jeux d'esprit*, and sometimes his *jeux d'esprit* turn out to stick as classics." But Connolly, as he himself readily admitted, was rather lazy and superficial. In October 1946, a few months after Wilson's review had appeared, Connolly, with mock modesty, compared himself to Wilson and said how much he had enjoyed their intellectual sympathy and conversational fireworks: "I wish I had your *grasp*. I am really only a napkin-folder. I very much miss our too-rare occasions together. There is something so exhilarating about any relationship in which the intellect succeeds in battering down the walls of nationalism."

Wilson and Connolly both produced children when they were middle-aged. On hearing that Connolly was to become a father, Wilson, speaking from personal experience, told a mutual friend: "I expect that baby will meet some heavy competition." Later on, in a self-interview in the *New Yorker*, Wilson hoped that Connolly would try something more ambitious than his weekly book reviews for the London *Sunday Times*. Wilson too was a frequent reviewer, but he had the ambition and energy to write many serious books. In his humorous poem "Enemies of Promise"—whose title alluded to Connolly's well known essay about the talk, drink and sex, the journalism, politics and worldly success that destroy talented writers—Wilson satirized his charming idleness:

> Cyril Connolly
> Behaves rather fonnily:
> Whether folks are at peace or fighting,
> He complains that it keeps him from writing.[3]

Connolly's great friend Evelyn Waugh—recently back from wartime service in Yugoslavia—was as short, stout, blunt and belligerent as Wilson. Though they were quite intimate during Wilson's trips to London, Waugh later tried to suggest that he scarcely knew him. In March 1944, a year before he arrived in London, Wilson put Waugh in a receptive mood by calling him "the only first-rate comic genius that has appeared in English since Bernard Shaw." When they met through Connolly, Waugh, who looked down on Americans, adopted the same teasing *faux naïf* role that Wilson had found so irritating in Maurice Bowra. Waugh began, Wilson noted, "by pretending to think that I was a 'simple man' from Boise, Idaho, and, alternately, that I was a Rhodes Scholar, preoccupied with Henry James. . . . I talked about the antagonism to Americans, and he acknowledged it with a wicked gleeful grin in his bright little hard eyes." As they were having a drink at

White's, Wilson retaliated by saying "some derogatory things about *Brideshead Revisited* [1945], and this really rocked him. When I quoted some absurd sentence, he said, 'That doesn't sound like me, does it?' He handed me the book," and, attempting to shift responsibility to Wilson, said "Find it."

A barbed exchange took place at Connolly's dinner party for Wilson, which Spender also attended. Waugh was particularly warned not to mention the guest of honor's *Memoirs of Hecate County*, which was considered pornographic and had just been rejected by Secker and Warburg. Seizing the first opportunity to bait Wilson, Waugh drew him out with exquisite cunning and then thrust in the barb:

> Evelyn: Mr. Wilson, are we to have the pleasure of reading some new work from your pen?
> Edmund: I have a new book but it's not going to be published in this country.
> Evelyn: Is that your decision or your publisher's?
> Edmund: My publisher's.
> Evelyn: Mr. Wilson, you must understand that there's a grave paper shortage in this country—
> Edmund: This has nothing to do with the paper shortage.
> Evelyn: But my dear Mr. Wilson, what other reason for withholding your book from your English admirers can there possibly be?
> Edmund: There is a different reason.
> Evelyn: Mr. Wilson, I have always hoped that one day we would have the privilege of reading a novel by you.
> Edmund: The book I've referred to is a novel.
> Evelyn: Then what possible reason can there be for your publisher not letting us read it?
> Edmund: They say it would be banned under the laws relating to pornography.
> [After a long pause] Evelyn: Mr. Wilson, in cases like yours, I always advise publication in Cairo.

Wilson must have taken all this rather well, for they left the party together in a taxi. Waugh remarked, in a lovely voice that redeemed his ugliness: "The Americans are politer than anyone else," to which Wilson, quickly learning the game, replied: "Only than the British."

But the following day, Waugh "chucked [his] appointment to show London to insignificant Yank named Edmund Wilson."[4]

Though he recognized Waugh's brilliance, Wilson found him off-putting and gleefully pointed out his faults and pretensions in a letter to Betty Huling: "he wallows in his snobbery to an unbelievable degree (having married a wife from the Catholic nobility), and shows off his inside knowledge of how things are done in the great houses, and his aristocratic friends were making him miserable by telling him that he had everything all wrong." In January and July 1946, Wilson followed up this letter with extremely hostile reviews of Waugh's work, which were provoked by Waugh's rudeness and condescension and by his slavish adoration of the Catholic Church. Wilson called *Brideshead Revisited* "a bitter blow" and said he was "cruelly disappointed" by the bathos and shameless snobbery. He later added that in *The Loved One*, Waugh's satire on burial customs in California, the "patrons and proprietors of Whispering Glades seem more sensible and less absurd than the priest-guided Evelyn Waugh."

In April 1946 Waugh defended himself against Wilson's onslaught, in *Life* magazine (which had a Catholic proprietor), by haughtily declaring: "I have already shaken off one of the American critics, Mr. Edmund Wilson, who once professed a generous interest in me. He was outraged (quite legitimately by his standards) at finding God introduced into my story." When asked, in his *Paris Review* interview of 1962, if Wilson's literary criticism had been of interest to him, Waugh, still clinging to his affectations, responded: "'Is he American?' 'Yes.' 'I don't think what they have to say is of much interest, do you?'" That same year Wilson, transcending his personal feelings about Waugh and his religious beliefs, praised his *Sword of Honour* trilogy. He also thought *The Ordeal of Gilbert Pinfold* (1957)—Waugh's own version of *The Crack-Up*—was "the greatest Protestant allegory since *Pilgrim's Progress*."[5]

For all their obvious differences, the English writer who had the most in common with Wilson, and who enjoyed a position in the London literary world comparable to Wilson's in America, was George Orwell. Wilson and Orwell dedicated themselves to literature and spent years in poverty before achieving success toward the end of their lives. Wide-ranging men of letters who wrote articles, reviews, travel essays, imaginary interviews, poems, satires, stories and novels, they were essentially autobiographical writers, best at nonfiction. They sought experience in exotic countries and were excellent reporters. They were Socialists who criticized Communism from the Left and were deeply concerned about the falsification of history in Soviet Russia. As foreign correspondents—for the *New Yorker* and the *Observer*—in the spring of 1945, they considered the moral problem of vengeance against the Germans and the proper treatment of a defeated enemy.

They were both interested in popular culture and what Orwell called "good bad books." They tried to promote clear and vivid English, free of cant, and had a direct, straightforward prose style. They approached literature from a historical and ideological point of view, and combined incisive literary criticism with a shrewd political analysis. They had similar literary interests—Dickens, Kipling, Yeats—and wrote major essays on the first two writers at almost the same time. *The American Jitters* and *The Road to Wigan Pier* reported on the condition of the industrial poor during the Depression. *Travels in Two Democracies* and *Animal Farm* showed the betrayal of the Russian Revolution. *The Little Blue Light* (1950) and *Nineteen Eighty-Four* (1949), set in the near future, portrayed the effects of thought police and mind control. Wilson and Orwell were hostile to religion, but longed for the lost world of their childhood. They shared a sympathy for the underdog, high principles and integrity of character.

Wilson also met Orwell—just before *Animal Farm* made him wealthy and famous—through Cyril Connolly, his contemporary at prep school and Eton. Orwell's wife had died suddenly, during an operation, on March 29; and Wilson, who had been through a similar experience with Margaret Canby, was especially sympathetic. For some reason, Wilson insisted on straightening out Orwell's misconception that in America all insects were indiscriminately known as "bugs." In May 1942, three years before they met, Orwell had favorably reviewed *The Wound and the Bow*. He wrote that Wilson had written "the best essay on Dickens that has appeared for some time," and had thrown "brilliant flashes of light on some very dark places" of the writer's psyche. Wilson was (like Orwell himself) "one of the few literary critics of our day who gives the impression of being grown up, and of having digested Marx's teachings instead of merely rejecting them or swallowing them whole."

Wilson did not include his three little-known reviews of Orwell's books in his collections of essays, but they are worth noting. Reviewing *Dickens, Dali and Others*, he praised Orwell as "the only contemporary master" of sociological criticism. Identifying his quintessential strengths, Wilson commended his "readiness to think for himself, courage to speak his mind, the tendency to deal with concrete realities rather than theoretical positions, and a prose style that is both downright and disciplined." In a rare accolade, Wilson called *Animal Farm* "absolutely first-rate," compared Orwell to Voltaire and Swift, and concluded that he is "likely to emerge as one of the ablest and most interesting writers that the English had produced" in the last decade. Stressing Orwell's unique and paradoxical qualities in his notice of the posthumously published *Shooting an Elephant*, Wilson placed him in the tradition of "middle-class British liberalism that depended on common sense and plain-speaking." His acquaintance with Orwell reinforced his literary judgments. Wilson's reviews reveal an ability to recognize a talented contemporary, define his special qualities and place him in his proper ideological context.

In 1948, between Wilson's second and third reviews, Orwell wrote four letters to Wilson asking for copies of his books, mentioning his disease and describing his life in a Scottish sanitorium: "I've been ill for several months and am likely to be in this hospital several months more. It is T.B., very unpleasant, but they seem to be confident of patching me up all right. I took the liberty of writing to you because apart from frequently reviewing one another I remember we did have lunch together" in 1945. Orwell's doctors, unfortunately, were too optimistic and he died in January 1950. Expressing sorrow about Orwell's death, Wilson associated him with the values of a lost world and observed: "I had a feeling that he wouldn't last, as if the things he represented were doomed to fade away, and it is disconcerting to have it gone."[6]

When evaluating contemporary British writers, Wilson told Roger Senhouse, whose firm published *Animal Farm*, that he reserved judgment on Connolly, liked the poetry of Edwin Muir and preferred the fiction of Orwell, Waugh and Greene. Greene, extremely impressed by *Memoirs of Hecate County*, tried to acquire the book for Eyre and Spottiswoode and later met Wilson in New York. Orwell, sensing Wilson's anglophobia before they met, had written in his review that "Wilson is one of those Americans who avoid visiting England lest their hatred for it should evaporate." Wilson's hostility was fortified by the arrogant behavior of the Englishmen he met in Italy and Greece. When he later asked himself what brought him to England, he replied that he wanted to dine at the Café Royal in Piccadilly and buy a set of Rudolph Ackermann's colored engravings of London (1795), after which he "need never come" to Britain again.

III

Visiting Naples in 1908, the thirteen-year-old Edmund had called it "a very dirty place, full of howling dagoes," and his opinion had not changed very much in 1945. He had started out for Naples in 1920, but cancelled his journey after being robbed in the train station in Florence. Now, at the end of the long war and the heavy fighting during the German retreat up the peninsula, the city was as ruined as Pompeii: "Naples is absolutely ghastly and makes the [bombed out] East End of London look relatively cheerful. I saw nothing but either ruined streets with fragments of walls rising like crumbled sand castles out of mounds of pulverized plaster or battered buildings with garbage strewn on the pavements, a few gruesome cuts in the butcher shops and thousands of dirty children running about the streets."

Wilson was happier (at first) on the balcony of his hotel on the Via Sistina in Rome. He had a splendid view of the city and was surrounded by memorials to illustrious writers—Stendhal, Keats, Gogol, D'Annunzio—who had lived in his quarter. But he was shocked to find the ruined parts of Italy more repugnant than anything he had ever seen. Appalled by the poverty and the prostitution, Wilson told Dos Passos that when he looked below the surface he found a "corrupt and stagnant swamp." His visit to Milan, shortly after Mussolini had been hanged upside down with his mistress in the Piazzale Loreto, affected him with horror. On his visit to the mountainous Abruzzi, east of Rome, with United Nations aid workers, he thought the devastation was unimaginable and saw that human life was cheap: "large towns with not a building left and the country still planted with mines, which the young men are getting killed digging up for 20 lire (20 cents) a day." Though Fascism had been defeated, feudal injustice remained. Wilson reported that when an unemployed stationmaster had begged a wealthy aristocrat (with whom Wilson had dined) for some corn for his starving family, the prince, despite the pleas of his cultured American wife, had callously refused.

William Barrett, an American writer who met Wilson in Rome, thought he had "great integrity, and also—something that usually has not been noted—kindness and good will." The eminent figures whom Wilson met—the handsome and voluptuous surrealist painter Leonor Fini, whom he found extremely attractive,[7] the novelists Alberto Moravia and Ignazio Silone, the critic Mario Praz, the English diplomat Sir Ronald Storrs and the Spanish-born Harvard philosopher George Santayana—all responded to these qualities. Wilson described Silone —who had a lively Irish wife, was a leading anti-Fascist and had spent the war years in exile—as "a queer mixture of priest and Communist underground worker."

Mario Praz, a professor of English at the University of Rome, became a good friend, and Wilson helped to arrange his State Department–sponsored trip to America in 1953. A short, heavy, wall-eyed and club-footed man, Praz lived in a flat that was oppressively embellished with Empire decor. Like Wilson, he was bookish, multi-lingual, cultured, energetic and prolific, and shared a taste for the mordant and macabre in literature. He had read everything, knew everything and had very nearly written about everything, and had the same stature as a man of letters in Italy as Wilson did in America. The two savants corresponded for many years and kept abreast of the latest writing in America and Italy, sent each other hard-to-find books and reviewed each other's works. Wilson called Praz's erudite study *The Romantic Agony* (1930) "one of the most truly original as well as one of the most fascinating works of our time," and warmly praised "his brilliant powers of description, his lyric interludes which are really prose poems, and his Proustian reflections on life."[8]

The cultivated, snobbish and apparently homosexual Storrs had recognized T. E. Lawrence's genius and supported him from Cairo during the Arabian campaign against the Turks in World War One. Lawrence had called him "the most brilliant Englishman in the Near East," but had hinted—in a passage deleted from the trade edition of *Seven Pillars of Wisdom*—that he was insidiously corrupt: "his eyelids were heavy with laziness, and his eyes dulled by cares of self, and his mouth made unbeautiful by hampering desires." Wilson was appalled by Storrs' preposterous vanity and considered him a prototypical British imperialistic agent. But he was also fascinated by him and thought it a pity that the old fossil could not be preserved in a museum.

The highlight of Wilson's stay in Rome was his visit to the frail but still lively eighty-two-year-old Santayana, who had spent the war years in the convent of the Blue Nuns. "He was slight and shrunken," Wilson recorded, "wore a brown bathrobe which did make him look rather like a monk." He had a mischievous smile, seemed slightly feline and feminine, but possessed remarkable dignity—as befitted a philosopher. He received Wilson with great politeness and amiability, and plunged directly into conversation about his Spanish background, his teaching at Harvard, the history of philosophy, Bertrand Russell and Jacques Maritain, his reading of religious works and of Charles Dickens, life in Rome, the virtues of the Fascist régime, English hostility to America and the role of the United States in the postwar world. Identifying, as he often did, with older, much admired figures, Wilson was delighted to hear that the aged Santayana "finds that he now knows his business better and is in full command of his forces. I have been feeling something of this as I have been coming closer to fifty."[9]

Wilson made his first trip to Greece in July 1945 and was delighted by Athens, the first illuminated city he had seen in darkened Europe. Unlike Rome, which was encrusted with ornate churches, it was a clean, well-swept city of simple and dignified buildings. After the excesses of densely-packed Italy, Greece seemed purer, grander and more mysterious: "In Italy, there was too much color, too much flesh and too much smell, too many things sprouting and swarming; Greece was lean and bare but somehow on a higher plane." In contrast to the noisy and demonstrative Italians, the Greeks seemed good humored, sensible and poised. Their children were rather serious—a great relief after the appalling gangs of street urchins in Naples and the "servile goblins" of Pescara.

The Greeks had fiercely resisted the Nazi occupation and suffered terribly in the war. One out of seven people had died, nearly two thirds of them from starvation. The educational system was in a disastrous state and seventy percent of the people were virtually illiterate. The Royalists and Communists, who had been fighting intermittently since the liberation of the country in 1944, were preparing for the ruthless three-year civil war that broke out in May 1946.

Wilson took language lessons in both Italian and Greek, went to outdoor performances of classical tragedies and often visited the Pavlides family, who were related by marriage to a Russian friend in New York. The highlight of Wilson's trip to Greece was his platonic love affair with the married interpreter Eva Siphraios, whom he calls "Eleni V." in *Europe Without Baedeker*. Smarter and prettier than any other Greek woman he had seen, she seemed to embody the spirit of the country and "had the special sort of elegance and fineness that is . . . part of some old kind of nobility, at once primitive and civilized, that still thrives in the Greek islands." Wilson, who loved to remember his romantic escapades and usually kept in touch with his lady friends, met Eva again on his second trip to Greece in 1954. Though she had lost the "Nausicaa look" that had once tempted Odysseus, she still re-minded him of some elemental creature: a siren or sea nymph.

IV

The ironic title of Wilson's account of his journey, *Europe Without Baedeker: Sketches Among the Ruins of Italy, Greece and England* (pub-lished by Doubleday in November 1947), alluded to the tourists who had used Karl Baedeker's factual guidebooks when viewing the sights of Europe, to Browning's poem "Love Among the Ruins" (1852) and to Eliot's satire "Burbank with a Baedeker: Bleistein with a Cigar" (1919).[10] Instead of sketching the charming classical ruins that had once attracted cultivated travelers, Wilson described the meaningless destruction of war and included England with the ruined empires of Greece and Rome. Like *Travels in Two Democracies, Europe Without Baedeker* was worked into a book from his contemporary diary, letters and essays. Wilson's vehement opposition to the war, the break-up of his marriage just before he left for Europe, his frustrated love in all three countries and the extremely depressing scene in postwar Europe accounted for his harsh and bitter tone.

Wilson's intense hostility to the English permeated the book, and he offered no substantial account of his generally friendly meetings with Greene, Connolly, Waugh and Orwell to mitigate his attacks. Wilson sharply criticized the austerity of England, the defects in the national character and the oppressive foreign policy. The shabby coun-try, whose restaurants served crow disguised as duck, was "bedevilled and bombed and deprived." Life was constricted by ration-books, food was inferior, housing scarce and unemployment high. The intolerably rude and voraciously greedy people lived in a thoroughly corrupt society that was characterized by "the passion for social privilege, the rapacious appetite for property, the egoism that damns one's neighbor, the dependence on inherited advantages, and the almost equally deep-fibered instinct, often not deliberate or conscious, to make all these appear forms of virtue."

Jealous of America's prosperity and resentful of their victorious role in the war, the English bitterly criticized the United States, which irritated Wilson and estranged him from his natural allies. Believing that the English tried to compensate for their loss of empire by accen-tuating their characteristic arrogance (exemplified by Maurice Bowra in

Oxford and Sir Ronald Storrs in Rome), Wilson maliciously suggested "that England might comfortably survive as a small agricultural country, with little industry and a reduced population; very sound and clean and trim like Denmark."

Wilson gave many examples of the Englishman's intolerable behavior in foreign countries—from refusing to pick up hitch-hiking American soldiers and stealing American food to telling Eva Siphraios that Athens was "an awful place" and kicking Arabs who seemed to be disrespectful. He also attacked the British for frustrating political development in southern Europe and for clamping a military government on Italy and Greece. He particularly condemned their brutal repression of the Communist National Liberation Front, "a genuine popular movement which had been able to recruit almost all that was generous, courageous and enlightened in Greece." The Communist partisans had fought against the Nazis. But Wilson failed to see that it would have been politically and economically disastrous if the Communists had seized power in Greece as they had done in Albania and Yugoslavia.

Fredric Warburg's internal report on *Europe Without Baedeker* was extremely negative. He noted the lack of structure and intemperate anglophobia, and suggested that Wilson had gone off the deep end: "It lacks all unity, save that bestowed upon it by the common ruin of war and the author's style and personality, including his bitter hatred of England. What must be noted is the violent envy which has produced these feelings, and the terrible frustrations which his ravings reveal. . . . [It is] a vile and vicious performance in which a man of brilliant talents and (in his own sphere) mature judgement, reveals himself as having just those characteristics which he attributes to the British." Nevertheless, Warburg was eager to keep Wilson on his list. Realizing the book would stir up controversy, he decided to publish it in 1948. Putting the best face on it, Warburg told Wilson that his attack might actually go over rather well in England: the "anti-British sections to which you have referred will almost certainly endear it to the British public who like really nothing better than to have rude remarks made about them," which they would confidently attribute "to the malice and ignorance of the 'bloody foreigner.'"[11]

Europe Without Baedeker marked the end of the American infatuation with England, which had reached its peak with Henry James' *Portrait of a Lady* (1881), and provoked many counter-attacks by the British popular press. Connolly told Wilson that the book, as Warburg had predicted, caused a considerable stir, and wittily explained that "the most charitable put it down to you being on the wagon." Richard Usborne, who reviewed the book for the B.B.C. European Service and may have heard some gossip about Wilson's *contretemps* with Bowra and Waugh, explained that "some English intellectual must have teased Wilson, or trodden on his corns."

Wilson had met W. H. Auden, who had spent the war years in America, during his second trip to London. Amused by Auden's gaucheness, he told Betty Huling that "without showing the least embarrassment, [Auden] complained about the coldness of English houses, and of other hardships of life in England, and told them that London hadn't really been bombed. They were speechless with indignation." Though Wilson did not go quite so far as Auden, he did seem to provoke the English more deeply than he intended. As the Oxford don A. L. Rowse indignantly observed, nearly fifty years after Wilson's visit: "It was extremely insensitive and *mean* of him to complain when he came over here after the war that a) the food was poor, and b) our rooms so cold. . . . How mean and *unimaginative* of E. W. not to realize the sacrifices this country made to defeat the Germans."[12]

A few people, however, realized that Wilson's book concerned more serious issues. William Hughes, a London lawyer whom Wilson had first met in Rome, perceptively wrote Wilson that the English critics, attacking the book for its anti-British animus, had completely ignored Wilson's "close and unexcited observation of our imperialistic ethos—or the strain which persists in odd perversions when the reality has ceased to exist." Stephen Spender, mildly ridiculed in the book, complained in the *Nation* that it left him "with a sense of betrayal." But Nicola Chiaromonte, writing in the *Partisan Review* and taking a loftier view, realized that Wilson's book concerned the effect of war on Europe and ranged "from the beastliness of modern man to the future of western civilization."[13] *Europe Without Baedeker* was stamped by Wilson's intense individuality and, for all its faults, has provided— along with Norman Lewis' *Naples '44* (1978)—the most vivid account of postwar Europe.

V

During his first visit to England in April 1945, Wilson fell profoundly and poignantly in love with a woman he could not capture. With Mamaine Paget, as with Edna Millay, he answered Yeats' crucial question—"Does the imagination dwell the most / Upon a woman won or a woman lost?"—by keeping his lost loves (in contrast to his four wives) on an ideal plane. Leonor Fini lived with a marquis in Rome, Eva Siphraios was married in Athens and Mamaine Paget was in love with the Hungarian émigré novelist Arthur Koestler. But Koestler was then in Palestine and Wilson, believing that he had a fighting chance, once again entered a competitive love triangle.

The beautiful, cultivated and frequently photographed Paget twins, Mamaine and Celia, were born in 1916 (twenty-one years after Wilson) and became the leading debutantes of the 1930s. Their mother had died a week after their birth and their clergyman father died when they were twelve. They had been educated first by a village schoolmaster in Suffolk and then at boarding schools in England and Lausanne, where they learned perfect French. After their presentation at Court they often appeared, dressed alike and with the same hairstyles, in gossip columns and glossy magazines. But Mamaine was not merely a beauty. She had read widely in English and French literature, was an accomplished pianist and wonderful mimic, and loved walking and bird-watching in the country. She could hold her own in high-powered conversation with writers, artists and intellectuals, and played a lively part in Cyril Connolly's circle of contributors to *Horizon*.

Wilson first met Mamaine in April 1945 at a dinner party with the Labour M.P. and future minister John Strachey and the journalist Humphrey Slater, and later took her home in a cab. She had an oval face, light brown shoulder-length hair, bright blue eyes, a *retroussé* nose and a small, slightly pouting mouth. Thin and frail, she made all her friends want to protect her. Arthur Schlesinger, Jr. found Mamaine (who was named for a French aunt) *gamine*, enchanting and terribly upper-class, and said that everyone adored her. Eleanor Perenyi, who met the twins in a German pension in Bavaria in 1938, said they were the two most attractive women she had ever known. Mamaine asked Wilson which film stars he fancied in order to determine the type of woman he liked—though it was abundantly clear that he liked *her*. When he offered to send her clothes from America, she gave her measurements: height: 5'3", waist: 24", bust: 32". Mamaine worked in the wartime department of economic propaganda, took lessons in Italian, Greek and Turkish, and persuaded Wilson to see Benjamin Britten's opera *Peter Grimes*, which he greatly admired.

In November 1947 Mamaine playfully told Celia: "do get Edmund's new book *Europe Without Baedeker* and read about me: unfortunately it is a bad book so my immortality is not assured; but perhaps that is after all just as well, particularly as he very clearly hints that I was his mistress, which God forbid! I am called 'G.'" Calling her "a London girl whom I very much liked," Wilson devotes nearly eight pages of his book to Mamaine. Though always high-strung and physically frail, with volatile moods and an enchanting expression, Mamaine, extremely bright and able, had a solid intellect and character. Wilson liked her because she had quiet manners and was pleased that she did not try to compete with men. She was beautiful in a feminine way, which he found a great relief after "the dashing and aggressive 'style'" of American women like Mary McCarthy. Wilson, who liked to keep his mistresses *au courant* about his affairs, told Betty Huling that he had been carried away in vulnerable middle age by Mamaine:

> I fell terribly in love in London with a young English girl —twenty-seven [*sic*] and one of the brightest I have ever known and—need I say?—rather neurotic. We talked about getting married and she was trying to join me in Italy.... I doubt now whether anything ever comes of it. I suppose, after my experience with Mary, I've been a lunatic to think of getting married to an even younger girl.... These last years have made me tinder for any real spark, and I haven't been so upset since my youth.[14]

Wilson's correspondence with Mamaine is fascinating. He tried hopelessly to persuade her to marry him; and though she tactfully and charmingly rejected him (which Mary McCarthy had been unable to do), she still managed to retain his adoration. When Wilson returned to America and continued his epistolary suit from Wellfleet, and Koestler came back to England to reclaim her, Connolly entered their correspondence (in yet another variant of the love triangle) and sent bulletins about her volatile relationship with Koestler.

Leaving London for Rome at the end of April, Wilson assumed Mamaine was in love with him rather than with his rival and begged her not to give her heart to anyone else before he returned. After he had left England Mamaine, acknowledging his liveliness and boundless curiosity, wrote: "I miss you a lot—Nobody I know here is half as much fun to be with as you"—but that was as far as she was prepared to go. Encouraged by her letters, Wilson made a formal proposal on May 28 in the same no-nonsense style he had once used with McCarthy. He emphasized their (that is, *his*) deep feelings and even set out the possible disadvantages in a fair-minded, lawyer-like way:

Why don't you marry me?—I am serious. I'm in love with you—though I've partly been trying to struggle against it. I don't expect you to decide at this distance, but please think about it very seriously till I see you again. You hardly know me, I suppose—I believe that I know you better than you do me; but I think that something fairly strong has been operating between us. I've never felt a natural understanding with any woman come so quickly as it has with you, and the month that I've been away from you, instead of diminishing my desire for you and this feeling of understanding, has made them stronger and stronger. I don't suppose you could care about me as much as I do about you and I know that marrying me would, from your point of view, have some pretty heavy disadvantages: step-children, who are always more of a problem than people think they are going to be, and my being enough older than you that I may be fading out while you are still in your prime. But there might be some good things about it for you, too—I'll tell you why when I see you. There are no practical obstacles on my side: I've called Mary suggesting that she get a divorce during the summer.—I've leased my house in New York for another year.

In mid-June Wilson flew back to London from Italy—laden with an antique veil and lace fan, two pairs of earrings, silk stockings, a carton of cigarettes, two bottles of sparkling wine, some Italian magazines and a book by Silone—to press his suit in person. But Mamaine, insisting that he did not know her very well, remained loyal to the still-absent Koestler and rejected his proposal: "I don't think I can marry you or do anything to make our relationship fit any conventional pattern, if it doesn't do so already."

Wilson took it all rather badly. When he had gone back to Rome, Mamaine said: "I was very glad to get your wire and discover that you don't hate me as much as your attitude on Saturday had led me to suppose." To which Wilson disconsolately replied, as he had to Mc-Carthy after their relations had soured: "I'm writing to you again, though I have nothing particular to say, because I still, despite our snappings and snarlings in London, feel closer to you than to anybody else (perhaps an illusion)."[15]

Wilson felt crushed after his romantic aspirations had been rejected by three enchanting European women. While living in the seedy Green Park Hotel, which resembled a "condemned brothel," he developed a Gladstonian obsession with prostitutes. He met a French whore —"a vigorous well-fitted-out brunette with a bright smile of strong white teeth"—who was doing overseas service, knew the business from the bottom up, and hoped to go back to Paris and open a lingerie shop. Like the prostitute he had once engaged with in New Orleans, Odette —whose purple girdle "left her black bush exposed"—stripped down to her shoes and dropped her stockings. She "produced a rubber condom, worked energetically and authoritatively," and gave him some welcome relief.

In September 1945, when Wilson was back in Wellfleet, Mamaine, eager for motherhood, unintentionally roused his hopes by writing that Koestler "firmly refuses to have children. . . so there seems no chance of getting married and not much point in doing so. . . . Arthur is a great fan of yours and was very crestfallen when I told him you'd never read any of his books"—though *Darkness at Noon* had attracted a great deal of attention in 1941. Wilson reported that he had found his house in terrible condition—ceilings fallen in, no hot water, spider webs all over his study—and desperately needed a woman's help. He flattered Mamaine by telling her that she was always in his mind, repeated his proposal and invited her over on a tour of inspection: "I think about you constantly and you still seem to me the only woman I really want to be with. Won't you think again about marrying me? Would you like to come over here for a while and look the situation over? I could send you the money for the trip and you could repay me by working as my secretary."[16]

Recalling the austerity of postwar England, Mamaine's enthusiastic response to his presents from Rome and, perhaps, Zelda Fitzgerald's belief that "having things, just things, objects, makes a woman happy. The right kind of perfume, the smart pair of shoes. They are great comforts to the feminine soul," Wilson, persistent as ever, sent another letter the following week with an offer he hoped she could not refuse: "I'm still in love with you and I still want to marry you. You don't sound as if you thought you and Koestler had much of a future together, and if you really do want to marry and have children, you probably ought to act fairly soon. . . . This is the time to come to America if you want me to outfit you at Saks Fifth Avenue."

Mamaine—always bright, witty, kind and responsive—knew she would not be able to hold out for very long while working off her debt in Wilson's rustic retreat. Though she very much wanted to come to America, she knew her situation would be impossible and had to reiterate her refusal: "I really thought I had told you I wouldn't marry you, but if not please accept herewith my official refusal. The idea of coming to the States and working for you is an excellent one, however, if I could do so without marrying you and feeling that you were being exploited, there is nothing I should like better." Seizing upon her interest in the bounty of America, Wilson put his cards on the table and tried to wriggle out of his painfully familiar role as paternal figure to a child-hood orphan: "I do need an intelligent secretary for a couple of months, but of course what I really want of you is YOU, and if you come—since you don't want to marry me—you ought to have a clear recognition of the practical and emotional problems involved. . . . I shan't feel that I'm being exploited unless you exploit me—which I'll probably feel that you're doing if you try to turn me into a Father substitute."[17]

Mamaine had moved into Koestler's remote Welsh cottage soon after he returned from Palestine in August 1945, though she did not marry him until 1950, and assumed the roles of cook, secretary, hostess and mistress. Connolly then told Wilson, who was eager for bad news, that Mamaine, though a glutton for punishment, might possibly be-come fed up with Koestler: "She is madly in love with him and doesn't care how he treats her. . . . She adores him but would like to be married and have children, which he wouldn't, and they might split up on that. . . . The only person who can break it up is A. K. himself. . . . I am told Koestler nags and bullies her rather, but she doesn't seem to mind and I think he is really devoted to her—but she may snap out of it suddenly, one never knows, with that kind of person." Keeping up his brisk correspondence with Connolly to get news about Mamaine, Wil-son condemned Koestler's harsh behavior and declared that he "carries obnoxiousness to a point where you realize that nobody can be as bad as that. . . . I suppose that he is a compulsive neurotic."[18]

In February 1951, when Mamaine and Koestler had moved to America and were living on an island in the Delaware River, she told Celia: "I saw Edmund in New York last week and met his wife, who is charming. He wants me to go up and spend a day with them, but God knows when I'll be able to get away owing to the impossibility of leaving K with nobody to look after him." That September, after six difficult years together, she finally decided to leave Koestler. Wilson and Mamaine met again in February 1954 when they were both staying at the Hôtel de Quai Voltaire in Paris. Wilson's wife, Elena, complain-ing that Mamaine always seemed to be around and that Wilson was always taking her out to lunch, made a jealous scene. Wilson explained that Mamaine, having just divorced Koestler, was feeling let down and lonely, and that he was merely trying to comfort her. Unlike the other women Wilson had once loved, Mamaine, years later, was still young and beautiful.

In March (just after Wilson saw her) Mamaine, who had always been in delicate health, became seriously ill. She spent April and May in the hospital, and on June 2, 1954, at the age of thirty-seven, she died. As Celia told Wilson, in an unbearably sad letter: "She had 5 *extremely* bad [asthma] attacks running within 3 months, and was never able to recover properly in between, and from the 5th she did not recover at all, as she was too weak by then. . . . She was in hospital of course, and I couldn't believe that they wouldn't be able to prevent any further bad attacks. But really there was nothing that they could do, try though they did, the drugs no longer had any effect on her."

Wilson kept in touch with Celia for the next decade by sending her valentines. In a recent letter, Celia explained Mamaine's attitude to Wilson and said that her sister had never seriously thought of marrying him: "Edmund's love for Mamaine *was* one-sided: she did not feel at all that way about him. She did not find him physically attractive but she liked him very much and enjoyed his company. She would certainly *not* have accepted his proposal of marriage, even if she had not been involved with Koestler."[19]

Wilson's attraction to Leonor Fini and Eva Siphraios and love for Mamaine Paget made him particularly responsive to European-born Elena Thornton, whom he had met in Wellfleet while still married to McCarthy. He had passionately wanted to marry Mamaine but, when she repeatedly refused him, married the charming Elena instead.

FIFTEEN

Elena Thornton, 1946–1949

I

When Wilson returned in September 1945 to his dilapidated house in Wellfleet, the scene of his unhappy marriage, he felt relieved to be liberated from Mary McCarthy. In a triumph of hope over experience, he courted three attractive younger women: Mamaine Paget by post, Anaïs Nin and Elena Mumm Thornton—who became his fourth wife —in person. The twenty-two-year-old Rosalind, living with him in Wellfleet, cooked gigantic turkeys and they entertained many friends whom he had not been able to invite to the house during the years with McCarthy.

None of Wilson's four very different wives came, as he did, from the Eastern establishment. Mary Blair was a Swedenborgian from Pittsburgh, Margaret Canby a Presbyterian from Santa Barbara, Mary McCarthy a Catholic from Seattle, and Elena Mumm Thornton (whose mother was Russian Orthodox) a Lutheran, born in France. Though none of his wives had been religious, Elena attended the Episcopal church on the Cape and often ended her letters to Wilson with "God bless you." Blair and McCarthy were artistic and intellectual; Thornton, like Canby, was aristocratic and elegant. All four wives had been previously married. Wilson had to persuade Margaret to leave Ted Paramore, Mary to leave Philip Rahv, Mamaine to leave Koestler and Elena to leave James Thornton. Wilson had been married for two years to Mary Blair, two years to Margaret and seven years to Mary McCarthy, but he remained married to Elena for twenty-five years, until his death.

Nabokov called the half-German, half-Russian Elena "a salad of racial genes." Her family had founded Mumm's champagne in the early 1800s and maintained the prosperous business for five generations. Elena (baptized Hélène-Marthe) was born in Rheims, in the province of Champagne, in 1906 and lived there until 1914. After World War One the French government confiscated the German-owned Mumm's. Elena's father—a champion ski-jumper—continued to produce the wine in Johannisberg, famous for its Riesling, on the Rhine, about ten miles west of Mainz. The family briefly regained the business in 1940, after the German occupation of France, and lost it again at the end of the war.

Elena's uncle, Walther Mumm, had a strong German accent and a weak sense of humor. David Chavchavadze recalled that Wilson loved to tease him: "'Walther,' he would say quite often, knowing what the result would be. 'What do you think of American champagne?' Uncle Walther always went into a slow, rapidly increasing burn. 'How many times do I have to tell you, Edmund, zere is no American champagne, only shparkling vine!'" When Wilson told Walther that Jesus was Jewish, he replied that He didn't look Jewish in His pictures.

Elena's grandfather had been the Russian ambassador to Japan, the Netherlands and the United States; the women in the family had been ladies-in-waiting at the Czarina's court. Her childhood home had a dozen servants; and one great-aunt, who lived in Paris after the Revolution, had never dressed herself. The eldest of four children, Elena was tutored at home, spent part of the year in Switzerland, and later studied art in Munich and Paris. Her parents had died before she married Wilson, and one brother had killed himself in Montreal.

Though Elena had never lived in or even visited Russia, she had learned the language in childhood and could speak and understand it very well. But, according to Simon Karlinsky, she wrote Russian like a small child—as it sounded and with many mistakes. Wilson later recalled that his own spoken Russian was poor when he married Elena and when he tried to speak to her in Russian, "I spoke so very badly and you with such easy fluency that we were unable to understand one another." She was also fluent in French and had a "formidable" knowledge of German. Elena spoke English with a slight and rather attractive German accent, or intonation. But Wilson, for all his praise, could also be sharp-tongued about her. When Charlotte Kretzoi, a Hungarian friend, asked, "What language does Elena think in," he said, "None!"[1]

Elena met her first husband, James Thornton, when he was working in Frankfurt, married him at Johannisberg in September 1931 and had a son, Henry, the following year. James' father, who had substantial interests in British, Canadian and American railroads, lived well and spent most of his fortune. Though both families had once been enormously wealthy, James and Elena did not have much money. She had lived in France, Germany, Switzerland, been dispossessed by the French and had become anti-Nazi before moving to the New World. "Sad to think," Wilson later wrote, "of Elena coming to America with eagerness, on account, as she says, of the Marx Brothers and of the idealization of the country, on the part of smart people in Paris, as the home of the *le jazz hot* and the vertiginous *gratte-ciels* [skyscrapers], and being landed in Montreal at its stuffiest."

Wilson first saw Elena swimming across Gull Pond and was immediately attracted to the tall, rangy, blue-eyed, brown-haired woman, who usually dressed in men's shirts, denim skirts and sandals. When he actually met Elena, a paying guest in the house of her childhood friend Nina Chavchavadze, Wilson was still married to McCarthy and Elena was living in the New York suburbs with her husband and son. After meeting her again in the fall of 1945 at *Town and Country*, where he published his story "Glimpses of Wilbur Flick" and where she worked as an assistant editor, he became more seriously interested in her. In October he proudly told Helen Muchnic (who was not pleased by the news) that he had already found a substitute for Mamaine: "I have a wonderful little half-Russian secretary who has been helping me buy things for my house as well as doing my correspondence and so forth."

In his first letter to Elena of April 16, 1946, Wilson said he was filled with joy and counting the days until he saw her again. A month later he gave his familiar line—"I think of you all the time" (women were always flattered to be lodged in that deep mind)—and hoped he would not become unreal to her when absent. In mid-May he also confessed that she had taken full possession of him and that if she really wanted him everything would be all right. On July 31 he wrote four separate letters to her. During July and August, after they had become lovers, Wilson pressed her to leave her husband. Elena advised him in a motherly way about how to bring up Reuel, and lamented that *her* son blamed Wilson for breaking up their family.

On October 25 Wilson and Elena took up residence in Nevada in order to obtain their divorces. They stayed at the Minden Inn—a square, three-story, yellow-brick building on the main street of Minden—south of Carson City and east of Lake Tahoe. In that debauched and dehydrated part of the world, far from Elena's turbulent marriage and alone for the first time, they amused themselves by walking around the pleasant town square, exploring the nearby desert, lakes and wildflowers, and doing a bit of gambling—which reminded Wilson of

Dostoyevsky at Baden-Baden. "I have been having a very quiet and not unpleasant, rather purgatorial, time out here," Wilson told Nabokov, who had often chased butterflies in the American West. "It is a queer and desolate country—less romantic than prehistoric and spooky."

They married in Reno on about December 11, 1946, while the scandalous trial of *Memoirs of Hecate County* was taking place in San Francisco. Unaccustomed to celebrity and not keen to appear as a blushing groom on his fourth try, the "short and stout" writer and "his six foot bride" dashed for the Reno–San Francisco train to avoid a mob of reporters. After a train chase out of a cowboy movie, Wilson tried some Hemingwayesque heroics to impress his new wife. According to a story that appeared the following day in the *San Francisco Chronicle:* "Newsmen climbed aboard and blocked the passageway in an effort to interview the newlyweds. While trying to escape, Wilson took an unsuccessful swing at a reporter for the *New York News* and tried to grab a camera pointed in his direction. A chase then ensued that embraced the length of five cars, and when the train pulled out, Wilson was noted staging a retreat—the imprint of a large foot clearly visible on his trousers." In the St. Francis Hotel in Union Square, where he had stayed with his parents during his first trip to California in 1915, Wilson noted the irony of his present situation: "I had wanted then to be famous as a writer: now I was, though the kind of fame that *Hecate County* was having at the moment in San Francisco was not very satisfactory."[2]

When they returned to Wellfleet in January 1947 Elena, much more of a *Hausfrau* than her predecessor, began redoing the place in her own style. "Elena is quietly transforming the house so that parts of it look already like Turgenev," he told Nabokov, "and I have had to rope off an American wing." But he was actually quite pleased by the way she changed his charming ruin into a nest of gentlefolk. As Elena later remarked, "Edmund's political views might be radical but there was nothing bohemian about the style in which he lived. Scratch the surface, and you'll find that underneath it's solid Red Bank." Louise Bogan, a frequent visitor, was enormously impressed by the handsome improvement of the house and by the creation of an environment that was perfect for his work:

> Elena has really effected a tremendous change in Edmund's way of living. She really *loves* him. . . . The house couldn't be more attractive; and Elena has evidently put real elbow grease into decorating

it: scraping floors and walls and making curtains. There is a "parlor" with a good deal of Federal mahogany (Edmund's mother's) upholstered in yellow; a dining room with more mahogany against blue walls, plus lovely blue Staffordshire and silver; a "middle room" with more blue walls and blue chintz and linen; and Edmund's magnificent study, with a bathroom attached, and a stairway to an attic, filled with overflow books. For the first time poor Edmund has attention, space and effectively arranged paraphernalia of all kinds—Mary never really helped in more practical ways; and Edmund has had a very scrappy kind of life, down the years. Now all moves smoothly: tea on a tray for his "elevenses"; absolute silence in his working hours, and good meals at appropriate intervals.

But Wilson was still subject to sudden rages. When he got angry at some changes she had made in his absence (as he had previously done when Mary had put blue sheets on the bed), he picked a quarrel with her. The more placid Elena refused to be provoked and merely said: "I hurt Jimmy [Thornton] and this is my retribution."[3]

Known for her excellent cooking as well as for her beauty, culture and devotion to Wilson, Elena did everything possible to tempt his appetite. Charlotte Kretzoi recalled that "she cooked 3-4 types of meals, because her husband drank heavily in the afternoon and in the evening, and she tried to feed him the next morning and noon." Michael Macdonald, a close friend of Reuel, was impressed—even in boyhood—by the delights of her table: "On Elena's trays would be steaks on toast even for lunch . . . or a good minute steak, with fine salad with French dressing and some Portuguese bread warmed in the oven. There was even cold lobster in the shell, with homemade mayonnaise." When Glyn Morris visited the Cape, Elena served a delicious baked fish with wild rice, followed by large plums swimming in an exotic sauce. Indulgent with the boys, she allowed Henry and Reuel to hold a contest during which they ate dozens of profiteroles.

Elena usually catered to Wilson's plain taste with basic, hearty fare: roast beef with roast potatoes and Yorkshire pudding, great desserts and puff pastries, and a fat goose for Christmas. Much of her fine cooking was rather wasted on Edmund, whose favorite dishes, according to his daughter, were leftover meat and mashed potatoes, a variant of this in shepherd's pie, and the apparently nauseous bacon and bananas.[4] To curb his girth, swollen by this heavy diet, Elena made him go for a walk every afternoon, "like a dog on a leash." During the summers they ventured farther afield to the Tanglewood music festival in western Massachusetts.

Elena, who gave up her editorial job at *Town and Country* when she married Wilson, "believed in that absolute obedience that a woman must give to the man she loves." Most of Wilson's friends thought him very fortunate indeed to have acquired such a wife. David Chavchavadze agreed with friends like Albert Guerard and Alison Lurie when he wrote: "Elena was a woman of extraordinary kindness, intelligence, and perception, and also wide interests, of which she had been largely deprived in her first marriage to the very conventional James Thornton. I think she was originally attracted to Wilson for his brilliance. The marriage was a stormy one. But she adored him to the end."

There were, however, a few dissenting opinions. Rosalind, inevitably jealous of a new rival, remarked that Elena had no sense of humor about herself, adopted a "German Herr Professor attitude" and became upset when Wilson read the comics. She would also exclaim in front of friends like Auden—as Wilson cringed—"Oh, dearest, you're so brilliant, you know so much." Wilson's step-daughter-in-law, Mary Canby, felt Elena lacked natural warmth and could be remote, austere and intimidating.[5] Stuart Hughes, who came from an eminent family and was a professor at Harvard, was also "scared" of Elena and thought she had a depth of anger, a belligerent way of speaking and a Germanic fierceness. But Wilson gave the orders and Elena, a substantial person in her own right, willingly became the housekeeper of a distinguished husband.

Loran and Mary Crosten, Wilson's summer friends in upstate New York, said that Elena liked to play the queen bee at Wellfleet and the lady of the manor at Talcottville. But when Mary asked what she did with her time, Elena, deflecting the question, replied: "I'm a mother. I go to P.T.A. meetings." Mary Struve—whose husband, a professor of Slavic at Berkeley, was distantly related to Elena—found Wilson much more difficult to get on with. Though she was born in Russia and had a doctorate in Slavic studies, Wilson lectured at her in an arrogant manner. He asked: "Who's the most interesting character in *War and Peace?*" and when she replied: "Prince Andrey Volkonsky," he "humphed" and declared: "Of course you'd say that, it's just the romantic thing for a young woman to say," and insisted that Pierre was in fact the most interesting character in the novel.[6]

The tall, impressively handsome, deep-voiced Elena and the short, swollen-faced, pot-bellied Wilson were bound together by an immensely satisfying sex life, which he elaborated, heightened and relived in his diaries. Wilson, who still had wet dreams at the age of fifty-one and never met a foot he did not like, gave a gratified top-to-toe description of Elena's body and their rapturous, resonant love-making:

> I loved her body, which I had first seen in a bathing suit. . . . Her breasts were low, firm and white, perfect in their kind, very pink outstanding nipples, no hair, no halo around them, slim pretty tapering legs, feet with high insteps and toes that curled down and out. . . .
>
> She would wind herself around me like an eel. . . . Would clasp her legs together very hard when I had my hand or my penis in her—seemed to have tremendous control of the muscles inside her vagina. . . .
>
> I would be delayed for a time, then gradually and comfortably come, but with a final terrific vibration, during which I could only hold it in her still and stiff, and while the tense charges would be shot into her in close succession, she, too, would vibrate, rigid, and sometimes fart in complete dedication that let all her bodily functions go. . . .
>
> Her frank and uninhibited animal appetite contrasted with her formal and gracious aristocratic manners.

Elena flattered Wilson about his sexual performance, and told him precisely what he wanted to hear ("You were so big!"). She also put his needs before her own: "unlike other women, she never wanted me to go on till she came—she thought this was not the thing." When Wilson was nearly seventy and no longer up to his old standard, he asked Elena (who was eleven years younger) if she still loved him now that he was old. She said, "'Old has nothing to do with it.' This touched me, she so seldom says anything like this."

Wilson was deeply in love with Elena, whose only fault (he said) was that she liked to have people dependent upon her. He therefore asserted his independence by drinking heavily and falling in love with younger women. Elena would hide the liquor; Wilson would search for it and get drunk, become abusive and indulge in what Rosalind called "bursts of sadism." According to Rosalind, he knew exactly how he was behaving—drunk or sober—and set out to destroy the woman he loved as if he were "possessed."

Elena indulged Edmund and tried to be philosophical about his other women, but was deeply hurt by his affairs. During the course of their marriage Wilson pursued the artist Mary Meigs, the editor Clelia Carroll, the student Frances Swisher, the actress Elaine May and his Hungarian teacher Mary Pcolar. In old age, he had affairs with Anne Miller and Penelope Gilliatt. Though Elena was resentful when he praised these attractive women, he continued to see (whenever possible) Mamaine Paget and Eva Siphraios, and kept in touch with most of his former mistresses. Referring to his drinking and frank interest in attractive young ladies, Elena wrote him with affectionate resignation: "I get terribly depressed about our disagreeing about some things so completely, but only very young people have illusions about being able to change the likes and dislikes of the people they love." When Wilson's behavior became intolerable her mood darkened. She told Rosalind: "I've gone to pieces since I married him" and described their life together as "hell with compensations."[7]

Elena endured his infidelities and Wilson wrote loving tributes to her at the beginning of their marriage and near the end of his life. "The White Sand" (1950), a charming love poem in long Whitmanesque lines, appeared originally as a privately-printed ten-page Christmas pamphlet (in an edition of only twelve copies) and was reprinted as the last poem in *Night Thoughts* (1961). Wilson describes his first sight of Elena, swimming at the beach in Wellfleet, characterizes her through Russian and German allusions ("Orchards and Chekhov and chess"; "Schubert's blue-coated Vienna") that suggest her cosmopolitan background. He eventually meets her for a Russian meal at the house of a mutual friend. As the seasons change to autumn and winter, he comes to know her and falls in love with her. She helps eradicate the bitter memories of his previous marriage and of McCarthy's flight to Gull Pond after their violent quarrel: "Oh, image that brightened / Seasons of barren spite—borne from the summer pond!" Elena's tenderness and affection provide a welcome refuge: "Suddenly turning my eyes, I find myself safe in your presence, / Rhine-daughter, northern princess, always with fresh surprise."

Wilson wrote a dedicatory letter to Elena in his posthumously published *A Window on Russia* (1972). In this grateful tribute he alludes to her dislike of Talcottville and offers thanks for "your undiscouraged patience with my effort to understand Russian customs and states of mind. You have never ceased to exemplify the most attractive Russian qualities: sensitivity, humor, human sympathy, capacity (with limitations) for adaptability to different milieux."[8]

II

Wilson had three children with three different wives, but his attitude toward them was problematical. His first child was conceived accidentally, he wanted Mary McCarthy to abort his second child and he had his third child with Elena when he was nearly fifty-three. Charlotte Kretzoi, who knew Wilson in Budapest and America, said: "As a husband he was rotten, as a father he was nice." But he did not bring up Rosalind or Reuel himself, and other friends (Richard Pipes, Eva Marcelin, Walter Edmonds and Jason Epstein) thought he was a poor father. He was absorbed with his own work, ill at ease with children, unsympathetic to their point of view, unable to express his affection and, as they grew up and he grew old, increasingly disconnected from them. Instead of playing with his children, Wilson tended to give them lectures and was disappointed that none of them was receptive to his tuition. As his Wellfleet neighbor Mary Meigs observed: "I think that he was an irascible father and could probably be a bully. . . . Personally I would *not* have liked to have him for a father and would have been frightened by his changes of mood, from gentleness to verbal brutality."

Yet Wilson—who felt his mother never loved him and was alienated from his morbidly depressed father—tried to be a good parent. When Rosalind was twenty years old and sharing an industrious life with Wilson and McCarthy in Wellfleet, he praised her achievements in a letter to the critic Maxwell Geismar: "My daughter Rosalind has just been having some sensational literary success: she has sold a story to *Mademoiselle* and *Harper's Bazaar* want to run a section of a novel she has been writing. During the morning we are all at our writing tables and desks working away like beavers." After dropping out of Bennington, Rosalind worked briefly as a nurse's aide in Bellevue Hospital, at the *New Yorker* and at the *New York Post*, before moving to Boston, where, as a reporter on the *Globe*, she once covered a magicians' convention. She began work at the publisher, Houghton Mifflin, in 1949, inherited money from her grandmother's trust in 1958, left the firm for a while and then returned. She frequently asked her father for money, even when she had a job, and he nearly always gave it to her.

Wilson felt that his uneasy marriage to McCarthy had hurt his relationship with Rosalind. It seemed to push her "back to child-hood—since Mary was herself so childish and competed in a childish way with Rosalind. . . . Mary did her best to crowd her out of my life—till toward the end, when she tried to make an ally of her."[9] He also felt guilty about his selfish behavior after his separation from McCarthy. When he and Rosalind lived together in Henderson Place, he made her sit in the Columbia University library while he bedded women at home. But when Rosalind went out on a date, Wilson, playing the protective father, would wait up for her and berate her for coming in late. Rosalind, once engaged to a young Greek student at Harvard, suffered "an awful blow" when the engagement was broken, and never married.

Wilson once told Louise Bogan that his great-grandfather had three wives and a dozen children. Carrying on this family tradition in a more modest way, Wilson had a third child, Helen Miranda, who was born in Boston on February 19, 1948. Named after her grandmother and mother, she also had, like Rosalind, the name of a Shakespearean heroine. When he held his new infant in his pudgy hands, he looked equally jowly, bald and baby-faced.

Wilson did not pay much attention to Helen in her infancy, but became more interested in her as she grew older. During their trip to Europe when Helen was six, he took her to the places that had pleased him in childhood: the Tower of London, the Christmas pantomime, Maskelyne's Temple of Magic and the Cirque Médrano in Paris. A few years later, he excused himself at Helen's bedtime and went upstairs to read *David Copperfield* to her. "How I envied her!" wrote Michael Macdonald. "How I wished that my father had read such books to me at such a tender age!" Wilson also told Leon Edel that he often made up stories, and had been telling Helen the fanciful adventures of a mermaid in the Adirondacks.

But Helen was mainly brought up by Elena, who doted on her and spoiled her. Friends of the family found Helen, the late child of older parents, bratty and rude, difficult and self-centered, baffling and impos-sible, resentful and strange. When crossed by Rosalind, she would exclaim, "I hate you!" But Wilson adored the pudgy Helen, his favorite child, and loved to record her precocious sayings. He treated her like a little doll, sometimes joked with her and made her uncomfortable.

When *he* misbehaved, she would assume a stern expression and disapprovingly declare: "There goes father!"[10]

The children gave Wilson the chance to indulge his lifelong passion for puppets and magic. "The first Punch-and-Judy show I ever saw—" he wrote in *Europe Without Baedeker*, "it must have been before 1900—was a sideshow in the Barnum & Bailey Circus in Madison Square Garden. . . . I was fascinated but also frightened, and when I revived the puppet theater for my children, I was afraid the real Punch and Judy would be too alarming for them, and, instead, gave them a kind of soap opera—improvised from night to night—in which the Punch and Judy were transformed into a comfortable domestic couple who never quarreled about anything but were plagued by a mischievous devil." Wilson identified with Punch, a fat, angry fornicator, who had "a big belly, a stick, a temperament of extreme truculence and a tendency to unscrupulous philandering." He loved the way the traditional Punch burst into jolly song after committing his crimes.

Wilson went to a great deal of trouble with his puppets, buying a special red light and putting a metal device in his mouth to make his voice sound squeaky. But Rosalind, who was hostile to the theater because of her mother's histrionics, disliked these entertainments as much as his lectures. Helen, who wanted to play with her own dolls instead of her father's, became bored with Punch and Judy. But she dutifully played her part in the shows as he wheezed out the lively songs. The children in the audience screamed with delight, and sometimes got so excited they wet their pants.

During his own childhood Wilson had wanted to be a magician and maintained this interest in adult life. He frequented Al Flosso's magic shop in Times Square, bought the latest tricks and, with his novelist friend Edwin O'Connor, attended magicians' conventions. He had fat but dextrous hands, loved theatrical effects, enjoyed performing for children and friends, and "saw magic as a kind of para-religion for his rationalistic mind."

Inspired by Edmund's enthusiasm, the family went in for elaborate birthday cards, sentimental valentines and April Fool's jokes, while Christmas was celebrated as a purely secular occasion. Wilson once sent Elena a telegram, apparently from her handsome young son Henry (then in England), unexpectedly announcing his engagement to a very rich, old and frog-like friend of the family. Elena was deeply concerned until Edmund, unable to hold back his laughter, was forced to reveal the joke. Wilson—who once drew a false beard on his passport photograph and was surprised when officials objected[11]—also inspired his grown-up friends to play card tricks, Authors, Chinese checkers and *bouts rimés*. He loved tricks, jokes, satires, backward rhymes (livid-devil), nonsense verse, limericks, anagrams, palindromes, clerihews and cartoons: the verbal toy as an embellishment of life.

III

During the first year of his marriage to Elena, Wilson formed a friendship with W. H. Auden (whom he had briefly met in wartime Rome), quarreled with his old comrade Dos Passos and paid a final visit to Edna Millay. In a fascinating review of *Upstate* (1971) Auden explained that their common background provided a solid foundation for their friendship, and modestly compared his own work habits to Wilson's: "Mr. Wilson and I belong to the same class, called in England Upper Middle Class Professional. One of his grandfathers was a Presbyterian Minister: both of mine were Anglican clergymen. His other grandfather was a physician as was my father. His own father was a lawyer like one of my uncles. Both of us received what was then an élite education: Mr. Wilson went to a boys' boarding school and Princeton, I to a boarding school and Oxford. . . . Mr. Wilson and I were both, thank God, brought up on the Protestant Work Ethic but, though I generally think of myself as fairly industrious, he makes me feel a lazybones."

In February 1946 Wilson—despite his inveterate anglophobia—told Mamaine that he admired Auden's stimulating conversation and independent character: "I've been seeing quite a lot of Auden and having a very good time with him. I find him very easy to talk to now and great fun. . . . He is really extremely tough, cares nothing about property or money, popularity or social prestige—does everything on his own and alone." One of the few homosexuals among Wilson's close friends, Auden liked to discuss his *louche* sexual experiences. He confided to Wilson that when his homosexual lovers cried "Stop! Stop!," he always obeyed orders, even though they really *wanted* to be whipped. Wilson later noted that Auden's face seemed as if it had been whipped, "crisscrossed with creases; it looks squarer than when I saw him last and like some kind of technical map."

Auden also expressed his admiration for two other works by Wilson. Before their first meeting, he had called *To the Finland Station* "a scholarly and beautifully written book," and observed: "we are not likely in our generation to see another study of the growth of the Socialist idea at once so concise, informative and readable." In his review of *Apologies to the Iroquois*, he noted Wilson's individuality and independence, and remarked that he "is a specimen of that always rare and now almost extinct creature, the Intellectual Dandy."[12]

Always generous with praise, Wilson appreciated Auden's extraordinary intelligence and technical skill, and recognized that he belonged—with friends like Fitzgerald, Hemingway, Nabokov, Malraux and Lowell—among the greatest writers of the century. Reviewing Auden's early work in February 1937, Wilson was at first irritated by his playful immaturity: he "has presented the curious case of a poet who writes an original poetic language in the most robust English tradition, but who seems to have been arrested at the mentality of an adolescent schoolboy." Nine years later he ranked Auden with Yeats and Eliot, calling him "one of the three first-rate poets writing in English in our time." Auden's impressive *New Year Letter* (1941) and *The Age of Anxiety* (1948) led Wilson to change his mind, in the revised edition of *The Triple Thinkers* (1948), about the lack of technique in contemporary poetry. In the mid 1950s, Wilson called Auden "the most accomplished poet in English since the great nineteenth-century masters . . . [and] one of the great Englishmen of the world." And in a surprising tribute to the English, he compared Auden to the philosopher and mathematician A. N. Whitehead, characterizing them as "the two Englishmen of genius I have known who have embodied most authentically the strong creative English qualities—stout character, self-dependence, stubbornness in following their intuitions, combination of practicality with poetic and metaphysical thinking."[13] In contrast to his rivalrous relationship with Nabokov, Wilson did not feel obliged to compete with Auden and cherished an unqualified admiration for both his character and his art.

In 1949, four years after Wilson's energetic assault on detective stories in "Who Cares Who Killed Roger Ackroyd?," he gently mocked Auden's notorious dishabille and taste for this subfusc genre:

> And Wystan Auden, with rigorous views
> But his necktie hanging around his shoes,
> Expounded his taste for detective stories,
> Which he reads to illumine the current mores.

The conclusion of Wilson's witty, didactic poem, "A message you'll expect my friends" (1953), was directly influenced by the conclusion of

Auden's "Under Which Lyre" (1946). Auden's poem ends with a contemporary "Decalogue" of instruction that parodies the Ten Commandments. Wilson concludes his poem in a similar fashion:

> So these the precepts are, my friends,
> The aging Wilson recommends:
> Beware of dogmas backed by faith;
> Steer clear of conflicts to the death;
> Keep going; never stoop; sit tight;
> Read something luminous at night.

Wilson, who wrote with Louise Bogan a sixtieth birthday poem for Auden, also collaborated with Stephen Spender on a sonnet for his sixty-fifth birthday. Since Wilson and Spender were then living five hundred miles apart, they had to send the successive lines back and forth by telegram. But they overcame this difficulty and completed the poem. Wilson "had a sense of grand style," Spender wrote, "as well as this acute literary conscience, which made him feel that a person like Auden ought to be honoured." Auden expressed his esteem for Wilson by dedicating *About the House* (1965) to "Edmund and Elena Wilson." Wilson sent one of his very last letters to Auden in Austria, congratulating him on the cottage he had been given by Oxford University and telling him he was pleased that Auden could now live comfortably and without financial worries.

At another of Auden's birthday parties in March 1955, Wilson met the preeminent English eccentrics Edith and Osbert Sitwell. They were enthroned side by side, with an empty chair next to Edith, to which people were led one by one. Wilson did not like their rather pretentious writing and felt that they demanded too much adulation. But his next meeting with them, at a party given by a curator of the Museum of Modern Art, was more eventful. According to one observer, Wilson "plucked a shrimp from the tray and dipped it in mayonnaise. He held it in the air as he sipped his whisky. I watched with frozen horror as the shrimp slid from its toothpick and gracefully landed on Miss Sitwell's coiffure. But Miss Sitwell ignored it and continued with serenity."[14]

Wilson and Dos Passos had been close friends and neighbors on the Cape since the early 1920s. But after the execution in Spain of his friend José Robles, Dos reacted against Communism and became increasingly conservative. Wilson, by contrast, maintained his Socialist principles, voted for the Democrats after 1948 and became intensely critical of American foreign policy during the Cold War and in Vietnam. The tragic death of Katy Dos Passos in September 1947 drew them together for a time. Driving through Wareham, Massachusetts, Dos, who had poor vision and was blinded by the afternoon sun, did not see a truck that had pulled off to the side of the road. He crashed into it, shearing off the top of the car and practically decapitating Katy. She died immediately and Dos lost his right eye. Visiting him in the hospital a few hours later, Wilson was moved by Dos' uncharacteristic show of emotion and wrote him a poignant letter about Katy's death. When Dos remarried and moved from the Cape to Virginia in 1949, Rosalind felt Wilson became "devitalized" by the loss of his companion.

In early 1950 Wilson and Elena visited Dos and his new wife Betty in Spence's Point, on the Potomac River in northern Virginia. Believing it was cheaper to hire than to own a car, Wilson asked Bill Peck, the Wellfleet taxi-driver, to take them five hundred miles south in his bottle-green Packard. Peck—nattily dressed in a Sam Snead straw hat, bow tie and clip-on sunglasses—posed something of a problem when they arrived. Dos Passos' biographer writes that

> Wilson refused to be seated at the table with Mr. Peck, and Martha Weldon, a black servant, refused "to serve a proper white man in the kitchen." Betty's solution was to serve the Wilsons in the library and Peck in the dining room. "We all felt curdled before the evening was up. Bunny pitched in about something, and since he was our guest, Dos couldn't react to it as strongly as he might have if he were in a club, for instance," recalled Betty. "It was a most peculiar visit. . . . Bunny had no interest in our life at Spence's Point and we could offer him no public entertainment. Dos and Bunny remained friends, but the Wilsons did not return. We confined our meetings to more neutral territory after that."

The problem was politics. Wilson felt that Dos had become a Marx-baiter for the Right-wing press and was just as unreliable in his extreme Right phase as he had been as an extreme Leftist. Betty later recalled that their argument "became very heated. Elena and I tried to calm the situation since it was unpleasant and embarrassing, but that was difficult to do. It was fortunate that they left the next morning." That Dos' literary reputation declined as Wilson's ascended made things even worse.

After a long cooling-off period, Wilson was as bluntly critical of Dos' lord-of-the-manor pretensions and reactionary political beliefs as he had once been of Allen Tate's. In a little squib on Dos in *Night Thoughts* he lamented:

> John Dos Passos
> No longer writes for the Masses,
> And when he returns to his Virginia estate, he
>   is greeted by a chorus of "Old Massa!"'s.

In 1964, when America was entering the war in Vietnam and Barry Goldwater was running against Lyndon Johnson for president, Wilson attacked the naiveté of Dos' report in the *National Review* on the Republican convention: "I don't understand how, at your age, you can continue to believe in these bugaboos [about Russia] and see everything in terms of melodrama. It seems to me that you are just as gullible as you ever were in the twenties. I get more and more sceptical myself. . . . I feel obliged to tell you that your article about the San Francisco convention sounded like a teenager squealing over the Beatles. What on earth has happened to you? How can you take Goldwater seriously?" Dos tried to smooth things over by saying that "two moderately reasonable people can reach diametrically opposite conclusions from the same set of facts."[15] But Wilson did not see it that way. Though they saw each other occasionally, their forty-year friendship was virtually dead.

On August 6, 1948, when Wilson and Elena were at the Tanglewood music festival in Lenox, Massachusetts, he decided to cross the state line to Austerlitz, New York, and visit Edna Millay, whom he had not seen for nineteen years. Wilson was always surprised when, after many years had passed, his friends looked so much older. But his visit to Millay, whose glamorous aura had remained fixed in his mind, was the most disillusioning experience of all. She was trying to pull herself out of some dark neurotic period and had aged so much that he scarcely recognized her. The nymph of Greenwich Village had now become heavy and dumpy. She was terribly nervous, her hands trembled, her bright green eyes looked frightened and her latest work was strangely dark: "She had changed terribly: her cheeks were fat and red, and she had flabby jowls. . . . Her old tension had turned into a form of the shakes. I thought that she showed badly the effects of drinking. . . . Her mouth and chin flapped like an old woman's. . . . At moments she would show signs of bursting into tears, becoming hysterical about not being able to find a poem."

Pressured by Millay for assurance, approval and praise, Wilson was unpleasantly reminded of their youthful love affair, and of her overwhelming egoism: "I felt, just as I had when she was young, that I was being sucked into her narrow and noble world, where all that mattered was herself and her poetry, and I felt the need to break away from it . . . so I had, when I had been in love with her, and experienced such relief, at one point, at putting her out of my mind."

Astonishingly popular in her youth, Millay had exhausted her poetic fire and was now a burnt-out case, a terrible reminder of the destruction and death of his talented friends of the 1920s and of the great loss in his own life: "I felt a certain satisfaction in the idea that I was outlasting her, but at the same time was troubled and depressed at finding the metamorphosis she had undergone. She seems to have ceased to care about her looks—one of the things that happens to the drinker. . . . At the same time, the strength of her character and her genius overcame me. . . . I reflected . . . on the tendency of the writers of my generation to burn themselves out or break down: Scott and Zelda, John [Bishop], Phelps Putnam (just dead), Paul Rosenfeld, Elinor Wylie, Edna."

After Millay's death, two years later, she spoke to him from beyond the grave. In 1950 Wilson finally received from her sister the letter she had sent him in March 1929 about *I Thought of Daisy*. He had always thought she had been offended by his portrayal of her as Rita Cavanaugh and had not answered his letters because she had disliked the novel. He now belatedly found, as he wrote in his memorial essay on Millay, that she had "made careful and copious notes and had good-naturedly undertaken to rewrite in what she thought a more appropriate vein the speeches assigned to the character partly based on herself."[16]

The break with Dos Passos and death of Millay seemed to cut off Wilson's vital contact with the 1920s. The connection to the *New Yorker* and marriage to Elena at the age of fifty-one seemed finally to stabilize his life. But the publication and suppression of *Memoirs of Hecate County*, which coincided with his courtship of Elena in 1946, led to unexpected scandal and notoriety, and to a series of trials for obscenity that culminated in the Supreme Court.

SIXTEEN

Memoirs of Hecate County, 1946–1948

I

Wilson's *Memoirs of Hecate County*, published by Doubleday in March 1946, contained five stories and the novella "The Princess with the Golden Hair," which was to provoke controversy and legal action. Though the conventional-sounding *Memoirs of . . .* suggests reflections of bourgeois old age, the narrator is actually a young art critic who works in New York and attacks the pretentious life of the suburbs.[1] In this book Wilson was as harshly critical of middle-class America as he was in *Europe Without Baedeker* of postwar Europe. As he told the lawyer who defended his work in the Supreme Court: "The book is a nightmarish satire on . . . the impotence and corruption of a certain milieu."

Wilson's stories—unified by a single narrator, a suburban setting, recurrent characters, and a satiric tone—were modeled on similarly structured collections: Kipling's *Plain Tales from the Hills* (1888), Mansfield's *In a German Pension* (1911), Joyce's *Dubliners* (1914) and Anderson's *Winesburg, Ohio* (1919). The five short stories are much less significant than the sensational novella which comprises half the book. When Wilson was living with Mary Blair in Brookhaven, Long Island, in the summer of 1923, their back yard "turned out to be a place of rendezvous for turtles" and Wilson liked to watch them copulating. "The Man Who Shot Snapping Turtles," the story of Asa Stryker, who at first tries to exterminate the turtles and then turns them into products that earn him a fortune, satirizes the capitalist system and the corrupting effect of advertising and money. "Ellen Terhune," the tale of a gifted musician who is cursed by an unhappy childhood and a failed marriage, illustrates Wilson's theme of the wound and the bow. "Surmounting her own despair," Ellen triumphs over "the coldness, the sickness, the quarreling, the bad birth" and composes a masterpiece.

"Glimpses of Wilbur Flick," a satire on a rich but empty drone who ends up performing magic tricks in a cabaret, synthesizes Wilson's fascination with magicians: his portrait of Bill McGee's father in *The Crime in the Whistler Room* and his essay on "John Mulholland and the Art of Illusion" (1944). "The Milhollands and Their Damned Soul" attacks the literary racket in magazines and book clubs, practiced by successful nonentities like Stephen Benét, the Van Dorens (on the *Nation*), Clifton Fadiman (Wilson's predecessor on the *New Yorker*) and Henry Seidel Canby (a cousin of Margaret's first husband, on the *Saturday Review*). "Mr. and Mrs. Blackburn at Home" is little more than the description of a party, given by wealthy, mysterious and vaguely European neighbors, broken up by a nine-page sequence in French about the Soviet purges and the Nazi terror. If the book had not contained the lively sexual scenes, the difficult-to-read French passage would have killed it.[2]

In the novella the dilettantish narrator courts the beautiful, upper-class, married suburbanite Imogen Loomis during a hot summer in New York. At the same time he has other sexual encounters, and continues his affair with the more earthy, carnal, working-class Anna Lenihan. Though Anna is the only woman he seems genuinely fond of, her poor background and lack of education preclude marriage. A sexual standby during his protracted attempt to seduce Imogen, Anna is as genuine as Imogen is fake. But the dose of the clap he gets from her delays his seduction of Imogen and increases his romantic longing. When he finally succeeds, he is shocked to discover that Imogen wears a back brace, and the contrast between its dark straps and her white skin is perversely exciting. At the end of the story the narrator, unable to decide between Imogen and Anna, rejects both of them for Jo Gates, a woman he has scarcely mentioned before, who lives in California.

Into the realistic and satiric settings of modern short stories Wilson wove other, more ancient themes. As his title suggests, his characters are bewitched by evil, and his narrator-hero is obsessed by physically attractive and wickedly repellent women. Hecate, the goddess of Hades in classical mythology, was associated with night, ghosts and magic. She haunted cross-roads, attended by hell-hounds, and was represented in statues in triple form. Wilson reproduced one of these ancient statues as the frontispiece of his book and used Hecate to suggest his demonic theme. His Connecticut-*Inferno* expresses, at the very beginning of the book, the Manichean belief that "the Devil is contending on equal terms with God and that the fate of the world is in doubt," that God cannot run the universe without letting in the forces of evil.

Wilson originally planned to quote on the title page a passage about magical transformation from Ovid's *Metamorphoses*. Instead, he used a long passage (in Russian, with an English translation) from Nikolai Gogol's hair-raising horror tale "Viy," the story of the destruction of an innocent man by a demonically possessed woman. In this Poe-like fantasy, a Kiev seminary student reads prayers for three nights next to the dead body of a beautiful Cossack girl. In life, she had taken the form of a witch and had possessed him. After death, she breaks out of her coffin at midnight, releases hellish spirits—including the enormous monster, Viy—and frightens the student to death.

Wilson also had in mind nineteenth-century French writers, like Gérard de Nerval and Pétrus Borel, who were precursors of Villiers' *Axel*. He was particularly interested in "the proud and perverse aristocrats of Barbey d'Aurevilly's *Diaboliques*, with their grandiose duels of sex," and wrote Helen Muchnic that the book "had something in common with the stories I am doing." The weird tales in *Les Diaboliques* (1874), which Wilson had read about in Mario Praz's study of Decadent literature, *The Romantic Agony* (1933), concern Satanism, the black arts and the diabolical influence of women who are "possessed." In *Against Nature* (1884), Huysmans suggested another theme that found its way into Wilson's stories: "In *Les Diaboliques* the author had surrendered to the Devil, and it was Satan he extolled. At this point there appeared on the scene that bastard child of Catholicism which for centuries the Church has pursued with its exorcisms and its *autos-da-fé* —sadism."[3] Asa Stryker gleefully decapitates the snapping turtles; the narrator is fascinated by the cruel brace that encloses Imogen's beauty.

Wilson intended his stories to be obviously "literary" and filled them with references and devices his audience would recognize. He said that his stories were "in the Hawthorne tradition," and introduced a supernatural element that showed the effect of evil on the Puritan conscience. "Ellen Terhune" combines a Jamesian style, atmosphere and theme of an emotionally obstructed life with a Kiplingesque use of the eerie and the occult. Wilson uses these two elements to show how the country house changes and how the narrator goes back in time from the present to the youth of Ellen's dead mother. Fitzgerald's fantasy "The Curious Case of Benjamin Button" (1922)—in which the hero is born an old man of seventy, gets progressively younger instead of older and finally becomes an infant—may also have suggested the reversal of time in this story.

In *Tender is the Night* (1934) the drunken Abe North wants to saw a French waiter in half "to know what was inside." Simon Delacy, the character based on Fitzgerald in *The Crime in the Whistler Room*, reappears in *Memoirs of Hecate County*, seizes one of the *garçons* at the Paris Ritz and declares that he "had always wanted to find out what was inside a waiter." Wilson told Morton Zabel that he "greatly admired that passage at the end of *The Great Gatsby*" (1925) where Nick Carraway decides to return to the West, evokes the dream of a primeval America and becomes "aware of the old island here that flowered once for Dutch sailors' eyes—a fresh, green breast of the new world." Similarly, at the end of Wilson's book, when the narrator finally unites with the California girl Jo Gates, he adapts this passage to emphasize his disgust with the decadence in Eastern life: "we turned West, as our fathers had done, for the new life we could still hope to find—we sought to regain that new world."[4]

Memoirs of Hecate County has a good deal in common with Wilson's earlier work of fiction, *I Thought of Daisy*. Both books have characters based on Edna Millay and on the Ukrainian waitress Frances, both have an intellectual narrator torn between upper- and lower-class women, and both include a liberating trip to Coney Island. Both books are written in flat, discursive prose, without suggestiveness or resonance. Both have long, static descriptions of houses, food, drink, of artistic and intellectual life, but lack dramatic action.

The unnamed first-person narrator and the leading characters are, like those in *I Thought of Daisy*, autobiographical. The narrator is tall and thin rather than short and fat, went to Yale instead of Princeton and is an artistic rather than a literary man; but he is clearly modeled on Wilson just as Hecate County is based on suburban Stamford. Mary McCarthy said Wilson's mother resented him because his large head had torn her body when he was born. Ellen Terhune also says that *her* mother "had a terribly bad time when I was born on account of my head's being so big, and I don't think she ever really recovered from it. . . . She used to talk about it sometimes in my presence. . . . I think she wanted me to feel that she had suffered and sacrificed herself for me." After reading *The Hysterical Element in Orthopaedic Surgery*, the narrator concludes that Imogen Loomis' spinal disease—like Helen Wilson's hysterical deafness—was a "neurotic sham."

The names of the leading characters in the stories allude to both personal friends and literary figures, suggest private jokes as well as thematic meanings. Jo Gates has the surname of both Paula Gates, whom Margaret Canby was living with when she first met Wilson, and of Sylvester Gates, his English lawyer-friend. Anna Lenihan recalls Frances' visit to the Minahan family (perhaps her in-laws) in upstate New York. Wilbur Flick, the subject of the third story, suggests both Millay's lover Arthur Ficke and Arthur Fiske, the hero of *This Room and This Gin and These Sandwiches*. The talented composer Ellen Terhune, based on Edna Millay, alludes to Dickens' mistress Ellen Ternan. The Milhollands in the fifth story suggest John Mulholland, "the distinguished scholar of magic and the author of *Beware Familiar Spirits*" (1938). Blackburn, in the sixth story, is another name for the devil.

The women in "The Princess with the Golden Hair" are a veritable portrait gallery of Wilson's mistresses in the 1930s. The tennis-playing Amazon Helen Hubbard was based on Betty Huling. The "stocky blond girl from Nebraska with a certain corn-fed sex appeal," whose white thighs the narrator admires while "pasturing on her ample breasts," was modeled on the Omaha-born Louise Fort. Jo Gates, who has to spend six months a year with her children in California and has visited New Mexico with the narrator, was based on Margaret Canby. In his diaries, Wilson recorded an incident with Margaret that he later transposed in the novel. Just before seeing Mozart's *Don Giovanni* (which nicely matches the demonic theme of the stories), they "overprepared on drinks, then I in my evening clothes had put her down on the couch and made love to her in her evening gown—after which we had been quite unfit to cope with the opera." At the end of *Memoirs of Hecate County* the narrator writes: "What gusto I expected to taste in the coarse enjoyment of Jo in her evening gown—the fierce sense of violating a woman at her most contrivedly attractive, when she is usually beyond our reach; just as my club seemed to burn and exult in liberation from the formality of my evening clothes."[5] Wilson had frequently dreamed of Margaret Canby during his love affairs with Frances and Elizabeth Waugh, and in this book the absent Jo Gates becomes part of the narrator's love triangle with Anna and Imogen.

The connection between Frances and Anna Lenihan, Elizabeth Waugh and Imogen Loomis are more elaborate. In "The Princess with the Golden Hair," as in real life, the narrator meets the reddish-haired Anna at the Tango Casino (or Gardens) on 14th Street. She lives with her impoverished family in Brooklyn. Her mother, who looks porcine, comes from Lemberg in the Ukraine, is married to her second husband and works in a fur factory. Anna had been sent to an orphanage as a two-year-old, has had an abortion and an ovarian cyst, and is the mother of a four-year-old girl. She is married to a brutish car thief who poses as an auto salesman, who has been sent to jail and who has had, while living in upstate New York, a blood clot on the brain. She holds the narrator's penis when she falls asleep with him and then infects him with gonorrhea. When she finds an ardent fiancé, she writes him a farewell letter—as Frances did in 1934.

When a passage from Wilson's diary about Elizabeth Waugh, his most intense and emotional mistress, is compared to the most notorious sexual description in the novella, the source of the fictional scene becomes clear. Both women have blond pubic hair, beautiful genitals, sweet and profuse female fluids, a smooth vaginal passage and deeply embedded clitoris, and both bring about their own climax.

In his diary for early 1937, Wilson described his secret encounter with Elizabeth at a hotel in Concord, Massachusetts:

> Her sex was ... the only genuinely beautiful, as distinguished from sexually stimulating one, that I had ever seen—she had the lighter hair of a blonde, and it was coppery so that I had to admit that her hair was ... that color naturally. ...
>
> Her vagina did its female work of making things easy with a honey-sweetly-smooth profusion. ... It was so smooth and open that after the first few moments I could hardly feel it. ... Her clitoris was also very feminine, deeply embedded. ... She made me stop my movement and did something special and gentle herself, seeming to rub herself in some particular way—and then climaxed with a self-excited tremor which also seemed to me strangely mild for a woman of so much energy and passion.

The corresponding passage in the novella similarly describes the woman's body as an aesthetic object that provides pleasure but evokes no depth of feeling in the narrator:

> All that lay between [her legs] was impressively beautiful, too, with an ideal aesthetic value that I had never found there before. ...
> The fleece, if not quite golden, was blond. ... [The portals] were doing their feminine work of making things easy for the entrant

with a honey-sweet sleek profusion. . . . She became, in fact, so smooth and open that after a moment I could hardly feel her. Her little bud was so deeply embedded that it was hardly involved in the play, and she made me arrest my movement while she did something special and gentle . . . rubbing herself somehow against me—and then came, with a self-excited tremor that appeared to me curiously mild for a woman of her positive energy.[6]

Wilson habitually used his diaries as a basis for his books, and the vividly erotic passages that created such controversy were virtual transcriptions—rather than transformations—of the diary entries. In his erotic fiction, Wilson extended the "objective" technique of his diary and relied on the power of details—rather than emotions—to create his effect.

Dylan Thomas once observed that "there are only three vocabularies at your disposal when you talk of sex: the vocabulary of the clinic, of the gutter, and of the moralist." Wilson thought it difficult to write about sex in English without making it seem unattractive, and agreed (in his review of *Lady Chatterley's Lover*) that technical words from biology and medicine were unsuitable for fiction while coarse, colloquial words were usually repulsive. "The truth is," Wilson told a lawyer involved in the trial of his book, "that in spite of Lawrence and Joyce, the treatment of sex in literature is still decades behind the treatment of every other aspect of life."[7]

Wilson's method was to use exaggeratedly impersonal diction to objectify both participants: "making things easy for the entrant," "arrest my movement," "a tremor that appeared to me curiously mild." Avoiding coarse language, he heightened the effect of his sexual scenes by combining objective language with metaphorical euphemisms: "fleece," "honey-sweet . . . profusion" and "little bud." Where Joyce was sensuous and comic, Lawrence solemn and exalted, Wilson tried to be amoral and clinically distant, keeping his eyes open and the light on, noting the inevitable awkwardness and the marine odor of the sexual act.

Both the diary and the novella lack real emotion. Though Wilson had passionate feelings for Elizabeth Waugh, he deliberately omitted them. In his diaries he records how women (including his wives) looked, felt, smelled and behaved. The effect of this objectivity, when describing the narrator's protracted pursuit of Imogen, is coldly anti-romantic. The frank and detailed descriptions of physical love in the novella suggest that the narrator's pleasure in seducing Imogen is more intellectual than sexual or emotional. This violation of a social and literary convention—that sexual descriptions should appear in the context of romantic love—got Wilson into trouble with the critics and the courts.

II

The reviewers were baffled and dismayed by Wilson's apparently random collection of stories, which were very different from the more traditional, realistic works of American fiction that appeared in 1946: *Mister Roberts, The Member of the Wedding, All the King's Men.* "It's been having a curious reception," Wilson told Mamaine, "selling, for me, pretty well, but I've been getting extremely sour reviews from most of my fellow critics and some horrified reactions from friends that I shouldn't have expected to be shocked." Alfred Kazin, for example, writing in the *Partisan Review*, declared "it is not a good book" and then tried to soften the blow: "The judgment is proportionate to Edmund Wilson's gifts, which are extraordinary and sometimes unpleasant, and to his peers, who are very few in this country." By "unpleasant" Kazin seemed to suggest that the tone of the stories, and especially of the sexual scenes, was offensively unfeeling and negative. Few critics praised Wilson's bold treatment of sex, and some considered his descriptions either too coldly clinical or too heatedly pornographic. Raymond Chandler, taking the opportunity to retaliate for Wilson's attacks on detective stories, remarked that he "made fornication as dull as a railroad timetable."

The response was not much better when the English edition finally appeared in 1951. The poet Stevie Smith, running against the current, praised it as "a book to enjoy and strike fire from the intelligent reader. . . . This masterly, sprawling book is a rich experience for wise readers." V. S. Pritchett called it "an absorbing failure" and Angus Wilson, whose works Wilson had consistently praised, was sharply critical about the *lack* of creative spark: "the intelligence and sophistication are all too advertisedly present; but without the imagination which swept through the essays, the sophistication seems a surface veneer to a naive sentimentalism, the intellect is arid and random."[8]

Wilson sent Connolly a copy of the American edition, and in June 1946 his secretary wrote Wilson that Cyril was fascinated by the book and planned to write a long letter about it. Though Connolly never wrote the letter, Wilson had every reason to believe his review would be favorable. But *Horizon* had folded, Connolly had not produced the masterpiece he had always intended to write and he resented Wilson's highly successful novel. When the review finally appeared in June 1951, Wilson was shocked by Connolly's harsh personal attack. "His *Memoirs* fail because he cannot conceal his contempt for all his personages," Connolly wrote. "The whole vocabulary sinks and the narrator is apt to appear prosaic and vulgar, a desiccated buffoon. . . . These [sexual] descriptions, mechanistic and almost without eroticism, achieve a kind of insect monotony." The main weaknesses are "cleverness becoming long-winded and sexual attraction ceasing to be attractive."

Wilson, who identified himself with his fictional narrator, objected to being called—especially by the childish and self-indulgent Connolly—"a desiccated buffoon." It was particularly galling, after being accused of obscenity and pornography in America, for an old friend to call him both vulgar and unerotic. He tried to rationalize "the hideously bad review" in a letter to Mamaine: "I try to think he is jealous of the sales—the first [English] printing seems to have sold out in a week—but am afraid this is not true and he honestly doesn't like the book." Wilson was probably right in thinking that Connolly's review was personally biased. He may have retaliated for Wilson's extremely negative review of Waugh's *Brideshead Revisited* in the *New Yorker* of July 1946 and—after Connolly's generous hospitality—for his hostile portrayal of the English in *Europe Without Baedeker* (1947).

Even John Updike, a great admirer of Wilson's work, could not summon up much enthusiasm when writing about his fiction in the 1980s. He, too, found a core of deadness in the heart of the novel: "He creates a solid world, has an unforced feel for the macabre and for moral decay, and allows eroticism its centrality in human doings. But away from the erotic episodes, something leaden and saturnine depresses our attentiveness." Alice Toklas saw the book as an example of inverted puritanism, of the need to rebel against conventional respectability, and sneered at Wilson for revealing his sexual practices (she had never dared reveal hers) while trying to break through the barriers of language and morality. In a letter to a friend she commented: "Edmund (ex. Bunny) Wilson—isn't he the Queen Victoria living on to point the moral that high minded clear thinking can land one in the ditch with one's private tastes exposed to the eyes of the casual passerby."[9]

The poet John Crowe Ransom, whose *Kenyon Review* was for Wilson the epitome of academic dullness, expressed a similar view. Writing to Arthur Mizener, a potential reviewer, Ransom sketched the schematic plot, characterized the intellectual narrator, and lamented Wilson's poor taste and damaged reputation:

> Here's the most amazing book for some time. . . . It's Wilson's *Memoirs of Hecate County.* . . . It consists in half a dozen little stories, or sketches, carrying an attenuated (i.e., it's spasmodic though sufficiently "hot") little romance forward, now and then, till on the last two or three pages the "I" marries the woman, and they have a little honeymoon that's no happier than it should be. But the I everywhere is a hero whose artiness is absolute and sticks out; he's the Great Aesthete of our times. There are two or three qualifications. He's rather Leftist, which is odd, and it seems a lukewarm attachment in view of his great love for the fineries of life. He's pretty good-natured, but he does love those drunken parties where they put poison in each other's ears, and he uses a good bit habitually in his ink. And if he's not the Great Lover, he's quite a performer, and he gives us the plainest description of the techniques he uses with the ladies that I've ever seen from an American with a high-brow reputation. I think he destroys himself, in fact; I can't see how he dared to do it; though everywhere in the book you can see how he is oriented to the literary circles in New York, and the foreign countries, and the hinterland of America just doesn't exist for him. But what a book! I have always defended Wilson, e.g., against youngsters who wrote scathing things against his literary dictatorship: I've thought he had good taste, and always knew a good deal about the pragmatic, or it may be the social, conditions, of the art-works. But this will do him in.

Ransom, a conservative Southerner writing from the Midwest, enjoyed being shocked by the "amazing" *Memoirs of Hecate County*, but voiced the same prudish disapproval of Wilson's "daring" subject matter that was to animate the prosecution of the book.

Ransom thought Wilson was out of touch with his audience. But contemporary readers, who had just been through the tremendous social changes of World War Two, were eager for books that realistically portrayed their own experience. Wilson gave readers what they wanted—and have since come to expect—in modern fiction. The negative reviews had no effect on the sales, and *Memoirs of Hecate*

County probably sold more copies than all his previous books put together. Wilson joked to Mamaine about his new public of sex maniacs and expressed amused alarm that he might be corrupting President Truman: "The White House, it seems, has bought a copy, and I've been feeling rather uneasy at the idea of Harry and Bess perhaps attempting to read it aloud in the evening." Delighted by his new role as popular author, Wilson, outrageous and articulate, read from the book at the 92nd Street YMHA in the late 1940s. He was remembered for "the lustiness of his rendition of the ranker scenes, and for the satisfaction he took in his creation."[10]

Wilson demanded and got better contracts than publishers usually gave: fifteen percent royalties on all sales, translation and film rights, fifteen (rather than ten) percent of the printer's costs for author's corrections and *all* (rather than half) the permission fees. His original contract with Houghton Mifflin, which had rejected the book, paid an advance of $500 against fifteen percent royalties. Doubleday, keen to acquire Wilson, offered a $2,000 advance against the same royalty. The book became a best-seller, sold more than 50,000 copies, earned $35,000 in 1946 and, with the English edition, a grand total of $60,000. Wilson used the unexpected money to pay for his divorce and Elena's, for his residence in Nevada and honeymoon in San Francisco, and for improving his house in Wellfleet. But the suppression of the book cut off the bounty, and between 1947 and 1951 his entire income subsided (he claimed) to only $2,000 a year.

III

Wilson knew there might be trouble as early as November 1943 when he wrote Morton Zabel that both Houghton Mifflin and Scribner's were scared to death of "The Princess with the Golden Hair." Three years later, alluding to the theme of his stories, he told the owner of the Grolier Book Shop in Cambridge that the forces of darkness were about to attack the book. Wilson's principal antagonist was the lean, grey-haired, bespectacled, seventy-year-old John Sumner, the executive secretary of the New York Society for the Suppression of Vice. Born in Washington, D.C., the son of a rear admiral, and trained as a lawyer at New York University, he had succeeded the founder, Anthony Comstock, in 1915. Sumner, who confessed to an occasional cocktail, boasted, with unctuous high-mindedness, that in its seventy-three years of existence his society had confiscated more than 200,000 pounds of obscene books. His prime targets had included many works by outstanding writers: Dreiser's *The "Genius"* (1915), Cabell's *Jurgen* (1919), Joyce's *Ulysses* (1922), Lawrence's *Lady Chatterley's Lover* (1928), Caldwell's *God's Little Acre* (1933) and Farrell's *A World I Never Made* (1936). Sumner's last, unsuccessful, attack had been on Lawrence's *The First Lady Chatterley* (1944). But he considered Wilson's stories "the most objectionable book I have ever read."

On July 8, 1946—four months after the book was published and while it was still a best-seller in Chicago, St. Louis, El Paso and Denver—plainclothes policemen, responding to Sumner's complaint, entered four Doubleday bookstores in Manhattan. Describing the book as "salacious and lascivious," they removed 130 copies. H. L. Mencken, who had always fought prudery and censorship, supported Wilson by writing: "I am convinced that *Hecate County* will survive the Comstocks—indeed, their attack, when the victim is really a good book, always does much more good than harm." Wilson had told the newly-converted Allen Tate that the Catholic Church had been suppressing serious literature. Later on, he explained to his current publisher, Roger Straus, that the Church had encouraged Right-wing newspapers like the *New York Journal-American* to incite the suppression of his book:

> Long after the final appeal I was told, by somebody in the Doubleday office ... that the book was suppressed at the instance of Cardinal Spellman, who got Sumner of the Anti-Vice Society after it. Spellman at that time was very thick with Hearst, who was making a great bid for the circulation of his papers among Catholics, and the prosecution of *Hecate County* was prominently reported in the Hearst press. ... A series of my [*New Yorker*] articles that were critical of Catholics—reviews of books by Evelyn Waugh and Graham Greene—had been appearing just before Spellman made his move against *Hecate County*. [11]

While the critics complained that Wilson's descriptions were not erotic, the lawyers for the prosecution argued that his book was designed to deprave and corrupt. Their underlying assumption was that fictional descriptions of sexual acts are intrinsically immoral and violate the canons of good taste. The prosecution emphasized that Wilson's book portrayed twenty different acts of sexual intercourse with four different women (which statistically surpassed both *Ulysses* and *Lady Chatterley's Lover*) and that it described, with precise anatomic detail, "disgusting embellishments" to "assorted acts of sexual debauchery."

While in Nevada to secure his divorce, Wilson could not testify in his own defense. But after the book was seized in New York, Dos Passos organized a committee to defend freedom of expression. He wrote to prominent authors: Thomas Mann, H. L. Mencken and James Farrell, and to leading English professors: Lionel Trilling and Newton Arvin, William York Tindall and Howard Mumford Jones, and all agreed to help.

On October 29, 1946, in the Court of Special Sessions in New York, Trilling took the stand for the defense. When questioned about a specific passage, he asserted the author's right to describe such experience and justified its literary merit: "If you would characterize it as a rather precise and literal account of a woman's sexual parts in the sexual act, and if you would go on to admit that the story is about sexuality, then I would say, yes, it added to the accuracy, precision of the story." Since one of the judges was hard of hearing, the "obscenities" put into evidence by the prosecution had to be shouted up to the bench. The court ruled two to one that the book was obscene, banned all sales in New York and fined Doubleday $1,000.

On November 27, 1946 the Appellate Division of the State Supreme Court upheld the lower court's decision. But a front page article in the *New York Times* quoted Judge Perlman's dissenting opinion. He cited the precedents of *Ulysses* and *Lady Chatterley's Lover*, and concluded that the book did not "have a tendency to deprave the young and immature." The suppression of Wilson's book abruptly ended the booming sales in New York, publicly stigmatized him as obscene, brought unwarranted notoriety, provoked his clash with reporters in Reno and—as publishers shied away from his work—concluded his career as a writer of fiction. The bad publicity also brought *Memoirs of Hecate County* to the attention of Senator Joseph McCarthy, who called it "pro-Communist."[12]

Doubleday bravely continued to fight the case and appealed to the Supreme Court on the ground that the suppression of the book was a violation of free speech. In October 1948 Doubleday's counsel Whitney Seymour, echoing Judge Perlman, argued that "No suppression of any utterance can be constitutionally justified unless that utterance gives rise to a clear and present danger to some substantial interest of the State. Public discussions of sex are not excluded from the general rule and *Memoirs of Hecate County* does not give rise to any danger, either clear or present, that it will subvert order or morality." After Felix Frankfurter had disqualified himself on the ground that he was Wilson's friend, the Supreme Court justices split four-four and the verdict of the lower court was sustained. On the Cape the following summer, Frankfurter confided to Wilson that he actually approved of the book and thought (as Trilling did) that the sexual "improprieties were justified by the social points [Wilson] wanted to make." Furious at Frankfurter's disloyalty, Wilson told the wife of Francis Biddle, Roosevelt's attorney general, that "Felix was an old faker and that [he] never wanted to see him again."

The conviction in New York prompted another trial in San Francisco, which Wilson fought and won. The key to Wilson's success here was his superb lawyer, James MacInnes, a massive man who looked like a football player, but assumed in court the role of a shy country boy. Born in 1914, a graduate of the University of San Francisco and Stanford Law School, he had been admitted to the bar in 1937. Mac-Innes, whose parents had died young, had been brought up as a Catholic by two middle-class maiden aunts but was not especially religious. An avid reader of the *New Yorker* (where he learned to respect Wilson), he frequented the best restaurants in the city and ate hearty meals between the sessions of his trials. One of the most imaginative and effective lawyers in San Francisco, MacInnes was a liberal in politics. He represented both the Right and the Left, and once defended the radical labor leader Harry Bridges. He loved all kinds of trials—criminal, paternity, divorce and personal injury—and was completely at ease in court. He took great pride in Wilson's case and was pleased that it received national attention.[13]

The first trial in San Francisco took place in September 1946 after a clerk, who became the defendant in the case, was arrested for selling the book to a plainclothes policeman. That trial ended in a hung jury. The second trial took place during the first two weeks of December. On December 6, the judge solemnly instructed the jury to read every word of the book, "regardless of how tedious the chore may be." Six days later, when Wilson arrived in San Francisco, the jury—in only eight minutes—unanimously found the book not salacious. The decision was made so rapidly that the court reporter, who had wandered off during the deliberations, could not be found for half an hour. Despite the vindication in San Francisco, *Memoirs of Hecate County* was still considered obscene in New York, Boston and Los Angeles.

IV

On June 27, 1945, while in postwar London, Wilson had signed a contract with Secker and Warburg for the English edition of *Memoirs of Hecate County* and received an advance of £500. While the American trials were taking place in 1946–47, Warburg, though eager to capitalize on the scandal and reap the profits, was unable to find a firm to print the potentially pornographic pages. He therefore pressured Wilson to modify the sexual passages and promised to sell between 10,000 and 25,000 copies. Wilson's contract specified that no changes could be made without his explicit permission. Despite Warburg's strenuous and sometimes piteous pleas, and the considerable loss of money on potential sales, Wilson refused.

Wilson realized his decision was based on self-interest as well as on principle. The trials might vindicate his book, persuade the printers to undertake the work and minimize the risk of publishing it in England. He knew that the book would do much better if the sexual passages remained intact and was prepared to wait until it could be published as he had written it. Exaggerating the American sales to whet Warburg's appetite, on January 10, 1947 he wrote: "The situation at the present is that it has been condemned in Los Angeles and New York, but cleared in San Francisco. . . . The prosecution is an Irish Catholic affair. . . . Before the case went against us in New York, almost 70,000 copies of the book had been sold."

Ten days later, Donald Elder of Doubleday complained about Wilson's ingratitude and told Warburg that he was behaving even more provocatively in America than in England: Wilson "is not particularly grateful for the large sums of money we spent defending the book, and has told us that his next book is going to have even more sex in it." Fed up at last with all the trouble Wilson had caused—though Elder himself was actually at fault for not foreseeing the legal consequences—he frankly told Wilson that he had no future with Doubleday and ought to find a different publisher.

Wilson once told the critic Irving Howe that "every self-respecting writer ought to die owing advances to publishers." But he enjoyed baiting publishers more than exploiting them. Once the advantage had been gained, he acted like a gentleman. In May 1947 he surprised Warburg by declaring: "I have just been examining our contract for

Hecate County and I see that it is no longer valid, since Secker & Warburg agreed to bring the book out in 1946. I do not, however, as I have written you, want you to lose by our arrangement, so I will offer you my new book *Europe Without Baedeker* on the same terms." Wilson was, to a certain extent, bluffing. Contracts do not become invalid if publishers fail to bring out a book on time because of circumstances (like printers refusing to print pornography) beyond their control. This letter shows, however, that Wilson *was* a tough negotiator and had seized the initiative from the frustrated Warburg. If he had wished to do so, he could have kept the £500 for *Memoirs of Hecate County* and offered *Europe Without Baedeker*, which was not under contract, to another publisher.

In October 1947, while continuing to fence with Warburg, the old magician revealed that he had yet another card—a rival publisher—up his sleeve. After a meeting in New York with Graham Greene, who asked him to allow Eyre and Spottiswoode to expurgate his book, Wilson gave Warburg his final and still intractable position: "I don't, however, see how any expurgation is possible. The physiological passages are important and would have to remain. It could only be a question of leaving blanks for certain words, if you think this would placate the printers."[14] After this pronouncement, Secker and Warburg gave up the book, which was eventually published in England by W. H. Allen in 1951.

In America the trials gave the book enormous publicity and generated considerable demand. But after the stalemated Supreme Court had upheld the suppression on grounds of obscenity, Doubleday could not reprint or sell it. Wilson thought of reprinting it himself in 1950 and actually got a printer's estimate, but decided not to take the financial risk. In 1959, when the moral climate had changed, the book was republished in forty-nine states by L. C. Page, a subsidiary of his current publisher, Farrar, Straus and Cudahy, and carried the provocative warning: "Not for sale in New York State."[15]

SEVENTEEN

Talcottville, 1950–1953

I

In April 1950 Wilson's eighty-five-year-old mother had an alarming collapse and spent two weeks in hospital. Both Helen Wilson and her doctor thought she was going to die, but the tough old lady held on until February 3, 1951. A few days after her death Wilson wrote Nabokov that his mother, surrounded by servants and comfort, had managed to evade the humiliations of old age: "My mother was nearly eighty-six, was completely deaf, nearly blind and so arthritic that she could hardly stand up. But it was impressive to see how well she kept up and how keen she still managed to be. When she died, she had a moment before been having coffee and joking with Rosalind and her nurse. That morning she had asked Rosalind about her beaux and said, 'I suppose they're a lot of writers. Don't marry one or you'll never have any money.'"

A year later, Wilson had finally moved the furniture and posses-sions out of Red Bank and stuffed it all into the Wellfleet house, which seemed like an anaconda trying to swallow a great meal. The miscella-neous loot included a large stuffed owl, an elaborate jigsaw clock, a broken plaster gargoyle from Notre-Dame and a whole depressing library on polar exploration. More welcome, after a thirty-year delay, was a trust fund of $200,000, which, at 4.25 percent, produced an income of $8,500 a year. This money, along with his earnings from the *New Yorker* and the short-lived but lucrative royalties from *Memoirs of Hecate County*, made him relatively prosperous for the first time in his life.

Wilson sold his mother's place in Red Bank but became passion-ately attached to the Old Stone House in Talcottville, New York, which he had first visited in childhood. It combined, in a fascinating way, both personal and national history. As his mother's death drew his thoughts back to the past, the ancestral pile took on a private aura of romance. He loved the physical setting—the rawness, the vast open spaces, the end-of-the-world feeling—that repelled Elena and so many of his friends. The earthy people who ran the big dairy farms in the foothills of the Adirondacks seemed more solid and good-natured than the rather dried-up and decadent writers on Cape Cod. He glamorized the region in a letter to Mamaine, who was then living with Koestler in a rugged and romantic corner of Wales: "When I go up there, I feel that I am returning to a remote and queer past as I never really do in visiting mediaeval towers or even Roman ruins. The country up there is wonderful and still a good deal of it very wild: mountains, waterfalls and forests."

Talcottville was closely interwoven with the memories and experiences of Wilson's early life, with his first delight in books and with the discovery of his literary vocation. Cut off from his parents by death, he felt closer to them when he returned to the Old Stone House and to the village of eighty souls that had changed much less than any other part of the country. He liked to occupy the largest and most distinguished house in town, to have everyone know and accept him, to play the lord of the manor and behave exactly as he pleased. He even had the cemetery close by so he could conveniently look up the family dates on the tombstones.

When he first came up to Talcottville, the village seemed rather empty. Then everything filled in around him and it became more real to him than Wellfleet. Wilson felt he belonged there. If he had inherited the Old Stone House when he was younger, he would have settled in upstate as a landowner and family man, and led an entirely different kind of life. Dos Passos, whose squirearchical pretensions Wilson had gently mocked, now produced his own squib:

> He says he's the Talcottville squire
> But the facts will prove him a liar
> He don't plow, he don't harrow
> He don't push no wheelbarrow
> He juss sits and holds forth by the fire.[1]

Despite its remoteness and harsh climate, Talcottville also had some practical advantages. During the summer in Wellfleet, the guests, visitors, crowds, noise and traffic had made work—always a primary consideration—increasingly difficult. But Talcottville was very quiet and had few distractions. Wilson escaped there during the hot months to concentrate on uninterrupted reading and writing. After finishing work in the late afternoon, he would take a long walk or swim in the nearby Sugar River. Then, dressed in his wrinkled linen suit and battered straw hat, he would visit friends or dine out in his favorite local restaurants: the Fort Schuyler Club in Utica, the Savoy in Rome, the Hurlbut House in Boonville and the Towpath Inn (still serving excellent food) in Turin.

Elena had a completely different attitude toward upstate New York. Her extreme reluctance to go there led, during Wilson's annual spring offensive, to the most serious quarrels of their marriage. She had no intimate associations with the place and found it difficult to perceive its merits. She loved the beach and swimming on the Cape, her house and friends in Wellfleet, and had nothing to do in Talcottville. Far from being attracted to the wild country, she was frightened and repelled by the primitive outback and felt, as a cultivated European, that Indians were still lurking in the woods. Everything seemed to her to be in an advanced state of decay: the old canals were broken up, the mansions ruined, the churches abandoned. She refused to swim in the polluted river and was even attacked by a herd of cows. She found the locals unfriendly, was spied on by a neighbor who saw her gulping a bottle of whiskey and disliked the women who fawned over her husband. The rugged landscape, the harsh climate and the altitude she found uncongenial and "inimical to women." The whole place made her feel uncharacteristically nervous and ill at ease.

To Elena the house—cold and damp even in the summer—was a tomb. The wiring was obsolete, the furnace and plumbing did not work properly, and the books became swollen and clammy when water from the bathroom leaked into the musty library. The kitchen was small and had no amenities; and every year she had to do a great deal of painting and repairing to keep the whole place from collapsing. She was repelled by the accumulation of family rubbish in the attic, disgusted by the piles of mouse turds scattered through the house and scared by the ghosts she swore she had actually seen. Raised in baronial splendor, she refused to become the mistress of a crumbling old pile that gave her the creeps, almost suffocated her and threatened her sense of identity. Even Wilson sensed the House of Usher syndrome and once sent Stuart

Hughes a postcard showing "a bear scavenging in an overturned gar-bage can. 'This will give you some idea,' Edmund wrote, 'of how I live here.'"

Some of the problems, Wilson had to admit, were not imaginary. The juvenile delinquents, bored to death in that town, bothered Wilson when he sat on his front porch (which was often warmer than the house). When he tried to chase the cheeky brats away with a Civil War rifle that did not fire, he seemed like a gruff old man played by W. C. Fields. During the winter they broke his windows and vandalized his home. Motorcycles roared aimlessly up and down the road. Later on, an ugly four-lane highway cut off a slab of his front lawn and (as in Wellfleet) left him exposed to the passing traffic. The townspeople nailed John Birch Society posters on the trees across the street. As if to substantiate the Red Menace, squadrons of air force pilots took off from their base in Rome, New York, and flew through the night, armed with nuclear weapons, in the direction of Russia.

At first, Elena regarded the forced march to Talcottville as one of her marital duties. But as the years passed, she put up a more stubborn resistance and refused to be uprooted from her friends and comforts in Wellfleet. She once became so exasperated by Wilson's glorification of the Old Stone House that she threatened him with an eggbeater and told him to "go and join your ancestors." During another brief but bitter scene about exile to Talcottville, she spat out: "I hate you!" (as Helen did to Rosalind). Driven to Draconian measures by Elena's "perfectly unreasonable" attitude, Wilson once rented the Wellfleet house for the summer to the editor Jason Epstein. Though Elena was present, she was unable to protest. Since she had no place to stay, she had to go to Talcottville.

Rosalind felt the pliable Elena never took a stand on anything. But in June 1959, after eight visits upstate, she dug in her heels and tactfully told Wilson, who had already "joined his ancestors," that she could not face another gloomy, nerve-wracked summer:

> Dearest: I am not going to come to Talcottville this year. . . . I feel as badly as I can about letting you down at this moment but I know that physically and morally we had better be separated for a while. I just cannot take one more drunken quarrel and your being right that it is just as much my fault as yours, makes it worse. I just become a crying, hysterical person with no self-control and first must pull myself together.

Two weeks later she wittily promised that when they moved to Cambridge in the fall, "I will do my best to be a Vera Nabokoff"—the perfect model of a dutiful and submissive wife.

The following year, Elena, now devising her own cunning strategies, promised to join him upstate and then, when he had left for the north, anchored herself to the Cape. She explained that she could never become enthusiastic about the place, and called his bluff about finding a mistress or getting divorced:

> I can't take these deadlines and ultimatums. I cannot take the scenes which are unavoidable if I come to Talcottville. . . . I have a feeling of guilt and failure at doing what you obviously consider is letting you down, but I just can't.
>
> I did come all the other years but that was obviously not enough because what you want is for me to share your feelings for Talcottville and that I cannot do, which you should understand. I know that I risk what you threatened the other day—that you would have to find somebody else if I let you down—but I just can't. Not even for Helen's sake or for Reuel's, who is upset enough about one more divorce [McCarthy and Bowden Broadwater] in the family.[2]

Rosalind believed that Wilson's fourth marriage lasted because he was separated from Elena for all or part of the summer during their last twenty-one years together. Wilson thought Elena's greatest fault was catering to people and making them depend on her. But he also saw some advantages in his independent existence: "At Wellfleet, she insists on doing everything, and is upset if I make any arrangements for myself. The result is that I become dependent on her and take no responsibility. Here I attend to everything and am quite free to make my own routine and thoroughly enjoy it. I drink less and get more work done." In a tender poem, reminiscent of Swift's verses to Stella, Wilson mentioned their conflicting views about the Old Stone House—which became one of the dominant themes of *Upstate:*

> I bring you to this dull old place,
> A cloud occludes your darling face:
> Your powers fail, your spirit sinks . . .
> And I am torn, I must admit,
> Between my loves for you and it.[3]

II

In his essay on Casanova in *The Wound and the Bow*, Wilson remarked that a mistress of the great lover had urged him to remember her by writing her name on their window with a diamond. Wilson imitated this practice in Talcottville and Wellfleet by encouraging friends to write poems on his window panes with a diamond pencil. Saint-John Perse (whom Wilson met through Francis Biddle in Wellfleet) and Philippe Thoby-Marcelin wrote in French, the Scottish poet Edwin Muir copied his translation of Hölderlin, Charley Walker wrote in Greek, Vladimir Nabokov wrote in Russian, Isaiah Berlin wrote in Hebrew and Louise Bogan, Dorothy Parker, W. H. Auden, Stephen Spender and John Wain all engraved their own work. The poems on the windows of the bedrooms described sleep; and the lines of Auden's nocturne—written, like Dorothy Parker's poem, after quite a few drinks—looked wobbly as well as dreamy:

> Make this night loveable,
> Moon, and with eye single
> Looking down from there
> Bless me, One especial
> And friends everywhere.

The panes inscribed by Bogan and Spender were later broken by teenage vandals and thrown away.

Wilson also had a more permanent circle of family members, doctors, servants and friends—including Loran Crosten, Walter Edmonds, Malcolm Sharp and Glyn Morris—who either lived upstate all year or came up for the summer. His cousin Otis Munn was a brawny, self-assured, substantial farmer with an ample stomach. Robert Smith, his Harvard-trained physician, was a model of the rural doctor, totally at the service of his patients. His housekeepers—first Elizabeth McGuire and then Mable Hutchins, who took over in Elena's absence —usually worked from eight to one and five to seven, unless Wilson (as he often did) went out for dinner. Unlike Elena, Mable, a hearty local girl, found the house quite manageable and warm enough—even in winter. She did the shopping, drove Wilson through the countryside and to nearby Boonville, and once took him all the way to Helen Muchnic's house in Cummington, Massachusetts. Mable spent the summer of 1970 working for Wilson on the Cape and living in the guest house—more as a guest than a maid. Her only problem occurred when she broke a stemmed goblet ("I didn't mean to do it," she said) and Wilson "growled a little." Though Wilson could be demanding and gruff, he knew the indispensable Mable would quit if he became too harsh. Mable had a pretty niece called Beverly, whom Wilson tried to kiss when he was drunk and who became expert at resisting his advances.

Loran Crosten, who taught music at Stanford, was one of the summer residents. When his day's work was completed, Wilson would be driven a few miles to the Crostens' house, swim in their lake, have a few drinks and stay (uninvited but welcome) for dinner. On one occasion, when Loran was absent, Wilson borrowed his bathrobe for swimming and then asked Mary: "What would people think if they saw me in your husband's bathrobe when he was away?" But Wilson always behaved with the utmost propriety. He once took Mary and her two daughters to see a violent and horrible Japanese war movie. When they left in the middle to have a drink, she said: "Why waste time on such trash?" Wilson, interested in the propagandistic element, replied: "I see something entirely different in it."[4]

In 1951, shortly after returning to Talcottville, Wilson telephoned Walter Edmonds—the charming, Utica-born author of the famous historical novel *Drums Along the Mohawk* (1936)—and asked: "Could you give me tea? I won't stay long." As they drank Edmonds' rare old bourbon, Wilson's speech became a little blurry and his crusty reserve began to dissolve. When Wilson (always a sweet tooth) smelled brownies cooking and asked if he might have some, Edmonds warmed up to his new neighbor. Wilson was a steamroller in argument, and when he got excited his jowls would puff up like a bullfrog's. He bluntly declared that Edmonds' books were rather juvenile and "incredibly dull," but praised his authentic descriptions of animals. Wilson joked that after a period of psychoanalysis, Edmonds had told him, "Now I'm mature," and then "wrote a book on the Seneca Indians for twelve year olds." In his diaries, Wilson, who could also be seignorial and whose own house was crumbling, punctured Edmonds' pretensions and smugness: "Walter is a museum piece: his feudal estate and establishment, his way of pronouncing *o* as *ao*, his ostentatious satisfactions in his brandies and wines 'laid down' by his uncle or father, his sense . . . of being remote, half dissociated, from the rest of the American world but supreme in his little domain."

The learned and liberal Malcolm Sharp, a law professor at the University of Chicago, was married to Wilson's cousin, Dorothy Furbish, and shared his interest in local history and the Iroquois Indians. Sharp helped defend Julius and Ethel Rosenberg, who were accused of selling atomic secrets to Russia. After they were convicted and executed, he argued in *Was Justice Done? The Rosenberg-Sobell Case* (1956) that their trial was unjust. Wilson thought that the Rosenbergs were guilty, but agreed that they should not have been executed. In his tribute to Sharp, published in the *University of Chicago Law Review*, Wilson praised his "complex, sensitive and acutely conscientious character" and wrote that he had a "subtle intellect, philosophic and literary interests, a long view of human history . . . and a combination of moral anxieties with an ironic sense of humor."[5]

Wilson's closest friend in upstate New York was the clergyman and public school administrator Glyn Morris. Born in Wales in 1905, he came to America at the age of six and earned his divinity degree from Union Theological Seminary and his doctorate in education from Columbia Teachers College. He taught school in Harlan County, Kentucky, during the 1930s, when Wilson reported the coal miners' strikes for the *New Republic*, was chaplain to an engineering combat group in World War Two and was a school superintendent in Wilson's home county for nearly twenty years. Wilson found Morris—who was interested in literature, theater and music—imaginative, intelligent and amusing.

Morris carefully observed Wilson and wrote vividly detailed accounts of their friendship in his two autobiographies. Wilson would suddenly phone and say (as he did with the Walkers and the Chavchavadzes on the Cape): "How would you like to have a guest for dinner tonight?" and then duly appear in his habitual white button-down oxford shirt and loosely-knotted red tie. His purposeful, almost military walk, Morris wrote, "consisted of short, rapid, sure-footed steps, as though he had something specific and urgent in his mind—and his stance, chin out, body straight as a grenadier's, staccato steps, all seemed to reflect Edmund's outlook toward life." When he entered Morris' house, Wilson always stroked the cat and asked: "How's dat old puddy cat tonight?" He loved the rich dishes prepared by Glyn's wife Gladys—beef Stroganoff or creamed chicken with pilaf rice—and when Morris gave the blessing the unregenerate atheist respectfully stood up, rolled his napkin in his hands and bowed his head.

Once seated, Wilson habitually scratched his left forefinger with the forefinger of his right hand. When he wished to emphasize a point, he would place both arms on the table, "bob his head several times from side to side, then, 'B-b-but, I tell you . . .' proceed with his emphatic qualifying statement." Professionally concerned with matters of conscience, Morris once asked his friend if he ever felt guilty. "No, never," Wilson replied. "I have regrets but no guilt." But he did have fine scruples. After challenging a Mennonite minister on a factual point, Wilson asked if he had been too hard on the poor fellow—then added that he liked to correct misinformation. At about ten in the evening, Wilson would simply announce "I must get me home" or "I must dispatch myself," and Morris would drive him from Lyons Falls back to Talcottville.

The traditional life in Talcottville made Wilson acutely aware that his life spanned different and conflicting eras. He had grown up in a secure world, dominated by Victorian values, and had lived well into the atomic age. He always felt he was a man of the Twenties, could talk most meaningfully with writers of his own era and, as he grew older, longed for the idealized past. He would tell younger friends, without believing they would fully understand, "Nothing's much fun any-more. . . . Don't you think everything is going to hell?" The ancestral memories of Talcottville, the nearby family graves, the very stones of the Old Stone House, encouraged his dissatisfaction with the present and his retreat into the past. This nostalgia for the past and for the civilized tradition of ancient country houses attracted him to the works of two authors he greatly admired: Yeats and Lampedusa.[6]

By the time he reached the age of sixty, in 1955, Wilson—still quite radical in his views—had adopted a reactionary public persona that gave a quite misleading impression of what he really thought. He told the *New Yorker* reporter Richard Rovere: "I should be completely happy if I never had to emerge from my library to see anything which is not part of the past. I don't particularly like a good deal of what is going on in this country and like still less what we are doing abroad." His dissatisfaction with the present led not only to a nostalgia for the past but also to a spirited and salutary criticism of the present. In his oft-quoted essay "The Author at Sixty," Wilson was pleased to portray himself as an eighteenth-century man (almost in tie-wig and knee-breeches), who disliked cars and would not drive one, almost never went to the movies, made no attempt to keep up with younger American writers and was rapidly turning into an old fogey. In fact, he knew how to drive a car as well as a motorcycle, and loved his long, chauffeured drives from Wellfleet to Talcottville and distant Virginia. He had reviewed cinema for the *New Republic* in the Twenties; regularly took his children to Disney movies and saw two films just before his death. Though he accused himself of ignoring contemporary American writers, he kept in very close touch with the current literary scene. He never abandoned his progressive beliefs and remained in old age as contentious and critical as ever.

Nevertheless, Wilson allowed this ultra-conservative persona to be publicized in Europe by granting a rare interview (one of only four in his entire life) to an Italian journalist. Encouraged by Wilson, Alberto Arbasino exaggerated his crustiness and—ignoring Wilson's nine months a year in Wellfleet and frequent trips to Boston and New York—naively portrayed him as a kind of troglodyte Samuel Johnson, who was locked in the past but had somehow managed to survive into the twentieth century. In Arbasino's portrait, Wilson becomes an elderly Roman poet, driven by *"amaro egoismo"* and rusticated to his villa:

> He was living in an old stone house in Talcottville, Lewis County, built by his mother's family more than a century ago, when the northwest of the state of New York was still "frontier"; and he always remains there, in a remote corner of his mythic "ideal" America, simple, isolated, rural, archaic, without going to the movies, or watching television, or reading new books, in the company of the classics and the memories of his legendary Twenties, extinct forever and betrayed by those who no longer have faith in the pure values of literary art. . . . I saw him isolated in his great aristocratic rejection of an America in which he does not believe and which he does not want to recognize, now rather vulgarly corrupted and lost and alienated from the virtues of his ancestors.[7]

III

Like many authors, Wilson was hostile to publishers, saw them as his natural enemy and emphasized their commercial greed. "You must get over the instinctive idea," he told the novice Helen Muchnic, "that the publishers are doing you a favor or have anything in mind but their own gain." The quest for the ideal reader as well as an efficient intermediary between the author and his public, the search for greater appreciation and more money, the movement of editors and shifts in taste, prompted the restless Wilson to change publishers as frequently as he changed houses and wives. He began in America with Knopf and the Boni brothers, then passed through Scribner's, Harcourt, Colt Press, Houghton Mifflin and Doubleday until—after the scandal of *Memoirs of Hecate County*—he finally settled on Oxford University Press and Farrar, Straus.

According to John Tebbel, the historian of publishing, John Farrar, hearing of his trouble with Doubleday, approached Wilson and in June 1950 brought out his play *The Little Blue Light*. This was the first of more than twenty of his books to be published by this firm—until the end of his life and for twenty years after his death. Farrar, Straus was a small, highbrow, independently-owned firm with a strong poetry list (including Lowell, Bishop, Berryman and Jarrell), many distinguished foreign writers and (as the years passed) an extraordinary number of Nobel Prize winners (Solzhenitsyn, Singer, Canetti, Golding, Brodsky, Walcott).

Wilson handled his own affairs and dealt directly with Roger Straus, who was born in New York in 1917 and was an heir to the Guggenheim fortune. Straus got a journalism degree from the University of Missouri, worked as a magazine and book editor, and founded the firm in 1945. He was an aggressive and often crude man, who, Wilson thought, could effectively advance his interests and increase his income. Though they had generally good business relations, and sometimes saw each other socially at Longchamps or the Princeton Club when Wilson was in New York, they had little in common and were not close friends. Wilson—undisturbed by writing blocks, change of residence, travels abroad, marriage problems, love affairs, personal quarrels, tax disputes, drinking, illness, old age and imminent death —poured out his new and reissued his old books. Straus, proud of his illustrious acquisition, brought them out, in hardcover and paperback, as fast as Wilson could produce them. Wilson wrote only two original books in the 1950s (his play and *The Scrolls from the Dead Sea*), but —through judicious recycling—brought out seven others from previously published (and some new) material.

Like all experienced authors, Wilson knew, once the book was written, that he had to supervise every detail of the production—or risk catastrophe. Inspired by the handy size of the Pléiade editions of French classics and by the early Viking Portable paperbacks, he dictated the format of and even the paper to be used in his books. "He was concerned," Straus recalled, "about the color of his bindings and jackets; helped with the blurbs; argued with his foreign publishers and in the main controlled them with a tight rein. He refused the services of the publicity department—no interviews, no autographs, no invasion of his privacy"—but insisted on an energetic sales force and as much advertising as possible. When things displeased him, as they often did, he tried to whip Straus into shape with characteristically blunt criticism. In May 1950 he rewrote and sent back the blurb for his play, condemning it as "a mass of inaccuracy, bad grammar, bad vocabulary and mixed metaphors."

Though Straus tried hard, the sales, at first, were disappointingly modest. By February 1951 *The Little Blue Light*, despite a production in Cambridge, sold only 162 copies, leaving a debit of $374; and his literary essays of the 1940s, *Classics and Commercials* (also published in 1950), sold 3,650 copies, earning $2,155. When negotiating *A Piece of My Mind* in March 1956, Wilson asked for an advance of $1,500 and twelve percent royalties (less than his usual percentage) on the first 3,000 copies, rising to fifteen percent if he was lucky enough to sell more than that. His satiric play *The Duke of Palermo* (1969), originally published in the *New York Review of Books* in January 1967, sold by mid-June 1969 a respectable 2,200 copies, while *Five Plays* (1954), an old dud that Wilson somehow persuaded Straus to reissue in 1969, pooped out with a sale of only 570. Wilson's modest earnings were also reduced—and sometimes extinguished—by costly charges for excessive author's corrections (he paid $226 for alterations to *Europe Without Baedeker*). None of Wilson's three biggest sellers—*Axel's Castle* (Scribner's), *Memoirs of Hecate County* (Doubleday) and *The Scrolls from the Dead Sea* (Oxford)—were published by Farrar, Straus. But in about 1966 Straus got a good deal when he bought all five volumes of Wilson's diaries for less than $100,000.[8]

Wilson, who was translated into twenty languages, handled his own complicated foreign rights. He often sought lawyers' advice, and threatened to sue foreign publishers for poor translations (which he carefully checked) and for breach of contract. In a fascinating letter to Straus, who wanted to take over the foreign rights, Wilson insisted he could cut a much better deal on his own:

You are mistaken, by the way, in thinking that anybody else could do better than I in selling my books abroad. My experience in the past has been—before I began handling this myself—that the people in publishers' offices (I am not thinking of yours) who deal in these sales abroad simply accept anything that is offered them from the first foreign publisher that offers. I have just succeeded in getting from [the Italian firm] Einaudi an advance of $1,000 for *Hecate County* (Feltrinelli would not go beyond, I think, $200) and have extracted from Allen for the *Iroquois* a sum far greater than they wanted to pay. I do not, as you seem to think, let any opportunity slip but keep a chart with the estimated book-buying population of every country in Europe and have conducted negotiations with Iceland, Finland and Jugoslavia. I have, I fear, been outwitted by the Japs, who have succeeded in translating a book and an article of mine without paying me a penny.

Wilson's relations with English publishers were even more varied than with American ones. His early books were never published in London. Scribner's brought out English editions of *Axel's Castle* and *The American Jitters* under their own imprint, and *The Triple Thinkers* appeared with Oxford in 1938. Secker and Warburg published his books in the 1940s, Gollancz brought out *The Little Blue Light* in 1951, and W. H. Allen—an inappropriate firm with very little prestige —took over his new books and reissued several old ones in the 1950s and 1960s. During these two decades he was also published by John Lehmann, André Deutsch and Rupert Hart-Davis. Macmillan and Routledge brought out his posthumous works, and Farrar, Straus published the English edition of *The Sixties*.

English sales were, quite typically for an American author, less than in the United States. By 1952 the Secker and Warburg editions of *To the Finland Station* had sold 2,681 copies, *The Wound and the Bow* 1,682, *Notebooks of Night* a respectable 1,547 (because of the demand for books in wartime) and the controversial *Europe Without Baedeker* 2,777. In May 1947, having already irritated Fredric Warburg by refusing to expurgate *Memoirs of Hecate County*, Wilson once again pulled the rug from under his feet when he offered him English rights of *The Wound and the Bow*. After Warburg asked, with scarcely restrained rage: "Have you forgotten that *we* are the publishers in England of *The Wound and the Bow?*," Wilson cunningly answered: "About *The Wound and the Bow:*

I have myself bought all the rights [including English] from Houghton Mifflin and have sold the American rights to Oxford, with the under-standing that the English Oxford shall have first refusal of the British rights."[9] After securing world rights, he then cheekily asked Warburg for a $500 advance on a book that Warburg thought he already owned!

The firm of W. H. Allen, who succeeded Secker and Warburg as his publisher, brought out the English editions of sixteen books by Wilson between 1951 and 1967. Wilson's editor Jeffrey Simmons recalled that in 1951 Mark Goulden, the managing director, "made a deal with Roger Straus to publish the controversial *Memoirs of Hecate County*. It was only because Mark was willing to take the risk that we prised the book away from one of the more obviously literary publish-ers. In the event, the police informed us that there would be no prosecution, and the book sold very well indeed." In 1953, after the firm had brought out his first few books and reissued *I Thought of Daisy* (later published by Penguin Books), Wilson told a friend that they had done better for him than any other English publisher. He liked the fact that W. H. Allen got on with publishing his books instead of wasting time and money on lavish publicity parties.

Simmons also gave a vivid account of negotiating foreign rights with the volatile and unpredictable Wilson:

> He would occasionally say no to an excellent offer without expla-nation, requiring me to write a second and more persuasive letter, which usually brought his agreement. On one memorable occa-sion, I received an offer from India for the Gujurati rights in one of his books: I think that it was *To the Finland Station*. The publisher, of whom I had never heard, offered the princely sum of £10! As a joke, I referred the offer to him, half expecting a rude response. Instead I received a cable—something I had never had before from him—expressing his great pleasure and asking me to proceed with all haste. I think he meant it seriously. The idea of being read in Gujurati doubtless appealed to him enormously.

W. H. Allen offered modest advances. But in 1951—when the pound was worth about five dollars—they brought out four books at one time and paid £300 for *I Thought of Daisy*, £180 for *The Wound and the Bow* (which Wilson had sold for the fourth time), £150 for *Classics and Commercials* and £100 for a new and never-to-be-writtten novel (perhaps *The Golden Air of Death*). *I Thought of Daisy* (out of print since 1929) sold 4,000 copies in 1952 and *Memoirs of Hecate County* (which could still not be exported to Australia) sold an impressive 20,000 copies in 1951.

Things went fairly smoothly with W. H. Allen until 1967, when Wilson quarreled with them about English rights of *O Canada* (1965). They felt he had accepted their advance and agreed to let them publish his book on Canadian literature and politics; he felt he had not done so and that they were trying to get two books for the price of one. The confusion arose because Wilson originally planned to include his Canadian pieces in a new collection of essays, and then decided to make them into an entirely new book. In the end, he broke with W. H. Allen and, after Rupert Hart-Davis had brought out the English edition of *O Canada* in 1967, Macmillan took over as his English publisher and brought out seven of his posthumous books between 1972 and 1986.

Wilson's success in the early 1950s with Farrar, Straus and W. H. Allen was complemented by his profitable connection with Jason Epstein, an editor at Doubleday, who founded the first quality paperback imprint in America, Anchor Books. Wilson called the brash and energetic Epstein, born in 1928 and educated at Columbia, "a highly intelligent boy, very well read and with a good deal of taste." Isaiah Berlin, who thought Wilson had his own misanthropic streak, said that Wilson particularly admired Epstein's phenomenal dislike of mankind. Wilson always visited Epstein when he came to New York. As Jason told him all the malicious literary gossip, tears of delight would roll down Wilson's cheeks.

Though Wilson saw himself as a "wolf pouncing on publishers," he accepted the best offer that Epstein could give in 1953: $750 for the paperback rights of *To the Finland Station*. As the new project took off, Epstein increased his advances and paid $2,500 for *Eight Essays*, $3,000 for *A Literary Chronicle* and $2,500 for a work on Russian literature, which never appeared as an Anchor Book and was eventually published by Farrar, Straus as *A Window on Russia* (1972). Epstein also brought out two other Wilson books: *A Piece of My Mind* and *The American Earthquake* (both 1958). The latter sold 4,000–5,000 copies and *To the Finland Station* earned $8,000 in the radical 1960s. In 1953 Wilson told Betty Huling that he was making money from his paperback editions and was beginning to feel, for the first time in his life, as if he were a real success. Epstein had a surprisingly hard time selling Wilson, who was never a popular author in America. But he felt that though Anchor had helped Wilson financially, Wilson's prestige had made Anchor a great success.[10]

IV

Wilson's play *The Little Blue Light* was published by Farrar, Straus in May 1950 and performed in Cambridge and in New York in 1950–51. It is an intellectual drama, like T. S. Eliot's *The Cocktail Party* (1949), an abstract yet melodramatic and fantastic attack on the tyrannical forces that are destroying civilization: the Catholic Church, criminal organizations, monopolistic corporations and fanatical political parties. It is set in the near future, like *Nineteen Eighty-Four* (1949), and the oppressive powers use the little blue light, a mysterious electric ray that originated in one of Wilson's nightmares, to liquidate their opponents. Its characters include Frank, a crusading liberal journalist; Judith, his egoistic and ambitious wife (based on McCarthy); Gandersheim, a neurotic mystical writer; Ellis, an idealistic young reporter; and a moralizing Gardener of indeterminate nationality, who offers sermons throughout the play and is finally revealed as the Wandering Jew. As in all Wilson's plays, the characters are torn by a desire to remain loyal to idealistic values and an urge to sell out for money and power. This static and talky drama ends more darkly than Wilson's previous plays, as the editor, his wife and the writer are all zapped by the little blue light.

The performances of Wilson's play, the first since *The Crime in the Whistler Room* in 1924, were more a tribute to his literary prestige than to his powers as a dramatist. *The Little Blue Light* first opened at the Brattle Theater in Cambridge on August 15, 1950, with Hume Cronyn as Gandersheim and Jessica Tandy as Judith. Cronyn recalled that Wilson—protected by his contract—was polite but adamant about forbidding any cuts in his long script. His attitude caused serious problems in staging the play; and Cronyn received a telegram from the frustrated director of both productions, Albert Marre, who played The Gardener in Cambridge: "We cut another 20 minutes. Wilson attacked me immediately saying perfectly furious things about these cuts. They also have to [be put] back. Seeing my lawyer."

Cronyn also described Wilson at the first-night party, dishevelled and numbed against failure by alcohol: "Bald-headed, flushed and perspiring, sitting on the floor, [he has his] back propped against the wall. . . . He is wearing a crumpled white suit with dark rings of nervous sweat around the armpits and is happily drunk, as well as being uncharacteristically benign." Friends who saw the play in Cambridge had antithetical responses. Harry Levin thought it was an undramatic and unsuccessful closet drama while Daniel Walker found it scary, interesting and effective on stage.

Wilson's fierce quarrel with the director and actors continued when the play was produced in New York. It opened on April 29, 1951 at the American National Theater and Academy (ANTA) playhouse with a strong cast: Burgess Meredith as Gandersheim, Arlene Francis as Judith and Melvyn Douglas as Frank. Two months before opening, *Variety* reported that Wilson was "irate at what he claims are unauthorized cuts in the script and has been threatening 'legal action.' . . . The same refusal to agree to any cuts or revisions was given as a reason for the Theatre Guild's decision to drop the script."[11]

The reviews of the book and of the New York production were generally negative, and seemed to justify the director's advice to cut the play. James Newman, writing in the *New Republic*, called the rather deadly book "earnest and derisive, serious and self-mocking," banal and "demonstrably superficial." The two most influential theater critics also disliked the play. Walter Kerr stated that it lacked "clarity and coherence," that Wilson's thought was "vague, if not downright flabby." Brooks Atkinson in the *New York Times* agreed that "Wilson's ideas are disembodied and he has no more talent for the stage than Henry James. . . . [The play is] not only insubstantial, but unreal and more and more confusing." Only Francis Fergusson, reviewing the book for the *New York Times Book Review*, was enthusiastic. Impressed by Wilson's ambitious attempt, he called the play "an intellectual thriller with a serious moral" and "entertainment at a high level."[12] The audiences, however, were not entertained. The play closed in New York, after only eight performances, before some of the late reviews had even been published. Wilson, who earned forty percent of the gross receipts after taxes, got only $154 from the Brattle Theater. But his more advantageous contract with ANTA stipulated a minimum of $1,000.

Farrar, Straus published *Classics and Commercials* (1950), Wilson's more up-to-date literary chronicle of the 1940s, before *The Shores of Light* (1952), his much stronger collection of essays and reviews of the 1920s and 1930s. Wilson had an extraordinary range of interests, but his literary studies were mainly confined to American, English, French and Russian works after 1800, and he rarely ventured outside that period. Though the narrator of *Memoirs of Hecate County* is an art historian, Wilson wrote very little on painting, sculpture and architecture. *Classics and Commercials* contains sixty-one essays, fifty from the *New Yorker* and the rest from the *New Republic, Nation* and *Partisan Review*. The pieces are arranged in order of publication, which scattered through the book the two essays each on Thackeray, Saintsbury, Joyce and Waugh, and the three on Van Wyck Brooks. He reprinted *The Boys in the Back Room* (with a postscript), memoirs of T. K. Whipple and Paul Rosenfeld, and the fine autobiographical piece "Thoughts on Being Bibliographed." The best essays were appreciations of Joyce, Nabokov and Connolly, and the provocative attacks on Kafka, Waugh, Maugham and detective stories.

The title of his second and best collection, *The Shores of Light*, echoed Lucretius and Virgil, and alluded to the classic rural order of the Mediterranean coast. Three quarters of the ninety-seven essays were originally published in the *New Republic*. The volume opened and closed with the great memorial tributes to Christian Gauss, who died in 1951, and to Edna Millay, who died in 1950. Their deaths, and his mother's, seemed to close off an early phase of his life. The volume also included studies of Sophocles and Persius, elegies on Elinor Wylie and Herbert Croly, and pioneering essays on his friends Fitzgerald and Hemingway, Dos Passos and Cummings, Anderson and O'Neill, Eliot and Malraux. In his Foreword Wilson wrote: "I have not arranged the pieces in strictly chronological order, but have sometimes grouped them in such a way as to put together pieces on the same subject." But they were not arranged either by subject or by order of publication, and even essays on the same subject (Wylie or Dos Passos) were not placed consecutively. It is difficult to understand why Dostoyevsky's *Diary* followed *Lady Chatterley's Lover* or Virginia Woolf came after George Washington Cable. The order seemed entirely random.

V

In 1939 Wilson had lectured on "Marxism and Literature" (an essay from *The Triple Thinkers*) at Princeton; and his historical criticism, as Leon Edel observed, opposed the current academic fashion for "ahistorical and aesthetic New Criticism." Gauss had wanted to bring Wilson back to Princeton to direct the Creative Arts Program, which began in 1939 with a grant from the Carnegie Foundation. But the genteel and idle English Department—threatened by a learned, energetic and productive candidate—opposed the appointment, claiming that Wilson drank too much, was too contentious and harbored an irrational dislike for his old university. "That was Allen Tate's opinion," wrote Russell Fraser. "In any case, it was Allen who got the job."

Tate loved to shoot barbs at Wilson. On November 19, 1949, when Tate was teaching at New York University but living in Princeton, he invited his old adversary to his fiftieth birthday party. They both had plenty to drink, and Wilson exchanged insults with the Southern squire. Finally, wrote Eileen Simpson (John Berryman's wife), Wilson "protested that he couldn't stay for another drink; he'd already kept his mother's chauffeur waiting too long and must get back to Red Bank. 'Chauffeur?' Allen sniffed through one nostril. Looking out the door to see who was behind the wheel of the Cadillac, he said disdainfully, 'That's not a chauffeur, Bunny. Why that's just an ordinary field negra.'"[13]

In 1952 Wilson was invited to Princeton to participate in the Gauss Seminars in Criticism, named in honor of the dean, which had been founded in 1949 to provide a forum for the exchange of ideas in the humanities. The Seminars attracted eminent scholars, were highly successful and eventually produced a number of distinguished books: Francis Fergusson's *Dante's Drama of the Mind*, Jacques Maritain's *Creative Intuition* and René Wellek's *History of Literary Criticism*. The director, E. B. O. Borgerhoff of the French Department, described the fairly light duties as "a series of six lectures followed by an hour's informal discussion, and attendance at the other seminars given during the term." Eager to entice Wilson, whose dislike of teaching was well known, Borgerhoff hastened to add that he would have no contact with students: "No undergraduates are involved, there are no papers to correct, there are no examinations. The majority of the audience at the seminars would consist of faculty members from various departments and guests." The generous fee was $5,000.

Since the other lecturers had not yet been selected, Wilson nominated six promising candidates: Nabokov and the German critic Erich Heller (both brilliant lecturers), the learned Mario Praz, the witty Cyril Connolly, the amiable V. S. Pritchett and, for old times' sake, his Cape Cod neighbor Waldo Frank. None of these recommendations was followed. But Borgerhoff did get three other good men: the German theologian Paul Tillich spoke on what became *Love, Power and Justice*, the biographer Leon Edel on *The Modern Psychological Novel* and the young critic Irving Howe on *Politics and the Novel*.

Once again short of money, Wilson asked for the first month's salary in advance so he could "pay the rent," and the director complied with a check for $1,000. Wilson lived in Princeton from October 1952 until mid-February 1953. The Seminar met in the Poetry Room of the library at eight in the evening and the listeners included Saul Bellow, the poets John Berryman and Delmore Schwartz, the novelist Monroe Engel, the critic R. W. B. Lewis and the German scholar Erich Kahler. In November Wilson wrote Waldo Frank that he was enjoying Tillich's talks even though his "interpretation of Christian theology in terms of German philosophy is not exactly my cup of tea."[14]

Wilson, who began the second series of lectures on December 11, spoke on "The Literature of the American Civil War," including Harriet Beecher Stowe, Civil War memoirs, John DeForest, Sidney Lanier and Ambrose Bierce. These lectures later became *Patriotic Gore*. His recommended reading included *Uncle Tom's Cabin*, Herndon's *Life of Lincoln*, Grant's *Personal Memoirs*, Francis Grierson's *The Valley of Shadows* and Bierce's *In the Midst of Life*. Leon Edel, giving a somewhat idealized view, recalled that Wilson, "calm, unruffled, hesitant in speech, delivered his papers in a low-keyed voice, pondering everything and never allowing his enthusiasm for his work to carry him away." Monroe Engel, also on the scene, gave a more realistic account of the chaotic sessions: "He'd read from a typescript for an hour (early portions of *Patriotic Gore*) making no concessions to performance, emit something between a sigh and a groan when he'd finish, and then allow an anarchic often bellicose discussion to go on for another hour with very little direction, guidance, or even efforts to keep the peace." Saul Bellow found the lectures "enlivened by the objections of John Berryman, who often told Wilson that he didn't know what he was talking about. Wilson was a heavy-breathing and even a groaning lecturer. I had attended his Dickens seminar at the University of Chicago and was prepared for this Troglodyte act."

While in Princeton the fifty-seven-year-old Wilson began to study Hebrew at the Theological Seminary, from which his paternal grandfather, a Presbyterian minister, had graduated in 1846. After his mother's death, he had found in the attic of the house his grandfather's Hebrew Bible, along with a dictionary and grammar, and had become fascinated by the heavy black alphabet, the short words and the quick, staccato language. He took Charles Fritsch's introductory course, studied *Essentials of Biblical Hebrew* and was the only layman among the prim young theological students: Antichrist as elderly seminarian.

The stern Jewish Deity was more appealing to Wilson than the milder Christian God. He liked to compare one language to another, and told his Jewish friend Waldo Frank: "The Hebrew verbs are more dynamic, more full of conviction and determination, than those of any other language we study. The sense of time, time by the clock, is vaguer than even in Russian—there are no real tenses of the Western sort." In his intellectually exciting essay "On First Reading *Genesis*" (1954) (the title of which alludes to Keats' sonnet about first reading Homer in George Chapman's Renaissance translation) Wilson declared: "To write out Hebrew vocabulary, with black ink and a stub pen, affords a satisfaction that may give one a faint idea of the pleasures of Chinese calligraphy, as well as a feeling of vicarious authority as one traces the portentous syllables."[15] When he became more proficient in the language, he liked to play Scrabble in Hebrew.

Wilson attended Leon Edel's seminars on the stream-of-consciousness novel, often dined with him and took late-afternoon walks with him almost every day. He called their leisurely strolls "the Edmund Wilson seminars for Lé-on" and reminisced about his early days in Princeton. In 1953 Edel published the first volume of his magisterial life of Henry James. Contrary to his established practice, Wilson later allowed Edel to use a passage from his personal letter of October 24, 1962 on the dust jacket of the second and third volumes. He admired Edel's lucidity and elegance, his exhaustive research and acute psychological insight, and wrote: "I don't know of any other American literary biography which is comparable to it or, in fact, anything like it. It is an altogether original work, which, inspired by Henry James, is not subordinate to him. I only await the last volume . . . to call it a masterpiece. It makes one realize that one never really knew before what sort of man James was or what his life was like."

Wilson also saw quite a lot of the alcoholic and often manic poet John Berryman, who was teaching at Princeton that year. He told Berryman that it was impossible to live by free-lance writing without some sort of financial backing, and advised him to "give up the notion. It will only cause you trouble." An expert in domestic discord, Wilson perceived, even before the Berrymans did, that their marriage was about to break up. "This man," wrote Eileen Simpson, "who often seemed so vague about people, and still didn't have my name straight, had a deeper insight into our marriage than our closest friends, for he saw in John the husband he had been in an earlier marriage [to McCarthy], and saw in me that wife."[16]

Well versed in contemporary poetry, Wilson had a high opinion of Berryman's *Dream Songs*. In his self-interview, he sensed Berryman's desperation and remarked: "These poems are the utterances of a writer who has arrived at his own idiom to express his self-mockery and panic, his moments of lyric grandeur and his relapses into infantilism." In 1971, the year before his suicide, Berryman, referring to Wilson's use of the Philoctetes myth in *The Wound and the Bow*, declared that "an alcoholic is no more responsible for his vices than a gangrene victim for his stench." In a draft of a late poem, "Defensio in Extremis," later published in *Delusions, Etc.* (1972), Berryman included Wilson, with his Columbia teacher Mark Van Doren and the poet John Crowe Ransom, as one of his three mentors—and then criticized them for disapproving of his chaotic and destructive life:

> O even Mark, great Edmund, fine John Ransom
> splinter at my procedures and my ends.
> Surely their spiritual life is not what it might be?
> Surely they are half-full of it?
> Tell them to leave me damned well alone with my insights.[17]

In mid-December 1952 Wilson met Berryman in the street and asked him if Theodore Roethke's poetry was any good. Berryman said, "He's brilliant." Wilson invited Roethke to his Christmas party and Ted—the son of a nurseryman—sent dozens of flowers beforehand. Despite this auspicious beginning, things did not go well at the party. The giant Roethke entered the dining room, wearing pinstriped trousers tied with a pajama cord, like a fighter coming into the ring. After helping himself to copious quantities of food and to a bunch of white grapes, Roethke—rather fat himself—squeezed next to Wilson on the couch. He stared at Wilson for a minute or two, then said, "Come on. Let's blow this and go upstairs and I'll show you some of my stuff." When Wilson properly replied, "I can't do that. I'm the host," Roethke took offense and said, "You hate all contemporary poets, don't you?" He then leaned over, grabbed one of Wilson's jowls in his massive hand and remarked, "Why, you're all blubber!" Wilson, recovering his composure, pointed to the bunch of grapes and came up with a classical allusion: "Who, uh, do you think you are? A half-baked Bacchus?"

—which drove the aggressor right out of the room.[18] It is astonishing that Roethke, especially while sober, would dare to attack such a dignified and distinguished older man, and choose such an abysmally poor way to cultivate an influential critic. His madcap behavior was probably provoked by his jealous rivalry with Wilson. Roethke resented the long-standing affection of his current mistress, Louise Bogan, for her old friend and lover.

EIGHTEEN

The Dead Sea Scrolls, 1954–1956

I

In 1954, nine years after his first trip to postwar Europe, Wilson returned for a four-month stay in a more positive frame of mind. His close friendship with Auden made him more sympathetic to the English, and his revulsion from Senator Joe McCarthy's hysterical witch-hunts made him eager to breathe a different air. Edmund, Elena and the nearly six-year-old Helen sailed on the *Ile de France* on December 30, 1953—accompanied by Jason and Barbara Epstein, who were on their honeymoon—and were delighted to find Buster Keaton aboard ship. They landed in England on January 5 and stayed at the Basil Street Hotel in Knightsbridge. After three weeks in London, Oxford and Edinburgh, they spent a week in Paris at the Hôtel du Quai Voltaire (on the Left Bank, opposite the Tuileries) and saw Mamaine Koestler for the last time. Wilson taught for a month at the Salzburg Seminar; then spent a week in Munich and Frankfurt before visiting Elena's family home in Johannisberg, on the Rhine. Leaving his own family in Germany, Wilson paid his respects to Max Beerbohm in Rapallo and sailed from Marseilles to Athens (where he saw Eva Siphraios) and to Israel, where he spent a month investigating the Dead Sea Scrolls. He flew back to his family in Paris on April 20, sailed to America a week later and arrived in New York on May 3.

Wilson was received enthusiastically in England, despite the harsh words in *Europe Without Baedeker*, and met even more literati than on his previous trip. The *London Magazine*, the *Listener* and the *New Statesman* all gave parties for the eminent visitor. Waugh was estranged, Greene was abroad and Orwell was dead. But Wilson saw his old friends Connolly, Spender and Sylvester Gates, and was introduced to Arthur Waley, John Betjeman, E. M. Forster and Angus Wilson. He traveled up to Edinburgh to see Compton Mackenzie and Edwin Muir, and through Isaiah Berlin met a number of academic stars in Oxford. It is not known whether Bunny Wilson ever met Bunny Garnett to dine off carrots and lettuce.

Ignoring Connolly's harsh attack and personal insult in his review of *Memoirs of Hecate County*, Wilson often met him at White's or at the houses of mutual friends. Though the obese Connolly, obsessed with food and wine, was unwilling to listen to any conversation but his own, Wilson actually enjoyed his extraordinary nastiness and malice. There was also some hostility in his relationship with Spender, whom Wilson considered a second-rate talent. In his diary he called Spender, who sometimes looked like a frightened antelope, a prima donna who really can't sing, a poet who has always been frustrated by the intellectual and artistic superiority of his friend and rival, Wystan Auden.

Wilson had first known the lawyer and financier Sylvester Gates —a friend of Connolly, Betjeman, Berlin and Mamaine Koestler —when Gates was attending Harvard Law School in the mid-1920s. Born in 1901, Gates went to Winchester and took a first at New College, Oxford. He was called to the Bar in 1928 and worked at the Ministry of Information during the war. Chairman of the National Westminster and director of several other major banks, he had elegant houses in Eaton Square and in Wiltshire. Isaiah Berlin called Gates "a man of exceptionally fastidious taste—indeed, one of the cleverest, most intellectual, most civilized men I had ever met." Wilson found Gates great fun, despite their very different ways of looking at the world, and was fascinated by the violent side of his personality:

> I had a very good time with Gates this trip, found him very genial, and we have reached a kind of old-crony basis, so that I do not have to bother with his cynicism nor he with my relatively idealistic notions. . . . [He has] neurotic outbursts of violence. At "21" in New York . . . he had picked up the whole table and thrown it into the middle of the room. On another occasion, he had told me, he had thrown a conductor out of a train (in the station, not when it was moving) when he had questioned his ticket or something. Mamaine said he had socked someone at the Gargoyle bar who had jostled him with his elbow.

Wilson had a hard time with Arthur Waley, the leading English translator of Chinese and Japanese literature, whom he met for drinks at Celia Paget's house. They discussed Hemingway's near-fatal plane crashes in Africa and whether Eliot (who had become a British subject) might become Poet Laureate. But Wilson found Waley extremely snooty and could not bear his devastating deadpan remarks. As Celia later told Elena: "Edmund was in cracking form, very interesting and funny, but Arthur was awfully sticky, as he could be on occasion, even though he liked Edmund so much and specially wanted to see him. Afterwards Edmund commented: 'I see what it is about Arthur, he's very Bloomsbury.'"[1]

He got on much better with the rubicund and avuncular John Betjeman, who actually became Poet Laureate in 1972. Betjeman fixed on his favorite subjects, church architecture and High Church ritual, and Wilson thought him "quite amusing; has a somewhat clerical look and a perpetual twinkle in his eye—you feel that both these features are deliberate and almost professional." Wilson admired light verse and had a high regard for Betjeman's poetry. He considered him superior to both Eliot and Robert Graves, and, since Dylan Thomas' death, "the best poet in England—a minor poet, perhaps, but a very, very good one."

The elusive and unprepossessing E. M. Forster was, like Waley, associated with the Bloomsbury Group. Wilson described him as "a tiny little man—who might, at first glance, be some kind of clerk or a man in an optician's shop—with spectacles and a small slightly sagged moustache." Having read Forster's *Aspects of the Novel* (1927), Wilson immediately told him, when they met at a party, that he shared Forster's enthusiasm for his three favorite books—*The Divine Comedy, The Decline and Fall of the Roman Empire* and *War and Peace*—and added that the six greatest writers in English (before the modern age) were Shakespeare, Milton, Swift, Austen, Keats and Dickens. A few minutes later, as Wilson was getting up a head of steam, Forster said he must not detain the guest of honor, and shyly slipped away. Forster declared (as Orwell had done in his review of *The Wound and the Bow*): "I must tell you that your essays have thrown a good deal of light for me on Kipling and other things."

Edmund found Angus Wilson the most interesting English novelist and, before their first meeting, had repeatedly praised his Forsterian invention and wit. Angus, who loved to expose academic careerists and frauds, had satirized many aspects of English society that Edmund had previously found so objectionable. "One shares in the malevolent gusto," Edmund wrote in an encouraging *New Yorker* review of *The*

Wrong Set in April 1950, "with which he invents detail, for he is a master of mimicry and parody and is as funny as anyone can be who never becomes exhilarated." The tall, pink-faced, animated Angus, still working in the Reading Room of the British Museum, was extremely lively and amusing. Edmund took to him at once. He admired Angus' interest in social problems—poverty, housing in the East End, homosexual rights—which were generally ignored in the literary world, and recorded that "he has positive opinions and a strong Scottish moral strain that gives vertebrae to his work."

Edmund kept in touch with Angus and maintained a high opinion of his work. They met again in England in 1956, just after the success of *Anglo-Saxon Attitudes*, when Angus had resigned his job and moved to the country. They discussed Dickens and Kipling (Angus would later write books about both of them), and argued about Zola. Edmund attended his talk at Harvard in January 1961 and told Mary McCarthy, with whom he was by then on friendlier terms: "Angus Wilson has been here and did a very good lecture, which received the greatest ovation I have heard anybody get since [Robert] Oppenheimer—I don't quite know why, except that he covered a great deal of ground —contemporary English fiction—quickly and rather amusingly and gave the students the impression that he was on the level."

Two years later, Angus took Edmund on a tour of Suffolk churchyards, where he discovered tombstones of the Kimball family, who had left England for America in the seventeenth century. Going to meet the Wilsons at the Basil Street Hotel, Angus had bought a large bunch of white tulips for Elena. Finding Edmund on his own, wrote Angus, led to a minor contretemps: "Some teasing quality in me led me to present him with the flowers in homage to himself. I have seldom seen a man so embarrassed. He accepted them with many ums, held them behind his back, reversed uneasily into the bedroom [and] got rid of them."[2] Angus' campy humor caught Edmund off guard and he felt awkward about entertaining a well known homosexual in his room.

Wilson also saw friends in Edinburgh and Oxford. In Scotland he visited for the last time his old teacher, Norman Kemp Smith, now in his eighties, and discussed G. E. Moore's *Principia Ethica*, which had profoundly influenced the outlook of the Bloomsbury Group. He lunched with the poet Edwin Muir, born in a poor family in the Orkney Islands, who had translated Kafka's novels into English; and visited Compton Mackenzie, whose novels had been popular when Wilson was at Princeton. Ill in bed, Mackenzie spoke with disarming candor about his own career and confirmed Fitzgerald's account (in a letter to Wilson) of their conversation on Capri in 1925. Wilson, who enjoyed their talk and wished it were longer, always retained his affection for Mackenzie's books.

At All Souls College, Oxford—where Wilson lunched with Spender and the philosopher Stuart Hampshire—he was put up in a dismal little cell that resembled a run-down New York rooming house. The shabby, crumbling buildings seemed to symbolize the decay of modern England, and Wilson was delighted to be "in at the kill." Though he enjoyed agreeable, stimulating talks with the historian A. J. P. Taylor and with the Judaic scholar Cecil Roth, Wilson was quite sickened by "the intramural spites and grudges, cliques and snobberies, celibate jealousies . . . [and] monastic staleness" of Oxford. At one party, he was listless and unresponsive, drank too much whiskey and seemed to despise everyone. Put off by John Bayley's distracting stutter, Wilson confused him with the Dickens scholar Humphrey House, and pronounced both Bayley and his wife Iris Murdoch, "boring"—a serious misjudgment. Iris Murdoch later recalled meeting Wilson with Isaiah Berlin "in a dark room. He was rather tough and forbidding and he frightened me."

Oxford, however depressing, was redeemed by Wilson's always invigorating encounters with the philosopher and historian of ideas Isaiah Berlin. Born in Russia in 1909, he came to England at the age of eight, had a distinguished career at All Souls and published books on Vico, Herder, Marx and Tolstoy. Wilson and Berlin had first met through the art critic Meyer Schapiro in February 1946. Berlin, a "devoted reader" of Wilson, had served in the British diplomatic service during the war and had recently been to Moscow, where he saw Boris Pasternak. Berlin's erudition, liveliness and charm made him an appealing companion. They soon became close friends and met as often as possible. Berlin wrote Elena that Wilson is "the most unsurrendering intellectual—the most unyielding keeper-up of standards—I have ever met." He told Mamaine that when he was with Wilson he "felt like an aeroplane that has to keep up so many revolutions to the minute or it will fall to the ground." He loved and respected Wilson, and "wanted [him] to have a good opinion of me."[3]

Wilson was equally impressed by Berlin. He "affected me," Wilson wrote, "like nobody else I had known; though he was not particularly handsome, I tended to react to him a little as if he were an attractive woman whom I wanted to amuse and please." He explained to Mamaine that Berlin "has a sort of double Russian-and-British personality. The combination is uncanny but fascinating. We spent the whole time talking brilliantly, covering rapidly, but with astonishing knowledge, sure intelligence, and breathtaking wit, an incredible variety of subjects." They talked, Berlin recalled, "about Hebrew tenses and the structure of the Hungarian language . . . about his intense admiration for the poetry of W. H. Auden, about the interesting position of the *New Yorker* in American cultural life, about the monstrously patronizing attitude of Europeans, not only the despicable English but the French and even the Italians, toward such great poets as Walt Whitman and such prose writers as Herman Melville and Henry James."

After Wilson's death, Berlin wrote Elena of their intensely emotional friendship and of their mutual desire to win each other's esteem: "I absolutely adored Edmund as you know: and felt more reverence for him . . . than for any living man. I felt Russian emotions in his presence: love, acute interest in every word, a sense of pride about knowing him at all and surprise and extreme pleasure at the fact that he liked me at all." Berlin remembered Elena as "charming, civilised and beautiful," her company delightful, Wilson's love for her "touching." He recalled, in an extraordinarily illuminating letter, Wilson's grasp of Russian and Hebrew, intellectual complexity and sense of humor:

> Wilson's knowledge of Russian was not perfect—in the famous controversy with Vladimir Nabokov, the latter came off best—but he knew it pretty well, and read Russian authors most easily. He did not talk it particularly well, but he did speak it—indeed, I was impressed by his extraordinary understanding of Russian idiom in nineteenth and twentieth [century] Russian literature, which made his essays on the subject perhaps the best I know published in my own lifetime. As for Hebrew, I have no idea how well he learnt it—I know that he dealt very expertly with the famous Scrolls, and he certainly pronounced the words in a good old-fashioned way, which he was taught, I think, in the Theological Seminary at Princeton, where he originally learnt it. He had a considerable feeling for Hebrew grammar, for tenses, cases, the rhythm and shape of sentences, both old and new—and took more interest, I think, in Hebrew of anyone I have ever known who was not himself a Jew.

He described Wilson's personality as combative, but not competitive; and noted how, despite his great experience in the literary world,
Wilson could be gullible and naive:

> He did not suffer critics gladly, and was extremely obstinate about
> defending his own views, attitudes, interpretations of literary
> texts; and on the whole had no great respect for most contempo-
> rary critics—save a few. He was in some ways biased—had vari-
> ous bees buzzing in his bonnet; a man of passionate loves and
> hates, likings and dislikes, admiration and contempt—but this did
> not seem to be derived from competitiveness so much as strongly
> held views, and certainly a conviction that he was right, and that
> he had a just appreciation of the qualities, both of writers and of
> human beings in general—which in a large number of cases was
> valid, or seemed so to me. But at the same time he could be rather
> naive, and was occasionally taken in by people who flattered him
> sufficiently skillfully, and certainly over-estimated their merits
> —and was innocent enough not to know about the malicious
> things which some of them certainly said behind his back. I was
> privy to various criticisms of that type, and was shocked at the
> disloyalty of some of the people to whom he was loyal—I never
> reported anything to him. No doubt he did discover such unkind
> behaviour in some cases, but he never spoke of this to me.

Wilson's delight in mocking pretensions, of his own or others, was
one of his most endearing traits. Berlin loved his clever jokes, remembering that

> He certainly sent me one or two spoof letters, imitating someone
> else's style, or a letter which on one page said that he had suffered
> a spiritual crisis and had undergone a deep change of views—and
> went on and on as if leading up to some tremendous renunciation
> or conversion or abandonment of his old views and positions in
> favour of some religious or reactionary or otherwise critical
> change in his beliefs—and when one turned the page, I cannot
> remember exactly but it said something like "I have therefore
> decided to take tea rather than coffee in the mornings," or some-
> thing of this kind. I remember showing this letter to Professor
> Harry Levin, whose face grew longer and longer as he read the

first page, anticipating the worst—but he burst into laughter at the first words overleaf. That was very typical—he liked practical jokes.[4]

Though Wilson, as always, found much to criticize in England, he did have immensely enjoyable meetings with Sylvester Gates, Cyril Connolly, Angus Wilson and, for all his hostility to English dons, with Cecil Roth and Isaiah Berlin. Gates, Spender, Muir, Angus Wilson and Berlin later visited him in America.

II

Of all the distinguished people Wilson knew, only four—Nabokov, Auden, Berlin and André Malraux (none of them American)—matched his intellect, achievement and international stature. Wilson had met Malraux—then married to his first wife, Clara Goldschmidt, who had shared his adventures in Indochina—after his trip to Russia in 1935, and would meet him again at the Kennedy White House when Malraux was De Gaulle's minister of culture. But their main encounters took place in Paris in February and April 1954, just before and after Wilson's visit to Israel, and sparked the same intellectual fireworks as his conversations with Berlin.

Always quick to recognize a new talent, Wilson had immediately praised Malraux's first major novel, *Man's Fate* (1933), about the Communist revolution in Shanghai. "The personalities of Malraux's characters are organically created and thoroughly explored," Wilson wrote in the *New Republic*. "We not only witness their acts and see them in relation to the forces of the social-political scene: we share their most intimate sensations." When the novel was published in English the following year, the translator Haakon Chevalier called Wilson the "father" of the book and thanked Wilson for alerting him to Malraux. Wilson particularly admired Malraux's ability to make perceptive and striking connections between different cultures, and called his highly original and provocative *The Psychology of Art* "one of the really great books of our time."

Wilson was perhaps the first critic in the English-speaking world to perceive that Malraux's *The Walnut Trees of Altenburg* (1943) was one of the greatest novels of the century. The hero's tribal warfare among the

Senussi of the Libyan desert and his relation to Enver Pasha and the Pan-Turk movement were closely based on T. E. Lawrence's achievements in the Arab Revolt. Malraux himself had led a squadron of French aviators in the Spanish Civil War, fought courageously in the French Resistance and, as a lieutenant-colonel, commanded the victorious Alsace-Lorraine brigade, which captured Stuttgart in February 1945. Attracted to his swashbuckling character, Wilson described Malraux, in a chapter of *Europe Without Baedeker* (1947), as an "international adventurer—part explorer of the ancient Oriental world . . . part Byronic egoist and actor, driven by an obscure compulsion to assert his will for its own sake." He also observed that one finds in the highly intellectual yet extremely exciting novel "passages of sinewy and searching thought, strokes of dramatic imagination, of which only a man of genius would have been capable."[5] Seven years later, he vainly urged the *New Yorker* to commission Malraux to write about T. E. Lawrence's *The Mint.*

Malraux's second wife, Josette Clotis, had (like Margaret Canby) died in an accident. She fell under a train in November 1944. Four years later, Malraux married the beautiful pianist Marie-Madeleine, the widow of his brother Roland, who had been killed in the war. In his diary Wilson described Malraux's home and new wife, alluded to Clara's infidelity, and noted the conflict in Malraux between politics and art:

> He now lives in a large house, rather modern and quite new, quite far from the center of the city [in Boulogne-sur-Seine]. I thought he was flourishing and happy in a way that he had not seemed when I saw him [last]. . . . The wife that I met then, Clara, is said to have treated him badly, and his present one . . . a very pretty brunette, seemed to both of us attractive and honest. I think that he is relieved, too, to be able to relax from politics, which he had on his mind when I saw him before, and had had constantly and more heavily on his mind ever since—the Spanish War, the Resistance, De Gaulle—and devote himself entirely to writing and art. The Gaullist movement, he said, had been the only chance for France to get a New Deal but De Gaulle had now *échoué* [run aground].

They spoke of Roman and French history, Malraux's view of America, the function of museums, western, oriental and primitive art, contemporary politics, Michelet's diaries, the poetry of Saint-John

Perse, the plays of Anouilh, Sartre and Genet. Malraux, in a characteristic *mot*, observed that "Genet was the Sartre character which Sartre himself had not the genius to invent." The intensely animated Malraux had a number of spasmodic tics—his legacy from the wars. He spoke standing up, jumping around and punctuating his expositions with *bon!* and *bien!*, then rushing on to the next point before Wilson could discuss the previous one.

Wilson enjoyed his second lunch with Malraux, in April 1954, even more than the first. Malraux, now more at ease with Wilson, seemed more likeable and human than before. He was, as always, full of enthusiasm. Wilson began by asking about Indochina, which Malraux analyzed at great length, and they went on to speak of the Dead Sea Scrolls, T. E. Lawrence, Stalin, the death of Maxim Gorky and Genet's instinctive, amusing theft of his publisher's cuff links. Exhausting and exhilarating, Malraux was "an intense, energetic, self-kindling, self-consuming force, whirling about without giving heat." Five years later Wilson told an interviewer, as he had once told Nabokov, that he "tremendously admired" Malraux and considered him "the greatest living European writer."

In mid-March 1954 Wilson stopped in Rapallo, en route to the ship in Marseilles, to see the eighty-two-year-old English artist and satirist Max Beerbohm—a startling contrast to Malraux and indication of Wilson's catholic tastes. In his appreciative essay in the *New Yorker* of May 1948, Wilson said he had been reading Beerbohm since his schooldays and that his respect for Max's writing had since then immensely increased. He was therefore delighted to accept the offer of Beerbohm's friend and future biographer, S. N. Behrman, to introduce him to the old man. Like Compton Mackenzie, Beerbohm belonged to the Edwardian age.

Wilson was struck by Beerbohm's distinguished appearance and manner: his round blue eyes with large rings around them, his long elegant fingers, sharpened at the ends like engraver's tools, his subtle "continental" personality. They spoke of Beerbohm's Edwardian contemporaries—James, Conrad, Housman, Shaw and the Webbs—and Wilson developed his theory that Max's work was a comic *Divine Comedy*. Beerbohm's self-confidence and strength of character reminded Wilson of Malraux. "He is quite sure of himself," Wilson told Behrman. "He knows the value of what he has done, both as a writer and as an artist." Wilson thought Max was "the greatest caricaturist of the kind—that is, portrayer of personalities—in the history of art."

In February, between his visits to Malraux and Beerbohm, Wilson taught at the Seminar in American Civilization in Salzburg, Austria. This teaching, and his articles on the Dead Sea Scrolls, paid for his trip. In 1948 the poet Randall Jarrell, on his first journey to Europe, had also taught at Salzburg and luxuriated in its fantastic setting, the marbled and mirrored Schloss Leopoldkron. This rococo château, which had Mozartian associations, had once belonged to the theatrical producer Max Reinhardt and had been German military headquarters during the war. The government-sponsored Salzburg Seminars brought over American lecturers to give courses in American culture to about a hundred select teachers and graduate students from all over Europe. Wilson's colleagues included the Chicago novelist Isaac Rosenfeld, Lawrance Thompson of Princeton and Roy Harvey Pearce of Ohio State University. Wilson lectured again on his long-standing project, the literature of the American Civil War.

Unlike Jarrell, who had been in his mid-thirties and loved teaching, the fifty-eight-year-old Wilson found the army beds and blankets uncomfortable, the food depressing, the Alpine weather gloomy. The castle, cold and still battered by the war, was full of heavy chandeliers, plaster cupids, pastry-like stucco ornaments and bogus portraits of ecclesiastics. He caught a cold and lectured, with rheumy eyes, through a series of hacking coughs. Worst of all, he felt alienated by the stifling academic atmosphere: "I think it is going to be rather fun, then find that it is mostly uncomfortable. In a college, one becomes only gradually aware of the at first invisible hierarchy; and even with professors from different places and far away from their communities, as here, you and they still belong to different worlds."

After a depressing February in Salzburg, Wilson spent a week of rest and recuperation in the Hotel Vierjahrezeiten in Munich and the Frankfurter Hof in Frankfurt—his first trip to Germany since his postwar duties in Trier in 1919. He enjoyed the excellent beds, baths and dinners; and had his first real introduction to Elena's family in Europe: broken-down Russian émigrés, dispossessed German vintners, and a pro-Nazi, anti-Semitic sister. He felt about Elena's ancestral residence, which she had not seen since before the war, pretty much as she did about Talcottville: "The Mumm place at Johannisberg was not quite so impressive or attractive as Elena's love for it had led me to expect. It was now rather faded, and the original furniture and decoration had been in rather bad German taste."[6] Wilson had a dull time with the Mumms, and was often exasperated by the family scandal—

Elena's French sister-in-law and her brash, omnipresent lover. Glad to escape from Johannisberg, Wilson left on March 15 for Rapallo and Israel.

III

While Wilson was traveling in Israel in April 1954 W. H. Allen loyally brought out the English edition of *Five Plays*, which included works written over a period of thirty years. *The Crime in the Whistler Room* had been performed by Mary Blair and the Provincetown Players in 1924 and first published two years later in *Discordant Encounters*. *The Little Blue Light* had been published separately in 1950 and performed in Cambridge and New York in 1950–51. *Beppo and Beth* and *This Room and This Gin and These Sandwiches* had been published (with *The Crime in the Whistler Room*) by the *New Republic* in 1937, but had never been acted on stage. *Cyprian's Prayer* was the only new play in this volume.

Wilson thought of himself as a dramatist, tried to promote his plays whenever he could and had a soft spot for these distinctly inferior works. In his Preface he said: "I have always been particularly suscepti-ble to the theater, and the stories that take shape in my imagination are likely to do so in dramatic form." He then attempted to impose some unity on the three plays originally published in 1937: "These three variations on the same theme represent three successive stages of the artistic and moral revolt which had its headquarters in New York after the War. . . . *The Crime in the Whistler Room* is a fantasy of our first liberation from the culture and convention of the previous era; *This Room and This Gin and These Sandwiches* . . . shows the movement con-solidated and concentrated in the Greenwich Village section of New York; and *Beppo and Beth* is a comedy of New York 'sophistication' reeling from the Stock Market crash." Like James, Conrad and Fitzger-ald, Wilson was a prominent man of letters whose theatrical ambitions were doomed to disappointment. His extremely talky and undramatic plays were punctuated by long, didactic, Shavian speeches. Adopting a defensive stance in his Preface, he admitted that "few people care to read printed plays unless they have been very successful. . . . So I dump the whole lot in your laps, at the risk of having you dump them right off. . . . Cuts supplied on application."

The title of the second play, which refers to a cosy, domestic scene, originated in *Travels in Two Democracies* when a Russian mentions "this little room, this vodka, this bread." In the last two plays of this trio the repressed, stuffy, ineffectual hero attempts to solve his social and ideological problems and save himself by marrying a pretty, down-to-earth girl. In *Beppo and Beth*, a Depression play, Beppo Miles—an artist who is about to sell out and do a comic strip for a commercial newspaper —gives a fashionable dinner party for his ex-wife Beth and several other guests. Bootleggers, drug dealers and gunmen intrude and, during an evening of fear and farce, Beppo and Beth decide to remarry and unite against a cruel and corrupt world: "gangsters on one side and Communists on the other!"[7]

In July 1950, after the publication of *The Little Blue Light*, Wilson alluded to the weakness of that play and told Dos Passos about an even more unpromising project: "I don't think that stories and plays that are supposed to take place in the future are ever quite satisfactory. I'm doing another one now that takes place in a fairy-tale fifteenth century—on a theme like *The Sorcerer's Apprentice*: a young magician who has to take over from the old magician before he has learned the business." *Cyprian's Prayer*, first conceived during his illness in Odessa in 1935, was concocted (as Wilson acknowledged in his Preface to the play) out of wildly disparate sources: Lucian, the *Arabian Nights*, Goethe, Cocteau, Michelet's volume on the reign of Louis XI (whose historical Tancarville was delightfully close to Talcottville) and a story by Frank Stockton in the *St. Nicholas* magazine.

In this play a reformed devil enables Cyprian to renounce his Faustian pact and helps save the world. This theme allowed Wilson to indulge himself with two of his favorite characters: devil and magician, to attack the futility and evils of Christianity, and to create his usual theatrical conclusion as the hero renounces worldly temptations and settles down in his castle with his recently exorcised bride. But Wilson's dialogue is either intolerably stilted, as when a peasant declares: "Your conceit is absolutely insufferable!" or unbearably awkward, as when a farmer says: "He hasn't even got the sense to have his dogs taught not to kill sheep!" His use of modern slang in a medieval French setting is as absurd as Fitzgerald's mock-medieval "Philippe, Count of Darkness" stories.

Wilson must have exercised some magic of his own. For he persuaded the uptown students' theater of New York University to put on four performances of *Cyprian's Prayer*—the third of his plays to achieve production—at the Hall of Fame Playhouse at the University Heights campus on February 21–24, 1957. On the day the play opened, the

Heights Daily News reported that Wilson had attended rehearsals and contributed as a program note his Preface to *Cyprian's Prayer*. Wilson undoubtedly advised the students about the magical effects, for the newspaper also promised: "This will be a show full of special effects. There will be multi-directional sound. A genie from the East will emerge turban and all from a bottle, a magician's assistant will have his head cut off and presented on a serving tray."[8]

IV

Though Wilson rejected the doctrines and ethics of Christianity, he had always been attracted to Jewish culture and impressed by the power of the Jewish moral vision. His Puritan forebears in seventeenth-century New England habitually identified themselves with the Jewish patriarchs of the Old Testament, and Cotton Mather thought of himself as the true heir of Abraham's covenant with God. The closest ally of Wilson's father in Red Bank, the only other man in town seriously interested in education, was Eisner, a Czech-born Jew, who had come to New Jersey as a peddler, opened a uniform factory and sent his sons to Harvard. One of Wilson's own tent mates in the army training camp in July 1916 was a "remarkably brilliant" Jew named Sakolsky. Influenced by the snobbishness he had acquired at Princeton, Wilson at first ignored Sakolsky, but soon came to regard him as a "most remarkable and amiable" companion.

In one of the great passages in *To the Finland Station*, Wilson discusses Marx in the context of modern Jewish thinkers—Freud, Proust and Einstein—and declares: "The characteristic genius of the Jew has been especially a moral genius. The sacred books of the people of Israel have served as a basis for the religions of three continents; and even in the case of those great men among the Jews who do not occupy themselves with religion proper, it is usually a grasp of moral ideas which have given them their peculiar force. . . . Nobody but a Jew could have fought so uncompromisingly and obstinately for the victory of the dispossessed classes." In *Patriotic Gore*, Wilson also placed the esteemed Justice Holmes in a Jewish context and observed that "through his intelligence and his love of learning, his sharpness of mind and his humor, he has obviously more in common with certain of his Jewish colleagues than with most of his Gentile ones." In a similar fashion—especially after he began to meet New York intellectuals,

both on the Cape and in Manhattan—Wilson established close rela-
tions with many Jewish friends: first Paul Rosenfeld, Gilbert Seldes,
Waldo Frank and Felix Frankfurter; then Helen Muchnic, Daniel
Aaron, Isaiah Berlin, Roger Straus, Leon Edel and Jason Epstein; in
Israel David Flusser and Yigael Yadin; and, later on, Richard Pipes,
Harry Levin, Alfred Kazin, Irving Howe and Lillian Hellman.

In the summer of 1953, after studying Hebrew at Princeton while
lecturing at the Gauss Seminars, Wilson heard from Paolo Milano—a
professor of Italian at Queens College in New York, who had just come
back from Jerusalem—about the controversy surrounding the recently
discovered Dead Sea Scrolls. Following his habitual practice, Wilson
read, as Thackeray said of Macaulay, "twenty books to write a sentence;
he traveled a hundred miles to make a line of description." Beginning
with accounts of the Roman occupation of Palestine in Josephus' *History of the Jews* and in the works of Philo Judaeus and Pliny the Elder, he
moved on to Edward Gibbon, the historian of the late Roman Empire,
whose work covered the period when the Scrolls had been hidden. This
was the time of the Jewish rebellions against the Romans, which ended
with the fall of Jerusalem in A.D. 70 and the final defeat of the Jewish
garrison at Masada three years later. Wilson also turned with renewed
interest to the work of Ernest Renan, the French historian and Biblical
scholar, whom he had first discussed in *To the Finland Station*. Renan's
textual studies led him to question the doctrines of revealed religion,
and later archeological work confirmed his view that Christianity originated, not in the divinity of Christ, but in a Jewish mystical sect.
Wilson studied these ideas in Renan's *Life of Jesus* (1863), the first
volume of his *Origins of Christianity* (1863–83). He then indefatigably
tackled the scholarly articles on the Dead Sea Scrolls themselves.

Wilson's intensive study of the Hebrew Bible and Jewish history
made the landscape come alive when he visited Israel, where the little
hills and valleys stood out as the scenes of savage Old Testament and
Roman wars. This trip (only six years after Israel's independence)
confirmed Wilson's hostility to the British, who, during and after the
war with Hitler, had restricted Jewish access to Palestine and then
abandoned the country in an unconscionable way. He noted that the
British authorities had refused to let Jews who were fleeing from the
Nazis "even land in a country which the British themselves had set
aside as a Jewish refuge, and finally left the Jews to the mercy of seven
Arab states." Wilson's sympathies were firmly with the Jews. He disliked the Arabs, who, living in squalor, leaped out at him and tried to

sell things for outrageous prices. He felt the Jews had succeeded, in only a few years, in doing more with that barren land than the Arabs had been able to do in more than a thousand. To Wilson, Israel represented a victory of the spirit, and his attitude toward the country inevitably influenced his views of the controversy surrounding the Scrolls.

He told Mamaine that except for a short trip to Tel Aviv and Tiberias, "I simply sat in the very comfortable King David Hotel, studying Hebrew and seeing the various intellectuals—professors, writers, officials—with whom I had a very good time."[9] He was not quite as inactive, however, as he suggested. Tel Aviv, then a pleasant little Mediterranean city with an esplanade along the sea, had theaters, coffee houses and bookshops that reminded him of Vienna. In the North he saw Nazareth, the old crusader town of Acre, and Safed, an artists' colony in the mountains above Galilee. He crossed the Allenby bridge into Jordan to visit the Old City of Jerusalem and the excavations of the remote caves that contained the Dead Sea Scrolls. He was attracted to the combination of luminosity and bareness of Jerusalem, but repelled by the Church of the Holy Sepulcher, where Christ was supposed to be buried. The façade was supported by a metal scaffolding, trimmed with barbed wire, which looked like the elevated train in New York, and the whole place had the "claustrophobia of vulgarity." In these sacred precincts, he took advantage of the coolness and defiantly amused himself by sitting down to read "Dick Tracy" in the *Herald Tribune*.

When the young Polish-Israeli journalist Dahn Ben-Amotz asked to interview Wilson for his weekly newspaper column (an imitation of the *New Yorker*'s "Talk of the Town") Wilson agreed to cooperate if they could meet in Dahn's house rather than in the hotel. Enormously interested in Israeli writers, Wilson reversed the interview, asked most of the questions himself and stayed all afternoon. Since there was very little to eat or drink in the flat, Dahn's American wife Ellen offered her honored guest the precious food packages sent by her family.

Wilson discussed his Hebrew course at Princeton and his study of the Old Testament, and was interested in Dahn's view of the differences between the ancient and modern language. Curious about the books in the flat, Wilson was fascinated by a volume in Dutch, which crankishly argued that the letters in the Hebrew alphabet represented the actual shape of the mouth and tongue as each letter was pronounced. Wilson did not ask about Ellen's background until late in the afternoon. He then said he had been trying to place her speech and decided that she had grown up near San Francisco, had gone to Bennington (like Rosalind) and had lived for a time in New York. The old magician could not have known any of this beforehand and Ellen was astonished by his precise and accurate diagnosis of her background.

Wilson had originally studied Hebrew for sheer love of the language. The discovery of the Scrolls gave his studies a focus, and he had spent many months acquiring a basic knowledge of Biblical archeology and mastering the complex scholarship in several languages. Now he inspected the desert site, examined the Scrolls and questioned the principal figures involved in their acquisition, translation and interpretation. Excited by the methods of modern archeology ("a veritable Gold-bug treasure hunt"), by the scholarly controversy and by the personalities of the participants, Wilson described, with a clear style and logical structure, and in a judicious and magisterial tone, the story surrounding the greatest manuscript discovery of modern times. While writing his book he corresponded with experts around the world and submitted his printed proofs for their corrections.

Found in the caves of Qumran by a Bedouin goatherd in the spring of 1947, some of these brownish fragments of Hebrew—written on strips of leather, wrapped in linen and placed in earthenware jars —turned out to be the earliest manuscripts of the Jewish Bible, a thousand years older than the previously known Hebrew manuscripts. Other Scrolls described the rules of the monastic, mystical and schismatic Essene sect, who lived, between 100 B.C. and A.D. 70, in the northwest corner of the Dead Sea. Some of these texts were apparently related to well-known apocryphal and apocalyptic writings, some referred to a specific Teacher of Righteousness, a Messianic figure. The Essene Manual of Discipline, outlining the sect's separate calendar and particular rituals—the sacred meal and baptism with water—suggested obvious links with the origins of Christianity. Scholars conjectured that John the Baptist had been an Essene and that Jesus had come to the desert monastery, the ruins of which were discovered near the caves of Qumran, to be baptized by him.

The discovery, sale and dispersal of the Scrolls, which became at different times the property of various people and nations, and were subject to various methods of preservation, is an interesting (and ongoing) story. The site was in Jordanian territory in 1947; some of the Scrolls remained in Jordan, others were sold to an antique dealer in Israel. Though damaged by looting during the 1948 Israeli-Arab war, the caves and the monastery were gradually excavated, and new items continued to turn up. The contentious work on the two groups of Scrolls went on throughout long years of sporadic guerrilla warfare and a major war in 1967, and news of discoveries on both sides came out slowly. Only recently, after international protests, have the Scrolls been made available to scholars outside the inner circle.

More important to Wilson, however, was not merely the struggle to possess, preserve, identify and decipher the Scrolls, but the task of interpreting them. Fierce debate raged in the scholarly literature about the date of the texts and their meaning. Scholars from different religious backgrounds—Christians, whether Catholic, Eastern or Protestant; Jews from various schools of thought; and those who had, like Wilson, no religious affiliation, but were steeped in Biblical texts and their history—all had sharply divergent views about what new light the Scrolls cast on Judaism and Christianity.

The amazing find, the sacred subject, the location in the Holy Land, the struggle to save the manuscripts during the savage fighting that followed the partition of Palestine, the secret mode of acquisition, the physical division of the Scrolls between Israel and Jordan, the difficulty of unrolling, reconstructing and deciphering the fragmentary texts, the enormous significance of the material, the eccentric scholars, the bitter battles, the explosive revelations—all these gave Wilson fascinating material. Though the French scholar André Dupont-Sommer had published the first books on the Scrolls, Wilson was the first to present the story to the general public. He produced the original instalment, a mixture of melodrama, adventure quest and detective story, in a long *New Yorker* article of May 14, 1955. One Jesuit priest recommended the essay to his students, but regretted that the adjacent bathing suit advertisements made it impossible to give it to the nuns.

In his major books, *To the Finland Station* and *Patriotic Gore*, Wilson portrays the leading historical figures (Marx and Engels, Lenin and Trotsky; Grant and Sherman, Lincoln and Holmes) more effectively than his own fictional characters. Since the principal actors in *The Scrolls from the Dead Sea* were very much alive and engaged in scholarly warfare, Wilson was able to meet them—in Israel, Europe and America—and describe them from personal experience. Like his hero Renan, Wilson cultivated a biographical approach to the history of ideas. The book gives us vivid portraits of the individuals at work on the Scrolls: the Catholic Father de Vaux, the academic Dupont-Sommer, the Jewish scholars Flusser and Yadin, and other participants. Wilson is especially interesting on how personalities influence the course of scholarship, and how such arcane disputes ultimately affect the religious beliefs of ordinary people.

Father Roland de Vaux, of the École Biblique in the old quarter of Jerusalem, was a leading player. He led the first archeological excavation at Qumran, was the chief member of the team of translators and kept a stranglehold on the manuscripts until his death in 1971. Wilson met the earthy yet elegant de Vaux in the Dead Sea wilderness—"monotonous, subduing and dreadful"—and described his "almost Jewish nose and eyes of the high-powered headlight variety behind the thick magnifying lenses of his glasses, teeth to match, long, regular, and always displayed, self-enjoyment, an eagerness almost greedy . . . white flannel Dominican robe, with leather belt . . . always, with a certain smartness, smoking cigarettes—climbed the ruins like a chamois."

André Dupont-Sommer, a former priest and professor of Semitic languages at the Sorbonne, first argued, in 1950, that the Scrolls proved the Jewish Essene sect had foreshadowed the birth and beginnings of Christianity. As William Albright, the leading American scholar of the Scrolls, pointed out in his review, the iconoclastic Dupont-Sommer somehow becomes in Wilson's book "a reincarnation of the famous Frenchman, Renan, in physical appearance, in outward life and academic career, as well as in his philosophic credo." Dupont-Sommer, like Renan, saw Judaism and Christianity as intimately related. The Scrolls provided a missing textual and historical link for Renan's original hypothesis that Jesus was not a divine figure, but a remarkable man who developed his teaching from a Jewish Messianic tradition. Wilson warmly espoused this view. He particularly disliked the Catholic theological tradition that claimed the Old Testament had predicted the coming of Christ, and was fascinated by evidence in the Scrolls that disproved the unique origins of the Christian religion. "The characteristic doctrines of Christianity," Wilson argued, "must have developed gradually and naturally, in the course of a couple of hundred years, out of a dissident branch of Judaism."[10]

The Scrolls also had implications for Judaism itself, which seemed to have contained a defiantly heterodox sect during the century that preceded the birth of Christ. Wilson was most intrigued by two Israeli scholars: the Prague-born David Flusser, professor of comparative religion at Hebrew University, and Yigael Yadin, the leading archeologist at Masada and former chief of staff of the Israeli army. Both, like Wilson himself, were extremely erudite and passionately involved in the subject. Wilson portrayed the short and stocky, dynamic and imaginative Flusser as a devilish figure, with "flaming hair brushed straight up and not parted, modestly Mephistophelian eyebrows, little cold green eyes, a dry and harsh laugh, complete detachment from everything." As tea was served and a Viennese string quartet played in the lobby of the hotel, Flusser, speaking voluble French and unconsciously influenced by the Danubian rhythms, sang rather than spoke some of his answers to Wilson's questions.

Flusser himself was impressed by Wilson's evaluation of Biblical scholarship, perception of the significant issues and major contribution to the subject. In an essay of 1978, he wrote that Wilson's book revealed "the negative qualities of the so-called method and 'systematic thinking' and writing of much modern scholarship." It also "raised questions which the scholars were forced to answer, and so it changed profoundly the course of research into Essenism and had an important impact upon the study of both ancient Judaism and the beginnings of Christianity." It was, in fact, "a turning-point in the research of the history of religions." Flusser later praised Wilson's mastery of ancient languages, which enabled him to penetrate to the intellectual core of the subject: "In his first visit to Jerusalem, I translated for him passages from the Scrolls in Greek (of that period), because I have seen that it is the most appropriate language for this purpose. Both Jews and early Christians developed a kind of Greek for translation from Hebrew (and Aramaic). I have *never* seen a human being, which is praise, who listened with high interest to *spoken* Greek from New Testament times!"

General Yadin, the son of Professor E. L. Sukenik (who was the first to realize the importance of the Scrolls and who purchased some of them for Israel) was, like T. E. Lawrence, both a soldier and archeologist. Wilson described Yadin as "tall, good-looking, and cosmopolitan. He speaks English incredibly well and has a great deal of charm. He held me spellbound for two hours and a half, talking about the Scrolls." Like Flusser, Yadin praised Wilson's grasp of the Scrolls and credited that "scholarly amateur" with making their importance known to the world at large. He "influenced some scholars in the way they dealt with the Scrolls, because he was very provocative in his writings. He was trying to define the views of some scholars more boldly than they themselves dared, perhaps, and this created fresh controversy. I would say, therefore, that Wilson's contribution was of real importance to the actual scholarly work on the Dead Sea Scrolls."[11] When the Israelis captured Bethlehem during the 1967 war, Yadin recovered more Dead

Sea manuscripts from Kando's antique shop. The owner had been the principal Arab intermediary between the Bedouin who had originally found the Scrolls in the caves and the scholars in Israel and Jordan who had acquired them.

Wilson told Dos Passos that he was the only outsider who knew anything about the subject and, using a striking analogy, compared his popular account of a specialized subject to Hemingway's exposition of bullfighting. Warming to his new role and alluding to Browning's poem, he thought of sending a Christmas card in 1954 to be called *The Wit and Wisdom of Rabbi Ben Edmund*. Dos Passos, in a spirited reply, told Wilson: "It's delightful to think of you in the role of aficionado egging on the rabbis and Jesuits and the bearded and beardless scholars to fresh combats. I just read your ["Notes on Gentile Pro-Semitism"] in *Commentary*. Carrying out the role of uncircumcised rabbi very well, I thought."

Wilson told the radical novelist Upton Sinclair that he thought his book would inspire a great deal of complaint and denunciation and "was somewhat disappointed at not having shocked people more!" *The Scrolls from the Dead Sea* had some interesting similarities to Robert Graves' provocative *The Nazarene Gospel Restored*, written with the Judaic scholar Joshua Pedro. Graves and Wilson, both born in 1895, learned Hebrew late in life and engaged in heated controversy with Biblical scholars. Graves, who argued, even more strongly than Wilson, that Jesus was first and foremost a Jew, was attacked from all sides when his book appeared in 1953. Graves' book may have made readers more responsive to Wilson's thesis, just as the evidence adduced in Wilson's book may have strengthened Graves' more radical argument.

After Wilson's exciting and erudite article had made a great splash in the *New Yorker*—sales were high and fan mail heavy—he decided to describe his experience in Israel in two separate books. The scholarly material from the *New Yorker* essay appeared in *The Scrolls from the Dead Sea* (published in October 1955); his travel writing comprised one quarter of *Red, Black, Blond and Olive* (published in April 1956). Wilson had signed a contract for *Patriotic Gore* with Oxford University Press in 1946, during the controversy about *Memoirs of Hecate County* and four years before he joined Farrar, Straus. Since Oxford had been waiting many long years for his ever-expanding Civil War book (which would not be delivered until 1961), he gave them *The Scrolls from the Dead Sea* and they also got *Red, Black, Blond and Olive* as a spin-off.

After his second trip to Israel in 1967, Wilson brought out an

expanded edition, *The Dead Sea Scrolls, 1947–1969* (published by Ox
ford in 1969), which contained *The Scrolls from the Dead Sea*, a new
section on the scholarly controversies between 1955 and 1967, and an
account of his second journey. This volume was reissued as *Israel and
the Dead Sea Scrolls* by Farrar, Straus in 1978, with a perceptive Foreword by Leon Edel and the "Olive" section from *Red, Black, Blond and
Olive*. Leading Biblical scholars—William Albright, Millar Burrows,
Frank Cross and Father de Vaux—had praised the earlier version of the
book. In his review of the second edition M. I. Finley, a professor of
Classics at Columbia, confirmed General Yadin's view that Wilson had
performed a double service: he brought knowledge of the Scrolls to a
wide audience and stimulated specialists to consider new ideas.[12]

The *Sunday Times* and *Observer* of London wanted to serialize the
book when W. H. Allen brought out the first edition in November
1955. But Wilson, who thought a condensation would distort his argument and provoke unnecessary controversy before publication, refused
their lucrative offer—just as he had refused to bowdlerize *Memoirs of
Hecate County*. W. H. Allen, which had paid an advance of £300 (or
about $1,000), sold 14,000 copies by February 1956. Oxford University
Press, which advanced $5,000 against royalties, sold an astonishing
75,000 copies in 1955. Wilson actually made the best-seller list for
several weeks and earned more than $37,000 from the first edition.
Oxford sold another 18,000 copies in 1968, which surpassed the sales of
Memoirs of Hecate County by about 35,000 copies, and made it Wilson's
most successful as well as his most interesting book.

V

Wilson's third and last travel book—*Red, Black, Blond and Olive. Studies
in Four Civilizations: Zuñi, Haiti, Soviet Russia, Israel* (1956)—contained
four unrelated essays (out of chronological order) published between
1936 and 1955. The Postscript, which explains his method and attempts to unify the book, should have come at the beginning rather
than at the end. If the chronological order of Wilson's journeys *had*
been maintained, the reader would have been guided more logically
from godless Russia, through the primitive Shalako religion of the Zuni
Indians and the voodoo of the Haitians, to the Judaism of ancient and
modern Israel.

In the Postscript Wilson wrote that "in each case, I visited a country for a few weeks or months, read it up, saw as much as I could of it, then came back home and wrote about it." In these chapters the unregenerate atheist and enemy of Christianity adopted an extremely sympathetic view of non-Christian religions. He praised their social cohesion, dynamic purpose, moral discipline and contemplative ecstasy, and endorsed "the supremacy of moral force and human will over the adventitious aspects of life."

The chapter on Russia, about half the book, was reprinted from *Travels in Two Democracies* (1936). But a number of passages, which would have endangered Russian friends and had been deleted from the earlier version, were now added in brackets. These included his statement that class distinctions in Russia were much greater than he had previously acknowledged; that Stalin had engineered the murder of Kirov in December 1934; that Wilson had visited the country during a relatively liberal period, before the start of the Purge Trials that executed or imprisoned ten percent of the population. He also described the torments by the secret police of a Russian woman friend who was married to an American. Most importantly, he gave the full story of the life and terrible death of the idealistic Prince Mirsky. Put on a blacklist after his book was published, Wilson was never allowed to return to Russia.

There is a striking difference between Wilson's sharp criticism of the ruins of postwar England, Italy and Greece in *Europe Without Baedeker* and his positive attitude toward the primitive cultures of the Zunis and Haitians nine years later. From December 12 to 20, 1947, Wilson observed the Zunis, forty miles south of Gallup, New Mexico, one of the toughest towns in the West. His interest in the Indians went back to his trip to the Southwest with Margaret Canby in July 1931 and to his three essays about the region, which he published in the *New Republic* in October and then included in *The American Earthquake*. In a witty letter to Max Perkins, Wilson had contrasted the wealthy and bogus bohemians of Santa Fe and Taos, which "have about the worst set of artists and writers to be found anywhere, as most of them have or have had t.b. in addition to their artistic disabilities," to the wild landscape of Bland, New Mexico: "This country out here is one of the greatest things I have ever seen. . . . It is way up in the mountains, 8,000 feet above sea level." Wilson's enthusiastic response was astonishingly similar to D. H. Lawrence's statement, made three years earlier, "I think New Mexico was the greatest experience from the outside world that I have ever had."

Lawrence had lived near Taos for several years in the mid-1920s and his account of the Indian rituals in *Mornings in Mexico* (1927) undoubtedly stimulated Wilson's interest in the Zunis. Lawrence's description of the Hopi Snake Dance, for example, inspired Wilson's 1931 account of the Indian Corn Dance. Lawrence, who wanted to put himself in touch with the primitive and regenerative powers of the Indians, identified with the cthonic ceremonies that seemed to embody his concept of blood consciousness: "With bodies bent a little forward, shoulders and breasts loose and heavy, feet powerful but soft, the men tread the rhythm into the centre of the earth. . . . It is the homeward pulling of the blood, as the feet fall in the soft, heavy rhythm, endlessly. . . . They are experiencing a delicate, wild inward delight, participating in the natural mysteries."[13] Wilson also followed Lawrence in his portrayal of the Shalako masked bird dances: "arising from no visible human source, scanning no human chant, yet filling the quiet air, the song seems the genuine voice of deities that are part of Nature. . . . It seems as if the dancer, by his pounding, were really generating energy for the Zunis; by his discipline strengthening their fortitude; by his endurance, guaranteeing their permanence."

In this eloquent passage Wilson suspends disbelief but does not (indeed, cannot) explain how this mysterious process takes place. In the end, his rational cast of mind, so different from Lawrence's, opposes the mystical element, sees it as an absurd "show": "something in me began to fight the Shalako, to reject and repulse its influence just at the moment when it was most compelling. One did not want to rejoin the Zunis in their primitive Nature cult." As ambivalent about the Zunis as he was about Russia, Wilson states that theirs "is supposed to be the most complicated religion that still exists in the world," but is also disgusted by their barbaric and nauseating practices: "they drink urine and eat excrement, chew up pieces of cloth and wood, swallow pebbles and handfuls of ashes, bite the heads off live mice and devour the entrails of dogs, which they have just torn to pieces alive."[14]

Wilson's interest in Haiti was directly inspired by his friendship with Philippe (Phito) Thoby-Marcelin, who wrote novels about that country with his brother Pierre. Both Dos Passos and Dawn Powell had known and liked Phito during their writing holidays in Port-au-Prince, and through them Wilson first met Phito when he came to Washington, with his American wife and translator Eva, to work for the Pan American Union. In September 1948 Wilson wrote Elena that Phito —born into an upper-class family in 1904—was, "though a mulatto, pretty dark and absolutely African in appearance, with intense and piercing black eyes." When Phito and Eva moved to her hometown of Cazenovia, New York, Wilson often saw them during his summers in Talcottville. Both men were extremely fond of Johnnie Walker Scotch, but the Haitian could not quite keep up with Wilson. "Don't let Phito drink as much as he'd like," he warned an upstate friend. "He becomes unintelligible—in English *and* in French."

Wilson, as usual, was very generous to his new friend; he introduced him to English-speaking readers and did everything he could to advance his career in America. He reviewed the French edition of *Canapé Vert* in the *New Yorker* of February 1944; reprinted his review of *The Pencil of God* as an Introduction to the Houghton Mifflin edition of 1951; and discussed Phito's work in the Haiti chapter of *Red, Black, Blond and Olive*. He compared his novels to Silone's, praised his clear intellect and unashamed humanity, emphasized his universal appeal and wrote that the "books of the Marcelins are distinguished performances. They deal with difficult subjects [voodoo]—material that is controversial in Haiti and unfamiliar abroad; and, presenting them, without sentimentality or political melodrama and with no explicit comment, they bring out in them a human poignancy that is communicated to readers anywhere." Partly through Wilson's enthusiastic efforts, the Marcelins' novel, *The Beast of the Haitian Hills* (1946), was published as a *Time* paperback edition in 1964 and sold 80,000 copies. Wilson provided Phito with introductions to influential writers in France and Italy, helped him get published in the Italo-American literary magazine *Botteghe Oscure*, and successfully recommended him for Yaddo and Guggenheim fellowships. In 1970 he concluded his quarter-century of interest in Phito's work by writing another Introduction to the Farrar, Straus edition of *All Men Are Mad*.

In November 1949, after the *New Yorker* had rejected his proposal, Wilson persuaded a new magazine, the *Reporter*, to send him to Haiti to write about its literature and politics. The magazine paid his fare, $100 a week expenses for one month and $2,000 for two substantial articles. On November 25 he left by train for Miami, and was appalled by its decadent luxury and blatant vulgarity. He then flew via Havana to Port-au-Prince, where he stayed at the Hotel Olaffson, later the sordid scene of Graham Greene's *The Comedians* (1966). Wilson was impressed by Haiti, which had been occupied by the United States from 1915 until 1934, and found it a fascinating mixture of West Africa and New Orleans. Alluding to the successful late eighteenth-century revolt against French domination, he told Elena that "it is the only place where you can see independent Negroes, with a tradition of victory behind them, trained in a highly developed culture." Despite the ravages of neglect, the country still had a seedy appeal.

Active as ever in Haiti, Wilson visited King Christophe's citadel at Cap-Haitien on the north coast and a UNESCO program to combat illiteracy near Jacmel on the south coast. He noted the beauty of the women and the charm of the people, the relation of skin color to social class and political power, the terrible government and horrible diseases. He saw a cockfight and a ritual sacrifice of fowl. But he did not witness any voodoo ceremonies, then enjoying an unprecedented popularity, and had to fill the gap with accounts from printed sources. Phito Thoby-Marcelin guided Wilson during his month on the island, where they cemented the friendship that had begun in Washington. "He is a very first-rate fellow," Wilson told Dos, "and most interesting to talk to when you get past his conventional politeness. He knows Haiti inside out and—when he is really speaking with candor—is very realistic and intelligent about it."[15]

Wilson introduced the chapter on Israel with his great essay "On First Reading Genesis" (originally published in the *New Yorker* in May 1954), in which he vividly conveys the unique qualities of the language, the experience of reading the Bible in Hebrew and the concept of God in the Old Testament. He also makes Jacob—who wrestled with God and saw Him face to face, managed to limp away and yet still lived—a hero out of *The Wound and the Bow*. To Wilson, Jacob represents the Jewish "idea that they had conquered, at a maiming cost, some share in the power of God."

Wilson concerned himself while in Israel with many other things beside the Dead Sea Scrolls, and was particularly interested in small, picturesque and extremist communities. He witnessed a Samaritan passover, in which sheep were slaughtered as dogs had been in the Zuni rituals. He visited the fanatical and ultra-Orthodox Guardians of the City, who do not recognize the state of Israel and believe that Zionist profanities are preventing the advent of the Jewish Messiah. He praised the fiction of S. Y. Agnon, who would win the Nobel Prize in 1966, and saw him "as a true representative of that great line of Jewish writers that begins with the authors of Genesis." Wilson read the Hebrew Bible every day (as he had studied the languages in Italy and Greece) and saw Israel in the context of three thousand years of history.

Red, Black, Blond and Olive, one of Wilson's most readable and interesting books, is as timely today as it was in 1956. Indian tribes in America are vitally concerned with the preservation of their cultural identity (an issue he would reconsider in *Apologies to the Iroquois*); Haitians live in poverty and terror, with no solution in sight; Russia is undergoing another political and economic convulsion; Israel faces hostile neighbors and sharp domestic conflicts. Reviewing the book in the *New Republic*, Robert Graves praised Wilson's "cantankerous, well-stocked mind, keen eye for the absurd as well as the essential" and his admirable sense of English prose.

Wilson focused on the precarious future of cultural minorities. He realized, from observing the Zunis, that "a highly developed and vividly imagined mythology" was valuable for binding a people together, yet felt "impatience at their exclusiveness and bigotry" toward outsiders. He believed that "the Christian mythology is obsolete, almost as impracticable for the modern man" as the Zuni religion, and yet wondered what other cohesive force could be found to hold society together. Atheist, humanist, pacifist, Wilson realized that traditional orthodoxies, however picturesque, could become dangerous fundamentalist movements, with the power to censor and coerce.

VI

On July 20, 1956—four months after the book appeared—Wilson, with Elena and Helen, took his eighth trip to Europe and celebrated the surprising financial success of *The Scrolls from the Dead Sea*. The Wilsons repeated the European part of the 1954 journey and, with no work to do, had a curiously uneventful holiday. They crossed on the *Media*, arrived in Liverpool and stayed at the Basil Street Hotel in London. He desperately missed Mamaine, who had died in 1954; but as usual saw Cyril Connolly, Sylvester Gates, Stephen Spender and Angus Wilson, and had lunch in Corpus Christi College, Cambridge, with Stewart Perowne, who had arranged his expedition to the Dead Sea. Wilson also met the difficult and reclusive Derek Lindsay (a friend of Connolly), who would write a very fine novel, *The Rack* (1958), under the name of A. E. Ellis. According to the poet Alan Ross, "Wilson and Connolly stared at each other like a pair of sumo wrestlers, not giving ground and sizing up the moment to strike. In between they exchanged desultory gossip." But the sexagenarian Wilson, once the fire-breathing enemy of England, had become much more gentle, and now saw the merits in the class system he had once attacked so ferociously. Coming to England, he recorded in his diary, "is always relaxing. In spite of the developments since the last war, the social system is still largely taken for granted, and it is soothing for an American to arrive in a place where everybody accepts his function along with his social status, and everything operates smoothly."[16]

The Wilsons reached the Hotel Lotti on the rue Castiglione in Paris by mid-August and saw the novelist Elizabeth Bowen (whom he had previously met in wartime London); Vladimir's cousin Nicolas Nabokov; Esther Arthur, the sister of Fitzgerald's close friend Gerald Murphy; Janet Flanner, who wrote for the *New Yorker* from Paris; and Joyce's devoted friend Maria Jolas. Wilson dined at Joyce's favorite restaurant, Fouquet's, and ordered his old favorites: homely chicken croquettes with tomato sauce and a bottle of Château d'Yquem. But the dish of his childhood now seemed insipid, and the sweet wine made him sick. After visiting Munich, which still had some Old World charm, they sailed back to America on the *Queen Mary*. Wilson arrived in New York on September 18, and was pitched into an unexpected crisis with the Internal Revenue Service.

NINETEEN

Fighting the IRS, 1957–1958

I

The publication of *A Piece of My Mind: Reflections at Sixty* in November 1956, two months after Wilson returned from Europe, marked a new phase in his career. His years of literary and political journalism, his notoriety as the author of *Memoirs of Hecate County* and the much wider readership achieved by his articles on the Dead Sea Scrolls made Wilson a public figure. Editors and interviewers sought his opinion on current issues, readers were interested in his personality and his life. Grouped under general headings, like "Religion" and "The United States," the essays were critical, analytic, persuasive and provocative. They combined autobiographical reflections with discussions of books, characters, historical eras and political systems, and revealed, in an erudite yet entertaining style, as much about the author as they did about the topic under discussion. Wilson concluded with an elegant, more narrowly focused chapter, "The Author at Sixty," a companion piece to "The Case of the Author" (1932). This piece—with his biographical essays on Marx and Holmes, Gauss and Millay—is one of the best things he ever wrote.

In this book Wilson took the opportunity to sum up, in a reflective and elegiac way, some of his familiar ideas about literature, history and his own life. In the section on Religion, he restated his atheist position, answered some of the critics of his *Dead Sea Scrolls*, and compared the Catholic dogma to its Communist equivalent. The Antichrist, though sympathetic to Judaism and to primitive religions, still believed, as he had told Kemp Smith in 1945, that "the word *God* is now archaic, and it ought to be dropped by those who do not need it for moral support."

The essay on the Jews was a masterpiece of Wilson's indirect style, building up a great deal of apparently irrelevant but interesting detail, and then vividly homing in on the main point. Wilson argued that the spirit of the ancient Jews, in the sacred Hebrew texts and the English translations, has become an intimate part of modern American consciousness. He traced the history of attitudes toward Jews in nineteenth-century America, and noted that admiration was entwined with fears that Jews were nearly supernatural and would take over the world. His conclusion movingly explained his respect for Judaism: its absence of ornament, saints and Messiah, its bleak but bracing outlook, "the power of the spirit, the authority of the moral sense."

Wilson concludes this section with a satiric story, "The Messiah of the Seder." In this rather schematic fable, four modern Jewish men and their womenfolk sit down to a Seder, during which the Prophet Elijah and the Messiah appear in answer to the traditional prayers. Each man reveals his own professional orthodoxy, his desire to exclude certain categories of Jew from the Promised Land, and the comic would-be Messiah is finally rejected by God Himself. The story revealed the way in which a religion may rest on aspirations that are comforting as long as they never come true, and mocked exclusive and self-righteous orthodoxies. This fable contained the kind of portentous Messianic character that Wilson first introduced with The Gardener, the Wandering Jew, in *The Little Blue Light* (1950), and continued with the Jonathan-Christ figure in his late playlet, *Dr. McGrath* (1967).

The United States, Wilson argued, is not a nation but " a society, a political system, which is still in a somewhat experimental state," and this explains our periodic panics and crises. We tend to have different types of president, who reflect the basic conflict in American life: the desire to make money for oneself and the desire to contribute to a better life for all people. Irritated by Europe's patronizing attitude to America, the man who had read "Dick Tracy" in the Church of the Holy Sepulcher adopted a deliberately philistine attitude. In a much-quoted passage, he defiantly proclaimed: "I have not the least doubt that I have derived a good deal more benefit of the civilizing as well as of the inspirational kind from the admirable American bathroom than I have from the cathedrals of Europe." He also mentioned the positive effect of having various means of protest at our disposal: "Instead of settling conflicts of interest by irrevocable dismissals and sweeping proscriptions, we give vent to our violence as we go along, relieve our crises of friction in innumerable limited contests."

"Reflections on the Teaching of Latin," first published in a prep school magazine, provided a useful complement to his discussion of the teaching of Greek in "Mr. Rolfe" (1943). It set forth his ideal curriculum, arguing for an emphasis on spoken, colloquial Latin and on reading poetry and plays rather than the dull grind of Caesar.

In his deliberately negative, provocative and unsexy essay on sex, Wilson urged the practice of eugenics, "the betterment of the race by breeding," since the old aristocracies are dead and we now have the means to avoid mediocrity. He dismissed "the hysterical orgasms of Lawrence" and "the biologically sterile relationships" in modern literature, misleadingly declared that at his age he had now almost put sex behind him and argued that romantic love has little to do with marriage. Wilson set aside his amorous past and adopted an amoral voice, challenging the reader's assumptions and urging him to be aware of how modern science can "improve" the world.

"The Author at Sixty" described his highly eccentric parents and defined himself in relation to his ancestors. Though he asserted that "Old Fogeyism is closing in," he also celebrated "the sense of my continuity" and realized that the sixty-year-old Wilson contained within himself all the different selves he had ever been. In a moving analogy between himself and the Old Stone House, he compared his place in American society to the house in its setting. Wilson asserted, in a classic statement of American individualism, that he was not in a pocket of the past but at the center of things, because "the center can be only in one's head."[1] This final chapter emphasized the historical and personal theme of the book: the force of the past in the present.

In an earlier interview of November 2, 1952, Harvey Breit of the *New York Times* had called Wilson "America's number one man of letters," and Wilson had discussed his function as a wide-ranging and truly international critic, and the first stage of his work on *Patriotic Gore*. Wilson had always cultivated his privacy, but soon after his emergence as a poised and witty oracle in *A Piece of My Mind*, he gave interviews to Alberto Arbasino and two other foreign journalists. Published during his humiliating struggle with the tax authorities, these interviews enhanced his battered public image at home and abroad. John Wain, an English novelist who traveled to Talcottville and wrote about Wilson in the *Observer* of November 3, 1957, called his piece "Edmund Wilson Eludes the Interviewer." Wilson had produced a list of typed questions for Wain to answer, and there was some confusion (as with Dahn Ben-Amotz) about who was interviewing whom. Wain emphasized the high quality of Wilson's work as a literary and social critic, and later edited and contributed to a collection of appreciative essays, *An Edmund Wilson Celebration* (1978).

Henry Brandon, in an interview for the London *Sunday Times* (reprinted in the *New Republic* of March 30, 1959), questioned Wilson about his attitude to Europe and America, his literary taste and his view of contemporary writers: Malraux and Genet, Kerouac and Salinger, Auden, Day Lewis and MacNeice. Contrary to normal practice, Wilson was paid £150 for this interview and did quite a bit of work on it. As he told Scottie Fitzgerald Lanahan, a Washington friend of Brandon: "I talked to him over highballs rather incoherently, and he took it all down on a tape-recorder. Later he sent me a typed-out version of this, which made no sense at all. I carefully rewrote the whole thing; then the *Sunday Times* published only selections from this, so that it is now incoherent again."[2]

The first feature article on Wilson, written by Eleanor Perenyi and based on interviews with his friends, was commissioned by *Esquire* and appeared in July 1963. Perenyi, a friend of Mamaine Paget, had published a memoir of her life on a prewar feudal estate in Hungary, which Wilson reviewed in the *New Yorker* in March 1946. Her piece, more personal than literary, described the tastes and habits of the charming old curmudgeon. The interviews and essay were a natural extension of *A Piece of My Mind*, which had whetted the public's appetite for Wilson's cunning mixture of nostalgic autobiography and contentious opinions.

II

In January 1957 the Wilsons rented a house in Cambridge for about four months. Reuel was a freshman at Harvard, Rosalind was working at Houghton Mifflin in Boston, and Edmund wanted to use the Harvard Library and frequent the bookshops in Harvard Square. Sixteen Farrar Street, in a quiet, leafy part of town, was a two-story house with shuttered windows, peaked gables, a steep-pitched roof and a fanlight above the front door. When Bambi died in April, Wilson buried the old dog in a shallow winter grave in the back yard. But he was forced to remove the corpse, much to his annoyance, after the spring thaw had revealed it to the indignant landlord.

Always aware that his old companions were dying off, Wilson now began to form close friendships with the younger generation. In the spring of 1957 he met Robert Lowell, the leading American poet of the postwar era, who was teaching a course at Boston University. Descended from an eminent New England family, Lowell had, like Wilson, roots in the Puritan past. After dropping out of Harvard, he had studied under Ransom at Kenyon College and come under the influence of Allen Tate. Lowell had once been married to the novelist Jean Stafford, who would become Wilson's good friend during their year at Wesleyan in 1964–65, and was currently married to the writer Elizabeth Hardwick. He had been a conscientious objector in World War Two and during the 1960s would become a leading opponent of the war in Vietnam. Lowell's sophisticated and urbane, learned and allusive mind was clouded by a long history of mental illness and by a series of tragic breakdowns.

Impressed by Lowell's range of reading and genuine feeling for literature, Wilson recorded, soon after they met: "I was so pleased to find someone who talked like an old friend of the Twenties . . . accelerating conversations, going off in all directions, interrupting one another, range of interest and reading, flares of imagination, general freedom of the world." But, Wilson observed, when Lowell fell into one of his manic moods, his startling wit became perverse and his talk accelerated right off the rails: "Cal [Lowell] at the dinner table was always as usual going off on a conversational tangent—though he often says brilliant things, this makes him rather difficult to talk to."

Lowell could be, Wilson learned, dangerous as well as difficult. When he was staying with Lowell in 1957, the poet, having discovered at breakfast that Wilson had never read Macaulay's huge *History of England*, suddenly appeared in Wilson's bedroom. Almost naked and covered with a pelt of black hair, he held an immense set of Macaulay over Wilson's head and then dropped it on top of him. But Lowell, as abject as Fitzgerald, always apologized for his out-of-control behavior. On one occasion he wrote: "I have a memory of being rather loud and drunk and rude to you the other night. I was feeling tired and trying to relax. This can be a pain in the neck to one's friends. Please trust in my love and admiration forever."[3]

Lowell etched an early poem, "Children of Light," on a window in the Wellfleet house, and later sent Wilson a manuscript of the revised version. He admired Lowell's imaginative strength, rhetorical force and technical skill. In his self-interview of June 1962, he compared Lowell with the leading poets of the century and declared: "the poetry never ceases to be noble, and the imagery, which is spikey and dark, is also in its way rich and brilliant. He is, I think, the only recent American poet—if you don't count Eliot—who writes successfully in the language and cadence and rhyme of the resounding English tradition. In some way that I find it rather hard to define, he and W. H. Auden stand distinctly apart from the other contemporary poets."

Lowell expressed his reverential attachment to Wilson in a letter to his editor Robert Giroux. Written a week after Wilson's death, on June 20, 1972, it praised Wilson's power to create vivid scenes: "My good angel must have told me to write Edmund, out of a blue sky, about three weeks before his death; I had an answer saying he had just had a stroke. He must have somewhat recovered to get to Talcottville. I'm re-reading almost all his books since I came to England—he's the best bridge maybe for an American in Europe, and so much of him reads like great short stories for novels. Good-bye, dear old man!" In "Our Afterlife, I," Lowell placed Wilson with his distinguished peers and lamented: "This year killed / Pound, Wilson, Auden."[4]

In the spring of 1958 Wilson became friendly with an intriguing upper-class lesbian couple, Barbara Deming and Mary Meigs (both born in 1917, the same year as Lowell), who had just bought Mary McCarthy's old house in Wellfleet. Deming, born in New York, the daughter of a singer and of an admiralty lawyer, was the second of four children. She attended Quaker schools, where she became an ardent pacifist, earned degrees from Bennington and from Case Western Reserve in Cleveland. After graduation, she wrote theater and film criticism, and published several books of poetry and social protest with small feminist presses. Deming shared Wilson's interest in the ecology of the Cape and was a follower of the peace activist A. J. Muste. Wilson had admired Muste since the labor struggles in the coal mines of Kentucky during the 1930s, published excerpts from *The Cold War and the Income Tax* (1963) in Muste's progressive journal *Liberation* and donated the proceeds of the book to his peace movement. Deming, more radical than Wilson, was rather naively enthusiastic about Castro and Cuba. He admired Deming's commitment to the Civil Rights movement and in June 1966 recommended her book, *Prison Notes*, to William Shawn, the editor of the *New Yorker:* "She spent twenty-seven days in jail in Albany, Georgia, for taking part in one of those marches, and her book is . . . a notably well-written document that throws more light than anything else I have read on the meaning of their non-violent protests."

Deming had had a two-year affair with Edna's sister, Norma Millay; another of Barbara's lovers had married her brother Quentin. She had been living since 1954 with Mary Meigs, who described her as "almost six feet tall, with long arms, a swinging gait and a deep voice, like a man's.... [She had a] serious face with kind, mournful eyes, framed by straight dark hair and bangs, and long hands in continual motion."[5]

Mary Meigs, who came from an old New England family, was born in Philadelphia and grew up in Washington, where her father was a prominent government official. Rich and elegant, she was also mysterious and dramatic. An amateur painter, writer and pianist, she reminded Wilson of the girls of his youth. Both men and women were always falling in love with her—as they had once fallen in love with Edna Millay. Though a lesbian, Meigs had slept with the homosexual Bowden Broadwater when he was married to Mary McCarthy. This brief liaison accounted for the sharp-edged satiric portrait of Meigs as Dolly Lamb in *A Charmed Life:* "She was tall and long-legged and curiously flattened out, like a cloth doll that had been dressed and redressed by many imperious mistresses. She had a neat round little face that came to a point unexpectedly in a firm, slightly jutting chin, short crisp blond hair, of a silvery cast, a silvery quiet laugh, and bright silver-blue eyes that shone with a high gleam, as if they had just been polished." Meigs later wrote that McCarthy had managed to zero in on her hidden weaknesses: "Mary [McCarthy], with unerring accuracy, had hit everything that was vulnerable in me: the indecisiveness of my life, the tightness of my work, my prudish habits. She had even let fly an arrow in the direction of Dolly's money and stirred up the old guilt in me."

Wilson, like many others, fell in love with Mary Meigs. Rosalind called her the great love of his later life and Elena agreed that Meigs was, since their marriage, the only woman who aroused his serious interest. He was intrigued by the fact that she had the same surname as the headmasters of The Hill School, that she shared his background and was a friend of Mary McCarthy. Most fascinating of all was her androgynous sexuality. In 1958, soon after they met, Wilson recorded that he was drawn to Meigs as if she were a beautiful boy—and she played Tadzio to his Aschenbach: "I began to feel a strange attraction exerted by Mary and a tendency, when sufficiently exhilarated, to kiss her.... I decided that her effect on me—with snub nose, her glittering blue eyes, her square face, boyish cheeks, straight up-and-down figure, and 'sensible' unfeminine shoes—was actually homosexual." When he asked Mary what it would be like to be married to her, she insisted: "I'd make a terrible wife." Though his declaration of love made her feel nervous and awkward, she also valued it. She remembered how

> my friendship with Edmund created in me a mixture of fear, shyness, humility, anger, uneasy love, pride, and a terrible anxiety that, through my unworthiness, I would lose his friendship. Our friendship was complicated (for me, at least) by the fact that, for several years, he believed himself to be in love with me. I was, in fact, one of a good many women he loved during this time, but I was close at hand, whereas they (except for Elena, his wife) were far away. I did not want Edmund to be in love with me; I could not believe he really was, yet I was afraid he would cease to be, knowing the indifference that follows on the heels of love.[6]

In the fall of 1963 Wilson introduced Marie-Claire Blais, who became the third member of their emotional triangle, to Deming and Meigs. Born into a poor family in bleak and bigoted Quebec City in 1939, she was educated for twelve years in a Catholic convent and later took courses in literature at Laval University. In her teens she had had an affair with her mentor, the Dominican monk Père René Lévesque, who later became premier of Quebec. Wilson first met her in Montreal in September 1962 when he was conducting interviews for his book on Canadian culture. In *O Canada* (1965), in which he introduced her to American readers (as he had done with the francophone Phito Thoby-Marcelin), he ecstatically declared that "Mlle. Blais is a true 'phenomenon'; she may possibly be a genius. At the age of twenty-four, she has produced four remarkable books of a passionate and poetic force." The following year he boosted her reputation in the United States by writing an Introduction to her novel *A Season in the Life of Emmanuel*.

Wilson was at first quite taken by Marie-Claire, who was forty years younger than himself, and twenty years younger than Barbara and Mary. "She is actually an attractive little woman," he wrote, "with well-developed breasts but tiny hands and feet, a sharp nose, a very small mouth and deep-thinking, gray-green eyes, with the good quiet manners and the very pure French that I suppose she learned from the nuns. . . . She is perfectly self-possessed and has an unusual simplicity and directness that are signs of a remarkable person." His friends were also intrigued by her. Roger Straus, her principal American publisher (thanks to Wilson), called her attractive and lively, both opinionated and shy. Barbara Epstein described her as a Canadian spitfire, self-dramatizing, temperamental and sometimes hysterical.[7]

In the winter of 1963 Blais had a serious accident while walking through the Wellfleet woods with Mary Meigs. Strolling ahead of her, Mary carelessly let a branch snap back into Marie-Claire's eye. She was blinded for a time, and could not read or write for months. While Barbara was away freedom-marching and getting jailed in the South, Marie-Claire moved in with the guilt-ridden Mary, stayed on and soon became a member of their family. In September 1965 Wilson told McCarthy that he had become very fond of the three women: "Mary and Barbara and their little French-Canadian protegée, the novelist Marie-Claire Blais, have been away in Maine and I miss them. They now have a strange ménage à trois, with a black Lesbian dog that tries to bite all the men."

According to Rosalind, Wilson initially thought Barbara and Mary "were a couple of nuns." He did not realize they were lesbians until he noticed their affectionate gestures and their sculptures of naked women. When Marie-Claire moved in, he remarked, "at last, they have a daughter with breasts." But he took a gloomy view of their relationship when Marie-Claire supplanted Barbara and formed a ménage à deux with Mary. As tormented and anguished as the heroines of Mauriac's dark novels, Marie-Claire, wrote Wilson, "makes terrific demands on people, attaches herself to women and won't let go. . . . I think that Marie-Claire has really settled down to suffering as a way of life, and that this involves making other people suffer—in fact, Mary and Barbara."[8] Adelaide Walker thought Blais was "a corrupting influence"; and by 1970 Wilson, who had turned angrily against her, agreed that the "little bitch" was a "*porte-malheur*," a bringer of evil. Marie-Claire, however, remained affectionately loyal to Wilson, emphasized the gentle side of his character, and recently wrote that "Edmund had a magical side that charmed children, the very young, a magical and amusing side, full of inventions of all sorts. These qualities were very simple and veiled by an exceptional wit. They were very seductive and always surprising."[9] In 1974 Blais dedicated *St. Lawrence Blues* "to the memory of Edmund Wilson."

III

Wilson's protracted battle with the Internal Revenue Service began in June 1958—just after he first met Deming and Meigs—when he received a notice from the IRS office in Utica asking when and where he had last filed a tax return. In fact, he had not filed any returns at all between 1946 and 1955, and the authorities had been very slow indeed to catch up with him. According to Wilson's distorted, inaccurate yet fascinating account in *The Cold War and the Income Tax: A Protest* (1963),[10] tax was withheld from his *New Yorker* salary and he had very little additional income until 1946, when he earned $35,000 from the American edition of *Memoirs of Hecate County*—plus $25,000 from the English edition of 1951 and another $25,000 for an option on the film rights in 1961. It was precisely in 1946, when the big money first started rolling in, that Wilson arbitrarily decided to stop paying taxes. His disingenuous explanation was that he thought "this obligation could always be attended to later" and that "before filing for the years since 1945, it would be better to wait until I was making more money." "Better" for Wilson, perhaps, but not for the IRS.

In the fall of 1955, after the publication of his second financially successful book, *The Scrolls from the Dead Sea*, Wilson, finally realizing he had been remiss, first contacted Judge Biggs, who recommended a lawyer in Brooklyn, and then sought help from his old Princeton friend John Amen. He had supervised the estate of Wilson's father, and had made his reputation during the trials of the Nazi criminals at Nuremberg. In Germany he operated brilliantly while on the verge of collapse: "Amen's intimidating investigatory technique and prosecutorial approach were straight out of *Gangbusters*. A womanizer and coping alcoholic whose work was seemingly unaffected by his addiction, he had his first drink while whipping up his shaving lather and seldom went an hour without another during the day. One of his legs tremored involuntarily and was given to occasional small kicks. [One colleague] dubbed him 'the glamorous knight of the bottle, the bed, and the ego.'"

Wilson had appropriately dedicated his poem "Highballs" to Amen, who had been overcome by alcoholism and fallen into a radical decline by the time he took over the case in 1955. Astonished and appalled by Wilson's reckless indifference to the tax laws, he advised his client to avoid prosecution by leaving America and becoming a citizen of some other country. Wilson seriously considered the possibility of moving to Canada or Switzerland. In July 1956, just before departing for a summer in Europe, Wilson signed his long overdue tax returns, told Amen to file them and gave him a check for $9,000 to pay the IRS. When he returned to America in mid-September, he learned that his lawyer had lost all the papers and had done nothing.

In June 1958 Wilson, who by then had very little cash, received his first notice of delinquency and the hunt began. Suddenly desperate, he got rid of Amen and was generously taken on by Francisco Penberthy, an old-time Utica ward-heeler. Penberthy suggested that Wilson might impress the tax authorities by going on poor relief, and actually kept him out of jail by threatening to put his client on welfare. Mary McCarthy—thinking of Lenin and Gandhi, and resenting her own incarceration in Payne-Whitney—thought Wilson in prison would be quite a good idea. "It would probably be quite peaceful," she told him, "and one could get a lot of writing done. Besides studying Conditions." On September 15, according to a newspaper story filed in Syracuse, Wilson was finally "Charged in Big Tax Case."[11]

The IRS informed Wilson that he was liable to prosecution for not paying taxes between 1953 and 1957 (they did not hold him liable for taxes before then), and took until 1963 to settle the case. During that time Wilson, as always, kept on with his writing, but was under severe emotional and financial strain. Jason Epstein recalled that Wilson "became involved in all kinds of messy paper-work; I remember his house was full of cancelled checks in those days, with lawyers and accountants coming and going. . . . It was his good wife Elena who pulled the whole thing together for him."

Penberthy's argument on Wilson's behalf was straightforward and fairly convincing. As he told Wilson: "you had employed outstanding New York counsel to prepare your returns, long before the IRS had started investigation of your case; that you had signed the returns and advanced money for the payment of the tax; and that for reasons not known to you or to me, the returns were not filed." On November 14, 1960 Wilson won a dismissal of three out of the four charges against him. But he pled guilty to failing to report an income of $17,000 in 1957 and was fined $7,500. The court accepted the rather unlikely story that Amen, now deceased, had not paid Wilson's taxes and was responsible for his delinquency. But the judge felt obliged to remark that a man of Wilson's intelligence and experience should have taken better care of his own affairs. In order to pay the fine Wilson borrowed money from Barbara Deming and his Russian friend Roman Grynberg.

Though the case was decided, it was far from settled. Wilson, who had still not paid his long overdue taxes, was penalized 96 percent for interest, fraud, delinquency, underestimating his income and failure to file. He still owed the government about $68,500 and did not have the money. But the IRS knew how to extract it. They froze his sources of income by seizing his trust fund of $8,500 a year and putting a lien on his royalties, which stopped all payments from his publishers. He was required each month to present an itemized account of all the money he received and spent; was reprimanded for owning two houses and renting a third one in Cambridge, for sending Helen to a private school, "for spending too much money on liquor, for taking my Italian translator to the theater, and for having bought a $6 mat for my dog."

In July 1961 Wilson raised some of the necessary money by selling his present and future papers to Yale for $30,000. Princeton had shown no interest in his archive; and though Texas had offered $75,000, Wilson disliked the dealer, Lew Feldman, who was buying for them and preferred to have the material near enough to consult. It is worth noting that Wilson could have made a great deal more money if he had been less intransigent about expurgating *Memoirs of Hecate County*, about cutting *The Little Blue Light*, which would have increased its chances of success and extended its run, about serializing *The Scrolls from the Dead Sea* in the English newspapers and about selling his papers to Texas instead of to Yale. Yale arranged to pay Wilson $10,000 down (of which he owed $7,500 to Deming and Grynberg) and annual increments of $5,000. The payments were later speeded up by mutual consent and Wilson got the final check in 1963.[12] (His letters to Elena were sold separately by her after his death; and the University of Tulsa bought his library of books in English.)

Wilson's main problem after the trial in November 1960 was to get the IRS to name a figure they would accept as an "offer of compromise." In May 1962 the Utica tax office told him to appear the next day and threatened to arrest him if he did not turn up. Wilson coolly replied that he was unable to come because of an invitation to the Kennedy White House. He maintained that the Utica tax man looked like Boris Karloff, and he would ask for him by that name when he telephoned the office. In August 1962, after four years of struggle and humiliation, he told Roger Straus: "I spent three hours in Syracuse yesterday with the income tax people, conducting most of the negotiations myself, which I should probably have done before and I have for the first time got them to suggest an offer which they would be willing to accept. . . . If I agree to their proposal, they will immediately lift all the levies" on his income.

Finally, in 1963, the IRS demanded $40,000 plus a collateral agreement that mortgaged his future literary earnings up to $30,000. This sum, slightly more than the $68,500 he owed, was no great bargain. He continued to negotiate and on a subsequent visit the authorities went down to $25,000 plus the $30,000 collateral agreement, which Wilson—eager to conclude the dispute—accepted. His legal bills came to another $16,000, and he continued to be plagued by financial troubles for many years. In his acceptance speech for the National Medal for Literature in June 1966, Wilson lamented that "he was still being penalized for previous tax delinquencies and was obliged to turn over 50 percent of his total income, in addition to his regular tax, which left him 'with about $100 in the bank.'"

More interesting than the factual details of the case are Wilson's reasons for not paying taxes for ten years. In his book he describes himself, when he first consulted Amen in the fall of 1955, as a Rip Van Winkle waking up to reality. He admits at the beginning that it was "naive, and even stupid" for a writer who had been concerned with public affairs during his long years on the *New Republic* to be so unaware "of how heavy our taxation had become or of the severity of the penalties exacted for not filing tax returns."[13]

He nevertheless felt that filling out tax forms was an unimportant waste of time. He could sometimes be naive about public affairs (he had swallowed the Soviet propaganda about Lenin and voted for the Communist candidate in the presidential election of 1932) and, as a humanistic anarchist, resolutely opposed the oppressive powers of government. When told that everybody had to pay taxes, he replied that it was wrong for them to do so. (But, unwilling to risk the loss of his houses, he paid his *local* taxes promptly.) He felt he had been misled by Amen (whom he could have sued for malpractice), and been unfairly persecuted and abused. There was also a grand seigneur side to Wilson's character. He believed, after all he had done for American culture, that he was a privileged person who ought to be treated differently from the ordinary man. Like many others, he had an inexplicable and irrational resistance to paying taxes. In 1946, as the money came in after a quarter century of hard struggle, he saw no reason to hand it over to a government that spent it on pointless weapons and reckless wars. In *The Cold War and the Income Tax*, his flawed but underrated book, he cleverly transformed a flagrant case of tax evasion into an effective political protest.

IV

In his humorous poem on Thoreau, "The Extrovert of Walden Pond," Wilson wrote that "He refused to pay his taxes / And they put him in the cooler." In *The Cold War and the Income Tax*, he evoked Thoreau's classic pamphlet *Civil Disobedience* (1849), to suggest that he had not paid his taxes for similarly principled reasons. Wilson subtly shifts from his flagrant tax delinquency to a condemnation of the oppressive methods of the tax authorities, the use of tax money for foreign wars and the American fight against Communism. Wilson knew that the connection between his not paying taxes and protesting against the Cold War was illogical, even spurious. He admitted, in a sentence that shattered his high-minded argument, that "my original delinquency was not due to principle but to negligence." Some of his familiar, hobby-horse arguments (carried on from the 1957 Postscript to *The American Earthquake*)—that the Japanese had been willing to negotiate peace before the attack on Hiroshima, that the atomic bomb was dropped without prior warning—were demonstrably false. He pointed out the absurdity of the arms race by observing that "the Soviets soon came to be as scared of us as we have come to be of them," yet did not argue against the strategy of deterrence.

Many of Wilson's arguments, however, now seem more forceful and salutary than they did thirty years ago. He argued that modern weapons cause "wholesale destruction and deliberate contamination" of the environment, that though education is our most pressing concern, 79 percent of the budget is used to pay for military needs, space programs and the cost of past wars. He cited the cancellation of an air force project after $500 million had been wasted. He opposed expenditure on the development and testing of nuclear weapons, and warned of the unknown but certain dangers of radioactivity. He documented the horrific production of chemical and biological weapons, of cholera and anthrax, and of the use in Vietnam of poison gas and napalm. Wilson was one of the first to challenge the Pentagon's claim that the widely-used defoliant, Agent Orange, was no more harmful than a gardener's weed-killer.

In *A Piece of My Mind* Wilson said he felt out of touch with contemporary American life and was more at home in the eighteenth century. Seven years later, in a frequently-quoted sentence in *The Cold*

War and the Income Tax, he declared: "I have finally come to feel that this country, whether or not I continue to live in it, is no longer any place for me." Wilson concluded, as America became fatally entrapped in Vietnam, that "the present image of the United States [is] homicidal and menacing."[14] Wilson's opposition to the war in Vietnam—which was not well received among the conservative population of upstate New York—had originally been provoked by his tax problems. But it was principled as well as personal. Though Mary McCarthy, Robert Lowell and the *New York Review of Books* (to which he frequently contributed) were leading opponents of the war, Wilson did not believe groups of writers could influence foreign policy, conducted his campaign independently and did not become involved in the public protests.

In 1963 both American and British critics were largely in the grip of the Cold War mentality, and few could imagine the consequences of intervening in Vietnam. Though Jason Epstein loyally defended Wilson's book in the first volume of the *New York Review of Books*, it was considered unpatriotic and received mostly negative reviews. In the *New Republic* Richard Gilman, consistently hostile to Wilson, called it naive and illogical. In a scathing article in the conservative *National Review*, Dos Passos passionately defended everything that Wilson had attacked: American anti-Communism, the war in Vietnam and the build-up of nuclear weapons. In his autobiography, *Out of Step*, the political philosopher Sidney Hook also criticized Wilson's "anti-Americanism." Cyril Connolly identified the spurious connection between Wilson's non-payment of taxes and his anti-war protest by writing in the *Sunday Times* that "Mr. Wilson's attack on atomic and biological warfare would have been more impressive if he had paid his taxes in the first place and then protested his indignation." But Connolly failed to answer Wilson's criticism of United States policy. Bertrand Russell, however, who later convened a tribunal to condemn American war crimes in Vietnam, whole-heartedly commended the book in a private letter to his fellow pacifist A. J. Muste. To Russell, the issue of Wilson's taxes seemed insignificant in comparison to his anti-war arguments, and he praised Wilson's "gradual, but very powerful, exposition of the evils we have to fear at present and the much greater evils that will be feared in the near future, unless there is a fundamental change in policy."

In *The Cold War and the Income Tax*, Wilson condemned the Soviet-style spying on its own citizens by the American government. But in the eyes of the IRS, the twice-divorced Wilson was a dubious character—well-known as an atheist and Communist, a labor agitator and defender of the Soviet Union, a fornicator and pornographer, a tax evader, a protester against the war in Vietnam and an unpatriotic American.

Despite Wilson's record, Herbert Mitgang, who has written a book on the FBI's surveillance of American writers, absurdly maintained that "Wilson seemed to me one of the least likely authors to have a file."[15] Wilson had in fact attracted the attention of the FBI and its director J. Edgar Hoover—his exact contemporary. His fourteen-page FBI file was opened in 1946, the year *Memoirs of Hecate County* was suppressed. The last thirteen pages repeat, in typical FBI fashion, what was originally stated on the first page. On July 2, 1951, Wilson gave the agents his views (previously quoted) on Marxism, Communism, the Russian Revolution and the Soviet Union. A second, smaller file, covering his notorious activities since then, would presumably be more interesting. As of October 1993, it remains classified and unavailable "in the interest of national defense."

TWENTY ❖

Harvard, 1959–1962

I

In September 1959 the Wilsons once again moved to Cambridge and Edmund took up a year's appointment as the Abbott Lawrence Lowell professor at Harvard. Their modest three-story house at 12 Hilliard Street—around the corner from the Brattle Theater, where *The Little Blue Light* had been performed in 1950—had a bay window on the second floor, an entrance on the side porch, a low front gate and a small garden in back. It reminded Wilson of his childhood home in Red Bank and was quite satisfactory: well-equipped, well-built, plain but solid, with dark woodwork and a carved banister. Accustomed to the milder climate of Wellfleet, he was oppressed by the dreary Cambridge winter: "Outside I can see nothing but a narrow Cambridge street—the gray snow and ice or slush are all over the sidewalks and road. There are ugly frame-houses opposite, all crowded up against one another. In the mornings, the garbage collectors bang around the big garbage cans that always stand in front of the houses—it's a feature of Cambridge life. Later on, you hear the gaspings and barkings of the cars that people are trying to start, trying to get them out of the snowdrifts—the streets there are never cleaned."

Wilson told James Thurber, his colleague on the *New Yorker*, that most people, surprised and disappointed by his physical appearance, somehow expected him to be more impressive. A stocky, short-legged, paunchy man, with a rolling gait and an owlish demeanor, his large square head was set on a short solid neck, his stubborn jawbone slung forward, his thin mouth like a letter slot. His rufous hair had become thin and grey, and his face, a friend noted, was "dangerously near to mortal crimson." In his mid-sixties, Wilson had evolved into a Churchillian figure with the finely chiseled features of a Roman senator. Sydney Greenstreet, it seemed, had escaped from *The Maltese Falcon* and turned up in the Harvard Yard.

Wilson himself was often unhappy with the iconographic insults of painters and photographers. He thought Seymour Shimin's portrait, which accompanied Eleanor Perenyi's article in *Esquire*, made him look like a New York businessman after a bad day, and the photo on the English dust jacket of *A Piece of My Mind* he found revolting enough "to discourage anyone from buying the book."[1] He preferred Douglas Glass' image of Wilson, the crafty magician, about to perform a clever trick with a deck of cards.

Wilson accepted the teaching position, for which he was paid "a substantial sum," because his resources had been choked off during his five-year battle with the IRS. English sales were also disappointing. Most of the books published by W. H. Allen in the 1950s had not earned their advance, and things did not improve much during the next decade. In 1965 he earned £63 for the Panther paperback edition of *Memoirs of Hecate County* and got an advance of £325 for the Hart-Davis edition of *O Canada;* but four hardcover books had earned only £183 in 1966 and royalties had trickled down to £10 in 1970. Wilson sometimes had Reuel pick up the small publisher's check and spend it while he was in London. There were, however, two other windfalls in the early Sixties. Julian Blumstein paid $25,000 for an option on the never-to-be-made film of *Memoirs of Hecate County;* and Wilson sold German and French rights of that book to Rowohlt and Gallimard for a total of $3,500.

II

Harry Levin, a Wellfleet friend and leading teacher of comparative literature at Harvard, arranged Wilson's appointment. The Lowell professorship had been filled the previous year by Louis Kronenberger —the kind of critic and anthologist, associated with *Time* magazine, whom Wilson had satirized in "The Milhollands and Their Damned Soul." Archibald MacLeish was teaching at Harvard during 1959–60. Though embittered by Wilson's satiric poem and by his refusal to shake hands when they met at the hospital after Dos Passos' car accident, MacLeish was too gentlemanly to oppose Wilson's nomination and deliberately abstained from the vote. After Wilson's year the chair, which had previously been offered to visitors, was absorbed by the permanent faculty of the English Department.

At Harvard, as at the Gauss and the Salzburg Seminars, Wilson read through his drafts of *Patriotic Gore*. English 175, his lecture course on "The Literature of the American Civil War," was offered in both the fall and spring terms and limited to a hundred students. According to the Harvard catalogue, it dealt with "the writings—novels, poetry, memoirs, diaries and speeches—of persons involved in the war or intimately connected with it, from Harriet Beecher Stowe to Justice Holmes. A study in the ideas and states of mind in the Union and the Confederacy before, during and after the war." In the spring term he also gave a seminar on this subject, with only five students.

Wilson's second course in the fall of 1959—Comparative Literature 290: "The Use of Language in Literature"—resembled the course, taught at Smith in the fall of 1942, on the representative powers of language. In the Harvard catalogue Wilson rather vaguely described it as "Studies in the use of language in poetry and prose for the representation of sights, sounds and movement, for the expression of character in dialogue and the creation of atmosphere. Some knowledge of Latin required, and one modern language."

Though the Harvard logician Willard Quine described Wilson's conversation as "vigorous, articulate, emphatic," Wilson (as at Chicago and Smith) was a lamentable teacher. He did not want to take the time from his writing and did the absolute minimum when preparing his classes. He usually read *Patriotic Gore* aloud—poorly, in a hesitating manner and with a slight stammer—and the students thought him a bit of a joke. Wilson was equally ineffective when he became excited. Donald Gallup wrote that "he spoke rapidly, his words spewing forth in torrents, accompanied by a good deal of wheezing that made it somewhat difficult to understand what he was saying."[2] Not surprisingly, Wilson began his "Language in Literature" course with twenty-five students and ended with six. He later told Glyn Morris that he had been "a downright failure" as a professor.

Three of Wilson's students have vivid memories of his performance in the classroom. Eliot Stanley, who audited his course on Civil War Literature, recalled that Wilson alienated the students with harsh criticism and could not unbend sufficiently to reach them:

> He was at that time short and rotund, a kind of Dickensian character who wore a straw hat in warmer months. . . . I recall that

he was irritated at the poor grammar and word usage in the papers he graded and would spend the better part of an hour when he returned those papers, complimenting those by name who did well and mercilessly criticizing those by name who did not! This must have been extremely humiliating to any student who came up for repeated criticism. . . . My overall impression of him was that he tended to "lord it over" the students in the class and that he was more pompous and pleased with himself than I expected to find. . . . I think that in fact he saw himself as a kind of Churchillian Zeus of the literary scene—and he resembled Churchill in some ways.

Philippe Radley, who later taught Russian at Amherst and became a lawyer, took Wilson's "Language in Literature" course. He too found Wilson disappointing and was sophisticated enough to spot his weaknesses:

I had read a great deal of Wilson by 1959. But I was not prepared then for someone who was physically unimpressive, overweight, and who often walked with difficulty. [The course on the literature of the Civil War] consisted entirely of his reading passages from the as yet unpublished *Patriotic Gore.* I never heard from anyone that it was a good course. . . .

Our course was to be devoted to an analysis of poetry and poetic language. . . . Wilson had no idea how to plan a course. He was, frankly, a poor teacher, who seemed happy just to talk, about Virgil, or Baudelaire, or Turgenev. There was no clear center of focus. . . . Since I was the only Slavist in the class, we would talk, before or after class, about Pushkin and Turgenev. When it came to Russian, he seemed to me incurably sentimental. Nor was his Russian as good as he would have had others believe. . . . Wilson was not at Harvard because he loved teaching. He was there to earn money to pay off the IRS.

Radley came to know Wilson much better than most other students. He visited Wilson's house on Hilliard Street a few times and found Elena, to whom he could speak Russian, "severe and removed." Despite Wilson's imperious manner, Radley felt he was sympathetic. After the course was over, he consulted Wilson about his own marriage problems. Wilson tried his best to be paternal. "He invited me to lunch at a café in Harvard Square," Radley wrote. "Before we had any food, he had had three martinis, after which he felt fortified enough to tell me that as he had gone through numerous unhappy relationships, he knew what misery was about, and that I should not worry, I would get through it too."

Radley's future wife, whom he had first met in Wilson's course and married the following December, was a Radcliffe undergraduate, Frances Nevada Swisher. Unlike Stanley and Radley, she found Wilson enthusiastic, exuberant and exciting to listen to, and was delighted to be in the presence of a great mind. There was no reading list, but Wilson gave out mimeographed sheets of poems. Students were asked to discuss an author of their choice, and Wilson was particularly interested in a young man who analyzed the use of *lambdas* and *rhos* in Greek poetry.

Elena usually did everything for Wilson, and he depended on her even more during his year of teaching at Harvard. But in his diary he complained that she had let him down on three occasions. Elena had left him alone in Red Bank after his mother's death in 1951 and when his mother's longtime maid Jenny Corbett went into hospital in 1957. She had also failed to help him "when we first came to Hilliard Street, and I had to get my lectures on the Civil War and my seminar on comparative literature under way at the same time that I was trying to finish my [Iroquois] Indian book—so that I should have had someone to stand by me, to see that I got out of the house with the books I had to have, etc."

Disappointed by Elena, and resenting his dependence, Wilson turned to another woman for help. He was so attracted to Frances Swisher and so delighted by her admiration that he invited her to be his secretary for a month during the summer preceding her marriage. In Wellfleet she typed and indexed the interminable *Patriotic Gore*, which Wilson called his "Johnson's *Dictionary.*" She found him very pleasant to work for and thought he was affectionate with his family. He and Elena seemed very close and took long walks around Gull Pond every afternoon. Frances remembered that Wilson, who had raised tadpoles as a boy, was very disappointed that the ones he kept died off in Wellfleet. She also got on well with the twelve-year-old Helen: they made fudge, played "ghosts" and swam together at the beach.

Though she believed Elena was too self-possessed and self-assured to be jealous of a young woman, Frances' presence caused a crisis in the household. Though Frances was then engaged to Philippe (Wilson went to their wedding and gave them an Audubon print of red squirrels)[3] and Wilson did not make any overtures, Elena, thinking he had designs on Frances, became "perfectly hysterical." In July 1960, just after Frances had left Wellfleet, both Wilsons were under extreme emotional and financial pressure from the IRS. Alone in Talcottville, Edmund wrote to Elena and complained, in the coldly rational tone he had once used with Mary McCarthy, of her irrational behavior:

> I don't think you realize how jealous you are and how difficult you make life for me by sabotaging or opposing a lot of things that are necessary for me or are already inextricable parts of my life. Your jealousy and opposition have extended to such varied objects as . . . Swisher, the Widener library, my mother's old Cadillac and Talcottville—as well as any woman, like Mamaine or Sofka [Winkelhorn, a close friend of Elena] with whom I have a kind of special rapprochement and with whom I enjoy talking (I should think that you would have had so much of my holding forth that you would be glad to let some other woman listen). . . . I should have been very happy with you [at Wellfleet] if you had not begun to have hysterics and driven me away before I intended to go. I am very sorry I had talked about [Swisher] so much. . . . I have always been fundamentally sure that you and I loved one another, and it does seem to me rather silly of you, after your [unfaithful] behavior for years when you were married to Jimmy, to get into such a state about non-existent infidelities.

Elena, trying to explain her reaction, expressed her intense shame and unhappiness. She replied that "one of our troubles . . . and advantages [is] that our relationship is much too emotional for our age. It is one of the reasons for my getting upset about Swisher.—I was hurt, jealous, insulted and still am. I know this will pass but am still so bitter that I know I could not control myself at the slightest provocation." Tormented by jealousy and rage when Wilson took her devotion for granted and flirted with a younger woman, she called him a destructive scorpion and accused him of trying to push her to breaking point. In the end, however, Wilson realized that he could not live without Elena and the crisis subsided when Swisher passed out of their lives.

Like most visiting professors, Wilson was disappointed by the lack of response from his colleagues. Elena felt that most of the English professors—enclosed in their own lives, intimidated by Wilson's fierce reputation and by his manifest hostility to academics—ignored or even snubbed him. Arthur Schlesinger, Jr. and Richard Pipes, who taught in the History Department, remembered his unhappiness, even misery, during his year at Harvard. The weather that winter was terrible, and he found only a few kindred spirits to satisfy his need for conversation and drink after a day of isolated writing. He disliked the deafening parties where he was served up to guests like roast beef and hated being, at the same time, both a literary trophy and a failure as a teacher. Pipes once invited Wilson, Schlesinger, Isaiah Berlin and the diplomat George Kennan for what was meant to be an exceptional intellectual feast. But each one of the guests remained quiet and self-absorbed; there was no general conversation and the promising evening was a total flop.

On most occasions, however, Pipes found Wilson a stimulating talker. Though the Polish-born Pipes was an expert on Russian history and politics, Wilson always questioned him about the minute details of Russian literature.[4] Other faculty members, like Perry Miller of the English Department, resented Wilson's persistent interrogations and felt they were being exploited by him. Though Miller had written a positive notice of *Classics and Commercials* in the *Nation*, he criticized Daniel Aaron for writing a favorable review of *Patriotic Gore*. By contrast, Kenneth Lynn, then teaching at Harvard, did not mind Wilson's rather blunt mode of discourse: "To me, his ruthlessness in this regard was simply a function of his marvelous eagerness to learn."

In the mid-1960s Wilson was invited to a Cambridge dinner-party with Mark DeWolfe Howe, who was an expert on Justice Holmes, the subject of the final chapter of *Patriotic Gore*. Mary Manning Howe recalled that "before dinner, during dinner, and after dinner he pumped my unfortunate husband. Nothing could stem the flood of questioning." As they were leaving, a young poet remarked: "That guy Wilson should qualify for the FBI. What an interrogator!" Wilson's alternation between asking questions and giving speeches was undoubtedly disconcerting. Some thought he tended to lecture at people—in what he called his "expository mode of conversation"—because he did not, like his colleagues, hold a permanent university chair. He desperately needed an outlet for his turbulent ideas, and talked, as Johnson said of Burke, "because his mind was full."

There was no one on the Harvard faculty as solicitous as Helen Muchnic had been at Smith. But, when he taught there and during the several winters he spent in Cambridge in the early 1960s, Wilson found a stimulating and respectful group of friends: Lowell, Schlesinger, Pipes and Lynn as well as Stuart Hughes, Monroe Engel, Albert Guerard and Harry Levin. Guerard met Wilson for drinks at Engel's house when all three lived on Hilliard Street. Lacking all small talk and never discussing personal matters, Wilson seemed to Guerard an unimpressive conversationalist who lacked the brilliance and wit of Nabokov. Nervous and uneasy in an academic setting, and aware that he was not getting through to his large class, Wilson insecurely asked: "Where do I look when lecturing?" Nobody actually told Wilson that he had to prepare his classes and stimulate his students instead of merely reading a text. The Guerards also noticed the "childish" side of Wilson—his love of games and tricks. When Macklin Guerard brought over some framed Confederate money as a gift, Wilson, eager to see it, came down the stairs in his underwear.[5]

Wilson's most complicated friendship at Harvard was with Harry Levin. He thought well of Levin's work, considered him the best of the younger critics and praised him in print from 1938 to 1965. He called Levin's introduction to Ben Jonson's works "brilliant," said he had written "brilliantly" on Joyce and also commended his essay on Malraux. Levin found Wilson an odd mixture of shyness and unintentional rudeness. The generally unhappy year at Harvard, Levin felt, catalyzed Wilson's prejudice against academics and hurt their friendship. As an amateur in comparative literature, Wilson had something of a rivalry with Levin, and could not take him as seriously as he wanted to be taken. Levin—who could sometimes be pompous and arrogant—would stand on his professorial dignity. When Wilson cavalierly dismissed Spanish literature, Levin countered with: "Harvard thinks very highly of Cervantes." Wilson preferred the company of more wide-ranging professors—Stuart Hughes ran for the U.S. Senate against Edward Kennedy, Arthur Schlesinger became Special Assistant to President John Kennedy—who were involved in public affairs.

Another source of tension was Wilson's half-hearted, semi-serious attempts to seduce his friends' wives. Despite his big belly and unromantic appearance, he made advances to many women and did not mind rejections if he could score a few hits. Seated at a dinner table with the Russian-born Elena Levin, the rather deaf Harry nearby, Wilson leaned over and whispered: "I'd like to go to bed with you." Stuart Hughes once gave Wilson a lift to Boston. He stopped en route to buy liquor and returned to find Wilson kissing his wife, Suzanne, in the car. She, at least, was not troubled by his advances and actually found them quite amusing.

Wilson's social relations were not confined to academics and their wives. In January 1960 he met the "jolly, amusing, even bubbling" Igor Stravinsky, who spoke Russian with Elena and looked like an insect. When offered a piece of cheese at a reception, he would lean forward and stick his tongue out to receive it. Wilson had become increasingly suspicious of T. S. Eliot's Old Possum persona and fenced a bit with him when they met again in Cambridge in 1959. I. A. Richards, also at Harvard, reported that "Tom, who seemed a little over gay, got off badly by telling Wilson that he looked more and more like Randolph Churchill—which Wilson didn't like: but after that they got on well enough. Wilson rather deferential, inquiring about Tom's metrics and so on."

In February 1960 Wilson heard Auden read his poetry in Sanders Theater. Even drunker than when he had etched his lines on Wilson's window pane, Auden kept leaning forward and pushing his papers off the edge of the lectern, and seemed surprised as they floated down into the crowd. There was considerable confusion as they were retrieved and handed back to him—upside down and out of order. Two months later Wilson attended Isaac Bashevis Singer's theatrically effective reading at the Divinity School. When they met, Singer remarked that he believed in some sort of survival after death, and Wilson said that he did not want to survive. "If survival has been arranged," Singer answered, "you will have no choice in the matter."[6]

In March 1961, during his second year on Hilliard Street, Wilson told Morton Zabel that Harvard, though livelier than Chicago and Princeton, still had severe limitations. It was more tolerable, however, if he could occasionally escape to Wellfleet: "We have been more or less enjoying our winters in Cambridge. The best of the faculty are brilliant, and a real exchange of ideas goes on; but it is a cramped claustrophobic place. This year, however, since I don't have a job, we quite often get away to the Cape." Looking back on his Cambridge years in a gloomy but humorous Christmas poem of 1970, Wilson criticized the rigid academic hierarchy and wrote:

> Like in nasty English common-rooms the dons are looking
>   deggers

Where department heads are princes and no-tenure men are
  beggers.
Our hound-dog has been poisoned, and our pussycat is preggers,
And we've got those Cambridge Blues![7]

III

Wilson had the ability to take on unusual subjects and make them
fascinating. In the mid-1950s, as he became increasingly alienated from
the modern world, he began to feel that he belonged to a half-obsolete
group of survivors from the Victorian age. Like D. H. Lawrence with
the Etruscans, he became particularly interested in vulnerable nations
who were struggling against oppressive powers, and made compassion
for cultural minorities a dominant theme of his late polemical works.
He had, as early as *The American Jitters* (1932), identified with innocent
Anarchists, the rural poor, exploited factory workers, striking coal
miners and the suicidal victims of the Depression. In October–November
1959, while teaching at Harvard, Wilson published his articles on
the Indians in the *New Yorker* and brought them out as *Apologies to the
Iroquois* the following March.

In *To the Finland Station* (1940), where he sympathized with the
exiled and imprisoned Russian revolutionaries, he wrote that Marx and
Engels, interested in the "communism of primitive societies," had read
the works of an American ethnologist on the Iroquois Indians. Wilson
wrote about the Zunis of New Mexico in 1947, the Haitians in 1951,
the Essenes in 1955, the Jews in 1956, the Iroquois in 1960, the
defeated Confederates in 1962, the persecuted tax resisters in 1963 and
the French Canadians in 1965.

In December 1957, two months after he first visited the Indian
reservation, Wilson told Van Wyck Brooks: "I have discovered, to my
great surprise, that I am surrounded at Talcottville by an Iroquois
national movement—not unlike Scottish nationalism and Zionism
—with a revival of the old religion and claims for territory of their
own." In August 1958 Wilson wrote Compton Mackenzie, who was
active in the Scottish nationalist movement, that his current inquiry
concerned the Iroquois. The title and jurisdiction of their reservations
"were supposed to be guaranteed to them by treaties with the federal

government made after the Revolution, when they were recognized as a sovereign nation. They have recently been deprived of certain rights, and are fighting [to retain] their reservations, which the New York or U.S. authorities are threatening to take for various public [power] projects." The Iroquois were the original inhabitants of upstate New York and Wilson was interested in them in the same way that he was absorbed in the history of his own family.

In his Foreword to *Apologies to the Iroquois*, Wilson acknowledges his debt to William Fenton, the leading authority on the upstate tribes, for "sponsoring me among the Senecas and arranging for me to attend their ceremonies." In October 1957, after visiting the Mohawks at St. Regis, Wilson suddenly appeared in Fenton's office at the Albany State Museum, carrying a cane and followed by a taxi-driver bearing his luggage. Wilson announced, "All paths lead to Fenton" and Fenton wondered, "Is this a crank or is it really Edmund Wilson?" A seminar was in progress that day, and Wilson joined the group and listened attentively. Fenton, impressed by his shrewd observations, liked the idea of a man of letters who was interested in the Indians and thought he would write well about them. He promised to let Wilson know about the ceremonies at the Indian New Year. Wilson thought Fenton was "brilliant and quite free from anthropological jargon." When his book appeared, he inscribed a copy, using the French formula, "To Bill and Olive Fenton, with the distinguished sentiments of Edmund Wilson, February 10, 1960."

Wilson had gained valuable experience as a theater reviewer in the Twenties and a labor reporter in the Thirties, and used the techniques of recording entire conversations and observing performances when interviewing the Indians and watching their ceremonies. Daniel Aaron, who accompanied Wilson when he reported on the Iroquois, said he interrogated them skillfully, was a good listener and took careful notes. Reuel Wilson, who drove his father to the reservations, said the Indians thought the hawk-nosed Aaron looked like one of their tribesmen. Reuel agreed that Edmund "always knew exactly what he wanted to see and what he wanted to know. . . . He was clearly motivated by a sense of revulsion about the ongoing history of government injustice against the Indians."[8]

Fenton, a trained anthropologist, was also impressed by Wilson's surprising ability to get on with the Indians. He enchanted them with his mouse and coin tricks, rapidly established rapport and gained their confidence. Wilson had a bad case of gout and thought he might be helped by Indian medicine, and they tried to cure him with natural remedies. To Wilson, who saw things the professional anthropologists had missed, Iroquois culture was complicated, interesting and dramatic. Arthur Parker had first described the Little Water Medicine ceremony as early as 1909. But Wilson, wondering how the Indians remembered all one hundred and sixty verses of their song, saw the ritual as part of the ballad and epic traditions. He thought it expressed the "theme of near-death and resuscitation." Fenton found Wilson receptive to criticism and willing to write as many as six drafts in order to achieve clarity and accuracy. He regarded Wilson's chapter on "The Little Water Ceremony" "as one of the finest pieces in the Iroquois literature" and wrote that his book "lifted the cause of Iroquois cultural autonomy into the realm of *belles lettres* . . . generated support for the Seneca case against the U.S. Corps of Army Engineers over Kinzua [Dam and] . . . was read by President Kennedy and discussed in the White House."[9]

Sympathizing with the Indians, Wilson offered "apologies" for his own previous unawareness of the Iroquois and for the way they had been treated from Colonial times to the present. His two goals in the book were to arouse the public's conscience on their behalf and to describe their traditional life. Wilson focused on the conflict between the New York State Power Authority, who wanted to build a dam to provide more electricity for the northern part of the state, and the Tuscarora Indians, whose land would be flooded to create the dam. The Authority's chairman, Robert Moses, believed that financial compensation and the public good should override the Indians' claim to the land. The Indians, by contrast, believed they could not be compensated, since their ancestral land, along with language and customs, was an integral part of their tribal identity. They rejected the idea that any public good could justify the destruction of their way of life.

Wilson used past history to discuss this contemporary issue and moved, in an effective way, from the Indians' current struggle to preserve their culture to a demonstration that their culture was worth preserving. Unlike most outsiders, he expressed the Iroquois' point of view and consistently emphasized their identity, their values and their rights. Wilson's book, which preceded the film *Little Big Man* (1970) and Dee Brown's *Bury My Heart at Wounded Knee* (1971), influenced the contemporary shift of sympathy toward the Indians.

Apologies to the Iroquois, another collaborative book, begins with a long chapter by Joseph Mitchell, "The Mohawks in High Steel," originally published in the *New Yorker* in September 1949. Mitchell showed that the Mohawks, who have an uncanny sense of balance and an outstanding coolness when working at great heights, were employed throughout the country in the dangerous construction of high bridges and skyscrapers. By co-opting Mitchell's essay into his own book, Wilson aroused sympathetic interest in the Indians. He then described their struggle against the systematic persecution by the aptly named Power Authority and linked them to anti-colonial movements in Asia and Africa.

In this book Wilson put aside his own beliefs and prejudices, and tried to be open-minded. In doing so, he accepted and endorsed several specious arguments whenever it suited his polemical purposes. In *To the Finland Station*, Wilson wrote that Enfantin "did not have the true fanatic's capacity, the capacity of Mrs. Eddy or Joseph Smith, for deceiving himself and others." Despite his previous scepticism about the founder of Mormonism, in the "St. Regis" chapter Wilson adopted an uncritical attitude toward the mystical writings of Joseph Smith. When describing the Zuni dances in *Red, Black, Blond and Olive*, Wilson was torn between acceptance and rejection of their ceremonies, but finally decided that "it was hardly worth while for a Protestant to have stripped off the mummeries of Rome in order to fall victim to an agile young man in a ten-foot mask." Though the Fish Dance of the Senecas was much less impressive than the Shalako dance of the Zunis, Wilson —suppressing his characteristic scepticism for the sake of his argument—suggested there was deep significance in their mechanical gyrations: "They take first a few steps to the right, and then a few steps to the left—which is supposed to represent the technique of salmon making their way upstream." Even the older Indians, he reported with astonishment, got bored with the ceremonies and watched television while the Senecan Dark Dance was being performed in the next room. At the beginning of the New Year's ceremonies, a leader preached ecological harmony and chanted: "Go and live with the trees and birds and beasts and fish, and learn to honor them as your own brothers." Just afterwards, Wilson wrote, without noting the contradiction, a dog from a special white breed that represents purity was "honored" by being "ritually strangled on the day that the ceremonies began."[10]

In February 1958, soon after he began his investigation, Wilson told Roger Straus that "the Indians in that part of the world are rich enough to have hired a smart Washington lawyer, and there is a chance that they may succeed in saving their reservation." In his book Wilson optimistically reported that "on February 2, 1959, the Federal Power Commission more or less astonished everybody by ruling, in a three-to-two decision, that the Tuscaroras could not be compelled to give up any part of their reservation." Just as *To the Finland Station* ignored the failure of Russian Communism after the Bolshevik Revolution, so *Apologies to the Iroquois* did not tell the whole story. The Indians, in fact, failed to save their ancestral lands from the depredations of the New York State Power Authority. In March 1960, the month Wilson's book appeared, the Supreme Court ruled six to three against the Tuscaroras, who lost a large portion of their land. In the end, the state authorities persuaded the courts that the public benefits of the Niagara electric power projects should prevail over the rights of the Indians.

The arguments in *Apologies to the Iroquois* inspired a curious counterblast in the form of an eight-page pamphlet published by Robert Moses, the villain of Wilson's book, on June 20, 1960: *Tuscarora Fiction and Fact: A Reply to the Author of "Memoirs of Hecate County" and to His Reviewers.* Addressing Wilson as the author of a suppressed and scandalous book, and opposing Fenton's authoritative opinion, Moses argued that Wilson's "research was in fact shockingly slipshod and careless." Ignoring the Tuscaroras' point of view, he maintained that "all nine Indian families displaced by the project have been relocated . . . to dwellings superior to those they had before." Moses praised the Supreme Court, which held that "there was no treaty whatever covering the Tuscarora land needed for the power project," and quoted the majority decision that concluded: "[taking] the lands of the Tuscaroras as are needed for the Niagara project does not breach the faith of the United States." Moses ended, with a show of impartiality, by stating: "Now that we have won, we will nevertheless treat the Indians with scrupulous fairness and do everything in our power to improve their lot." Wilson retaliated with a kick at Moses in *Patriotic Gore* and linked him in his self-interview with three of his *bêtes noires* (a millionaire who bought political office, a magnate who corrupted journalism and a priest who helped suppress *Memoirs of Hecate County*) when he declared, "If New York were bombed, Nelson Rockefeller and Henry Luce and Cardinal Spellman and Robert Moses might be quickly eliminated."[11]

Those who understood the cultural issues valued Wilson's plea for decent treatment of the Indians. Bette Mele, a Senecan who recognized Wilson's work in her community, wrote that "*Apologies to the Iroquois* presented us with dignity and intelligence, as contemporary people in conflict with the value system of the dominant society." In 1965 she named her son Antonio Edmund Wilson in order to put Edmund's name on the Seneca tribal rolls. Mad Bear—who made a prominent appearance in the Tuscarora chapter, and whose dress and behavior, Wilson thought, "tended to confirm the rumor that he was homosexual"—sent him "many thanks for the wonderful article that you had in the *New Yorker*. . . . I just know that you have successfully brought our problems before thousands of people in such a way that it just cannot be misunderstood." William Sturtevant, reviewing the book for the *American Anthropologist*, called Wilson "a superb reporter" and concluded, "This is an original contribution; the information is new, and the topic has been little investigated by ethnologists."[12]

IV

In September 1960—just after his year at Harvard and in the midst of his battle with the IRS—Wilson's friend Newton Arvin, whom he had first met at Smith College in 1942, was (like the Iroquois) persecuted by oppressive authorities. Born in Valparaiso, Indiana, in 1900, Arvin had graduated from Harvard and had taught at Smith since 1922. Arvin had written enthusiastic notices of *Classics and Commercials* and *A Piece of My Mind* in the *New York Times Book Review*, and had won the National Book Award in 1951 for his biography of Melville. In his review of Arvin's book on Longfellow, Wilson said that he "has a charm of style—a curious kind of radiance, which is a personal emanation—and the ability to renew stale subjects."

Arvin, once briefly and unhappily married to a Smith student, had been through several emotional and spiritual crises, and sought comfort in religion. Gentle and charming, as well as neurotic and difficult, he had cruised for pick-ups in Springfield, but was unhappy about his secret homosexuality and had made three attempts at suicide. At the Yaddo writers' colony in the summer of 1946, Arvin met the twenty-two-year-old Truman Capote—whom Wilson called "a not unpleasant little monster, like a fetus with a big head"—and, quite improbably, became his lover. Capote's biographer describes Arvin as "bald, bespectacled, slight, shy, anemic, a victim of depression, vertigo and a score of other psychological ailments—almost a parody, in short, of the popular image of the mousy college professor."[13]

Toward the end of the Eisenhower administration the Postmaster

General, Arthur Summerfield, had initiated a campaign to stamp out smut and begun to search for pornography that was sent through the mail. After a raid on a publishing plant in Kansas City, the postal authorities discovered that Arvin had ordered photographs of naked men. On September 3 the police raided Arvin's apartment in North-ampton. They found "thousands of pornographic pictures," which he had displayed in his home and traded with three other faculty members, and charged him with being "a lewd and lascivious person." The reserved, decorous and deferential Arvin caved in under interrogation and gave the police "the names of other faculty members who had been involved in his activities." The shock and scandal, compounded by the shameful betrayal of his colleagues, propelled Arvin into a nervous breakdown, and he voluntarily committed himself to the local insane asylum, Northampton State Hospital. On September 21, after cooper-ating with the police and pleading guilty to a felony—lewdness and possession of obscene pictures—he received a suspended sentence of one year, was placed on probation for two years and fined $1,200. Though Arvin posed no danger to the students at the women's college, he was forced by Smith to retire on half-salary and ended his distin-guished career in disgrace.[14]

Remembering the recent suppression of *Memoirs of Hecate County* by the "censor morons" and his current struggle with the IRS, Wilson was enraged by the persecution of his harmless homosexual friend. His strong anti-academic feeling was reinforced by the abject cowardice of the officials at Smith, who (he felt) should have stood by Arvin instead of brutally dismissing him. The fact that the president of Smith, Tho-mas Mendenhall, was the son of his esteemed cousin Dorothy Reed made things even worse. On September 12, between Arvin's arrest and trial, Wilson naively but loyally dashed off a letter, apparently sent to the *Times* but never published, exclaiming: "I am unable to believe the charges against him which have been printed in a story in the *New York Times* and which sound like a fantasy of the local police distorted by an incompetent reporter."

Two months later he tried to comfort the despondent Arvin by insisting, "the way you were treated was gratuitously insulting and outrageous." Wilson thought that the unfortunate episode might in the long run prove stimulating and emphasized that it would not detract in any way from Arvin's literary reputation. He offered to help him place his work in American and English magazines, and furiously concluded, "Goddam all this interference with people's personal affairs! I had to submit to a [tax] interrogatory covering my whole life." Arvin replied that "it has been a pretty grueling experience. . . . I feel very much as if I had been involved in a violently destructive automobile accident that had no intelligible meaning, only a shattering one."[15]

V

In his diary for 1961 Wilson mentioned his yearning for attractive women: Mary Meigs, Frances Swisher, Suzanne Hughes as well as three very recent interests: Elaine May, Clelia Carroll and Mary Pcolar. All these women were born between 1928 and 1932, and were younger than Rosalind. But, he cautiously added, "I am too sexually fond of Elena to try to start a new love affair; and I am also, I suppose, too old: I could not be attractive to younger women and should only make myself ridiculous." For all his misgivings, Wilson *did* try to start new liaisons; despite old age and the danger of looking foolish, he actually had two love affairs in his late seventies.

Elaine May wrote and acted in a successful comic and satiric show with her partner Mike Nichols. Wilson first heard their records, then saw their Broadway show several times and finally went backstage to meet them. "They are extremely interesting young people," he told Mary McCarthy, "he immensely intelligent, she something of a genius." Emphasizing his age and vulnerability in order to rein in his feelings, Wilson recorded: "She is extremely handsome, with powerful black eyes—probably passionate and strong-willed. . . . It is a good thing I am too old to fall in love with her. I've always been such easy game for beautiful, gifted women and she is the most so I've seen since Mary McCarthy in the Thirties. I imagine that she, too, would be rough going."[16]

If Elaine May followed the passionate theatrical tradition of Edna Millay, Clelia Carroll, who came from a wealthy and distinguished family, belonged to the same well-bred background as Mary Meigs. A beautiful and enthusiastic socialite, she was married to a descendant of Charles Carroll of Carrollton, Maryland, who had signed the Declaration of Independence, and lived on an estate outside Baltimore. Clelia was co-editor, with the artist Edward Gorey, of the Looking Glass Library of children's books, and Wilson saw her socially through Jason Epstein, their publisher. Wilson told Clelia that her chatty, flattering letters were "always vibrant and interesting"; and emphasized their similarity by co-opting her, like the Edna Millay figure in "Ellen Terhune" who moves backward in time, into his own tradition and culture: "I've always thought ... that you were like a girl of my own generation who had somehow turned up in a later one, and I found that your parents were much like the parents of my friends of my own generation." When he learned that Clelia had an Italian strain in her family, he understood why she had been given the name of the heroine of Stendhal's *The Charterhouse of Parma* and was able to understand her "peculiar kind of attractiveness." A few years later, however, when his romantic feelings had subsided, he was struck by her cold eyes and sharp nose.

Wilson's late interest in Hungarian led to a more serious involvement with a very different kind of woman, Mary Pcolar, in upstate New York. Though Wilson was preeminently a critic, he always wanted to be considered an imaginative writer. In 1959, when Péter Nagy wanted to translate Wilson's work into Hungarian but could not publish his "ideologically charged" essays under the Communist regime, he fixed on two of Wilson's weaker plays of the 1930s: *Beppo and Beth* and *This Room and This Gin and These Sandwiches,* which were never produced, in Hungary or any other country.

Always fascinated by foreign languages, Wilson had studied Russian when he was forty, learned Hebrew in his late fifties and took up Hungarian in his mid-sixties. After reading George Borrow's *Wild Wales* during the last year of his life, he studied Glyn Morris' Welsh dictionary and grammars. Enchanted by an exhibition of Chinese calligraphy, he regretted that he was too old to fulfill his long-standing ambition to learn Chinese. During the last year of his life, like Marx, Wilson studied Old Church Slavonic. Announcing to Mary Meigs in August 1960 that he had taken up the study of Hungarian—a difficult Altaic tongue, unrelated to the Indo-European languages—Wilson wrote: "In the volume [of plays], the translator explains that they know nothing of my other work in Hungary, but that I am obviously a first-rate dramatist. I was so pleased with this that I think of starting soon for Budapest."[17] Though he did not reach Budapest until April 1964, he got into contact with the Hungarians near Talcottville and with Mary Pcolar. She became his tutor, typist, secretary, driver, companion and amorous substitute for the absent Elena.

Born near Talcottville, the daughter of Hungarian immigrant farmers, Mary—a respectable later model of the Ukrainian Frances —was married to George Pcolar, a Slovak steel worker, and had three teenaged children. Mary, then working in a Boonville drugstore, first knew Wilson as "the rude old man who kept coming into Kramer's and demanding the *New York Times*, which he believed, by some act of God, was being put aside for him." She had heard that he might be "a dangerous character," who had a cellar filled with wine and had been married four times, and was wary of Wilson until she realized he was a famous and important figure.

In *Upstate* and in letters to Celia Paget Goodman, Wilson (who always liked to write to one woman about another) praised Mary's blond hair, extraordinary complexion and exotic looks: "She is a very handsome girl in whom the Mongolian stock is evident: high cheek-bones, slightly slanting gray eyes, set rather wide apart, a figure erect and well built." Mary Crosten, speaking more objectively, remembered her as a pleasant and good-looking woman, who wore pink store uniforms, had a "put-on sweetness" and was overwhelmed by her association with Wilson.

Wilson was also impressed by Mary's talents, energy and ambition. An able seamstress and carpenter, she also wrote poetry, painted pictures, delivered babies during snowstorms—and was even a champion bowler. After she left Kramer's, Mary sold surgical appliances, held conversation classes for women and ran a "charm school," where she taught teenagers the correct way to drink from a water fountain. Though Wilson had said, "I almost never go to the movies," he began to go to all the mediocre films in Rome and Utica in order to spend more time with Mary. When he mentioned Oscar Wilde, whom she had never heard of, Mary thought he was referring to the actor Cornel Wilde, whom he had never heard of. When asked if her husband ever complained about his friendship with Mary, Wilson replied: "She's had him lashed to the mast years ago." "My Hungarian superwoman still calls to console my solitude," he told Clelia Carroll. "Having long ago tamed her husband, she now has got her boss muffled."[18]

Mary—whom Elena bitterly called "the Madame Bovary of Boon-ville"—had a tremendous desire to improve herself, transcend her humble origins and succeed in the world. "She wants something more," her mother told Wilson, "but she can't reach it." Never able to mold his children as he had wanted to, Wilson began to form the more receptive and pliable Mary. Flattered by the attention of an attractive young woman who "saw him as a celebrity and went after him," he opened a new world for her, offered much more than her husband could give and enabled her to achieve her ambitions. He helped send

Mary through Utica College and paid for her trip to Hungary in the summer of 1970. When Wilson received the National Medal for Literature in Utica in June 1966, Mary took pictures of the celebrities and got into the photographs with Wilson. Jealous of her upstate rival, Elena reproached Wilson for taking more interest in Mary than in his own daughters.

Wilson's letters to Mary (which were saved and later sold to Yale) are characteristically unromantic. He wrote about his daily life and frequent travels, offered paternal advice about her studies and career, and discussed—sometimes in schoolboy Hungarian—their common interest in Magyar language and culture. On Valentine's Day, always for Wilson a special occasion, he expressed his feelings more openly. In February 1966 he sent a flowery valentine with a pasted-in photo of an ice-cream concoction and an equally saccharine message: "I should like to eat you some day / Because you are a great big sundae." Three years later, when he was nearly seventy-four, the message, though playful, was more serious: "Ödön Bácsi [Uncle Edmund]'s old and dark / But his heart still has a spark."

The spark was finally ignited in September 1969 when Wilson, no longer able to contain himself, made his first sexual overtures. "I found out what her personality was like when she was excited and being made love to: 'U-n-n-no!—It would make me feel guilty. . . .' When I told her that I wanted to see the rest of her body, she said with conscious humor: 'I'm perfectly beautiful, but no.' I took out my cock, and she felt it." When he kissed Mary and grappled with her armored underwear, she whispered: "I want to, but I won't. . . . I'm afraid you'd have a heart attack."

Though grateful for Wilson's assistance and sentimental about their friendship, genuinely fond of the distinguished old man and willing to grant a few sexual favors, Mary resisted his attempts to seduce her and preferred platonic relations. In the fall of 1971, after she had achieved minor fame through her appearance in *Upstate*, Mary rapturously wrote: "How can I thank you for all you've done for me? I have known the world's greatest man and only gradually have I learned how great. . . . Remember that you are dearly loved by me and many others. . . . [I can only] say 'thanks' to someone who has immortalized me in print. . . . *We* have bridged the generation gap and the sex barriers were not involved. It's love in the purest sense."

Elena's likening Mary Pcolar to Emma Bovary was tragically accurate. During an upstate winter in the 1970s, her car skidded off the road. She broke three ribs, her face was badly disfigured and she nearly died. Her close friendship with Wilson inevitably made her dissatisfied with the constrictions of her marriage, and she eventually divorced her husband and left her children. She remarried and moved to a trailer in Florida, and in 1982 was burned to death, with her new husband, when their can of kerosene exploded.[19]

VI

In December 1961, a few months after Mary began to teach Wilson Hungarian, he published his third and final book of poetry, *Night Thoughts*. The title came from Edward Young's "graveyard school" poem of 1745. Wilson included his two previous books, *Poets, Farewell!* and *Notebooks of Night*, and added twenty-five satiric and humorous poems from pamphlets he had privately printed between 1950 and 1955. Wilson satirized the Catholic Church in two poems with many topical allusions: "The Mass in the Parking Lot" and "Cardinal Merry de Val" (the cardinal had been Secretary of the Holy Office between 1914 and his death in 1930). The best poems in the book were the parody of MacLeish (1939), the elegy on Fitzgerald (1942) and the love poem to Elena, "The White Sand" (1950).

Four months later Wilson's longest and most ambitious book, the 800-page *Patriotic Gore: Studies in the Literature of the American Civil War*, which he had been working on since 1946, was finally published by Oxford University Press. During his long years of research, which ended in the Harvard library, Wilson—despite his disdain for the academic world—had corresponded with and met many scholarly specialists on minor American writers. He also had fruitful discussions with friends who were interested in that period: Tate, Edel, Schlesinger and Lowell as well as Faulkner and Robert Penn Warren. When Robert Linscott, Faulkner's editor at Random House, introduced them in March 1953, the two writers naturally discussed George Washington Cable, Southern generals and Civil War literature. Wilson also liked the gentle and charming Warren, and thought he had one of the best minds of his generation. Warren later recalled that when they occasionally met at parties, Wilson would come up to him and say: "Red, let's go and sit in the corner and talk about the Civil War."

The Shock of Recognition (1943) had provided a remarkably clear picture of American thought in the nineteenth century. But it had dealt with major American writers and excluded minor figures between the Revolution and the time of Henry James. Wilson now filled in the gap, as he wrote in his Introduction, by analyzing the "speeches and pamphlets, private letters and diaries, personal memoirs and journalistic reports . . . [of] some thirty men and women who lived through the Civil War, either playing some special role in connection with it or experiencing its impact in some interesting way." In *To the Finland Station* he treated historical writing as literature; in *Patriotic Gore* he treated literature as history and offered a penetrating picture of the streams of American history that flowed into the Civil War. In April 1961, the year before the book appeared, Wilson told Sheldon Meyer, his editor at Oxford, about its vast scope: "I want to show the *whole career* of all my major subjects, how they lived, what they thought about and what their personalities were. . . . My themes [are] the corruption of the post-war period (Grant's later career), the psychology of the men committed to war (the Shermans)."

Wilson's eyes held up during the fifteen-year gestation period, though he wore old-fashioned, metal-rimmed glasses for reading. But as he reached the homestretch in the spring of 1961 he developed a strange occupational ailment: "a nose and throat infection from reading old books and bound periodicals that give out clouds of dust." Paul Roazen, then a student at Harvard, remembered that Wilson seemed to wheeze every time he turned a page in a book.[20]

In *Patriotic Gore* Wilson tried to rescue many inferior writers from well-deserved neglect. As he wrote from personal experience about Van Wyck Brooks' account of a third-rate romance: his hollow words cannot disguise the fact that these books "are quite unreadable for anyone who is not under a scholar's obligation to allow himself to be steadily bored." Having to plow through so many mediocre works made him receptive to distractions and frequently delayed the progress of his *magnum opus*. Using a Homeric allusion, Wilson told Lowell that the book, which had devoured years of his life, was getting out of control: "I keep adding more and more people and things and am now having difficulty to prevent the book's bursting at the seams. . . . My Civil War book has become a Penelope's web—longest and most complicated thing I've ever attempted." After he had finally finished it, he confessed to Daniel Aaron: "I had the book around so long that I finally got bored and depressed by it." One reviewer shrewdly noted: "one gets the impression that Wilson *enjoys* plodding through notably boring and long-winded material just to be able to show that he has done it."

Readers were grateful that Wilson had gone through these books so that no one else would ever have to do so.

Covering a vast amount of material caused difficulties for both Wilson and his audience. He deliberately gave very little space to Melville's war poetry and Whitman's *Specimen Days* and, since Crane had no direct experience in battle, excluded the best novel about the Civil War, *The Red Badge of Courage*. Since most of the admittedly dull books he considered had never been read by anyone but academic specialists—the only fairly well known works were *Uncle Tom's Cabin* and some stories by Ambrose Bierce—Wilson had to provide long and sometimes quite deadly descriptive summaries in order to make his points intelligible.

Though Farrar, Straus had been Wilson's American publishers since 1950, he had signed the contract for *Patriotic Gore*—after the *débâcle* of *Memoirs of Hecate County* and when he was drifting between publishers—with Oxford University Press. Wilson's sales figures, except for his scandalous stories, had never been impressive, but he demanded and received a $2,000 advance and a straight fifteen percent royalty for *Patriotic Gore*. Oxford also republished two earlier collections of his essays: *The Wound and the Bow* in 1947 and *The Triple Thinkers* in 1963. In October 1958 an exasperated editor at Oxford, referring to the long-awaited *Patriotic Gore*, declared: "two thousand dollars in advance royalties were paid eleven years ago for a book eight years overdue and for which we do not even have now a firm delivery date."[21] Wilson, like many authors, had to promise a book in order to get money; then, as it expanded into a massive project, was unable to meet the deadline. But, unlike numerous academics with long-standing Oxford contracts, Wilson finally *did* complete his magisterial and well-executed work.

Wilson preferred to deal with the head of the Press, the Englishman John Brett-Smith, but was actually edited by a younger man, Sheldon Meyer. When Meyer told Wilson that he was descended from the Puritan Jonathan Edwards, he irritably replied: "Do you know that his grave is in a shocking condition?" Wilson had been Meyer's personal literary hero ever since the editor had written his Princeton senior thesis on American Left-wing intellectuals in the 1930s. Wilson, he felt, was almost the only Leftist literary figure who had emerged from that period "with his integrity and dignity intact." He thought Wilson was "the most important figure Oxford had ever published in the United States."

Meyer found his hero quite disappointing in person. Wilson considered Farrar, Straus his true publishers and his old contractual connection with Oxford an inconvenience. Meyer thought he was a "self-absorbed individual with virtually no small talk and no interest in anyone (especially his editor) unless he had some information he needed." When Wilson finally handed in *Patriotic Gore*, he spoke in "lugubrious terms about the manuscript and said he was sick and tired of the book." He admitted that several chapters were rather lumpy, that there were some *longueurs* of quotation and that the book would be much more readable if he deleted the discussion of unimportant works. "He knew it needed to be cut," Meyer recalled, "but didn't have the inclination or energy to do it. He then made a fervent appeal to me for help. Would I do the cutting of the manuscript for him?"

Imagining himself as a young Max Perkins who would achieve literary glory by editing Edmund Wilson, Meyer carefully cut two hundred pages and returned the manuscript. A few days later, "in the furious voice that Wilson characteristically used, he phoned me and roared, 'Meyer, you've ruined me. Put back in everything you've taken out. The book is fine the way it is." Wilson later called Oxford University Press "the worst-organized and most irritating publishing house that I have ever done business with."[22]

Meyer, too, found Wilson difficult to deal with. Though he always questioned the royalty statements, he was sometimes right about them. For all his complaints, Wilson actually did quite well with Oxford. In addition to his spectacular success with *The Scrolls from the Dead Sea*, *Red, Black, Blond and Olive* sold 6,126 copies and *Patriotic Gore* sold 12,732. Even the reprints went briskly: *The Wound and the Bow* (which had three printings) sold 11,632 copies, *The Triple Thinkers* sold 10,467. Six months after the publication of *Red, Black, Blond and Olive*, copies returned to the publisher by the bookstores had surpassed sales, leaving a depressing debit of $345. But by late 1962 *Patriotic Gore* and his other Oxford books had earned Wilson a substantial $8,677; and in 1967 he received from Oxford an additional $3,000 against fifteen percent royalties for the enlarged second edition of *The Scrolls from the Dead Sea, 1947–1969*. In January 1954 Wilson had signed a contract for the English edition of *Patriotic Gore* with a small publisher, Derek Verschoyle. When Verschoyle folded, André Deutsch took over the contract. In January 1963 Deutsch published an edition of 1,500, but there was little interest in this subject in England and only about 1,000 copies were sold.

The twenty-four-page Introduction—which Arthur Schlesinger, Jr., Stuart Hughes and Daniel Aaron advised Wilson to cut—was the most controversial part of the book. When writing about Michelet in *To the Finland Station* (1940), Wilson, emphasizing the relation of men to animals, had declared: "the doings of human beings begin to seem to have more and more in common with the doings of insects and birds"; when writing about Steinbeck in *The Boys in the Back Room* (1941), Wilson had mentioned his tendency "to present human life in animal terms." In a similar, Darwinian fashion, he wrote in the final chapter of *Europe Without Baedeker* (1947) that humanity "has been demonstrating its closeness to the brute and making its pretentions to divine origin ridiculous." In *Patriotic Gore* he repeated his analogy of the 1940s even more forcefully and placed man lower down on the phylogenic scale. Rejecting all idealistic motives, and equating the North's opposition to the South in the Civil War with America's confrontation of Russia in the Cold War, Wilson portrayed the United States as a cruel devourer, driven by blind lust for power and heading in the same direction as the European dictatorships: "our panicky pugnacity as we challenge [the Soviet Union] is not virtue but at bottom the irrational instinct of an active power organism in the presence of another such organism, of a sea slug of vigorous voracity in the presence of another sea slug."

Repeating the arguments of the 1957 Postscript to *The American Earthquake* and *Apologies to the Iroquois*, and anticipating those of *The Cold War and the Income Tax*, Wilson attacked America's treatment of the Indians, its participation in World War Two, its saturation bombing of civilians in German cities, its frantic industrializing, its extortion of staggering taxes for nuclear weapons, its surveillance of citizens "by an extensive secret police" and its misguided hostility to Fidel Castro. He warned—six months before the Cuban missile crisis—that we were heading "for a blind collision with the Soviet Union."[23]

Worst of all, from the viewpoint of the patriotic reader, was Wilson's witty crack about Carl Sandburg's biography: "the cruellest thing that has happened to Lincoln since he was shot by Booth," and his equation of the revered Lincoln with two European tyrants: Bismarck and Lenin. Wilson shocked people, who expected the usual Sandburgian panegyric about Lincoln, by declaring: "Each of these [three] men, through the pressure of the power which he found himself exercising, became an uncompromising dictator, and each was succeeded by agencies which continued to exercise this power and to manipulate the peoples he had been unifying in a stupid, despotic and unscrupulous fashion." The Introduction—a strategic error which alienated readers before they began to read the main part of the book—had the honor of being denounced in editorials in *Life* and *American Heritage*. The latter also rejected Daniel Aaron's favorable review of the book, explaining that "if they printed it, they would be taking the bread out of their mouths."

Patriotic Gore, like most of Wilson's late polemical books, was extremely timely. It appeared during the centenary commemorations of the Civil War and in the midst of the Civil Rights movement. Wilson touched deep emotions when he wrote that the novelist George Cable's "campaign for Negro civil rights and study of the Negro problem which was unique in Cable's own era is of special interest today." But Wilson's portrayal of Lincoln angered the North as much as his progressive views on civil rights offended the South. He maintained that Lee had always disapproved of slavery and quoted Lincoln's surprising statement in his debate with Douglas: "I have no purpose to introduce political and social equality between the white and black races. There is a physical difference between the two, which, in my judgment, will probably forever forbid their living together on the footing of perfect equality." Strongly sympathetic to the South—the striking anti-war title of the book came from a Confederate song—Wilson argues that it would "have been a good deal less disastrous if the South had been allowed to secede."[24]

The sometimes sluggish book gains considerable momentum when Wilson, using his own experience in war, dramatically describes actual battles in the brilliant sections on Grant, Sherman and the guerrilla leader John Mosby—the T. E. Lawrence of the Civil War. Mosby is "a will-o'-the-wisp, a lurking and mocking spirit, an unseizable force [?source] of frustration." Sherman, in Brady's horrendous photograph, "would not relax his fierce and obdurate frown or subdue the almost animal hackles of his fiery red hair and beard." Wilson effectively concludes the chapter on Grant with a periodic sentence of some 170 words that convincingly synthesizes his whole career.

Wilson offers concise and convincing judgments on the poetry of Sidney Lanier, who is sensitive and commands our admiration, though he "is limited, sometimes a little stupid"; on G. W. Harris' novel, *Sut Lovingood*, "by far the most repellent book of any real literary merit in American literature"; on Kate Chopin, whom Wilson had introduced to American readers and whose novel *The Awakening* "anticipates D. H. Lawrence in its treatment of infidelity"; and on Ambrose Bierce, who "lacks the tragic dimension; he was unable to surmount his frustration, his contempt for himself and mankind, through work of the stature of Swift's."

The concluding chapter on Justice Holmes—who "stands alone as one who was never corrupted, never discouraged or broken, by the alien conditions that the war had prepared"—is a covert self-portrait and the most powerful part of the book. The vitally important theme of *Patriotic Gore*, and of most of Wilson's late books, concerns "the exercise of power, of the backing up of power by force, the issue of the government, the organization, as against the individual. . . . The issue presses hard on our time. There are moments when one may wonder today . . . [whether] the cause of the South is the cause of us all."[25]

Robert Lowell, who shared Wilson's sympathy for the South, was one of the first to read the completed typescript. In March 1961 he alluded to Wilson's fine chapters on men like Lincoln and Holmes, and sent a heartening response: "One might use this phrase: *moral aristocrats* for them. By this I mean some queer tense twist of principle, changed to virtue by having been lived through the undefinable multiplicity of experience. . . . Let me salute you, dear old fellow-questioning Calvinist, on your triumphant book." Defining Wilson's strengths as a writer in the *New Republic*, Leon Edel had credited him with "an intelligent, critical mind, luminescent, curious, cosmopolitan in range yet on occasion parochial in attitude, unceasing in inquiry, tireless in speculation." The leading reviews recognized Wilson's achievement, and agreed with the judgments of Lowell and Edel. C. Vann Woodward, a prominent American historian, wrote in the *American Scholar* that "no single work goes deeper into the meaning and implications of the Civil War experience for its more articulate participants."[26]

Unlike most critics, the Kentucky-born Robert Penn Warren praised the contentious Introduction: "Dramatically, it is a splendid way to begin the book—to throw the reader back on his heels, to make him come gasping for breath to the story of Americans of the past trying to find and justify their roles in a great crisis." The English critic George Steiner welcomed the attacks on American aggression and convincingly placed the book in the context of Wilson's thought. It expressed, Steiner observed, "the disillusion of a populist radical, the outrage felt by the champion of the decimated Iroquois, the scorn of a Tory anarchist and aristocrat of the mind for the rainbow slogans of American foreign policy."

Despite the overwhelming praise, Wilson inevitably felt let down when the book was finally published in April 1962. In the middle of that month, in the middle of the night, he had a physical and mental crisis that recalled his nervous breakdown after completing *I Thought of Daisy* in 1929. At 2 A.M. Monroe Engel, who lived opposite Wilson, heard through his open window "a series of wordless bellows that the common forms of anger couldn't account for. This wasn't simply anger, it was rage." "I had a paroxysm of exasperation with Elena," Wilson wrote, "combined with an acute heart attack and smashed her filing cabinet, her typewriter and something else made of glass. She was frightened and called Monroe Engel, who got me a doctor"—and a sedative that put Wilson to sleep. Elena told Engel that "Edmund had been in pain for some hours; that in the course of the evening he'd had quite a lot to drink, which hadn't helped."[27] The long Cambridge winter, the emotional strain of his tax problems, his physical ailments (heart, teeth, gout) and his attempts to drink himself out of depression, which made his black mood worse, had led to a sudden explosion, with Elena the victim of his rage.

TWENTY-ONE ❖

Europe and Wesleyan, 1963–1965

I

As Wilson entered his seventh decade, he was increasingly alienated and increasingly honored. His career, instead of declining with old age, actually peaked toward the end of his life. Like Oliver Wendell Holmes, Wilson was now an intellectual touchstone and cultural icon who exposed the threats to freedom in American life. He was certainly thinking of his own career when he paid eloquent tribute to Holmes in *Patriotic Gore:*

> The old Justice begins to appear—as he has never in his life done before—in the light of an established sage, a god of the national pantheon. His books are reprinted and read; his minor papers collected and published. . . . In the reaction against the gentility, the timidity, the sentimentality of American cultural life, he is seen to have been a humanist, a realist, a bold and independent thinker, who has required of himself from the first to meet the highest intellectual standards and who has even, with little public encouragement, succeeded in training himself to become also a distinguished writer.

Wilson did not set out to win honors and (as his "Edmund Wilson Regrets" card indicated) never participated in self-promoting extramural activities. Like Henry James, he maintained his integrity and "lived retired, never making any bid for publicity." When Wilson heard that Eliot had turned up for the Nobel Prize with the Order of Merit around his neck, he expressed strong disapproval. He adopted a consistently ironic attitude toward his own honors, and accepted them with a fine discrimination. They began to accumulate on his sixtieth birthday; and once he got on the honors circuit, the awards and medals kept pouring in. He was given the Gold Medal of the American Acad-

414

emy in 1955, an honorary degree from Princeton in 1956, the Presidential Medal of Freedom in 1963, the Edward MacDowell Medal in 1964, the Emerson-Thoreau Medal and the National Medal for Literature in 1966, the Aspen Award in 1968 and the Golden Eagle Award in 1971. Wilson wrote first-rate books until the very end, but his energy and self-confidence began to wane in the mid-1960s, when he would sit on the toilet and read old reviews of his books in order to raise his morale. Though he was wary of the honors that came his way, they bucked up his ego and encouraged him to continue his work during periods of depression and poor health.

Wilson managed, at the same time, to belong to the literary establishment and remain apart from it. He agreed with Flaubert, who had asked, when Renan was elected to the French Academy, "When one is *someone*, why should one want to be *something?*" Like Groucho Marx, he refused to belong to any club that would have him as a member. He accepted the Gold Medal from the American Academy of Arts and Letters on May 25, 1955. But he refused to make a speech at the ceremony just as he had refused to be a member of that organization, which included mediocrities like Henry Seidel Canby and Archibald MacLeish, when they elected him in the 1940s. "I can't see that [the Academy] serves any good purpose," he told Van Wyck Brooks in 1957, "except for its handouts to writers and artists—and I don't want to have to lobby and vote about them. Still less do I want to have to worry about who is or is not admitted." "Not to have been a member," he caustically added, "is the only distinction in my life that I can be sure of."[1]

Wilson refused honorary degrees from UCLA and from Harvard, and told Stanley Dell that he did not plan to attend his fortieth class reunion at Princeton. But he still felt loyalty to his old teacher and his old university, and on June 12, 1956, three years after lecturing at the Gauss Seminars, he accepted an honorary Doctor of Letters degree. Alluding to the dedication of *Axel's Castle*, the citation read: "Freely acknowledging his debt to such great teachers as Christian Gauss, he has himself gone over from their precepts to become, through the immense range of his interests and by his power of expression on the printed page, a great teacher in his own right."

Wilson's most prestigious award, the Presidential Medal of Freedom, had an interesting history. He had voted for the Democratic presidential candidates since 1952 and really loathed the Republicans. Nixon, he thought, was "dumber than Harding, except Harding knew he was dumb" and Goldwater, about whom he had quarreled with Dos Passos, was "surely one of the biggest asses in our asinine country." When Arthur Schlesinger, Jr. left Harvard to become Special Assistant to President Kennedy, Wilson suddenly acquired great prestige in the White House. He was invited to Kennedy's inauguration in January 1961, but refused to go. Having attended two previous inaugurations, he knew how boring they were and was very glad to have missed Robert Frost read his "terrible poem," "The Gift Outright."

Though Wilson admired Kennedy, he was critical of his belligerent foreign policy. The FBI, keeping a watchful eye, noted that Wilson, along with many distinguished members of the Harvard faculty, had signed "An Open Letter to President Kennedy" in the *New York Times* of May 10, 1961, protesting United States' policy toward Cuba and advising him to "reverse the present drift towards American military intervention." In 1965 and again in 1966, Wilson signed a "Writers' and Artists' Protest" against the continuation of the American war in Vietnam.

At the request of his old friend André Malraux, De Gaulle's Minister of Culture and guest of honor at a state banquet, Wilson was invited to dinner at the White House on May 11, 1962. The one hundred sixty-eight guests at the "big cultural blow-out" included Tate, Warren, Thornton Wilder, Saul Bellow and Robert Lowell. After dinner Kennedy made his famous remark that "there were more brains assembled that evening in the dining room of the White House than [at] any time since Thomas Jefferson dined alone." The President had read *Apologies to the Iroquois* and made a point of asking Wilson about the recently published *Patriotic Gore*. In his diplomatic speech, Malraux said that the United States had "never been oriented toward conquest," which prompted Wilson to whisper irascibly to Malraux's wife: "Tell him that I don't believe it."

Both Bellow and Lowell were impressed by Wilson's Holmesian honesty on this state occasion. Bellow "was deeply amused at the White House by the presence of Wilson who had had a tax problem, by Charles Lindbergh who had been a Nazi sympathizer and by Irwin Shaw who had established residence abroad in order to avoid taxes." He wrote ironically that "it would be a pity to waste Mr. Wilson's fine old rumblings on a lousy republic and that his eccentricities deserved at least an imperial setting." Lowell also praised his frankness: "I meant to write you a little fan note after Washington. Except for you, every one there seemed addled with adulation at having been invited. . . . I thought, of all the big names there, only you acted like yourself."[2]

During the White House dinner Wilson consulted Schlesinger about his tax problems. Kennedy, hearing from Schlesinger about Wilson's plight, instructed the IRS to arrange a settlement and conclude the case. "It was only through President Kennedy's intervention," Wilson informed Glyn Morris, "that the matter was settled as favorably as it turned out to be."

He once told Tom Matthews that Fitzgerald had said, "when the revolution came, [Wilson] should inevitably be made Secretary of State." In November 1962, while his tax case was pending and his financial affairs in disarray, Wilson still seemed destined for high office. As he jokingly told an academic friend, Cecil Lang: "I do seem to be popular with the Kennedys. Bobby reads me, and Jack read me and insisted on my being given one of those freedom medals, though they tried to fob off Archie MacLeish on him. I saw Arthur Schlesinger yesterday and told him that you expected me to be Secretary of State in the next Kennedy cabinet. He said he had been thinking of me rather for Secretary of the Treasury."

Schlesinger, now a powerful government official, had great admiration for Wilson. "One feels in him above all," he wrote in his review of *The American Earthquake*, "a sense of old-fashioned American rootedness, of an organic relationship with the American past, of a deep-running belief in national dignity and a national identity." He conveyed his admiration to Kennedy and proposed Wilson for the Presidential Medal. As Schlesinger explained in *A Thousand Days*, the Medal was to honor "those whose talent enlarges the public vision of the dignity with which life can be graced and the fullness with which it can be lived."[3]

Informed of the impending award and sensing there might be trouble, Wilson honorably told Schlesinger that Kennedy ought to read his fiery Introduction to *Patriotic Gore*, and warned him that he was currently writing an attack on the income tax and defense budget. The IRS, learning of the proposed award, expressed strong opposition in a sixteen-page memorandum. In Congress, Senator Milward Simpson of Wyoming agreed with the tax authorities and asked: "What justification exists for honoring by a Presidential Freedom Medal a man of Edmund Wilson's philosophy and temperament?" But Kennedy, who had accepted Schlesinger's recommendation and personally added Wilson's name to the list, stood firm. Advised of Wilson's tax troubles and radical politics, he declared: "This is not an award for good conduct but for literary merit." On July 1, 1963 Kennedy confirmed in a telegram to Wilson: "I am happy to inform you of my intention to award you on July 4th the Presidential Medal of Freedom. This is the highest civilian honor conferred by the President of the United States for service in peacetime." The less illustrious winners that year included Thornton Wilder and the *New Yorker* writer E. B. White.

Wilson wrote Kennedy that he would be in Europe and could not attend the ceremony on December 3, 1963. After the President was assassinated in November, Wilson told Robert Kennedy, "I very much appreciate receiving the medal, and all the more because I understand it was given at the insistence of the late President." On March 6, 1964 Charles Bohlen, the American Ambassador to France, wrote Wilson that President Lyndon Johnson had asked him to present the Medal as "recognition for the invaluable contributions you have made to the literary arts."[4] Wilson, who disliked Johnson, also managed to evade the second ceremony by replying that he was about to leave for Rome and would not be in Paris on April 2, the date proposed by Bohlen. Ignoring the gravity of the occasion, he added, "I suggest you simply send it to me."

On August 16, 1964 Wilson was awarded the Edward MacDowell Medal, named in honor of the American composer, for his outstanding contribution to literature. When he accepted the medal at the Mac-Dowell Colony in Peterborough, New Hampshire, Wilson alarmed the chairman by rolling it between his palms as if to conjure it out of existence. He tried not to take his honors too seriously, and replied to Alfred Kazin's introductory talk by saying: "I was a little nervous for fear he would get to the point, which sometimes happens, that he would wake up some morning and decide I was an old fraud. I am very glad he got through today without revulsion of feeling." After the ceremony Wilson, like a trapped animal, whispered to Richard Pipes, "Let's get out of here," and they fled to Pipes' nearby country house.

On June 14, 1965, as America became more deeply enmeshed in the disastrous war in Vietnam, President Johnson tried to court the literati and improve his image with an ill-fated White House Festival of the Arts. The by-now-familiar cultural representatives were to include, in addition to Wilson, E. B. White, Mark Van Doren, John Hersey, Saul Bellow, Robert Lowell and, to lamely represent the ladies, Phyllis McGinley and Catherine Drinker Bowen. Lowell, who would man the barricades in 1967, expressed Wilson's feelings as well as his own when he wrote, in a letter to Johnson that was published on the front page of the *New York Times*, that he was "conscience-bound" to refuse the invitation: I "can only follow our present foreign policy with the greatest dismay and distrust. . . . We are in danger of imperceptibly becoming an explosive and suddenly chauvinistic nation, and may even be drifting on our way to the last nuclear ruin." Johnson's advisors had never read *The Cold War and the Income Tax.* They were shocked—and Johnson quite furious—when Wilson refused the invitation, as Eric Goldman wrote, "with a brusqueness that I have never experienced before or after in the case of an invitation in the name of the President and First Lady."[5]

II

Though honored in public, in private Wilson was troubled. As he grew older and his health deteriorated, he became more and more irascible, and sometimes put an intolerable strain on his family. The Christmas holiday, which made him depressed and bad-tempered, was always a poisonous time. Elena, for the sake of their teenaged daughter, tried to make the best of things and maintained a jolly Germanic schedule: 8 to 9: breakfast and unpacking the stockings; 11 to 12: champagne and distribution of presents under the tree; 5 to 9: dinner, to which (Edmund regretted) their boring old friends were invited. Parodying the Victorian devotion to the Bible, he claimed that every Christmas he read aloud to the family Pauline Réage's *Histoire d'O* (1954), a pornographic novel about female masochism and bondage.

Wilson occasionally enlivened the holidays by getting Thomas Todd of Boston to print on good quality paper about two hundred copies of ten- to twenty-page booklets. They contained mostly humorous verse sprinkled, like plums in a pudding, with many foreign words and exotic alphabets, attenuated drawings and fanciful forms. *The White Sand* (1950), *Three Reliques of Ancient Western Poetry* (1951), *Wilson's Christmas Stocking* (1953) and *A Christmas Delirium* (1955) were included in *Night Thoughts* (1961), and contained some amusing couplets on American expatriates:

> Said Lieutenant Henry to Henry James
> "They tell me you're not very hot with the dames."

> Said Rudolph Steinach to Gertrude Stein,
> "As a glandular freak you're all very fine."

After a hiatus of eleven years Wilson's friends were again pleased to receive his *Holiday Greetings* of 1966, which included illustrated limericks, poems on Italian and Hungarian themes, a set of puzzle clues that produced "fabulous word squares" and in "Homecoming" a satiric blast against the things he hated in the modern world: Texas chauvinism, sex talk, oppression of blacks, deadbeat beatniks, crude advertising, boring television and mindless bureaucracy. The five dark poems in Wilson's last and best pamphlet, *Holiday Greetings and Desolating Lyrics* (1970), express the mournfulness of old age and impending death: gloomy verses on Talcottville, "The Boston and Cambridge Blues," "On Excavating My Library" (a depressing companion to "Thoughts on Being Bibliographed," 1944), "Tristes Tropiques" (a satire on Jamaica, with a title borrowed from Lévi-Strauss) and "By Dark Cocytus' Shore," a tale in Poesque rhythm of frustrated love.

During his last decade Wilson could be rude to strangers as well as harsh and domineering with his family. Interrupted by a visitor in Talcottville, he exclaimed: "Since you admire my work so much, why don't you go away and let me get on with it?" When an obscure Polish critic lamented to Wilson that no one in America seemed to know who he was, Wilson asked, "But who *are* you?" Friends agreed that the willful, spoiled, only child knew what he wanted and wanted it right away. When he went too far, Elena would call him, with a strong French accent, an *"ee-dee-óh"*—an idiot.[6] The trouble was, wrote Mary Meigs, "no one had ever effectively challenged *his* power, his right to command, to shout orders to his wife, his children, like a master sergeant in the Marines."

Rosalind bitterly complained that her father "would hold things against [her] for years and never let go." But when a crisis erupted on September 4, 1963, two days before he planned to leave for a year in Europe, Wilson (who feared his imminent departure might have precipitated her collapse) responded admirably and did everything in his power to help her. After he had flown up from Wellfleet and Rosalind had failed to meet him at the Boston airport, he called her up and she made absolutely no sense. He asked what was wrong and she alarmingly replied: "I don't know. . . . I don't know what's real any more." He then rushed to her "horribly ill-kept and dirty" apartment and found Rosalind, unmarried at forty, "in a strangely exalted state, full of delusions—she thought someone who was going to marry her was communicating with her" through special wiring on the radio, and had suffered this delusion on three previous occasions.

Remembering his father's recurrent breakdowns, his own crack-ups in 1929 and his recent "paroxysm of exasperation" in April 1962, Wilson (as he had once done with Mary McCarthy) summoned a doctor who put Rosalind in the psychiatric ward of Massachusetts General Hospital. He postponed his departure and Elena, with Helen, who had to enroll in school in Switzerland, sailed to Europe without him. Wilson later learned that Rosalind had been behaving irresponsibly at Houghton Mifflin and that her work had been deteriorating for many weeks before her breakdown. She could not concentrate on reading manuscripts and her hand constantly trembled. While in hospital, Rosalind told him that she thought the physicians were all actors pretending to be doctors.

Fortunately, Rosalind seemed to make a remarkably rapid recovery. On September 15 Wilson wrote Elena that Rosalind was evidently much better. She called up and assured him, "I'm not crazy any more," and said the doctors were moving her out of the locked ward. On September 18, after she had spent only two weeks in hospital, Wilson prematurely concluded that "she has completely cleared up" and brought her back to Wellfleet to recuperate with him. She had lost her job at the publisher's, but was taking tranquilizers, getting better and "touchingly apologetic about having caused so much trouble." Wilson finally flew to Europe on October 4, a month after Rosalind's breakdown. Two weeks later her doctor informed him that he was putting her back in hospital. Though she no longer had delusions and misconceptions, she was still anxious and bewildered.[7]

After Rosalind moved permanently to Talcottville in 1969, Wilson saw more of her. The only time he seemed close to her and Reuel, he regretfully remarked, was when they drove him around the countryside and had long conversations in the car. But, friends recalled, Wilson was as difficult with Rosalind upstate as he was with Elena and Helen on the Cape. Though he was sometimes mean to her, ordered her about in his raspy voice and treated her like a house serf, she did not talk back when he yelled at her and always adored him. Even the gentle and devoted Glyn Morris disapproved of Wilson's "truculent and almost tyrannical" behavior when Rosalind put out the wrong wine glasses. The long-suffering Rosalind agreed that her intensely critical father would sit silently glowering and could be "damned disagreeable."[8]

Abandoned by Elena, who remained on the Cape, Wilson resented his dependence on Rosalind in Talcottville, treated her like a child and was sometimes severe with her. He was partly supporting her, at a cost of $5,000 a year (she had also inherited money from his mother) and was sadly disappointed that she had not fulfilled her promise as a writer and editor. She appeared to have no close friends, serious ambitions or realistic plans. Her entire life, he felt, seemed to be ending in a "blind alley." Rosalind could be temperamental, even hysterical, which provoked Wilson and led to bitter quarrels: "Sometimes she gets on my nerves—her always high-pitched voice, due to living with her deaf grandmother, and her habitual laugh that sounds like whooping cough —then I speak sharply to her and she flares up childishly. . . . With me, she is partly still infantile, begins to squeal and shriek when I complain or ask her to do something she does not want to do." Once, when Wilson was playing solitaire and being "perfectly awful" to Rosalind, she threw all his cards on the floor and said: "Why don't you play '52 pick-up'?"

A characteristic incident took place in early September 1965 when Rosalind's behavior once again forced Wilson into the role of stern father. She was arrested, Wilson wrote, on her way back from an evening with the Chavchavadzes, "for blocking traffic, with her lights off, stalled in the middle lane and half pointed in the wrong direction. The [police] saw that she had been drinking and put her in the Provincetown jail. She called me up in the middle of the night, boohooing like a baby. . . . I am not sure she knew what happened. . . . I am depressed and worried about her." Desperately contrite and apparently seeking punishment, Rosalind confessed she was fed up with herself and had made a mess of her life.[9]

Wilson also had troubled relations with Reuel and Helen. Both children, much closer to their mothers than to their father, were angry about the way he had treated Mary and Elena. Brought up by and sympathetic to Mary, Reuel may have resented Wilson's attempts to persuade his mother to abort him. The continuing discord between his parents, the contrast between his summer and winter households, made him insecure. He became rebellious and had a number of misadventures. Wilson recorded that in the summer of 1957, when Reuel was eighteen, he was "getting somewhat out of hand." During his trip with a borrowed vehicle through the Abruzzi, where he had gone against Mary's wishes, he had "come to grief, been robbed and smashed up the car." Three years later he was caught speeding in upstate New York and spent several hours in a local jail, with a tree surgeon who had not paid his alimony, until William Fenton bailed him out. And in January 1962, when Reuel was a graduate student in Slavic at Berkeley, he had too much to drink, tried to jump into a Japanese garden and fell eight feet. He broke his jaw, lost a tooth and had to have an operation.

In the summer of 1963 Reuel married a divorced woman whom Wilson instantly disliked: "I thought she was neurotic and had an ominous resemblance to Mary. Reuel told me that she had [abandoned her] three children. . . . This somewhat shook both me and Elena. She is evidently a hypochondriac and has Reuel lashed to the mast." Sensing his father's hostility, Reuel defended his wife and gave Edmund a wigging. He criticized Edmund's lack of cordiality, interest and respect for both himself and his wife, and said that he would have to change his attitude if he wanted to see them in the future. Edmund rejected this fiat and did not change his attitude. In October 1966 he told McCarthy that he had not seen Reuel for a year. After his first marriage broke up, Reuel married an Asian woman and had a second child, who, McCarthy said, looked "like a Jap with Edmund's jaw."[10]

Handicapped by his eminent parents, and by Edmund's expectations that he would become an important writer and great man, Reuel did not get into the Foreign Service and had an unimpressive academic career. Several professors at Harvard considered him a serious yet boring fellow, neither bright nor talented. After many years in various graduate schools, he finally retreated to the University of Western Ontario in provincial Canada.

Though he felt closest to Rosalind, Helen—the only child who lived with Wilson—was his favorite. But Wilson, prematurely old when Helen was born, did not pay much attention to her. Once, when baby-sitting for Stuart Hughes, she burst into tears and exclaimed: "We don't have a family. Daddy's always drunk." Wilson lectured at Helen's girlfriends, "more or less interested victims," and disapproved of her beaux, whose long hair and ragged garb gave him "the creeps."

Helen graduated from the Cambridge School in 1966, went to Barnard to study Russian and—reacting against Wilson as Rosalind had done—dropped out, or failed out, of college. In 1967 Elena told Wilson that Helen was going to Dr. Wormer, a psychiatrist, and was "trying to pull herself together as far as the compulsive eating is concerned, which is her main worry—the example of Rosalind is frightening." Helen, once quite fat, became fanatical about vegetarian diet and weight control, and turned into a thin, ascetic young woman. She disliked being kissed when greeted by her friends and was eccentric, reclusive and severe.

After leaving Barnard, Helen studied painting at the Skowhegan

Art School in Maine. Mary Canby was surprised to find that Helen, as a teenager, owned an expensive Porsche. In the summer of 1970 she had a serious car accident in Skowhegan, went through the windshield and needed twenty-three stitches in her head. While in art school Helen met a young sculptor, Tim Woodman, a grandson of Edmund's college classmate, and has lived with him since then. More indulgent with Helen than he had ever been with Rosalind, Wilson moved with the times and tolerated her unconventional arrangement. "Helen likes to manage people," Wilson told Glyn Morris, "and the boy doesn't seem to object to it. Elena approves and so do I."[11] According to Adelaide and Daniel Walker, close observers of the family, Helen resented Wilson's alcoholism, harsh treatment of Elena and late love-affairs. He represented "trauma" to Helen, who disliked, even "hated" him.

III

Depressed by four harsh winters in Cambridge, the Wilsons decided to spend the academic year of 1963–64 in Europe. The tax torments were finally resolved and his sources of income were released. Elena had arranged to sell her stock in the champagne company for (she vaguely told Edmund) "twenty or thirty thousand dollars." Though still in debt, they now had more money. After Rosalind had apparently recovered from her nervous breakdown, Wilson met Elena in London and spent three weeks at the Basil Street Hotel. On October 26 they crossed the Channel and lived for four months at the Hôtel de Castille on the rue Cambon in Paris. They took a freezing trip to the Vosges during the second week of December, visiting his World War One haunts: Nancy, Vittel and Lunéville as well as Rheims, where Elena had spent her childhood. He returned to England for a week at the beginning of March to see the Hebrew scholar John Allegro and the English professor Marcus Cunliffe in Manchester. They stayed for the rest of March at the Hotel Victoria in the Via Campania in Rome, and he spent most of April at the Hotel Gellert in Budapest. While in Hungary he visited Debrecen, near the Romanian border in the eastern part of the country, and took a short trip to Vienna, where he met Elena and Auden, who owned a country house in Austria. They returned to America via London and flew home on May 12, 1964. The seven-month trip was fairly uneventful. He went back to his favorite European cities, saw old friends, discovered Hungary and worked on his next book, *O Canada*.

Britain seemed to have declined, as Wilson had predicted in 1945, from imperial splendor to relative insignificance. "It has been a great relief to be in England," he told Mary Meigs, "which seems so quiet after America. Instead of being all keyed up, they seem to be slowly subsiding from their position as a great power." He made a pilgrimage to Rochester to see Dickens' house at Gad's Hill and to Gravesend to visit an old man who made traditional Punch and Judy puppets. He saw, as usual, Auden and Spender, Compton Mackenzie and Isaiah Berlin, Connolly, Betjeman and Angus Wilson. Edmund had dismissed the handsome novelist Anthony Powell, who had served in the war and was married to the daughter of an earl, as "a watered-down British Proust." Powell, equally condescending to Wilson, remembered meeting him at a party at Lord and Lady Glenconnor's: "His appearance was very typical of the American 'college type,' a distinct cut above the average American (or British) journalist. . . . He had always shown himself as unfriendly towards myself, so far as I could see for no particular reason, and I taxed him with this. We had a drink quite happily together. He was an odd fish who never had the smallest idea what the British, or life in the U.K. was like, but was, I think, intelligent in his way."

In Paris Wilson saw the composer Nicolas Nabokov, the conductor Erich Leinsdorf, the Hebrew scholar André Dupont-Sommer and the poet Saint-John Perse, who had won the Nobel Prize in 1960. He also saw the *New Yorker* correspondent Janet Flanner, Fitzgerald's mistress Sheilah Graham, whom Wilson now found coarse, unscrupulous and "as amoral as Moll Flanders," the Surrealist painter Leonor Fini, at forty-five "no longer opulent and handsome, but aging and somewhat shrunken," and Mary McCarthy, now married to her fourth husband. Though Wilson was comfortably lodged and well fed, the winter in Paris was not a success. He found the government hostile, the city cold and depressing. As he told Dawn Powell in March 1964:

> Paris is very unpleasant now. The air is bad, the people are drab, and De Gaulle, though entirely out of touch with the people, makes himself everywhere felt as a repressive and oppressive presence. . . . The cops are everywhere and beat up student demonstrations. And then there is always the awful winter weather, which Paris has always had. But we couldn't get away from Paris, because I had had to bring a whole library to do a long *New Yorker* piece about Canada, and I couldn't travel with it. Now at last we have come to Rome, which is full of sun and cheerful activity.[12]

Wilson thought the Italians were the friendliest and most convivial people in Europe. In Rome he saw the journalist Alberto Arbasino, the leading novelists: Elsa Morante, Alberto Moravia and Ignazio Silone, and Mario Praz, still "sympathetic in spite of his streak of malignity." At dinner with the Silones and Count Morra, the bastard son of the former king, Wilson awkwardly asked if he knew that Edith Wharton was supposed to be illegitimate. The count gracefully evaded the question and Wilson, questioning his own motives, wondered if "such remarks come from unconscious malice."

The high point of his trip to Europe—eight years after the Russians had brutally suppressed the Hungarian revolution—was his first visit to Budapest. He pursued his interest in exotic cultures and oppressed minorities (Cardinal Mindzenty was still living in the American Embassy, where he had sought refuge), satisfied his intense curiosity about all aspects of the country and continued the language studies he had begun with Mary Pcolar. Wilson refused to be discouraged by the negative aspects of Hungary, whose principal exports, he said, alluding to Bela Lugosi and Edward Teller, were "vampires and atomic scientists." After the luxury of western Europe, he found Budapest a sad, empty, "spiky and bristling city—churches with high sharp spires, towers with needles like stings." The anti-Semitism was still appalling. His Communist translator Péter Nagy completely distorted his views and explained in a note to the plays that Wilson was "depicting the decay of the capitalist world and indicating the correct line of escape through following the Party line."[13]

Wilson was mainly interested in the outlandish language, in which *fog* means "take" and *tart* means "hold." Eleanor Perenyi, who spoke Hungarian, said the country did not have a great literature. She thought their leading poets, Ady and Petöfi, were minor writers and could not understand why Wilson wanted to "suffer through the language." Wilson, she said, saw rather than heard the language and could write simple letters. His knowledge of Hungarian, "insofar as a language can be mastered from books, was extensive. But he couldn't speak it, and was unfamiliar with nuances of usage." Wilson himself was delighted to find, by the time he had left the country, that he could read almost all the signs as well as the inscriptions under the paintings in the art museum.

Wilson's principal guide and teacher in Hungary was the thirty-six-year-old Charlotte Kretzoi (the same age as Mary Pcolar), who taught American literature at Debrecen University. She was, he wrote, "a handsome [married] woman, though for me without sex appeal: rather tall, blue eyes with dark discolorations under them." Charlotte said that Wilson, who called himself *Ödön Bácsi* (Uncle Edmund) with Mary Pcolar, "really behaved with the kindness of a self-adopted uncle." Following his habitual practice, Wilson took language lessons. "I read some Hungarian texts with him," she recalled. "His understanding of a written text was excellent, sometimes almost eerie; I don't think he could speak much. . . . I felt honored to be able to work with him, since I was moved—impressed—by the fact that he had taken the trouble to study our difficult language."

Charlotte, hurt by the way Wilson portrayed her in his posthumously published diaries, had some bitter words about his character and about the accuracy of the enlarged edition of *Europe Without Baedeker* (1966): "His account of his visit to Budapest was not accurate. Full of misunderstandings. . . . He *asked* for my comments. There were factual errors. I pointed them out. He didn't change them. . . . His vanity could not accept it. . . . You either had to admire Edmund Wilson unconditionally or you were an enemy—but he didn't show his malice openly."[14] Wilson certainly made a serious error (not mentioned by Kretzoi), when attempting to make the Hungarians more sympathetic, by stating that in 1945 "the Russians got rid of the Nazis; the Hungarians were grateful to them for this." In fact, during World War Two Fascist Hungary, an ally of the Axis powers, had actively collaborated with the Nazis in eastern Europe and participated in their invasion of Russia.

On May 16, 1964, four days after he returned to America, Wilson contrasted the various countries he had visited and summarized his journey in a letter to his childhood friend Margaret Edwards Rullman:

> [We spent] four months in Paris—which is not at all attractive now: bad weather, which they have always had, but now almost unbreathably bad air, terrible prices and the French badly dressed and kind of morose and depressed. In March we went to Rome —which was a good deal more cheerful—for Helen's Easter vacation, and Rosalind joined us there. Then I spent a month in Budapest. Hungary is green and uncomfortable, but was a good deal more interesting to me than the other countries, which I already knew.

Wilson published three sections of his "Notes from a European Diary: 1963–1964"—on Paris, Rome and Budapest, but not on London—first in the *New Yorker* and then in a new edition of *Europe Without Baedeker*. These lively if relatively unexciting chapters on the contemporary cultural scene were closely based on his diaries and not nearly as dramatic as the description of his journey to postwar Europe in 1945. He described his congenial travels and comfortable hotels, and discussed the latest work of Paul Claudel, Simone de Beauvoir and Christiane Rochefort, of Bertolt Brecht, Rolf Hochhuth and Günter Grass. He also offered a first-rate analysis of the biographical background and literary antecedents of Lampedusa's stories and magnificent novel, *The Leopard*, a "half-nostalgic, half-humorous picture of a declining but still feudal princely family in Sicily in the sixties of the last century."[15]

IV

In September 1964 Wilson began a year's appointment as a fellow in the Center for Advanced Studies at Wesleyan University in Middletown, Connecticut. He had been selected by the president of the university, Victor Butterfield, the trustee Henry Allen Moe (of the Guggenheim Foundation) and the novelist Paul Horgan, director of the Center. Horgan had originally approached Wilson through their mutual publisher, Roger Straus. Though there were no teaching duties, Wilson was initially sceptical and hesitant about involving himself once again in academic life. He seemed, Horgan said, "somewhat nervous and concerned about what might be expected of him in return for the fellowship." Nevertheless, the offer was attractive and Wilson accepted the grant of "$15,000 for two semesters, along with rent-free house, [office], secretarial aid, and transportation to and from Middletown."

"They supply you with everything from a house to postage stamps," Wilson told Jacob Landau (a New Jersey tavern-owner with whom he corresponded about Hebrew), "and pay you for being here."[16] Wilson lived at 131 Mount Vernon Street, a two-story, white shingle house with a bay window (whose furnishings reminded Elena of a dentist's waiting room), a steep front lawn and a large back garden. The other fellows that year included the novelist Jean Stafford, the English Jesuit Martin D'Arcy, the classicist Moses Hadas, the Italian journalist Luigi Barzini, the critic Sir Herbert Read, the logician Willard Quine and several others.

Wilson was well paid for doing hardly anything except being "accessible"—perhaps, he told Celia Paget Goodman, an "ominous word." As with the Gauss Seminars, he gave formal lectures—on Canadian literature and on the Marquis de Sade (both published in 1965)—to a Monday night private audience of twelve to fourteen people, half fellows, half invited faculty. During talks by the other fellows he blissfully fell asleep. Horgan thought there was no actor in Wilson—except in his magic and puppets—no sense of drama or self-projection that was essential for effective teaching. He read his paper in a rapid, toneless voice, husky and clouded, kept his eyes on the lectern and killed his own presentation.

The local and student newspapers reported Wilson's response to questions when he met with the general public in March 1965. He said "the only ambition I ever had as a child was to be a magician" and then discussed the relationship between conjuring and literature: "Both involve creating a 'false direction.' You deceive the audience into thinking what you want them to think and conceal what you're actually doing." Asked about his meetings with Fitzgerald after they had left Princeton, he encouragingly replied, "they were literary, but we did quite a lot of drinking." In a strange response to a query about his collaboration on *The Undertaker's Garland* with John Bishop, who had fought in the war, Wilson recalled: "I have rather macabre tendencies. I got him to write about death, something he had never thought about before." He disagreed that he had the power to make or break the reputation of an author, but admitted that he had once tried to "ambush best sellers" like Anya Seton's *The Turquoise* (1946). Though he had very recently reported on current European literature, Wilson was pleased to remark that he no longer read current books or attempted to keep up with contemporary trends.

Both reporters complained that Wilson answered curtly, often with a single negative word, and was not nearly as helpful nor as personally impressive as they expected him to be. He clearly disliked to perform in public, to be treated like a historical relic and to have to answer what he considered to be fatuous questions. As Paul Horgan observed: "He hated being conspicuous. Ordinary courtesies, little amenities recognizing his high position in the world of letters annoyed him. He became self-conscious. Intruded upon, he tended to become rude."[17]

The *New Yorker* writer Brendan Gill and the *Commentary* editor, Norman Podhoretz, who met Wilson in New York during the 1960s, have described his mode of conversation as off-putting and intimidating, and helped to explain why his year at Wesleyan—as at his previous posts—was not a great success. Gill, who has a nasty streak, enjoyed satirizing Wilson and felt there was nothing to learn from him. He remarked that "it was just as well to avoid him at a party; his shyness caused him to be overbearing and garrulous, and he would speak on and on, in a penetrating, high-pitched voice, leaving his auditors with little to do but plan the least impolite means of escaping him." Podhoretz, who admired him, recalled that Wilson's conversation did not (perhaps could not) match his listener's high expectations:

> Lucid and sane in his writings, he seemed odd and befuddled in person (even when he was sober, I hasten to add). And I for one always found him as hard to talk to as he was easy to read. In fact, in my experience conversation with him was almost impossible; the best you could hope for was that he would use you as the interlocutor for a monologue. In my case, the monologue as often as not was about Hebrew or something pertaining to Jews or Judaism, but literary subjects came up as well. We once, for example, had a long "talk" about the Beat Generation, prompted by a piece of mine in *Partisan Review* called "The Know-Nothing Bohemians." . . . He thought I should have placed Ginsberg and the others in the tradition of the *poète maudit.* . . . On the whole, I would say that Edmund was one of those writers who are so much better on paper than in person that to know them tends to make one think less of them.

Wilson considered Horgan, his temperamental antithesis, a snob and a name-dropper, "an endearing and slightly ridiculous figure . . . a bachelor of the type who wants to be the beloved friend and is full of sympathetic consideration." Wilson did not get on well with Horgan or with the Wesleyan faculty. Anxious to defend their "field" from outsiders, and either sycophantic toward or awed by the distinguished fellows, the professors resented their special treatment. They routinely snubbed Wilson as well as all the others. They rarely invited him to participate in intellectual activities or (though he offered to do so) to meet any students.[18] Bored to death in provincial and primitive Middletown, Wilson wanted intellectual companionship but unintentionally discouraged it.

It was also lonely for Elena, who had no one to talk to and spent her free time teaching local schoolchildren to read. The Wilsons escaped whenever possible on weekends and, "after the blind little backwater of Middletown," found the parties and gossip of Boston and New York quite exhilarating. In January 1965, as the penetrating dampness blew off the Connecticut River, Wilson complained to Mary Pcolar, snowbound in the tundra of upstate New York:

> You can't imagine how dull it is. There is nothing in Middletown but the little college. The town itself is so dismal that it makes Boonville look like a lively attractive city. . . . Usually, at the end of the day, we don't know what to do with ourselves. I come home from my office and say, "Well, what's happened?" and Elena answers, "Nothing." We simply have a drink and read.

The town had no decent restaurants and the Center had no dining room in which the fellows could gather for meals and conversation. Most of them, in any case, were absorbed in their work, unresponsive and often away from Wesleyan. But Wilson did find two kindred spirits, Jean Stafford and Father D'Arcy. Stafford, a talented writer, had been unhappily married to Robert Lowell in the 1940s and spent hours discussing that brilliant maniac. Her beloved second husband, the *New Yorker* writer A. J. Liebling, had died in 1963. She was depressed and drinking heavily, her writing had deteriorated and her reputation was in decline. But her ironic pessimism, her bitter mood and her scathing attitude toward academics matched Wilson's. She could be as wickedly funny as Dorothy Parker and Dawn Powell, and liked to call Middletown the "Slough of Despond"—a fearful, miry place in Bunyan's *Pilgrim's Progress*. The poet Richard Wilbur, then teaching at Wesleyan, remembered that Wilson and Stafford would get drunk together, exchange barbed comments "like Nichols and May," and engage in "free and continuous detraction." Stafford planned a "mammoth air tragedy" in which all her enemies crashed in flames.[19]

Father D'Arcy, seven years older than Wilson, had taken a first at Oxford, taught at a Catholic school, worked at the Jesuit Headquarters in London, been Master of Campion Hall, Oxford, and had become Provincial (or head) of the English Society of Jesus. He published many theological works, including studies of Augustine and Aquinas. An amusing and learned literary man, with a subtle mind, D'Arcy had a great social influence and was famous for bringing distinguished converts into the Catholic Church. But he was considered too worldly, had been recalled to Rome and relieved of his duties. D'Arcy reminded Wilson of Bertrand Russell: "Small and frail, very old, almost nonexistent chin like Russell's, but without his strong aristocratic nose." Having served a term together in Middletown, Wilson felt, was almost like having been comrades in the army. Though himself an atheist, Wilson was deeply impressed by D'Arcy's unusual mixture of sophistication and spirituality. Wilson was rather reassured, he told Clelia Carroll, "to see somebody as intelligent as he is who has himself the appearance of unshakeable faith and the strength of an institution to which he has devoted his life."

Brisk and brief in his summary of the year at Wesleyan, Wilson officially told Horgan: "I have finished my book on Canada and another longer book [*The Bit Between My Teeth*] that is made up of my articles of the last fifteen years, some of them written at the Center. . . . I have been seeing individual students who are interested in literature and have read a paper to the faculty of the Russian department."[20]

V

O Canada: An American's Notes on Canadian Culture, serialized in the *New Yorker* and published as a book in May 1965 (when he was completing his year at Wesleyan), is one of Wilson's least known and least successful works. Wilson had taken idyllic childhood trips to Canada with his father. Margaret Canby's mother had come from Canada and Elena had spent the early years of her marriage there. His interest in Canada was closely related to his origins in upstate New York and to his passionate defense of the Israelis, the Iroquois and the Confederacy. Like the French Canadians, Wilson argued in *O Canada*, all these persecuted minorities fought to protect their individual identity "against the proddings and encroachments of centralized power" and opposed "official domination that can so easily become a faceless despotism."

In September 1964 Wilson wrote Celia Paget Goodman that the book was "not one of my best, but informative," and then explained his interest in Canada: "for the first time in history since the early French and English wars [of the eighteenth century], it is beginning to become interesting, and people ought to be instructed about what is going on up there." Two years earlier, when his income had been cut off by the IRS, Wilson had traveled to Toronto, Montreal and Quebec at the *New*

Yorker's expense, staying in luxurious hotels while buying drinks and dinners for Canadian writers. Wilson found Quebec a "queer but beautiful city: gray seventeenth-century buildings, huge convents and priests in black gowns," yet was repelled by the denizens of the old *maisons seigneuriales* who "exist in a damp and murky atmosphere of Jansenist religion and incestuous relationships." Though Quebec was more interesting than the rest of Canada, he told Louise Bogan it was "still not very interesting."[21]

Wilson anticipated the weakness of his book when he wrote William Shawn, the editor of the *New Yorker*, that he could not control and focus the material: "I found the subject of Canada extremely difficult to handle, because the country itself is so uncoordinated, and it is hard to present the French and English sides in any unified way." Wilson's problems, in fact, were formidable. The authors and books he discussed in *O Canada* were even more obscure to American readers than those in *Patriotic Gore*. Just as the best Civil War novel had been written long after the war by Stephen Crane, so the best Canadian novel, *Self-Condemned* (1955), was written by Wyndham Lewis, an Englishman—and both novels were excluded from Wilson's books. Many of the most talented Canadians—Saul Bellow, John Kenneth Galbraith, Leon Edel, Donald Greene and Hugh Kenner—had left the country and had distinguished careers in American universities. Of those who remained, Wilson named but did not discuss the novelist Robertson Davies, the critic Northrop Frye and the poet Irving Layton. He did not even mention important Jewish-Canadian writers like Mordecai Richler and Leonard Cohen, or the extremely influential Marshall McLuhan; and Margaret Atwood did not publish her first book until 1966.

O Canada has no table of contents, Introduction or index, and the structure is even more wobbly than usual. The "Notes" in the subtitle suggested Wilson's random approach to the subject. Part way through the book he indicated his method, when he casually and rather apologetically mentioned: "I am not pretending here to do more than try to call attention to some writers who have attracted my own attention. My ignorance of the subject is still immense." Though Wilson stated that the literature "cannot fully be understood without some knowledge of Canadian history," he discussed the fiction and poetry first, did not clearly show how the literature reflected the political issues and did not provide the historical context until the end. Even the title, which came from a French anthem, "*O Canada, terre de nos aïeux*," and should have been used as an epigraph, was not explained until well into the book. In old age Wilson had clearly become rather tired and careless about planning, and his editors and publisher accepted what he wrote instead of trying to improve it.

Wilson began with an essay on Morley Callaghan, first published in November 1960, which claimed that he was the "most unjustly neglected novelist in the English-speaking world." Wilson's analysis, continued in 1964, did not substantiate his argument. Callaghan remains known, not for his fiction, but for his friendship with Hemingway and Fitzgerald in 1929 and for his memoir *That Summer in Paris* (1963). When discussing a score of little-known writers, including Marie-Claire Blais, Wilson found it difficult to arouse the reader's interest and made them all seem rather unappealing. French Canadian poets come from a stifling milieu that makes them all neurotic; French Canadian novelists cannot present a genuine woman and their whole literature is filled with "unillumined gloominess." Callaghan, his prime exhibit, is "too bleak," Hugh MacLennan "discourages the modern reader," Blais is "unrelievedly painful," Albert Lozeau is monotonous and insipid, and André Langevin is "lugubrious and leaden." Emile Nelligan went insane and Roger Lamelin gave up literature to manufacture sausages. Wilson concluded the book with an analysis of the cultural movements in French Canada and, sympathetic to the separatists, argued that the French should be allowed to break away and become an independent nation. Always sensitive to new cultural currents, Wilson anticipated by more than two years De Gaulle's demand for *Québec libre* and the flowering of Canadian literature during the next decade.

Despite the manifest faults of the book and Wilson's French bias, which alienated many English-speaking Canadians, *O Canada* provided a valuable introduction. It was, as Anthony Burgess wrote in the *Spectator*, "the only useful handbook in existence on the whole complex political and intellectual situation in Canada." A positive review in *Commentary* justly called the book "rambling and discursive, based upon wide but unsystematic reading . . . and liberally spiced with the author's Johnsonian wit and prejudice. . . . He summarizes the plots of a number of Canadian novels so brilliantly that to read the originals is rather anticlimactic."[22] Wilson's most striking work of 1965 was not *O Canada*, but his contentious review of Nabokov's edition of Pushkin's *Eugene Onegin*.

TWENTY-TWO

Quarrel with Nabokov, 1965–1966

I

In January 1964, during their year in Europe, the Wilsons visited the Nabokovs in Switzerland. The extraordinary success of *Lolita* had enabled Nabokov to give up teaching at Cornell, and he now lived permanently in a suite in the Montreux Palace Hotel. They exchanged friendly lunches and dinners, and neither of them knew this would be their last meeting. Nabokov, later on, felt wounded and betrayed when he discovered that Wilson had written an attack on his translation of and elaborate commentary on *Eugene Onegin*, but never mentioned it.

Wilson's harsh review of Nabokov's four-volume edition of Pushkin's poem, published in the *New York Review of Books* on July 15, 1965, destroyed a friendship that had lasted, through minor storms, since Nabokov first arrived in the United States in 1940. An acrimonious correspondence between the two ensued in the *New York Review of Books*, and in February 1966 Nabokov published in *Encounter* his "Reply to My Critics," which responded to all the attacks, including Wilson's, on his edition. Wilson later reopened the wound with an account of his visit to Nabokov's home in *Upstate* (1971). Nabokov retaliated with a final, ferocious letter in the *New York Times Book Review* of November 1971. Wilson revised his *Onegin* review, adding a critique of Nabokov's novels, in his posthumously published *A Window on Russia* (1972), which concluded the most notorious literary quarrel of the century.

Though Nabokov could be as touchy as a Samurai, he had enjoyed their energetic literary disagreements in person and in letters, and put up with Wilson's frank criticism of his work as long as it was off-the-cuff (or off the Nabokov). But by 1965 his novels in English had established him as a major figure in American culture, and he was shocked by Wilson's review. He considered it condescending, ill-informed, even vindictive. For his part Wilson—despite his quarrel with Waugh after his review of *Brideshead Revisited*—did not foresee that his critical review would wound Nabokov so deeply. Though he was usually generous and tactful in reviewing fiction and poetry by friends, and often promoted their work, judging a translation presented a rather different task. Accustomed to the potshots of their private disputes, and not fully aware of his own destructive impulse, Wilson felt free to attack Nabokov's translation in what he claimed was an objective spirit. But Wilson's biographical and Freudian critical approach made him far from objective, and he could not resist relating his criticisms of the writer to his intimate knowledge of Nabokov's life, art and opinions. Wilson considered their dispute a literary and critical polemic; Nabokov believed it was a betrayal of their friendship.

II

The controversy began with a preliminary skirmish between Nabokov and Walter Arndt, who had published a verse translation of Pushkin's narrative poem in 1963. *Eugene Onegin* portrays a bitter and cynical young man who kills his friend and rival, Lensky, in a duel. The novel in verse is Pushkin's masterpiece and inspired an opera by Tchaikovsky. Like Byron's *Don Juan*, which influenced the poem, *Eugene Onegin* is written in vivid, dramatic, swift-moving verse. Arndt's translation imitated the form of the original by preserving in English the rhymed stanzas in iambic tetrameter. The result, though a tour de force, inevitably lapsed into inaccuracy and padding.

Like Nabokov, Arndt was an ardent anti-Fascist and cosmopolitan exile, who became an academic in America.[1] But these similarities did not save him from a savage review in the *New York Review of Books* of April 30, 1964. Announcing his own long-gestated and soon-to-be-published translation, Nabokov mercilessly flayed the verbal gobbets of the "pitiless and irresponsible paraphrast," who had just won the Bollingen Prize for translation. He attacked Arndt's anachronisms, absurd scansion, burlesque rhymes, crippled clichés, vulgarisms, howlers, lamentable Russian and wobbly English.

After his attack on Arndt, Nabokov was under considerable pressure to produce a superior version when he published his own edition in 1964. But his word-for-word translation was generally condemned by the critics. The root of the problem was Nabokov's curious theory of translation. His goal was to produce a literal "rendering, as closely as the associative and syntactical capacities of another language allow, [of] the exact contextual meaning of the original. Only this," he insisted, "is true translation." Nabokov, the greatest Russian prose stylist of the century, was willing to sacrifice everything—"elegance, euphony, clarity, good taste, modern usage, and even grammar"—on the altar of literalism.[2] He felt he would reap his greatest reward if students used his deliberately dull version of Pushkin's sparkling stanzas as a lame trot. Yet Nabokov's version was not even useful as an aid to students. Deliberately cast in recondite English and eccentric syntax, it drew attention to the translator instead of conveying the sense and spirit of the original.

Virtually all the Slavic experts agreed that the translation was a failure. Robert Conquest said that it was "too much a transposition into Nabokovese, rather than a translation into English." Edward Brown, writing in the *Slavic Review* about the revised edition of 1975, was even more severe. He asserted that "this translation of *Eugene Onegin* by one of the great craftsmen of our time is execrable. . . . [He] systematically abandons poetry and does so on the basis of a shallow and spurious 'theory' of translation." The cultured Harvard economist Alexander Gerschenkron, in what Wilson considered the most intelligent review, perceived that "what Nabokov sacrifices so lightheartedly and so disdainfully is not his own elegance and clarity, and euphony, but Pushkin's." Even Nabokov's partisan biographer, Brian Boyd, later explained: "Unquestionably Nabokov's lines are not only unrhymed but often flat and gracelessly awkward, unlike Pushkin's, and it was this that many reviewers found a cruel betrayal of Pushkin and sufficient reason to prefer Arndt's nonsense jingles." Nabokov's friend Gleb Struve believed that Wilson "was right in criticizing Nabokov's translation . . . for the use of rare, unfamiliar, outlandish and . . . *un-Pushkinian* words."

Nabokov's translation was accompanied by a great Gothic cathedral of commentary, full of superfluous detail, in which he venomously criticized many famous writers (Stendhal, Balzac, Zola) as well as previous translators and commentators on Pushkin. It also contained a ninety-two-page Appendix on Russian and English prosody. For most critics, the eccentricity and arrogance of the commentary complemented the failings of the translation. Gerschenkron concluded his review with a convincing catalogue of Nabokov's defects: "It is indeed deplorable that so much of Nabokov's great effort is so sadly distorted by the desire to be original at all cost, by confused theorizing, by promises that never could be redeemed, by spiteful pedantry, unbridled emotions, and, last but not least, by unrestrained egotism. All this is bound to annoy some readers; it will revolt others."[3]

All the verbal artistry that should have been applied to the translation Nabokov lavished on his learned commentary. He surpassed his academic colleagues—who had been reluctant to recognize either his creative or his scholarly achievements—with his vast scholarly apparatus. Applying to the text of Pushkin the minute taxonomic details he had so ably used in his scientific study of butterflies, he observed that in chapter three of *Eugene Onegin*, the "vigorous flow of events constitutes a most harmoniously constructed entity with a streamlined body and symmetrical wings."

Nabokov's extremely digressive commentary not only mimicked the Byronic digressions in Pushkin's poem but, as Clarence Brown has observed, imitated and recreated the satiric tone and scholarly structure of his brilliant novel *Pale Fire* (1962): "This work consists of an introduction by [Dr.] Kinbote, a narrative and ruminative poem entitled "Pale Fire" by John Shade, a much longer, very detailed, even more ruminative, certainly more narrative, and I think more poetic commentary by Kinbote, and, finally, a hilarious index to the whole book."[4]

Nabokov's commentary made two significant references to Wilson. In the first, friendly reference (2.391), Nabokov recalled a Russian actress reading Pushkin on "a wonderful record (played for me in Talcottville by Edmund Wilson)." In the second, slightly critical reference (2.474)—mentioned by Wilson in his review—he stated that Pushkin's famous "description of the coming of winter . . . is well translated (with a few minor inexactitudes)" by Edmund Wilson. Wilson's brief translation, in his essay on Pushkin, had remained unchanged since its publication in 1936. But it seemed to deteriorate, in Nabokov's view, between his original edition of 1964, which provoked Wilson's hostile review, and his revised edition of 1975. In the later edition Wilson's description of winter was "translated" (rather than "well translated") with "a number of inaccuracies" (rather than "a few minor inexactitudes"). The later, retaliatory note lumped Wilson with the rest of the dunces in the commentary.

III

Battered by the professional Slavicists, Nabokov hoped that Wilson would respond favorably in the influential *New York Review of Books* to the edition that had cost so much time, thought and labor. But in August 1964 Nabokov warned his editor that the Bollingen Foundation—which had supported and co-published his edition, but also awarded the translation prize to Arndt—"keeps looking forward to the Edmund Wilson article; but as I have mentioned before his Russian is primitive, and his knowledge of Russian literature gappy and grotesque." He also quite accurately told his first biographer, Andrew Field, that "there were the two mirages of Wilson. That he knew Russian history better than I because of his Marxism, and that he knew at least as much about Russian literature as I." But Wilson had confidently disputed Marxist philosophy with Sidney Hook, and believed he could hold his own with any authority when discussing a subject he had carefully studied. In his review he now displayed, according to Clarence Brown, "the almost unbelievable *hubris* of reading Nabokov several petulant little lessons about Russian grammar and vocabulary, himself blundering all the while."[5]

Wilson's immediate response matched that of other critics. As he told Barbara Epstein, his editor at the *New York Review of Books:* "Just looking through it, I can see that Volodya's translation, sometimes in the same way, is almost as much open to objection as Arndt's. It is full of flat writing, outlandish words, and awkward phrases. And," he added ominously, "some of the things he says about the Russian language are inaccurate." Though Wilson realized he did not like the book, he could not resist the challenge to beat Nabokov at his own game. Despite his imperfect knowledge of Russian, he scored several direct hits in his lengthy attack.

Wilson's measured opening paragraph established the severely critical tone of the review, and allowed himself the same freedom that Nabokov had previously taken with rival critics and translators.

> Vladimir Nabokov's translation of Pushkin's *Evgeni Onegin* is something of a disappointment; and the reviewer, though a personal friend of Mr. Nabokov—for whom he feels a warm affection

sometimes chilled by exasperation—and an admirer of much of his work, does not propose to mask his disappointment. Since Mr. Nabokov is in the habit of introducing any job of this kind which he undertakes by an announcement that he is unique and incomparable and that everybody else who has attempted it is an oaf and an ignoramus, incompetent as a linguist and scholar, usually with the implication that he is also a low-class person and a ridiculous personality, Nabokov ought not to complain if the reviewer, though trying not to imitate Nabokov's bad literary manners, does not hesitate to underline his weaknesses.

Wilson indicated his ambivalence about Nabokov the man ("warm affection . . . chilled by exasperation") and condemned Nabokov's ill-mannered attack on Arndt and other unfortunate predecessors. Rhetorically balancing "does not propose to mask his disappointment" with "does not hesitate to underline his weaknesses," he suggested his own view would be more objective. His magisterial tone, more appropriate to dealing with inept translators and doltish scholiasts than judging the work of an intimate friend, asserted his critical and scholarly superiority. Like most other critics, Wilson found the "bald and awkward language" of Nabokov's translation, "which has nothing in common with Pushkin's or with the usual writing of Nabokov . . . more disastrous than Arndt's heroic effort." He gave examples of his uneven and at times banal translation:

> You will agree, my reader
> That very nicely did our pal
> act toward melancholy Tatiana.

and

> Winter! the peasant celebrating
> in a flat sledge inaugurates the track;
> his naggy, having sensed the snow,
> shambles at something like a trot.

He also criticized Nabokov's "perverse-pedantic impossible" style, his addiction to unfamiliar and inappropriate words. He spent several pages comparing the words and phrases used by various translators, and defended his own translation of some Pushkin stanzas. But Wilson carried his criticism one step further. He related Nabokov's perverse verbal virtuosity to his desire to punish himself and the reader, to his "sado-masochistic Dostoevskian tendencies so acutely noted by Sartre," and compared Nabokov's review of Arndt to "one of Marx's niggling and nagging attacks."[6] In his blurb for *The Real Life of Sebastian Knight* Wilson had compared his friend to three writers that Nabokov greatly admired: Gogol, Proust and Kafka. Now he deliberately wounded Nabokov by comparing him to writers that he particularly disliked: Marx and Dostoyevsky, and quoted with approval the criticism of his work by Sartre, whom Nabokov regarded as an enemy.

Wilson disagreed with Nabokov's view that Pushkin did not know English and had not read Byron in the original, and accused him of "lack of common sense" in his tedious and interminable appendices about Pushkin's African ancestor and Pushkin's prosody. They had been heatedly arguing about Russian versification since the early 1940s, when Nabokov sent Wilson an eight-page lesson, complete with charts and diagrams. At one point he tried to tell Wilson "you are as wrong as can be," and in 1950 Wilson had told Nabokov, "you are all off, as usual." By now Wilson was weary of arguing about this stale and stalemated subject, on which they each had firm and unshakeable views.

But Nabokov's edition revived their dispute. In his appendix Nabokov explained his own system of prosody which, he insisted, would apply equally to Russian and English verse. Although Nabokov certainly knew more about Russian versification than Wilson, it is clear that his system could not apply to English metrics, which Wilson claimed Nabokov did not understand. Both loved to instruct others, and Nabokov had much to teach Wilson, since his English was far superior to Wilson's Russian. But, according to Simon Karlinsky, Wilson was right—and Nabokov wrong—when Pushkin came to shovekin: Pushkin *did* know English, and English versification operates differently from Russian.[7] Once again, however, Wilson was not content simply to argue with Nabokov's ideas about English verse. He resorted to a psychological explanation of Nabokov's theories, arguing that Nabokov's attempt to find a system that would apply to both languages was part of an effort to reconcile his Russian heritage with his English education.

Wilson called the parodic commentary "overdone" and overloaded with pedantic detail. It showed, he thought, "remarkably little sensitivity to the texture and rhythm of [Pushkin's] writing, to the skill in manipulating language." At the same time, he recognized its occasional brilliance, and conceded that if one skipped the *longueurs*, it makes "very pleasant reading, and represents an immense amount of labor." Toward the end of the review Wilson summarized the psychological theme of his whole essay by remarking of Nabokov's *déraciné* style: "what he writes is not always really English. On the other hand, he sometimes betrays . . . that he is not quite at home with Russian." Concluding, however, on a more positive note, Wilson portrayed Nabokov in the role he himself had assumed—that of cultural interpreter and intermediary: "In spite of his queer prejudices, which few people share—such as his utter contempt for Dostoyevsky—his sense of beauty and his literary proficiency, his energy which never seems to tire, have made him a wire of communication which vibrates between us and that Russian past."[8]

Wilson's most radical criticism of Nabokov's commentary focused on the most dramatic event in Pushkin's poem: the fatal duel between Onegin and Lensky. In his 1936 essay on Pushkin, Wilson had observed: "Evgeny has killed in the most cynical fashion a man whose friend he had believed himself to be and whom he had thought he did not want to kill. . . . Evgeny had been jealous of him, because Lensky has been able to feel for Olga an all-absorbing emotion, whereas Evgeny, loved so passionately by Tatyana, has been unable to feel anything at all." In his review Wilson returned to this episode to criticize Nabokov's "most serious failure," his inability to understand the central situation: "He finds himself unable to account for Evgeni Onegin's behavior." Wilson then repeated his original interpretation: Onegin "thinks Lensky a fool yet he envies him. He cannot stand it that Lensky . . . should be fired by ecstatic emotion. So, taking a mean advantage—raising slowly, we are told, his pistol, in malignant cold blood—he aims to put out that fire." Nabokov's commentary, in contrast, emphasizes the instinct that makes Lensky challenge his dearest friend: "In modern Russia little remains of the idea of honor—pure personal honor." Lensky's course of action, in challenging the friend who had recklessly flirted with Lensky's fiancée, "far from being a temperamental extravaganza, is the only logical course an honorable man could have taken."[9]

Pushkin's duel takes on new meaning in the context of the quarrel between the intellectual critic (Onegin-Wilson) and the passionate artist (Lensky-Nabokov), whose interpretation of the duel revealed their own motivation. Both authors, engaged in an intellectual duel, believed their personal honor was involved. Just as Wilson's review

inadvertently revealed his own "malignant cold blood" and unconscious wish to "kill" their friendship, so Nabokov's understanding of
Lensky and lack of sympathy for Onegin reflected his instinctive urge
to defend his artistic honor (almost extinct in modern Russia) and
retaliate against his old friend. In "Reply to My Critics" Nabokov
noted that "Pushkin stresses the fact that Onegin 'sincerely loves the
youth' but that *amour propre* is sometimes stronger than friendship."

Nabokov considered the review a personal insult. Wilson's offensive tone, Nabokov explained to Barbara Epstein, "compels me to be
quite ruthless in regard to his linguistic incompetence." He did not
directly confront the fundamental source of his anger: Wilson's biographical and psychological critique of his edition. He decided, at first,
to limit his letter in the *New York Review of Books* of August 26, 1965 to
refuting only the "Russian"—or weakest—part of Wilson's review,
adding that "though well aware of the real reason behind this attack, I
consider this reason far too sad and private to be aired in print."[10]
Wilson's reply, in the same issue, while responding to Nabokov's
specific points, suggested that he had miscalculated both the severity of
his review and the effect it would have on Nabokov. He now conceded
that it sounded to him "more damaging" than he had intended.

In the spring campaign of 1966, unwilling to leave the battlefield to
the apparently victorious Wilson, Nabokov changed the venue to England (where few readers would have closely followed their controversy)
and replied once more at great length in the February 1966 issue of
Encounter. He began his "Reply to My Critics" by stating that Wilson's
attack was a "polemicist's dream come true" and that he would be a
"poor sportsman to disdain what it offers." He also, like Wilson,
mentioned their friendship and conceded that Wilson had verbally
expressed admiration for his work but had avoided writing about his
fiction: "I have always been grateful to him for the tact he showed
in not reviewing any of my novels while constantly saying flattering
things about me in the so-called literary circles where I seldom re-
volve."

His strategy, however, remained similar to the one he adopted in
his first letter to the *New York Review of Books:* he wanted to discredit
Wilson's knowledge of Russian and of Pushkin. He continued in this
personal vein by mocking Wilson's absurd attempt to pronounce Pushkin's poetry and seriously questioning his competence on this subject:
"Upon being challenged to read *Evgeniy Onegin* aloud, he started to
perform with great gusto, garbling every second word, and turning

Pushkin's iambic line into a kind of spastic anapest with a lot of jaw-twisting haws and rather endearing little barks that utterly jumbled the rhythm and soon had us both in stitches." Carrying his argument one step further, Nabokov absurdly claimed that Wilson was "incapable of comprehending the mechanism of verse—either Russian or English."

Nabokov's tone became venomous as he shifted the attack from Wilson himself to his review of *Eugene Onegin*. He resented Wilson's insinuation that he had read neither Theocritus nor Virgil; jeered at Wilson's ignorant Russianisms; insisted that Wilson "knows nothing" about Pushkin's knowledge of English; condemned Wilson's "ludicrous display of pseudo-scholarship"; and defended his own savage digs at established reputations—including Wilson's. In 1949 he had told Wilson that "I liked your book [*The Triple Thinkers*] very much." But in his *Encounter* "Reply," he emphasized their different approach to literature and mocked "the old-fashioned, naive, and musty method of human-interest criticism championed by Mr. Wilson . . . [and exemplified by] Wilson's extraordinary misconceptions [about Pushkin and other writers] in *The Triple Thinkers*."

Nabokov concluded by referring to Wilson's letter in the *New York Review of Books* of August 26, 1965, and loftily withdrew from the conflict: "Mr. Wilson says that on rereading his article he felt it sounded 'more damaging' than he had meant it to be. His article, entirely consisting, as I have shown, of quibbles and blunders, can be damaging only to his own reputation—and that is the last look I shall take at this dismal scene."[11] Ignoring Wilson's praise of his wit, insight and knowledge, and obscuring once more the "real reasons" for his anger, Nabokov tried to reduce Wilson's review to a collection of errors in Russian.

The contentious Mary McCarthy, amused and delighted by the sparks of Wilson's polemic, urged him to continue the controversy. But Isaiah Berlin, writing from Oxford, gave Wilson some very different tactical advice. He pointed out the weakness of Nabokov's egoistic translation and told Wilson to curtail the dispute:

> People will of course assume that he is an impeccable Russian scholar, and knows far more than any non-Russian could; this they will assume whether you are right or wrong; the more you answer, the more he will counter-reply; the point to make, I am sure, is that the translation as such is nothing but a curiosity of literature

... that he has all the faults of a self-intoxicated virtuoso with a vast narcissistic talent and no capacity for conveying other works of art, which needs the negative capability of which he is totally devoid; the notes are an idiosyncratic collection of a typical Russian nineteenth-century amateur of culture and knowledge, but the whole thing is part of the work of Nabokov and not of Pushkin. . . . You are right—he *is* a little dotty.[12]

IV

Wilson did not reply to Nabokov's "Reply," and their lively and affectionate correspondence inevitably ceased. But five years later, on March 2, 1971, Nabokov responded to news from their mutual friend Harry Levin that the nearly seventy-six-year-old Wilson was seriously ill with heart disease. In his last letter to Wilson, Nabokov made a magnanimous gesture of conciliation: "A few days ago I had the occasion to reread the whole batch . . . of our correspondence. It was such a pleasure to feel again the warmth of your many kindnesses, the various thrills of our friendship, that constant excitement of art and intellectual discovery. . . . Please believe that I have long ceased to bear you a grudge for your incomprehensible incomprehension of Pushkin and Nabokov's *Onegin*."

Wilson, usually the more belligerent of the two, was glad to get Nabokov's letter. In *his* last letter, written on March 8, Wilson warned his old comrade-in-arms that he would soon have two pieces about him in press. He was revising his old review of *Eugene Onegin* for *A Window on Russia*—correcting his own errors in Russian and "citing a few more of your ineptitudes"—and had included an account of his 1957 visit to the Nabokovs in Ithaca in the forthcoming *Upstate*. "I hope it will not again impair our personal relations," he told Nabokov—but seemed to fear that it would. But he suspected Nabokov's motives for reviving their friendship, considered his letter insincere and thought it was yet another example of his notorious *Schadenfreude*, or malicious pleasure. Ten days later, Wilson bitterly informed Helen Muchnic: "Nabokov has suddenly written me a letter telling me that he values my friendship and that all has been forgiven. He has been told that I have been ill, and it always makes him cheerful to think that his friends are in bad shape."[13]

The two peacocks had always been hypersensitive about each other's behavior. In the early 1940s, when Wilson and Mary McCarthy were in the front seat of a car and the Nabokovs in the rear, Vladimir "leaned forward and nimbly removed Wilson's awful brown hat." Ignoring Nabokov, and sounding as huffy as his father, Wilson turned to Vera and remarked: "Your husband has a rather strange sense of humor." On another occasion, when Mary McCarthy had gone to great trouble to prepare cherries jubilee for the Nabokovs, Vladimir had mocked the absurdly hot and cold American confection. Though testy himself about Nabokov's behavior, Wilson noted in the 1971 addition to his review of *Eugene Onegin:* "Like all persons who enjoy malicious teasing and embarrassing practical jokes, [Nabokov] is invariably aggrieved and indignant when anyone tries anything of the kind on himself."[14]

Wilson's visit to Ithaca in late May 1957 got off to a bad start. He had a painful attack of gout and Nabokov met the wrong train. In his account of this visit in *Upstate* (1971), Wilson noted that his friend was exhausted from overwork, that his nerves were on edge and that he suddenly shifted from a benign to an aggressive temper. Nabokov told Wilson that Onegin was going to marry Lolita, whom he had met at the University of Alaska. He "was at first amusing and charming, then relapsed into his semi-humorous, semi-disagreeable mood, when he is always contradicting and always trying to score, though his statements may be quite absurd." The devoted Vera, as usual, sided with her husband and became hostile if anyone argued with him. Wilson's gout forced him to eat dinner on the couch, with his leg on a footstool; and he thought "it irked Vera a little to have to serve me thus. She so concentrates on Volodya that she grudges special attention to anyone else." Since Vera was rather prudish, she did not like Wilson giving Nabokov pornographic books like *Histoire d'O.*

Wilson not only mildly criticized Nabokov's moods, hospitality and wife (about whom Nabokov felt very protective). He also offered the Freudian theory (which Nabokov particularly disliked) about Nabokov's years in exile in order to account for the unpleasant aspect of his fiction: "I always enjoy seeing them—what we have are really intellectual romps, sometimes accompanied by a mauling—but I am always afterwards left with a somewhat uncomfortable impression. The element in his work that I find repellent is his addiction to *Schadenfreude.* Everybody is always being humiliated. He himself . . . must have suffered a good deal of humiliation." Despite this criticism, Wilson concluded his description with a tribute to Nabokov's personal courage and dedication to his work: "He is in many ways an admirable person, a strong character, a terrific worker, unwavering in his devotion to his family, with a rigor in his devotion to his art which has something in common with Joyce's. . . . The miseries, horrors and handicaps that he has had to confront in his exile would have degraded or broken many, but these have been overcome by his fortitude and his talent."

The aristocratic Nabokov had always controlled his interviewers and biographers by demanding that they submit their questions in writing and in advance, and by revising whatever they had written about him. The suggestion—in Wilson's ambivalent though essentially sympathetic memoir—that he was rude and inhospitable was, he believed, an invasion of his privacy, an insult to his wife, an affront to his honor. Vera may also have been offended by *Upstate* and urged Nabokov to retaliate. He felt that after forgiving Wilson's review and renewing their friendship—as Wilson himself should have done—he had once again been subjected to an unprovoked assault. Nabokov had not, in fact, taken his last look at the "dismal scene."

As he explained to the editor of the *New York Times Book Review*, which published his corrosive letter on November 7, 1971, he was not merely "airing a grievance but firmly stopping a flow of vulgar and fatuous invention on Wilson's part." Believing that he had been victimized by Wilson's "conjecture, ignorance and invention," he once again rejected Wilson's views on Russian versification, defended his wife against Wilson's criticism and condemned his psychological theory:

> His muddleheaded and ill-informed description of Russian prosody only proves that he remains organically incapable of reading, let alone understanding, my work on the subject. Equally inconsistent with the facts—and typical of his Philistine imagination —is his impression that at parties in our Ithaca house my wife "concentrated" on me and grudged "special attention to anyone else." A particularly repulsive blend of vulgarity and naiveté is reflected in his notion that I must have suffered "a good deal of humiliation," because as the son of a liberal noble I was not "accepted (!) by the strictly illiberal nobility."

Wilson's published diary was so "vindictive and fatuous," Nabokov exclaimed, that—had he known Wilson was nourishing such hostile feelings—he would have immediately ordered him out of the house. Returning to the concept of honor that defined Lensky's character,

Nabokov bitterly concluded: "I am aware that my former friend is in poor health but in the struggle between the dictates of compassion and those of personal honor the latter wins."[15]

Nabokov had consistently praised Wilson's books; and in letters written to Nabokov between 1945 and 1953 Wilson repeatedly mentioned that he planned to write a long essay about Nabokov for the *Atlantic* or the *New Yorker*. Though Wilson liked *The Real Life of Sebastian Knight*, he was "disappointed" (his favorite word about Nabokov's works) by *Bend Sinister* and the later novels. Wilson disliked the elaborate artifice and lack of social context in Nabokov's work. He was unsympathetic to the satiric portrayal of a series of fictional heroes who were, like Wilson himself, highly intellectual and emotionally repressed. Since he could not help Nabokov by giving his frank opinion, he thought it best not to review his books.

But Wilson had the last word in their quarrel—after his death in June 1972. He did not make restitution, as he had done with Fitzgerald, but finally delivered—in the form of a critical time bomb—the judgment of his work that Nabokov had awaited for thirty years. In *A Window on Russia*, Wilson doggedly attacked, for the last time, Nabokov's belief that Pushkin knew almost no English and remarked on Nabokov's surprisingly limited knowledge of Russia. He "despises the Communist regime and, it seems to me, does not even understand how it works or how it came to be." Turning to Nabokov's works, Wilson ignored his early masterpiece *The Gift*, found the other Russian novels —*Mary; King, Queen, Knave; Invitation to a Beheading;* and *The Defense*, which ache with pain for the loss of Russia—static and disappointing, and dismissed them all in less than two pages. When examining the English novels (in only one page), he ignored the dazzling *Pale Fire* (which Mary McCarthy called "one of the very great works of art of this century"), revived the *Schadenfreude*-humiliation theory he had first expressed in *Upstate*, casually dismissed *Bend Sinister*, *Pnin* and *Lolita*, and found *Ada* boring.

In a letter of 1976 to the English novelist John Wain, Nabokov alluded to the real reasons for Wilson's attack. The Pushkin controversy, Nabokov wrote, "revealed not only ignorance of Russian on EW's part, but also a bizarre animosity that he appears to have been nursing since the late nineteen-fifties." Since he dates Wilson's animosity from the time of his own success with *Lolita*, the possibility that Wilson envied Nabokov cannot be dismissed. But success had made Nabokov intolerably egoistic, and Wilson may have wanted to chasten him. Wilson had said of Stravinsky: "He has triumphed over exile and displacement, the disruption of Russia and Europe, the temptations, on the one hand, of patronage and, on the other, of popular applause."[16] The same could not be said of Nabokov.

But Wilson's behavior was not inspired merely by animosity or envy. He loved controversy and thought that Nabokov would actually enjoy their dispute. Though well aware of Nabokov's "insatiable and narcissistic vanity," Wilson certainly underestimated the "damaging" effect of his review and naively thought their friendship could somehow survive it. As late as 1971 he tried to minimize his own responsibility and claimed that his "attempts to tease Nabokov were not recognized as such but received in a virulent spirit, and his retaliation was protracted."

The remark of another touchy beneficiary, Edward Dahlberg, illuminates Wilson's generous yet patronizing attitude to Nabokov: "He never ceased to show me kindnesses . . . and [was] quite ready to help a writer provided that he felt he was superior to him."[17] When Wilson had all the advantages (an established reputation, extensive contacts, an editorial position and considerable power in the literary world), he could afford to be generous to the proud Nabokov, who had come from an immensely rich family and had been forced, at first, to live on charity in America. But when Nabokov refused to become his disciple and then surpassed him—as Fitzgerald had done—in art, wealth, fame and reputation, Wilson felt obliged to put him in his place.

Wilson had the "intellectual arrogance and unconscious assumption of superiority" that he attributed to Lincoln in *Patriotic Gore;* and his "impulse to wound," as he said of Ambrose Bierce, "was involved with a vulnerable pride." The intensely competitive Wilson, who always (as Hannah Arendt told Mary McCarthy) wanted to prove how intelligent he was, boldly challenged Nabokov on his own scholarly turf. Wilson's friend Lillian Hellman, though not discussing his relations with Nabokov, penetrated to the core of their quarrel when she observed that Wilson was always gallant with women, but "if you were a man and not prepared to pay him proper obeisance, he would have to knock you down intellectually by demonstrating that he knew more about your subject than you did, had read key books that you hadn't in languages you didn't know, and otherwise establish himself as the brightest guy on the block."

The real beneficiaries of the *Eugene Onegin* quarrel were the literary editors who got all the controversial letters and profitable publicity for nothing (Robert Lowell also jumped into the fray on Wilson's behalf), and the readers who delighted in the cut and slash, the revelations and insults, of two great literary figures. But when the dust had settled, the lives of Wilson and Nabokov had been sadly diminished by the loss of a treasured and irreplaceable friend. In July 1972, a month after Wilson's death, Vera tried to calm the troubled waters of the past by writing to Elena: "I would like to tell you . . . how fond Vladimir has always been of Edmund despite the unfortunate turn in their late relations. We always think of Edmund in terms of past friendship and affection; not of the so unnecessary hostilities of recent years." In May 1974, when Elena was gathering their letters for publication, Nabokov, saddened by their quarrel, wrote: "I need not tell you what agony it was rereading the exchanges belonging to the early radiant era of our correspondence."[18]

TWENTY-THREE

The Middle East and the MLA, 1967–1969

I

The publication in November 1965 (four months after his review of Nabokov's *Onegin*) of Wilson's third volume of collected essays, *The Bit Between My Teeth: A Literary Chronicle of 1950–1965*, affords a retrospective view of his critical tastes, interests and reputation. The forty-three essays by the old workhorse—mainly for the *New Yorker*, *Nation*, and *New York Review of Books*—included three important autobiographical pieces; memoirs of John Bishop, Max Beerbohm, Dawn Powell and Mario Praz; a superb chapter on Malraux's art criticism as well as essays on other friends: Eliot, Auden, Newton Arvin, Angus Wilson and Morley Callaghan; four articles expressing his interest in words and language plus a major work: "My Fifty Years with Dictionaries and Grammars"; and unusually long essays on De Sade, Swinburne and James Branch Cabell. Wilson wrote about new writers (J. R. R. Tolkien, Kingsley Amis and Boris Pasternak) and tried to rescue old ones who had been unjustly forgotten (George Ade, Logan Pearsall Smith and Trumbull Stickney).

Wilson's shrewd observations on the drawings and illustrations of Max Beerbohm and Edward Gorey revealed his interest in graphic art with literary and social content. In 1946 he had exchanged letters with the émigré artist, George Grosz, after reviewing his autobiography in the *New Yorker*. Wilson told Grosz that he had been inspired by his satiric pictures of the Weimar Republic and called him "the historian of tragic modern Germany as well as the carrier-on of the noblest German traditions." Grosz, who had to establish his reputation anew in America, was especially grateful for Wilson's appreciation and praised his insight: "To me you belong to the very few who really do understand my work and the 'ideas' involved. I treasure your words more than all the writings of the professional art critics."

Wilson's own poems, plays, stories and novel gave to his criticism the authority of an artist. But, as Wilson noted of George Saintsbury, "he made a few rather queer evaluations, as every good critic does." He was usually unresponsive to German literature. He took great pleasure in studying Heine with Louise Bogan, but concluded, after reading Goethe with Elena, and perhaps thinking of her family, that the poet "has all the characteristics of the Germans—egoism, blind self-assertion, pomposity, lack of consideration for others." He praised Rolf Hochhuth's *The Deputy* and the works of Günter Grass in the second edition of *Europe Without Baedeker*; and in his essay on Grosz had defined the quintessence of Ernst Jünger and then dismissed his novels, in which "the excitement of war is raised to a pitch of barbaric ecstasy."[1]

Ignoring Fontane's *Effie Briest*, Mann's *Buddenbrooks*, and Döblin's *Berlin-Alexanderplatz*, Wilson informed Silone that "the Germans had no literature of social observation." This criticism was at the heart of his notorious essay "A Dissenting Opinion on Kafka" (July 1947). Though Wilson admired the great modern masters (Flaubert, Proust and Joyce), told Fitzgerald about Kafka and planned to include a chapter about that pre-eminent example of the lacerated artist in *The Wound and the Bow*, he disapproved of Kafka's as well as of Axel's castle. Impatient with the weak-willed and psychologically crippled Kafka, with the "pusillanimity in remaining in bondage" to his father and the pitiful religious doubts of a "soul trampled under," the critic who could not bear indecision and went to pieces when he could not make up his mind rejected Kafka's stories as "realistic nightmares that embody in concrete imagery the manias of neurotic states."

Wilson's view of Mann was equally misguided. He had read only a few short stories and essays by the writer whose children had also called him the Magician. He had begged off reviewing *Joseph and His Brothers* and—as if to apologize for his own imperception—had a character in *Memoirs of Hecate County*, "who was always delighted at a pretext for belittling a distinguished contemporary," exclaim: "The Joseph series is one big snore." Ignoring (once again) writers like Hermann Hesse, Gottfried Benn and Paul Celan as well as Mann's greatest work, *Doctor Faustus* (1947), Wilson declared, during his interview with Henry Brandon, that "German literature seems to have been non-existent by the time the war was over, except for Jünger and Brecht."[2]

Though Wilson had written an innovative chapter on French Symbolist poets in *Axel's Castle*, he found Baudelaire, another wounded artist and the greatest French poet of the nineteenth century, "personally unsympathetic and rather uninteresting." Wilson argued with Morton Zabel about Conrad, the most "Russian" of English novelists, just as he had with Gauss about Baudelaire. In *The Wound and the Bow* Wilson favorably compared Conrad to Kipling and called the hero of *Under Western Eyes* "a tormented and touching figure, confused in his allegiances by the circumstances of his birth." Twenty years later, when Zabel finally persuaded him to read *Lord Jim*, he called it "a wonderful book." But he thought *The Secret Agent* "very boring" and full of "old-fashioned psychologizing," and found the Jamesian shifts in chronology made *Nostromo* "one of the most labored and tedious novels ever written."[3] In his late essay on Turgenev, Wilson criticized Conrad's strained and awkward style.

Wilson's dislike of MacLeish's poetry and persona were well founded. But he had the same objections to a far greater poet, Robert Frost. He had dismissed him as early as June 1926 by writing that Frost "has a thin but authentic vein of poetic sensibility; but I find him excessively dull, and he certainly writes poor verse." Nearly forty years later, when the poet's reputation was solidly established and Louise Bogan tried to persuade Wilson that Frost was indeed a great poet, he was still disappointed by Frost's "flat and uninteresting" work. He was intensely irritated by Frost's appearance as a cultural icon at Kennedy's inauguration. To Wilson, Frost was self-satisfied and fake; he had (like Kafka) an overrated reputation and was the "most self-inflated poet in American literary history."

Like Eliot and Betjeman, Wilson cultivated his own public image and even played the country squire in rural Talcottville. But he was disgusted by the contrast between Frost's folksy wisdom and his ruthless ambition. Wilson, who would kick at Carl Sandburg in *Patriotic Gore*, in August 1959 told Lionel Trilling: "Frost is partly a dreadful old fraud and one of the most relentless self-promoters in the history of American literature. The general acceptance of him as 'a symbol of America'—a dear old sturdy simple New Englander—has become absolutely revolting. . . . Certainly the effect of his work is chilling, and whatever is authentic there is not buckwheat cakes and maple syrup."[4]

Wilson was usually respectful to major authors, positive about contemporaries and generous to friends. Though he tried to avoid inferior books in his reviews for the *New Yorker*, he could be savage about mediocre writers who were taken quite seriously and puffed up by the press. He wrote that Kay Boyle's *Avalanche* was "a piece of pure rubbish"; that the once respected and now forgotten Louis Bromfield "has gradually made his way into the fourth rank, where his place is now secure"; that Somerset Maugham's "language is such a tissue of clichés that one's wonder is finally aroused at the writer's ability to assemble so many and at his unfailing inability to put anything in an individual way." By focusing on a weak historical novel, *Then and Now*, and ignoring first-rate works like *Cakes and Ale*, Wilson was certainly unfair to Maugham.

Wilson once wrote that "the reputation of Ernest Hemingway has . . . reached such proportions that it has already become fashionable to disparage him." By 1948, when he had published *Axel's Castle* and *The Wound and the Bow*, taken over the book section of the *New Yorker* and was generally considered to be the greatest critic in America, it had also become fashionable to disparage Wilson. His whole approach to literature was out of fashion with the prevailing New Criticism. Pascal's observation—"When we see a natural style we are quite surprised and delighted, for we expected to see an author and we find a man"—suggests how Wilson's clear, vigorous prose expressed his character as well as his ideas.[5] By contrast, the critics most esteemed in academic circles—F. R. Leavis and William Empson, Kenneth Burke and R. P. Blackmur—obscured their meaning in crabbed and convoluted sentences, and seemed more profound than they actually were.

Stanley Edgar Hyman launched the first major attack, "Edmund Wilson and Translation in Criticism," in *The Armed Vision* (1948). He conceded that Wilson had "a special insight into the minds and work of disillusioned radicals" like Malraux, Silone and Koestler, but condemned him as a superficial introducer and popularizer who "specializes in plot-synopsis and summary," "interprets or 'translates' the content of literature" and has no real value for the informed reader. Hyman criticized Wilson's "skillful use of other men's researches and insights, sometimes without credit," and also claimed that he separated form and content, analyzed and judged poetry "badly," showed a "weakness of taste" by admiring writers like Poe and reduced Marxist doctrine to the sum total of Marx's physical illnesses. Hyman mentioned the weak structure of Wilson's compilations and concluded that "he has not actually written any critical books (or, with the exception of *I Thought of Daisy* and *To the Finland Station*, any organic books at all), but merely collections of magazine articles." Hyman thought that Wilson enjoyed "an abnormally inflated reputation."

Hyman concentrated on Wilson's apparent weakness and ignored his obvious strengths. Though he was right about the structural flaws of the critical books, he eventually realized that Wilson's "translations" and summaries were in fact analytical; that he had a great deal to say to the more specialized reader; that he was highly original rather than derivative; that he was an excellent judge of poets like Rimbaud and Valéry, Yeats and Eliot, Auden and Lowell, Berryman, Bishop and Jarrell; that he was one of the first modern critics to recognize the genius of Poe; and that it was precisely his ability to place authors in their biographical and historical context that revealed his strength as a critic. By the time Hyman brought out the second edition of *The Armed Vision* in 1955, he had completely changed his mind and omitted the misguided but damaging chapter. Wilson, who did not bear grudges, shrugged off the assault and told Brendan Gill: "That fellow Hyman is bad news."[6]

Hyman's attack suggested the contrary impulses of modern literary criticism. Wilson wanted to encourage people to read serious books with discrimination and pleasure. The academic critics wanted to make their writing even more complex and difficult than the modern authors (Joyce, Pound, Eliot) they most admired. Wilson was the best, and one of the last, of the learned democratic critics who expressed a genuine love of literature.

Richard Gilman, who had written a negative review of *The Cold War and the Income Tax*, wrote an even more hostile review of *The Bit Between My Teeth* in the *New Republic* of July 1966. Gilman argued that Wilson, once in the vanguard of criticism, has now "become increasingly detached from the central life of culture in this country" and has "not for the past twenty years written about the period's significant writers except Pasternak"—though Wilson's book contained essays on Eliot, Malraux, Dawn Powell, J. R. R. Tolkien, Auden, Stephen Potter, Angus Wilson and Kingsley Amis. Emphasizing his "decline from originality and forcefulness," he did not judge Wilson by what he chose to write about, but rather by what Gilman thought he should have written about.

Gilman's claim that Wilson was out of touch with current writers originated in Wilson's own misleading statement, in *A Piece of My Mind*, that he had rejected contemporary life, ignored current literature and lived "more or less in the eighteenth century." It was reinforced by Wilson's self-interview in *The Bit Between My Teeth* when he asked himself: "What contemporary American writers do you think most highly of?" and was pleased to reply: "I don't read them very much nowadays." This criticism was first voiced by Gore Vidal, who maintained that Wilson "has shown virtually no interest in the writing of the last fifteen years." One can search the "'Literary Chronicle of the 1940s' without coming upon any but the most cursory mention of the decade's chief talents." Though Wilson, it is true, did not discuss Gore Vidal, he did, in *Classics and Commercials* (to which Vidal refers), write about a number of contemporary writers: Sartre, Waugh and Connolly, Faulkner, Steinbeck and Wilder, Saroyan, Dorothy Parker and Katherine Anne Porter.

Wilson's uncollected reviews, interviews, diaries and letters reveal, on the contrary, that he kept in very close touch with contemporary authors. Though Wilson turned to other cultures when he became disillusioned with America during the Cold War in the 1950s and the Vietnam war in the 1960s, Gilman's criticism is absurd. He had a far wider range of interests than any other critic in America and his artistic judgment in *The Sixties* was still characteristically sound. He condemned as bogus and boring the films of Antonioni and Resnais, the plays of Hellman, the novels of Susan Sontag.[7]

II

Wilson had maintained contact with the Dead Sea Scrolls scholars, especially the renegades, and kept up with the latest Biblical scholarship. In New York he met Malachi Martin, a witty Irishman and drop-out Jesuit. Formerly a professor at the Pontifical Institute in Rome and currently translating the *Encyclopaedia Britannica* into Arabic, he gave him the latest gossip on the leading players. Wilson thought John Allegro's *The Dead Sea Scrolls* (1955) was the best book on the subject in English and in the *New Statesman* of October 1956 called it "important and fascinating." He looked up the irreverent and brash Allegro—who had once studied for the Methodist ministry and then lost his faith—in Manchester in March 1964. But Wilson changed his mind about Allegro when he claimed, in sensational and "quite fantastic" statements to the press and radio, that the Essenes' Teacher of

Righteousness had been crucified and that the four Gospels were actually an Essene document.

In April and May 1967, just before his seventy-second birthday, Wilson took his tenth and last journey to Europe, and on to the Middle East, to catch up on the latest developments in Jordan and Israel. On April 27 he flew from New York to Rome, and three days later from Rome to Jordan, where he stayed at the American School of Oriental Research. He crossed the Allenby Bridge into Israel on May 10, and three weeks later flew from Tel Aviv to Paris, where he saw Elena's family, his French publishers, Dupont-Sommer, Janet Flanner and Mary McCarthy. On May 29 he returned to Boston.

In Rome Wilson took an expedition with Darina Silone, who surprised Wilson by revealing that her husband was impotent and they had never had sexual relations. Having heard from Mario Praz about a wild park in Bomarzo, southeast of Orvieto in Umbria, that was filled with surrealistic statues, Wilson hired a car and took Darina to see it. According to the legend, in 1560 a hunchbacked Duke of Orsini, having discovered that his wife had slept with her handsome younger brother, killed the brother and then, to express his anguish, built the monstrous park. Wilson's descriptive essay on Bomarzo appeared in the *New York Review of Books* in February 1972 and in *The Devils and Canon Barham* the following year.

In Israel, Wilson visited two new places. The road to Bethlehem, he told Elena, was "the most frightening I have ever been driven on: mostly on the edge of abysmal drops, with no guards to keep cars from falling off, and full of abrupt loopings—in going round one of these, you may suddenly be confronted with a huge bus." At Masada—"a huge, butte-like rock that, thirty miles south of Qumrân, rears itself a sheer thirteen hundred feet from the west shore of the Dead Sea"—the Jews, after the fall of Jerusalem, had made their last suicidal stand against the Romans. Treated as a celebrity in Israel, Wilson was introduced to S. Y. Agnon, who had won the Nobel Prize in 1966. Agnon admired his intellectual power and wrote that Wilson "has been graced by God with an eye to see and a heart to understand."

Israel had fought the Suez War in 1956, two years after Wilson's first visit, and another war threatened to break out while he was there. Troops and tanks were massed on both sides of the border, and Nasser was menacing Israeli shipping in the Gulf of Aqaba. If the Egyptians established a blockade, General Yadin told Wilson, "there will be war."

Alluding to the Essene document, David Flusser rushed up to Wilson in the King David Hotel and exclaimed: "This is the War of the Children of Darkness against the Children of Light!" Twelve days after Wilson left Israel, the Six-Day War began.

In the second, enlarged edition of his book on the Dead Sea Scrolls, Wilson devoted one part to the Scrolls and one to his personal experiences in Israel in 1967. In the first part, he clearly and concisely discussed the newly discovered manuscripts and those that had been (with great difficulty) recently unrolled and read, as well as the latest theories about these documents. He considered the continuing scholarly polemics and forgeries, and the resistance of the various churches to the revelations in the published texts of the Scrolls, and concluded with a chapter on Masada.

The title of the second part, "On the Eve" (of war), alludes to a novel of 1860 by Turgenev about Russia on the eve of reform. Wilson described a military tattoo on the night before Independence Day, the old and new sections of Jerusalem, the Shrine of the Book (dedicated to the Scrolls) in the new Israeli National Museum, and related his lively conversations with Yadin and Flusser. Though the second edition inevitably lacked the freshness and excitement of the original volume, and covered some of the same ground, it was still valuable and extremely interesting. Wilson concluded the book on a sceptical note by emphasizing the abysmal gap between Christian doctrine and behavior: "the myth of the all-forgiving, the all-suffering and redeeming demigod [took] shape after his death and endured through the subsequent centuries, coexistent with that name of Jesus in which so many horrors and hatreds have been justified."[8]

III

In the fall of 1965, after six winters in Cambridge, Paris and Middletown, Wilson was very glad to return to his own house and his own books in Wellfleet—though he still had intense bursts of social and cultural life during his brief visits to Boston and New York. Friends like Arthur Schlesinger, Jr., Edwin O'Connor, Daniel Aaron and Alfred Kazin had bought or rented houses in Wellfleet. In the summer they congenially assembled in the afternoons on what Stuart Hughes called *la plage des intellectuels*, and met afterwards, in various combinations, for drinks and dinner. Kazin remembered the eccentrically attired Squire

Wilson, "in a stained old Panama hat, the long white dress shirt that he wore everywhere—'I have only one way of dressing'—brown Bermuda shorts that bulged with his capacious middle, and carrying a handsome straight gold-topped cane that had long been in his family."

In the late 1960s, before he was overcome by serious illness, Wilson—with sufficient money from recent cash awards, a wide circle of friends, an enviable reputation and no great pressure to produce—had finally found a modicum of contentment. His life was orderly, conducive to work and almost idyllic. His daily routine remained much the same as it had been when he first moved to Wellfleet in 1941, except that he now worked somewhat less than before. After a hearty breakfast at 8:15, he read a bit and then began to write, taking a light lunch at his desk. At three he and Elena strolled into the village for the newspaper, the mail and his daily pint of whiskey. He bathed and shaved to classical music on the phonograph, then followed the libretto of an opera and played solitaire, while drinking before and after his well-cooked dinner. He always played with the cat Lulu and then read himself to sleep.

There were always, of course, distinguished visitors and new friends. Paul Chavchavadze, who translated a memoir by Stalin's daughter, Svetlana Alliluyeva, introduced her to Wilson. He was quite taken with that conscientious and curious, good-looking and good-humored woman, who had a sound command of English. Wilson reviewed two of Svetlana's books, overpraising *Only One Year* (1969) as "a unique historical document" that would take its place "among the great Russian autobiographical works" by Herzen, Kropotkin and Tolstoy.

He had originally met the New Orleans–born playwright Lillian Hellman, who had been an ardent Stalinist and mistress of the detective-story writer Dashiell Hammett, when Nathanael West was running the Sutton Club Hotel on East 56th Street in the early 1930s. After she had introduced Wilson to Mike Nichols, who was then directing a new production of her play *The Little Foxes*, their friendship revived, in New York and on Martha's Vineyard, where Hellman held court. Though Wilson had no illusions about the quality of Hellman's popular plays, he gave her vital encouragement. In her memoir *Pentimento* she gratefully recalled: "Edmund asked why [a friend] didn't write anymore. I mumbled something about writing blocks, I had one myself, all of us, and so on. Edmund said, 'Foolishness. A writer writes. That's all there is to it.' For anybody of my generation, so eager for the neurosis, yours if you could manage it, if desperate somebody else's, the hardheaded sense of that was good stuff. . . . The next day after Edmund said it I went to work on *Toys in the Attic*."

William Styron remembered that when Wilson visited Hellman on the Vineyard in September 1966, he was appalled by the frivolity of the guests. Rejecting their company, he devoted himself to serious study: "Everyone at dinner wanted to watch the Miss America pageant on television, while Wilson, apparently thinking this was a waste of time, made his way upstairs with a big book—Pushkin in Russian—rather disdainful in his expression."[9]

IV

In his late years, Wilson could occasionally be persuaded to give a public lecture. On January 31, 1966, for a fee of $500, he returned to the 92nd Street YMHA, where he had read from *Memoirs of Hecate County* in the late 1940s, and appeared with Jean Stafford. In order to support cultural programs in upstate New York, he accepted Thomas O'Donnell's invitation to speak about Harold Frederic on October 19, 1967 (for which he also received $500) at nearby Utica College. Richard Costa wrote that Wilson gave an unusually sinking performance: "Head buried in script, he gripped the lectern as if it would at any moment slip from his hands. In forty-five minutes he looked up from his paper [only] four times. . . . The audience grew restive as the high-pitched drone varied only to accommodate an occasional fluff." Wilson rescued the evening by inviting Glyn Morris, Mary Pcolar, Phito Thoby-Marcelin and the tax lawyer Francisco Penberthy to be his guests at a party in the Fort Schuyler Club. Though Wilson had bombed in Utica, he loyally returned on October 16, 1968, along with Thomas O'Donnell and William Fenton, and read his chapter on the Little Water ceremony from *Apologies to the Iroquois*.

Wilson also continued to gather important honors. To his great delight they now brought in substantial amounts of tax-free money and provided a public forum for his radical views. On May 11, 1966 the American Academy of Arts and Sciences in Boston awarded him the Emerson-Thoreau Medal and $1,000. He refused to give a public lecture and instead read his translation of Pushkin's *The Bronze Horseman*. He still found it difficult to appear before an audience. On this occasion, imagining that he heard mocking laughter, he became extremely nervous and started to sweat.

The following month, on June 3, the National Book Committee gave Wilson the National Medal for Literature and $5,000. They asked him to give the keynote address at a PEN conference in New York. But, wanting to curb the publicity and control the number of people, Wilson claimed ill health, insisted the presentation be made at his own luncheon at the Fort Schuyler Club and, as he told Costa, "escaped all the fuss and got the money, too." Before an audience that included William Fenton, Roger Straus, John Brett-Smith of Oxford University Press and Mary Pcolar (revelling in the publicity and taking snapshots of the guests), Wilson repeated the arguments he had made in *The Cold War and the Income Tax* in Utica, the scene of his battles with the IRS. Combining remarks about his personal finances with an attack on the war in Vietnam, he said: "I am of course delighted to be so honored, and the award has for me the special significance that the $5,000 that goes with it happens to be a financial lifesaver." The money, he concluded, was "all the more welcome for being, as I understand, tax-free, so that not a penny of it will be demanded for the infamous war in Vietnam."[10]

The ceremony for Wilson's greatest windfall, the $30,000 Aspen Award from the Aspen Institute of Humanistic Studies in Colorado, was awkward and unpleasant. The money came from the chairman of the Atlantic-Richfield Oil Company and was presented by William Stevenson, the president of the Institute, who had been the American ambassador to the Philippines. The previous winners included Albert Schweitzer, Thomas Mann and José Ortega y Gasset. Wilson's doctors told him that his heart could not bear the strain of the 8,000-foot altitude of Aspen, so a "small dinner" was held at the Waldorf-Astoria on June 12, 1968.

The dinner turned out to have forty-eight guests, including an IBM executive, a stockbroker and a dress designer. The only people Wilson knew were Henry Moe, Paul Horgan and Roger Straus, and he had "horrors on either side." One of these "crushing and aggressive bores" talked so much that he finally had to ask her to be quiet. The oil millionaires who gave the award did not know why he had won it and circulated *Who's Who* under the table to find out who he was. The president's wife, vaguely recalling that one of his works had something to do with the Baltic, asked if he had written *Finlandia*.

Wilson drank a great deal to numb the boredom and spoke with blurred diction. But the guests also had a lot to drink and would not in any case have understood what he was talking about. In the Waldorf, as in Utica two years before, Wilson made his familiar attacks and declared that he was "immensely gratified that not a penny of the money this institute is awarding me will have to contribute to the $8.9 billion which are going for this disgraceful war." Recalling C. P. Snow's *The Two Cultures and the Scientific Revolution* (1959), which had provoked a caustic response from F. R. Leavis, Wilson went on to criticize "donnish" hostility to science and provincialism in literature:

> At the present time this gap is made to draw a line between what are called the liberal arts, on the one hand, and every kind of science, on the other. In certain academic communities, it is rather disturbing to find that a certain hostility has arisen on the part of the faculty that represents the humanities toward the departments that represent the sciences. They accuse them of narrow specialization when they are often narrowly specialized themselves.

At the end of the evening, when William Stevenson asked Wilson to sign a copy of *The Shores of Light*, he irritably exclaimed, after months of corresponding with his patron, "Oh, all right. What name?"—and then asked him to spell it. Wilson used the money to pay off his tax debts, buy a new car, improve the Wellfleet house and prop up the manor at Talcottville. The Aspen Award was discontinued by the trustees the following year. Wilson, first nominated in 1966, got it just in time.

Wilson's last major honor (which he accepted *in absentia*) was the Golden Eagle, with $5,500, awarded by the city of Nice on June 1, 1971 to celebrate its third International Festival of Books. The jury—which included the French-Canadian novelist Anne Hébert (whom he had praised in *O Canada*), his former wife Mary McCarthy (whom he later thanked for "the plug at Nice"), his old friend Stephen Spender and his great fan James Baldwin—was favorably disposed toward him. Ten years earlier, Baldwin had written a gratifying letter to Wilson: "Your work has meant something tremendous for me for many years. I mean, I admire your range, your courage, and your depth, and what I've admired in you I've tried to dig out of myself. . . . *To the Finland Station* was a very important book for me. It stretched my mind and it broke my heart." The $41,500 handed out to Wilson between 1966 and 1971—the equivalent of nearly one and a half years' income—provided financial security for the last years of his life.

Wilson did not, however, get all the awards for which he had been nominated. During the National Book Award deliberations in 1963, the historian Walter Lord wanted to give the prize to Barbara Tuchman's *The Guns of August*, but the critic Harry Moore and the science writer William Lawrence held out for the second and third volumes of Leon Edel's elegantly written biography of Henry James. The judges had ruled out *Patriotic Gore*, Moore said, "because it was rather shapeless, a hodge-podge of various articles."[11]

In 1971 Wilson, a great friend of Israel, was awarded the biannual Jerusalem Prize for the "Freedom of the Individual in Society." The $5,000 prize, awarded by the Jerusalem Municipality at their International Book Fair, had been previously won by Bertrand Russell, the Swiss novelist Max Frisch, the French writer André Schwarz-Bart and, most recently, Ignazio Silone, who probably recommended Wilson. The Israeli ambassador told him that the prize was conditional on his receiving it in person. Jerusalem needed Wilson to promote their book fair and enhance their cultural image, and would not—unlike the National Book Committee and the Aspen Institute—accept his quite valid excuse. When Wilson maintained that he was too ill to travel, they took back the prize and gave it to Borges who, Wilson remarked, had never done anything "for the Jews."

Never pompous, Wilson maintained a humorously ironic attitude toward his cascade of respectable honors. Referring to the previous winner of the National Medal for Literature, he recorded: "These awards I am getting make me rather nervous. They mean I am an O.K. character like Thornton Wilder." He defensively told Walter Edmonds that "these medals make me feel like a stuffed shirt, but the checks came at a time when they were badly needed" for his tax debts. When Jimmy and Mary Canby visited Wilson in Wellfleet in 1967, he showed them his medals (now at Yale) and, picking out a smaller one, said: "This is for your pajamas." After receiving the Aspen Award, Wilson was not inclined to accept anything that paid less than four figures. He refused the Friends of Newport (Rhode Island) Library, who offered him the Sarah Josephson Hale Award: a bronze medal plus $50. "I appreciate your offering me that award," he wrote, "but I feel that I now have all the medals that I'll ever be able to use—and I really don't regard it as much of an honor to be associated with that list of second- and third-rate writers (among whom I include Robert Frost)."[12]

V

The Duke of Palermo, first published in the *New York Review of Books* in January 1967, satirized those aspects of academic life that Wilson had despised at Harvard and Wesleyan as well as the pseudo-scholarship he attacked in *The Fruits of the MLA*. The play condemned the illiterate students, the tyrannical college hierarchy, the brown-nosing careerists, the envy of successful teachers and talented colleagues, the stultifying Ph.D. degree, the mindless policy of "publish or perish," the absurd interpretations of texts and complete lack of feeling for literature. Wilson mocked the textual scholar Fredson Bowers, "the great Demiurge" behind the MLA editions, as Dr. Edgar J. Creech, who exposes a textual forgery. He alludes to Robert Lowell, who taught at Harvard while being treated for mental disorders at McLean Hospital, and to Newton Arvin, who was dismissed from Smith, when an administrator exclaims: "Something rather alarming has broken about Ned Simms. . . . That's one thing I can't stand for. We had a scandal here six years ago."

One of Wilson's earliest stories, "Edward Moore Gresham: Poet and Prose-Master," which appeared in the *Nassau Lit.* in May 1915, concerned a literary hoax. His new play—"a kind of 'breakthrough' of high spirits from the Civil War and other depressing matters"—was a clever and amusing tour de force about a professor in a small New England college who forges and stages a pseudo-Elizabethan play in order to arouse the interest of his students. Inspired by the play within the play in *Hamlet*, it not only parodied Elizabethan tragedy, but also revealed the personalities of the actors and the conflicts in the college through the roles they play in the bloody revenge drama. Though Wilson's play was filled with verbal wit, it lacked dramatic action and could not have been effectively performed. When he read it to the Crostens and John Gaus in Talcottville, they resented his satire on academics and found the language of the students inappropriate, inept and absurd. Though stunned by their hostile reaction, Wilson did not attempt to defend his work.[13]

The other two plays, published with *The Duke of Palermo* in 1969, were insignificant. *Dr. McGrath* (1967) continued Wilson's assault on the menacing theology of Calvinism that began with his story "Galahad" (1927). In this one-act play a Calvinist minister, persuaded to behave like a Christian by an atheist and a Messianic Jew, confesses that he has committed incest with his sister and fornicated with his maid, and finally agrees to clear his conscience by attending his sister's funeral. *Osbert's Career* (1969)—a tedious fantasy, like *Cronkhite's Clocks*, on four decades of American life—originated in the 1920s and incorporated Wilson's early playlet, "Beautiful Old Things" (1930). In the "Open Letter to Mike Nichols," he mentioned American plays—like *Uncle Tom's Cabin* and David Belasco's *The Girl of the Golden West* —which were worth reviving.

In a chapter called "What About American Literature?" in *The Cold War and the Income Tax* (1963), Wilson had argued that some of the tax money now spent on military weapons ought to be used "to encourage the national literature" and to bring out "a series of complete editions of the principal American classics in convenient form and at a moderate price." Five years later—first in the *New York Review of Books* of September and October 1968, then as a separate pamphlet brought out in December—Wilson's hostility to academics boiled over in the ironically titled *The Fruits of the MLA*. He now attacked the Modern Language Association (a group of college English and foreign language teachers) as vigorously as he had once condemned the IRS. His fiery polemic followed the great tradition of Swift, Tom Paine and Thoreau.

Wilson's pamphlet was inspired by Lewis Mumford's review of the Harvard University Press edition of Emerson's *Journals* and *Notebooks*. It had appeared in the *New York Review of Books* in January 1968 and had condemned the "totally unreadable text" and the superfluous diacritical marks that "made it look like something between an uncoded Morse message and a cuneiform inscription." Wilson felt "they order this matter better in France." In an open letter to Jason Epstein of August 18, 1962, he suggested they follow the splendid "example of the Editions de la Pléiade, which have included so many of the French classics, ancient and modern, in beautifully produced and admirably printed thin-paper volumes, ranging from 800 to 1,500 pages," with limp leather covers and two silk ribbons for markers.

Having defined his plan and model, Wilson enlisted the support of thirteen eminent men of letters—including Auden, Lowell, Tate, Trilling, Warren—and (through Arthur Schlesinger, Jr.) President

Kennedy, and applied for a grant to the Bollingen Foundation. When they decided the project was not within their scope, he applied to the National Endowment for the Humanities. That government foundation rejected his proposal and instead supported the MLA, which had its own project for reprinting the American classics and, Wilson wrote, "apparently had ours suppressed." Thoroughly sick of all the inferior books he had forced himself to read when doing research for *Patriotic Gore* and *O Canada*, Wilson launched a spirited assault on the MLA-sponsored editions of absolutely worthless works by Howells and Twain, encumbered by a monstrous "textual apparatus." Wilson considered this "ill-judged, quite sterile" republication of "the writer's rejected garbage" a complete "waste of money and time."

The Fruits of the MLA sold 1,489 copies in the first eighteen months, earned $223 and provoked a pamphlet from John Fisher, executive secretary of the MLA, just as *Apologies to the Iroquois* had done from Robert Moses. After wounded laments about the "ill-tempered attack," Fisher claimed that Wilson had "proposed reprinting James A. Harrison's [1902] edition of Poe," which was neither reliable nor complete. But Fisher, desperate to win a point, had distorted Wilson's argument. In fact, Wilson had said that Harrison's unreliable edition "should be checked with the materials of the late Thomas Mabbott," who had been establishing superior texts of Poe's works, and that "the whole subject should be brought up to date."[14] Wilson's original idea was eventually realized when in 1982 the Library of America began to publish the works of classic American authors in single volumes.

Wilson, unfortunately, lost most of the battles he fought. *Memoirs of Hecate County* was suppressed, the Iroquois' land was flooded, the IRS fined him for tax evasion, the French-Canadian separatists fizzled out, his precious friendship with Nabokov was destroyed, the MLA got the grant money and the Vietnam war raged on.

VI

In 1969 Wilson made two attempts to palliate old age and illness: he went on holiday in Jamaica in February and in October began a love affair with an attractive younger woman in upstate New York. Though Wilson had liked Haiti because of its history of independence and French culture, he loathed the neighboring Caribbean island of Jamaica. Soon after he arrived he was poisoned by the food, began vomiting violently and, in "agony and chaos," was too weak to summon Elena from the next room. He found Jamaica a sad and horrible little country, overwhelmed by problems after the English had pulled out, torn between exploitation by the tourists and utter poverty. He felt he was in an intellectual vacuum, and was debilitated by the torpid climate and the squalid atmosphere. He joked that, if he stayed long enough, he would begin to write in the superficial style of Noël Coward and Ian Fleming, who owned expensive villas on the island. He summed up his feelings about the place in "Tristes Tropiques" (misdated "Jamaica 1968"):

> The palms that stand flapping their foolish fronds;
> The phantom of Fleming diffusing James Bonds;
> The almond trees dropping inedible nuts;
> On lawns that are littered with cigarette butts;
>   White beaches, coconut debris,
>   The wide and calm unquiet sea.

On October 1, 1969, only a few days after Mary Pcolar began to respond to his kisses, Wilson was invited to lunch by his dentist, Edgar Miller. He was immediately attracted to Miller's petite, dark-haired, black-eyed wife Anne. She was forty-one, the same age as Mary, had been married for twenty-one years and had four children. Like Mary, she was intellectually curious and longed for something better than small town provincial life; but Anne had a creative urge, made ceramics and wrote poetry. Wilson began by discussing her metrics and soon focused on her feet. She was pleasantly flirtatious and sensual, "so lively, bright and quick—and so tempting with her bare little legs, arms and her pretty slim figure" in shorts or mini-skirts. After years of sexual frustration with Mary, Anne was a welcome relief. Always romantic and attracted to warm, vivacious women, Wilson fell in love with her and proudly told Eva Marcelin: "You see, I can always find the pretty ones."

In contrast to Mary, who felt constrained by her husband and three children, Anne was uninhibited. According to Rosalind, she eagerly pursued Wilson and turned up at his house "in heat." She did not realize how ill he was—though he was constantly taking nitroglycerin and digitalis for his heart condition—and, ignoring all the dangers, was "drunk with the idea of Wilson." Aware that Anne was his mistress, Elena referred to her as "Madame la Slut."[15]

Edgar Miller confirmed that Anne had pursued Wilson. She was a great reader, he had known two of her favorite writers, Fitzgerald and Nin, and she was enthralled by him. The Millers had practiced wife-swapping in the 1960s, her infidelity did not bother her husband and he would certainly not give up Wilson as a patient because of his affair with Anne. Wilson gleefully recorded that "the situation had comic possibilities. Three of my upper row of false teeth came out, and Ned [Miller] had to put them back. I don't want to spoil, by my attentions to his wife, the best dentist I have ever had."

Wilson had been delighted by Lampedusa's story "Lighea," about a Greek scholar who has an ecstatic affair with a siren. In his mid-seventies he believed, as Yeats wrote, that sex would revitalize and inspire him:

> You think it horrible that lust and rage
> Should dance attendance upon my old age;
> They were not such a plague when I was young;
> What else have I to spur me into song?

He considered himself free to seek other women when Elena abandoned him in Talcottville and felt as unrestrained as Anne did about embarking on a love affair. He had no wish to remain celibate and could not resist the last chance of sexual pleasure. He hoped to keep the liaison secret from Elena and felt, in any case, that he needed women to look after him, divert him and stimulate his work.

As eager for fame and recognition as Mary Pcolar, tremendously impressed by a recent article in *Esquire* of April 1970 that included Wilson among the hundred most important people in the world, Anne excited and seduced him. During their courtship she took off her white tennis dress, which enhanced her suntan, and swam naked while he watched. They then proceeded to kisses and "further intimacies." Anne, who had been having a love affair for the past two years with a clergyman, confessed, "I am a very warm person." She allowed Wilson to touch her, but at first refused "the final favor." She admitted she was neglected by her husband and "underkissed," and Wilson insisted that she was also "underfucked." He suggested fellatio and she demurely replied, "I'm a lady." In his house, she again undressed and remarked that he did not take off his socks in bed. He answered that some men did not even take off their shoes. He found it wonderful to feel her "wet, gluey, reeking" parts—so different from the way he had described Elena's idealized and poetic "lovely little rose" in his diary of twenty years before. In October 1971, two years after they first met, Anne announced, in one of her poems, the end of the affair—and opted, like Mary, for a platonic relationship:

> I think I have made love with you
> For the last time.
> Not because it was unpleasant.
> Not because you were demanding.
> Not because of strength of virtue.
> And not because I want to hurt you—
> Just because you are my friend and not my lover.[16]

TWENTY-FOUR

The Dark Defile, 1970–1972

I

In his last years Wilson deliberately placed his own life and family background at the center of his work. He had begun this process with the polished autobiographical essay in *A Piece of My Mind* (1956), and continued to explore this theme in *A Prelude* (1967) and *Upstate* (1971). He carefully maintained his diary until the end, and made plans for its future publication. Swift's self-dramatization, Wilson once observed, "is really one of his most brilliant achievements." Though Wilson recognized that he had limited success at portraying himself in fiction and drama, he knew that his literary criticism and social commentary were stamped with his mind and character. As he grew older and more reflective, he more consciously identified his values with those of his family.

Just after his marriage to Elena he visited an elderly cousin in California. Looking at her photograph album, with pictures of his mother's side of the family, made him feel "most poignantly" that as a writer he had a certain duty "to tell about them so that they should be expressed and should not die out without their goodness, their enjoyments, and their pathos being put on record." Regretful that he did not have their strength of character, he determined to "make up for it by concentrating on my literary ability, not merely to tell about them, but to bring their virtues into my writing, make my writing exemplify their virtues."[1] These qualities, in Wilson's mind, were inseparable from the destiny of America. Just as his family had helped create a new society, so Wilson saw his life as a continuation of their efforts. If he recorded them, he felt, they would endure.

A Prelude: Characters and Conversations from the Earlier Years of My Life, Wilson's first volume of selective and impressionistic memoirs, was based on his diaries. It covered the years 1908 to 1919 and included his family history, childhood trip to Europe, years at The Hill School and Princeton, life at the army camp in Plattsburgh, work on the *Evening Sun* in New York and military experiences in France and Germany. It "aimed to catch *sur le vif* things that struck [him] as significant or interesting," and showed the dark side of his family: his father's neurotic depression, his Uncle Reuel's incapacitating alcoholism. Written with Wilson's characteristic "lucidity, force and ease," *A Prelude* connected his old and young selves. It showed how the young Bunny evolved from a conventional and privileged background, through an elite education, belated exposure to ordinary life and confrontation with the horrors of war into the sexually liberated, socially conscious and intellectually formidable Edmund Wilson.

When Wilson started spending summers in Talcottville, he shifted the center of his interests from Cambridge and Manhattan to upstate New York, from the natives of the Algonquin Hotel to the tribes of the Iroquois, and wrote his loosely connected trilogy of the northern frontier: *Apologies to the Iroquois, O Canada* and *Upstate*. Wilson used his Talcottville diaries of the 1950s and 1960s, with later additions, as the basis for his second volume of memoirs, *Upstate: Records and Recollections of Northern New York*. In *Upstate* he portrayed his intellectual life in a rural setting. He explained what the Old Stone House meant to him and why Elena disliked the place; described his work and reading; portrayed his family, neighbors and friendship with Mary Pcolar; and had sections on his older cousin Dorothy Reed, on his upstate lawyer friend Malcolm Sharp and on his own unhappy visit to Nabokov in Ithaca. He reflected on the life and death of Hemingway, gave an account of his distinguished visitors and told about the poems they inscribed on the windows of his house. Wilson also described the local Indians, the Oneida Community (a nineteenth-century religious and sexual cult) and the origins of Mormonism, founded just north of the Finger Lakes by Joseph Smith, whom he later condemned as "a swindler, a charlatan and an unscrupulous and insatiable lecher." Finally, he merged—in a proud, nostalgic, Yeatsian fashion—personal ancestral and regional history. In a rapturous passage in *Patriotic Gore*, Wilson had defined the mode and mood he would eventually adopt in *Upstate*:

> The tempo of secluded lives [allows] men in a position to live by themselves, usually in the country, to write about country man-

ners which they try to think traditional and stable; to idealize historical episodes; to weave fantasies out of their dreams; to reflect upon human life, upon man's relation to Nature, to God and the Universe; to speculate philosophically or euphorically, to burst into impetuous prophecy on the meaning and the promise of the United States."[2]

Wilson's self-portrait as a Victorian gentleman, his idealized account of rural American life, his juncture of intellectual Manhattan with the upstate wilderness and his description of what Lawrence called the spirit of the place appealed to sophisticated readers and led to a quite unexpected success. He told Rosalind: "I have sold *Upstate* for twenty-five thousand dollars to the *New Yorker* and regard it as the highlight of my journalistic career." By the end of 1971, the penultimate year of his life, the book—which had been selling at the rate of a thousand copies a week and earning a thousand dollars a week—had sold 38,000. Even the little bookstore in Boonville had sold a brisk one hundred forty copies.

But Wilson's portraits provoked a bitter response, not only from Nabokov but also from his relative, the farmer Otis Munn. He resented Wilson's condescending portrayal of his household and was stung by what he took to be Wilson's demeaning remarks: "Otis asked me whether he was 'stunk up' from the cow barn—they got used to it and didn't notice it." Otis angrily and effectively hit back at Wilson in a letter to the *Boonville Herald:* "I am apparently relegated to the role of the country cousin with dirt under my fingernails. . . . I feel that my cousin Edmund is a little unfair in his portrayal of us as a family which has lost its education. In fact I think my education is more complete than his, which is confined to the literary field, and he seems completely helpless when faced with any problem outside his chosen profession."[3]

II

Upstate was also Wilson's modern version of Cicero's *De Senectute,* a philosophical discussion about how to bear the burdens of old age. On one occasion, when he complained of his age to Glyn Morris, who pointed out that Wilson was only ten years older than he was, he replied, "Yes, old boy, but you've still got lots ahead of you." In "The Children's Hour," written when he was sixty, Wilson described his illnesses and waning powers in humorous terms:

> Well, first you see, I'm growing stout:
> I pant, and suffer pangs of gout. . . .
> [The] constant pain must be subdued
> By stiffish drinks, when dining out,
> Which then result in further gout. . . .
> When monster projects loom and lure,
> When powers seem at last mature,
> The wretched old physique decays.
> One smoulders in a slump for days.

Eleven years later, on Memorial Day in 1966, Wilson's mood had become much darker. Playing solitaire on a dismal rainy day, amidst the ghostly presences of the Old Stone House, he expressed regrets about lost opportunities and the threat of death:

> Cities I'll never visit, books that I'll never read,
>   Magic I'll never master. In a cage,
> I stalk from room to room—lose heat and speed,
>   Now entering the dark defile of age.

At the age of seventy-one, Wilson felt, like Mallarmé: *"La chair est triste, hélas! et j'ai lu tous les livres."*[4]

In the late 1950s, Wilson began to suffer from high blood pressure and gout, and as he grew older he developed acute heart disease. As early as 1961, Louise Bogan commented on his severe cardiac pain and told a friend: "He looked ghastly: and has *angina*. A little Johnnie Walker helped, but when we went out for the taxi, he could hardly *walk*." During the last years of his life Wilson suffered from lost teeth, deafness, eye hemorrhage, fractured vertebrae, diabetes, arthritis, tropical fever, infarcts, two strokes and two coronaries. A difficult and temperamental patient, he refused to accept advice or orders that displeased him. His doctors regretted that Wilson could never be kept in the hospital long enough to find out what was wrong with him. Elena complained: "Both at home and in the hospital he becomes petulant; wants service at once and exactly right." Rosalind wittily agreed: "Father is very demanding. He screams frequently, and no one knows whether he's dying or whether there's no pepper on his tray."

Wilson's declining health forced him into hospitals five times during the last four years of his life. In late July 1969, about five months after returning from his disappointing trip to Jamaica, Wilson, thinking he had contracted malaria, entered Beth Israel Hospital in Boston. After enduring five days of tedious tests, during which they found no evidence of tropical fever, he discharged himself and left the hospital feeling much worse than when he went in. In April 1970 he entered Cape Cod Hospital in Hyannis—where John Bishop had died in 1944—after his first serious heart attack. The doctor told him that he had a blocked artery and that it would be dangerous for him to leave the hospital. As usual, Wilson discharged himself before they could complete the diagnosis and celebrated a very slight improvement in health by consuming a quart of whiskey.

In February 1971 Wilson spent a week in Doctors Hospital in New York with a throat and lung infection. Six months later, a second heart attack put him back in the Boston hospital. The doctors recommended a pacemaker to regulate and sustain his weak heart, and to prolong his life. But, as a man of the nineteenth century, deeply sceptical of modern technology, he firmly rejected their advice. In August 1943 he had told Maxwell Geismar: "I'm suspicious of tonsilectomies myself—my impression is that they're a medical fashion that is sometimes unnecessary and sometimes does harm instead of good. In general, I think it's a good thing to avoid resorting too much to doctors." He had refused a hearing aid and, though his life was threatened, remained suspicious of mechanical devices: "I don't want electrodes attached to my heart, and I suspect that this is simply the latest medical fad."[5]

Certain modes of life were for Wilson much worse than death. His mother had taken three years to die and he did not want to prolong his own life in order to become a permanent invalid. He was afraid, if he accepted the pacemaker, that he would be left with a beating heart and a blank mind. He had an even greater, Poesque fear that he might lapse into a coma and be buried alive, and told both Rosalind and Glyn Morris that "he wanted to be sure that he was really gone before anything was done to him." Knowing his heart disease was serious and anticipating the loss of intellectual powers, Wilson loosened his grip on the world, ready, as he put it, "to call my life a day." The dying D. H. Lawrence, accepting his death as part of a natural process, explained to his wife in 1930: "Do you see those leaves falling from the apple tree? When the leaves want to fall you must let them fall." Wilson felt his time was near, but rejected the comforts of religion and stoically accepted the inevitable. "There'll be no begging for Absolution from me," he told Mary Pcolar, "when I have one foot in the grave."[6]

III

Just as Wilson had sought rest in Jamaica and pleasure with Anne Miller in 1969, so he had his last love affair in 1970 and his last season in the sun in 1972. Wilson had met the *New Yorker* film critic Penelope Gilliatt in 1967, through her lover Mike Nichols. Born Penelope Connor in London in 1932, the daughter of a judge, she had come to America to attend Bennington College but dropped out during her first year. Twice divorced, she had been married to an English surgeon and to the playwright John Osborne, who had left her. In 1971 she wrote the successful screenplay *Sunday, Bloody Sunday*. She responded to Wilson's irascible but gallant persona; and he found her amusing and attractive, with black eyes and bright red hair: "She laughs at all my jokes and plays up to what she thinks is the 'image' I want to project—and one could easily become addicted to her. . . . The trouble has been that she has wanted to *please* her men too much."

By 1969, after Nichols had left her, Wilson felt Penelope's attentions were excessive. She embarrassed him by kissing and caressing him at every opportunity. But she was exactly the type of woman he had always been attracted to: good-looking and talented, divorced, neurotic and a heavy drinker. In October 1970—between his second and third confinements in hospitals and just after his summer encounters with Anne Miller—the seventy-five-year-old Wilson was seduced by Penelope at the Princeton Club.

Wilson's deft dramatic sketch of his encounter with "O." (an allusion to the pornographic novel) recalled his diaries of the 1930s and *Memoirs of Hecate County*. He set the scene in the lounge, and recorded their frank dialogue, her eagerness to please and his initial disappointment. He then delayed the action and moved up to his room. Finally, he catalogued the fine points of her naked body and sexual organs, and captured their last verbal exchange, which repeated what he had told Anne Miller the previous summer. His conversation with Gilliatt, a talented writer, had a liveliness and wit completely lacking in his talk with Pcolar and Miller:

> [We] were soon kissing on one of the couches. I turned off the lights. The club was deserted. "I want to go down on you"; but I couldn't feel much. She said, "We'll soon be fucking. We'd better stop." . . . I took her up to my room, and got her to take off her clothes. Her body was prettier than I had expected. Firm but not large breasts; cunt small and charming and pink, but rather far back, with a little fringe of hair. Beautiful sheer ivory white skin, the kind that goes with her [red] hair. She disillusioned me about my conquest by saying that she had two other "fucking friends." . . . She said, "People will know that I've just been fucked. I look like a woman who's just been fucked." "Not enough," I said.

In amusing and flirtatious letters to Wilson, Penelope said that she thought of him and sent "lots of love." Happy and gratified just after the seduction, she wrote: "It was wonderful to see you. I've missed you. I'd like to come up again soon." The following April she revealed that their affair had continued after the first meeting and attempted to alleviate his guilt: "I don't think there's any call to distress yourself about hurting [Elena] or angering her. Storm in a teacup. It'll pass. . . . Perhaps you should destroy this note."

Wilson's trips to Santa Barbara in the 1920s had established, early on, his attitude to tropical resorts. He hated Miami and Jamaica, and was bored to death during his holiday, from January to March 1972, in Naples, Florida—one of the nicest towns on the Gulf Coast. In Naples, Wilson read Balzac and observed the human comedy. "It is largely populated," he told Glyn Morris, frozen in the harsh upstate winter, "by elderly parties who are delighted to get away from the blizzards and winds of the Great Lakes and who are shocked and uncomprehending when you say you find it dull." Though not himself elegantly shaped, Wilson was even more savage about his fellow escapees: "It is a paradise of the retiring middle class, and of an emptiness I should hardly have thought possible. . . . I said that it was like living in prison, and Elena said, 'A sanitarium.' . . . Monotony. . . . Retired executives with potbellies, their dumpy rather dowdy wives." Things got even worse when an elderly party crashed into Elena's car, which had to be replaced at a cost of $2,000. Alluding to Henry Miller's 1945 satire on the American scene, Wilson called Naples an "air-conditioned nightmare."[7]

IV

Despite extremely poor health, Wilson managed to complete an impressive amount of work during his final years. His publishers kept him in the minds of his readers by bringing out eleven books after his death. Farrar, Straus published a reprint of *To the Finland Station*, with his new Introduction, that modified his earlier views about Lenin and the Soviet Union, in August 1972, and *A Window on Russia* in September 1972; *The Devils and Canon Barham* in July 1973, *Letters on Literature and Politics* in 1977 and the five volumes of his diaries. Harper published *The Nabokov-Wilson Letters* in 1979 and Viking brought out the *Portable Edmund Wilson* in 1983. Wilson had always thought the *New York Times Book Review* superficial and middlebrow, and refused to contribute to it. In 1971, for the first time, a few of his pieces were rejected by the *New Yorker*. But beginning in May 1963, and during the last decade of his life, he published eleven essays in the newly-established and intensely intellectual *New York Review of Books*. His support of the journal contributed significantly to its success.[8]

The title and epigraph of *A Window on Russia: For the Use of Foreign Readers* came from Wilson's old favorite, Pushkin's *The Bronze Horseman*. The book included all his previously uncollected articles, written between 1943 and 1971, on Russian literature. Three of the essays—on Pushkin, Tolstoy and the review of Nabokov's *Eugene Onegin*—were originally published in the *New York Review of Books*. There were also two pieces on the Russian language, a second essay on Pushkin and others on Gogol, Turgenev, Chekhov, Solzhenitsyn, Svetlana Stalin and two other obscure writers. Though this book was extremely uneven, all the essays were lively and readable. Two of them were major works: the review of Nabokov and the long survey of the life, career, themes and translations of Turgenev, "the first Western writer of fiction to perfect the modern art of implying social criticism through a narrative that is presented objectively, organized economically, and beautifully polished in style."

Wilson's last collection, *The Devils and Canon Barham: Ten Essays on Poets, Novelists and Monsters*, included works published in the *New Yorker*, the *New York Review of Books* and the *Atlantic* between 1968 and 1972. In addition to two major essays: "The Fruits of the MLA" and a review of Hemingway's *Islands in the Stream*, there were others on

Mencken and on Eliot (in which Wilson states that Pound was a better editor of Eliot's works than of his own), on three minor writers: Maurice Baring, Henry Fuller and Harold Frederic (on whom Wilson spoke at the Utica conference in October 1967) and on three fantastic subjects: Barham's *The Ingoldsby Legends*, the sculptures of Bomarzo, the unfinished magician story "Baldini," accompanied by an affectionate memoir of his friend and collaborator, Edwin O'Connor.

Wilson's *Letters on Literature and Politics*, intended to balance the confessional side of the diaries, was planned by Leon Edel and edited by Elena. Her selection (deliberately excluding personal and family correspondence) from more than three thousand letters was judicious; but the letters were poorly annotated and placed out of chronological order. By contrast, *The Nabokov-Wilson Letters*, for which Harper paid an advance of $12,500, was superbly edited by the Russian scholar Simon Karlinsky.

Wilson's five volumes of diaries, published between 1975 and 1993, were his most important posthumous work. Written by hand in forty-one well-worn, black ledger notebooks, totaling more than two thousand pages, the sketchy, spontaneous, anecdotal journals, to which he usually turned late at night, were a relief and relaxation from his logical, systematic daytime work as reporter, editor, reviewer and writer. He faithfully kept his diary, even when on the move and anxious about public issues and private problems. Everything in Wilson's life revolved around reading and writing, and no experience was quite real to him until he had recorded it. The diaries were a repository of acutely observed details and valuable material, which he often summoned up for formal presentation in books and essays. They were written for his own perusal and enjoyment, both to examine his thoughts and behavior, and to relive the pleasurable days of his youth. He also wrote about his experiences to depersonalize and objectify them, to detach himself from what had happened and to see his life more clearly. He thought that expressing his personality was just as important as writing criticism, and regretted that he had not portrayed himself effectively in his fiction. In his diaries, as in his late memoirs, he himself was the main character.

In his last years he had begun to revise and edit his diaries, but, having used the material in so many other ways, had difficulty deciding what to omit. When Leon Edel suggested that Wilson was free to revise them, he replied: "I don't want to cut any corners"—even though the corners were his own. In his will he ordered his executors to publish them in their entirety, without changing a word. Since he believed that the "records of writers of genius are one of the only ways we have of finding out how life was really lived in any given time or place," Wilson had to be absolutely honest. Editing Fitzgerald's works had shown him how posthumous publication could significantly enhance a writer's reputation. He had survived most of his old friends, had acquired a good deal of inside knowledge and wanted to have the last word. He liked the idea of prolonging his literary career from beyond the grave and of publishing, when dead, more copiously than his living rivals.

In *The Fruits of the MLA* he quoted Mark Twain's statement: "When a man is writing a book dealing with the privacies of his life—a book which is to be read while he is still alive—he shrinks of speaking his whole frank mind." But, Twain added, "from the grave he can at last 'speak freely.'"[9] Wilson did not flinch from hurting others' feelings. No doubt the prospect of future publication of his diaries gave him a sense of power: to criticize and expose his friends, to denigrate or condemn his enemies when they could no longer retaliate. He saw himself in the tradition of literary and social diarists, like the Goncourts and Gide, and considered the fidelity of the record more important than individual feelings.

He told Rosalind that the diaries "will make a lot of people mad," and his family and friends all wondered if they would escape censure. His cousin Esther Kimball was hurt and angry when he included revelations about her brother, Sandy. Though Wilson had promised not to discuss certain aspects of Sandy's life, he recorded that his cousin spoke "with a certain amount of enthusiasm of his homosexual experiences" in prep school. Rosalind, Harry Levin, Daniel Aaron, Alfred Kazin, Paul Horgan and Charlotte Kretzoi all felt wounded by Wilson's harsh comments in his diaries.

It was also difficult for Elena and Helen to authorize publication of Wilson's frank descriptions of sex, but they followed his wishes.[10] These descriptions were the most surprising and provocative part of the diaries, and the surprise was not entirely pleasant. His accounts of sexual experience were often more clinical than erotic, and the tone is especially disturbing when his partner was a woman he loved. But these episodes contributed to the full portrait of himself he wished to leave behind. They revealed the sensual man beneath the cold public persona, and the steady gaze at the absurdities of life, his own included.

They now have a wider historical interest, reflecting the changes in social and sexual behavior in America from 1920 to 1970.

Wilson was predictably severe about the scholarly books on his work. In January 1966 he told William Fenton that Sherman Paul's study "is factually rather unreliable about matters that would have been easy to check and I rather resent his impertinence at trying to guess the originals of my characters and the personal origins of my views. His guesses are usually wrong." "His response to my book," Paul wrote, "was to send it back corrected in his hand," and Paul later published these corrections in a pamphlet. Wilson also wrote a sharp letter to Leonard Kriegel. Referring to both Paul and Kriegel, he told Glyn Morris: "They don't know what they're talking about."[11] The respect and admiration, even love (and sometimes hate) that friends felt for Wilson were reflected in the books dedicated to him and in the poems, stories and novels written about him.[12]

Wilson's will, drawn up in Utica, left the Wellfleet house to Elena and, after her death, in equal shares to Reuel and Helen; the Talcottville house to Rosalind, with its foreign books to Reuel; the Wellfleet library to Reuel, except for the Hungarian books, which went to Mary Pcolar, and the books on magic, to Daniel Walker; the portrait of Wilson by George Hartman to Roger Straus; the royalties of his books to Elena, and then to Helen. He named Elena as his literary executrix; recommended Leon Edel and Daniel Aaron as the editors of his papers. Henry Thornton was appointed guardian if Helen inherited her share before she was twenty-one. Reuel eventually traded his half-interest in the Wellfleet house and its contents for the separate guest house in the back.[13]

V

Wilson had a slight stroke, which affected his right hand, in late December 1970, and a more serious one, two months after his rest cure in Florida, in mid-May 1972. Right after his second stroke he phoned Roger Straus, said that he was waiting for an ambulance to take him to Cape Cod Hospital and—fearful that his mind as well as his speech was impaired—asked if Straus understood what he was saying. Escaping from the hospital as quickly as possible, Wilson went to the circus, fell down, "badly injured his back" and remained in great pain. He could now move about only with the aid of a walker, "and had sufficient difficulty with his arms and hands as well to make eating a meal a clumsy and uncertain process." He found it too difficult to dress, remained in his pajamas and bathrobe, and for the first time fell into periods of silence. He moved permanently downstairs in both houses, accompanied by two alarming green bottles of oxygen. He had Moses' exhortation to Israel in Deuteronomy 31:6—"Be strong and of a good courage"—written out in bold Hebrew letters and tacked up behind the oxygen tanks in his bedroom-study. As he wrote in his poem "On Excavating My Library," "over my chair I have nailed, for tomorrow, / A high tonic slogan I stole from the Torah."[14]

Wilson left the hospital late that month and reached Talcottville on May 31. He was close to death, but Elena remained in Wellfleet. Though he claimed to dislike the movies, he was desperate for distraction during the last days of his life and tried to amuse himself with his girlfriends. On June 8 he had dinner with Mary Pcolar in Rome and saw Marlon Brando as the aging patriarch in *The Godfather.* On June 10, two nights before his death, he went to Utica with Anne Miller to see a film about drug smuggling, *The French Connection.* In his last photograph, taken three days before his death, Wilson, his papers spread before him, wears rumpled pajamas and grasps a sturdy cane. Slumped in a soft chair between two well-lit corner windows of the Old Stone House, he gazes stoically out toward nothingness. Unable to shake hands with Robert Stabb because of his painful arthritis, he lamented: "I never thought I'd come to this." On his last Sunday he drank white wine, played Ravel on the phonograph and read Housman's elegiac, almost morbid Preface to *Last Poems* (1972), which moved him deeply: "I publish these poems, few though they are, because it is not likely that I shall ever be impelled to write much more. I can no longer expect to be revisited by the continuous excitement under which in the early months of 1895 I wrote the greater part of my other book [*A Shropshire Lad*], nor indeed could I well sustain it if it came."

Wilson may well have wished to end his days in the Old Stone House. According to his nurse, Elizabeth Stabb, on the morning of Monday June 12 the seventy-seven-year-old Wilson got up by himself, went to his chair in the front room, picked up one of the books from the piles scattered around the house and began to read. Elizabeth asked if he wanted his bath or breakfast first, and Wilson asked for his breakfast. She went to the kitchen to prepare the meal, and heard a rasping noise. He was having great difficulty in breathing. At 6:20 she connected him to one of the cylinders of oxygen. She called Dr. Smith and told Rosalind, who was asleep in her nearby house, "Your father is having a bad spell." Rosalind rushed over in her nightclothes. Wilson had two convulsions, slumped over and—successfully evading the doctors and hospitals—went quickly and painlessly out of existence.

Rosalind phoned Mary Crosten, who came to the house and, at Rosalind's request, held Edmund's still-warm hand. Rosalind—moaning, "Oh, the poor boy!"—gathered up most of his papers, his glasses and his personal possessions in order to prevent Elena, absent in Wellfleet, from getting them. Rosalind informed Elena and Reuel that Edmund had died. Glyn Morris picked up Elena at the airport at 2 P.M. According to Rosalind, "when Elena came in the house, the first thing she did was to walk to the card table and scoop the papers off it, saying 'Where are the diaries? Where are the diaries?'"[15]

Dressed in his pajamas and bathrobe, Wilson was laid out on his big brass bed in the library. He still had traces of his florid complexion and, according to Walter Edmonds, looked more like a Roman bust than a dead body. At 6 P.M. Wilson's friends gathered around him for a brief, simple traditional service. It was conducted, according to his will, by the Presbyterian minister Glyn Morris. Before Elena and Rosalind, Mary Crosten, Walter and Kay Edmonds, Mary and George Pcolar, Anne and Edgar Miller, Elizabeth and Robert Stabb, Mable Hutchins and her niece Beverly, and a few other neighbors, Glyn Morris read the ninetieth Psalm and the twelfth chapter of Ecclesiastes:

> The days of our years are threescore years and ten; and if by reason of strength they be fourscore years, yet is their strength labour and sorrow; for it is soon cut off, and we fly away.

> Of making many books there is no end; and much study is a weariness of the flesh. Let us hear the conclusion of the whole matter: Fear God, and keep his commandments; for this is the whole duty of man.

After the service, Wilson was cremated and Elena carried the ashes back to Wellfleet.

On June 15, a bright, windy day, the funeral took place in the far corner of the Rose Hill cemetery in Wellfleet. Jason Epstein wrote: "There were moments of humor that I had not anticipated: the young Orleans curate, like a scrubbed Beatle, shyly adjusting his lacy canonicals beside his blue Volkswagen in the Wilsons' driveway, as if he were hanging curtains; Edmund's daughters, Rosalind and Helen, his son, Reuel, and Elena's son, Henry, smiling as they took turns shoveling sand back into the grave where Edmund's ashes had been placed, like children playing at the beach." Charley Walker, his oldest friend, gave the funeral oration. When he declared, "Edmund Wilson was a religious man," Elena protested, "That's absurd, Charley!" Walker ended his speech by saying, "*Shalom*, Edmund."[16] Helen's companion, Tim Woodman, cut the Hebrew letters of Wilson's motto, "Be strong, be strong," into his white marble tombstone. After Elena's death in July 1979 her tombstone, next to Edmund's, was incised with a cross and phrase in Greek: ΑΘΑΝΑΤΟΣ Η ΨΥΧΗ, the immortal soul.

Straightforward and unpretentious in style, indifferent to fashionable taste, receptive to original work, generous to young and little known writers, Wilson's criticism had great integrity and could be read with pleasure by any educated person. His friend Isaiah Berlin explained the power of his organic work:

> His aim and practice were to consider works of literature within a larger social and cultural frame—one which included an absorbed, acutely penetrating, direct, wonderfully illuminating view of the author's personality, goals, and social and personal origins, the surrounding moral, intellectual, and political worlds, and the nature of the author's vision—and to present the writer, the work, and its complex setting as interrelated, integrated wholes.

As Wilson grew older, he thought about his ancestors and wished to emulate their virtues in his writing. The most intelligent and most cosmopolitan figure in American literature, Wilson dominated the literary scene for half a century by combining great learning with an acute sense of the American past. He upheld the highest standards, towered above his contemporaries and represented what the aged Tolstoy meant to Chekhov in 1900:

> Tolstoy stands solid as a rock. . . . As long as he remains alive bad taste in literature, all vulgarity, be it insolent or tearful, all coarse, irascible vanities will be held at a distance, deep in the shadows. His moral authority alone is capable of keeping literary moods and trends at a certain high level.[17]

Notes

ONE: RED BANK

1. Edmund Wilson, *Patriotic Gore: Studies in the Literature of the American Civil War* (New York, 1962), pp. 8, 41; Edmund Wilson, *Memoirs of Hecate County* (Garden City, New York, 1946), p. 261; Letter from Wilson to Alberto Arbasino, February 11, 1961, Beinecke Library, Yale University.

2. Edmund Wilson, *Classics and Commercials: A Literary Chronicle of the Forties* (1950; New York, 1962), p. 17; "Edmund Wilson Dead," *Red Bank Register*, May 16, 1923, p. 1; Edmund Wilson, "The Case of the Author," *The American Jitters* (New York, 1932), p. 305.

3. Edmund Wilson, "The Author at Sixty," *A Piece of My Mind: Reflections at Sixty* (1956; New York, 1958), pp. 213–215; Edmund Wilson, *The Triple Thinkers: Twelve Essays on Literary Subjects*, revised and expanded edition (1948; London, 1962); Wilson, *A Piece of My Mind*, p. 207.

4. Edmund Wilson, *A Prelude: Landscapes, Characters and Conversations from the Earlier Years of My Life* (New York, 1967), p. 31; Rosalind Baker Wilson, *Near the Magician: A Memoir of My Father, Edmund Wilson* (New York, 1989), p. 39; Edmund Wilson, *The Sixties: The Last Journals, 1960–1972*, edited with an Introduction by Lewis Dabney (New York, 1993), p. 492.

5. Wilson, *A Piece of My Mind*, p. 208; Edmund Wilson, *I Thought of Daisy* (1929; London, 1963), p. 105; Wilson, *A Piece of My Mind*, pp. 211, 209; Phone conversation with Dr. Allen Jackson, otologist at the University of California Medical Center in San Francisco, September 28, 1993.

6. Letter from Nathaniel Hartshorne to Jeffrey Meyers, February 3, 1994; Edmund Wilson, "A House of the Eighties," *Night Thoughts*

(1961; New York, 1964), p. 103; Wilson, *A Piece of My Mind*, p. 86; Wilson, *A Prelude*, pp. 168, 22; Mary McCarthy, *Intellectual Memoirs: New York, 1936–1938*, Foreword by Elizabeth Hardwick (New York, 1992), p. 110.

7. Edmund Wilson, "Woodrow Wilson of Princeton," *The Shores of Light: A Literary Chronicle of the Twenties and Thirties* (1952; New York, 1961), p. 301; Wilson, *A Piece of My Mind*, p. 154; Edmund Wilson, *The Wound and the Bow: Seven Studies in Literature* (1941; New York, 1965), p. 237.

8. Wilson, "At Laurelwood," *Night Thoughts*, p. 177; Jane Foderaro, "Red Bank: Birthplace of Edmund Wilson," *Daily Register* (Red Bank), April 17, 1967, p. 9; Valentine card from Wilson to Mary Edwards Rullman, no date, Yale.

9. Wilson, *A Piece of My Mind*, p. 227; T. S. Matthews, *Name and Address* (London, 1961), p. 194; Edmund Wilson, *Letters on Literature and Politics, 1912–1972*, ed. Elena Wilson, Introduction by Daniel Aaron, Foreword by Leon Edel (New York, 1977), p. 596; "A School Boys' Reunion," *Red Bank Register*, August 31, 1910, no page.

10. Edmund Wilson, "The Case of the Author," *The American Jitters*, p. 306; Letter from Wilson to Louise Bogan, July 19, 1933, Amherst College; Wilson, *The Sixties*, p. 141; Wilson, *A Prelude*, p. 5.

TWO: THE HILL SCHOOL AND PRINCETON

1. Wilson, "Mr. Rolfe," *The Triple Thinkers*, pp. 269, 262, 268; Letter from Edmund Wilson to Helen Wilson, February 28, 1910, Yale.

2. Quoted in Glyn Morris, *Less Traveled Roads* (New York: Vantage, 1977), p. 375; Edmund Wilson, *Galahad and I Thought of Daisy* (New York, 1967), p. 27; Wilson, *A Prelude*, p. 60; Letter from Wilson to John Lester, November 20, 1950, Yale.

3. Edmund Wilson, *The Twenties*, edited with an Introduction by Leon Edel (New York, 1975), p. 58; Wilson, "Mr. Rolfe," *The Triple Thinkers*, pp. 262, 273, 263, 265; Letter from Larry Noyes to Wilson, June 26, 1942, Yale. Rolfe edited a school text of Xenophon's *Anabasis* in 1897, and in the mid-1930s, a few years before his death in 1942, published *Old Testament Rhymes*, *Songs of Saints and Sinners* and *A Little Book of Charades*. See Boyd Edwards, ed., *Mr. Rolfe of The Hill* (Pottstown, Pennsylvania, 1930).

4. Edmund Wilson, "The Problem of English" [Preface to an excerpt from *A Piece of My Mind*], *Hill School Bulletin*, March 1958, p. 3; Alfred Bellinger, "A Reply to Edmund Wilson," *Hill School Record*, April 1960, p. 5; Edmund Wilson, "The Library," *Hill School Record*, 21 (June 1912), 271; Quoted in Harvey Breit, "Edmund Wilson," *The Writer Observed* (1956; New York, 1961), p. 174.

5. F. Scott Fitzgerald, "Princeton," *Afternoon of an Author*, Introduction and Notes by Arthur Mizener (New York, 1957), p. 72; Edmund Wilson, "These United States—v. New Jersey: The Slave of Two Cities [Philadelphia and New York]," *Nation*, 114 (June 14, 1922), 714; Wilson, *A Prelude*, p. 140.

6. John Peale Bishop, "Princeton," *Collected Essays*, edited with an Introduction by Edmund Wilson (New York, 1948), p. 398; Wilson, *A Prelude*, p. 103; Edmund Wilson, *The Bit Between My Teeth: A Literary Chronicle of 1950–1965* (New York, 1965), p. 551.

7. Bishop, "Princeton," p. 396; Wilson, "Disloyal Lines to an Alumnus," *Night Thoughts*, p. 90; Wilson, "John Jay Chapman," *The Triple Thinkers*, p. 170; Wilson, *Memoirs of Hecate County*, p. 55; Wilson, *A Prelude*, pp. 179; 86, 85.

8. Wilson, "Christian Gauss as a Teacher of Literature," *The Shores of Light*, pp. 23–24; Edmund Wilson, *The Thirties*, edited and with an Introduction by Leon Edel (New York, 1980), pp. 697–698; Wilson, *The Twenties*, p. 61.

9. Christian Gauss, "Edmund Wilson, The Campus and the *Nassau Lit.*," *Princeton University Library Chronicle*, 5 (February 1944), 43, 50, 45; Edmund Wilson, *Axel's Castle* (New York, 1931), dedication.

10. Wilson, "Woodrow Wilson at Princeton," *The Shores of Light*, p. 314; Wilson, *A Prelude*, p. 148; Bishop, "Princeton," p. 395.

11. Wilson, "T. K. Whipple," *Classics and Commercials*, p. 71; Edmund Wilson, *The Fifties*, edited with an Introduction by Leon Edel (New York, 1986), p. 61.

12. Gauss, "Edmund Wilson, The Campus and the *Nassau Lit.*," pp. 49–50; F. Scott Fitzgerald, *This Side of Paradise* (New York, 1920), p. 50; Quoted in Fred Millett, "John Peale Bishop," *Contemporary American Authors* (New York, 1940), p. 252.

13. Quoted in Jeffrey Meyers, *Scott Fitzgerald: A Biography* (New York, 1994), p. 32; Wilson, *A Prelude*, p. 148; Wilson, *Letters*, p. 22.

14. Letter from Edmund Wilson to Stanley Dell, June 29, 1916, Yale; Wilson, *A Piece of My Mind*, pp. 220–221.

THREE: WAR

1. Wilson, *A Piece of My Mind*, p. 47; Interview with Adelaide Walker and her son Daniel Walker, Wellfleet, Massachusetts, July 31, 1993; Wilson, *Letters*, p. 29; Wilson, *A Prelude*, pp. 156, 155.
2. Wilson, "The Case of the Author," *The American Jitters*, p. 306; Wilson, *Letters*, p. 33; Quoted in Enid Starkie, *Arthur Rimbaud in Abyssinia* (Oxford, 1937), p. 132; Wilson, *Letters*, pp. 31–32.
3. Letter from Wilson to Stanley Dell, October 13, 1917, Yale; Wilson, *Letters*, pp. 32–33; Wilson, "At Laurelwood," *Night Thoughts*, p. 173.
4. Wilson, *Letters*, pp. 34–35; Letter from Edmund Wilson to Helen Wilson, December 23, 1917, Yale.
5. Wilson, *A Prelude*, pp. 207, 225; Wilson, *I Thought of Daisy*, p. 38; Wilson, *Letters*, pp. 36–37.
6. Letter from Ninette Fabre to Wilson, February 13, 1922 (my translation), Yale; Wilson, *Letters*, pp. 43–44.

   The publishing history of this story was characteristically Wilsonian. It originally appeared in *Travels in Two Democracies* (1936), though it had no connection to his experiences in America and Russia described in that book. It was omitted when Wilson included the first half of *Travels* in *The American Earthquake*, but was reprinted in the *New Yorker* of May 1967 and in *A Prelude* later that year.
7. Wilson, *Letters*, p. 41; Wilson, *The Twenties*, p. 11.
8. Edmund Wilson, Jr., "The Death of a Soldier," *The Undertaker's Garland* (New York, 1922), p. 100; Edmund Wilson, *This Room and This Gin and These Sandwiches* (1937), in *Five Plays* (New York, 1954), p. 218; Wilson, "The Case of the Author," *The American Jitters*, p. 307.

FOUR: *VANITY FAIR* AND EDNA ST. VINCENT MILLAY

1. Edmund Wilson, [Introduction] to Phelps Putnam, *Collected Poems*, ed. Charles Walker (New York, 1971), p. vii; Wilson, *Letters*, p. 134; Putnam, "To Some Sexual Organ: Male," *Collected Poems*, p. 143.
2. Matthew Josephson, "Encounters With Edmund Wilson," *Southern Review*, 11 (October 1975), 733; Matthew Josephson, *Life Among the Surrealists* (New York, 1962), p. 249; Matthews, *Name and Address*, p. 192.

3. Quoted in Wilson, *The Twenties*, p. 209; Wilson, *This Room and This Gin and These Sandwiches*, in *Five Plays*, p. 219; Quoted in Matthews, *Name and Address*, p. 201.

4. Wilson, *The Sixties*, p. 48; Wilson, *Letters*, pp. 53–54; Burton Rascoe, "The Monkeyshines of Edmund Wilson," *A Bookman's Daybook* (New York, 1929), pp. 28–29; Josephson, *Life Among the Surrealists*, p. 367.

5. Letter from Margaret de Silver to Wilson, no date, Yale; Letter from Lyle Saxon to Wilson, August 11, 1926, Yale; Edmund Wilson, *To the Finland Station: A Study in the Writing and Acting of History* (New York, 1940), p. 14; Edmund Wilson, *The American Earthquake* (Garden City, New York, 1958), pp. 146–147.

6. Henry Brandon, "A Conversation with Edmund Wilson: 'We Don't Know Where We Are,'" *New Republic*, 140 (March 30, 1959), 14; Edmund Wilson, *Europe Without Baedeker: Sketches Among the Ruins of Italy, Greece and England*, revised and enlarged edition (New York, 1966), p. 349.

7. Wilson, *The Twenties*, p. 32; Quoted in Wilson, "Morose Ben Jonson," *The Triple Thinkers*, p. 253; Interview with Alfred Kazin, New York, July 28, 1993; Stephen Spender, *Journals, 1939–1983*, ed. John Goldsmith (New York, 1986), p. 411; Wilson, *The Fifties*, p. 329.

8. Wilson, *Memoirs of Hecate County*, p. 331; *Conversations with Graham Greene*, ed. Henry Donaghy (Jackson, Mississippi, 1992), p. 114; Wilson, "An Interview with Edmund Wilson," *The Bit Between My Teeth*, p. 544.

9. Frederick Hoffman, *The Twenties* (New York, 1962), pp. 108–109; Wilson, *The Twenties*, pp. 34, 42; Frank Crowninshield, "Crowninshield in the Cubs' Den (part 2)," *Vogue*, November 1, 1944, p. 158.

10. Wilson, *Letters*, pp. 55, 596; Wilson, *The Bit Between My Teeth*, p. 10; Wilson, *Letters*, p. 95; Letter from Edmund Wilson to T. C. Wilson, August 2, 1931, Yale; *The "Hound & Horn" Letters*, ed. Mitzi Hamovitch, Foreword by Lincoln Kirstein (Athens, Georgia, 1982), p. 38.

11. F. Scott Fitzgerald, "My Lost City," *The Crack-Up*, ed. Edmund Wilson (New York, 1945), pp. 24–25; F. Scott Fitzgerald, *Letters*, ed. Andrew Turnbull (1963; London, 1968), p. 345.

12. Wilson, *Letters*, pp. 45–46; Wilson, "F. Scott Fitzgerald," *The Shores of Light*, pp. 27, 29; Wilson, *The Twenties*, p. 60; Quoted in Arthur Mizener, *The Far Side of Paradise: A Biography of F. Scott Fitzgerald*, revised edition (Boston, 1965), p. 132.

13. F. Scott Fitzgerald, *The Beautiful and Damned* (New York, 1922), p. 285; Wilson, *Letters*, pp. 56, 78–79; Edmund Wilson, "Gorgonzola: or

the Failure of Literary Criticism," *Whither, Whither, or After Sex, What?*, ed. Walter Hankel (New York, 1930), pp. 85–86; Fitzgerald, *Letters*, p. 350; Wilson, "F. Scott Fitzgerald," p. 34.

14. Quoted in Wilson, *The Twenties*, p. 79; Thomas Wolfe, *The Web and the Rock* (New York, 1937), p. 482; Rosamond Lehmann, quoted in Sarah Bradford, *Splendours and Miseries: A Life of Sacheverell Sitwell* (New York, 1993), p. 169; Virginia Woolf, *Letters: Volume III, 1923–1928*, ed. Nigel Nicholson and Joanne Trautmann (New York, 1977), p. 280.

15. Wilson, *Night Thoughts*, p. 75; Letter from Elinor Wylie to Wilson, August 14, [mid-1920s], Yale; Nancy Hoyt, *Elinor Wylie: The Portrait of an Unknown Lady* (Indianapolis, 1935), p. 64; Edmund Wilson, Review of Elinor Wylie's *Black Armour*, *Vanity Fair*, 20 (July 1923), 19; Edmund Wilson, *Discordant Encounters: Plays and Dialogues* (New York, 1926), p. 11.

16. Wilson, *The Twenties*, p. 79; Wilson, *Letters*, p. 157; Wilson, *Travels in Two Democracies* (New York, 1936), pp. 216–217. The best works on Wylie are John Gordan, "A Legend Revisited: Elinor Wylie," *American Scholar*, 38 (Summer 1969), 459–468 and Stanley Olsen, *Elinor Wylie: A Life Apart* (New York, 1979).

17. Wilson, "Edna St. Vincent Millay," *The Shores of Light*, p. 749; John Dos Passos, *The Best Times* (New York, 1966), p. 173; Max Eastman, "My Friendship with Edna St. Vincent Millay," *Great Companions* (New York, 1959), pp. 77–78, 83.

18. Edna St. Vincent Millay, *Letters*, ed. Alan Macdougall (New York, 1952), p. 99; Quoted in Wilson, *The Sixties*, p. 168; Wilson, *The Twenties*, p. 64.

19. Edmund Wilson, *The Forties*, edited with an Introduction by Leon Edel (New York, 1983), pp. 223–224; Wilson, *The Twenties*, pp. 334, 63; 52.

20. Quoted in Elizabeth Spindler, *John Peale Bishop: A Biography* (Morgantown, West Virginia, 1980), pp. 52, 50–51; Delmore Schwartz and James Laughlin, *Selected Letters*, ed. Robert Phillips (New York, 1993), p. 74; Millay, *Letters*, pp. 98–99, 153, 115; Edna St. Vincent Millay, "Portrait," *Buck in the Snow* (New York, 1928), pp. 46–47.

21. Wilson, *Letters*, p. 67; Wilson, *The Twenties*, pp. 92, 94.

22. Wilson, *The Forties*, p. 25; Wilson, *The Twenties*, pp. 284, 190; Wilson, *The Thirties*, pp. 252, 623.

23. Wilson, *This Room and This Gin and These Sandwiches*, in *Five Plays*, p. 215; Wilson, *I Thought of Daisy*, p. 80. For the foot-fetishism

of Wilson's close friend, see Meyers, *Scott Fitzgerald*, pp. 12–14.

24. Wilson, *Letters*, p. 63; Quoted in Wilson, *The Twenties*, pp. 86, 109; Wilson, *Letters*, pp. 75–76.

25. Wilson, *The Twenties*, pp. 15–16; Wilson, *Letters*, pp. 73–74.

FIVE: THE *NEW REPUBLIC* AND TED PARAMORE

1. Wilson, *Letters*, p. 56; Fitzgerald, *The Beautiful and Damned*, p. 265; Wilson, *The Twenties*, pp. 29, 31; Letters from Ted Paramore to Wilson, August 12 [1922] and July 19, 1922, Yale.

2. Wilson, *The Twenties*, pp. 132, 278; Letter from Paramore to Wilson, February 9, 1954, Yale.

   While driving across the country in May 1956, Paramore died of a skull fracture in a freak accident. He remained in his car when it was lifted on a cylinder so the mechanic could work underneath it, and when the elevator suddenly collapsed, he was killed.

3. Quoted in Wilson, *The Twenties*, pp. 205–206; Dos Passos, *The Best Times*, p. 139.

4. Allen Tate, Introduction to John Peale Bishop, *Selected Poems* (London, 1960), p. vii; Wilson, *I Thought of Daisy*, pp. 103, 6.

5. Quoted in Andrew Field, *Djuna: The Life and Times of Djuna Barnes* (New York, 1983), p. 63; Wilson, "A Modest Self-Tribute" (1952), *The Bit Between My Teeth*, pp. 2, 5; Wilson, *Classics and Commercials*, pp. 368–369; Edmund Wilson, "George Saintsbury," *New Republic*, 73 (February 8, 1933), 339.

6. Edmund Wilson, *Upstate: Records and Recollections of Upstate New York* (New York, 1971), p. 182; Letter from H. L. Mencken to Wilson, January 21, 1925, Yale; Wilson, *The Bit Between My Teeth*, pp. 31, 33; Letter from H. L. Mencken to Harold Ross, November 26, 1943, Yale.

7. Edmund Wilson, Preface to *The Confessions of Jean-Jacques Rousseau* (New York, 1923), p. v; John Updike, "Edmund Wilson," *Odd Jobs* (New York, 1991), p. 104; *The Nabokov-Wilson Letters, 1940–1970*, ed. Simon Karlinsky (New York, 1979), p. 243.

8. Morris, *Less Traveled Roads*, p. 357; Wilson, "A Miscellany of Max Beerbohm," *The Bit Between My Teeth*, p. 57; Morris, *Less Traveled Roads*, p. 367; Wilson, "An Interview with Edmund Wilson," *The Bit Between My Teeth*, p. 541.

9. Edmund Wilson, "How Not to Be Bored by Maurice Baring," *The*

Devils and Canon Barham: Ten Essays on Poets, Novelists and Monsters (New York, 1973), p. 78; Wilson, "Thoughts on Being Bibliographed," *Classics and Commercials*, p.113.

Five Plays (1954) includes *The Crime in the Whistler Room* (1924), previously published in *Discordant Encounters*, three plays from *This Room and This Gin and These Sandwiches* (1937) and *The Little Blue Light* (1950). *Eight Essays* (1954) includes two essays from *The Triple Thinkers* (1938) and two from *The Wound and the Bow* (1941). *Red, Black, Blond and Olive* (1956) includes the Russian half of *Travels in Two Democracies* (1936). *A Literary Chronicle, 1920–1950* (1956) is made up of selections from *Classics and Commercials* (1950) and *The Shores of Light* (1952). *A Piece of My Mind* (1956) includes an inappropriately inserted chapter on science from *Discordant Encounters* (1926). *The American Earthquake* (1958) includes almost all of *The American Jitters* (1932) and the American half of *Travels in Two Democracies* (1936). *Night Thoughts* (1961) includes *Poets, Farewell!* (1929) and *Note-Books of Night* (1942). *A Prelude* (1967) includes "The Death of a Soldier" from *The Undertaker's Garland* (1922) and "Lieutenant Franklin" from the American half of *Travels in Two Democracies* (1936). *The Fifties* (1986) and *The Sixties* (1993) include most of *Upstate* (1971).

In addition to this professionally effective though often lumpy self-cannibalizing, Wilson reprinted revised editions, often with new introductions, of *I Thought of Daisy* (1929 and, with *Galahad*, 1967), *To the Finland Station* (1940 and 1972) and *Memoirs of Hecate County* (1946 and 1958) as well as considerably expanded editions of *The Triple Thinkers* (1938 and 1948), *Europe Without Baedeker* (1947 and 1966) and *The Scrolls From the Dead Sea* (1955), second edition published as *The Dead Sea Scrolls, 1947–1969* (1969), third edition (with the "Olive" section from *Red, Black, Blond and Olive*) published as *Israel and the Dead Sea Scrolls* (1978).

10. James Joyce, *Letters*, ed. Stuart Gilbert (New York, 1957), p. 185; "Joyceiana," *New York Times*, December 14, 1929, p. 18; Edmund Wilson, Review of *The Waste Land*, *Vanity Fair*, 19 (January 1923), 92; Wilson, *Letters*, p. 94.

11. Edmund Wilson, Review of T. S. Eliot's *Ash Wednesday*, *New Republic*, 64 (August 20, 1930), 24–25; *The "Hound & Horn" Letters*, p. 170.

Wilson wrote favorable notices of books by the following friends: Léonie Adams, Newton Arvin, W. H. Auden, the artist Peggy Bacon, John Bishop, Marie-Claire Blais, Louise Bogan, Morley Callaghan, his

Russian neighbor Paul Chavchavadze, Cyril Connolly, E. E. Cummings, John Dos Passos, Sheilah Graham, André Malraux, Edna Millay, Helen Muchnic, Anaïs Nin, Eleanor Perenyi (who wrote a biographical essay about him), Dawn Powell, Mario Praz, Phelps Putnam, Burton Rascoe, Philippe Thoby-Marcelin, Lionel Trilling, Evelyn Waugh and Elinor Wylie.

12. Letter from Wilson to Malcolm Cowley, January 5, 1951, Yale; Edmund Wilson, "The Decline of the *Dial*," *New Republic*, 52 (October 12, 1927), 211; Wilson, *The Twenties*, p. 417; Wilson, *The Shores of Light*, pp. 751–752.

13. *Friends of a Lifetime: Letters to Sydney Carlyle Cockerell*, ed. Viola Meynell (London, 1940), p. 326; Letter from Horace Gregory to Wilson, July 26, 1937, Yale.

14. Wilson, *Letters*, p. 83; Quoted in James Mellow, *Invented Lives: F. Scott and Zelda Fitzgerald* (Boston, 1984), p. 203; Fitzgerald, *Letters*, p. 317; Allen Tate, "John Peale Bishop," *Memories and Essays, Old and New: 1926–1974* (Manchester, 1976), p. 72.

15. Wilson wrote poems—sometimes to celebrate the birthday of a mutual friend—with Elinor Wylie, Allen Tate, the poet John Hall Wheelock, the critic Morton Zabel, Louise Bogan, Mary McCarthy and Stephen Spender. He also wrote an unfinished play with Ted Paramore, gave Barbara Deming and Evgenia Lehovich collaborative credit for the serialized version of his essay on *Doctor Zhivago*, included Joseph Mitchell's chapter on "The Mohawks in High Steel" in *Apologies to the Iroquois*, translated Pushkin's short play *Mozart and Salieri* with Nabokov, and published "Baldini," a fragment of a novel, with alternate chapters by himself and the popular Boston novelist Edwin O'Connor.

16. Wilson wrote admiring essays on De Sade, William Beckford, Barham's *Ingoldsby Legends*, Poe, Gogol, Swinburne's novels, H. P. Lovecraft and the sixteenth-century sculpted "Monsters of Bomarzo."

17. Lucretius, *The Nature of the Universe*, trans. R. E. Latham (Baltimore, 1962), Book III, p. 128; Dante Alighieri, "Inferno," *The Divine Comedy*, trans. and ed. Charles Singleton (Princeton, 1980), Canto VII, p. 77. The epigraph in Greek from Homer comes from Book XXI of the *Odyssey* and suggests the destruction of the drunken centaur in Wilson's poem "The Death of the Last Centaur": "Wine was the downfall of Eurytion the famous Centaur, in the house of brave Peirithous, during his visit to the Lapithae. The wine took away his senses and maddened him so that he did terrible things in Peirithous' house. The

heroes went wild with rage and flung him out of doors after slicing his ears and nose with their cruel weapons; and away with shattered wits he went, hag-ridden by the burden of his folly" (trans. T. E. Lawrence, 1932; New York, 1965, p. 288).

18. Bishop and Wilson, *The Undertaker's Garland*, pp. 56, 22; Quoted in *The Twenties*, p. 66. [See H. L. Mencken, "Adventures Among Books," *Smart Set*, 70 (March 1923), 144]; Gilbert Seldes, Review of *The Undertaker's Garland*, *Dial*, 73 (November 1922), 578; Letter from Nathaniel Hartshorne to Jeffrey Meyers, February 3, 1993; Wilson, *Letters*, p. 112.

SIX: MARY BLAIR

1. Wilson, *The Twenties*, p. 92; Louis Shaeffer, *O'Neill: Son and Artist* (Boston, 1973), p. 42; Martin Duberman, *Paul Robeson* (New York, 1988), p. 58; Quoted in Shaeffer, *O'Neill*, p. 345.

2. Wilson, *This Room and This Gin and These Sandwiches*, in *Five Plays*, pp. 218–219, 306; Rosalind Wilson, *Near the Magician*, pp. 32, 43; Interview with Rosalind Wilson, Talcottville, New York, August 6, 1993.

3. Wilson, *Upstate* p. 234; Wilson, *Letters*, p. 87; Wilson, *The Twenties*, pp. 110–112.

4. Wilson, *The Crime in the Whistler Room*, in *Five Plays*, p. 156; Wilson, *A Prelude*, p. 277; Wilson, Preface to *Five Plays*, p. 8; Wilson, *A Prelude*, p. 46.

5. Wilson, *The Crime in the Whistler Room*, in *Five Plays*, pp. 202, 143, 159, 200–201. See Jeffrey Meyers, "Poe and Fitzgerald," *London Magazine*, 31 (August-September 1991), 67–73.

6. Joseph Wood Krutch, "Drama: Two Experiments," *Nation*, 119 (October 29, 1924), 475; Stephen Vincent Benét, "Is the Costume Drama Dead?," *Bookman*, 60 (December 1924), 484.

7. Wilson, *The Twenties*, p. 354; Rosalind Wilson, *Near the Magician*, p. 32; Wilson, *The Twenties*, p. 545; Letter from Lois Blair Jansen to Rosalind Wilson, [late 1947], Yale.

8. Wilson, *A Piece of My Mind*, p. 226; Wilson, *Letters*, pp. 215, 107.

9. Rosalind Wilson, *Near the Magician*, p. 44; Glyn Morris, *Nights and Days with Edmund Wilson: An Upstate Friendship*, unpublished typescript, courtesy of Barbara and the late Glyn Morris; Wilson, *Memoirs of Hecate County*, p. 195.

10. Quoted in Stanley Kunitz and Howard Haycraft, eds., *Twentieth Cen-*

tury Authors (New York, 1942), p. 1529; Interview with Rosalind Wilson.

11. Wilson, *Letters*, p. 117; Wilson, *The Twenties*, p. 158; D. H. Lawrence, "The Gods! The Gods!" *More Pansies* (1932), in *Complete Poems*, ed. Vivian de Sola Pinto and Warren Roberts (New York, 1964), 2: 651.

12. Letter from Ted Paramore to Wilson, March 10, 1924, Yale; Letter from Paula Gates to Wilson, March 5, 1924, Yale.

13. Wilson, *The Shores of Light*, pp. 270, 50; Wilson, *Letters*, p. 168; Wilson, "e. e. cummings," *Night Thoughts*, p. 196.

14. Letter from Paul Rosenfeld to Wilson, February 18, 1929, Yale; Wilson, "Paul Rosenfeld: Three Phases," *Classics and Commercials*, p. 503. See also *Paul Rosenfeld: Voyager in the Arts*, ed. Jerome Mellquist and Lucie Wiese (New York, 1948).

15. Wilson, *The Twenties*, pp. 149–150; Edmund Wilson, ed., *The Shock of Recognition: The Development of Literature in the United States Recorded By the Men Who Made It* (Garden City, New York, 1943), p. 906; Wilson, *The Shores of Light*, p. 405; Wilson, *I Thought of Daisy*, p. 152.

16. Sherwood Anderson, *Letters to Bab: Sherwood Anderson to Marietta Finley, 1916–33*, ed. William Sutton (Urbana, Illinois, 1985), p. 249; Wilson, *Letters*, pp. 130–131; Wilson, *The Twenties*, p. 255.

17. Ernest Hemingway, *Selected Letters, 1917–1961*, ed. Carlos Baker (New York, 1981), pp. 104–105; Quoted in Jeffrey Meyers, *Hemingway: The Critical Heritage* (London, 1982), pp. 63–64, 12; 113–114; Hemingway, *Letters*, pp. 326, 360, 418.

18. In addition to *The Evil Eye*, eight plays and the four dialogues in *Discordant Encounters*, Wilson used the dramatic form in many short works: "The Critics: A Conversation" (1925), *The Shores of Light*, pp. 248–253; "The Age of Pericles: An Expressionist Play" (1926), *The American Earthquake*, pp. 164–166; "Prologue: The Man in the Mirror" (1935) and "Illinois Household" (1936), *Travels in Two Democracies*, pp. 3–8, 32–38; "Karl Marx: A Prolet-Play" (1938), *To the Finland Station*, pp. 477–483; "An Interview with Edmund Wilson" (1962) and "Every Man His Own Eckermann," (1962), *The Bit Between My Teeth*, pp. 534–550, 576–597.

19. Wilson, *Letters*, p. 133; "The Poet's Return" and "The Delegate from Great Neck" were reprinted in *The Shores of Light*, pp. 125–155; "In the Galapagos" in *A Piece of My Mind*, pp. 165–187; *The Crime in the Whistler Room*, in *This Room and This Gin and These Sandwiches*, pp. 1–86 and in *Five Plays*, pp. 129–210.

20. Wilson, *Discordant Encounters*, p. 64; Wilson, *Letters*, p. 82.

21. T. S. Matthews, "Edmund Wilson: An American Original," *Saturday Review*, 2 (May 17, 1975), 19; Wilson, *Letters*, p. 127; Wilson, *The Twenties*, pp. 321, 331; 315–316.

22. Louise Bogan, *What the Woman Lived: Letters, 1920–1970*, ed. Ruth Limmer (New York, 1973), p. 24; Leon Edel, in *The Twenties*, p. 199.

23. Wilson, *The Shores of Light*, pp. 243, 206; Telephone interview with William Jay Smith, October 2, 1993; Bogan, *Letters*, p. 48.

24. Letter from Léonie Adams to Wilson, December 12, 1925, Yale; Wilson, *Letters*, p. 153; Wilson, *The Twenties*, p. 442.

    I owe the connection between "Winifred" and Léonie, and many other insights, to Leon Edel.

25. Letter from Léonie Adams to Wilson, 1929, Yale; Wilson, *The Sixties*, p. 197.

    For more on Adams, about whom very little has been written, see: Tony Redd, "Léonie Adams," *Dictionary of Literary Biography, Volume 48: American Poets, 1880–1945*, Second Series (Detroit, 1986), pp. 3–9; Wallace Fowlie, "Remembering Léonie Adams," *New Criterion*, 7 (October 1988), 16–20; and Bruce Bawer, "Léonie Adams, Poet," *New Criterion*, 7 (October 1988), 21–26.

SEVEN: NERVOUS BREAKDOWN

1. Wilson, *Letters*, pp. 371–372; Wilson, *The American Earthquake*, p. 275.

2. Wilson, *Letters*, p. 84; Wilson, "A Selection of Bric-à-Brac," *Vanity Fair*, 20 (June 1923), 18.

3. Wilson, *Letters*, p. 121. Wilson, *Discordant Encounters*, p. 57; Wilson, "A Weekend at Ellerslie" (1952), *The Shores of Light*, pp. 373, 379–380; Letter from Wilson to Scottie Fitzgerald Lanahan, c. February 1959, Yale; Wilson, *Letters*, p. 478.

4. Wilson, "A Weekend at Ellerslie," pp. 382–383; Wilson, *The Bit Between My Teeth*, p. 522.

5. Wilson, *The Thirties*, p. 424; Letter from Frances to Wilson, February 21, 1933, Yale; F. Scott Fitzgerald, "May Day" (1920), *Stories*, ed. Malcolm Cowley (New York, 1951), p. 117.

6. Quoted in Wilson, *The Twenties*, p. 524; Letters from Frances to Wilson, August 1932; November 20, 1933; December 7, 1932; July 20, 1934; November 2, 1928; August 25, 1932, Yale.

7. Wilson, *The Twenties*, pp. 413, 446, 518; Wilson, "Infection," *Night*

Thoughts, p. 29; Letters from Frances to Wilson, June 25, 1934; June 28, 1934; September 28, 1934, Yale.

8. Wilson, *Beppo and Beth*, in *Five Plays*, p. 321; Wilson, *Travels in Two Democracies*, pp. 250–251; Wilson, "Home to Town: Two Highballs," *Night Thoughts*, p. 111.

9. Edward Dahlberg, *Confessions* (New York, 1971), p. 245; Wilson, *The Shores of Light*, pp. 201–202, 241; 201, 207; Quoted in Susan Brown, *Robber Rocks: Letters and Memories of Hart Crane, 1923–1932* (Middletown, Conn., 1969), p. 74.

10. Wilson, *Classics and Commercials*, p. 60; Lionel Trilling, "Edmund Wilson: A Backward Glance" (1952), *A Gathering of Fugitives* (Boston, 1956), pp. 49–50; Quoted in Hans Bak, *Malcolm Cowley: The Formative Years* (Athens, Georgia, 1993), p. 420.

11. Leon Edel, in *The Twenties*, p. 388; Wilson, *Letters*, p. 154. For more on the background of Wilson's story, see Felix Frankfurter, *The Case of Sacco and Vanzetti* (Boston, 1927).

12. Wilson, *Letters*, p. 148; Wilson, Foreword (1953) to *Galahad and I Thought of Daisy*, pp. v–vi; Letter from Wilson to Mary McCarthy, December 2, 1937, Vassar College Library; Stanley Edgar Hyman, "Edmund Wilson: Translation in Criticism," *The Armed Vision* (New York, 1948), p. 43.

13. Wilson, *The Twenties*, p. 373; Wilson, *I Thought of Daisy*, p. 30; Millay, *Letters*, p. 230; Wilson, *I Thought of Daisy*, pp. 64, 133, 220.

14. Quoted in Cyril Connolly, "Edmund Wilson: An Appreciation," *Sunday Times*, June 18, 1972, p. 40; George Painter, "New Novels," *New Statesman*, 43 (March 22, 1952), 354; Fitzgerald, *Letters*, p. 325; Letter from Wilson to Phelps Putnam, September 3, 1929, Yale.

15. Wilson, "Copper and White," and "The Lido," *Poets, Farewell!* (New York, 1929), reprinted in *Night Thoughts*, pp. 46–47, 16; Bogan, *Letters*, p. 48; Allen Tate and John Peale Bishop, *The Republic of Letters in America: Correspondence*, ed. Thomas Daniel Young and John Hindle (Lexington, Kentucky, 1981), p. 27; Wilson, *The Shores of Light*, p. 599.

16. Wilson, *A Prelude*, p. 172; Wilson, *Memoirs of Hecate County*, p. 35; Rosalind Wilson, *Near the Magician*, p. 31; Quoted in Glyn Morris, *Nights and Days with Edmund Wilson*, p. 78.

17. Wilson, *The Twenties*, pp. 492–493; Quoted in Jeffrey Meyers, *Manic Power: Robert Lowell and His Circle* (London, 1987), p. 117; Wilson, *Letters*, p. 159; Letter from Allen Tate to Wilson, March 8, 1943, Yale. See Matthew Arnold, "Thomas Gray," *Essays in Criticism: Second Series* (1888; London, 1906), p. 70.

EIGHT: MARGARET CANBY

1. Interview with Margaret's daughter-in-law and granddaughter, Mary Canby and Catherine Canby Day, Carpinteria, California, October 6, 1993; Interview with Adelaide Walker and Daniel Walker; Wilson, *The Twenties*, pp. 440, 29.

2. Wilson, *The Twenties*, pp. 178–179; Wilson, *The Thirties*, p. 413; Letters from Ted Paramore to Wilson, September 28, 1922 and January 15, 1924, Yale; Wilson, "The Men from Rumpelmayer's," *The American Earthquake*, pp. 158–159.

3. Letter from Ted Paramore to Wilson, March 10, 1924, Yale; Wilson, *Letters*, p. 158; Wilson, *Memoirs of Hecate County*, pp. 302–303.

4. Malcolm Cowley, "Edmund Wilson on the *New Republic*," *New Republic*, 167 (July 1972), 25; Matthew Josephson, "Encounters with Edmund Wilson," p. 746; Harold Clurman, *All People Are Famous* (New York, 1974), p. 106; Wilson, *The Thirties*, pp. 236, 249.

5. Wilson, *The Thirties*, p. 193; Letter from Frances to Wilson, August 25, 1932, Yale; Wilson, *The Thirties*, p. 249.

6. The details of the acccident came from an interview with Mary Canby; Margaret's characteristically heavy drinking at the party from an interview with Jason Epstein (who got this information from Wilson), New York, July 21, 1993; "Mrs. Edmund Wilson Dies. Wife of Writer Fractured Her Skull in Fall at Santa Barbara, Cal.," *New York Times*, October 1, 1932, p. 15; "Mrs. Edmund Wilson is Called by Death as Result of a Fall," *Santa Barbara News Press*, October 1, 1932, p. 8.

7. Wilson *The Thirties*, p. 226; Rosalind Wilson, *Near the Magician*, p. 76; Letter from Wilson to Upton Sinclair, October 19, 1932, Indiana University Library; Edel, in *The Thirties*, p. 227.

8. Wilson, *The Thirties*, pp. 235–236, 241, 252, 368, 252.

9. Wilson, *The Thirties*, p. 368; Wilson, *The Fifties*, p. 231; Wilson, *Letters*, pp. 448–449; John Dos Passos, *The Fourteenth Chronicle: Letters and Diaries*, ed. Townsend Ludington (Boston, 1973), p. 582.

10. Wilson, *The Thirties*, p. 239; Interview with Mary Canby.

11. Letter from Wilson to Katherine Anne Porter, April 7, 1931, University of Maryland Library; Tate and Bishop, *The Republic of Letters in America*, p. 21; Caroline Gordon, *The Southern Mandarins: Letters of Caroline Gordon to Sally Wood, 1924–1937*, ed. Sally Wood (Baton Rouge, 1984), p. 73.

12. Wilson, "The Tennessee Agrarians," *The American Earthquake*, pp. 330–331; Quoted in *The Lytle-Tate Letters: The Correspondence of Andrew Lytle and Allen Tate*, ed. Thomas Daniel Young and Elizabeth Sarcone (Jackson, Miss., 1987), pp. 367–368; Letter from Allen Tate to Wilson, May 17, 1944, Yale.

13. Jacob Landau, "Be Strong, Be Strong and We Shall Strengthen Ourselves," *Forward*, November 6, 1992, p. 15; Wilson, *Letters*, p. 495; Allen Tate, "Causerie (1925)," *Poems* (Denver, 1961), p. 79.

14. Wilson, *Letters*, 496; Letter from Wilson to Malcom Cowley, January 5, 1951, Yale; Letters from Allen Tate to Wilson, January 12, 1951 and April 4, 1951, Yale.

15. Wilson, *Axel's Castle*, pp. 21–22; Diana Trilling, *The Beginning of the Journey* (New York, 1993), p. 76; *The Papers of Christian Gauss*, ed. Katherine Gauss Jackson and Hiram Haydn (New York, 1957), p. 273.
    In the 1919 edition, Symons added chapters on Balzac, Merimée, Gautier, Flaubert, Baudelaire, the Goncourts and Zola.

16. Other books influenced by *Axel's Castle* were Charles Fiedelson, *Symbolism and American Literature* (1953), William York Tindall, *The Literary Symbol* (1957), Harry Levin, *The Power of Blackness* (1958), Maurice Beebe, *Ivory Tower and Sacred Founts* (1964) and Anna Balakian, *The Symbolist Movement* (1967). Wilson's long analytical summary of Proust, which explained the characters, themes, techniques and structure of his novel, was elaborated in F. C. Green, *The Mind of Proust* (1949).

17. Edmund Wilson, *Red, Black, Blond and Olive. Studies in Four Civilizations: Zuñi, Haiti, Soviet Russia, Israel* (New York, 1956), p. 497; Wilson, *Letters*, p. 94; T. S. Eliot, *The Use of Poetry and the Use of Criticism* (1933; London, 1964). pp. 126–127; Wilson, *Axel's Castle*, pp. 203, 218.

18. Wilson, *Upstate*, p. 62; Wilson, *Axel's Castle*, pp. 239, 243; Quoted in Elizabeth Sprigge, *Gertrude Stein: Her Life and Work* (New York, 1957), p. 169; Wilson, *The Shores of Light*, p. 585; Wilson, *Letters*, p. 257.

19. Allen Tate, "Post-Symbolism," *Hound & Horn*, 4 (July-September 1931), 620; Hyman, "Edmund Wilson and Translation in Criticism," p. 19; Frank Kermode, "Edmund Wilson and Mario Praz," *Puzzles and Epiphanies* (London, 1962), p. 56; Karl Shapiro, "The Making of Edmund Wilson," *Washington Post: Book World*, June 25, 1967, p. 5.

20. Wilson, *Letters*, pp. 277, 151.

NINE: MARXISM AND RUSSIA

1. Wilson, *The Thirties*, pp. 316–317; Quoted in Virginia Spencer Carr, *John Dos Passos* (Garden City, New York, 1984), p. 339; Waldo Frank, *Memoirs*, ed. Alan Trachtenberg, (Amherst, Mass., 1973), p. 196; Josephson, "Encounters with Edmund Wilson," p. 753.

2. Wilson, *Letters*, pp. 312; 322; Wilson, "The Case of the Author," *The American Jitters*, p. 308.

3. Daniel Aaron, *Writers on the Left* (1961; New York, 1965), p. 212; Wilson, *The Shores of Light*, p. 498; Quoted in Richard Kennedy, *Dreams in the Mirror: A Biography of E. E. Cummings* (New York, 1980), p. 323.

4. Wilson, *The Shores of Light*, p. 532; Letter from Wilson and Malcolm Cowley to Theodore Dreiser, August 4, 1932, University of Pennsylvania Library; Tate and Bishop, *The Republic of Letters in America*, pp. 23, 46; Quoted in Spindler, *John Peale Bishop*, p. 167.

5. Edmund Wilson, "I Expect to Vote for Norman Thomas," *New Republic*, 103 (September 30, 1940), 445; Wilson, *Patriotic Gore*, p. 700; Quoted in Wilson, *The Thirties*, p. 170; Cowley, quoted in *The Thirties*, p. 178; Wilson, *Letters*, p. 222.

6. Michael Gold, *The Hollow Men* (New York, 1941), p. 68; James Farrell, "The End of a Literary Decade," *American Mercury*, 48 (December 1939), 409–410; Wilson, "The Jumping-Off Place," *The American Jitters*, reprinted in *The American Earthquake*, p. 420.

7. Quoted in Bak, *Malcolm Cowley*, p. 385; Letter from Wilson to Malcolm Cowley, October 26, 1927, Yale; Letter from Malcolm Cowley to Wilson, April 18, 1939, Yale; Edmund Wilson, Review of Christopher Isherwood's *Goodbye to Berlin*, *New Republic*, 99 (May 17, 1939), 51.

8. Wilson, "A Libel on Malcolm Cowley" [1939], Yale; *Conversations with Malcolm Cowley*, ed. Thomas Daniel Young (Jackson, Miss., 1986), p. 212.

9. Wilson, *Letters*, p. 245; Letter from T. S. Eliot to Wilson, January 11, 1923, Yale; Quoted in Meyers, *Scott Fitzgerald*, p. 226.

10. Wilson, *Letters*, p. 230; Letter from Wilson to Louise Bogan, July 19, 1933, Amherst; Wilson, *Letters*, pp. 383; 548–549.

11. Wilson, "My Fifty Years with Dictionaries and Grammars," *The Bit Between My Teeth*, pp. 598, 608.

Wilson translated Petronius and Housman from Latin; Flaubert, Maxime du Camp, Renan, Verlaine, Cocteau and Tzara from French; Giovanni Papini from Italian; Engels from German; Pushkin and Chekhov from Russian.

12. Wilson, *The Bit Between My Teeth*, p. 655; Wilson, *To the Finland Station*, pp. 327–328; Interview with Loran and Mary Crosten, Stanford, California, May 6, 1993; Interview with Richard Pipes, Chesham, New Hampshire, July 18, 1993; Interview with Harry and Elena Levin, Wellfleet, Mass., July 31, 1993.

13. Letter from David Chavchavadze to Jeffrey Meyers, June 10, 1993 (Chernokhvostov is one of the names for the devil in *Memoirs of Hecate County*, p. 301); David Chavchavadze, *Crowns and Trenchcoats: A Russian Prince in the CIA* (New York, 1990), pp. 227–228; *Annual Report of the Guggenheim Foundation, 1935–1936*.

14. See John Reed, *Ten Days That Shook the World* (1919), Max Eastman, *Since Lenin Died* (1925), Theodore Dreiser, *Dreiser Looks at Russia* (1928), John Dewey, *Impressions of Soviet Russia and the Revolutionary World* (1929), Henri Barbusse, *Stalin* (1929), Bernard Shaw, *The Rationalization of Russia* (1931), Lincoln Steffens, *Autobiography* (1931), Julian Huxley, *A Scientist Among the Soviets* (1932), Waldo Frank, *Dawn in Russia* (1933), E. E. Cummings, *Eimi* (1933), John Dos Passos, *In All Countries* (1934) and *Journeys Between Wars* (1938), André Gide, *Back from the U.S.S.R.* (1936), Sidney and Beatrice Webb, *Soviet Communism: A New Civilization* (1936).

15. John Dos Passos, "Russian Visa: 1928," *Journeys Between Wars* (New York, 1938), p. 246; Dos Passos, *The Fourteenth Chronicle*, pp. 461–462; Robert Conquest, "The Kirov Murder," *The Great Terror* (New York, 1990), p. 37.

16. Wilson, *Letters*, p. 273; Edmund Wilson, "Comrade Prince: A Memoir of D. S. Mirsky," *Encounter*, 5 (July 1955), 12, 10; Bogan, *Letters*, p. 112.

17. Leon Edel, in *The Thirties*, p. 589; Wilson, *Travels in Two Democracies*, pp. 208, 243, 179, 215.

18. Wilson, *Travels in Two Democracies*, pp. 212, 304, 321; Letter from T. S. Eliot to Wilson, April 24, 1936, Yale; Tate and Bishop, *The Republic of Letters in America*, p. 133.

19. André Gide, *Back from the U.S.S.R.*, trans. Dorothy Bussy (1936; London, 1937), pp. 62–63; Wilson, Review of *Retouches à mon retour de l'U.R.S.S.*," *Nation*, 145 (November 13, 1937), 531; Leon Edel, "The Critic as Wound-Dresser," *Stuff of Sleep and Dreams* (New York,

1982), pp. 100–101; Quoted in Nathan Halper, "Conversations with Edmund Wilson," *Journal of Modern Literature*, 7 (September 1979), 548.

20. Wilson, *Letters*, pp. 311; 286, 288; 357–358; FBI file on Wilson, July 2, 1951.

   For more on José Robles, see Jeffrey Meyers, *Hemingway: A Biography* (New York, 1985), pp. 307–308, 602–603.

TEN: MISTRESSES

1. Rosalind Wilson, *Near the Magician*, p. 94; Bogan, *Letters*, p. 140.
2. Wilson, *The Triple Thinkers*, pp. 87; 159; Letters from John Jay Chapman to Wilson, May 18, 1929 and September 29, 1931, Yale.

   Even in the revised edition Wilson gives the wrong birth and death dates for Flaubert and says the old farm worker in *Madame Bovary* is awarded a medal for forty-five—rather than fifty-four— years of service.

3. Wilson, *The Triple Thinkers*, pp. 121, 123, 102, 141; A. J. A. Waldock, "Mr Edmund Wilson and *The Turn of the Screw*," *Modern Language Notes*, 62 (May 1947), 333–334.
4. Wilson, *The Triple Thinkers*, pp. 84; 38–39; F. O. Matthiessen, Review of *The Triple Thinkers*, *New Republic*, 94 (April 6, 1938), 280; Wilson, *The Triple Thinkers*, pp. 235, 230; Frederick Dupee, Review of *The Triple Thinkers*, *Partisan Review*, 4 (May 1938), 51.
5. Lionel Trilling, "Edmund Wilson: A Backward Glance," p. 51; Edmund Wilson, Review of Trilling's *Matthew Arnold*, *New Republic*, 98 (March 22, 1939), 199–200; Quoted in Philip French, ed., "Edmund Wilson: 1895–1972," *Three Honest Men: Edmund Wilson, F. R. Leavis, Lionel Trilling* (Manchester, 1980), p. 18; Wilson, "The Mass in the Parking Lot," *Night Thoughts*, p. 181; Quoted in French, "Edmund Wilson: 1895–1972," p. 25.
6. Wilson, *Letters*, p. 307; Letter from Archibald MacLeish to Wilson, October 10, 1938, Yale; Wilson, "The Omelet of A. MacLeish," *Night Thoughts*, pp. 84–88; Robert Penn Warren, Review of Wilson's *Note-Books of Night*, *Nation*, 155 (December 5, 1942), 625.
7. Archibald MacLeish, *Letters, 1907–1982*, ed. R. H. Winnick (Boston, 1983), p. 298; Wilson, "Archibald MacLeish and the Word," *Classics and Commercials*, pp. 3, 6. At the beginning of *Europe Without Baedeker*,

p. 5, Wilson again attacked MacLeish and called his speech of 1945 "sheer verbalizing nonsense."

8. Quoted in Scott Donaldson, *Archibald MacLeish: An American Life* (Boston, 1992), p. 170; MacLeish, *Letters*, p. 123; Archibald MacLeish, *Reflections*, ed. Bernard Drabeck and Helen Ellis (Amherst, Mass., 1986), p. 99.

9. Edmund Wilson, "Letter to the Russians about Hemingway," *New Republic*, 85 (December 11, 1935), 135–136, reprinted in the Soviet journal *International Literature* in February 1936; Edmund Wilson, Review of *The Fifth Column and the First Forty-Nine Stories*, *Nation*, 147 (December 10, 1938), 628, 630; Letter from Ernest Hemingway to Wilson, after December 10, 1938, John F. Kennedy Library, Boston, Mass.; Wilson, "Hemingway: Gauge of Morale" (1939), *The Wound and the Bow*, pp. 184, 195.

10. Wilson, *Letters*, p. 387; Charles Scribner, Jr., *In the Company of Writers: A Life in Publishing* (New York, 1991), p. 82; Wilson, *Memoirs of Hecate County*, pp. 68, 323.

11. Hemingway, *Letters*, p. 694; Quoted in Bernice Kert, *The Hemingway Women* (New York, 1983), p. 88; Letter from Wilson to Morley Callaghan, September 16, 1960, Yale.

12. Wilson, *Letters*, pp. 602, 607; Wilson, *Upstate*, p. 342; Wilson, Review of Hemingway's *Islands in the Stream*, *New Yorker*, 46 (January 2, 1971), 59–62.

13. Tape from Rosalind Wilson to Jeffrey Meyers, August 31, 1993; Wilson, *Memoirs of Hecate County*, p. 85.

14. Letter from Mary Blair-Eakin to Wilson, January 24, 1946, Yale; Letter from Paul Rosenfeld to Wilson, September 4, 1936, Yale; Wilson, *The Sixties*, pp. 743–744.

15. Quoted in a letter from Henrietta Fort Holland to Wilson, January 7, 1963, Yale; Wilson, *The Thirties*, p. 373; Letter from Louise Fort Connor to Wilson, March 23, 1935, Yale; Wilson, *The Thirties*, p. 622. In these entries, Louise is disguised as "K."

16. Letter from Louise Fort Connor to Wilson, February 24, 1937, Yale; Wilson, *The Forties*, p. 298; Letter from Louise Fort Connor to Wilson, July 22, 1960, Yale.

17. Wilson, *The Fifties*, p. 81; Letters from Helen Augur to Wilson, January 26 and 27, 1937, Yale; Wilson, *Upstate*, pp. 96–97.

18. Wilson, *The Thirties*, pp. 673, 513, 673; Letters from Elizabeth Waugh to Wilson, September 30, 1937; January 23, 1937; March 4, 1937.

19. May Sarton, "Louise Bogan," *A World of Light: Portraits and Celebrations* (New York, 1976), p. 225; Letter from Mary Blair-Eakin to Wilson, January 24, 1946, Yale; Rosalind Wilson, *Near the Magician*, p. 93; Wilson, *Letters*, p. 118.

20. Wilson, *Letters*, pp. 205, 207; 269, 271; Bogan, *Letters*, pp. 111; 140; 150; Wilson, *Letters*, p. 289.

21. Letter from Morton Dauwen Zabel to Wilson, July 17, 1937, University of Chicago Library; Edmund Wilson, Review of Louise Bogan's *Body of This Death*, *Vanity Fair*, 21 (November 1923), 26; Louise Bogan, *Journey Around My Room: The Autobiography of Louise Bogan*, ed. Ruth Limmer (New York, 1980), p. 132.

Wilson and Bogan's poem on Auden's forty-eighth (not forty-ninth) birthday is printed in Wilson's *The Fifties*, pp. 295–296.

ELEVEN: MARY McCARTHY

1. Quoted in Carol Brightman, *Writing Dangerously: Mary McCarthy and Her World* (New York, 1992), p. 152; Mary McCarthy, "Our Critics, Right or Wrong," *Nation*, 141 (December 18, 1935), 719.

2. William Phillips, *A Partisan View: Five Decades of the Literary Life* (New York, 1983), p. 63.

3. Mary McCarthy, *A Charmed Life* (1955; New York, 1974), pp. 4–5, 171; McCarthy, *Intellectual Memoirs*, p. 89; Letter from Donald Ogden Stewart to Wilson, June 24, 1942, Yale; Letter from Wilson to McCarthy, September 22, 1942, Vassar; Interview with Arthur Schlesinger, Jr., New York, July 28, 1993.

4. Wilson, "Uncomfortable Casanova," *The Wound and the Bow*, p. 153; McCarthy, *Intellectual Memoirs*, pp. 99, 107, 65, 102; Leon Edel, in *The Thirties*, p. 704.

5. Mary McCarthy, "Ghostly Father, I Confess," *The Company She Keeps* (1942; London, 1966), pp. 203, 219, 206.

6. Mary McCarthy, "The Weeds," *Cast a Cold Eye* (1950; New York, 1963), pp. 13, 28; Mary McCarthy, *The Groves of Academe* (1952; New York, 1963), pp. 13–14; Bogan, *Letters*, p. 302; *Nabokov-Wilson Letters*, p. 273.

7. Quoted in Morris, *Nights and Days with Edmund Wilson*, p. 149; Mary McCarthy, *A Charmed Life* (1955; New York, 1974), pp. 35, 34, 52, 102, 108, 73, 103.

8. McCarthy, *A Charmed Life*, pp. 39, 117; Quoted in *New York Times*,

February 16, 1980, p. 12; Letter from McCarthy to Wilson, December 10, 1955, Yale; Quoted in Doris Grumbach, *The Company She Kept: A Revealing Portrait of Mary McCarthy* (New York, 1967), p. 121.

9. Quoted in Carol Gelderman, *Mary McCarthy: A Life* (New York, 1988), pp. 186–187; McCarthy, *Intellectual Memoirs*, p. 90; Interview with Eleanor Perenyi, Stonington, Conn., July 24, 1993; Norman Mailer, *Cannibals and Christians* (New York, 1966), p. 228.

10. Mary McCarthy, *Theatre Chronicles, 1937–1962* (New York, 1963), pp. vii, ix; McCarthy, *Intellectual Memoirs*, pp. 99–100.

11. Letter from Wilson to McCarthy, [November] 1937, Vassar; Letters from McCarthy to Wilson, December 1, 7, 14 and 20, 1937, Yale.

12. Letters from McCarthy to Wilson, January 7, 19, 24 and 26, 1938, Yale; Quoted in Brightman, *Writing Dangerously*, p. 194.

13. Quoted in Alexander Bloom, *Prodigal Sons: The New York Intellectuals and Their World* (New York, 1986), p. 124 (only the last sentence appears in Wilson's *Letters*, p. 360); Wilson, *The Twenties*, pp. 78–79; Rosalind Wilson, *Near the Magician*, p. 100; Quoted in Anaïs Nin, *Diary, Volume Four, 1944–1947*, ed. Gunther Stuhlman (New York, 1971), p. 88; Quoted in Brightman, *Writing Dangerously*, p. 175.

14. Interview with Harry and Elena Levin; Quoted in Gelderman, *Mary McCarthy*, pp. 107–108; Tate and Bishop, *The Republic of Letters*, pp. 159, 192.

15. Quoted in Brightman, *Writing Dangerously*, pp. 265, 174; Three letters from McCarthy to Wilson, June 1938, Yale; Interview with Rosalind Wilson, and Rosalind Wilson, *Near the Magician*, p. 81.

16. Quoted in Gelderman, *Mary McCarthy*, p. 93 and in Brightman, *Writing Dangerously*, p. 177; Letters from Wilson to McCarthy, July 31 and August 14, 1939, Vassar; Quoted in Brett Millier, *Elizabeth Bishop: Life and the Memory of It* (Berkeley, 1993), p. 58; McCarthy, *Intellectual Memoirs*, p. 105; Letter from Wilson to McCarthy, August 19, 1939, Vassar.

17. Quoted in Meyers, *Hemingway*, p. 350; Interviews with Harry and Elena Levin, and with Rosalind Wilson; Letter from McCarthy to Wilson, September 10, 1942, Yale.

18. Letter from Leon Edel to Rosalind Wilson, November 1, 1990; Wilson, *The Sixties*, pp. 174–175; Quoted in Brightman, *Writing Dangerously*, pp. 264, 266; Wilson, deleted paragraph from the typescript of *The Forties*.

19. McCarthy, *Theatre Chronicles*, p. 83; Quoted in Grumbach, *The Company She Kept*, pp. 117–118; Quoted in Brightman, *Writing Danger-*

ously, p. 261: Tape from Rosalind Wilson to Jeffrey Meyers, March 25, 1994; Quoted in Brightman, *Writing Dangerously*, pp. 253–254; Letter from Wilson to McCarthy, July 13, 1944, Vassar.

20. Telephone interview with Anna Paramore Brando, October 24, 1993; Letter from John Biggs III to Jeffrey Meyers, July 9, 1993; Quoted in Gelderman, *Mary McCarthy*, p. 91.

21. John Golden, "Letters Paint a Portrait of a Great Man of Letters," *Watertown Daily Times* (New York), September 1, 1991, p. C-2; Wilson's legal deposition, c. September 1945, Yale; Quoted in Brightman, *Writing Dangerously*, pp. 252, 256.

22. Rosalind Wilson, *Near the Magician*, p. 114; Quoted in Brightman, *Writing Dangerously*, p. 264; Letter from Adelaide Walker to Wilson, September 12, 1947, Yale.

23. Quoted in Gelderman, *Mary McCarthy*, p. 131; Interview with Arthur Schlesinger, Jr.; Interview with Stuart Hughes, La Jolla, Calif., October 7, 1993; Quoted in Richard Costa, *Edmund Wilson: Our Neighbor from Talcottville* (Syracuse, 1980), p. 105.

24. Letter from Katy to John Dos Passos, November 8, 1945, quoted in Gelderman, *Mary McCarthy*, p. 115–116; Wilson, *The Little Blue Light* (1950), in *Five Plays*, pp. 484, 537, 536.

25. Quoted in Brightman, *Writing Dangerously*, p. 598; Quoted in Gelderman, *Mary McCarthy*, p. 90.

   Wilson met McCarthy in 1937, they married in 1938 and separated in 1945. Hemingway met Gellhorn in 1936, they married in 1940 and separated in 1944.

26. Wilson, *The Sixties*, p. 322.

TWELVE: WELLFLEET

1. Edmund Wilson, "Donmanship," *The Bit Between My Teeth*, p. 476; Letter from Austin Briggs to Jeffrey Meyers, September 7, 1993; Interview with William Fenton, Albany, New York, August 5, 1992.

2. Quoted in Gauss, *Papers*, p. 329; Saul Bellow, *It All Adds Up* (New York, 1994), p. 25; Quoted in Gelderman, *Mary McCarthy*, p. 95; Interview with Rosalind Wilson; Letter from Wilson to McCarthy, August 26, 1939, Vassar; Telephone interview with Ruth Schorer, August 16, 1993.

3. Interview with Daniel Aaron, Cambridge, Mass., July 17, 1993; Wilson, *Letters*, p. 401.

4. Wilson, *The Thirties*, p. 298; Wilson, *To the Finland Station*, p. 468; Bogan, *Letters*, p. 79; Wilson, *Letters*, p. 249.

5. Wilson, *To the Finland Station*, pp. 80, 85; 237; 270; 465; 118; 157.

6. Wilson, *Letters*, p. 293; Wilson, *To the Finland Station*, p. 392; Edmund Wilson, Introduction to *To the Finland Station* (New York, 1971), p. v; Letter from Wilson to Louise Bogan, October 10, 1939, Amherst.

7. V. J. Jerome, "To the Munich Station," *New Masses*, 31 (April 4, 1939), 23; Sidney Hook, "Thinkers Who Prepared for Revolution," *New York Herald Tribune Books*, September 29, 1940, p. 5; Leonard Woolf, "Lenin Turns the Key," *New Statesman and Nation*, 22 (September 6, 1941), 234; Edmund Wilson, "On Excavating My Library," *Holiday Greetings and Desolating Lyrics* ([Boston], privately printed, 1970), [p. 5].

8. Wilson, *Letters*, pp. 313–314; Fitzgerald, *Letters*, p. 368; Budd Schulberg, "Old Scott: The Myth, the Masque, the Man," *Four Seasons of Success* (Garden City, New York, 1972), p. 126.

9. Letter from Wilson to Maxwell Geismar, July 23, 1944, Boston University; Wilson, *Letters*, p. 369–370; 337; Edmund Wilson, Foreword to Fitzgerald's *The Last Tycoon* (New York, 1941), n.p.; Edmund Wilson, Foreword to Fitzgerald's *The Last Tycoon, The Great Gatsby and Selected Stories* (New York, 1945), p. xi.

10. Wilson, *Letters*, p. 343; Letter from Sheilah Graham to Wilson, June 30, 1941, Yale; Wilson, *Letters*, p. 337.

    In her edition of Wilson's *Letters*, his fourth wife, Elena, confuses William Matson Roth with the unscrupulous Samuel Roth, who pirated *Ulysses* and *Lady Chatterley's Lover*. The Colt Press papers became available at the Bancroft Library of the University of California, Berkeley, in December 1993.

11. Letter from Wilson to John Biggs, August 10, 1943, Yale; Letter from Wilson to Edward Dahlberg, November 3, 1954, Humanities Research Center, University of Texas; Letter from James Laughlin to Wilson, August 17, 1943, Yale.

12. Letter from Wilson to John Biggs, May 21, 1942, Yale; Edmund Wilson, "Dedication," to Scott Fitzgerald, *The Crack-Up*, pp. 8–9; Letter from Wilson to Arthur Mizener, February 21, 1950, Maryland; Letter from Wilson to Dorothy [de Santillana] at Houghton Mifflin, March 3, 1950, Yale.

    Though Mizener followed Wilson's advice, he must have been wounded by his criticism and did not thank him in the Foreword to the biography.

13. Morris, *Less Traveled Roads*, p. 378. Scottie agreed that Sheilah had had a positive effect on Fitzgerald. In a letter to Wilson of January 26, 1959 (Yale), she alluded to one of Scott's favorite poems, "Ode on a Grecian Urn," and expressed unwarranted guilt about her troubled relations with her parents: "Daddy's fame has given me a kind of eternal youth, being fixed, like Keats' maidens, in posterity forever as 'the daughter of'. . . . I contributed to the tragedy by being a constant drain on the finances, and benefitted in the end from the fame and fortune and lavish care, whereas all Sheilah did was to keep him alive for five [i.e., 3½] years."

14. Letter from Wilson to Maxwell Geismar, November 9, 1943, Boston University; Letter from Wilson to Lionel Trilling, August 31, 1953, Columbia University; Wilson, *Letters*, pp. 335, 328; Quoted in Charles Todd, "Upstate with Edmund Wilson," *New York History*, 54 (1973), 54.

15. Letter from Wilson to Mamaine Paget, September 9, 1946, Yale; Wilson, *The Forties*, p. 221; Wilson, *The Sixties*, p. 583; Interview with Rosalind Wilson.

16. Letter from Michael Macdonald to Jeffrey Meyers, November 4, 1993; Interview with Richard Pipes; Interview with Adelaide and Daniel Walker; Interview with Henry Thornton, Sheffield, Mass., August 4, 1993.

17. Interview with Jason Epstein; Wilson, "On Excavating My Library," *Holiday Greetings and Desolating Lyrics*, [p. 4]; "The Rats of Rutland Grange," *Night Thoughts*, p. 253; *New York Times*, September 18, 1951, p. 8.

18. Letter from Michael Macdonald to Jeffrey Meyers, November 4, 1993; Letter from David Chavchavadze to Jeffrey Meyers, June 10, 1993; Alfred Kazin, *New York Jew* (New York, 1978), pp. 67, 65.

19. Interview with Harry and Elena Levin; Letter from Wilson to McCarthy, June 19, 1946, Vassar; Quoted in Gelderman, *Mary McCarthy*, p. 117.

20. Wilson, *The Forties*, p. 29; Quoted in Brightman, *Writing Dangerously*, p. 234; Wilson and Tate, unpublished poem, summer 1940, Yale; Wilson, "Edna St. Vincent Millay," *The Shores of Light*, p. 786; Wilson, *The Forties*, p. 300.

21. Rosalind Wilson, *Near the Magician*, p. 15; Interview with Adelaide and Daniel Walker; Telephone conversation with Alfred Kazin, June 22, 1993 and letter from Alfred Kazin to Jeffrey Meyers, June 18, 1993.

22. Leon Edel, in *The Forties*, p. 10; Wilson, *The Forties*, p. 19; Roger Straus, report on Wilson's *The Story of the Three Wishes*, Yale.

23. Quoted in John Tebbel, *A History of Book Publishing in the United States* (New York, 1978), 4: 436; Telephone interview with William Matson Roth, August 17, 1993; Wilson, "The Boys in the Back Room," *Classics and Commercials*, p. 21; Letter from Wilson to William Matson Roth, June 23, 1941, University of California, Berkeley.

24. Edmund Wilson, *Note-Books of Night* (San Francisco, 1942), pp. 14, 59.

25. Wilson, *The Twenties*, pp. 423, 428; Wilson, *The Wound and the Bow*, pp. 240, 136; Quoted in James Atlas, *Delmore Schwartz* (1977; New York, 1978), p. 174; Wilson, *Letters*, p. 361.

26. Letter from Wilson to Morton Zabel, November 6, 1936, Yale; Wilson, *The Shock of Recognition*, pp. vii–viii; 79, 1155, 906.

THIRTEEN: AT THE *NEW YORKER*

1. Michael Straight, *After Long Silence* (New York, 1983), p. 159; Letter from Wilson to Gilbert Harrison of the *New Republic*, November 30, 1954, Yale; Wilson, "Postscript of 1957," *The American Earthquake*, p. 567; Arthur Schlesinger, Jr., "From the Golden Days of Boom to the Desperation of Bust," *New York Times Book Review*, February 9, 1958, p. 3.

2. Letter from Wilson to Sheldon Meyer of Oxford University Press, August 5, 1961, Yale; Interview with Arthur Schlesinger, Jr.; Wilson, Introduction to *Patriotic Gore*, p. xxvi; Wilson, *The American Earthquake*, pp. 569–570; Alfred Kazin, "Zeal for the Hidden Detail," *Atlantic*, 251 (April 1983), 126.

3. Letter from Wilson to Alyse Gregory, November 10, 1944, Humanities Research Center, University of Texas; Brendan Gill, *Here at the New Yorker* (New York, 1975), p. 283; Edmund Wilson, "Doubts and Dreams: *Dangling Man*," *New Yorker*, 20 (April 1, 1944), 78.

4. Virginia Spencer Carr, *The Lonely Hunter: A Biography of Carson McCullers* (Garden City, New York, 1976), p. 268; Edmund Wilson, Review of Charles Jackson's *The Lost Weekend*, *New Yorker*, 19 (February 5, 1944), 78; Letter from Charles Jackson to Wilson, February 11, 1944, Yale; Rolfe Humphries, *Poets, Poetics and Politics*, ed. Richard Gillman and Michael Novak (Lawrence, Kansas, 1992), pp. 194–195.

5. Letter from Wilson to Harold Ross, November 24, 1947, Yale; Letter from Wilson to James Thurber, March 22, 1958, Yale.

6. Wilson, *Letters*, pp. 407, 690; Letter from Wilson to Charles "Cap" Pearce of the *New Yorker*, December 20, 1940, Yale; Letter from Wilson to Houghton Mifflin, January 3, 1945, Harvard University.

7. Letters from Maxwell Geismar to Wilson, March 1, 1942 and September 9, 1943, Yale. Wilson's successful candidates included Conrad Aiken, W. H. Auden, Saul Bellow, John Berryman, Elizabeth Bishop, Marie-Claire Blais, Hart Crane, John Dos Passos, Leon Edel, Irving Howe, Randall Jarrell, Alfred Kazin, Harry Levin, Arthur Mizener, Vladimir Nabokov, Katherine Anne Porter, Phelps Putnam, Allen Tate and Charley Walker. Among his unsuccessful candidates were: James Agee, Helen Augur, Paul Chavchavadze, Anaïs Nin and Nathanael West.

8. The information on Muchnic comes from Golden, "Letters Paint a Portrait of a Great Man of Letters," pp. C1–C2; *Smith Alumnae Quarterly*, August 1969, p. 23; Interview with Rosalind Wilson; Interview with Charlee (Muchnic's former pupil) and Richard Wilbur, Cummington, Mass., August 4, 1993.

9. Interview with Simon Karlinsky, Berkeley, Calif., May 13, 1993; Letter from Rosalind Wilson to Edmund Wilson, June 1, 1945, Yale; Interview with Daniel Aaron; Interview with Harry and Elena Levin.

10. *Nabokov-Wilson Letters*, p. 92; Wilson, *Letters*, p. 411; Edmund Wilson, Review of Helen Muchnic's *Introduction to Russian Literature*, *New Yorker*, 18 (June 21, 1947), 72; Letter from Edmund to Elena Wilson, August 30, 1956, Yale.

11. Edmund Wilson, *A Window on Russia: For the Use of Foreign Readers* (New York, 1971), p. 276; Letters from Wilson to Helen Muchnic, May 20, 1946 and October 25, 1968, Yale.

12. Edmund Wilson, Review of Anaïs Nin's *Under a Glass Bell*, *New Yorker*, 20 (April 1, 1944), 81; Anaïs Nin, *Diary*, p. 5; Edmund Wilson, Review of Anaïs Nin's *This Hunger*, *New Yorker*, 21 (November 10, 1945), 101; Edmund Wilson, Review of Anaïs Nin's *Ladders to Fire*, *New Yorker*, 22 (November 16, 1946), 130; Nin, *Diary*, p. 165.

13. Letter from Wilson to Clelia Carroll, August 1, 1967, Yale; Letter from Wilson to Mary Meigs, May 23, 1966, Yale; Nin, *Diary*, pp. 41, 79; 83–84. Noel Riley Fitch, *Anaïs: The Erotic Life of Anaïs Nin* (Boston, 1993), p. 272, describes her affair with Wilson.

14. Nin, *Diary*, pp. 89, 93, 90; 106, 116; Letter from Wilson to Anaïs Nin, February 12, 1966, Yale; Wilson, *The Sixties*, pp. 503–504; Gore Vidal, "The Fourth Diary of Anaïs Nin," *Homage to Daniel Shays: Collected Essays, 1952–1972* (1972; New York, 1973), p. 408.

15. Wilson, *The Forties*, p. 288; Matthew Josephson, "Dawn Powell: A Woman of Esprit," *Southern Review*, 9 (January 1973), 20; Letter from Dawn Powell to Wilson, August 23, 1962, Yale.

16. Wilson, *The Forties*, p. 304; Wilson, *The Sixties*, p. 489; Edmund Wilson, Review of Dawn Powell's *My Home is Far Away*, *New Yorker*, 20 (November 11, 1944), 93; Wilson, "Dawn Powell: Greenwich Village in the Fifties," *The Bit Between My Teeth*, p. 527. For a superb appreciation of Powell's work, see Gore Vidal's "Dawn Powell: The American Writer," *At Home: Essays, 1982–1988* (New York, 1988), pp. 241–271.

17. Simon Karlinsky, Introduction to *Nabokov-Wilson Letters*, p. 2; Wilson, quoted in a New Directions publicity release on Nabokov's *The Real Life of Sebastian Knight*, Yale; Gauss, *Papers*, p. 331; Quoted in Brian Boyd, *Vladimir Nabokov: The American Years* (Princeton, 1991), pp. 40, 26.

18. Quoted in Andrew Field, *V N: The Life and Art of Vladimir Nabokov* (New York, 1986), p. 261; *Nabokov-Wilson Letters*, pp. 149, 96, 210; Quoted in Field, *V N*, p. 357.

19. Wilson, "Vladimir Nabokov on Gogol," *Classics and Commercials*, pp. 218, 216; Wilson, *Letters*, p. 409; *Nabokov-Wilson Letters*, p. 97; Herbert Gold, "Vladimir Nabokov," *Writers at Work: The "Paris Review" Interviews: Fourth Series*, ed. George Plimpton (1976; New York, 1977), p. 100.

20. Wilson, *The Fifties*, p. 393; *Nabokov-Wilson Letters*, pp. 211, 298; Vladimir Nabokov, ed., Alexander Pushkin's *Engene Onegin* (1964; Princeton, 1981), 2: 151; Vladimir Nabokov, *Selected Letters, 1940–1977*, ed. Dmitri Nabokov and Matthew Bruccoli (New York, 1989), p. 293. Wilson's two essays on *Doctor Zhivago* appeared in *The Bit Between My Teeth*, pp. 420–472.

21. *Nabokov-Wilson Letters*, pp. 178–179; Letter from Michael Macdonald to Jeffrey Meyers, November 4, 1993; *Nabokov-Wilson Letters*, pp. 165, 288; 185, 304.

22. Quoted in Boyd, *Vladimir Nabokov*, p. 20; Wilson, Introduction to *To the Finland Station* (1971), p. vii; *Nabokov-Wilson Letters*, p. 304.

FOURTEEN: POSTWAR EUROPE
AND MAMAINE PAGET

1. Letter from Wilson to Alberto Arbasino, February 11, 1961, Yale; Letter from Noel Annan to Jeffrey Meyers, June 15, 1993; Wilson, *The Forties*, pp. 127, 156.

2. Ezra Pound, "Hugh Selwyn Mauberley," *Selected Poems* (London, 1977), p. 64; Wilson, Introduction to *Patriotic Gore*, p. xxv; Letter from V. S. Pritchett to Wilson, April 26, 1965, Yale; Letters from Roger Senhouse to Hamish Hamilton and to Secker and Warburg, June 28 and July 3, 1945, Secker and Warburg papers, University of Reading Library.

3. Wilson, *Europe Without Baedeker*, pp. 14, 178, 14; Wilson, *Classics and Commercials*, p. 285; Letter from Cyril Connolly to Wilson, October 23, [1946], Yale; Letter from Wilson to Celia Paget Goodman, January 25, 1950, Yale; Wilson, *Night Thoughts*, p. 195.

4. Wilson, *Classics and Commercials*, p.140; Wilson, *The Forties*, p. 151; Christopher Sykes, *Evelyn Waugh: A Biography* (Boston, 1975), pp. 284–285; Wilson, *The Forties*, p. 157; Evelyn Waugh, *Diaries*, ed. Michael Davie (1976; New York, 1979), p. 625.

5. Wilson, *Letters*, p. 429; Wilson, *Classics and Commercials*, pp. 298–299, 304; Evelyn Waugh, "Fan-Fare" (1946), *The Essays, Articles and Reviews of Evelyn Waugh*, ed. Donat Gallagher (Boston, 1984), p. 302; Julian Jebb, "Evelyn Waugh," *Writers at Work: The "Paris Review" Interviews: Third Series*, ed. George Plimpton (New York, 1967), p. 113; Wilson, *The Bit Between My Teeth*, p. 537.

6. George Orwell, "An American Critic," *Observer*, May 10, 1942, p. 3; Wilson, *New Yorker*, May 25, 1946, September 7, 1946 and January 13, 1951, reprinted in Jeffrey Meyers, *George Orwell: The Critical Heritage* (London, 1975), pp. 226, 224; 205; 310; Letter from George Orwell to Wilson, 1948, Yale; Wilson, *Letters*, p. 486.

7. Wilson, *A Prelude*, p. 5; Wilson, *Letters*, p. 417, 421; William Barrett, *The Truants* (Garden City, New York, 1983), p. 64.

   Leonor Fini, born in Buenos Aires of Spanish and Italian parents and brought up in Trieste, was indeed very beautiful. Wilson complained to Fini that the Italians were boorish and rude. He grumbled in the restaurant, but she liked him anyway (Letter from Leonor Fini to Jeffrey Meyers, March 15, 1994). For her photograph and paintings, see Whitney Chadwick, *Women Artists and the Surrealist Movement* (New York, 1985), pp. 80–83.

8. Wilson, *Letters*, p. 421; Wilson, *The Bit Between My Teeth*, pp. 152, 656.

9. T. E. Lawrence, *Seven Pillars of Wisdom* (Garden City, New York, 1935), p. 57 and *Seven Pillars of Wisdom* (Oxford: privately printed, 1922), p. 11. In *Red, Black, Blond and Olive*, p. 480, Wilson quotes Storrs' autobiography, *Orientations* (1937), on a ceremony at the church of the Holy Sepulcher in Jerusalem in 1918; Wilson, *The Forties*, pp. 57, 66–67.

In "For George Santayana," *Life Studies* (New York, 1959), p. 51, Robert Lowell described the postwar discovery of the reclusive philosopher by American intellectuals:

> In the heydays of 'forty-five
> bus-loads of souvenir deranged
> G.-I.'s and officer-professors of philosophy
> came crashing through your cell,
> puzzled to find you still alive.

10. Wilson, *Europe Without Baedeker*, pp. 267, 292. Evelyn Waugh would satirize the Welfare State in *Love Among the Ruins* (1953).

11. Wilson, *Europe Without Baedeker*, pp. 32, 172, 259–260; Fredric Warburg's internal report, September 4, 1947 and letter from Warburg to Wilson, May 14, 1947, University of Reading.

12. Letter from Cyril Connolly to Wilson, January 18, 1949, Yale; Richard Usborne, Review of *Europe Without Baedeker*, B.B.C. European Service, December 1938, Reading; Wilson, *Letters*, p. 429; Letter from A. L. Rowse to Jeffrey Meyers, August 29, 1993.

13. Letter from William Hughes to Wilson, February 10, 1947, Yale; Stephen Spender, "Wilson Among the Ruins," *Nation*, 165 (November 29, 1947), 592; Nicola Chiaromonte, "Wilson Among the Ruins," *Partisan Review*, 15 (February 1948), 247.

14. W. B. Yeats, "The Tower," *Collected Poems*, Definitive Edition (New York, 1956), p. 195; Celia Goodman, ed., *Living With Koestler: Mamaine Koestler's Letters, 1945–1951* (London, 1985), p. 62; Wilson, *Europe Without Baedeker*, pp. 179, 181; Letter from Wilson to Betty Huling, July 4, 1945, Yale.

15. Letter from Mamaine Paget to Wilson, May 6, 1945, Yale; Letter from Wilson to Mamaine Paget, May 28, 1945, Yale; Mamaine Paget,

quoted in *The Forties*, p. 106; Letter from Mamaine Paget to Wilson, July 6, 1945, Yale; Letter from Wilson to Mamaine Paget, July 22, 1945, Yale.

16. Wilson, *Europe Without Baedeker*, p. 192; Wilson, *The Forties*, p. 109; Letter from Mamaine Paget to Wilson, September 7, 1945, Yale; Letter from Wilson to Mamaine Paget, September 11, 1945, Yale.

17. Zelda Fitzgerald, in F. Scott Fitzgerald, *In His Own Time*, ed. Matthew Bruccoli and Jackson Bryer (1971; New York, 1974), p. 262; Letter from Wilson to Mamaine Paget, September 17, 1945, Yale; Letter from Mamaine Paget to Wilson, September 16, 1945, Yale; Letter from Wilson to Mamaine Paget, October 4, 1945, Yale.

18. Letters from Cyril Connolly to Wilson, November 15, [?1945] and January 31, 1946, Yale; Letter from Wilson to Connolly, December 15, 1948, Yale.

19. Quoted in Iain Hamilton, *Koestler: A Biography* (New York, 1982), p. 220; Letter from Celia Paget Goodman to Wilson, June 11, 1954, Yale; Letter from Celia Paget Goodman to Jeffrey Meyers, June 29, 1993.

FIFTEEN: ELENA THORNTON

1. David Chavchavadze, *Crowns and Trenchcoats*, pp. 227–228; Interview with Simon Karlinsky, who worked with Elena while editing *The Nabokov-Wilson Letters*; Wilson, Dedication to Elena, *A Window on Russia*, p. 1; Letter from Charlotte Kretzoi to Jeffrey Meyers, August 31, 1993.

2. Wilson, *The Sixties*, pp. 130–131; Letter from Wilson to Helen Muchnic, October 2, 1945, Yale; *Nabokov-Wilson Letters*, p. 179; "Author Wilson, Bride in S. F.," *San Francisco Chronicle*, December 12, 1946, p. 3; Wilson, *The Forties*, pp. 193–194.

3. *Nabokov-Wilson Letters*, p. 187; Quoted in Eileen Simpson, *Poets in Their Youth* (New York, 1982), p. 182; Bogan, *Letters*, pp. 288–289; Quoted in Rosalind Wilson, *Near the Magician*, p. 130.

4. Letter from Charlotte Kretzoi to Jeffrey Meyers, August 31, 1993; Letter from Michael Macdonald to Jeffrey Meyers, November 4, 1993; Interview with Henry Thornton; Interview with Rosalind Wilson.

5. Marie-Claire Blais, *Parcours d'un écrivain* (Montreal, 1993), p. 36 (my

translation); Letter from David Chavchavadze to Jeffrey Meyers, June 10, 1993; Interview with Rosalind Wilson; Interview with Mary Canby.

6. Interview with Stuart Hughes; Interview with Loran and Mary Crosten; Telephone interview with Mary Struve, May 10, 1993.

7. Wilson, *The Forties*, pp. 161–162, 185; 210; Wilson, *The Sixties*, p. 228; Letter from Elena Wilson to Edmund Wilson, June 19, 1955, Yale; Interview with Rosalind Wilson.

8. Wilson, *Night Thoughts*, pp. 273–274; Wilson, *A Window on Russia*, p. 2.

9. Letter from Charlotte Kretzoi to Jeffrey Meyers, August 31, 1993; Letter from Mary Meigs to Jeffrey Meyers, August 28, 1993; Letter from Wilson to Maxwell Geismar, June 30, 1944, Boston University; Wilson, *The Fifties*, p. 406.

10. Letter from Michael Macdonald to Jeffrey Meyers, November 4, 1993; Interviews with Mary Canby, Arthur Schlesinger, Jr., Daniel Walker, Richard Pipes and Rosalind Wilson; Interviews with Loran and Mary Crosten, Daniel Aaron and Jason Epstein.

A photograph of Wilson holding the baby Helen appears in *The Forties*, opposite p. 273.

11. Wilson, *Europe Without Baedeker*, pp. 412–413, 406; Letter from Michael Macdonald to Jeffrey Meyers, November 4, 1993; Interview with Henry Thornton; Interview with Alfred Kazin.

12. W. H. Auden, "Wilson's Sabine Farm," *Books and Bookmen*, 17 (June 1972), 7–8; Wilson, *Letters*, p. 430; Wilson, *The Sixties*, p. 12; W. H. Auden,"Who Shall Plan the Planners?," *Common Sense*, 9 (November 1940), 22; W. H. Auden, Review of *Apologies to the Iroquois*, *Mid-Century* [Book Society], 9 (February 1960), 2.

13. Wilson, *The Shores of Light*, p. 669; Letter from Wilson to William McPhee, October 10, 1946, Yale; Wilson, *The Bit Between My Teeth*, pp. 362–363; Wilson, *The Fifties*, p. 298.

14. Wilson, "The Mass in the Parking Lot" and "A message you'll expect, my friends," *Night Thoughts*, pp. 181, 217; Quoted in French, "Edmund Wilson: 1895–1972," p. 40. (In *Memoirs of Hecate County*, p. 275, Wilson parodies Auden's poems of the 1930s: "The doors broken down, the methodical search of the files / The waste-baskets captured, the commands against looting sent out."); Frederic Prokosch, *Voices: A Memoir* (New York, 1983), p. 289.

15. Carr, *John Dos Passos*, p. 487; Letter from Elizabeth Dos Passos to Jeffrey Meyers, June 25, 1993; "John Dos Passos, Esq.," *Night*

Thoughts, p. 196; Wilson, *Letters*, pp. 643, 653; Dos Passos, *The Four-teenth Chronicle*, p. 626.

16. Wilson, *The Forties*, pp. 287, 289; Wilson, *The Shores of Light*, p. 791.

SIXTEEN: *MEMOIRS OF HECATE COUNTY*

1. The title of the book was influenced by the classical Greek "Deux Hymnes à Hecate," *Mésures*, 15 avril 1937, pp. 201–204, in Wilson's papers at Yale, and by Châteaubriand's *Mémoires d'autre-tombe* (1849–50). The title of the most important story, "The Princess with the Golden Hair," came from the proposed title of Wilson's unfinished novel, *The Golden Air of Death*, and from the last line of his poem on Ted Paramore, "The Playwright in Paradise" (1939), *Night Thoughts*, p. 94.

2. Letter from Wilson to Whitney Seymour, [1948], Yale; Wilson, *The Twenties*, p. 141; Wilson, *Memoirs of Hecate County*, pp. 51–52.

   The long, untranslated passage in French neither disguised ob-scenities nor, like the French conversations in Mann's *The Magic Mountain*, had an aesthetic justification. It recalled Wilson's quotation of French poetry in *Axel's Castle*, of Latin poetry in *The Triple Thinkers*, of the long Greek epigraph in *The Undertaker's Garland* and of the long Russian epigraph in *Memoirs of Hecate County*.

3. Wilson, *Memoirs of Hecate County*, p. 3; Interview with Richard Wilbur (on Nerval and Borel); Wilson, *Classics and Commercials*, p. 190; Wilson, *Letters*, p. 378; J.-K. Huysmans, *Against Nature*, trans. Robert Baldick (London, 1959), p. 162.

4. Scott Fitzgerald, *Tender is the Night* (New York, 1934), p. 32 and Wilson, *Memoirs of Hecate County*, p. 127; Wilson, *Letters*, pp. 369–370; Scott Fitzgerald, *The Great Gatsby* (New York, 1925), p. 182 and Wilson, *Memoirs of Hecate County*, p. 338.

5. Wilson, *Memoirs of Hecate County*, pp. 21–22; Wilson, *Upstate*, p. 361; Wilson, *Memoirs of Hecate County*, p. 207; Wilson, *The Thirties*, p. 241; Wilson, *Memoirs of Hecate County*, p. 330.

6. Wilson, *The Thirties*, pp. 669–670; Wilson, *Memoirs of Hecate County*, pp. 190–191.

7. Dylan Thomas, *Collected Letters*, ed. Paul Ferris (New York, 1985), p. 50; Letter from Wilson to Carl Rachlin, January 26, 1947, Yale.

8. Wilson, *Letters*, p. 438; Alfred Kazin, "Le Misanthrope," *Partisan*

Review, 13 (Summer 1946), 375; Raymond Chandler, *Selected Letters*, ed. Frank MacShane (New York, 1981), p. 238; Stevie Smith, "Puzzled Young Man," *John O'London's Weekly*, March 28, 1952; Angus Wilson, "A Critic's Failure," *Observer*, March 16, 1952.

9. Cyril Connolly, "A Satirist at Sea," *Sunday Times* (London), June 10, 1951, p. 2; Wilson, *Letters*, p. 440; Updike, "Edmund Wilson," *Odd Jobs*, p. 103; Alice Toklas, *Staying on Alone: Letters*, ed. Edward Burns (New York, 1973), p. 242.

10. John Crowe Ransom, *Selected Letters*, ed. Thomas David Young and George Core (Baton Rouge, 1985), pp. 326–327. (Mizener, pre-empted by Ransom's letter and unwilling to offend Wilson, never reviewed the book for the *Kenyon Review*); Wilson, *Letters*, p. 438; Brightman, *Writing Dangerously*, p. 495.

11. Quoted in Tebbel, *A History of Book Publishing in the United States*, 4: 697; Letter from H. L. Mencken to Wilson, July 25, 1946, Yale; Letter from Wilson to Roger Straus, July 1954, Yale.

12. Lionel Trilling, quoted in John Updike, Afterword to Wilson's *Memoirs of Hecate County* (Boston: Godine-Nonpareil, 1980), p. 451; William O'Neill, *A Better World: The Great Schism: Stalinism and the American Intellectuals* (New York, 1982), p. 300.

13. Supreme Court of the United States, October term 1948. Doubleday vs. State of New York. Brief for Appellant, Whitney North Seymour, Counsel [52-page pamphlet], p. 14; Wilson, *The Forties*, pp. 312, 314; Telephone interview with MacInnes' former partner, Nicholas Alaga, August 17, 1993.

14. Letter from Wilson to Fredric Warburg, January 10, 1947, Reading; Letter from Donald Elder to Fredric Warburg, January 10, 1947, Reading; Irving Howe, "A Man of Letters," *Celebrations and Attacks* (London, 1979), p. 224; Letters from Wilson to Fredric Warburg, May 9 and October 13, 1947, Reading.

15. Despite all the problems, the book has done very well. It was reprinted in paperback by Zephyr in 1947, by Signet in 1961 and 1962, by Noonday in 1965, by Ballantine in 1967, by Bantam in 1976 and by Nonpareil in 1980. There were also two book club editions. In England the book was reissued by W. H. Allen in 1958 and reprinted in paperback by Panther in 1960, 1963 and 1964.

SEVENTEEN: TALCOTTVILLE

1. *Nabokov-Wilson Letters*, p. 256; Letter from Wilson to Mamaine Paget, March 26, 1946, Yale; Quoted in Carlos Baker, "Edmund Wilson," *A Princeton Companion*, ed. Alexander Leitch (Princeton, 1978), p. 512.

2. Quoted in Stuart Hughes, *Gentleman Rebel: Memoirs* (New York, 1990), p. 249; Interview with Rosalind Wilson; Letters from Elena Wilson to Edmund Wilson, June 21, 1959, July 8, 1959, July 19, 1960, Yale.

3. Wilson, *The Fifties*, p. 628; Wilson, poem to Elena, no date, Yale.

4. W. H. Auden, No. 5 of "Five Songs," *Collected Shorter Poems, 1927–1957* (London, 1966), p. 274; Interview with Mable Hutchins, Talcottville, New York, August 7, 1993; Interview with Loran and Mary Crosten.

5. Interview with Walter Edmonds, Concord, Massachusetts, July 17, 1993; Quoted in Glyn Morris, *Nights and Days with Edmund Wilson*, p. 79; Wilson, *The Fifties*, p. 562; Edmund Wilson, "Conversing with Malcolm Sharp," *University of Chicago Law Review*, 33 (Winter 1966), 198, 200.

6. See "Former NNY Educator and Writer Glyn Morris Dies in Pa. at Age 88," *Watertown Times*, October 12, 1993; Morris, *Nights and Days with Edmund Wilson*, pp. 12, 19, 22, 5, 30.

7. Letter from Wilson to Richard Rovere, May 16, 1958, Yale; Alberto Arbasino, "America senza querce" [America without Oaks], *L'Illustrazione Italiana*, aprile 1960, p. 84 (my translation).

8. Wilson, *Letters*, p. 380; Roger Straus, "A Flow of Work," *New York Times*, June 18, 1972, IV: 4; Letter from Wilson to Roger Straus, May 24, 1950, Yale; Interview with Jason Epstein.

9. Letter from Wilson to Roger Straus, May 29, 1960, Yale; Letter from Fredric Warburg to Wilson, May 14, 1947 and letter from Wilson to Fredric Warburg, May 26, 1947, Reading.

10. Letter from Jeffrey Simmons to Jeffrey Meyers, July 2, 1993; *Nabokov-Wilson Letters*, p. 288; Interview with Jason Epstein.

11. Hume Cronyn, *A Terrible Liar: A Memoir* (New York, 1991), pp. 219, 218; Interviews with Harry Levin and Daniel Walker; "Wilson Squawks Over *Light* Cuts, Claims Play is Now 'Nonsensical,'" *Variety*, March 2, 1951, p. 69.

12. James Newman, "Allegorical Melodrama," *New Republic*, 123 (August

21, 1950), 21–22; Walter Kerr, *"The Little Blue Light,"* *Commonweal*, 54 (May 18, 1951), 141–142; Brooks Atkinson, "At the Theater," *New York Times*, April 30, 1951, p. 17; Francis Fergusson, "Thriller Plus Moral," *New York Times Book Review*, June 25, 1950, p. 14.

13. Leon Edel, in *The Thirties*, p. 714; Russell Fraser, *A Mingled Yarn: The Life of R. P. Blackmur* (New York, 1981), p. 192; Simpson, *Poets in Their Youth*, p. 198.

14. Letter from E. B. O. Borgerhoff to Wilson, April 24, 1952, Yale; Wilson, *Letters*, p. 521. See David Blair, "The Gauss Seminars," *Princeton Alumni Weekly*, December 7, 1956, pp. 10–14.

15. Leon Edel, in *The Fifties*, p. 47; Letter from Monroe Engel to Jeffrey Meyers, July 31, 1993; Letter from Saul Bellow to Jeffrey Meyers, March 30, 1994; Wilson, *Letters*, p. 522; Wilson, "On First Reading Genesis," *Red, Black, Blond and Olive*, pp. 394–395.

16. Wilson *Letters*, p. 630. (Wilson also provided a blurb for Waldo Frank's *The Prophetic Island: A Portrait of Cuba*, 1961); Simpson, *Poets in Their Youth*, p. 228.

17. Wilson, *The Bit Between My Teeth*, p. 549n; John Berryman, *Henry's Fate* (New York, 1977), p. xiv; Quoted in John Haffenden, *The Life of John Berryman* (London, 1982), p. 390.

18. Simpson, *Poets in Their Youth*, p. 221 and Allan Seager, *The Glass House: The Life of Theodore Roethke* (New York, 1968), pp. 206–207.

EIGHTEEN: THE DEAD SEA SCROLLS

1. Isaiah Berlin, *Personal Impressions* (1980; New York, 1982), p. 83; Wilson, *The Fifties*, pp. 116–117; Letter from Celia Paget Goodman to Elena Wilson, September 26, 1977, Yale.

2. Wilson, *The Fifties*, pp. 114–115; 117–118; Wilson, *The Bit Between My Teeth*, p. 272; Wilson, *The Fifties*, p. 113; Letter from Wilson to Mary McCarthy, January 22, 1961, Vassar; Angus Wilson, "Edmund Wilson," *An Edmund Wilson Celebration*, ed. John Wain (Oxford, 1978), p. 33.

3. Wilson, *The Fifties*, p. 139; Letter from Iris Murdoch to Jeffrey Meyers, late March 1993; Letters from Isaiah Berlin to Elena Wilson, June 3, 1949 and to Mamaine Paget, May 10, 1953, Yale; Isaiah Berlin, "Edmund Wilson at Oxford," *Encounters*, ed. Kai Erikson (New Haven, 1989), p. 21. This essay, the best on Wilson, was reprinted from the *Yale Review*, 76 (Winter 1987), 139–151; *New York Times Book*

Review, April 12, 1987, pp. 1, 40, 42–43; and the *Guardian*, October 12, 1989, pp. 25, 47.

4. Wilson, *The Fifties*, p. 114; Wilson, *Letters*, p. 454; Berlin, "Edmund Wilson at Oxford," p. 20; Letter from Isaiah Berlin to Elena Wilson, June 19, 1972, Yale; Letter from Isaiah Berlin to Jeffrey Meyers, June 14, 1993.

5. Wilson, *The Shores of Light*, p. 570 (this pioneering essay was reprinted at least four times); Wilson, *The Bit Between My Teeth*, p. 137; Wilson, *Europe Without Baedeker*, pp. 82, 88.

6. Wilson, *The Fifties*, pp. 157, 162, 159; Quoted in Brandon, "A Conversation with Edmund Wilson," p. 13; Quoted in S. N. Behrman, *Portrait of Max* (New York, 1960), p. 262; Wilson, *The Fifties*, pp. 172; 180.

7. Wilson, *Five Plays*, pp. 7–8; Wilson, *Travels in Two Democracies*, p. 233; Wilson, *Five Plays*, p. 403.

8. Wilson, *Letters*, p. 487; Wilson, *Five Plays*, pp. 20, 16; "Hall of Fame Players Stage *Cyprian's Prayer*," *Heights Daily News*, February 21, 1957.

9. Wilson, *To the Finland Station*, pp. 306–307; Wilson, *Patriotic Gore*, pp. 784–785; William Makepeace Thackeray, "Nil Nisi Bonum," *Roundabout Papers*, in *Works* (New York, 1899), 12: 178; Wilson, *Red, Black, Blond and Olive*, p. 461; Letter from Wilson to Mamaine Paget Koestler, May 5, 1954, Yale.

10. Interview with Ellen Ben-Amotz Lifschutz, Berkeley, Calif., August 16, 1993; Wilson, *The Fifties*, p. 236; William Albright, "New Light on the Biblical Past, in Scrolls from Dead Sea Caves," *Herald Tribune Book Review*, October 16, 1955, p. 3; Edmund Wilson, *Israel and the Dead Sea Scrolls*, Foreword by Leon Edel (New York, 1978), p. 191.

11. Wilson, *The Fifties*, p. 234; David Flusser, "Not Obliged to Any Religion," *An Edmund Wilson Celebration*, pp. 112–114; Letter from David Flusser to Jeffrey Meyers, September 9, 1993; Wilson, *Letters*, p. 673; Yigael Yadin, quoted in French, "Edmund Wilson: 1895–1972," pp. 27–28.

12. Dos Passos, *The Fourteenth Chronicle*, p. 609; Wilson, *Letters*, p. 531; Interview with Sheldon Meyer, Berkeley, Calif., February 25, 1994; M. I. Finley, "Storm Over Qumran," *Washington Post: Book World*, September 21, 1969, p. 5.

    Woody Allen's contribution to the scholarly debate, "The Scrolls," in *Without Feathers* (New York, 1976), p. 24, begins: "Scholars will recall that several years ago a shepherd, wandering in the Gulf of Aqaba, stumbled upon a cave containing several large clay jars and also two tickets to the ice show. . . ."

13. Wilson, *Red, Black, Blond and Olive*, pp. 495; 498–499; Wilson, *Letters*, pp. 210, 209; D. H. Lawrence, "New Mexico," *Phoenix*, ed. Edward McDonald (London, 1936), p. 142; D. H. Lawrence, *Mornings in Mexico* (1927; London, 1974), pp. 58, 60.

14. Wilson, *Red, Black, Blond and Olive*, pp. 26, 38, 41; Wilson, *The Forties*, p. 230; Wilson, *Red, Black, Blond and Olive*, p. 57.

15. Letter from Wilson to Elena Wilson, September 29, 1948, Yale; Quoted in Costa, *Edmund Wilson*, p. 52; Wilson, *Red, Black, Blond and Olive*, p. 124; Wilson, *Letters*, pp. 467, 470.

   Philippe Thoby-Marcelin's *Poèmes* were brought out in 1986 by Eva in a beautiful privately printed edition and dedicated to "Edmund Wilson *In Memoriam.*"

16. Wilson, *Red, Black, Blond and Olive*, pp. 409, 449; Robert Graves, "Religion: None; Conditioning: Protestant," *Five Pens in Hand* (Garden City, New York, 1958), p. 129; Wilson, *Red, Black, Blond and Olive*, p. 67; Letter from Alan Ross to Jeffrey Meyers, March 10, 1994; Wilson, *The Fifties*, pp. 369–370.

NINETEEN: FIGHTING THE IRS

1. Wilson, *A Piece of My Mind*, pp. 6; 104; 21; 59; 67; 201; 196; 232.

2. Breit, *The Writer Observed*, p. 173; Letter from Wilson to Scottie Fitzgerald Lanahan, [c. March, 1959], Yale. For Brandon's account of the interview, see *Special Relationships: A Foreign Correspondent's Memoirs from Roosevelt to Reagan* (New York, 1988), pp. 377–381.

3. Interview with Harry and Elena Levin; Wilson, *The Fifties*, p. 452; Wilson, *The Sixties*, p. 580; Letter from Robert Lowell to Wilson, November 5, 1967, Yale.

4. Wilson, *The Bit Between My Teeth*, p. 547; Robert Giroux, "Homage to a Poet" (1979), in *Robert Lowell: Interviews and Memoirs*, ed. Jeffrey Meyers (Ann Arbor, 1988), p. 260; Robert Lowell, "Our Afterlife, I," *Day by Day* (New York, 1977), p. 21. Wilson and Pound died in 1972, Auden in 1973.

5. Information on Deming comes from the Barbara Deming Collection, Schlesinger Library, Radcliffe College, Cambridge, Mass.; Wilson, *Letters*, p. 600; Mary Meigs, *Lily Briscoe: A Self-Portrait: An Autobiography* (Vancouver, 1981), p. 85. The title of Meigs' book alludes to her alter-ego, the heroine of Virginia Woolf's *Mrs. Dalloway*. It is dedi-

cated to Barbara Deming and Marie-Claire Blais, and includes photographs of these women and the author.

6. McCarthy, *A Charmed Life*, p. 109; Meigs, *Lily Briscoe*, p. 159; Wilson, *The Fifties*, p. 518; Meigs, *Lily Briscoe*, pp. 19, 13–14.

7. Edmund Wilson, *O Canada: An American's Notes on Canadian Culture* (New York, 1965), p. 148. (Meigs' charming portrait of Blais appears opposite p. 150 in this book); Wilson, *The Sixties*, pp. 152–153; Interview with Roger Straus, New York, July 21, 1993; Interview with Barbara Epstein, New York, July 5, 1993.

8. Letter from Wilson to Mary McCarthy, September 1, 1965, Vassar; Interview with Rosalind Wilson; Wilson, *The Sixties*, pp. 407, 664.

9. Interview with Adelaide Walker; Wilson, *The Sixties*, pp. 872, 825; Letter from Marie-Claire Blais to Jeffrey Meyers, November 9, 1993 (my translation).

10. It is impossible, in the absence of Wilson's bank statements and confidential tax returns, to give an exact account of his finances. But one can note significant contradictions in his book and, using other sources, provide a general but still accurate picture. On page 7 Wilson states that he first consulted an old friend and extremely able New York lawyer (the unnamed John Amen) after the successful publication of *The Scrolls from the Dead Sea* in the *New Yorker* (on May 14, 1955) and as a book (in October 1955). On page 25 he mistakenly says he first consulted Amen, two and a half years earlier, in March 1953. On pages 10–11 he says that he was liable to prosecution for not paying taxes during the years 1953–57 and that the tax authorities brought "an information" against him for willful failure to file in 1957; in the same paragraph he says that he *had* paid $16,000 in taxes for 1956 and 1957.

In a desperate attempt to win his argument against the IRS (not one of our most beloved institutions), Wilson minimizes his income and exaggerates his debts. He also failed to mention that he did not pay taxes on his earnings from *Memoirs of Hecate County*, that in 1951 he inherited a substantial estate from his mother: houses with valuable contents in Red Bank and Talcottville and a trust fund of $200,000, and that in 1961 he sold his papers to Yale for $30,000. He claims on page 6 that his average yearly income during 1947–51 was only $2,000, which seems far too low for a period when he sold many articles to the *New Yorker* and the *Reporter*, published three new books, and earned a certain amount of money from royalties and reprint fees. In 1951, between the suppression of the American edition of *Memoirs of Hecate County* and the publication of the English edition, he did tell Nabokov that he was badly in debt. Yet his income in 1954, only three years later and before the publication of *The Scrolls from the Dead Sea*, shot up to $27,000.

11. Edmund Wilson, *The Cold War and the Income Tax: A Protest* (New York, 1963), pp. 4, 6; Robert Conot, *Justice at Nuremberg* (New York, 1983), p. 38; Letter from Mary McCarthy to Wilson, February 11, 1959, Yale; "Edmund Wilson Charged in Big Tax Case," Syracuse, September 15, [1958], no citation, in the Wilson file at the Guggenheim Foundation. This news story states that Wilson had a "gross income of $27,156 in 1954; $25,229 in 1955; $39,918 in 1956; and $16,949 in 1957."

12. Jason Epstein, quoted in French, "Edmund Wilson: 1895–1972," p. 30; Letter from Francisco Penberthy to Wilson, July 5, 1962, Yale; Wilson, *The Cold War and the Income Tax*, p. 12; Donald Gallup, "Edmund Wilson, 1961–1975," *Pigeons on the Granite* (New Haven, 1978), pp. 311–316.

13. Interview with Walter Edmonds; Interview with William Fenton; Letter from Wilson to Roger Straus, August 12, 1962, Yale; "Edmund Wilson Honored in Utica," *New York Times*, June 4, 1966, p. 27; Wilson, *The Cold War and the Income Tax*, pp. 4–5.

14. Wilson, "The Extrovert of Walden Pond," *Night Thoughts*, p. 80; Wilson, *The Cold War and the Income Tax*, pp. 115; 62; 92; 115; 118.

15. Cyril Connolly, "The Artist and His Taxman," *Sunday Times* (London), March 8, 1964; Letter from Bertrand Russell to A. J. Muste, October 9, 1963, Yale; Herbert Mitgang, *Dangerous Dossiers* (1988; New York, 1989), p. 135.

   Mitgang interviewed me in the *New York Times* of March 11, 1983, p. C–27, just after my article "Hemingway: Wanted by the FBI!" had appeared in the *New York Review of Books*. He later appropriated my discovery that the FBI consistently spied on leading American writers, paraphrased the material I had found in Hemingway's FBI file and published it under his own name—without giving me credit—in his *New Yorker* article of October 5, 1987 and in his book the following year.

TWENTY: HARVARD

1. Wilson, *The Bit Between My Teeth*, pp. 541–542; Letter from Wilson to Jeffrey Simmons of W. H. Allen, March 24, 1957, Yale.
2. Letter from Willard Quine to Jeffrey Meyers, July 21, 1993; Interview

with Stuart Hughes; Gallup, "Edmund Wilson: 1961–1975," p. 313.

3. Letter from Eliot Stanley to Jeffrey Meyers, August 25, 1993; Letter from Philippe Radley to Jeffrey Meyers, November 19, 1993; Wilson, *The Sixties*, p. 127; Telephone interview with Frances Nevada Swisher, September 25, 1993.

4. Letter from Edmund Wilson to Elena Wilson, July 21, 1960, Yale; Letter from Elena Wilson to Edmund Wilson, [late July 1960], Yale; Interviews with Arthur Schlesinger, Jr. and with Richard Pipes.

5. Letter from Kenneth Lynn to Jeffrey Meyers, August 5, 1993; Mary Manning, in her review of *The Sixties*, "Mr. Know-It-All," *Irish Times*, October 11, 1975; James Boswell, *Life of Johnson*, (London, 1961), p. 1196; Interview with Albert and Macklin Guerard, Stanford, Calif., May 6, 1993.

6. Interviews with Harry and Elena Levin and with Stuart Hughes; I. A. Richards, *Selected Letters*, ed. John Constable (Oxford, 1990), p. 151; Wilson, *The Sixties*, p. 72.

   During 1959–60 I was a twenty-year-old, first-year graduate student at Harvard and, like Wilson, attended the readings by Auden and Singer. I knew Wilson was at the university, but had no interest in the literature of the Civil War and could find no reason to see him.

7. Wilson, *Letters*, p. 602; Wilson, "The Boston and Cambridge Blues," *Holiday Greetings and Desolating Lyrics*, [p. 2].

8. Wilson, *Letters*, pp. 553; 562; Interview with William Fenton; Wilson, *The Fifties*, p. 456; Interview with Daniel Aaron; Letter from Reuel Wilson to Jeffrey Meyers, January 15, 1994.

9. Interview with William Fenton; Edmund Wilson, *Apologies to the Iroquois* (New York, 1960), p. 310; William Fenton, "The Iroquois in the Grand Tradition of American Letters: The Works of Walter D. Edmonds, Carl Carmer and Edmund Wilson," *American Indian Culture and Research Journal*, 5 (1981), 36–37.

10. Wilson, *To the Finland Station*, p. 100; Wilson, *Red, Black, Blond and Olive*, pp. 41–42; Wilson, *Apologies to the Iroquois*, pp. 235; 217, 224.

11. Wilson, *Letters*, p. 554; Wilson, *Apologies to the Iroquois*, p. 156; Robert Moses, *Tuscarora Fiction and Fact* (New York, 1960), pp. 1–4, 7; Wilson, *The Bit Between My Teeth*, p. 544.

12. Bette Crouse Mele, "Edmund Wilson and the Iroquois," *An Edmund Wilson Celebration*, p. 36; Wilson, *The Fifties*, p. 601; Letter from Mad Bear to Wilson, December 5, 1959, Yale; William Sturtevant, Review of *Apologies to the Iroquois*, *American Anthropologist*, 64 (1962), 1116.

13. Wilson, *The Bit Between My Teeth*, p. 555; Wilson, *The Sixties*, p. 438; Gerald Clarke, *Capote: A Biography* (New York, 1988), p. 105.

14. "2 Smith Teachers Held in Vice Case," "2 More Arrested in Smith Vice Case," "3 At Smith Accept Finding of Guilty" and "Morals Case is Lost by Smith Professor," *New York Times*, September 4, 1960, p. 54; September 6, 1960, p. 70; September 21, 1960, p. 31; October 12, 1960, p. 36; Interview with Daniel Aaron (Arvin's friend and colleague at Smith).

15. Letter from Wilson to *New York Times* (?), September 12, 1960, Yale; Wilson, *Letters*, pp. 599–600; Letter from Newton Arvin to Wilson, December 1, 1960, Yale.

16. Wilson, *The Sixties*, p. 46; Letter from Wilson to Mary McCarthy, April 14, 1961, Vassar; Wilson, *The Sixties*, pp. 36, 39.

17. Interview with Jason Epstein; Wilson, *Letters*, pp. 660; 598.

18. Quoted in Costa, *Edmund Wilson*, p. 144; Wilson, *Upstate*, p. 214; Interview with Loran and Mary Crosten; Interview with Rosalind Wilson; Letter from Wilson to Clelia Carroll, June 3, 1965, Yale.

19. Quoted in Wilson, *Upstate*, p. 234; Interview with William Fenton; Wilson, *The Sixties*, p. 816; Letters from Mary Pcolar to Wilson, September 30 and November 19, 1971, Yale; Interview with Loran and Mary Crosten, and letter from Leon Edel to Jeffrey Meyers, December 3, 1993.

20. Quoted in *Talking About Robert Penn Warren*, ed. Floyd Watkins (Athens, Georgia, 1990), p. 135; Wilson, *Patriotic Gore*, pp. ix–x; Wilson, *Letters*, p. 615; Letter from Wilson to Margaret Edwards Rullman, July 8, 1961, Yale; Letter from Paul Roazen to Jeffrey Meyers, November 10, 1993.

21. Wilson, *The Bit Between My Teeth*, p. 283; Wilson, *Letters*, pp. 601; 616; Louis Rubin, "Edmund Wilson and the Despot's Head," *The Curious Death of the Novel* (Baton Rouge, 1967), p. 123; Letter from Oxford University Press to Wilson, October 9, 1958, Yale.

22. Interview with Sheldon Meyer; Sheldon Meyer, "Wilson," an unpublished address delivered at Oxford University Press (courtesy of Mr. Meyer); Wilson, *The Sixties*, p. 798.

23. Interview with Sheldon Meyer; Wilson, *To the Finland Station*, p. 31; Wilson, *Classic and Commercials*, p. 36; Wilson, *Europe Without Baedeker*, p. 345; Wilson, *Patriotic Gore*, pp. xxxii, xxix, xxxi.

24. Wilson, *Patriotic Gore*, pp. 115; xviii; Wilson, *The Sixties*, p. 88; Wilson, *Patriotic Gore*, pp. 554; 114; 124.

25. Wilson, *Patriotic Gore*, pp. 308; 197; 461; 509; 590; 632; 782; 434.
26. Letter from Robert Lowell to Wilson, March 31, 1961, Yale; Leon Edel, "Am I, Then, in a Pocket of the Past?," *New Republic*, 135 (December 17, 1956), 25–26; C. Vann Woodward, "A Stance of Moral Neutrality," *American Scholar*, 31 (Autumn 1962), 640.
27. Robert Penn Warren, Review of *Patriotic Gore*, *Commentary*, 34 (August 1962), 152; George Steiner, "The Angry American," *Sunday Times* (London), June 24, 1962; Monroe Engel, "An Exemplary Edmund Wilson," *Encounters*, ed. Kai Erikson (New Haven, 1989), 128–129; Wilson, *The Sixties*, p. 71.

TWENTY-ONE: EUROPE AND WESLEYAN

1. Wilson, *Patriotic Gore*, p. 779; Wilson, *The Fifties*, p. 204; Quoted in Wilson, *To the Finland Station*, p. 37; Wilson, *Letters*, p. 667; Letter from Wilson to Gilbert Seldes, March 8, 1963, Yale.
2. Princeton University, citation for Wilson's honorary degree, June 12, 1956, Yale; Quoted in Morris, *Less Traveled Roads*, p. 373; Wilson, *Letters*, p. 642; FBI file on Wilson, May 28, 1963 and August 13, 1965; Wilson, *The Sixties*, pp. 77–78; Saul Bellow, "White House and Artists," *Noble Savage*, 5 (1962), 5; Quoted in Ian Hamilton, *Robert Lowell: A Biography* (New York, 1982), p. 299.
3. Quoted in Morris, *Nights and Days with Edmund Wilson*, p. 84; Wilson, *Letters*, pp. 596, 632; Schlesinger, *New York Times Book Review*, February 9, 1958, p. 3; Interview with Arthur Schlesinger, Jr.; Arthur Schlesinger, Jr., *A Thousand Days: John F. Kennedy at the White House* (Boston, 1965), p. 733.
4. *Congressional Record*, April 3, 1964, p. 6597; Quoted in Wilson, *Upstate*, p. 251; Telegram from President John Kennedy to Wilson, July 1, 1963, Yale; Letter from Wilson to Robert Kennedy, [mid-December 1963], Yale; Letter from Ambassador Charles Bohlen to Wilson, March 6, 1964, Yale.
5. Quoted in "Colony Awards Medal to Critic Edmund Wilson," *Peterborough Transcript*, August 20, 1964; Interview with Richard Pipes; Robert Lowell, "To President Lyndon Johnson" [June 3, 1965], *Collected Prose*, ed. Robert Giroux (New York, 1987), 371; Eric Goldman, *The Tragedy of Lyndon Johnson* (New York, 1969), p. 423. The Lyndon Johnson Presidential Library in Austin, Texas, cannot find this letter.
6. Wilson, *Night Thoughts*, pp. 228, 229; Quoted in C. J. Fox, "The Old

Stone House," *London Magazine*, 32 (June-July 1992), 76; Interview with Richard Pipes; Interview with Robert and Elizabeth Stabb, Talcottville, N.Y., August 7, 1993; Interview with Alfred Kazin.

7. Meigs, *Lily Briscoe*, p. 23; Rosalind Wilson, *Near the Magician*, p. 46; Wilson, *The Sixties*, pp. 252; 887; 889; Letter from Dr. Jacob Schwartz to Wilson, October 17, 1963, Yale.

8. Interviews with Loran and Mary Crosten and with Daniel Aaron; Morris, *Nights and Days with Edmund Wilson*, p. 66; Interview with Rosalind Wilson.

9. Wilson, *The Sixties*, pp. 727–728, 653; 478; Letter from Rosalind Wilson to Edmund Wilson, [c. 1965–1966], Yale.

10. Wilson, *The Fifties*, p. 532; Wilson, *The Sixties*, p. 250; Letter from Reuel Wilson to Edmund Wilson, [mid-1960s], Yale; Interview with Eleanor Perenyi.

11. Interview with Stuart Hughes; Letter from Elena Wilson to Edmund Wilson, [c. 1967], Yale; Interview with Adelaide and Daniel Walker; Quoted in Morris, *Days and Nights with Edmund Wilson*, p. 136.

12. Wilson, *Letters*, p. 641; Wilson, *The Fifties*, p. 363; Letter from Anthony Powell to Jeffrey Meyers, June 10, 1993; Wilson, *The Sixties*, pp. 299, 304; Letter from Wilson to Dawn Powell, March 18, 1964, courtesy of Jacqueline Rice.

13. Wilson, *The Sixties*, pp. 325; 333; 347; 364n.

   In the summer of 1972 Praz told me that in the Hungarian edition of his *Gusto neoclassico*, translated without his permission and adapted to the Party line, his thesis was reversed and "Comrade Praz" was made to denounce the aristocratic society that had produced "decadent" neo-classical taste.

14. Interview with Eleanor Perenyi; Letter from Eleanor Perenyi to Jeffrey Meyers, June 14, 1993; Wilson, *The Sixties*, pp. 338–339; Letter from Charlotte Kretzoi to Jeffrey Meyers, August 31, 1993.

15. Wilson, *Europe Without Baedeker*, p. 426; Letter from Wilson to Margaret Edwards Rullman, May 16, 1964, Yale; Wilson, *Europe Without Baedeker*, p. 391.

16. Memo from Paul Horgan to Victor Butterfield, April 16, 1963, Wesleyan University Library; Letter from Paul Horgan to Jeffrey Meyers, May 18, 1993; Wilson, *Letters*, p. 653.

17. Interview with Paul Horgan, Middletown, Conn., July 29, 1993; Quoted in J. G. Escher, Jr., "Edmund Wilson: Students Quiz Writer-Critic," *Middletown Press*, March 18, 1965, pp. 1, 19 and James McEnteer, "Wilson Review: Discordant Encounter," *Wesleyan Argus*, March

23, 1965, p. 4; Paul Horgan, "Wilson at Wesleyan," *Tracings: A Book of Partial Portraits* (New York, 1993), p. 220.

18. Brendan Gill, *A New York Life* (New York, 1990), p. 317; Letter from Norman Podhoretz to Jeffrey Meyers, June 26, 1993; Wilson, *The Sixties*, p. 425; Interview with Paul Horgan.

19. Wilson, *The Sixties*, p. 444; Letter from Wilson to Mary Pcolar, January 25, 1965, Yale; Interview with Richard Wilbur.

20. Wilson, *The Sixties*, p. 449; Letter from Wilson to Clelia Carroll, April 4, 1967, Yale; Final Report from Wilson to Paul Horgan, May 24, 1965, Wesleyan.

21. Wilson, *O Canada*, pp. 241, 245; Wilson, *Letters*, p. 636; Wilson, *The Sixties*, pp. 142; 240; Wilson, *Letters*, p. 276.

22. Letter from Wilson to William Shawn, October 3, 1964, Yale; Wilson, *O Canada*, pp. 84; 47; 9; Anthony Burgess, "Et Ego in Arcadia," *Spectator*, 219 (August 4, 1967), 134; Neil Compton, "The Northern Light," *Commentary*, 40 (August 1965), 75.

TWENTY-TWO: QUARREL WITH NABOKOV

1. Born in Constantinople of German parents, Arndt was educated in Germany, England and Poland, where he learned Russian. He volunteered for the Polish army, was captured by the Germans and escaped from a prisoner of war camp, fought with the Polish Underground and made his way to Istanbul, where he worked for the OSS. After the war he taught at Roberts College in Turkey, came to America, earned his doctorate at the University of North Carolina and became a professor of Russian there.

2. See Vladimir Nabokov on Arndt, "Pounding the Clavichord" (1964), *Strong Opinions* (New York, 1973), pp. 231–240; Nabokov, Foreword to *Eugene Onegin*, 1: viii, x.

3. Robert Conquest, "Nabokov's *Eugene Onegin*," *Poetry*, 106 (June 1965), 238; Edward Brown, "Round Two: Nabokov vs. Pushkin," *Slavic Review*, 36 (March 1977), 101; Alexander Gerschenkron, "A Manufactured Monument?," *Modern Philology*, 63 (May 1966), 336; Boyd, *Vladimir Nabokov*, p. 327; Gleb Struve, "The Moralist as Magician," *Times Literary Supplement*, May 2, 1980, p. 510; Alexander Gerschenkron, "A Manufactured Monument?," p. 347.

4. Nabokov, ed., *Eugene Onegin*, 1: 36. See also 2: 110 for a striking poetic

gloss on Pushkin's rainbows; Clarence Brown, "Nabokov's Pushkin and Nabokov's Nabokov," *Nabokov: The Man and His Work*, ed. L. S. Dembo (Madison, 1967), p. 204.

5. Nabokov, *Selected Letters*, p. 358; Quoted in Field, *V N*, p. 263; Clarence Brown, "Pluck and Polemics" [review of Wilson's *A Window on Russia*], *Partisan Review*, 40 (February 1973), 313.

6. Wilson, *Letters*, p. 652; Wilson, "The Strange Case of Pushkin and Nabokov" (1965), *A Window on Russia*, pp. 209, 210, 213, 210, 209.

7. Interview with Simon Karlinsky. In a letter of January 26, 1937, at Yale, the Russian scholar Ernest Simmons told Wilson that "Pushkin certainly knew considerable English after 1828; his library had many English books in it and he read them with some care."

8. Wilson, "The Strange Case of Pushkin and Nabokov," pp. 228, 224, 230–231.

9. Wilson, "In Honor of Pushkin" (1936), *The Triple Thinkers*, pp. 50–51; Wilson, "The Strange Case of Pushkin and Nabokov," pp. 223–224; Nabokov, ed., *Eugene Onegin*, 3: 16.

10. Vladimir Nabokov, "Reply to My Critics" (1966), *Strong Opinions*, p. 264; Nabokov, *Selected Letters*, p. 374.

11. Vladimir Nabokov, "Reply to My Critics," pp. 247, 248, 263, 262; *Nabokov-Wilson Letters*, p. 218; Nabokov, "Reply to My Critics," pp. 263, 266.

12. Letter from Isaiah Berlin to Wilson, January 25, 1966, Yale.

13. *Nabokov-Wilson Letters*, pp. 332–333; Wilson, *Letters*, p. 733.

14. Boyd, *Vladimir Nabokov*, p. 72; Wilson, "The Strange Case of Pushkin and Nabokov," p. 231.

15. Wilson, *Upstate*, pp. 159, 161–162; Nabokov, *Selected Letters*, p. 492; Nabokov, "Reply to My Critics," pp. 218–219.

16. Wilson, *A Window on Russia*, p. 235; Mary McCarthy, "A Bolt from the Blue" (1962), *The Writing on the Wall* (1969; London, 1973), p. 37; Nabokov, *Selected Letters*, p. 553; Wilson, "Stravinsky," *The American Earthquake*, p. 111.

17. *Nabokov-Wilson Letters*, p. 150; Wilson, *A Window on Russia*, p. 232; Dahlberg, *Confessions*, p. 246.

18. Wilson, *Patriotic Gore*, pp. 119, 630; Quoted in Joseph Epstein, "Never Wise—But Oh, How Smart" [review of *The Fifties*], *New York Times Book Review*, August 31, 1986, p. 3; Letter from Vera Nabokov to Elena Wilson, July 12, 1972, Yale; Quoted in Karlinsky, Introduction to *Nabokov-Wilson Letters*, p. 2.

TWENTY-THREE: THE MIDDLE EAST
AND THE MLA

1. Letter from Wilson to George Grosz, October 25, 1946, Harvard; Letter from George Grosz to Wilson, November 7, 1946, Yale; Wilson, *Classics and Commercials*, p. 309; Wilson, *The Sixties*, p. 508; Wilson, *Classics and Commercials*, p. 346.

2. Wilson, *The Forties*, p. 74; Wilson, *Classics and Commercials*, pp. 389, 392, 385; Wilson, *Memoirs of Hecate County*, p. 279; Brandon, "A Conversation with Edmund Wilson," p. 15.

3. Quoted in Gauss, *Papers*, p. 351; Wilson, *The Wound and the Bow*, p. 122; Wilson, *The Sixties*, p. 831; Wilson, *Upstate*, p. 280.

4. Wilson, *The Shores of Light*, p. 240; Letter from Wilson to Alfred Kazin, March 31, 1962, Yale; Letter from Wilson to Lionel Trilling, August 25, 1959, Columbia.

5. Wilson, *Classics and Commercials*, pp. 128, 153, 321; Edmund Wilson, Review of Hemingway's *Men Without Women*, *New Republic*, 53 (December 14, 1927), 102; Blaise Pascal, *The Pensées*, trans. and Introduction by J. M. Cohen (London, 1961), p. 38.

6. Hyman, "Edmund Wilson: Translation in Criticism," pp. 45, 25, 19, 21, 23, 24, 46, 44; Quoted in Gill, *Here at the New Yorker*, p. 270.

7. Richard Gilman, "Edmund Wilson: Then and Now," *New Republic*, 155 (July 2, 1966), 23–24; Wilson, *A Piece of My Mind*, p. 205; Wilson, *The Bit Between My Teeth*, p. 545; Vidal, "Novelists and Critics of the 1940's," *Homage to Daniel Shays*, p. 8.

    Vidal's misleading criticism was repeated not only by Gilman but also in Frederick Crews' review of *The Bit Between My Teeth*, *New York Review of Books*, 5 (November 25, 1965), 4; in Leonard Kriegel's *Edmund Wilson* (Carbondale, Illinois, 1971), p. 88; in Saul Bellow's "An Interview with Myself" (1975), *It All Adds Up*, p. 85; and in Richard Costa's *Edmund Wilson*, p. xvi.

    Wilson's uncollected *New Yorker* essays included reviews of Siegfried Sassoon, Graham Greene, Christopher Isherwood, Arthur Koestler, Albert Camus, Carson McCullers and Saul Bellow. Despite the disclaimer in his self-interview, he offered in that essay his opinion of Lawrence Durrell, J. D. Salinger, James Baldwin and Edwin O'Connor. Wilson extensively discussed Genet—"at once the final degradation and triumph of French culture"—in his letters and journals, wrote about a dozen foreign writers in *Europe Without Baedeker*, about S. Y. Agnon in *Red, Black, Blond and Olive*, about most of the important English and French Canadian writers in *O Canada*, and about Solzhenitsyn and Eugenia Ginzburg in *A Window on Russia*. He knew the work of William Burroughs and Jack Kerouac, read books by Wilfrid Sheed and Joan Didion, and admired the novels of Alison Lurie.

8. Wilson, *Letters*, p. 673; Wilson, *Israel and the Dead Sea Scrolls*, p. 306; Wilson, *The Sixties*, p. 615; Wilson, *Israel and the Dead Sea Scrolls*, pp. 362, 402.

9. Kazin, *New York Jew*, p. 236; Wilson, *A Window on Russia*, p. 259; Lillian Hellman, *Pentimento*, Introduction by Richard Poirier (New York, 1979), p. 507; Letter from William Styron to Jeffrey Meyers, July 29, 1993.

10. Costa, *Edmund Wilson*, p. 73; Interview with Richard Pipes; Quoted in Costa, *Edmund Wilson*, p. 59; Quoted in Harry Gilroy, "Edmund Wilson Honored in Utica," *New York Times*, June 4, 1966, p. C-27.

11. Quoted in Alden Whitman, "Edmund Wilson Criticizes War As He Accepts the Aspen Prize," *New York Times*, June 13, 1968, p. 44; Horgan, "Wilson at Wesleyan," p. 236; Letter from James Baldwin to Wilson, November 15, 1961, Yale; Harry Moore, Preface to Kriegel, *Edmund Wilson*, p. viii.

12. Quoted in Barry Callaghan, "Edmund Wilson," *Exile* (Toronto), 1 (1972), 107; Wilson, *The Sixties*, p. 529; Letter from Wilson to Walter Edmonds, June 10, 1966, courtesy of Walter Edmonds; Interview with Mary Canby; Letter from Wilson to Friends of the Newport (Rhode Island) Library, June 6, 1965, Yale.

13. Edmund Wilson, *The Duke of Palermo and Other Plays, with an Open Letter to Mike Nichols* (New York, 1969), p. 82 (this book has an impressive dust jacket by Edward Gorey); Letter from Wilson to Robert Lowell, January 5, 1961, Harvard; Interview with Loran and Mary Crosten.

14. Wilson, *The Cold War and the Income Tax*, p. 53; Edmund Wilson, *The Fruits of the MLA* (New York, 1968), pp. 3, 4, 7, 35, 20, 13; John Fisher and others, *Professional Standards and American Editions* (New York: MLA, 1969), p. 24; Wilson, *The Fruits of the MLA*, p. 37.

15. Wilson, "Tristes Tropiques," *Holiday Greetings and Desolating Lyrics*, [p. 6]; Wilson, *The Sixties*, p. 849; Interview with Eva Marcelin, Cazenovia, New York, August 5, 1993; Interview with Rosalind Wilson.

Rosalind, who began by describing Anne's cute face and plump tan thighs, ended by emphasizing her drinking and by calling her a "bitch."

16. Interview with Edgar Miller. Miller gave up his dental practice in the 1970s, went to India and became a red-robed disciple of the late Indian guru Bhagwan Shree Rajneesh; Wilson, *The Sixties*, p. 847; Yeats, "The Spur," *Collected Poems*, p. 309; Wilson, *The Sixties*, pp. 844, 859–863, 588; Poem by Anne Miller in a letter to Wilson, October 20, 1971, Yale.

According to Edgar Miller, Anne and her grown children allowed publication of the passages about her in Wilson's diaries. When the book appeared in 1993 and caused a scandal in upstate New York, her second, extremely jealous husband was mortified and furious. Anne then regretted her laissez-faire attitude, adopted a coy and demure role, and refused to be interviewed by newspapers or biographers.

TWENTY-FOUR: THE DARK DEFILE

1. Wilson, *The Shores of Light*, p. 699; Wilson, *The Forties*, pp. 198–199.
   Wilson's autobiographical essays include: "The Case of the Author" (1932), "The Old Stone House" (1933), "At Laurelwood" (1939), "Thoughts on Being Bibliographed" (1944), "A Modest Self Tribute"(1952), which alludes to Swift's "A Modest Proposal," "On First Reading Genesis" (1954), "The Author at Sixty" (1956), "An Interview with Edmund Wilson" (1962) and "Every Man His Own Eckermann" (1963).

2. Wilson, *A Prelude*, p. 1; Wilson, *Israel and the Dead Sea Scrolls*, p. 389; Wilson, *Patriotic Gore*, p. 637.

3. Rosalind Wilson, *Near the Magician*, p. 247; Wilson, *Upstate*, p. 92; Otis Munn, "My Answer to the Talcottville Diary," *Boonville Herald*, September 15, 1971, p. 3.

4. Morris, *Nights and Days with Edmund Wilson*, p. 129; Wilson, "The Children's Hour" (a title borrowed from a poem by Longfellow and a play by Lillian Hellman), *Night Thoughts*, pp. 221, 223; Wilson, "Talcottville 1966," *Holiday Greetings and Desolating Lyrics*, [p.1]; Stéphane Mallarmé, "*Brise Marine*," *The Penguin Book of French Verse: The Nineteenth Century*, ed. Anthony Hartley (London, 1957), p. 188.

5. Bogan, *Letters*, p. 328; Quoted in Morris, *Nights and Days with Edmund*

Wilson, pp. 166, 158; Letter from Wilson to Maxwell Geismar, August 18, 1948, Boston University; Wilson, *The Sixties*, p. 873.

6. Glyn Morris, *Less Traveled Roads*, p. 381; Wilson, *The Fifties*, p. 559; Quoted in Frieda Lawrence, *Not I, But the Wind* (New York, 1934), p. 200; Quoted in Costa, *Edmund Wilson*, p. 150.

7. Wilson, *The Sixties*, pp. 672; 864; Letters from Penelope Gilliatt to Edmund Wilson, October 22, [1970] and April 12, 1971, Yale; Wilson, *Letters*, p. 739; Wilson, *The Sixties*, p. 878.

8. Wilson's contributions to the *New York Review of Books* include: "Every Man His Own Eckermann" (May 1963), Review of Nabokov's *Eugene Onegin* (July 15, 1965), *The Duke of Palermo* (January 12, 1967), "An Open Letter to Mike Nichols" (January 4, 1968), "The Fruits of the MLA" (September 26, 1968 and October 10, 1968), Introduction to Philippe Thoby-Marcelin's *All Men Are Mad* (March 26, 1970), "Notes on Pushkin" (December 3, 1970), "Notes on Tolstoy" (February 25, 1971), Review of the facsimile edition of *The Waste Land* (November 18, 1971), "The Monsters of Bomarzo" (February 10, 1972).

9. Wilson, *A Window on Russia*, p. 74; Quoted by Leon Edel, in *The Thirties*, p. xxix; Wilson, *Letters*, p. 70; Wilson, *The Fruits of the MLA*, p. 23.

10. Quoted in Rosalind Wilson, *Near the Magician*, p. 11; Letter from Esther's son, Nathaniel Hartshorne, to Jeffrey Meyers, February 3, 1994; Wilson, *The Twenties*, p. 12; Interview with Roger Straus.

11. Letter from Wilson to William Fenton, January 10, 1966, St. Lawrence University; Letter from Sherman Paul to Jeffrey Meyers, June 19, 1993. See Edmund Wilson, *Corrections and Comments for the Benefit of Sherman Paul* (Iowa City: Windhover Press, 1976); Quoted in Morris, *Nights and Days with Edmund Wilson*, p. 1.

12. The dedications are: Scott Fitzgerald, *The Vegetable* (1923); Louise Bogan, *Sleeping Fury* (1937); John Udmark, *The Road We Have Covered* (1940); W. H. Auden, *About the House* (1965); Helen Muchnic, *Russian Writers: Notes and Essays* (1971); Marie-Claire Blais, *St. Lawrence Blues* (1974); Lewis Dabney, *The Indians of Yoknapatawpha* (1974); Alfred Kazin, *Contemporaries* (revised edition, 1982) and Philippe Thoby-Marcelin, *Poèmes* (edited by Eva Marcelin,1986).

The poems are: Elinor Wylie, "Impromptu Sonnet" and "To Bunny"; Allen Tate, "Causerie"; Edna Millay, "Portrait"; John Bishop, "No More the Senator"; Archibald MacLeish, squib, after Wilson's "Omelet"; Delmore Schwartz, verse on Wilson and Dickens; Rolfe Humphries, "To Edmund Wilson"; John Dos Passos, quatrain on Talcottville; Ted Paramore, "A Yuletide Riposte"; John Berryman, "Defensio in Extremis" and Robert Lowell, "Our Afterlife, I."

The stories are: Mary McCarthy, "Ghostly Father, I Confess" (1942) and "The Weeds" (1950). The novels are: Fitzgerald, *The Beautiful and Damned* (1922); McCarthy, *The Groves of Academe* (1952), *A Charmed Life* (1955) and *The Group* (1963); George Zuckerman, *The Last Flapper* (1969), in which Delano Fredericks is based on Wilson; and Alison Lurie, *The Truth About Lorin Jones* (1979), in which Garrett Jones is modeled on Wilson.

13. In a letter to me of January 15, 1994, Reuel explained that the guest house

> actually was Elena's property. She had bought the wing of the nineteenth-century house across the road (slated for demolition because of road expansion) and had it moved to our side. . . . After my father's death, Elena and Helen felt that they had been shortchanged by his will and were aggressively urging me to renounce my eventual half interest in his house (where Elena had lifetime tenancy). When EW died he left Elena a large debt—money he had borrowed from Farrar Straus against future earnings. This was the ostensible reason they wanted to acquire the whole Wellfleet property for Helen.

14. Interview with Roger Straus; Engel, "An Exemplary Edmund Wilson," p. 132; Wilson, "On Excavating My Library," *Holiday Greetings and Desolating Lyrics*, [p. 4].

15. Interview with Robert Stabb; A. E. Housman, Preface to *Last Poems* (London, 1922), n.p.; Interview with Elizabeth Stabb; Interview with Mary Crosten; Rosalind Wilson, *Near the Magician*, p. 263.

16. Jason Epstein, "EW: 1895–1972," *New York Review of Books*, 19 (July 20, 1972), 6; Interview with Stuart Hughes.

Arthur Schlesinger, Jr., Harry Levin, Stuart Hughes, Daniel Aaron, Barbara Epstein, Roger Straus, Morley and Barry Callaghan, Penelope Gilliatt and Lillian Hellman also attended the ceremony.

17. Berlin, "Edmund Wilson at Oxford," p. 22; Anton Chekhov, *Selected Letters*, edited with an Introduction by Lillian Hellman, trans. Sidonie Lederer (New York, 1955), pp. 262–263.

Bibliography

I. WORKS BY EDMUND WILSON

The Evil Eye: A Comedy in Two Acts. Princeton: Triangle Club, 1915. Lyrics by Scott Fitzgerald.

The Undertaker's Garland. New York: Knopf, 1922. With John Peale Bishop.

Discordant Encounters: Plays and Dialogues. New York: Boni, 1926.

I Thought of Daisy. New York: Scribner's, 1929. Revised, with a Foreword, 1967.

Poets, Farewell! New York: Scribner's, 1929.

Axel's Castle: A Study in the Imaginative Literature of 1870–1930. New York: Scribner's, 1931.

The American Jitters: A Year of the Slump. New York: Scribner's, 1932.

Travels in Two Democracies. New York: Harcourt Brace, 1936.

This Room and This Gin and These Sandwiches: Three Plays. New York: New Republic, 1937.

The Triple Thinkers: Ten Essays on Literature. New York: Harcourt Brace, 1938. Revised and enlarged edition, 1948.

To the Finland Station: A Study in the Writing and Acting of History. New York: Harcourt Brace, 1940. Reissued, with a new Introduction, 1972.

The Boys in the Back Room: Notes on California Novelists. San Francisco: Colt Press, 1941.

The Wound and the Bow: Seven Studies in Literature. New York: Houghton Mifflin, 1941.

Note-Books of Night. San Francisco: Colt Press, 1942.

The Shock of Recognition: The Development of Literature in the United States Recorded by the Men Who Made It. Garden City, New York: Doubleday, 1943.

Memoirs of Hecate County. Garden City, New York: Doubleday, 1946. Revised edition, 1958.

Europe Without Baedeker: Sketches Among the Ruins of Italy, Greece, and England. Garden City, New York: Doubleday, 1947. Revised and enlarged edition, 1966.

The Little Blue Light: A Play in Three Acts. New York: Farrar, Straus, 1950.

Classics and Commercials: A Literary Chronicle of the Forties. New York: Farrar, Straus, 1950.

The Shores of Light: A Literary Chronicle of the Twenties and Thirties. New York: Farrar, Straus and Young, 1952.

Five Plays. New York: Farrar, Straus and Young, 1954.

Eight Essays. Garden City, New York: Anchor, 1954.

The Scrolls from the Dead Sea. New York: Oxford University Press, 1955. Enlarged editions: *The Dead Sea Scrolls, 1947–1969*, 1969; *Israel and the Dead Sea Scrolls*, 1978.

Red, Black, Blond and Olive. Studies in Four Civilizations: Zuñi, Haiti, Soviet Russia, Israel. New York: Oxford University Press, 1956.

A Literary Chronicle: 1920–1950. Garden City, New York: Anchor, 1956.

A Piece of My Mind: Reflections at Sixty. New York: Farrar, Straus and Cudahy, 1956.

The American Earthquake: A Documentary of the Twenties and Thirties. Garden City, New York: Anchor, 1958.

Apologies to the Iroquois. New York: Farrar, Straus and Cudahy, 1960.

Night Thoughts. New York: Farrar, Straus and Cudahy, 1961.

Patriotic Gore: Studies in the Literature of the American Civil War. New York: Oxford University Press, 1962.

The Cold War and the Income Tax: A Protest. New York: Farrar, Straus, 1963.

O Canada: An American's Notes on Canadian Culture. New York: Farrar, Straus and Giroux, 1965.

The Bit Between My Teeth: A Literary Chronicle of 1950–1965. New York: Farrar, Straus and Giroux, 1965.

Galahad and I Thought of Daisy. New York: Farrar, Straus and Giroux, 1967.

A Prelude: Landscapes, Characters and Conversations from the Earlier Years of My Life. New York: Farrar, Straus and Giroux, 1967.

The Fruits of the MLA. New York: New York Review of Books, 1968.

The Duke of Palermo and Other Plays, With an Open Letter to Mike Nichols. New York: Farrar, Straus and Giroux, 1969.

Upstate: Records and Recollections of Northern New York. New York: Farrar, Straus and Giroux, 1969.

A Window on Russia for the Use of Foreign Readers. New York: Farrar, Straus and Giroux, 1972.

The Devils and Canon Barham: Ten Essays on Poets, Novelists and Monsters. Foreword by Leon Edel. New York: Farrar, Straus and Giroux, 1973.

The Twenties: From Notebooks and Diaries of the Period. Edited with an Introduction by Leon Edel. New York: Farrar, Straus and Giroux, 1975.

Letters on Literature and Politics, 1912–1972. Edited by Elena Wilson. Introduction by Daniel Aaron. Foreword by Leon Edel. New York: Farrar, Straus and Giroux, 1977.

The Nabokov-Wilson Letters, 1940–1971. Edited with an Introduction by Simon Karlinsky. New York: Harper and Row, 1979.

The Thirties: From Notebooks and Diaries of the Period. Edited with an Introduction by Leon Edel. New York: Farrar, Straus and Giroux, 1980.

The Forties: From Notebooks and Diaries of the Period. Edited with an Introduction by Leon Edel. New York: Farrar, Straus and Giroux, 1983.

The Portable Edmund Wilson. Edited with an Introduction by Lewis Dabney. New York: Viking-Penguin, 1983.

The Fifties: From Notebooks and Diaries of the Period. Edited with an Introduction by Leon Edel. New York: Farrar, Straus and Giroux, 1986.

The Sixties: The Last Journal, 1960–1972. Edited with an Introduction by Lewis Dabney. New York: Farrar, Straus and Giroux, 1993.

II. MEMOIRS OF WILSON

Aaron, Daniel. Introduction to Edmund Wilson. *Letters on Literature and Politics, 1912–1972.* Ed. Elena Wilson. New York, 1977. Pp. xv–xxix.

Arbasino, Alberto. "America senza querce," *L'Illustrazione Italiana*, aprile 1960, pp. 32–38, 82–89.

Berlin, Isaiah. "Edmund Wilson at Oxford," *Yale Review*, 76 (Winter 1987), 139–151. Reprinted in *New York Times Book Review*, April 12, 1987, pp. 1, 40, 42–43; *Guardian*, October 12, 1989, pp. 25, 47; and in *Encounters*, ed. Kai Erikson. New Haven, 1989. Pp. 12–22.

Brandon, Henry. "A Conversation with Edmund Wilson: 'We Don't Know Where We Are,'" *New Republic*, 140 (March 30, 1959), 13–15.

Breit, Harvey. "Edmund Wilson." *The Writer Observed.* 1956; New York, 1961. Pp. 173–176.

Brunauer, Dalma. "A Day with Edmund Wilson," *Prairie Schooner*, 49 (Winter 1975–76), 343–352.

Callaghan, Barry. "Edmund Wilson," *Exile* (Toronto), 1 (1972), 107–110.

Connolly, Cyril. "Edmund Wilson: An Appreciation," *Sunday Times* (London), June 18, 1972, p. 40.

Costa, Richard. *Edmund Wilson: Our Neighbor From Talcottville*. Syracuse, 1980.

Cowley, Malcolm. "Edmund Wilson on the *New Republic*," *New Republic*, 167 (July 1, 1972), 25–28.

Edel, Leon. Introduction to Edmund Wilson. *The Twenties*. New York, 1975. Pp. xvii–xlvi.

————. Introduction to Edmund Wilson. *The Thirties*. New York, 1980. Pp. xv–xxix.

————. Introduction to Edmund Wilson. *The Forties*. New York, 1983. Pp. xiii–xxvi.

————. Introduction to Edmund Wilson. *The Fifties*. New York, 1986. Pp. xiii–xxx.

Engel, Monroe. "An Exemplary Edmund Wilson," *Yale Review*, 76 (Spring 1987), 323–333. Reprinted in *Encounters*, ed. Kai Erikson. New Haven, 1989. Pp. 124–132.

Epstein, Jason. "Edmund Wilson: 1895–1972," *New York Review of Books*, 19 (July 20, 1972), 6–8.

Exley, Frederick. *Pages from a Cold Island*. New York, 1974.

French, Philip, ed. "Edmund Wilson: 1895–1972." *Three Honest Men: Edmund Wilson, F. R. Leavis, Lionel Trilling*. Manchester, 1980. Pp. 17–23.

Gauss, Christian. "Edmund Wilson, the Campus and the *Nassau Lit.*," *Princeton University Library Chronicle*, 5 (February 1944), 41–50.

Gill, Brendan. "Homage to Edmund Wilson," *Princeton University Library Chronicle*, 34 (Spring 1973), 158–167.

Halper, Nathan. "Conversations with Edmund Wilson," *Journal of Modern Literature*, 7 (September 1979), 545–548.

Horgan, Paul. "Edmund Wilson at Wesleyan," *American Poetry Review*, 22 (September-October 1993), 37–43. Reprinted in *Tracings: A Book of Partial Portraits*. New York, 1993. Pp. 211–236.

Josephson, Matthew. "Encounters with Edmund Wilson," *Southern Review*, 11 (October 1975), 731–765.

Kazin, Alfred. *New York Jew*. New York, 1978. Pp. 64–68, 232–234, 238–249.

Levin, Harry. "Edmund Wilson: The Last American Man of Letters," *Times Literary Supplement*, October 11, 1974, pp. 1128–1130. Reprinted in *Memories of the Moderns.* 1980; London, 1981. Pp. 184–197.

Matthews, T. S. *Name and Address.* London, 1961. Pp. 192–204. Reprinted in *Spectator,* 233 (August 17, 1974), 208–210; *Saturday Review,* 2 (May 17, 1975), 19–23; *Adam International Review,* 385–390 (1975), 76–80; *Spectator,* 236 (January 3, 1976), 15–16.

McCarthy, Mary. "Edmund Wilson," *Paris Review,* 33 (Summer 1991), 10–37. Reprinted in *Intellectual Memoirs: New York, 1936–1938.* New York, 1992. Pp. 89–114.

Meigs, Mary. *Lily Briscoe: A Self-Portrait.* Vancouver, 1981. Pp. 13–28.

Morris, Glyn. *Less Traveled Roads.* New York, 1977. Pp. 352–386.

———. *Nights and Days with Edmund Wilson: An Upstate Friendship.* Unpublished typescript.

Perenyi, Eleanor. "Wilson," *Esquire,* 60 (July 1963), 80, 82–85, 118.

Pritchett, V. S. "My Friend Edmund Wilson," *New Statesman,* 84 (July 7, 1972), 28.

Rowse, A. L. "An Evening with Edmund Wilson," *Yale Literary Magazine,* 148 (February 1981), 52–61.

Sayre, Joel. "Edmund Wilson, 1895–1972: A Reminiscence," *Washington Post: Book World,* June 18, 1972, pp. 3, 10.

Sayre, Nora. "Growing Up with Edmund Wilson," *New York Times Book Review,* April 29, 1984, pp. 1, 55–57.

Sheed, Wilfrid. "Edmund Wilson: 1895–1972," *New York Times Book Review,* July 2, 1972, pp. 2, 16.

Straus, Dorothea. "The House of Letters." *Palaces and Prisons.* Boston, 1976. Pp. 148–163.

Straus, Roger. "A Flow of Work," *New York Times,* June 18, 1972, IV:4.

Todd, Charles. "Upstate with Edmund Wilson," *New York History,* 54 (1973), 52–58.

Wain, John. "Literature and Life—6: Edmund Wilson Eludes the Interviewer," *Observer,* November 3, 1957, p. 3.

———, ed. *An Edmund Wilson Celebration.* Oxford, 1978.

Wilson, Rosalind Baker. *Near the Magician: A Memoir of My Father.* New York, 1989.

III. CRITICISM ON WILSON

Berthoff, Werner. *Edmund Wilson.* Minneapolis, 1968.

Castronovo, David. *Edmund Wilson.* New York, 1984.

Douglas, George. *Edmund Wilson's America*. Lexington, Kentucky, 1983.

Frank, Charles. *Edmund Wilson*. New York, 1970.

Groth, Janet. *Edmund Wilson: A Critic for Our Time*. Athens, Ohio, 1989.

Kriegel, Leonard. *Edmund Wilson*. Carbondale, Illinois, 1971.

Paul, Sherman. *Edmund Wilson: A Study of Literary Vocation in Our Time*. Urbana, Illinois, 1965.

Ramsey, Richard David. *Edmund Wilson: A Bibliography*. New York, 1971.

Index

compiled by Valerie Meyers